POSTTRAUMATIC STRESS DISORDER
A COMPREHENSIVE TEXT

EDITED BY

PHILIP A. SAIGH

*Graduate School and University Center
of the City University of New York*

J. DOUGLAS BREMNER

*Yale University School of Medicine
and Veterans Administration
Connecticut Health Care System
West Haven Campus*

ALLYN AND BACON

Boston • London • Toronto • Sydney • Tokyo • Singapore

Series editorial assistant: Susan Hutchinson
Marketing manager: Joyce Nilsen
Manufacturing buyer: Suzanne Lareau

Library of Congress Cataloging-in-Publication Data

Posttraumatic stress disorder : a comprehensive text / edited by
  Philip A. Saigh, J. Douglas Bremner.
     p. cm.
    Includes bibliographical references and index.
    ISBN 0-205-26734-3 (hardcover)
    1. Post-traumatic stress disorder. I. Saigh, Philip A.
  II. Bremner, J. Douglas, [date–].
    [DNLM: 1. Stress Disorders, Post-Traumatic. WM 170P85715   1999]
  RC552.P67P664   1999
  616.85'21–dc21
  DNLM/DLC
  for Library of Congress   98-38799
                                       CIP

Printed in the United States of America
10 9 8 7 6 5 4 3 2 1   02 01 00 99 98

Contents

PREFACE

Information involving the effects of traumatic stress has been chronicled for centuries. Reports dating from the Great Fire of London (1666) attest to the posttraumatic symptoms of children, adolescents, and adults. Since the DSM-III recognized posttraumatic stress disorder (PTSD) as an independent psychiatric classification in 1980, an exponential amount of research has focused on the disorder. Although a number of books have dealt with PTSD in recent years, these books have not provided a conceptual synthesis between research and practice. In view of this, this work was developed in order to present an empirical approach to science and practice. In so doing, psychiatrists and psychologists with sustained records of scholarly achievement in the field of traumatic stress studies review the history, epidemiology, etiology, assessment, and treatment of PTSD.

As editors, we owe a considerable debt of gratitude to Anastasia Yasik, Ph.D., for her assistance throughout the editorial process. Our appreciation goes also to Bonnie L. Green, Ph.D., Georgetown University, for her comments on the manuscript. Of course, the kind efforts of the chapter authors are appreciated. The support of our spouses and children is also appreciated.

Philip A. Saigh, Ph.D.
New York

J. Douglas Bremner, M.D.
New Haven

Biographical Sketches

Philip A. Saigh, Ph.D., is a Professor at the City University of New York's Graduate School and the Director of the Ph.D. Program in School Psychology. His research involves the epidemiology, etiology, assessment and treatment of child-adolescent PTSD. He is also the Director of the Child-Adolescent PTSD Clinic at Bellevue Hospital. This clinic provides assessment and referral services for inner city child-adolescent victims of physical/sexual assault as well as pediatric accident victims. Professor Saigh has published more than 80 articles or book chapters and has developed eight psychological tests. He was a member of the American Psychiatric Association's Advisory Committee on PTSD for the *Diagnostic and Statistical Manual of Mental Disorders* (4th edition). He is a Fellow of the American Psychological Association and has served on the editorial boards of 12 journals. Professor Saigh is currently investigating the effects of sexual assault, physical assault, or serious accidents on the cognitive, affective, and behavioral parameters of urban youth.

J. Douglas Bremner, M.D., is an Assistant Professor of Diagnostic Radiology and Psychiatry at Yale University School of Medicine. He is a Research Scientist at the National Center for PTSD and the Yale-Veterans Administration (VA) PET Center at the Veterans Administration Connecticut Health Care System. Dr. Bremner is also the Director of the Trauma Assessment Unit at the Yale Psychiatric Institute. Dr. Bremner received his medical degree from Duke University School of Medicine and his clinical training in psychiatry and nuclear medicine at the Yale School of Medicine. Dr. Bremner is internationally recognized for his research in neuroimaging and the neurobiology of PTSD with veteran and childhood abuse populations. He has published over 50 articles and book chapters on PTSD and recently received the Chaim Danielli Award for outstanding research in the field of traumatic stress studies. He

has developed instruments for the assessment of childhood trauma as well as dissociation. His clinical experiences range from working as an inpatient director for a specialized VA inpatient unit to providing psychotherapy for adult incest survivors. He is currently directing an active research effort at Yale involving the neurobiology of PTSD in women with histories of childhood sexual abuse and in the veterans with PTSD.

Ron Acierno, Ph.D., is an Instructor in the Department of Psychiatry and Behavioral Sciences at the Medical University of South Carolina. Dr. Acierno is also Co-Director of the Older Adult Crime Victims Center, located within the National Crime Victims Research and Treatment Center. He has authored over 25 articles and book chapters, with his primary area of research interest being the assessment and treatment of anxiety-based disorders, particularly PTSD, in older adults. Dr. Acierno's primary research interest involve differentiating response differences to trauma as a function of age and developing treatments as a function of these differences.

Edward B. Blanchard, Ph.D., is currently a Distinguished Professor of Psychology at the University of Albany-SUNY, and Director of its Center for Stress and Anxiety Disorders. He began work on the psychophysiology of PTSD in Vietnam veterans with Larry Kolb in 1981. More recently, he has been studying survivors of serious motor vehicle accidents. Dr. Blanchard is co-author of *After the Crash: Assessment and Treatment of Motor Vehicle Accident Survivors.*

Todd C. Buckley, B.S., is a fourth year doctoral student in the clinical psychology program at the University of Albany, State University of New York. He has co-authored eight peer-reviewed journal articles in the area of trauma studies during his first three years of graduate school. His primary areas of interest involve the information processing mechanisms associated with PTSD and psychophysiological assessment of anxiety disorders, including psychophysiological predictors of treatment outcome for exposure based therapies and long term follow-up.

Juesta M. Caddell, Ph.D., is a clinical psychologist with more than 10 years of experience in designing and conducting mental health, behavioral medicine, and substance abuse research. She has been a member of research teams conducting clinical trials, large-scale epidemiologic research, evaluation research, and multisite cooperative studies. Dr. Caddell also has been a direct service provider to psychiatric patients (including patients with co-morbid substance related disorders) and behavioral medicine patients in both inpatient and outpatient settings. She has particular expertise in the areas of trauma related psychiatric disorders, inlcuding Postraumatic Stress Disorder (PTSD), and other anxiety disorders. She is a recipient of the International Society for Traumatic Stress Studies Chaim Danieli Young Professional Award and serves as a book review editor for *Stress Points,* the newsletter for the International Society for Traumatic Stress Studies. She is currently a Senior Research Clinical Psychologist in the Mental and Behavioral Health Research Program at the Research Triangle Institute, and an adjunct faculty member in the Department of Psychiatry and Behavioral Sciences at Duke University Medical Center.

Dennis D. Charney, M.D., is Professor and Deputy Chair for Research and Education, Department of Psychiatry, Yale University School of Medicine, Director of the National Center for PTSD, Division of Clinical Neurosciences-VA Connecticut Healthcare System, and Editor of Biological Psychiatry. Dr. Charney is on the editorial boards for several psychiatry research journals as well as National Institute of Mental Health committees. Dr. Charney is internationally known for his research in PTSD anxiety and depression, and has over 300 publications in these fields, including co-editorship of *Neurobiological and Clinical Consequences of Stress: From Normal Adaptation to PTSD* (1995, Friedman, M. J. Charney, D. S. & Deutch, A. Y. (Eds.)). Dr. Charney has won several awards for his work, including the

Young Investigator Award from the American College of Neuropharmacology.

Jonathan Davidson, M.D., is a professor in the Department of Psychiatry and Behavioral Science at Duke University Medical Center in Durham, North Carolina, where he is also director of the Anxiety and Traumatic Stress Program. Dr. Davidson is a member of the American Psychiatric Association, the Board of Directors of the Anxiety Disorders Association of America, for which he serves as chairperson of the Publication Committee. In addition, he serves as a reviewer for 18 professional journals in the United States and the United Kingdom, including the *American Journal of Psychiatry, New England Journal of Medicine, Journal of Clinical Psychopharmacology, Archives of General Psychiatry,* and *Alternative Therapies in Health and Medicine.* Dr. Davidson has participated in numerous studies of selective serotonin reuptake inhibitors in social phobia, posttraumatic stress disorder (PTSD), and generalized anxiety disorder. He is currently involved in several National Institutes of Health–sponsored trials, including investigations of family risk factors in posttraumatic stress disorder, the use of maintenance fluoxetine in the treatment of PTSD, and the use of hypericum perforatum in the treatment of depressive disorders. Dr. Davidson co-chaired the DSM-IV Advisory Committee on PTSD.

Lori Ebert, M.A., is a Research Scientist at Research Triangle Institute in North Carolina. She is a Ph.D. candidate in clinical psychology at the University of Illinois. Her professional interest span a range of topics in the area of traumatic stress, including clinical services and research involving adult survivors of childhood sexual abuse.

John A. Fairbank, Ph.D., in an Associate Professor of Medical Psychology in the Department of Psychiatry and Behavioral Sciences at Duke University Medical Center and Associate Professor in the Department of Psychology: Social and Health Sciences at Duke University. He serves on the editorial board of the *Journal of Traumatic Stress* and on the Board of Directors for the International Society for Traumatic Stress. Dr. Fairbank is recipient of the Vietnam Veterans of America Special Commendation Award for his contributions to the National Vietnam Veterans Readjustment Study. He is the author of over 75 professional papers and book chapters on topics including PTSD, substance abuse, and mental health epidemiology. Dr. Fairbank served on the DSM-IV Advisory Committee on PTSD.

Edna Foa, Ph.D., is a professor at Allegheny University of the Health Sciences (formerly Medical College of Pennsylvania and Hahnemann University). She is an internationally renowned authority on the psychopathology and treatment of anxiety and is the Director of the Center for the Treatment and Study of anxiety. Her research aiming at delineating etiological frameworks and targeted treatment has been highly influential and she is currently one of the leading experts in the area of posttraumatic stress disorder. She has published several books and over 200 articles and book chapters, has lectured extensively around the world, and was the co-chair of the PTSD work group of the DSM-IV. Dr. Foa is the recipient of numerous awards and honors, including the *Distinguished Scientist Award* for the Scientific section of the American Psychological Association, the *First Annual Outstanding Research Contribution Award* from the Association for the Advancement of Behavior Therapy, the *Distinguished Scientific Contributions to Clinical Psychology Award* from the American Psychological Association and the *Lifetime Achievement Award* from the International Society for Traumatic Stress Studies.

Subhash C. Inamdar, M.D., is currently a Clinical Associate Professor of Psychiatry at the New York University School of Medicine. At present, Dr. Inamdar's clinical and research interest have involved childhood psychopathology and group dynamics. The assessment and treatment of child-adolescent posttraumatic stress disorder has been his most recent research focus.

B. Kathleen Jordan, Ph.D., is Senior Research Sociologist in the Health and Social Policy Division at the Research Triangle Institute and is an Adjunct Professor in the Department of Psychiatry and Behavioral Sciences at Duke Medical Center. Dr. Jordan has more than 16 years of professional research experience in the fields of psychiatric epidemiology and etiology, psychological and social functioning, criminal justice and drug abuse and drug abuse treatment. She has played key roles in the National Institute of Mental Health's Epidemiologic Catchment Area (ECA) Study and Department of Veterans' Affairs National Vietnam Veterans Readjustment Study (NVVRS). She conducted the first major psychiatric epidemiology study of women prison inmates. The Women Inmates' Health Study, and is currently conducting a similar study of women probationers. Her publications include three reports published in the *Archives of General Psychiatry*. Dr. Jordan shared the 1991 Robert S. Laufer, Ph.D. Memorial Award for Outstanding Scientific Achievement in the Field of PTSD, and received the Vietnam Veterans of America (VVA) Special Commendation Award for her research on Vietnam Veterans.

Terence M. Keane, Ph.D., is Professor and Vice Chairman of Psychiatry at the Boston University School of Medicine. He is also the Chief of Psychology and the Director of the National Center for PTSD at the Boston VA Medical Center. The Past President of the International Society for Traumatic Stress Studies, Dr. Keane has published extensively on the assessment and treatment of PTSD. His contributions to the field have been recognized by many honors including the Robert Laufer Award for Outstanding Scientific Achievement from ISTSS, a Fulbright Scholarship, and Outstanding Research Contributions from the Division of Public Sector Psychology of the American Psychological Association. Dr. Keane is a Fellow of the American Psychological Association and the American Psychological Society. Dr. Keane was a member of the DMS-IV Advisory Committee on PTSD.

Dean G. Kilpatrick, Ph.D., is a professor of Clinical Psychology and the Director of the National Crime Victims Research and Treatment Center at the University of South Carolina in Charleston. For the past 24 years, he has been involved in the crime victims' rights movement, having served as a founding member of South Carolina's first rape crisis center in 1974 and of the South Carolina Victim Assistance Network in 1984. Dr. Kilpatrick and his colleagues have received several grants from the National Institute on Drug Abuse, supporting their research on the scope of violent crime and its psychological impact on victims. He has over one hundred publications to numerous state, national, and international groups. In 1985, he was given the National Organization of Victim Assistance Stephen Schafer Award for Outstanding Contributions to Victims Research. Dr. Kilpatrick was recently appointed Editor of the *Journal of Traumatic Stress.* In 1990, President George Bush presented Dr. Kilpatrick with the President's Award for Outstanding Contributions on Behalf of Victims of Crime. Dr. Kilpatrick on the DSM-IV Advisory Committee on PTSD.

Harold S. Koplewicz, M.D., is the director of the New York University Child Study Center and the Division of Child and Adolescent Psychiatry at NYU/ Bellevue Hospital Center. As Professor of Clinical Psychiatry and Pediatrics and Vice Chairman of the Department of Psychiatry at the New York University School of Medicine, Dr. Koplewicz has been recognized as one of America's leading mental health experts. He is the author of *It's Nobody's Fault: New Hope and Help for Difficult Children and Their Parents* (Times Books/Random House, 1996) and over 50 articles on child and adolescent mental health.

Daniel J. Madden, J.D., received a Bachelor of Arts degree from Boston College in 1993 and Juris Doctor degree from Southern Methodist University in 1997. He is currently in private practice with the law firm of Thornton, Summers, Bicchlin, Dunham, & Brown, L.C. in Corpus Christi, Texas and practices in the area of civil litigation.

John S. March, M.D., M.P.H., is Director of the Programs in Psychopharmacology and Child and Adolescent Anxiety Disorders at Duke University Medical Center. In 1994, Dr. March received the Norbert and Charlotte Reiger Service Award from the American Academy of Child and Adolescent Psychiatry for research on the diagnosis and treatment of pediatric PTSD. Dr. March's research interests focus on the development and evaluation of cognitive-behavioral and medication treatments for pediatric mental disor-

ders; instrument development and psychometric evaluation; and development and elaboration of clinical trial methods in pediatric psychiatry. Dr. March was a member of the DSM-IV Advisory Committee on PTSD.

Alexander McFarlane, M.D., was appointed as the Foundation Professor of Community and Rehabilitation Psychiatry at the University of Adelaide, South Australia in 1990. A major interest is in the area of posttraumatic stress disorder. He has also conducted a study with a colleague, looking at the immediate reactions to motor vehicle accidents and their role in predicting long-term psychiatric morbidity. He has an active research interest in the categorization, description and measurement of disability in both psychiatric physical illness. Dr. McFarlane served as a member of the DSM-IV Advisory Committee on PTSD.

Elizabeth A. Meadows, Ph.D., is an Assistant Professor of Psychology at Central Michigan University. Her clinical and research interests include assessment and treatment of anxiety disorders, responses to trauma, prevention of psychopathology, and the relationships between psychological and medical problems. She has published a number of articles and chapters involving panic disorder and PTSD.

James F. Munroe, Ed.D., has been with the Department of Veterans Affairs Outpatient Clinic in Boston for almost 25 years. He is Clinical Director of the Veterans Improvement Program, Deputy Director of the outpatient PTSD Clinic, and an Associate Clinical Staff member of the National Center for PTSD Behavioral Science Division in Boston. His primary interests include clinical work with severe or complex PTSD, secondary or vicarious trauma in clinicians, and how interactive system effects of therapists and clients can be used to enhance the therapeutic process.

Yuval Neria, Ph.D., is a faculty member at the Tel-Aviv University, Bob Shapell Social Work School. He is a clinical psychologist and earned his Ph.D. in Psychology at the University of Haifa, Israel (1994). Dr. Neria is involved in research involving combat reactions and the aftermath of war captivity. He has published several articles and chapters on these issues.

Richard A. Oberfield, M.D., is currently a Clinical Associate Professor of Psychiatry at the New York University School of Medicine. At present, he is the Chief of the Pediatric Psychiatry Liaison Unit at Bellevue Hospital, as well as the Director of the Family Therapy Unit. Dr. Oberfield recently served as President of the New York Council on Child and Adolescent Psychiatry (1996–97) and is a delegate to the Assembly of the American Academy of Child and Adolescent Psychiatry. He also currently serves on the Child and Adolescent Committee of the American Academy of Psychiatry and Law. Dr. Oberfield's clinical and research interests have focused on the interface between pediatrics and child psychiatry, often from a family/systems perspective. The identification, clinical description, and treatment of children and adolescents suffering from posttraumatic stress disorder has been his most recent research endeavor.

Roger K. Pitman, M.D., is currently Coordinator for Research and Development at the VA Medical Center, Manchester, NH and Associate Professor of Psychiatry at Harvard Medical School, Boston, MA. Since 1985, he has been conducting and publishing research into the psychophysiology and psychobiology of PTSD funded by the Department of Veterans Affairs, National Institute of Mental Health, and U.S. Army. He is a Fellow of the American Psychiatric Association, a Fellow of the American Psychopathological Association, a Member of the American College of Neuropsychopharmacology, and a Member of the National Institute of Mental Health's Violence and Traumatic Stress Initial Review Group. In 1994, he received the International Society for Traumatic Stress Studies' Robert S. Laufer Memorial Award for Outstanding Scientific Achievement in the Field of PTSD. Dr. Pitman served on the DSM-IV Advisory Committee on PTSD.

Nicholas L.D. Potts, M.D., did his medical training in Australia then went overseas and did his Psychiatry Residency Training at Duke University Medical Center in Durham, North Carolina followed by a two year Psychopharmacology Research Fellowship. He is currently working as a lecturer in the Department of Psychiatry at the University of Adelaide in South Australia. He has been involved in research in the area of anxiety disorders with a specific interest in social phobia and posttraumatic stress disorder. Dr. Potts' research has included studies focused on biological disturbances associated with these disorders and treatment for these disorders using psychopharmacological agents whether alone or in combination with various psychotherapies such as CBT.

Heidi S. Resnick, Ph.D., is an Associate Professor of Clinical Psychology at the National Crime Victims Research and Treatment Center (NCVC) at the Medical University of South Carolina. The NCVC is a division of the Department of Psychiatry and Behavioral Sciences at MUSC. Dr. Resnick received her B.A. from the University of Wisconsin-Madison in 1980 and her Ph.D. in clinical psychology from Indiana University in 1987. Her major research interest is the study of factors involved in the development of post-traumatic stress following civilian trauma. Recent research has included the study of rape victims' immediate post-rape biological and psychological response profiles in association with specific assault characteristics and as predictors of long term PTSD outcome. Ultimately this line of research may lead to strategies for prevention of PTSD as early as the initial emergency medical care contacts. In addition, she is studying rape victims' concerns about their physical health following rape, and development of appropriate medical care and health care counseling for rape victims, including information about HIV and risk reduction. Dr. Resnick was a member of DSM-IV Advisory Committee on PTSD.

William Sack, M.D., Emeritus Professor of Psychiatry and Emeritus Associate Professor of Pediatrics at the Oregon Health Sciences University, Portland, Oregon, was Director of the Division of Child and Adolescent Psychiatry at the institute from 1975 to 1997. He was a member of the Committee on Certification for the American Board of Psychiatry and Neurology from 1987 to 1993. His research interest include the mental health of the American Indian child and the effects of war trauma on Southeast Asian refugee youth.

Glenn Saxe, M.D., is Chairman of the Department of Child Adolescent Psychiatry at Boston University School of Medicine. Dr. Saxe studied medicine at McMaster University Medical School in Hamilton, Ontario (1988). He completed a residency in adult psychiatry at Harvard Medical School/Massachusetts Mental Health (1992) and two post-residency fellowships: a PTSD Fellowship at Harvard Medical School/Massachusetts General Hospital (1993), and a Child and Adolescent Psychiatry Fellowship at Harvard Medical School/The Cambridge Hospital (1995). He is a specialist in the area of childhood trauma and PTSD. His current research concerns how children adapt to the stress of burn injury and on the long term consequences of child abuse.

William E. Schlenger, Ph.D., is Director of the Mental and Behavioral Health Research Program at the Research Triangle Institute, Research Triangle Park, NC. In addition, he is Adjunct Professor of Psychology at North Carolina State University, and Adjunct Assistant Professor of Medical Psychology in the Department of Psychiatry and Behavioral Sciences at Duke University Medical Center, Durham NC. Dr. Schlenger's research interests involve psychiatric and substance abuse epidemiology, services research, and evaluation. He has conducted applied research projects that include large scale community epidemiologic studies, randomly controlled trials of treatment and preventive interventions, and evaluations of major Federal demonstration programs in mental health and substance abuse. He served as coprincipal investigator of the National Vietnam Veterans Readjustment Study (NVVRS), a landmark study of the prevalence of post-traumatic stress disorder (PTSD) and other adjustment problems among Vietnam veterans, and has published widely on the epidemiology of PTSD. In 1991 he was a recipient of the Robert S. Laufer Memorial Award for Outstanding Achievement from the International Society for Traumatic Stress Studies. Dr. Schlenger received a Special Commendation Award from the Vietnam Veterans of America for his research on Vietnam veterans. He was a member of the DSM-IV Advisory Committee on PTSD.

Jonathan Shay, M.D., is a psychiatrist for the Department of Veterans Affairs in Boston. His patients are combat veterans. He is the author of *Achilles in Vietnam: Combat Trauma and the Undoing of Character.* His book is part of the Marine Corps professional reading program for "all hands" under the heading "Character, Values, and Ethics." In addition to clinical work, he speaks frequently with active duty armed services audiences on prevention for psychological and moral injury in military service. He is a Clinical Instructor in the Department of Psychiatry at Tufts Medical School.

Daniel Shuman, J.D., is a Professor of Law at Southern Methodist University School of Law. He teaches Torts, Evidence, Law and Social Science, and Mental Health Law, and is an adjunct Professor of Psychiatry at the University of Texas, Southwestern Medical School. He has authored many books— *Psychiatric and Psychological Evidence* (winner of the 1988 American Psychiatric Association Manfred S. Guttmacher Award), *Law, Mental Health, and Mental Disorder, Law and Mental Health Professionals: Texas, Doing Legal Research: A Guide for Social Scientists and Mental Health Professionals,* and *The Psychotherapist Patient Privilege*—and more than 50 articles and book chapters. He is a member of the American Law Institute and former chair of the Association of American Law Schools' sections on Law and Mental Disability, and Law and Medicine. Prior to joining the faculty of the SMU School of Law, he served as an Assistant Attorney General for the State of Arizona and a Legal Services attorney in Tucson, Arizona.

Zahava Solomon, Ph.D., is a Professor of Psychiatric Epidemiology and Social Work at the Tel Aviv University and the Head of the Adler Research Center for Child Welfare and Protection. Professor Solomon is internationally known for her research in the field of traumatic stress and the psychological sequelae of combat stress reactions, war captivity, and the Holocaust. She has published two books on psychic trauma related issues: *Combat Stress Reaction: The Enduring Toll of War* and *Coping With War-Induced Stress: The Gulf War and the Israeli Response.* She has also published over 160 articles and 30 chapters. Professor Solomon is a member of the editorial board of the *Journal of Traumatic Stress* and

The Journal of Personal and Interpersonal Loss. She was a member of the DSM-IV Advisory Committee for PTSD, and has earned many awards and research grants including the Robert S. Laufer Memorial Award for Outstanding Scientific Achievements from the International Society for Traumatic Stress Studies. Dr. Solomon was a member of the DSM-IV Advisory Committee on PTSD.

Steven M. Southwick, M.D., is Professor of Psychiatry, Yale University School of Medicine, Clinical Director of the National Center for Posttraumatic Stress Disorder, Division of Clinical Neurosciences, and Director of the PTSD Program-VA Connecticut Healthcare System. Dr. Southwick is on the VA Merit Review committee and Board of Directors of the International Society for Traumatic Stress Studies. Dr. Southwick is internationally known for his research in PTSD, and has over 75 publications in this field. He also is internationally recognized as an expert in the pharmacological treatment of combat veterans with PTSD.

Landy F. Sparr, M.D., M.A., is Associate Professor of Psychiatry at Oregon Health Sciences University and is the Acting Clinical Director of the Mental Health Division at the Portland VA Medical Center. Dr. Sparr has served as Director of Psychiatric Outpatient Services at the Portland VAMC and as Psychiatry Service Chief and Assistant Chief. Dr. Sparr is a Fellow in the American Psychiatric Association. He has received the Distinguished Service Award from the Oregon Psychiatric Association for his extensive work in organizing statewide psychiatry CME events. He has been a leader in the development of the hospital-wide security management programs. He is also a national expert and has written extensively about forensic issues associated with PTSD, stress disability claims, and the VA disability system. Dr. Sparr was a member of the VA Central Office Task Force on PTSD research and afterward served as an intramural reviewer for VA Merit Review PTSD research proposals. In addition, he is a reviewer for numerous scholarly journals and has delivered many peer-reviewed regional and national scientific CME presentations. Dr. Sparr has a long

record of successful administration of psychiatric programs and of organizing both psychiatric care delivery and educational programs.

Suzanne Sutherland, M.D., is Assistant Clinical Professor of Psychiatry and Behavioral Sciences at Duke University Medical Center, where she teaches and supervises residents in the Outpatient Clinic and Family Studies Program and serves as psychiatric consultant for the Diet and Fitness Center. She has published primarily in anxiety disorders, especially posttraumatic stress disorder and social phobia, and continues to do research in anxiety and depression. Dr. Sutherland has an active practice, utilizing psychopharmacology, individual, family and group psychotherapies, as well as the fine arts, in her work with trauma victims. A special interest is working with performance anxiety in musicians.

William R. True, Ph.D., is a Professor of Community Health in the Epidemiology Division of the St. Louis University School of Public Health. He and Seth A. Eisen, M.D, developed the Vietnam Experience Twin Registry, which has been the source of a number of studies relating to mental health. Dr. True was an officer on the USS Columbus (CG-12) from 1965-66 and continued his interest in veterans by working for the Department of Veterans Affairs Medical Center in St. Louis. He is continuing research on genetic issues in PTSD susceptibility and is funded by the NIAAA to study health services utilization and children of alcoholics.

Frank W. Weathers, Ph.D., is an Assistant Professor of Psychology at Auburn University. He received his B.A. from Butler University in 1984 and his Ph.D. in clinical psychology from Indiana University in 1990. After completing his internship at the Boston VA Medical Center, he served as a clinical research psychologist at the National Center for PTSD until 1997. His research and clinical interests are in the assessment and treatment of PTSD and the classification of psychopathology. Much of his work has focused on the development and evaluation of the Clinician-Administered PTSD Scale, the PTSD Checklist, and other measures of trauma and PTSD.

Jessica Wolfe, Ph.D., is the Director of the Women's Health Sciences Division, National Center for Posttraumatic Stress Disorder, at the Veterans Affairs Medical Center, Boston. She is also Director of Mental Health for VA's comprehensive Women's Health Center at that facility. In addition, she serves as Co-Associate Director for the Department of Health and Human Services' Center of Excellence in Women's Health at Boston University Medical Center. Dr. Wolfe is an Associate Professor of Psychiatry and Psychology at Boston University School of Medicine and an instructor in Psychiatry at Harvard Medical School. Dr. Wolfe is the recipient of numerous grant awards from various agencies including the Department of Veterans Affairs Medical Research Service and Health Services Research and Development Service, the Department of Defense, and the National Institute of Mental Health. Her research interests include PTSD, violence, health, and gender.

Anastasia E. Yasik, Ph.D. is currently a postdoctoral fellow in the Psychiatric Epidemiology Training Program at Columbia University. Her research and clinical interest in child-adolescent psychopathology include the cognitive and academic functioning of urban youth with PTSD and comorbid affective disorders, the application of a systems perspective to the families of traumatized youth, and the assessment and treatment of child-adolescent PTSD.

Gary A. Zarkin, Ph.D., is the Director of Research Triangles Institute's Health and Human Resource Economics Program in the Center for Economics Research. Dr. Zarkin is currently the principal investigator of an NIAAA-funded grant that develops, implements, and evaluates the impact of an enhanced employee assistance program (EAP) worksite intervention directed at women and minorities. Dr. Zarkin is also leading the economic component of a project that evaluates the effect of screening for risky alcohol use in managed care organizations. Dr. Zarkin was previously an Assistant Professor of Economics at Duke University and a Research Associate Professor in Duke University's Institute of Statistics and Decision Sciences.

Chapter 1

THE HISTORY OF POSTTRAUMATIC STRESS DISORDER

PHILIP A. SAIGH, PH.D.
Graduate School and University Center
of the City University of New York

J. DOUGLAS BREMNER, M.D.
Yale University School of Medicine and Veterans Administration
Connecticut Health Care System West Haven Campus

HISTORICAL ACCOUNTS OF REACTIONS TO EXTREME STRESS

Information involving the effects of traumatic experiences have been chronicled for centuries. An early example is evident in the 1666 diary of Samuel Pepys. Six months after Pepys survived the Great Fire of London, he reported that "it is strange to think how to this very day I cannot sleep a night without great terrors of the fire; and this very night could not sleep to almost two in the morning through great terrors of the fire" (quoted in Daly, 1983, p. 66). Da Costa (1871), an American physician treating casualties of the American Civil War (1861–1865), described increased arousal, irritability, and elevated heart rate in soldiers exposed to combat. This cluster of symptoms came to be known as "Da Costa's Syndrome," or "Soldiers Irritable Heart," and was felt to reflect a physiological disturbance related to exposure to the stress of combat (Trimble, 1981). Kraepelin, the nineteenth-century German nosologist, subsequently coined the term "schreckneurose," or fright neuroses, to describe a psychiatric condition "composed of multiple nervous and psychic phenomena arising as a result of severe emotional upheaval or sudden fright which would build up great anxiety; it can therefore be observed after serious accidents and injuries, particularly fires, railway derailments or collisions"

(Kraepelin, 1896, translated by Jablensky, 1985, p. 737).

During the First World War, medical practitioners documented the effects of war-related stressors across a wide range of combatants (Freud, 1917; Hurst, 1916; Mott, 1919; Southard, 1919). Freud theorized that war trauma "presents the mind with an increase of stimulus too powerful to be dealt with or worked off in the normal way, and this must be result in permanent disturbances" (p. 275). Southard (1919) recounted the psychiatric morbidity of 589 combatants who suffered from "shell shock." Among these cases was a French corporal who was buried after a shell hit his trench. Although the man escaped without physical injury "his pulse was variable; at rest it stood at 60; if a table nearby was struck suddenly, it would go up to 120" (Southard, 1919, p. 309). In a similar vein, Mott (1919) recorded the following autobiographical description of a British lieutenant who was hospitalized in Great Britain after being trapped behind enemy lines in France:

During the five days spent in the village of Rouex, I was continually under our own shell fire and also continually liable to be discovered by the enemy, who was also occupying the village. Each night I attempted to get through his lines without being observed, but failed. On the fourth day my sergeant was killed by a shell. During this time I had nothing to drink or eat, with the exception of about a pint of water. On the fifth day I was rescued by our own troops while I was unconscious. At the present time I am subject to dreams in which I hear these shells bursting and whistling through the air. I continually see my sergeant, both alive and dead, and also my attempts to return are vividly pictured. I sometimes have in my dreams that feeling of intense hunger and thirst which I had in the village. When I awaken I feel as though all the strength had left me and am in a cold sweat. For a time after awaking I fail to recognize where I am, and the surroundings take on the form of the ruins in which I remained hidden for so long. Sometimes I do not think that I thoroughly awaken, as I seem to doze off, and there are conflicting ideas that I am in the hospital, and again that I am in France. During the day, if I sit doing nothing in particular and find myself dozing, my mind seems to immediately begin to fly back to France (pp. 126–127).[1]

In 1934, Prasard provided a general account of the psychological distress that occurred in India following a devastating earthquake. In contrast to early reports involving traumatized adults, Bender and Blau (1937) published one of the first articles involving the psychiatric distress of sexually abused youth (age range 5–13 years). Bender and Blau made direct reference to the children's fears, nightmares, avoidance, irritability, trauma reminiscent re-enactments, and hypervigilance. Adler (1943) went on to make reference to the "post-traumatic mental complications" of the survivors of Boston's Coconut Grove nightclub fire.

During the Second World War, mental health practitioners evaluated and treated thousands of psychiatric casualties (Grinker & Spiegel, 1945; Hastings, Wright, & Glueck, 1994; Kardiner, 1941; Lewis, 1942; Raines & Kolb, 1943; Solomon, 1942; Vernon, 1941). In their salient work *Men Under Stress*, Grinker and Spiegel (1945) described the symptoms of a B-24 gunner with "combat neuroses." According to Grinker and Spiegel, the man's aircraft was hit by flack over Germany. One motor was knocked out and

the wings were perforated by shrapnel. This induced the gradual loss of gasoline that was essential for the crew's return. Over the English Channel, the airplane ran out of fuel and the pilot crash-landed. Although the gunner could not swim, his pilot assisted him, and the two were able to escape the sinking craft. Unfortunately, the rest of the crew did not escape. As the gunner had survived without physical injury, he was given a furlough and subsequently assigned to another air crew. Shortly thereafter, he began to evidence stress-related symptoms. According to Grinker and Spiegel:

The night before his first scheduled mission he was very restless and had difficulty in falling asleep. In a terrifying nightmare he dreamed he was back in the plane with his crew, preparing to ditch. It was more frightening than the actual event. He saw himself in the plane, under the water, trying to find a way out. The bombardier appeared and showed him a hole in the plane, motioning to him to get out. He awoke suddenly crying, with the realization that the bombardier never got out. After that he could not go back to sleep but lay quietly, smoking cigarettes, until it was time for the briefing. He could not eat breakfast and during the briefing felt strangely cold. His hands shook and he could not concentrate on the details of the raid to come. He tried to shake off a growing feeling of dread and forced himself to get into the plane with an assumed nonchalance.

On the way out to the target, everything worried him. He mistrusted the pilot, with whom he had never flown before, and worried about every unexpected bump and shudder of the plane. He had a feeling of imminent catastrophe which kept him rigidly tense, listening to any change in the pitch of the motors for signs of failure, constantly looking for an indication that his fears would be realized. When the plane passed over the sea on the way to the target, he fought off rising panic by crouching on the floor of the plane with his head clenched between his fists. Over the target, he felt more controlled and was able to stand by his guns and look for fighters, though his knees shook and his hands trembled. On the way back he continued to feel helpless, trapped, doomed, but still determined that he must not show how he felt to his crewmates. The mission was uneventful, but on his return he was weak and exhausted from the prolonged tension. He went immediately to his tent to lie down, hoping to get some relief from the iron grip of dread and fear. He had not eaten

---

[1]Mott, F. W. (1919). *War neuroses and shell shock.* London: Oxford University Press. Reprinted by permission.

that day and wanted nothing except sleep and relief. But he slept only fitfully, each time being awakened by the dream of his bombardier showing him how to get out of the sinking plane. Instead of being at peace, the night was as full of anxiety as the day's mission.[2]

While the aforementioned accounts involved traumatized adults, a number of war-related papers described similar symptoms of distress among children and adolescents. Bodman (1941), for example, surveyed British youth and observed that approximately 8 percent of the sample presented with psychological symptoms that were associated with air raids. These symptoms involved nightmares, war-specific fears, psychophysiological reactivity on exposure to war-related stimuli, avoidance behaviors, and misconduct. Mercer and Despert (1943) chronicled a similar pattern of posttraumatic emotional morbidity among French youth who were exposed to war-related events. Bradner (1943) documented how Finnish families were forced to leave their homes during the Russio-Finnish War, crowded into unheated railroad cars, moved to unspecified areas at night, and repeatedly strafed by Soviet aircraft. Bradner's report made direct reference to the children's posttraumatic fears, nightmares, blunted affect, avoidance, and psychological arousal on exposure to war-related stimuli. He also indicted that "even a year after the war, the sight of ruins had a profoundly depressing effect upon the children...war films, saddening war pictures in illustrated magazines, reports of war of any kind, still caused such symptoms of wartime to return at any given moment" (Bradner, 1943, p. 319).

Following World War II, a number of investigators described the emotional and psychophysiological distress of prisoners of war (Chadoff, 1963; Etinger, 1962; Friedman, 1948; Nadler & Ben-Shushan, 1989; Wolf & Ripley, 1947). Friedman (1948) used the term the Buchenwald Syndrome to describe the symptom pattern that he observed among Jewish youth who survived the Nazi death camps. Based on medical and psychiatric evaluations that were conducted at a detention center on the island of Cyprus, Friedman determined that 50 to 60 percent of the children had physical complaints without an organic etiology. He also reported that majority of these youth suffered from sleep disorders, subjective fears, hypervigilance, and "affective anesthesia."

Shortly following the surrender of Japan, Wolf and Ripley (1947) described the psychopathology of a sample of U.S. prisoners who had been held captive by the Japanese for approximately three years. In addition to having been forced to subside on inadequate rations and experiencing a number of diseases (e.g., beriberi, malaria, and dysentery), these men were subjected to forced labor, beatings, and more elaborate forms of torture. Wolf and Ripley reported that 22.9 percent of these cases evidenced war-related nightmares and fears, blunted affect, memory impairment, anger, and depression. Analogously, Etinger (1962) examined 100 Norwegian survivors of the German concentration camps and determined that 85 cases presented with chronic fatigue, impaired concentration, and irritability. He also reported that most of these subjects experienced "painful associations" that could occur in "any connection whatsoever, from seeing a person stretching his arms and associating this with his fellow prisoners hung up by their arms under torture, to seeing an avenue of trees and visualizing long rows of gallows with swinging corpses" (Etinger, 1962, p. 372).

Compelled by the prevalence of war-related psychiatric morbidity, the American Psychiatric Association's (APA) Committee on Nomenclature and Statistics included the classification *gross stress reaction* in the *Diagnostic and Statistical Manual of Mental Disorders* (DSM-I) of 1952. According to the 1952 manual, gross stress reaction was indicated in cases involving exposure to "severe physical demands or extreme stress, such as in combat or civilian catastrophe (fire, earthquake, explosion, etc.)" (APA, 1952, p. 40). The DSM-I also acknowledged (contrary to the prevailing psychodynamic view) that "in many instances this diagnosis applies to previously more or less 'normal' persons who experience intolerable stress" (APA, 1952, p. 40). While recognizing that exposure to extreme stress may induce significant psychological distress, the DSM-I did not provide

---

[2]Grinker, R. G., & Spiegel, J. P. (1945). *Men under stress.* Philadelphia: Blackstone. Copied with permission from Ayer Co., Inc. North Stratford, NH 03590.

operational criteria for formulating a gross stress re-action diagnosis.

Studies involving American veterans of the Korean conflict (Edwards & Peterson, 1954; Glass, 1954; Glass, Ryan, Lubin, Reddy, & Tucker, 1956; Lifton, 1954; Nobel, Roudebush, & Prince, 1952) further served to illustrate the unique distress that may be observed following exposure to traumatic events. Within this context, Nobel et al. (1952) examined a sample of wounded Korean conflict veterans and reported that 55 percent of the subjects presented with "startle reactions, occasional combat dreams, slight stammering, and other evidences of tension that had arisen during their combat experiences" (p. 496).

The 1950s and 1960s were marked by a great deal of pioneering research involving the psychological status of civilians who experienced natural and industrial disasters (Quarantelli, 1985; Saigh, 1992a). As it was assumed that information denoting the effects of civilian disasters (e.g., floods, hurricanes, tornados, and earthquakes) may be used to predict the psychiatric effects of war-related events (e.g., nuclear explosions), the National Academy of Sciences funded investigations that sought to assess the mental health of civilian disaster survivors (Saigh, 1992a). By way of example, Bloch, Silber, and Perry (1956) interviewed 185 youth who survived a tornado that devastated the town of Vicksburg, Mississippi, in 1953. Bloch et al. (1956) reported that many of these youth manifested nightmares, trauma-related reinactments (e.g., "tornado games"), irritability, and avoidance behaviors that were associated with tornado-related stimuli. Subsequent reports involving survivors of the sinking of the *Andrea Doria* (Friedman & Linn, 1957), the 1962 Alaska earthquake (Langdon & Parker, 1964), and the Bristol floods (Bennet, 1968) served to underscore the unique distress of traumatized survivors.

In 1968, the APA's Committee on Nomenclature and Statistics published the DSM-II. Whereas the DSM-I gross stress reaction classification had achieved a measure of recognition in the mental health circles (Anderson, 1985), the classification was omitted from the 1968 manual. In lieu of the former classification, *transient situational disturbance* was introduced. According to the DSM-II, this classification encompassed "transient disorders of any severity (including those of psychotic proportions) that occur in individuals without any underlying mental disorders and that represent an acute reaction to overwhelming environmental stress" (APA, 1968, p. 48). The DSM-II diagnostic category also listed a number of age-related sub-classifications (e.g., adjustment reaction of childhood). As in the case of the earlier gross stress reaction category, the transient situational disturbance classification did not include operational criteria for formulating a psychiatric diagnosis.

In 1972, Lacy examined 400 British students who survived a mud slide that engulfed an elementary school. Two years after the incident, he reported that the students were experiencing "sleeping difficulties, unwillingness to go to school or out to play, instability and enuresis" (Lacy, 1972, p. 259). He also observed that "bad weather, wind, rain and snow were very frightening for some children" (Lacy, 1972, p. 259) as an interval of inclement weather had preceded the mud slide.

Burgess and Holmstrom (1974) subsequently published an influential report involving *"rape trauma syndrome."* Their article was based on clinical interviews with 146 female rape victims. Burgess and Holmstrom's analysis led them to conclude that rape victims experience acute and long-term phases of distress. The acute phase involved symptoms of physical soreness, tension headache, insomnia, nightmares, genitourinary disturbance, anxiety, anger, and guilt. The long-term phase was associated with rape-related nightmares and thoughts, avoidance behaviors (46 percent relocated), subjective fears, and sexual dysfunction.

Also within the context of crime-related research, Kilpatrick, Veronen, and Resick (1979) conducted an analysis of postrape psychopathology over time. The authors administered the Modified Fear Survey (MFS; Veronen & Kilpatrick, 1979) to a sample of rape victims and a sample of non-stress exposed controls. The authors determined that the MFS scores of the rape victims at 6–10 days and 1 month significantly exceeded the scores of the control group. Kilpatrick et al. (1979) went on to perform an item discrepancy analysis and determined that the rape victims were significantly more fearful of specific rape-related stimuli (i.e., emergency rooms, strangers, naked men, and being alone).

While initial reports involving the adjustment of American troops in Vietnam were very favorable (Bloach, 1969; Bourne, 1970), Albert Glass (1973), the noted military psychiatrist, advised that the "reported low rates of neuropsychiatric casualties from Vietnam may be questioned until all categories of non-combat losses are stated" (p. 998). Later research involving the mental health of Vietnam veterans (Horowitz & Solomon, 1975; Panzarella, Mantell, & Bridenbaugh, 1978; Shatan, 1978; Strayer & Ellenhorn, 1975) lent a good deal of support to Glass's concern. For example, Horowitz and Solomon's (1975) assessment of Vietnam veterans who were receiving psychiatric treatment led them to conclude that these patients suffered from *delayed stress response syndrome.* This syndrome was said to involve "nightmares, painful moods and storms, direct or symbolic behavioral repetitions and concomitant secondary signs such as impaired social relationships, aggressive and self-destructive behavior, and fear of loss of control over hostile impulses" (Horowitz & Solomon, 1975, p. 72).

Given this history, it is evident that traumatized individuals of all ages can develop pervasive and chronic psychological problems. It is also evident that a host of terms such as "schreckneurose," "gross stress reaction," and "rape trauma syndrome" have been used to describe very comparable forms of pathology. Unfortunately, the use of a wide range of competing terms to describe the same phenomenon veiled clinical parallels and hindered practice and research (Saigh, 1992a). Recognizing the extent of confusion within the area of traumatic stress studies, Kardiner (1969) lamented that "it is hard to find a province in psychiatry less disciplined than this one. There is practically no continuity to be found anywhere…the literature can only be characterized as anarchic. Every author has his own frame of reference" (p. 246). Obviously, the situation was clinically and theoretically unsound, and the need for an operational and widely recognized nosology was acutely apparent.

PTSD AND THE DSM-III, DSM-III-R, AND THE DSM-IV

DSM-III. Given the DSM-II's dearth of operational criteria, impoverished reliability data, and limited coverage (only 108 classifications were included) (Morey, Skinner, & Blashfield, 1986; Saigh, 1992a), the APA appointed a task force to amend the manual. Working under the stewardship of Robert Spitzer, M.D., mental health practitioners prepared symptomological profiles for 265 psychiatric classifications. The DSM-III (APA, 1980) Reactive Disorders Committee (Nancy Anderson, M.D., Robert Lifton, M.D., Chaim Shatan, M.D., Jack Smith, M.D., Robert Spitzer, M.D., and Lyman Wynne, M.D.) went on to draw on their clinical experience and the existing literature to formulate the diagnostic criteria for what came to be called *posttraumatic stress disorder* (PTSD). According to the DSM-III, PTSD was indicated by the "development of characteristic symptoms following a psychiatrically traumatic event that is generally beyond the realm of normal human experience" (APA, 1980, p. 236). The DSM-III also indicated that the "stressor producing this syndrome would evoke significant symptoms of distress in most people and is generally outside the range of such common experiences as simple bereavement, chronic illness, business losses or marital conflict" (APA, 1980, p. 236). The adoption of this perspective clearly served to integrate theory and practice as it acknowledged that divergent stressors (e.g., sexual assault, war-related events, serious accidents, or disasters) could induce comparable patterns of psychiatric morbidity.

The DSM-III included four sets of polymorphic symptom clusters for making a PTSD diagnosis. In addition to the mandatory exposure to extreme stress (Criterion A), Criterion B required the presence of one of three reexperiencing symptoms (distressing trauma-related thoughts, nightmares, or a sudden feeling that the traumatic event was reoccurring). Criterion C required the presence of at least one of three psychic numbing symptoms (diminished interest in significant activities, detachment or estrangement from others, and constricted affect). Criterion

D required the presence of at least two of six symptoms that were not apparent before the trauma (hyper alertness or exaggerated startle response, sleep disturbance, guilt, memory/concentration impairment, avoidance, and exacerbation of symptoms on exposure to traumatic stimuli). While the DSM-III PTSD classification provided a fairly discrete set of diagnostic symptoms and four pages of explanatory text, it did not offer information relative to the unique expression of symptoms by stress exposed children or adolescents.

DSM-III-R.   Despite the widespread acceptance of the DSM-III, revisionary efforts were begun in 1983 and the DSM-III-R was published in 1987 (Saigh, 1992a). In keeping with the precedent that was set by the DSM-III, the 1987 nosology indicated that PTSD may occur after a "psychologically distressing event that is outside the range of normal human experience" (APA, 1987, p. 247) (Criterion A). On the other hand, Criterion B was modified to require the presence of a minimum of one of four reexperiencing symptoms (recurrent and intrusive, distressing recollections and dreams of the stressful event, recurrent distressing about the trauma, sudden acting or feeling that the traumatic event was reoccurring, and intense psychological distress upon exposure to trauma reminiscent stimuli). Criterion C was also broadened to include at least three of seven avoidance or numbing symptoms (avoidance of activities or places that induce traumatic recollections, efforts to avoid thoughts or feelings about the trauma, inability to recall significant details about the trauma, feeling detached or estrangement from others, constricted affect, and a sense of foreshortened future). Criterion D was revised to exclude feelings of guilt and required at least two of six increased arousal symptoms (difficulty in falling or staying asleep, irritability or anger outbursts, concentration impairment, hypervigilance, exaggerated startle response, and physiological reactivity on exposure to events that reflect an aspect of the traumatic event). In a significant departure from the DSM-III, the DSM-III-R provided information involving age-specific features of PTSD (e.g., "young children may not have the sense that

they are reliving the past; reliving the trauma occurs in action, through repetitive play," [APA, 1987, p. 249]). Whereas the DSM-III-R text made reference to the expression of symptoms under the heading of age-specific features (e.g., "In younger children, distressing dreams of the event may, within several weeks, change into generalized nightmares of monsters, of rescuing others, or of threats to self or others" (APA, 1987, p. 249). The list of diagnostic symptoms offered scant information relative to the expression of symptoms in youth.

DSM-IV.   The APA subsequently initiated a programmatic series of efforts toward the development of the fourth edition of the DSM in 1988. As the DSM-III and DSM-III-R had engendered a significant amount of scientific research (Widiger, Frances, Pincus, Davis, & First, 1991), the development of the DSM-IV primarily relied on literature reviews and a number of clinical trials (Saigh, Green, & Korol, 1996). Viewed along these lines, the DSM-IV PTSD work group (under the co-chairmanship of Jonathan Davidson, M.D., and Edna Foa, Ph.D.) reviewed the available literature (Davidson & Foa, 1993) relative to clinical phenomenology (course, subtypes, and symptomatic manifestations), epidemiology (prevalence, features, and risk factors), and relation to other disorders (e.g., phobias and dissociative disorders). The PTSD work group also performed a series of multisite clinical and community trials (Kilpatrick, Resnick, & Freedy, 1993). The actual field trials (under the direction of Dean Kilpatrick, Ph.D.) were conducted at 5 sites and involved 128 community subjects and 400 patients. The primary goal of these trials was to empirically examine relations between different stressors and PTSD symptoms. Practically speaking, these trials sought to establish if low magnitude stressors such as bereavement could induce PTSD. In addition, the likelihood that divergent stressful events could lead to symptoms of varying onset and duration was also explored. The work group further sought to ascertain if the inclusion of additional symptoms would effect the prevalence of the disorder. Finally, event characteristics (e.g., actual physical injuries or perceptions in response to various forms of stressful experiences) were assessed to identify variables that might be independently associated with PTSD without reference to the type of event that was experienced.

As earlier studies demonstrated that stressors that could induce PTSD (e.g., sexual assaults and motor vehicle accidents) were relatively common in the United States (Breslau, Davis, Andereski, & Peterson, 1991; Resnick, Kilpatrick, Dansky, Saunders, & Best, 1993), the DSM-IV PTSD work group withdrew the DSM-III-R provision that the stressor which induced the disorder must have been "outside the range of normal human experience" (APA, 1987, p. 247). In its place, Criterion A was amended to require that a person "experienced, witnessed, or been confronted with an event or events that involve actual or threatened death or serious injury, or a threat to the physical integrity to oneself or others" (APA, 1994, p. 428). Criterion A was also revised to state that responses must have "involved intense fear, helplessness, or horror" (APA, 1994, p. 428).

The DSM-IV text specifies that traumatic events may be directly experienced in a number of ways. Direct traumatic experiences encompass "military combat, violent personal assault (sexual assault, physical assault, robbery, mugging)" (APA, 1994, p. 424). The DSM-IV text also indicates that "being kidnapped, being taken hostage, terrorist attack, torture, incarceration as a prisoner of war or in a concentration camp, natural or manmade disasters, severe automobile accidents, or being diagnosed with a life-threatening disease" (APA, 1994, p. 424) constitute examples of directly experienced traumatic events. With reference to youth, the DSM-IV specifically states that "sexually traumatic events may include developmentally inappropriate sexual experiences without threatened or actual violence" (APA, 1994, p. 424). As such, incestuous behaviors that are perpetrated on youth without physical violence are clearly recognized as traumatic events that may lead to the development of the disorder.

The DSM-IV further denotes that PTSD may be induced by observing events such as the "serious injury or unnatural death of another person due to violent assault, accident, war, or disaster or unexpectedly witnessing a dead body or body parts" (APA, 1994, p. 424). A third avenue of traumatization involves receiving information (i.e., verbal mediation) about the stressful experiences of others such as "personal assault, serious accident, or serious injury experienced by a family member or a close friend; learning about the sudden, unexpected death of a family member or close friend; or learning that one's child has a life threatening disease." (APA, 1994, p. 424).

Within the context of the Lebanese conflict, Saigh (1991) described the verbally induced traumatization and subsequent PTSD in an 11-year-old schoolgirl. The girl's problems developed after her parents told her that her uncle died during a war-related shelling incident. The girl also inadvertently overheard a parental conversation wherein it was reported that her uncle's body had been mutilated by shrapnel and that his remains were claimed on the basis of the identity papers that he had carried. Two years after learning about the sudden and insidious death of her uncle, the girl presented with PTSD at a university outpatient clinic. In a related study, Saigh (1992b) demonstrated that the levels of anxiety, depression, and misconduct of the adolescents with verbally mediated PTSD were similar to the levels of distress that were evidenced by adolescents who developed the disorder through direct experience or by observing the traumatic experiences of others. Interestingly, Saigh (1992b) also reported that the anxiety, depression, and misconduct ratings of the PTSD groups (i.e., subjects who developed the disorder through verbal mediation, direct experience, or observation) significantly exceeded the levels of emotional morbidity of a stress-exposed PTSD negative group.

The DSM-IV PTSD work group also rearranged a few of the DSM-III-R symptom clusters and adjusted diagnostic thresholds. Physiological reactivity on exposure to traumatic stimuli was removed from the arousal cluster (Criterion D) and added to the reexperiencing cluster (Criterion B). Criterion B was revised to require the presence of a minimum of one of five reexperiencing symptoms (recurrent thoughts of the traumatic event, recurrent dreams about the traumatic event, intense psychological discomfort at exposure to trauma-reminiscent stimuli, sudden acting or feeling that the traumatic event was reoccurring, and physiological reactivity on exposure to trauma-reminiscent stimuli). As in the case of the DSM-III-R, Criterion C requires the presence of at least three of seven avoidance or numbing symptoms (e.g., efforts to avoid thoughts, discussions or feelings involving the trauma, avoidance of people, places, or actions that induce recollections of the trauma, significantly reduced interest in significant activities, feelings of detachment, blunted affect, and a sense of a foreshortened future). With the exception of the deletion of physiological reactivity, the symptoms that make up Criterion D in the DSM-IV are identical to the symptoms that appeared in the DSM-III-R. According to the DSM-IV, Criterion D requires the presence of two of five increased arousal symptoms (e.g., outbursts of anger, hypervigilance, difficulty concentrating, sleep impairment, and exaggerated startle response).

The DSM-IV also added a new stipulation (Criterion E) that requires the duration of the symptoms listed under Criteria B, C, and D to be apparent for at least one month. Finally, the DSM-IV maintains that the disturbance must cause "clinically significant distress or impairment in social, occupational, or other important areas of functioning" (Criterion E) (APA, 1994, p. 429). By way of example, Saigh, Mroueh, and Bremner (1997) reported that Metropolitan Achievement Test scores (a predictor of scholastic performance) of adolescents with PTSD were significantly lower than the scores of a stress-exposed comparison group that did not develop the disorder. Table 1.1 presents the diagnostic criteria for PTSD that appear in the DSM-IV.

Associated Features

According to the DSM-IV, individuals with PTSD may experience feelings of guilt. They may also blame themselves for surviving when others did not. Calhoun and Resick (1993) provide a graphic example of the guilt and despondence that was verbalized by an adult rape victim. The victim reported that "I kept it inside and blamed myself for all that happened. I was probably a slut. Nothing mattered anymore" (Calhoun & Resick, p. 71). Individuals with PTSD may also manifest phobic avoidance that severely interferes with daily activities and social interactions. Saigh (1987) described the phobic avoidance of an 11-year-old girl who witnessed the deaths of two pedestrians during a shelling incident. In addition to presenting with trauma-related recollections and nightmares, the girl consistently avoided the intersection where the incident occurred.

Also within the context of associated features, the DSM-IV indicates that interpersonal stressors such as childhood sexual abuse, domestic violence, being held as a hostage or a prisoner of war may be associated with a constellation of symptoms involving:

> *impaired affect modulation; self-destructive and impulsive behavior, dissociative symptoms; somatic complaints; feelings of ineffectiveness; shame; despair; or hopelessness; feeling permanently damaged; a loss of previously sustained beliefs; hostility; social withdrawal; feeling consistently threatened; impaired relationships with others; or a change from the individual's previous personality characteristics.*[3]

The DSM-IV indicates that there may be an increased risk for comorbid anxiety disorders (i.e., agoraphobia, panic disorder, obsessive-compulsive disorder, social phobia, and specific phobia) as well as major depressive disorder, somatization disorder, and substance-related disorders. As will be noted in chapter 2, Sack and his colleagues (1994) examined the psychiatric comorbidity of Cambodian adolescents who emigrated to America after the fall of the brutal Pol Pot regime. Between the ages of 8 to 12 years, the subjects were exposed to exceptional stress (e.g., they were forcibly separated from their parents, made to perform hard labor, given starvation rations, and forced to participate in the execution of civilians). Sack and his colleagues reported that stress exposed Cambodian subjects who developed PTSD were 4.3 times more likely to have a comorbid depressive disorder than stress-exposed youth that did not develop PTSD. These authors also reported that adolescents with PTSD were 3.5 times more likely to have a

---

[3]Reprinted with permission from the *Diagnostic and Statistical Manual of Mental Disorders,* Fourth Edition. Washington, D.C: American Psychiatric Association, 1994.

TABLE 1.1   DSM-IV Criteria for Posttraumatic Stress Disorder[1]

A. The person has been exposed to a traumatic event in which both of the following have been present:
   1. the person has experienced, witnessed, or been confronted with an event or events that involve actual or threatened death or serious injury, or a threat to the physical integrity to oneself or others.
   2. the person's responses involved intense fear, helplessness, or horror. **Note:** In children it may be expressed by disorganized or agitated behavior.

B. The traumatic event is reexperienced in at least two of the following ways:
   1. recurrent and intrusive distressing recollections of the event, including images, thoughts, or perceptions. **Note:** In young children, repetitive play may occur in which themes or aspects of the trauma are expressed.
   2. recurrent distressing dreams of the event. **Note:** In young children, there may be frightening dreams without recognizable content.
   3. acting or feeling as if the traumatic event were recurring (includes sense of reliving the experience, illusions, hallucinations, and dissociative flashback episodes, including those that occur on awakening or when intoxicated). **Note:** In young children, trauma-specific reenactment may occur.
   4. intense psychological distress at exposure to internal or external cues that resemble an aspect of the traumatic event.
   5. physiological reactivity upon exposure to internal or external cues that symbolize or resemble an aspect of the traumatic event.

C. Persistent avoidance of stimuli associated with the trauma and numbing of general responsiveness (not present before the trauma), as indicated by at least three of the following:
   1. efforts to avoid thoughts, feelings, or conversations associated with the trauma.
   2. efforts to avoid activities, places, or people that arouse recollections of the trauma.
   3. inability to recall an important aspect of the trauma.
   4. markedly diminished interest or participation in significant activities.
   5. feeling of detachment or estrangement from others.
   6. restricted range of affect.
   7. sense of foreshortened future (e.g., does not expect to have a career, marriage, children, or a normal life span).

D. Persistent symptoms of increased arousal (not present before the trauma), as indicated by at least two of the following:
   1. difficulty in falling or staying asleep.
   2. irritability or anger outbursts.
   3. difficulty concentrating.
   4. hypervigilance.
   5. exaggerated startle response.

E. Duration of the disturbance (symptoms in B, C, and D) is more than one month.

F. The disturbance causes clinically significant distress or impairments in social, occupational, or other important areas of functioning.

   Specify if:

   Acute: if duration of symptoms is less than three months.

   Chronic: if duration of symptoms is three months or more.

   Specify if:

   With Delayed Onset: onset of symptoms at least three months or more.

[1]Reprinted with permission from the *Diagnostic and Statistical Manual of Mental Disorders,* Fourth Edition. Copyright 1994 American Psychiatric Association

comorbid anxiety disorder. Likewise, Kesseler, Sonnega, Bromet, Hughes, and Nelson's (1992) national comorbidity survey determined that approximately 48 percent of the men and women with PTSD had a lifetime history of major depression. In contrast, 11.7 percent of the PTSD negative males and 18.8 percent of the PTSD negative females had a lifetime history involving major depression. In terms of substance-related disorders, 51.9 percent and 28 percent of the respective PTSD males and females abused alcohol in contrast to 34.4 precent and 13.5 percent of the PTSD negative males and females. Agoraphobia was observed in 18 percent of the males and 22.4 percent of the females with PTSD, compared to 4.1 percent and 7.8 percent of PTSD negative males and females.

Specific Culture and Age Features

The DSM-IV cautions that individuals who recently immigrated from areas of social unrest or conflict may have elevated rates of PTSD. In a methodologically rigorous series of longitudinal studies that will be described in chapter 2, Kinzie, Sack, and their colleagues (Kinzie, Sack, Angell, & Mason, 1986; Kinzie, Sack, Angell, Clarke, & Ben, 1989) observed PTSD prevalence estimates that ranged from 18.2 percent to 50.0 percent among Cambodian youth who immigrated to the United States. Ekbald (1993) also observed high levels of psychiatric morbidity among Bosnian youth who immigrated to Sweden.

The DSM-IV indicates that younger children may experience trauma-related nightmares that may revert to generalized nightmares over time. It is also indicated that "young children usually do not have the sense that they are reliving the past; rather, the reliving of the trauma may occur through repetitive play" (APA, 1994, p. 426). Hendriks, Black, and Kaplan (1993) provide a vivid description of the trauma-specific play of a 3-year-old British school boy who actually saw his mother kill his father. The authors reported that the boy reenacted the murder by using doll figures to symbolize his parents. According to Hendriks et al. (1993), "He picked up a toy scalpel belonging to a set of toys that we use for children being helped to prepare for a surgical operation and putting it in the hand of the mother doll, he used it as a hammer, repeatedly hitting the face of the father doll" (pp. 95–96).

In addition, the DSM-IV reports that "in children the sense of a foreshortened future may be evidenced by the belief that life will be too short to include becoming an adult" (APA, 1994, p. 426). It is also indicated that children may present with "omen formation" or the ability to foresee negative events in the future.

Course and Prevalence

The DSM-IV indicates that the disorder may occur at any age (including childhood). It is reported that symptoms generally become evident within the first three months following the trauma. On the other hand, it is also indicated that there may be a delay of several months or years before symptoms are evident. The DSM-IV further indicates that PTSD is frequently preceded by acute stress disorder (a rather similar disorder that may occur immediately after stress exposure and may last from 2 days to 4 weeks). In addition, the DSM-IV states that the symptom expression may vary over time and that "the duration of symptoms varies, with complete recovery occurring within three months in approximately half of the cases" (APA, 1994, p. 426). On the other hand, it is cautioned that PTSD symptoms may persist for more than 12 months in many cases. Among a sample of combat veterans that developed the disorder, Bremner, Southwick, Darnell, and Charney (1996) reported that symptoms occurred within a few years of stress exposure. These authors also reported that symptoms remained chronic and unrelenting five years following the initial stress exposure (see Figure 1.1).

As will be seen in chapters 2 through 5, the prevalence of the disorder is marked by great variance. For the time being, it may be said that the child, adolescent, and adult PTSD literature reflects differential levels of psychiatric morbidity.

Case Examples

Examined from a clinical perspective, Table 1.2 presents case illustrations that reflect the expression of PTSD symptoms in a 12-year-old female and a 50-

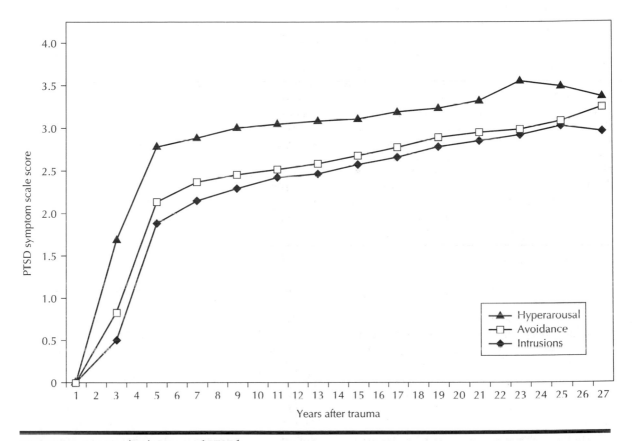

FIGURE 1.1   Longitudinal Course of PTSD[1]

[1]From Bremner, D. J., Southwick, S. M., Darnell, A., & Charney, D. S. (1996). Chronic PTSD in Vietnam combat veterans: Course of illness and substance abuse. *American Journal of Psychiatry, 153,* 369–375. Copyright American Psychiatric Press. Reprinted with permission.

year-old Vietnam veteran. Despite the variations in their developmental and stress exposure histories, the cases serve to underscore the unique constellation of symptoms that are indicative of the disorder. The illustrations also serve to illustrate that PTSD may occur in conjunction with other disorders.

SUMMARY

Information pertaining to the effects of extreme stress has been chronicled for centuries. Accounts dating from the Great Fire of London have repeatedly documented the unique symptoms of what the DSM-III Reactive Disorders Committee came to call posttraumatic stress disorder. According to the

DSM-III, PTSD was indicated by the "development of characteristic symptoms following a psychiatrically traumatic event that is generally beyond the realm of normal human experience" (APA, 1980, p. 236). The DSM-III PTSD classification also indicated that the "stressor producing this syndrome would evoke significant symptoms of distress in most people and is generally outside the range of such common experiences as simple bereavement, chronic illness, business losses or marital conflict" (APA, 1980, p. 236). The adoption of this perspective clearly served to integrate theory and practice as it acknowledged that divergent stressors (e.g., sexual assault, war-related events, serious accidents, or disasters) could induce comparable patterns of psychiatric morbidity.

TABLE 1.2

Clinical Examples of PTSD

Maria, a 12-year-old youth, was sexually assaulted by her 40-year-old uncle. Prior to the incident, she had maintained a B average and had been actively involved in soccer and softball leagues. Although she had been a popular and outgoing youth, Maria had not dated or experienced a sexual relation. According to Maria's testimony, her uncle visited her home when her parents were away. After he learned that her parents were out, he began to hug and fondle her. Although she attempted to stop him, she was unable to prevent him from pinning her down, pulling off her garments, and forcing his penis into her vagina. Maria experienced a great deal of pain during the assault. She felt terrified and helpless as her uncle forced himself into her. At times, she felt as though the assault was part of an awful nightmare. Afterwards, her uncle said that he had always cared for her. He told her that "these things happen all the time between adults." He also told her that her reputation would be ruined if others were to learn about what had happened. Before leaving, he cautioned that "If you ever tell, I'll have to deny it. Telling others will only cause a lot of trouble for you. Just keep this between us and everything will be fine."

For more than a year, Maria did not tell anyone about the rape. She blamed herself for allowing the incident to occur. In the days and months that followed, she constantly thought about the incident. She also worried about the possibility of having contracted HIV. These thoughts were associated with increased psychophysiological arousal (her heart beat faster and she perspired). Rape-related thoughts and mental images occurred in a variety of contexts and stimuli associated with the assault (e.g., the music that had been playing when the rape occurred) exacerbated her symptoms. She also began to experience very graphic rape-related nightmares. Maria frequently woke to find herself breathing rapidly and perspiring. She was not able to go back to sleep after these nightmares. Maria also avoided situations or places that reminded her of the assault. She avoided men and destroyed the dress that she had worn on the day of the assault. She also began to blame herself for what had happened. Maria reasoned that the assault would not have happened if she had not let her uncle into the house or if she had resisted in a more forceful manner. In addition, she began to experience pervasive feelings of sadness. She experienced difficulty in formulating decisions and began to lose weight. She felt less and less energetic.

While Maria did not inform her parents, they noticed that something was very wrong. Whereas she had been a sociable youth, she began to avoid friends and relatives. She lost interest in playing soccer and softball. Her parents noticed that Maria was becoming increasingly irritable and frequently remained in her bedroom for hours at a time. Although she had been a good student, her school grades deteriorated. Her arithmetic, spelling, and science scores were significantly below grade level as denoted by standardized exams. Her younger sister reported that Maria was crying and calling out in her sleep. One year after the assault, one of her teachers presented a lesson on sexual and physical abuse. Maria was surprised to learn that assault victims frequently suffer in silence because they harbor unjustified feelings of shame and guilt. Three days later, Maria told the teacher that she had been raped. While the teacher attempted to comfort her, she also said that she had to advise Maria's parents and the authorities about the allegation.

Maria's parents were shocked when they learned about the assault. Although they attempted to comfort their daughter, her distress was compounded when she was questioned by a child welfare caseworker. Her discomfort was further exasperated when she was reinterviewed by a prosecutor from the district attorney's office. Her uncle (who was interviewed in the presence of his lawyer) was not arraigned due to a perceived lack of evidence.

PETER

Peter, a 50-year-old Army veteran, was born and raised in a small town in Connecticut. He played on the high school football team and graduated with a C average in 1966. He had a pleasant childhood and enjoyed a warm relationship with his parents and two brothers. While in school, Peter served as an altar boy, and his parish priest later described him as "a fine young man, good, kind, and happy." He subsequently went to work in the construction industry and dated a woman that he had known in high school. Shortly after his high school graduation, Peter received a draft notice and was inducted into the U.S. Army on August 7, 1967.

He received his basic training at Fort Jackson, South Carolina and went on to attend artillery training at Fort Sill, Oklahoma. Following a 21-day leave, he was sent to a field artillery company on March 18, 1968. In this capacity he served as an artilleryman and was called on to provide fire support for U.S. and South Vietnamese forces. Peter was involved in multiple close engagements with the enemy. During one of these engagements, his unit had been providing support fire for a special forces South Vietnamese company. At the time, his unit's perimeter was being guarded by a company of U.S. 101st Airborne. Peter recalls that his captain warned that "Something is wrong. It's too quiet, we are going to get hit." He further recalls that at sunset trip flares went off and that a bleeding soldier ran into his hootch and said that he had been hit. Peter indicated that

Next, rounds were being fired and all hell broke loose and M-16s were going off all over. Then I realized that this was it and we all grabbed our M-16s. The Viet Cong had gotten through the Airborne guys guarding the perimeter. After a while our captain called for "bee hives" to be used. We use them when you are about to be over run. We readjusted the rounds and our gun was set to fire at point blank range. Anyone in front would be blown away. Our Airborne guys heard us yell that we were going to fire beehives and they knew what that meant. We tried to warn as many as we could and wait as long as possible before using them. Finally, we used one round after the other as it was really getting crazy at this point. The Viet Cong had already gotten through the perimeter and were coming for us. We ended up killing and wounding a lot of the enemy and many of our own men. I was the assistant gunner which meant I actually fired the gun. I pulled the trigger. At one point during the attack, I was standing at a wall made of sandbags and the captain yelled to me "Get your head down." He made everyone get out of the communication bunker and called for air support and medivacs. The enemy blew up the communication bunker with him inside. All

that remained was a charred body. You would never have believed that it was once a human being. We kept firing bee hives for most of the night. When fighting stopped at dawn, you could see bodies all over the ground. Before the assault, there were 47 men in my battery, afterwards, we had 14 left. Fourteen. We walked around dazed, confused, and depressed for days.

After 11 months in Vietnam, Peter was put on a helicopter and transported out of the field. Within a matter of days, he was flown back to San Francisco and given an honorable discharge. He returned to Connecticut and was given a warm welcome by his family. Although he had only been away for two years, Peter felt uncomfortable at home. He found it difficult to sleep and began to have nightmares about Vietnam. He also began to experience repeated and intrusive trauma-thoughts about his combat experiences. When his parents and former friends asked Peter about Vietnam, he declined to discuss his experiences.

Peter began to avoid the company of many of his former friends. He felt "different" and could not relate to many of the people that he had grown up with. He dated his former high school girlfriend and married after a brief engagement. Two years later, his wife requested and received a divorce. Peter experienced difficulty in concentrating and evidenced a startle response. He was always on guard and constantly checked his residence for intruders. Peter also began to experience sudden and overwhelming feelings of panic. While these episodes spontaneously remitted, he experienced palpitations, sweating, shortness of breath, chest pains, nausea, a fear of dying, and paresthesia during the attacks. Although he was repeatedly seen by a number of physicians, he consistently received negative diagnoses for physical ailments.

Shortly after his discharge, he went to work for his former employer. After six months on the job, a co-worker made a disparaging remark about Vietnam veterans. Peter recalled that he "seemed to snap." He subsequently learned that several workmen had to physically restrain him after he pummeled his verbal assailant. While charges were not filed, Peter lost his job. He went on to gain and lose employment with a number of firms. Peter has not been gainfully employed since 1987. He receives assistance from the Veteran's Administration for a service-connected disability (PTSD).

In addition to stress exposure, the DSM-III included four sets of polymorphic symptom clusters for making a PTSD diagnosis.

In keeping with the precedent that was set by DSM-III, the 1987 nosology indicated that PTSD may occur after a "psychologically distressing event that is outside the range of normal human experience" (APA, 1987, p. 247). While expanding the number of symptoms that were necessary to make a diagnosis and rearranging a number of diagnostic thresholds, it may be said that the DSM-III-R PTSD classification was quite analogous to its DSM-III predecessor.

The APA subsequently initiated a programmatic series of efforts toward the publication of the fourth edition of the DSM in 1988. Within this context, the DSM-IV PTSD work group reviewed the available literature relative to clinical PTSD phenomenology, epidemiology, and its relation to other disorders. This work group also performed a series of multisite clinical and community trials. The primary goal of these trials was to empirically examine relations between different stressors and PTSD symptoms. These trials also sought to establish if low magnitude stressors such as bereavement could induce PTSD. In addition, the likelihood that divergent stressful events could lead to symptoms of varying onset and duration was also explored. The research further sought to ascertain if the inclusion of additional symptoms would effect the prevalence of the disorder. Finally, event characteristics were assessed to identify variables that might be independently associated with PTSD without reference to the type of event that was experienced.

As earlier studies demonstrated that the stressors that could induce PTSD were relatively common, the DSM-IV PTSD work group withdrew the DSM-III and DSM-III-R provision that the stressor that induced the disorder must have been "outside the range of normal human experience." In its place, Criterion A was amended to require that a person had "experienced, witnessed, or been confronted with an event or events that involve actual or threatened death or serious injury, or a threat to the physical integrity to oneself or others" (APA, 1994, p. 428). The DSM-IV also rearranged a few of the DSM-III-R symptom clusters and adjusted diagnostic thresholds. Finally, the classification was revised to indicate that the disturbance must cause "clinically significant distress or impairment in social, occupational, or other important areas of functioning" (APA, 1994, p. 429).

While it is expected that the DSM-IV will not be amended for at least a decade, it is anticipated that future case-control studies that control for the confounding effects of comorbid disorders will be conducted. Over time, it may become evident that the DSM-IV PTSD criteria may not encompass the entire spectrum of symptoms that are associated with reactivity to traumatic stressors. In the future, there may be an increased focus on how symptoms of PTSD relate to other stress-related symptoms such as depression, personality disturbances, anxiety, dissociation, and substance abuse.

REFERENCES

Adler, A. (1943). Neuropsychiatric complications in victims of Boston's Coconut Grove disaster. *Journal of the American Medical Association, 123,* 1098–1101.

American Psychiatric Association. (1952). *Diagnostic and statistical manual of mental disorders.* Washington, DC: Author.

American Psychiatric Association. (1968). *Diagnostic and statistical manual of mental disorders* (2nd ed.). Washington, DC: Author.

American Psychiatric Association. (1980). *Diagnostic and statistical manual of mental disorders* (3rd ed.). Washington, DC: Author.

American Psychiatric Association. (1987). *Diagnostic and statistical manual of mental disorders* (3rd ed. Rev.). Washington, DC: Author.

American Psychiatric Association. (1994). *Diagnostic and statistical manual of mental disorders* (4th ed.). Washington, DC: Author.

Bender, L., & Blau, A. (1937). The reaction of children to sexual relations with adults. *American Journal of Orthopsychiatry, 7,* 500–518.

Bennet, G. (1968). Bristol floods of 1968: Controlled survey effects on health of local community disaster. *British Medical Journal, 298,* 454–458.

Bloach, H. S. (1969). Army clinical psychiatry in a combat unit. *American Journal of Psychiatry, 126,* 401–406.

Bloch, D. A., Silber, E., & Perry, S. E. (1956). Some factors in the emotional reaction of children to disaster. *American Journal of Psychiatry, 112,* 481–488.

Bodman, F. (1941). War conditions and the mental health of the child. *British Medical Journal, 11,* 486–488.

Bourne, P. G. (1970). Military psychiatry and the Vietnam experience. *American Journal of Psychiatry, 127,* 481–488.

Bradner, T. (1943). Psychiatric observations among Finnish children during the Russio-Finnish War of 1939–1940. *Nervous Child, 2,* 313–319.

Bremner, D. J., Southwick, S. M., Darnell, A., & Charney, D. S. (1996). Chronic PTSD in Vietnam combat veterans: Course of illness and substance abuse. *American Journal of Psychiatry, 153,* 369–375.

Breslau, N., Davis, G. C., Andreski, P., & Peterson, E. (1991). Traumatic events and posttraumatic stress disorder in an urban population of young adults. *Archives of General Psychiatry, 48,* 216–222.

Burgess, A. W., & Holmstrom, L. L. (1974). *American Journal of Psychiatry, 131,* 981–986.

Calhoun, K. S., & Resick, P. A. (1993). Posttraumatic stress disorder. In D. A. Barlow (Ed.), *Clinical handbook of psychological disorders: A step by step treatment manual* (pp. 48–80). New York: Guilford.

Chadoff, P. (1963). Late effects of the concentration camp syndrome. *Archives of General Psychiatry, 8,* 323–333.

Da Costa, J. M (1871). On irritable heart: A clinical study of a form of functional cardiac disorder and its consequences. *American Journal of Medical Science, 161,* 17–52.

Daly, R. J. (1983). Samuel Pepys and posttraumatic stress disorder. *British Journal of Psychiatry, 143,* 64–68.

Davidson, J. R. T., & Foa, E. B. (1993). Introduction. In J. R. T. Davidson & E. B. Foa (Eds.), *Posttraumatic stress disorder: DSM-IV and beyond* (pp. ix–xiii). Washington, DC: American Psychiatric Press.

Diamond, R., Saigh, P. A., & Fairbank, J. A. (in press). An analysis of internalizing and externalizing problems in preschool children with PTSD or ADHD. *Journal of Traumatic Stress.*

Edwards, R. M., & Peterson, D. B. (1954). Korea: Current psychiatric procedures and communication in the combat theater. *American Journal of Psychiatry, 110,* 721–724.

Ekbald, S. (1993). Psychological adaptation of children while housed in a Swedish refugee camp: Aftermath of the collapse of Yugoslavia. *Stress Medicine, 9,* 159–166.

Etinger, L. (1962). Concentration camp survivors in the postwar world. *American Journal of Orthopsychiatry, 32,* 367–375.

Freud, S. (1917) Fixation to traumas-the unconscious. In J. Strache (Ed.), (1966) *The complete introductory lectures on psychoanalysis* (pp. 274–275). New York: Norton.

Friedman, P. (1948). The effects of imprisonment. *Acta Medica Orientalia, 7,* 163–167.

Friedman, P., & Linn, L. (1957). Some psychiatric notes on the *Andrea Doria* disaster. *American Journal of Psychiatry, 113,* 426–432.

Glass, A. J. (1954). Psychotherapy in the combat zone. *American Journal of Psychiatry, 110,* 725–731.

Glass, A. J. (1973). Lessons learned. In W. S. Mullins (Ed.), *Neuropsychiatry in World War Two.* Volume 2 (pp. 989–1027). Washington, DC: Office of the Surgeon General, Department of the Army.

Glass, A. J., Ryan, F. J., Lubin, A., Reddy, C. V., & Tucker, A. C. (1956). *Psychiatric prediction and military effectiveness.* Washington, D.C.: Walter Reed Army Institute of Research, Walter Reed Army Medical Center.

Grinker, R. R., & Spiegel, J. P. (1945). *Men under stress.* Philadelphia: Blakiston.

Hastings, D., Wright, D., & Glueck, B. (1994). *Psychiatric experiences in the Eighth Air Force.* New York: Josiah Macy Foundation.

Hendriks, J. H., Black, D., & Kaplan, T. (1993). *When father kills mother: Guiding children through grief and trauma.* London: Routlidge.

Horowitz, M. D., & Solomon, G. F. (1975). A prediction of delayed stress response syndrome in Vietnam veterans. *Journal of Social Issues, 4,* 67–79.

Hurst, A. F. (1916). *Medical diseases of the war.* London: Edward Arnold.

Jablensky, A. (1985). Approaches to the definition and classification of anxiety and related disorders in European psychiatry. In A. H. Tuma & J. D. Masser (Eds.), *Anxiety and the anxiety disorders* (pp. 223–254). Hillsdale, NJ: Erlbaum.

Kardiner, A. (1941). *The traumatic neuroses of war.* New York: Hober.

Kardiner, A. (1969). Traumatic neuroses of war. In S. Arieti (Ed.), *American handbook of psychiatry* (pp. 246–257). New York: Basic Books.

Kesseler, R. C., Sonnega, A., Bromet, E., Hughes, M., & Nelson, C. B. (1995). Posttraumatic stress disorder in the *National Comorbidity Survey of General Psychiatry, 52,* 1048–1060.

Kilpatrick, D. G., Resnick, H. S., & Freedy, J. R. (1993). *DSM-IV post-traumatic stress disorder field trial:*

Criterion A and other stressor event histories associated with PTSD in clinical and community samples. Charleston, SC: Crime Victims Center, Medical University of South Carolina.

Kilpatrick, D. G., Veronen, L. J., & Resick, P. A. (1979). Assessment of the aftermath of rape: Changing patterns of fear. *Journal of Behavioral Assessment, 1,* 133–147.

Kinzie, J. D., Sack, W. H., Angell, R. H., Clarke, G., & Ben, R. (1989). A three year follow-up of Cambodian young people traumatized as children. *Journal of the American Academy of Child and Adolescent Psychiatry, 28,* 501–504.

Kinzie, J. D., Sack, W. H., Angell, R. H., & Mason, S. M. (1986). The psychiatric effects of massive trauma on Cambodian children. *Journal of the American Academy of Child and Adolescent Psychiatry, 25,* 370–376.

Kraepelin, E. (1896). *Psychiatrie Vol. 5: Auflage.* Leipzig: Barth.

Lacy, G. N. (1972). Observations on Aberfan. *Journal of Psychosomatic Research, 16,* 257–260.

Langdon, J. R., & Parker, A. H. (1964). Psychiatric aspects of the March 27, 1964 earthquake. *Alaska Medicine, 6,* 33–35.

Lewis, A. (1942). Incidence of war neurosis in England under war conditions. *Lancet, 2,* 175–183.

Lifton, R. J. (1954). Home by ship: Reactions of American prisoners of war repatriated from North Korea. *American Journal of Psychiatry, 110,* 732–739.

Mercer, M. H., & Despert, J. M. (1943). Psychological effects of the war on French children. *Psychosomatic Medicine, 5,* 266–272.

Morey, L. C., Skinner, H. A., & Blashfield, R. K. (1986). Trends in the classification of abnormal behavior. In A. R. Cimenaro, K. S. Kalhoun, & H. E. Adams (Eds.), *Handbook of behavioral assessment* (2nd ed.) (pp. 47–78). New York: Wiley.

Mott, F. W. (1919). *War neuroses and shell shock.* London: Oxford University Press.

Nadler, A., & Ben Shushan, D. (1989). Forty years later: Long term consequences of massive traumatization as manifested by holocaust survivors from the city and kibbutz. *Journal of Counseling and Clinical Psychology, 57,* 287–293.

Nobel, D., Roudebush, M., & Prince, D. (1952). Studies of Korean War combat casualties. Part I: Psychiatric manifestations of wounded men. *American Journal of Psychiatry, 108,* 495–499.

Panzarella, R. F., Mantell, D. M., & Bridenbaugh, R. H. (1978). Psychiatric symptoms, self-concepts, and Vietnam veterans. In C. R. Figely (Ed.), *Trauma and Its Wake* (pp. 148–172). New York: Brunner/Mazel.

Prasard, J. (1934). Psychology of rumors: A study of the great Indian earthquake of 1934. *British Journal of Psychology, 26,* 1–15.

Quarantelli, E. L. (1985). Assessment of conflicting values of mental health: The consequences of traumatic events. In C. R. Figely (Ed.), *Trauma and Its Wake* (pp. 173–218). New York: Brunner/Mazel.

Raines, G. N., & Kolb, L. C. (July, 1943). Combat fatigue and war neurosis. *U.S. Navy Medical Bulletin,* 923–926, 1299–1309.

Resnick, H. S., Kilpatrick, D. G., Dansky, B. S., Saunders, B. E., & Best, C. L. (1993). Prevalence of civilian trauma and posttraumatic stress disorder in a representative national sample of women. *Journal of Consulting and Clinical Psychology, 61,* 984–991.

Sack, W. H., McSharry, S., Kinney, R., Seeley, J., & Lewinson, P. (1994). The Khmer Adolescent Project I: Epidemiological findings in two generations of Cambodian refugees. *Journal of Nervous and Mental Diseases, 182,* 387–395.

Saigh, P. A. (1987). In vitro flooding of childhood posttraumatic stress disorder: A systematic replication. *Professional School Psychology, 2,* 135–146.

Saigh, P. A. (1991). On the development of posttraumatic stress disorder pursuant to different modes of traumatization. *Behaviour Research and Therapy, 29,* 213–217.

Saigh, P. A. (1992a). History, current nosology, and epidemiology. In P. A. Saigh (Ed.), *Posttraumatic stress disorder: A behavioral approach to assessment and treatment* (pp. 1–27). Boston, MA: Allyn & Bacon.

Saigh, P. A. (1992b). Verbally mediated childhood posttraumatic stress disorder. *British Journal of Psychiatry, 161,* 704–707.

Saigh, P. A., Green, B., & Korol, M. (1996). The history and prevalence of posttraumatic stress disorder in children and adolescents. *Journal of School Psychology, 34,* 107–132.

Saigh, P. A., Mroueh, M., & Bremner, D. J. (1997). Academic impairments among traumatized adolescents. *Behaviour Research and Therapy, 35,* 429–436.

Shatan, C. F. (1978). Stress disorders among Vietnam veterans. In C. R. Figely (Ed.), *Trauma and Its Wake* (pp. 43–56). New York: Brunner/Mazel.

Solomon, J. (1942). Reactions of children to blackouts. *American Journal of Orthopsychiatry, 12,* 361–364.

Southard, E. E. (1919). *Shell shock.* Boston: Leonard.

Strayer, R., & Ellenhorn, L. (1975). Vietnam veterans: A study exploring adjustment patterns and attitudes. *Journal of Social Issues, 31,* 81–93.

Trimble, M. R. (1981) *Post-traumatic neurosis. From railway spine to whiplash.* New York: Wiley.

Vernon, P. (1941). Psychological effects of air raids. *Journal of Abnormal and Social Psychology, 36,* 457–476.

Veronen, L. J., & Kilpatrick, D. G. (1979). Self-reported fears of rape victims: A preliminary investigation. *Behavior Modification, 4,* 383–396.

Widiger, T. A., Frances, A. J., Pincus, H. A., Davis, W., & First, M. (1991). Toward an empirical classification in the DSM-IV. *Journal of Abnormal Psychology, 100,* 280–288.

Wolf, S. & Ripley, H. (1947). Reactions among allied prisoners of war subjected to three years of imprisonment and torture by the Japanese. *American Journal of Psychiatry, 104,* 180–192.

CHAPTER 2

CHILD–ADOLESCENT POSTTRAUMATIC STRESS DISORDER: PREVALENCE, RISK FACTORS, AND COMORBIDITY

PHILIP A. SAIGH, PH.D.
City University of New York Graduate Center
New York University Medical Center

ANASTASIA E. YASIK, PH.D.
Columbia University School of Public Health

WILLIAM H. SACK, M.D.
Oregon Health Sciences University

HAROLD S. KOPLEWICZ, M.D.
New York University Medical Center

CHILD–ADOLESCENT POSTTRAUMATIC STRESS DISORDER: PREVALENCE AND RISK FACTORS

Epidemiology involves the study of health and morbidity in human populations (Fairbank, Schlenger, Saigh, & Davidson, 1995; Friedman, 1987; Klienbaum, Kupper, & Morgenstein, 1982). Typically, epidemiology focuses on the frequency of diseases in groups of people and specific factors that influence the distribution of illnesses among populations. Historically, this includes studies denoting the prevalence of disorders in populations, research that seeks association between a disorder of interest and other disorders, and the identification of particular factors that confer increased risk for the development of the disorder (Fairbank et al., 1995; Friedman, 1987; Klienbaum et al., 1982).

Within the context of psychiatric epidemiology, reliable information involving the prevalence of posttraumatic stress disorder (PTSD) among the general population as well as among populations that may be particularly vulnerable may facilitate our understanding of the nature and scope of the disorder (Saigh, Green, & Korol, 1996). Information involving the prevalence of PTSD may be of value to researchers who are interested in factors involving the etiology of the disorder. Prevalence estimates may also be used by policy makers who formulate decisions regarding the allocation of resources for prevention and intervention. Practical information regarding the prevalence of child-adolescent PTSD may also be of utility to clinicians who advise parents, teachers, and affected youth regarding the potential long-term sequela of highly stressful events.

Whereas community studies have not assessed the prevalence of PTSD among school-age populations, studies denoting the prevalence of child-adolescent PTSD following exposure to specific stressors have been conducted. In this chapter, we will examine the current epidemiological knowledge regarding child-adolescent PTSD. We will successively discuss research findings regarding exposure to extreme stress, the reported prevalence of PTSD, the comorbidity of PTSD with other disorders, and associated risk factors.

EPIDEMIOLOGY OF CHILD–ADOLESCENT EXPOSURE TO TRAUMATIC EVENTS

A number of surveys have investigated the prevalence of child–adolescent exposure to traumatic events (e.g., criminal victimization, serious accidents, and disasters) in the United States. For example, Hernandez (1992) surveyed randomly selected ninth graders from 94 percent of the schools in the Minnesota public school system. Of the 3,178 students that were interviewed, 10 percent said that they experienced some type of sexual abuse; 3 percent reported having been sexually abused within and outside their family; 2 percent reported only having experienced incest and 6 percent reported only having experienced extrafamilial sexual abuse. Hernandez also reported that sexually abused adolescents were more likely to report consumption of alcohol and drug use than nonabused youth. In a similar study, Bell and Jenkins (1993) surveyed 536 black elementary school students who were attending the second, fourth, sixth, or eighth grades at three inner city Chicago schools. Twenty-six percent of the students reported that they saw someone being shot and 30 percent said that they witnessed a stabbing. In the same study, Bell and Jenkins also interviewed 1,035 students who were attending four high schools and two middle schools within Chicago's east side. The Bell and Jenkins survey revealed that approximately 75 percent of the students reported witnessing one or more violent crimes. Twenty-three percent witnessed a murder, 39 percent witnessed a shooting, and 35 percent observed a stabbing. In terms of personal victimization, 11 percent reported having been shot at and 3 percent reported that they had been shot. Four percent of the youth said that they had been stabbed and 2.5 percent acknowledged that they had been sexually assaulted.

Also within the framework of adolescent exposure to crime in the United States, Singer, Anglin, Song, and Lunghofer (1995) administered an anonymous self-report questionnaire to 3,735 randomly selected students who were attending six schools in Ohio and Colorado. Singer et al.'s multisite data revealed that 33 percent to 44 percent (estimates varied across schools) of the male youth said that they had been punched, slapped, or hit at school. Three to 22 percent reported that they had been beaten or mugged in their neighborhoods. Moreover, 3 percent to 33 percent of the male youth indicated that they were shot at or shot within the preceding year and 6 percent to 16 percent reported being assaulted or stabbed by a knife. Male adolescents also reported high rates of witnessing violent events. Nine to 21 percent said that they saw someone being sexually abused or assaulted; 32 percent to 82 percent indicated that they witnessed others being beaten or mugged at school; 11 percent to 72 percent reported seeing someone being beaten or mugged within their neighborhood; 11 percent to 72 percent reported seeing someone attacked or stabbed with a knife; and 5 percent to 62 percent said they saw others shot at or actually shot.

Analogously, 34 percent to 56 percent of the female adolescents reported that they had been punched, slapped, or hit at home; 34 percent to 56 percent reported that they were attacked or actually stabbed with a knife; 0 percent to 9 percent said that they were shot at or actually shot; and 12 percent to 17 percent acknowledged being sexually abused or assaulted. Fifteen to 20 percent of the adolescent females said that they saw others being sexually abused or assaulted; 15 percent to 20 percent reported witnessing a beating or mugging in her neighborhood (incidence of witnessed neighborhood assault was not reported); 24 percent to 82 percent reported seeing others attacked or stabbed with a knife; 5 percent to 49 percent reported that they saw others being shot at or actually shot. Singer et al. (1995) further indicated that with the exceptions of physical victimization at home and sexual assault/abuse, the self-reported victimization rates among female adolescents were lower than the rates that were observed among adolescent males.

Although these surveys do not represent a systematic analysis of child–adolescent criminal victimization across the United States, the findings are concordant with the United States Department of Justice's national crime statistics (1994). These data indicate that approximately one and one-half million youth (ages 12–17) were assaulted, robbed, or raped in 1992. Whereas juveniles accounted for 10 percent of the U.S. population, 25 percent of all violent crimes involved juvenile victims in 1992. In terms of probability, one juvenile in 13 was the victim of a violent crime.

While the prevalence of child-adolescent exposure to accidents and disasters has received less study, the United States Department of Transportation (1993) reported that 894,000 United States youth (ages birth–20 years) were injured in motor vehicle accidents in 1992. In a similar vein, the United States Centers for Disease Control and Prevention reported that 8,714,000 youth under the age of 15 years made injury-related visits to hospital emergency departments in 1992 (Burt, 1995).

Given the child–adolescent stress exposure studies, it may be said that a sizable percentage of young people have been exposed to inordinate stress. Although community surveys involving the prevalence of PTSD have not been conducted with child–adolescent populations, a number of studies have been conducted with adults (Saigh et al., 1996). Breslau, Davis, Andreski, and Peterson (1991) administered the Diagnostic Interview Schedule (DIS; Robins, Helzer, Croughan, & Ratcliff, 1981) to 1,007 young adults (age range 21–30 years) within the Detroit metropolitan area. These authors reported that seeing others killed, injured, or experiencing an actual life threat produced a lifetime PTSD rate of approximately 25 percent. Rape-induced PTSD among 80 percent of the victims, and accidental injury resulted in a point prevalence of 12 percent among exposed subjects. The authors estimated that the lifetime rate of PTSD in the general population of young adults was approximately 9 percent. Similar investigations have estimated the prevalence of PTSD among more specialized populations. Kulka et al. (1990) reported lifetime PTSD rates of 31 percent (for males) and 27 percent (for females) among a representative national sample of Vietnam veterans. Resnick, Kilpatrick, Dansky, Saunders, and Best (1993) employed a random digit-dial procedure to sample 4,008 adult women in the southeastern United States. Resnick and her colleagues reported that 12.3 percent of the subjects had PTSD at one time in their lives (i.e., life-

time prevalence) and that 4.6 percent of the sample currently met criteria for PTSD.

PTSD PREVALENCE RATES AMONG CLINICAL SAMPLES OF STRESS-EXPOSED CHILDREN AND ADOLESCENTS

To date, a number of investigations have reported PTSD prevalence estimates among stress-exposed samples. The majority of this literature involves child or adolescent samples that were exposed to criminal victimization, war-related events, and industrial or natural disasters. Within this context, a review of the prevalence literature by stressor category will be presented. As structured interviews are generally more reliable than clinical interviews (Saigh, 1992; Spitzer, Endicott, & Robbins, 1978), the review will be limited to investigations that employed this assessment modality to identify cases. Given that different systems of classification influence morbidity estimates (Schwarz & Kowalski, 1991), the systems of classification that were employed will be specified by study. The interval between exposure to extreme stress and data collection will also be reported as the historical literature suggests that stress reactions generally remit over time (Carey-Trefzer, 1949; Kettner, 1972; Lewis, 1942; Rachman, 1990).

Crime-Related PTSD

Given the observed pervasiveness of criminal victimization among children and adolescents in America, it is not surprising to report that a number of investigators have described the prevalence of PTSD among affected youth. Taken in this context, Pynoos and his colleagues (1987) assessed a sample of children at a Los Angeles elementary school that experienced a sniper attack (one youth was killed and 13 were injured). One month after the incident, the DSM-III based Reaction Index (Frederick, 1985) was administered to 159 children. The authors determined that 60.4 percent of the subjects had PTSD. Nader, Pynoos, Fairbanks, and Frederick (1990) also performed a 14-month follow-up involving 100 of the

159 youths that were initially examined by Pynoos et al. (1987). Using the DSM-III Reaction Index, Nader and her colleagues observed a 19.0 percent point prevalence.

Following the World Trade Center bombing, Koplewicz et al. (1994) administered the Reaction Index (Frederick, Pynoos, & Nader, 1992) to 22 second, third, and fifth graders who were trapped in an elevator or stranded on the building's observation deck. The former group were ensconced in a dark elevator for several hours. The later group were forced to descend 107 flights in order to exit the building. Assessments were conducted at three and nine months after stress exposure. Of the 9 youth trapped in an elevator, 66 percent met criteria for PTSD three months following the incident. Nine months later, the authors determined that 55 percent met criteria. Of the 13 youth stranded on the observation deck, 69 percent met criteria for PTSD at three months and 53 percent met criteria for PTSD at nine months.

Burton, Foy, Bwanausi, Johnson, and Moore (1994) used the Foy, Sipprelle, Rueger, and Carroll (1984) Symptom Checklist to formulate DSM-III PTSD diagnoses among 91 male juvenile offenders who were incarcerated in Los Angeles. All of the subjects had evidenced a pattern of serious and consistent criminal behavior. Burton et al. reported that 22 (24.2 percent) of the subjects had PTSD. More recently, Pennoyer and Ellenhorn (1995) administered the DSM-III-R based Posttraumatic Supplement Module Interview Schedule for the Diagnostic Interview Schedule for Children 2.4 (DISC; Fisher, 1994) to 134 adolescents at two New York City public schools. Pennoyer and Ellenhorn reported that 32 subjects (23.9 percent) developed PTSD after experiencing and or observing incidents involving community or family violence.

McLeer, Deblinger, Atkins, Foa, and Ralphe (1988) screened 32 sexually abused children at a university-based outpatient child-adolescent psychiatry clinic. Although the interval between stress exposure and assessment was not reported, McLeer and her associates estimated that 48.4 percent of the subjects met criteria for PTSD as indicated by an author-constructed DSM-III-R PTSD checklist. Also within the context of child abuse, Deblinger, McLeer, Atkins,

Ralphe, and Foa (1989) used an author-devised DSM-III-R symptom checklist to formulate retrospective chart diagnoses. The subject pool consisted of 29 sexually abused, 29 physically abused, and 29 nonabused demographically matched children who attended a university child–adolescent inpatient psychiatric unit. Although the interval between stress exposure and assessment was not reported, the authors reported an overall PTSD point prevalence of 13.8 percent for the stress exposed inpatient samples combined. Famularo, Kinscherff, and Fenton (1989) also conducted a retrospective analysis of the symptomology of maltreated youth. Chart reviews of the court records of 115 children led to the identification of 22 sexually abused, 63 physically abused, and 30 sexually and physically abused subjects. An author-devised DSM-III-R PTSD symptom checklist was used to retrospectively diagnose PTSD. Famularo et al. subsequently reported that 24 youth (20.9 percent) had PTSD.

McLeer, Deblinger, Henry, and Orvaschel (1992) administered the Kiddie Schedule for Affective Disorders and Schizophrenia for School-Age Children Epidemiological Version (K-SADS-E; Orvaschel, Puig-Antich, Chambers, Tabrizi, & Johnson, 1982) and an author-developed DSM-III-R based PTSD checklist to 92 sexually abused children. Subjects were examined at a university hospital-based child sexual abuse center. McLeer and her colleagues reported that 39 subjects (42.4 percent) had been abused by their father or stepfather. Thirty-three subjects (35.9 percent) were abused by a trusted adult, 10 (19.9 percent) were abused by a stranger, and nine (9.8 percent) were abused by an older youth. Given this information, McLeer et al. reported PTSD point prevalence estimates of 53.8 percent, 42.4 percent, 10.0 percent, and 0.0 percent for the respective cohorts. In terms of the overall subject pool, 43.9 percent met criteria for PTSD.

In a related study, Famularo, Kinscherff, and Fenton (1992) used the DSM-III-R version of the Diagnostic Interview for Children and Adolescents (DICA-6-R; Reich & Welner, 1988) to assess 96 children (61 maltreated youth and 35 controls). The maltreated youth were drawn from an urban juvenile court and an outpatient pediatric clinic. The court sample involved youth whose parents were compelled to appear in court following petitions of child abuse. The hospital sample consisted of youth with two recently substantiated child abuse/neglect reports that had been filed with the Massachusetts Department of Social Services. The form of abuse (physical or sexual) and the interval between exposure and assessment were not specified. The control group were pediatric outpatients without a history of abuse or neglect. Famularo et al. (1992) observed a point prevalence of 39.3 percent among the maltreated youth and a 0.0 percent prevalence among the control group. In a related effort, Fitzpatrick and Boldizar (1993) administered the DSM-III-R based Purdue PTSD Scale (Figley, 1989) to 221 low income black youth who had experienced or witnessed criminal violence in Washington, D.C. Although the interval between stress exposure and assessment was not specified, Fitzpatrick and Boldizar determined that 54 children (27.1 percent of the sample) met DSM-III-R criteria for PTSD.

Livingston, Lawson, and Jones (1993) also used the DSM-III-R version of the DICA to evaluate 41 children. Twenty-six had been sexually abused and 15 had been physically abused. All of the subjects were the victims of repeated parental abuse that occurred within a year of the assessment. Livingston and his co-authors reported that 41.3 percent of the subjects met diagnostic criteria for PTSD. Pelcovitz et al. (1994) administered the DSM-III-R PTSD module of the Structure Clinical Interview (SCID; Spitzer, Williams, & Gibbon, 1987) to 27 court-referred adolescents with legally documented histories of intrafamilial physical abuse. The authors also administered the SCID to 27 demographically matched randomly selected controls. While three (11.1 percent) of the physically abused subjects received a PTSD diagnosis, their condition was attributed to incidents other than intrafamilial abuse (all of them developed PTSD following extrafamilial sexual assaults). Although three of the control subjects had been exposed to extreme stress (i.e., one was assaulted by a gang, a second saw the body of her brother following his suicide, and a third was the victim of a sexual assault), none of these subjects evidenced sufficient symptoms to warrant a PTSD diagnosis.

Also within the context of child abuse research, Merry and Andrews (1994) conducted a methodologically rigorous assessment of sexually abused youth in New Zealand. The DSM-III-R version of the Diagnostic Interview for Children-2 (DISC-2; Shaffer, Fisher, Piacenti, Schwab-Stone, & Wicks, 1989) was administered to 66 children. The subjects were recruited from child welfare agencies and examined three to six months after stress exposure. Data analysis revealed that 63.5 percent of the sexually abused children had at least one psychiatric disorder relative to the national base rate of 17.6 percent. In terms of PTSD prevalence, Merry and Andrews reported that 18.2 percent of their sample met PTSD criteria. In a related study, McLeer, Callaghan, Henry, and Wallen (1994) administered the epidemiological version of the K-SADS to 26 sexually abused children and 23 psychiatric controls. Both groups were receiving outpatient psychiatric services at university-based clinics. McLeer et al. reported that 42.3 percent of the sexually abused subjects and 8.7 percent of the psychiatric controls met DSM-III-R criteria for PTSD.

Wolfe, Sas, and Wekerle (1994) also administered an author devised DSM-III-R checklist to 90 Canadian children with court documented histories of sexual abuse. Data analysis determined a PTSD point prevalence of 48.9 percent. In a study involving preschool youth, Diamond, Saigh, and Fairbank (in press) administered the DSM-III based Children's PTSD Inventory (Saigh, 1989b) to 24 documented or suspected cases of physical abuse as denoted by the New York Social Services Law. The mean duration between stress exposure and assessment was six months. Seventeen children or 70.8 percent of the referred youth met criteria for PTSD on two independent administrations of the Children's PTSD Inventory.

Table 2.1 presents an overview of the crime-related child-adolescent PTSD studies. It is apparent that the point prevalence estimates ranged from 0.0 percent to 70.8 percent. Based on the six studies that reported the interval between stress exposure and data collection (Diamond et al., in press; Koplewicz et al., 1994; Livingston et al., 1993; Merry & Andrews, 1994; Nader et al., 1990; Pynoos et al., 1987), it may be seen that these intervals ranged from one month to one year.

TABLE 2.1 Prevalence of Criminal Victimization-Related PTSD

| STUDY | MEASURE | SUBJECTS | | ELAPSED TIME | PTSD PREVALENCE |
		GENDER	AGE		
Terrorist Acts					
Pynoos et al., 1987	DSM-III Reaction Index	80 males; 79 females	5–13 years	1 month	60.4%
Nader et al., 1990	DSM-III Reaction Index	100 youth; Gender not reported	Not reported	14 months	19.0%
Koplewicz et al., 1994	DSM-III-R Reaction Index	15 males; 34 females	Grades 2, 3, & 5	3 & 9 months	66% High Exposure (3 mos.) 69% Low Exposure (3 mos.) 55% High Exposure (9 mos.) 53% Low Exposure (9 mos.)
Criminal Victimization					
Fitzpatrick & Boldizar, 1993	DSM-III-R Purdue PTSD Scale	102 males; 119 females	mean age = 11.9 years	Not reported	27.1%
Burton et al., 1994	DSM-II Symptom Checklist	91 male offenders	mean age = 16 years	Not reported	24.2%
Pennoyer & Ellenhorn, 1995	DSM-III-R DISC 2.4	63 males; 71 females	mean age = 15 years	Not reported	23.9%
Sexual &/or Physical Abuse					
McLeer et al., 1988	DSM-III-R Author-devised interview	6 males; 25 females	mean age = 8.4 years	Not reported	48.4%
Deblinger et al., 1989	DSM-III-R Author-devised interview	46 males; 41 females	mean age = 8.8 years	Not reported	13.8%

Continued

TABLE 2.1 Continued

| STUDY | MEASURE | SUBJECTS | | | ELAPSED TIME | PTSD PREVALENCE |
		GENDER	AGE		
Famularo et al., 1989	DSM-III-R Author-devised interview	65 males; 50 males	mean age = 8.2 years	Not reported	20.9%
McLeer et al., 1992	DSM-III-R Author-devised interview & K-SADS-E	21 males; 71 females	mean age = 8.9 years	Not reported	43.9% Overall 53.8% Father 42.4% Adult 10.0% Stranger 0.0% Youth
Famularo et al., 1992	DSM-III-R DICA-C	27 males; 34 females	5–10 years	Not reported	39.3%
Livingston et al., 1993	DSM-III-R DICA-C	23 males; 18 females	mean age = 10.2 years	<1 year	46.3%
Pelcovitz et al., 1994	DSM-III-R SCID-PTSD	12 males; 15 females	mean age = 15.1 years	Not reported	11.1%
Merry & Andrews, 1994	DSM-III-R DISC-2	11 males; 55 females	mean age = 8 years	3–6 months	18.2%
McLeer et al., 1994	DSM-III-R K-SADS-E	17 males; 9 females	mean age = 9 years	Not reported	42.3%
Wolfe et al., 1994	DSM-III-R Author-devised interview	21 males; 69 females	mean age = 12.4 years	Not reported	48.9%
Diamond et al., in press	DSM-III Children's PTSD Inventory	14 males; 10 females	mean age = 4.98 years	mean = 6 months	70.8%

War-Related PTSD

Within the context of research that occurred during the Lebanese conflict, Saigh (1988a) conducted a prospective study involving 12 female students at the American University of Beirut. The course of PTSD (as measured by an author-devised DSM-III based structured interview) was charted 63 days before the subjects were exposed to a devastating artillery bombardment as well as 37 and 316 days later. While none of the subjects had PTSD before the bombardment, nine (75 percent) received an acute PTSD diagnosis when they were examined 37 days after the incident. Only one subject (or 8.3 percent of the sample) remained symptomatic 316 days after the bombardment. Clinical interviewing determined that the individual who developed PTSD (unlike her peers) was the only examinee to experience secondary trauma exposures. Saigh went on to note that this subject was aware of the fact that her neighborhood could have been shelled at any time. It was subsequently suggested that the initial trauma exposure coupled with secondary traumatic episodes may have served to prompt her aversive thought processes and the realization that her neighborhood could be shelled at any time may have maintained this distress.

As part of a study that examined the discriminant validity of the PTSD classification as it applies to adolescents, Saigh (1988b) administered the DSM-III version of the Children's PTSD Inventory to 92 Lebanese 13-year-olds. The subjects reportedly developed psychological and or academic difficulties after being exposed to war-related stressors. While the interval between stress exposure and assessment was not reported, Saigh determined that 27 subjects or 29.3 percent of the sample met criteria for PTSD. In a similar vein, Saigh (1989a) administered the DSM-III based Children's PTSD Inventory to 840 Lebanese children. These youth were referred for clinical evaluations by Red Cross personnel, physicians, mental health practitioners, and educators after exposure to extreme forms of war-related stress (e.g., an 11-year-old male indicated that "My arms, hands, legs were hit by shrapnel. I bled a lot and I had to go to the hospital."). Although the interval between stress exposure and assessment ranged from one to two years after the subjects' stressful experiences, 231 subjects, or 32.5 percent of the sample, met diagnostic criteria for PTSD.

Also within the context of Lebanese war-related research, Saigh, Fairbank, and Gross (1990) administered the DSM-III version of the Children's PTSD Inventory to 200 Lebanese children with a mean age of 9.6 years. The investigators reported that 93 children (46.5 percent of the sample) had PTSD. Saigh, Mroueh, Zimmerman, and Fairbank (1995) also administered the same instrument to 85 non-referred students at four Lebanese schools. Although 20 subjects had histories involving exposure to extremely stressful war-related events, only 10 cases (8.5 percent of the overall sample or 50.0 percent of the stress-exposed subjects met criteria for PTSD. More recently, Saigh, Mroueh, and Bremner (1997) examined the prevalence of PTSD among 95 non-referred Lebanese adolescents that were enrolled in six Lebanese secondary schools. The authors administered the DSM-III Children's PTSD Inventory and the DSM-III-R Severity of Psychological Stress Scale: Children and Adolescents (APA, 1987) to these youth. Saigh et al. (1997) determined that 30 subjects had been exposed to extreme war-related stressors. Fourteen adolescents met DSM-III criteria for PTSD (46.7 percent of the subjects that were exposed to extreme stress or 14.7 percent of the entire subject pool).

Examined from the perspective of the Cambodian conflict, Kinzie and his colleagues (Kinzie, Sack, Angell, Clarke, & Ben, 1989; Kinzie, Sack, Angell, Mason, & Ben, 1986) described the psychiatric morbidity of a sample of Cambodian adolescents who emigrated to America after the fall of the violent Pol Pot regime (1975–1979). Between the ages of 8 to 12 years, the subjects suffered "catastrophic trauma caused by separation from their families, forced labor, starvation, personal injuries, and the witnessing of many deaths and executions" (Kinzie et al., 1989, p. 501). Kinzie et al. (1986) administered the DIS to 40 subjects approximately 2.5 years after their immigration to the United States and observed that 50 percent met criteria for PTSD. Three years later, Kinzie et al. (1989) located and re-examined 27 of the Cambodian subjects. Of these, 13 (48 percent) met criteria for PTSD as measured by the DSM-III-R version of the DIS. Interestingly, 61.5 percent of the subjects that initially met criteria for PTSD continued to do so at the three-year follow-up.

In a six-year follow-up, Sack et al. (1993) administered the DSM-III-R version of the DICA (Welner, Reich, Herjanic, Jung, & Amando, 1987) to 19 of the 40 original Pol Pot survivors. Of the 19 subjects who were examined across assessment dates, 52 percent had PTSD in 1984, 47 percent in 1987, and 32 percent in 1990. In a similar study, Realmuto et al. (1992) administered the DSM-III-R version of the Reaction Index (Pynoos et al., 1987) to 47 Cambodian refugees who were residing in Minnesota. Realmuto and his colleagues went on to observe that 37 percent of the subjects met criteria for PTSD. Analogously, Hubbard, Realmuto, Northwood, and Masten (1995) administered the DSM-III-R SCID to 59 Cambodian refugees also residing in Minnesota. A point prevalence of 24 percent was observed for PTSD and a lifetime prevalence of 59 percent was also noted. Also within the context of Cambodian adolescent survivors of the Pol Pot, Clarke, Sack, Ben, Lanham, and Him (1993) administered the DSM-III-R version of the DICA to 39 Khmer youth. Although these youth had resided in America for 6.3 years, 46.2 percent had war-related PTSD. Sack et al. (1994) also conducted an elegant investigation wherein DSM-III-R version of the DICA was administered to 209 Pol Pot survivors who had resided in the United States for three to nine years (approximately 13 years after stress exposure). In this study, subjects were randomly selected and examined for PTSD as well as comorbid conditions. A point prevalence of 18.2 percent was observed for PTSD and a lifetime prevalence of 21.5 percent was also noted.

In an effort to establish the incidence of war-related PTSD of Cambodian refugees without the confounding effects of resettlement stress, Savin, Sack, Clarke, Meas, and Richart (1996) administered a Khmer version of the DSM-III-R DICA to 99 Khmer youth. Although the subjects had resided in the uncertain safety of a Thai refugee camp for 10 years, 26.3 percent of the subjects met diagnostic criteria for Pol Pot related PTSD and 31.3 percent had a lifetime prevalence of the disorder. Subjects who had experienced refugee camp trauma tended to show subthreshold symptoms of PTSD.

Within the context of the Persian Gulf War, Nader et al. (1993) administered the DSM-III-R version of the Reaction Index to 51 subjects who were attending a Kuwait summer school. Data collection took place five months after Iraqi forces withdrew from Kuwait. Nader et al. reported that 70 percent of the subjects met criteria for PTSD. Also within the context of the Gulf War, Weisenberg, Schwarzwald, Waysman, Solomon, and Klingman (1993) administered a modified version of the DSM-III-R Reaction Index to 492 Israeli children who were enrolled in grades 5 through 10. Many of the subjects that were examined had remained in hermetically sealed rooms and worn gas masks during Iraqi missile attacks. It was estimated that 24.9 percent of the children had PTSD as based on assessments that occurred three weeks after the war. In a very similar study that was conducted six weeks after the Gulf War, Schwarzwald, Weisenberg, Waysman, Solomon, and Klingman (1993) administered a DSM-III-R Hebrew adaptation of the Reaction Index to 225 Israeli youth who enrolled in grades 5, 7, and 10. These authors reported that 22.1 percent of the subjects had PTSD. In a comparable study that occurred one year after the Gulf War, Schwarzwald, Weisenberg, Solomon, and Waysman (1994) administered the Hebrew adaptation of the DSM-III-R Reaction Index to 144 Israeli youth who enrolled in grades six through eleven. In this instance, Schwarzald and his colleagues (1994) reported a point prevalence of 12.0 percent.

Table 2.2 presents an overview of epidemiological data relative to war-related child-adolescent PTSD. Examined in this context, it is apparent that the point prevalence estimates ranged from 8.3 percent to 75 percent. Based on the studies that reported the interval between stress exposure and data collection (Clarke et al., 1993; Kinzie et al., 1986, 1989; Nader et al., 1993; Sack et al., 1993, 1994; Saigh, 1988a, 1989a; Saigh et al., 1990, 1995, 1997; Savin et al., 1996; Weisenberg et al., 1993), it may be seen that the intervals ranged from 37 days to 18 years.

Although prevalence estimates varied between studies, the reported PTSD rates that were observed by 13 of the 18 war-related investigations that were reviewed exceed the 30.6 percent overall lifetime prevalence that was observed by the methodologically

TABLE 2.2 Prevalence of War-Related PTSD

| STUDY | MEASURE | SUBJECTS | | ELAPSED TIME | PTSD PREVALENCE |
		GENDER	AGE		
Lebanese Conflict					
Saigh, 1988a	DSM-III Author-devised interview	12 females	mean age = 18.2 years	37 & 316 days	75% at 37 days 8.3% at 316 days
Saigh, 1988b	DSM-III Children's PTSD Inventory	42 males; 50 males	13 years	Not reported	29.3%
Saigh, 1989a	DSM-III Children's PTSD Inventory	403 males; 437 females	9–12 years	1–2 years	32.5%
Saigh et al., 1990	DSM-III Children's PTSD Inventory	98 males; 102 females	mean age = 9.6 years	mean = 1.8 years	46.5%
Saigh et al., 1995	DSM-III Children's PTSD Inventory	48 males; 37 females	mean age = 13 years	mean = 1.8 years	8.5% overall sample 50% stress-exposed
Saigh et al., 1997	DSM-III Children's PTSD Inventory	48 males; 47 females	mean age = 17.5 years	mean = 4.2 years	46.7% stress-exposed 14.7% overall sample
Cambodian Conflict					
Kinzie et al., 1986	DSM-III DIS	25 males; 15 females	mean age = 17 years	mean = 2.5 years	50%
Kinzie et al., 1989	DSM-III-R DIS	16 males; 17 females	mean age = 20 years	mean = 5.5 years	48%

(continued)

TABLE 2.2 Continued

STUDY	MEASURE	SUBJECTS			ELAPSED TIME	PTSD PREVALENCE
		GENDER	AGE			
Sack et al., 1993	DSM-III-R DICA	N=19; gender not reported	mean age = 23 years		12–18 years	52% at 12 years 47% at 15 years 32% at 18 years
Realmuto et al., 1992	DSM-III-R Reaction Index	37 males; 10 females	mean age = 17.5 years		Not reported	37%
Hubbard et al., 1995	DSM-III-R SCID	29 males; 30 males	mean age = 20 years		15 years	24% Point prevalence 59% Lifetime prevalence
Clarke et al., 1993	DSM-III-R DICA	Not reported	mean age = 17.7		6.3 years	46.2%
Sack et al., 1994	DSM-III-R DICA	104 males; 105 females	13–25 years		13 years	18.2% Point prevalence 21.5% Lifetime prevalence
Savin et al., 1996	DSM-III-R DICA	89 males; 10 females	18–25 years		10 years	26.3% Point prevalence 31.3% Lifetime prevalence
Persian Gulf War						
Nader et al., 1993	DSM-III-R Reaction Index	16 males; 35 females	8–21 years		5 months	70%
Weisenberg et al., 1993	DSM-III-R Reaction Index	227 males; 265 females	grades 5–10		3 weeks	24.9%
Schwarzwald et al., 1993	DSM-III-R Reaction Index	162 males; 65 females	grades 5, 7, & 10		Not reported	22.1%
Schwarzwald et al., 1994	DSM-III-R Reaction Index	86 males; 58 females	grades 6–11		Not reported	12.0%

rigorous national survey of Vietnam veterans (Kulka et al., 1990).

Disaster-Related PTSD

To date, a number of investigations have examined the prevalence of PTSD among youth who were exposed to industrial hazards, earthquakes, floods, hurricanes, fires, or serious accidents. Within the context of industrial hazards, Handford et al. (1986) administered an author-developed PTSD inventory to 35 children approximately one and one-half years after the Three Mile Island nuclear accident. Whereas the subjects resided within 30 miles of the damaged reactor, none met DSM-III criteria for PTSD. Analogously, Korol (1990) administered an abbreviated version of the DSM-III-R Reaction Index to 120 youth who resided within a five mile radius of a weapons facility that was exposed to nuclear contamination. Assessments were conducted approximately five years after the residents were told that the area had been affected. Korol reported that 5.0 percent of the sample had PTSD. While the aforementioned investigations involved stressors that were relatively inconspicuous, the prevalence of child-adolescent PTSD has been reported following more discernable disasters.

Earls, Smith, Reich, and Jung (1988) administered the DSM-III version of the DICA to 32 youth who were exposed to a flood and dioxin contamination. Based on assessments that took place one year following exposure, it was determined that none of the subjects qualified for a PTSD diagnosis. In a similar vein, Green et al. (1991) reanalyzed data that had been collected following the tragic Buffalo Creek dam collapse. Green and her colleagues reviewed the case files (recorded two years after the incident) of 179 children and determined that 37 percent of the overall sample met "probable" criteria for PTSD (PTSD was not recognized as a psychiatric disorder when the data were collected).

A number of researchers have also examined the emotional morbidity that may occur after an earthquake. Bradburn (1991) administered the DSM-III-R Reaction Index to 22 children six to eight months after the 1989 San Francisco earthquake. Bradburn reported that 63 percent met criteria for PTSD. One and

one-half years after the 1988 Armenian earthquake, Goenjian et al. (1995) administered the DSM-III-R Reaction Index to 218 youth who resided in three cities that were located at varying distances from the epicenter of the earthquake. The first cohort lived in Spitak, a city very near the epicenter that was virtually destroyed. In terms of traumatic stressors, 14 percent lost a parent, 25 percent lost a nuclear family member, and 90 percent experienced the loss of their homes. The second cohort resided in Gumri, a city 20 miles from the epicenter. In this instance 16 percent reportedly lost a parent, 31 percent lost a nuclear family member, and 76 percent lost their homes. The third cohort resided in Yerevan, a city 47 miles from the epicenter. These subjects were exposed to less traumatic events as none of them lost a parent, nuclear family member, or their homes. Of the combined sample, 65.1 percent met DSM-III-R criteria for PTSD. Although the youth from Spitak and Gumri reportedly experienced approximately similar percentages of parental and nuclear family loss, Goenjian and his colleagues reported that 95 percent, 71 percent, and 26 percent of the respective cohorts met criteria for PTSD.

Two and one-half years after the same earthquake, Najarian, Goenjian, Pelcovitz, Mandel, and Najarian (1996) conducted a similar study wherein the DSM-III-R DICA-R-A (Kaplan & Reich, 1991) was administered to three groups of children. The first group continuously resided in the city of Gumri. The second group were residents of Gumri that were relocated with their families to the less damaged city of Yerevan. The third group consisted of subjects who were permanent residents of Yerevan. Najarian and his colleagues determined that 30.6 percent of the current and former residents of Gumri met criteria for PTSD. It was also reported that only one of the Yerevan subjects (4 percent of the sample) had PTSD.

A score of studies have investigated the effects of hurricanes on children and adolescents. Three months after Hurricane Hugo, Shannon, Lonigan, Finch, and Taylor (1994) administered the DSM-III-R version of the Reaction Index to 5,687 school-age children who resided in areas of South Carolina that had been extensively damaged by the hurricane. Data analysis determined that 5.4 percent of the sample exhibited

PTSD. Analogously, Garrison, Weinrich, Hardin, Weinrich, and Wang (1993) conducted a school-based investigation at three South Carolina high schools. Two of the schools were located in areas that experienced a great deal of hurricane damage and 328 injuries. The third school was located in an area that experienced less damage and 30 injuries. The authors developed and administered a DSM-III-R PTSD questionnaire to 1,264 subjects. They went on to report that 5 percent of the subjects met criteria for PTSD.

Eight weeks following Hurricane Andrew, Shaw et al. (1995) administered the DSM-III-R Reaction Index to 144 children who resided in two areas of southern Florida. The first group had resided in Homestead and were exposed to severe hurricane-related stressors (e.g., 56.5 percent reported that their roofs had blown away or caved in and 16.1 percent reported that someone in their family had been hurt). The second group resided in North Miami and were exposed to less severe stressors (e.g., 4.6 percent reported that their roofs had blown away or caved in and 0.0 percent reported that someone in their family had been hurt). Shaw and his colleagues (1995) determined that 87 percent of the children from the high impact area and 80 percent of the children from the less affected area had PTSD. LaGreca, Silverman, Vernberg, and Prinstein (1996) administered the DSM-III-R version of the Reaction Index to 442 children who resided in southern Dade county. Data collection occurred 3, 7, and 10 months after the hurricane struck the area. LaGreca et al. reported that 29.8 percent, 18.1 percent, and 12.5 percent of the children met PTSD criteria during the respective assessments. Interestingly, a somewhat lower prevalence was reported by Garrison et al. (1995). In this instance the DIS (Kilpatrick, Resnick, Saunders, & Best, 1989) was administered to 400 adolescents and a point prevalence of 7.3 percent was observed. Also within the context of longitudinal research involving Hurricane Andrew, Shaw, Applegate, and Schorr (1996) readministered the Reaction Index to 30 of the subjects that were previously examined. Data collection occurred 21 months post hurricane and a point prevalence of 70.0 percent was reported.

McFarlane (1987) conducted a longitudinal assessment of 808 Australian children who were exposed to a rural brush fire. In terms of reported exposure to traumatic events, 32 percent sustained property damage; 25 percent of the fathers, 13 percent of the mothers, and 8 percent of the children had an intense exposure to the fire or came close to death; 27 percent were bereaved; and 25 percent of the children had been separated from their parents for up to three days after the fire. McFarlane administered DSM-III adaptations of Rutter's Parent Questionnaire (Rutter, Tizard, & Whitmore, 1970) and Teacher Questionnaire (Rutter & Graham, 1967) 8 and 26 months after the fire. As based on parental ratings, PTSD point prevalence estimates of 52.8 percent and 57.2 percent were observed during the first and second assessment. The teacher ratings that were made during the same intervals yielded estimates of 29.5 percent and 26.3 percent.

With regard to accident research, Milgram, Toubiana, Klingman, Raviv, and Goldstein (1988) administered a Hebrew version of DSM-III Reaction Index to 410 Israeli seventh graders. Data collection occurred one week and 9 months after a catastrophic school bus accident. Milgram and his coauthors reported that one of several buses that were on route to a school outing was struck by a train. The accident claimed the lives of 19 children and 3 adults. The authors examined 108 youth who witnessed the catastrophic aftermath of the accident from an accompanying bus. Milgram et al. also examined 302 children that were on buses that had been stopped and diverted to the school. One week after the incident, they determined that 52.0 percent of the students who were at the scene of the accident and 58.6 percent of the students that were on the diverted buses had acute PTSD. In terms of total prevalence, 57.1 percent had acute PTSD. Eight months later, 19.7 percent of the combined subjects evidenced PTSD.

Stoddard, Norman, and Murphy (1989) administered the child and parent versions of the DSM-III based DICA (Herjanic & Reich, 1982) to 30 pediatric burn victims. All of the subjects were electively hospitalized at a pediatric burn center for reconstructive surgery. Stoddard and his colleagues reported that the mean interval between burn injury and data collection was 8.9 years. Using a consensual diagnosis model that was based on the child and parent DICA interviews as well as clinical interviews, Stoddard et al. reported a lifetime PTSD prevalence of 53.3 percent and a current prevalence of 6.7 percent. Stoddard and his colleagues also reported that 26.7 percent of the subjects had subthreshold PTSD symptoms.

Table 2.3 presents an overview of epidemiological data relative to disaster-accident child-adolescent PTSD. Examined in this context, it is apparent that the point prevalence estimates ranged from 0.0 percent to 95 percent. The interval between stress exposure and data collection ranged from 7 days to 8.9 years.

COMORBIDITY

With respect to psychiatric diagnoses, comorbidity refers to the co-occurrence of two or more psychiatric conditions in the same individual. Whereas information relative to comorbidity could have implications relative to understanding the etiology, course, and treatment of PTSD (Fairbank et al., 1995), a number of studies to date have examined the prevalence of comorbid conditions (e.g., substance abuse, major depression, and anxiety disorders) in adult patients with PTSD (Kulka et al., 1990). Considerably fewer studies have reported on the prevalence of comorbid conditions (e.g., ADHD, major depression, and conduct disorder) among children and adolescents with PTSD. In effect, 9 of the 51 (17.6 percent) studies reviewed utilized structured clinical interviews to determine the prevalence of comorbid psychiatric diagnoses among youth with PTSD.

Using the K-SADS-E, McLeer et al. (1994) reported that 23.1 percent of the sexually abused youth had PTSD and attention deficit hyperactive disorder (ADHD); 15.4 percent had PTSD and conduct disorder (CD); and 11.5 percent had PTSD, ADHD, and CD. Similar clusters were not observed among a psychiatric comparison group. The authors also reported that PTSD was not the most frequently diagnosed disorder among the sexually abused subjects as 46.0 percent met diagnostic criteria for ADHD. Merry and Andrews (1994) employed the DISC-II and reported that only 16.7 percent of the sample had PTSD without a comorbid condition. Separation anxiety was evidenced among 41.6 percent of the youth with PTSD. Twenty-five percent of the youth with PTSD met cri-

teria for oppositional defiant disorder and 25 percent had PTSD and ADHD. Major depression was denoted among 16.7 percent of the youth with PTSD. Overanxious disorder, functional enuresis, and depressive disorder (NOS) were noted among 8.3 percent of the PTSD sample. In a similar study, Diamond et al. (in press) utilized the DICA-R-P (Reich, Shayka, & Taibleson, 1991) to examine comorbidity among 17 physically abused preschool youth who met criteria for PTSD. One (5.8 percent) subject met criteria for ADHD and another (5.8 percent) met criteria for a speech disorder.

Kinzie and his colleagues (1986) administered the Schedule for Affective Disorders and Schizophrenia (SADS; Spitzer & Endicott, 1979) to Cambodian youth and determined that 85 percent met criteria for PTSD and unspecified affective disorders. Kinzie et al. (1986) also reported that 15 percent had panic disorder and 35 percent had unspecified anxiety disorders. None of the subjects received a positive diagnosis for schizophrenia, drug or alcohol abuse, or antisocial conduct. Kinzie et al. (1989) also employed the SADS and determined that 76.9 percent of the Cambodian subjects who meet criteria for PTSD also met criteria for unspecified affective disorders. Comorbid panic disorder was observed among 7.7 percent of the sample.

Sack et al. (1994) administered the DSM III-R Kiddie Schedule for Affective Disorders and Schizophrenia for School-Age Children (K-SADS; Puig-Antich, Orvaschel, Tabrinzi, & Chambers, 1980) to a sample of Cambodian youth with PTSD as well as a matched cohort of stress-exposed PTSD negatives. Their analysis established that the PTSD subjects had a significantly greater prevalence of unspecified depressive disorders (62 percent versus 27 percent), unspecified anxiety disorders (22 percent versus 6 percent) and overanxious disorder (11 percent versus 3 percent) relative to the stress exposed PTSD negatives. In addition, 10.5 percent of the youth with PTSD met criteria for panic disorder or conduct disorder. Sack et al. (1993) employed the K-SADS-E in a six-year follow-up study and reported that none of the Cambodian subjects with PTSD met criteria for conduct disorder, substance-related disorders or major psychoses. Sixty percent of the subjects with

TABLE 2.3 Prevalence of Disaster/Accident-Related PTSD

| STUDY | MEASURE | SUBJECTS | | | ELAPSED TIME | PTSD PREVALENCE |
		GENDER	AGE			
Nuclear Contamination						
Handford et al., 1986	DSM-III Author-devised Inventory	16 males; 19 females	6–19 years		1.5 years	0.0%
Korol, 1990	DSM-III-R Reaction Index	120 females	7–15 years		5 years	5.0%
Flooding						
Earls et al., 1988	DSM-III DICA	16 males; 16 females	6–17 years		1 year	0.0%
Dam Collapse						
Green et al., 1991	Author-devised checklist	179 youth; Gender not reported	2–15 years		2 years	37% "Probable" PTSD
Earthquakes						
Bradburn, 1991	DSM-III-R Reaction Index	12 males; 10 females	10–12 years		6–8 months	63%
Goenjian et al., 1995	DSM-III-R Reaction Index	82 males; 136 females	mean = 13 years		1.5 years	95% Hi-Impact 71% Moderate-Impact 26% Lo-Impact
Najarian et al., 1996	DSM-III-R DICA-R-A	37 males; 37 females	11–13 years		2.5 years	30.6% Moderate-Impact 5.0% Lo-Impact
Hurricanes						
Shaw et al., 1995	DSM-III-R Reaction Index	71 males; 73 females	mean = 8.2 years		8 weeks	87% Hi-Impact 80% Lo-Impact

Study	Measure	Sample	Age	Assessment	Prevalence
Shannon et al., 1994	DSM-III-R Reaction Index	2787 males; 2900 females	9–19 years	3 months	5.4%
Garrison et al., 1993	DSM-III-R Author-devised interview	600 males; 664 females	11–17 years	1 year	5.0%
LaGreca et al., 1996	DSM-III-R Reaction Index	187 males; 255 females	Grades 3–5	3, 7, & 10 months	29.8% at 3 months, 18.1% at 7 months, 12.5% at 10 months
Shaw et al., 1996	DSM-III-R Reaction Index	30 youth; Gender not reported	7–13 years	21 months	70%
Garrison et al., 1995	DSM-III-R DIS	189 males; 211 females	12–17 years	6 months	7.25%
Fires					
McFarlane, 1987	DSM-III Rutter Parent & Teacher Questionnaire	427 males; 381 females	mean age = 8.2 years	8 & 26 months	52.8% at 8 months (Parent), 57.2% at 26 months (Parent), 29.5% at 8 months (Teacher), 26.3% at 26 months (Teacher)
Stoddard et al., 1989	DSM-III DICA	13 males; 17 females	mean age = 13.3 years	8.9 years	53.3% Lifetime prevalence, 6.7% Current prevalence, 26.7% Subthreshold PTSD
School Bus Accident					
Milgram et al., 1988	DSM-III Reaction Index	Gender not reported	Grade 7	1 week & 9 months	57.1% at 1 week, 52.0% direct witness, 58.6% diverted buses, 19.7% at 9 months

PTSD also met criteria for major depression and 15 percent met criteria for unspecified anxiety disorders. Clarke et al. (1993) reported 13.5 percent of their sample of Cambodian subjects with PTSD also met criteria for major depression as generated through DICA-R diagnoses. Also within the context of the Cambodian conflict, Hubbard et al. (1995) used the SCID to assess comorbid disorders among youth with PTSD. Major depression, generalized anxiety disorder, and social phobia were respectively evidenced among 21 percent of youth with PTSD. Somatoform pain was observed among 29 percent of the youth that were sampled.

Table 2.4 presents an overview of the epidemiological data involving comorbidity.

RISK FACTORS

A number of studies have explored the association between a variety of risk factors and child-adolescent PTSD. To date, these variables have involved: (a) the intensity of the stressor, (b) interval between stress exposure and evaluation, (c) variations in type and mode of traumatic exposure, (d) duration and number of stress exposures, (e) pre- and post-trauma exposure to traumatic stress, (f) age, (g) gender, (h) ethnicity, (i) resettlement stress or relocation, (j) relation between the victims or perpetrators, and (k) parental psychopathology.

Intensity of Stressor.   Within the context of the California school shooting, Pynoos et al. (1987) reported that the prevalence of PTSD increased as a function of the severity of stress exposure as children who were in the area where the incident occurred had a higher prevalence of PTSD (94.3 percent) than youth who were in the school building (88.9 percent), at home (44.2 percent) or on vacation (45.1 percent). In contrast, Koplewicz et al. (1994) reported that level of stress exposure was not predictive of PTSD as prevalence rates among youth who experienced high and low life threat during the World Trade Center bombing were comparable (66 percent and 69 percent). Schwarzwald et al. (1994) also reported that Israeli youth who resided in areas that were hit by Scud missiles had a higher prevalence of PTSD (24.9 percent)

than youth who resided in areas that escaped the bombardment (12.9 percent). Analogously, Schwarzwald et al. (1993) reported that youth whose homes had been hit had a higher prevalence of PTSD (23.8 percent) than youth whose homes had not been hit (9.1 percent). Saigh et al. (1997) also drew an association between stressor intensity and the development of PTSD among Lebanese adolescents.

Bradburn (1991) determined that PTSD was significantly associated with the intensity of exposure to the 1989 San Francisco earthquake as children who resided within a mile of a collapsed freeway were more likely to have PTSD (50.0 percent) than youth who lived further away (8.3 percent). Goenjian et al. (1995) also reported that Armenian child-adolescent earthquake survivors from high and moderate impact areas had a higher prevalence of PTSD (80.6 percent) than youth residing in a less affected area (26.0 percent). Comparable findings were reported by Najarian and his colleagues (1996) as these authors determined that youth who resided in a city that was severely damaged by the Armenian earthquake had a higher prevalence of PTSD (30.6 percent) than youth who resided in the city that experienced very little damage (4 percent). While not reporting prevalence data, Garrison and her colleagues (1993) as well as LaGreca et al. (1996) reported that intensity of hurricane exposure and the extent of life threat were predictive of PTSD. Analogously, McFarlane (1987) determined that the intensity of children's exposure to an Australian bush fire was highly correlated with the diagnosis. Green et al. (1991) also reported that severity of life threat among the survivors of the Buffalo Creek flood was predictive of PTSD.

On the other hand, Shaw et al. (1995) failed to observe a significant difference between the prevalence estimates of the youth that resided in areas that received high and low exposures to Hurricane Andrew. Also contrary to expectations, Milgram et al. (1988) reported that being at the scene of the Israeli school bus accident conferred no greater psychological threat for developing PTSD (43.5 percent) than being on the buses that were diverted away (40.7 percent).

Time Interval.   While Pynoos et al. (1987) reported that 60.4 percent of the youth who experienced the

TABLE 2.4 Prevalence of Comorbid Psychiatric Diagnoses with PTSD

STUDY	DIAGNOSTIC MEASURE	COMORBID PSYCHIATRIC DIAGNOSES	PREVALENCE OF COMORBIDITY WITH PTSD
Crime-Related PTSD			
McLeer et al., 1994	DSM-III-R K-SADS-E	Attention Deficit-Hyperactivity disorder (ADHD)	23.1%
		Conduct disorder	15.4%
		Both (ADHD & conduct disorder)	11.5%
Merry & Andrews, 1994	DSM-III-R DISC-2	Separation anxiety	41.6%
		Oppositional defiant disorder	25.0%
		ADHD	25.0%
		Major depression	16.7%
		Overanxious disorder	8.3%
		Functional enuresis	8.3%
		Depressive disorder—NOS	8.3%
Diamond et al., in press	DICA-P	ADHD	5.8%
War-Related PTSD			
Kinzie et al., 1986	DSM-III SADS	Affective disorder	85.0%
		Panic disorder	15.0%
		Unspecified anxiety disorders	35.0%
		Schizophrenia	0.0%
		Substance abuse (drug or alcohol)	0.0%
		Antisocial conduct	0.0%
Kinzie et al., 1989	DSM-III-R SADS	Affective disorder	76.9%
		Panic disorder	7.7%
Sack et al., 1994	DSM-III-R K-SADS-E	Depressive disorder	62.0%
		Unspecified anxiety disorders	22.0%
		Overanxious disorder	11.0%
		Panic disorder	10.5%
		Conduct disorder	10.5%
Sack et al., 1993	DSM-III-R K-SADS-E	Major depression	60.0%
		Anxiety disorders	15.0%
		Conduct disorder	0.0%
		Substance abuse (drug or alcohol)	0.0%
		Schizophrenia	0.0%
Hubbard et al., 1995	DSM-III-R SCID	Major depression	21.0%
		Generalized anxiety disorder	21.0%
		Social phobia	21.0%
		Somatoform pain	29.0%
Clarke et al., 1993	DSM-III-R DICA-R	Major depression	13.5%

California school shooting had PTSD one month after the incident, Nader et al. (1990) determined that 19.0 percent of the same subjects continued to be symptomatic 14 months later. Koplewicz et al. (1994) reported that 68.2 percent and 54.5 percent of children who were exposed to the World Trade Center bombing had PTSD at three and nine month post bombing assessments. Thirty-seven days after a severe shelling incident, Saigh (1988a) determined that 75 percent of Lebanese youth that were sampled had PTSD. A 317 day follow-up established that only 8.3 percent of these subjects continued to evidence the disorder. Similar findings were observed among Cambodian (Kinzie et al., 1989; Sack et al., 1993) and Israeli (Schwarzwald et al., 1994) children and adolescents who were exposed to war-related stressors. Milgram et al. (1988) also determined that 57.1 percent of the Israeli youth that were sampled had acute PTSD seven days after the school bus accident. Eight months later, the rate decreased to 19.7 percent. The studies that examined the prevalence of PTSD among children and adolescents who were exposed to Hurricane Andrew also reported a reduction in the prevalence of the disorder over time (LaGreca et al., 1996; Shaw et al., 1995, 1996).

On the other hand, research examining the impact of Hurricane Hugo failed to reflect a decreased prevalence over time. Assessments conducted at three months (Shannon et al., 1994) and one year (Garrison et al., 1993) after the hurricane successively yielded an approximate prevalence of 5 percent. Analogously, McFarlane's (1987) 8 and 21 month post fire assessments determined that the prevalence of the disorder was essentially unchanged over time.

Type and Mode of Stress Exposure. Deblinger and her coauthors (1989) reported that 20.7 percent, 6.9 percent, and 10.3 percent of their respective sexually, physically, and nonabused inpatient sample met criteria for PTSD. Famularo et al. (1989) reported that 27.3 percent of the sexually abused, 12.7 percent of the physically abused, and 33.3 percent of the combined sexual-physical abuse cases that they examined met criteria for PTSD. Analogously, Livingston et al. (1993) compared the PTSD prevalence estimates of sexually abused subjects to the PTSD prevalence estimates of physically abused subjects. Their analysis

determined that 51.7 percent of the sexually abused and 33.3 percent of the physically abused youth met criteria for PTSD.

The manner in which the traumatic event was experienced may also present as a risk factor. Saigh (1991) reported that 25.2 percent, 55.6 percent, 5.6 percent, and 13.5 percent of the 230 stress-exposed Lebanese youth that met criteria for PTSD had been traumatized through direct experience (e.g., being shot), observation (e.g., witnessing the execution of a parent or sibling), information transmission (e.g., learning about the traumatic experiences of a parent or sibling) or combinations thereof.

Duration and Number of Stress Exposures. Wolfe et al. (1994) reported that youth with PTSD were more likely to have been abused for longer intervals (more than one year) and stress-exposed PTSD negatives tended to have experienced singular episodes of abuse. Livingston et al. (1993) also indicated that the number of stressors experienced (other than abuse) was significantly related to PTSD.

Pre- and Post-trauma Exposures. Garrison et al. (1993) determined that a pre-hurricane history of exposure to extreme stress (i.e., abuse or assault) was predictive of PTSD among the child-adolescent survivors of Hurricane Andrew. In terms of post-trauma experiences, Saigh (1988a) reported a strong association between secondary exposures to traumatic war-related events and PTSD. Sack et al. (1993) also determined that Cambodian subjects with PTSD experienced significantly more first year resettlement stress than subjects who did not develop the disorder.

Age. Wolfe et al.'s (1994) assessment of Canadian children with documented histories of sexual abuse determined that youth above the age of 12 years had a significantly higher prevalence of PTSD (56.5 percent) than younger youth (32.1 percent). In contrast, a number of victimization studies reported nonsignificant differences in the distribution of children with PTSD by age (Fitzpatrick & Boldizar, 1993; Livingston et al., 1993; Nader et al., 1990; Pynoos et al., 1987). Nader et al. (1993) reported that older Kuwati youth (age range 8 to 21 years) had a higher prevalence of PTSD than younger youth. However, Nader and her colleagues did not provide information regarding the comparative ages of the subjects in question. Sack et al. (1994) reported that older Cambodian youth (age range 24 to 25 years) were significantly more likely to be PTSD positive than younger youth (age range 13 to 14 years). In contrast, Weisenberg et al. (1993) and Schwarzwald et al. (1994) reported that younger children (fifth and sixth graders) had significantly greater prevalence of PTSD than older youth (seventh, eighth, tenth, and eleventh graders). Nonsignificant age differences were reported by two of the war-related PTSD studies (Realmuto et al., 1992; Saigh et al., 1990).

Gender. Although Fitzpatrick and Boldizar (1993) determined that males experienced and or witnessed more community violence, they also indicated that females reported significantly more PTSD symptoms. Wolfe et al.'s (1994) research with sexually abused Canadian children also indicated that females presented with a higher prevalence of PTSD (56.5 percent) than males (32.1 percent). On the other hand, Merry and Andrews (1994) reported that 18.2 percent of their sexually abused female cohort and 18.2 percent of their sexually abused male cohort received a PTSD diagnosis. In a similar vein, several victimization studies reported nonsignificant relationships between PTSD and gender (Livingston et al., 1993; Nader et al., 1990; Pynoos et al., 1987).

All of the war-related studies that attempted to examine for gender differences relative to PTSD diagnostic status (Hubbard et al., 1995; Realmuto et al., 1992; Sack et al., 1994; Saigh, 1988b, 1989; Saigh et al., 1990, 1995, 1997; Schwarzwald et al., 1994; Weisenberg et al., 1993) did not observe significant variations by gender. In contrast, Green et al. (1991) disaster research determined that female flood victims had a higher prevalence of PTSD (44 percent) than male victims (30 percent). Garrison et al. (1995) also reported that female survivors of hurricane Andrew experienced a higher prevalence (9.2 percent) than males (2.9 percent). Likewise, Shannon et al. (1994) established that female hurricane survivors had a higher prevalence (6.9 percent) than males (3.8 percent). While Milgram et al. (1988) reported that

female survivors of the school bus collision presented with a higher prevalence than males, the respective point prevalence estimates were not specified. In a similar vein, Goenjian et al. (1995) reported that females had a significantly higher prevalence than males. Goenjian and his colleagues did not report prevalence by gender data.

Ethnicity. LaGreca et al. (1996) reported that Hispanic and black youth had significantly higher levels of PTSD than white children. On the other hand, Garrison et al. (1993) and Shannon et al. (1994) reported nonsignificant differences when race was examined as a risk factor.

Resettlement/Relocation Stress. Savin and his colleagues (1996) compared the prevalence of PTSD among two cohorts of Cambodian youth who survived the brutal Pol Pot regime. The first group had resettled in Thai refugee camps and the second group were resettled in America. Whereas the point prevalence among the survivors who remained in Thailand (38.5 percent) was somewhat higher than the prevalence that was seen in the United States (32.8 percent), the difference was not significant. Savin and his colleagues concluded that the diagnosis of war-related PTSD was a direct product of the original trauma and not a byproduct of contextual or resettlement stress.

LaGreca et al. (1996) reported that loss of material objects and relocation following Hurricane Andrew was predictive of PTSD. On the other hand, the destruction of personal residence was not significantly correlated with the disorder. Bradburn (1991) also determined that the degree of earthquake damage to the homes of the children that were tested was not predictive of PTSD. In terms of post disaster resettlement stress, Najarian et al. (1996) reported that the prevalence of PTSD among highly stress-exposed youth who remained in the city of Gumri (32 percent) and former residents who relocated to the less damaged city of Yerevan (28 percent) were not significantly different.

Relationship between Victims or Perpetrators. McLeer et al. (1988) reported that 75 percent of the youth that were abused by natural fathers developed the disorder. They also indicated that 25 percent of the subjects that were abused by a trusted adult and 10.0 percent of those abused by a stranger evidenced PTSD. In considerable contrast, none (0.0 percent) of the children who were abused by an older youth met diagnostic criteria for the disorder.

Milgram et al. (1988) also observed that Israeli children who were personally acquainted with the victims of the school bus accident had a significantly higher prevalence of PTSD than youth who were not acquainted with the victims. Milgram and his coauthors did not specify prevalence estimates for the aforementioned groups.

Parental Psychopathology.   Koplewicz et al. (1994) reported a significant relationship between parental symptomology and child-adolescent PTSD 9 months after the World Trade Center bombing. Likewise, Sack et al. (1994) determined that the prevalence of PTSD among stress-exposed Cambodian youth increased as a function of parental PTSD. When neither parent had PTSD, 12.9 percent of their offspring met criteria. When one parent had the disorder, the prevalence rate increased to 23.3 percent. The point prevalence of the disorder increased to 41.2 percent when both parents had PTSD. McFarlane (1987) also determined that child-adolescent PTSD was highly correlated with the prevalence of parental PTSD as well as having overprotective parents. He also reported that PTSD was correlated with separation from one or both parents during or after the Australian bush fire. Likewise, Green et al. (1991) reported that parental psychopathology and the degree of family cohesion contributed to the prediction of PTSD among child-adolescent flood victims.

SUMMARY

Whereas it is clear that exposure to an extremely distressing event was usually not sufficient to induce PTSD in most of the youth that were examined, it is also apparent that the overriding majority of stressors described were capable of inducing the disorder among a subset of the subjects. Indeed, it may be concluded that children and adolescents (as in the case of adults) evidenced varying degrees of psycho-

logical morbidity after exposure to extremely stressful events.

As may be noted from Tables 2.1–2.3, the prevalence of PTSD among youth has been associated with considerable variability within and between stressor categories. Viewed across categories, point prevalence estimates ranged from 0.0 percent to 95.0 percent. It may also be said that war-related events, criminal victimization and exposure to earthquakes, floods, hurricanes, fires, or serious accidents were usually associated with higher estimates of PTSD than less deliberate acts or events. "Silent" stressors such as exposure to nuclear or chemical contamination were associated with lower levels of morbidity. While only 19.6 percent of the studies that were reviewed assessed for comorbidity, it is apparent that PTSD frequently presents in conjunction with affective disorders, anxiety disorders, ADHD, conduct disorder, and enuresis.

The variability in the literature may be explained in part by realizing that substantial differences were evident relative to the type and intensity of the precipitating stressors. Moreover, extensive variability was apparent relative to the duration between stress exposure and the assessment of PTSD (e.g., 1 week to 18 years). Sampling techniques also varied across studies. Analogously, a great deal of variability was apparent with respect to the demographic characteristics of the subjects that were sampled.

It is also important to note that variability was evident in the way PTSD was determined. A more comprehensive review of the assessment literature is provided in this book in the chapter by John March (1998). However, it is to be noted that 18 different tests or methods were used to diagnose PTSD (e.g., non-structured interviews, structured clinical interviews, parental ratings, teacher ratings, and self-report inventories) and that many of the assessment vehicles that were employed have different or undetermined psychometric properties. As such, psychometric variations relative to the specificity and sensitivity of the instruments that were used most probably significantly contributed to the observed variability. As three different sets of diagnostic criteria have appeared in the formal nomenclature since 1980, it is reasonable to assume that the divergent diagnostic criteria may have contributed to variations in reported prevalence (Schwarz & Kowalski, 1991).

A number of consistencies and inconsistencies are apparent among the most frequently explored risk factors. Five of the six longitudinal investigations evidenced lower prevalence estimates over time. Indeed, it appears that the duration between stress exposure and evaluation is predictive of PTSD. It is very apparent that the intensity of stress exposure is predictive of PTSD among 13 out of 16 investigations that explored this question. The four studies that explored the relationship between child-adolescent PTSD and parental psychopathology consistently reported significant findings. While only two investigations examined the duration and frequency of stress exposure, both reports determined that these factors are predictive of PTSD. One report established the personal relationship between victims and perpetrators was predictive and another study determined that the degree of personal acquaintance with victims presented a significant risk. One study reported that premorbid psychopathology was predictive of PTSD and another study identified secondary traumatization as a risk factor.

On the other hand, there are inconsistencies in the literature relative to gender, age, and ethnicity. With respect to gender, seven studies reported significantly higher prevalence estimates among females and 13 reported nonsignificant differences. Six studies reported that age was not predictive of PTSD and five reported the opposite. Of the studies that observed significant age effects, two determined that younger children had a higher prevalence and three indicated that older youth had a higher prevalence. One study reported that resettlement stress was predictive of PTSD and three did not. One investigation determined that ethnicity was predictive of PTSD and two failed to do so.

IMPLICATIONS FOR FUTURE RESEARCH

Whereas the studies that were reviewed generally measured PTSD through the administration of a single measure (e.g., the Children's PTSD Inventory or the Reaction Index), researchers may wish to go beyond the one-shot approach to case identification and employ multi-method multi-score approaches to PTSD case determination that draw on self-report, cognitive, behavioral, and psychophysiological indicators. Moreover, efforts should be made to collect data from multiple sources such as the affected youth, his or her parents/guardians, siblings, teachers, mental health practitioners, medical staff as well as school, hospital, and juvenile justice records.

There is a very clear need to systematically identify comorbid conditions inasmuch as only 9 of the 51 studies that were reviewed actually reported information about comorbidity. These comorbid conditions may pose a significant challenge to the resources of clinicians and researchers. Epidemiological research involving children and adolescents should also strive to go beyond the current cross-sectional approach to case identification and description by conducting more prospective investigations (Saigh et al., 1996). It is also recommended that future studies assess the frequency of symptoms and their impact on age-appropriate levels of functioning. As in the case of research involving other child adolescent disorders (Shaw, Keenan, & Vondra, 1994; Statin & Magnusson, 1989; White, Moffitt, & Silva, 1989), prospective studies may enhance our appreciation of the unique pathology of traumatized youth by providing much needed data that is essential to understand the complex associations between premorbid conditions, stress exposure, PTSD, comorbid disorders, and a variety of risk factors.

REFERENCES

American Psychiatric Association. (1987). *Diagnostic and statistical manual of mental disorders* (3rd ed. Rev.). Washington, DC: Author.

Bell, C. B., & Jenkins, E. (1993). Community violence and children on Chicago's south side. *Psychiatry, 56,* 46–54.

Bradburn, I. S. (1991). After the earth shook: Children's stress symptoms 6–8 months after a disaster. *Advances in Behavior Research and Therapy, 13,* 173–179.

Breslau, N., Davis, G. C., Andreski, P., & Peterson, E. (1991). Traumatic events and posttraumatic stress disorder in an urban population of young adults. *Archives of General Psychiatry, 48,* 216–222.

Burt, C. W. (1995). *Injury related visits to hospital emergency departments: United States, 1992.* Vital and Health Statistics of the Centers for Disease Control and Prevention/ National Center for Health Statistics. Number 261. Hayatsville, MD: United States Department of Health and Human Services.

Burton, D., Foy, D., Bwanausi, C., Johnson, J., & Moore, L. (1994). The relationship between traumatic exposure, family dysfunction, and post-traumatic stress symptoms in male juvenile offenders. *Journal of Traumatic Stress, 7,* 83–93.

Carey-Trefzer, C. J. (1949). The results of a clinical study of war-damaged children who attended a child guidance clinic. *Journal of Mental Science, 95,* 535–559.

Clarke, G. N., Sack, W. H., Ben, R., Lanham, K., & Him, C. (1993). English language skills in a group of previously traumatized Khmer adolescent refugees. *Journal of Nervous and Mental Diseases, 181,* 454–456.

Deblinger, E., McLeer, S. V., Atkins, M. S., Ralphe, D., & Foa, E. (1989). Post-traumatic stress in sexually abused, physically abused, and non-abused children. *Child Abuse and Neglect, 13,* 403–408.

Diamond, R., Saigh, P. A., & Fairbank, J. A. (in press). An analysis of internalizing and externalizing problems in preschool children with PTSD or ADHD. *Journal of Traumatic Stress.*

Earls, F., Smith, E., Reich, W., & Jung, K. G. (1988). Investigating psychopathological consequences of a disaster in children: A pilot study incorporating a structured diagnostic interview. *Journal of the American Academy of Child and Adolescent Psychiatry, 27,* 90–95.

Fairbank, J. A., Schlenger, W. E., Saigh, P. A., & Davidson, J. R. T. (1995). An epidemiological profile of post-traumatic stress disorder. Prevalence, comorbidity and risk factors. In M. J. Friedman, D. S. Charney, & A. Y. Deutch (Eds.), *Neurobiological and Clinical Consequences of Stress: From Normal Adaptation to PTSD.* Philadelphia: Lippincott-Raven Publishers.

Famularo, R., Kinscherff, R., & Fenton, T. (1989). Post-traumatic stress disorder among maltreated children presenting to a juvenile court. *American Journal of Forensic Psychiatry, 10,* 33–39.

Famularo, R., Kinscherff, R., & Fenton, T. (1992). Psychiatric diagnosis of maltreated children: Preliminary findings. *Journal of the American Academy of Child and Adolescent Psychiatry, 31,* 863–867.

Figley, R. C. (1989). *Helping traumatized families.* San Francisco, CA: Jossey-Bass.

Fisher, P. (1994). *Manual for the DISC 2.4 Post-traumatic Stress Disorder: Child and Adolescent Version.* New York State Psychiatric Institute.

Fitzpatrick, K. M., & Boldizar, J. P. (1993). The prevalence and consequences of exposure to violence among African-American youth. *Journal of the American Academy of Child and Adolescent Psychiatry, 32,* 424–430.

Foy, D. W., Sipprelle, R. C., Rueger, D. B., & Carroll, E. M. (1984). Etiology of post-traumatic stress disorder in Vietnam veterans: Analysis of premilitary, military, and combat exposure influences. *Journal of Consulting and Clinical Psychology, 52,* 79–87.

Frederick, C. J. (1985). Selected foci in the spectrum of posttraumatic stress disorders. In J. Laube & S. A. Murphy (Eds.), *Perspectives on disaster recovery.* (pp. 110–130). East Norwalk, CT: Appleton-Century-Crofts.

Frederick, C. J., Pynoos, R., & Nader, K. (1992). *Child Post-traumatic Stress Reaction Index.* Unpublished instrument.

Friedman, G. D. (1987). *Primer of epidemiology* (3rd. ed.). New York: McGraw-Hill.

Garrison, C. Z., Bryant, E. S., Addy, C. L., Spurrier, P. G., Freedy, J. R., & Kilpatrick, D. G. (1995). Posttraumatic stress disorder in adolescents after Hurricane Andrew. *Journal of the American Academy of Child and Adolescent Psychiatry, 34,* 1193–1201.

Garrison, C. Z., Weinrich, M. W., Hardin, S. B., Weinrich, S., & Wang, L. (1993). Posttraumatic stress disorder in adolescents after a hurricane. *American Journal of Epidemiology, 138,* 522–530.

Goenjian, A. D., Pynoos, R. S., Steinberg, A. M., Najarian, L. M., Asarnow, J. R., Karayan, I., Ghurabi, M., & Fairbanks, L. A. (1995). Psychiatric comorbidity in children after the 1988 earthquake in Armenia. *Journal of the American Academy of Child and Adolescent Psychiatry, 34,* 1174–1184.

Green, B., Korol, M., Grace, M., Vary, M., Leonard, T., & Gleser, G. (1991). Children and disaster: Age, gender, and parental effects on PTSD symptoms. *Journal of the American Academy of Child and Adolescent Psychiatry, 30,* 945–951.

Handford, H., Mayes, S., Mattison, R., Humphrey, F., Bagnato, S., Bixler, E., & Kales, J. (1986). Child and parent reactions to the Three Mile Island nuclear accident. *Journal of the American Academy of Child and Adolescent Psychiatry, 25,* 346–356.

Herjanic, B., & Reich, W. (1982). Development of a structured psychiatrist interview for children: Agreement between child and parent on individual symptoms. *Journal of Abnormal Child Psychology, 10,* 307–324.

Hernandez, J. T. (1992). Substance abuse among sexually abused adolescents and their families. *Journal of Adolescent Health, 13,* 658–662.

Hubbard, J., Realmuto, G. M., Northwood, A. K., & Masten, A. S. (1995). Comorbidity of psychiatric diagnoses with posttraumatic stress disorder in survivors of childhood trauma. *Journal of the American Academy of Child and Adolescent Psychiatry, 34,* 1167–1173.

Kaplan, L. M., & Reich, W. (1991). *Manual to accompany Diagnostic Interview for Children and Adolescents-Revised: DICA-R, DSM-III-R version.* St Louis, MO: Washington University Division of Child Psychiatry.

Kettner, B. (1972). Combat strain and subsequent mental health. *Acta Psychiatrica Scandinavica, 22,* 5–107.

Kilpatrick, D. G., Resnick, H. S., Saunders, B. E., & Best, C. L. (1989). *The National Women's Study PTSD Module.* Charleston: Crime Victims Research and Treatment Center, Department of Psychiatry and Behavioral Sciences, Medical University of South Carolina.

Kinzie, J. D., Sack, W. H., Angell, R. H., Clarke, G., & Ben, R. (1989). A three year follow-up of Cambodian young people traumatized as children. *Journal of the American Academy of Child and Adolescent Psychiatry, 28,* 501–504.

Kinzie, J. D., Sack, W. H., Angell, R. H., Mason, S. M., & Ben, R. (1986). The psychiatric effects of massive trauma on Cambodian children. *Journal of the American Academy of Child and Adolescent Psychiatry, 25,* 370–376.

Kleinbaum, D. G., Kupper. L. L., & Morgenstein, H. (1982). *Epidemiological research: Principles and quantitative methods.* New York: Van Nostrand Reinhold.

Koplewicz, H. S., Vogel, J. M., Solanto, M. V., Morrissey, R. G., Alonso, C. M., Gallagher, R., Abikoff, H. B., & Novick, R. M. (1994, October). *Child and parent response to the World Trade Center bombing.* Poster presented at the Annual Meeting of the American Academy of Child and Adolescent Psychiatry, New York.

Korol, M. (1990). *Children's psychological responses to a nuclear waste disaster in Fernald, Ohio.* Unpublished doctoral dissertation, University of Cincinnati, Cincinnati, Ohio.

Kulka, R. A., Schlenger, W. E., Fairbank, J. A., Hough, R. L., Jordan, B. K., Marmar, C. R., & Weiss, D. (1990). *Trauma and the Vietnam War generation: Report of findings from the National Vietnam Readjustment Study.* New York: Brunner/Mazel.

LaGreca, A. M., Silverman, W. K., Vernberg, E. M., & Prinstein, M. J. (1996). Symptoms of posttraumatic stress in children after Hurricane Andrew: A prospective study. *Journal of Consulting and Clinical Psychology, 64,* 712–723.

Lewis, A. (1942). Incidence of neurosis in England under war conditions. *Lancet, 2,* 175–183.

Livingston, R., Lawson, L., & Jones, J. G. (1993). Predictors of self-reported psychopathology in children abused repeatedly by a parent. *Journal of the American Academy of Child and Adolescent Psychiatry, 32,* 948–953.

March, J. (1998). Pediatric assessment of posttraumatic stress disorder. In P. A. Saigh & J. D. Bremner (Eds.), *Posttraumatic stress disorder: A comprehensive textbook.* Boston, MA: Allyn and Bacon.

McFarlane, A. C. (1987). Posttraumatic phenomena in a longitudinal study of children following a national disaster. *Journal of the American Academy of Child and Adolescent Psychiatry, 26,* 764–769.

McLeer, S. V., Callaghan, M., Henry, D., & Wallen, J. (1994). Psychiatric disorders in sexually abused children. *Journal of the American Academy of Child and Adolescent Psychiatry, 33,* 313–319.

McLeer, S. V., Deblinger, E., Atkins, M. S., Foa, E. B., & Ralphe, D. L. (1988). Post-traumatic stress disorder in sexually abused children. *Journal of the American Academy of Child and Adolescent Psychiatry, 27,* 650–654.

McLeer, S. V., Deblinger, E., Henry, D., & Orvaschel, H. (1992). Sexually abused children at high risk for posttraumatic stress disorder. *Journal of the American Academy of Child and Adolescent Psychiatry, 31,* 875–879.

Merry, S., & Andrews, L. K. (1994). Psychiatric status of sexually abused children 12 months after disclosure of abuse. *Journal of the American Academy of Child and Adolescent Psychiatry, 33,* 939–944.

Milgram, N. A., Toubiana, Y. H., Klingman, A., Raviv, A., & Goldstein, I. (1988). Situational exposure and personal loss in children's acute and chronic stress reactions to a school bus disaster. *Journal of Traumatic Stress, 1,* 339–352.

Nader, K., Pynoos, R., Fairbanks, L., & Frederick, C. (1990). Children's PTSD reactions one year after a sniper attack at their school. *American Journal of Psychiatry, 147,* 1526–1530.

Nader, K., Pynoos, R., Fairbanks, L., Frederick, C., Al-Ajeel, M., & Al-Asfour, A. (1993). A preliminary study of PTSD and grief among the children of Kuwait following the Gulf crisis. *British Journal of Clinical Psychology, 32,* 407–416.

Najarian, L. M., Goenjian, A. K., Pelcovitz, D., Mandel, F., & Najarian, B. (1996). Relocation after a disaster: Posttraumatic stress disorder in Armenia after the earthquake. *Journal of the American Academy of Child and Adolescent Psychiatry, 35,* 374–383.

Orvaschel, H., Puig-Antich, P., Chambers, W., Tabrizi, M., & Johnson, R. (1982). Retrospective assessment of child psychopathology with the Kiddie-SADS-E. *Journal of the American Academy of Child and Adolescent Psychiatry, 21,* 392–397.

Pelcovitz, D., Kaplan, S., Goldenberg, B., Mendel, F., Lehane, J., & Guarrera, J. (1994). Post-traumatic stress disorder in physically abused adolescents. *Journal of the American Academy of Child and Adolescent Psychiatry, 33,* 305–312.

Pennoyer, K. I., & Ellenhorn, T. J. (1995, August). *Exposure to community violence, post-traumatic stress and aspects of psychosocial functioning in adolescents living in inner-city neighborhoods.* Paper presented at the meeting of the American Psychological Association.

Puig-Antich, J., Orvaschel, H., Tabrinzi, M. H., & Chambers, W. (1980). *The schedule for affective disorders and schizophrenia for school age children (Kiddie SADS).* New York Psychiatric Institute and Yale University School of Medicine.

Pynoos, R. S., Frederick, C., Nader, K., Arroyo, W., Steinberg, A., Eth, S., Nunez, F., & Fairbanks, L. (1987). Life threat and posttraumatic stress in school-age children. *Archives of General Psychiatry, 44,* 1057–1063.

Rachman, S. J. (1990). *Fear and courage.* (2nd ed.) New York: W. H. Freeman.

Realmuto, G. M., Masten, A., Carole, L. F., Hubbard, J., Grotelushen, A., & Burke, C. (1992). Adolescent survivors of massive childhood trauma in Cambodia: Life events and current symptoms. *Journal of Traumatic Stress, 5,* 589–599.

Reich, W., Shayka, J. J., & Taibleson, C. (1991). *Diagnostic Interview for Children and Adolescents-Revised-Parent Version (DICA-R-P).* St. Louis: Washington University.

Reich, W., & Welner, Z. (1988). *DICA-R-C (DSM-III-R version) revised version 5-R.* St. Louis: Washington University.

Resnick, H. S., Kilpatrick, D. G., Dansky, B. S., Saunders, B. E., & Best, C. L. (1993). Prevalence of civilian trauma and posttraumatic stress disorder in a representative national sample of women. *Journal of Consulting and Clinical Psychology, 61,* 984–991.

Robins, L. N., Helzer, J. E., Croughan, J., & Ratcliff, K. (1981). National Institute of Mental Health Interview Schedule. *Archives of General Psychiatry, 38,* 381–389.

Rutter, M., & Graham, P. (1967). A children's behaviour questionnaire for completion by teachers: Preliminary findings. *Journal of Child Psychology and Psychiatry, 8,* 1–11.

Rutter, M., Tizard, J., & Whitmore, K. (1970). *Education, Health and Behaviour.* London: Longman.

Sack, W. H., Clarke, G., Him, C., Dickason, D., Goff, B., Lanham, K., & Kinzie, J. D. (1993). A six year follow-up of Cambodian adolescents. *Journal of the American Academy of Child and Adolescent Psychiatry, 32,* 3 15.

Sack, W. H., McSharry, S., Clarke, G. N., Kinney, R., Seeley, J., & Lewinsohn, P. (1994). The Khmer adolescent project I. Epidemiological findings in two generations of Cambodian refugees. *Journal of Nervous and Mental Disease, 182,* 387–395.

Saigh, P. A. (1988a). Anxiety, depression, and assertion across alternating intervals of stress. *Journal of Abnormal Psychology, 97,* 338–342.

Saigh, P. A. (1988b). The validity of the DSM-III posttraumatic stress disorder as applied to adolescents. *Professional School Psychology, 3,* 283–290.

Saigh, P. A. (1989a). The validity of the DSM-III posttraumatic stress disorder classification as applied to children. *Journal of Abnormal Psychology, 98,* 189–192.

Saigh, P. A. (1989b). The development and validation of the Children's Posttraumatic Stress Disorder Inventory. *International Journal of Special Education, 4,* 75–84.

Saigh, P. A. (1991). On the development of posttraumatic stress disorder pursuant to different modes of traumatization. *Behaviour Research and Therapy, 29,* 213–216.

Saigh, P. A. (1992). Structured clinical interviews and the inferential process. *Journal of School Psychology, 30,* 221–226.

Saigh, P. A., Fairbank, J. A., & Gross, A. (1990, August). *A logit analysis of the symptoms of traumatized adolescents.* In P. A. Saigh (Chair). International research on childhood posttraumatic stress disorder. Symposium conducted at the meeting of the American Psychological Association, Boston, MA.

Saigh, P. A., Green, B. L., & Korol, M. (1996). The history and prevalence of posttraumatic stress disorder with special reference to children and adolescents. *Journal of School Psychology, 34,* 107–131.

Saigh, P. A., Mroueh, A., & Bremner, J. D. (1997). Scholastic impairments among traumatized adolescents. *Behaviour Research and Therapy, 35,* 429–436.

Saigh, P. A., Mroueh, A., Zimmerman, B., & Fairbank, J. A. (1995). Self-efficacy expectations among traumatized adolescents. *Behaviour Research and Therapy, 33,* 701–705.

Savin, D., Sack, W. H., Clarke, G. N., Meas, N., & Richart, I. (1996). The Khmer Adolescent Project: III. A study of trauma from Thailand's Site Two refugee camp. *Journal of the American Academy of Child and Adolescent Psychiatry, 35,* 384–391.

Schwarz, E. D., & Kowalski, J. M. (1991). Posttraumatic stress disorder after a school shooting: Effects of symptom threshold selection and diagnosis by DSM-III, DSM-III-R, or proposed DSM-IV. *American Journal of Psychiatry, 148,* 592–597.

Schwarzwald, J., Weisenberg, M., Solomon, Z., & Waysman, M. (1994). Stress reaction of school-age children to the bombardment by SCUD missiles: A 1-year follow-up. *Journal of Traumatic Stress, 7,* 657–667.

Schwarzwald, J., Weisenberg, M., Waysman, M., Solomon, Z., & Klingman, A. (1993). Stress reaction of school-age children to the bombardment of SCUD missiles. *Journal of Abnormal Psychology, 102,* 404–410.

Shaffer, D., Fisher, P., Piacenti, J., Schwab-Stone, M., & Wicks, J. (1989). *DISC-2 Parent Version.* New York: Division of Child and Adolescent Psychiatry, New York State Psychiatric Institute.

Shannon, M., Lonigan, C., Finch, A. J., & Taylor, C. M. (1994). Children exposed to disaster: I. Epidemiology of posttraumatic stress disorder and symptom profiles. *Journal of the American Academy of Child and Adolescent Psychiatry, 33,* 80–92.

Shaw, D. S., Keenan, K., & Vondra, J. I. (1994). Developmental precursors of externalizing behavior: Ages 1 to 3. *Developmental Psychology, 30,* 355–364.

Shaw, J. A., Applegate, B., & Schorr, C. (1996). Twenty-one-month follow-up study of school-age children exposed to Hurricane Andrew. *Journal of the American Academy of Child and Adolescent Psychiatry, 35,* 359–364.

Shaw, J. A., Applegate, B., Tanner, S., Perez, D., Rothe, E., Campo-Bowen, A. E., & Lahey, B. L. (1995). Psychological effects of Hurricane Andrew on an elementary school population. *Journal of the American Academy of Child and Adolescent Psychiatry, 34,* 1185–1192.

Singer, M. I., Anglin, T. M., Song, L., & Lunghofer, L. (1995). Adolescents' exposure to violence and associated symptoms of psychological trauma. *Journal of the American Medical Association, 8,* (276), 477–482.

Spitzer, R. L., Endicott, J., & Robins, E. (1978). Research diagnostic criteria: Rational and reliability. *Archives of General Psychiatry, 23,* 45–55.

Spitzer, R. L., Williams, J. B., & Gibbon, M. (1987). *Structured Clinical Interview for the DSM-III-R* (SCID). Biometrics Research Department, New York State Psychiatric Institute.

Statin, H., & Magnusson, D. (1989). The role of early aggressive behavior in the frequency, seriousness, and types of later crime. *Journal of Consulting and Clinical Psychology, 57,* 710–718.

Stoddard, F. J., Norman, D. K., & Murphy, J. M. (1989). A diagnostic outcome study of children and adolescents with severe burns. *Journal of Trauma, 29,* 471–477.

United States Department of Justice. (1994). *Juvenile victimization: 1987–1992.* Office of Juvenile Justice and Delinquency Prevention. Fact sheet 17. Washington, DC: Author.

United States Department of Transportation. (1993). *Traffic safety facts.* National Highway Traffic Safety Administration. Report DOT HS 808 022. Washington, DC: Author.

Welner, Z., Reich, W., Herjanic, B., Jung, K. G., & Amando, H. (1987). Reliability, validity, and parent-child agreement studies: The diagnostic interview for children and adolescents (DICA). *Journal of the American Academy of Child and Adolescent Psychiatry, 26,* 649–653.

White, J. L., Moffitt, T. E., & Silva, P. (1989). A prospective replication of the protective effects of IQ in subjects at high risk for juvenile delinquency. *Journal of Consulting and Clinical Psychology, 57,* 719–724.

Wiesenberg, M., Schwarzwald, J., Waysman, M., Solomon, Z., & Klingman, A. (1993). Coping of school-age children in the sealed room during SCUD missile bombardment and postwar stress reactions. *Journal of Consulting and Clinical Psychology, 61,* 462–467.

Wolfe, D. A., Sas, L., & Wekerle, C. (1994). Factors associated with the development of posttraumatic stress disorder among child victims of sexual abuse. *Child Abuse and Neglect, 18,* 37–50.

CHAPTER 3

POSTTRAUMATIC STRESS DISORDER IN ADULTS RELATIVE TO CRIMINAL VICTIMIZATION: PREVALENCE, RISK FACTORS, AND COMORBIDITY

RON ACIERNO, PH.D.
Medical University of South Carolina

DEAN G. KILPATRICK, PH.D. and HEIDI S. RESNICK, PH.D.
University of South Carolina, Charleston

Rates of violent crime continue to rise in countries across the globe (Rosenberg & Fenley, 1991; Reiss & Roth, 1993). However, assaultive violence appears to be most problematic in the United States, which has the highest violent crime incidence of any industrialized nation. Indeed, the annual rate of successful homicides in the United States (7.9 per 1,000) is many times that of European countries (1.5 per 1,000) (this despite one of the most advanced emergency medical systems in the world). At least 20 percent of the population will experience some form of physical or sexual assault during their lifetime (Kilpatrick, Acierno, Resnick, Saunders, & Best, 1997; Resnick, Falsetti, Kilpatrick, & Freedy, 1996), making violent crime a public health emergency (Koop, 1992; Novello, 1992). Annual costs of the 2.2 million known injuries due to violent crime, measured in terms of lost work, lost wages, decreased productivity, and required medical and mental health care exceed $6,000,000,000 (Harlow, 1989). Not surprisingly, fear of violent crime is widespread. Over 82 percent of Americans indicate that they are very concerned about violence (Kilpatrick, Seymour, & Boyle, 1991) and more than half state that violence is a greater problem in their community now than it was 10 years ago, a sentiment supported by the FBI Uniform Crime Report (UCR) (1995).

PTSD is one of the most commonly observed mental health outcomes of violent crimes such as rape and aggravated assault (Breslau, Davis, Andreski, & Peterson, 1991; Green, 1994; Kilpatrick & Resnick, 1993). The Diagnostic and Statistics Manual (4th ed.) (DSM-IV) (American Psychiatric Association (APA), 1994) permits a diagnosis of PTSD when an individual has been exposed to a traumatic event that both presents actual or threatened death or serious injury to oneself or others, and elicits intense fear, helplessness, or horror. Experience of violent crime clearly satisfies this stipulation, known as "Criterion A." Symptom parameters of the PTSD diagnosis include re-experiencing, avoidance, and hyperarousal. In order to assign the PTSD diagnosis, these symptoms must follow a Criterion A event, persist for at least one month, and cause functional impairment in interpersonal or vocational spheres. Re-experiencing may take the form of recurrent recollections of the event, nightmares, flashbacks, or reactivity upon exposure to traumatic cues. Avoidance is typically manifest as behavioral or cognitive escape from thoughts, feelings, individuals, or places associated with the trauma, as well as the experience of feelings of de-

Preparation of this manuscript was supported by National Institute on Drug Abuse Grant Number DA 05220, and by National Institute of Mental Health Training Grant Number MH 18869.

tachment, foreshortened future, and restricted affect. Finally, hyperarousal is indicated by elevated startle response, sleep disturbances, hypervigilance, and concentration difficulties.

Criterion A of this disorder has been revised to reflect the relevance of subjective trauma characteristics (e.g., an individual's perceptions of the traumatic event) to outcome. Additionally, and in contrast to the previous DSM version, recognition of the high rate of trauma in the general population (e.g., Resnick, Kilpatrick, Dansky, Saunders, & Best, 1993; Kessler, Sonnega, Bromet, Hughes, & Nelson, 1995) has prompted authors of DSM-IV to drop the specification that Criterion A events be rare and "outside the range of usual human experience" (APA, 1987, p.250). PTSD is one of the only psychiatric disorders for which the DSM specifies an etiological antecedent, and intuitively, it would seem that the objective occurrence of a traumatic event would facilitate diagnostic processes. However, detection of trauma, particularly criminal trauma such as rape, appears to be far more complicated than originally presumed.

In order to provide insight into actual prevalence rates, this chapter describes issues in victimization assessment and then reviews several of the major epidemiological studies in some detail to allow readers to make judgements regarding validity of specific study findings relative to their population of interest. This literature is then summarized, and general risk factors for victimization are reviewed. Following this, a review of the prevalence and risk factors for PTSD in relation to criminal victimization for relevant subgroups is provided. Finally, findings relating to PTSD comorbidity are described.

PREVALENCE ESTIMATES: METHODOLOGICAL ISSUES

One cannot diagnose PTSD if one cannot ascertain that a traumatic event has occurred. Hence, accuracy of PTSD prevalence estimates is in large part determined by the adequacy of traumatic event assessment. Since a large proportion of PTSD-related trauma is associated with criminal victimization, assessment of this experience is essential. However, rates of criminal victimization, including sexual assault, physical as-

sault, and domestic violence may vary widely according to assessment methodology, including assessment context, assessment structure, assessor characteristics, and trauma definition (Breslau et al., 1991; Hanson, Kilpatrick, Falsetti, & Resnick, 1995; Kessler et al., 1995; Kilpatrick, Saunders, Amick-McMullan, Best, Veronen, & Resnick, 1989; Koss, 1993; Resnick et al., 1993; Resnick, 1996). For example, definitions of rape in a particular survey may be confined to instances of forced vaginal intercourse; or they may include forced penetration of any orifice; or they may include unforced penetration while intoxicated; or they may include attempted forced intercourse; or they may include intercourse, forced or otherwise with a female below a certain age (Koss, 1993). Clearly, asking "Have you ever been raped?" means different things to different people and will produce inaccurate estimates of rape prevalence if used in survey research. In addition to definitional inconsistency, research yielding violent crime prevalence estimates has been narrowly focused, utilizing univariate or limited multivariate analyses. Thus, observed differences across some variables may actually result from the influence of other, untested variables. For example, the propensity of Caucasian female college students to report high rates of rape and sexual assault might be due to (1) actual increased rates of victimization in this group; *or rather to* (2) increased willingness or capacity to recognize assault as such; (3) increased proclivity to report assault; (4) increased personal resources to deal with ramifications of internalizing a trauma experience, resulting in increased willingness to report, etc. As a consequence of methodological variance and limitations, simple comparison or aggregation of prevalence rates across studies is inappropriate.

Violent crime, particularly that type of crime associated with interpersonal, psychological, or cultural stigma (e.g., rape) is not readily reported by all victims. Indeed, in order to report to an investigator that a particular type of crime has occurred, a victim must: (a) recall the assault, (b) label the assault as such, (c) be queried by an investigator who is using a similar label/definition, (d) be willing and psychologically able to disclose the assault, and (e) be able to safely disclose the assault (e.g., when the perpetrator lives with the respondent). While straightforward, these factors must not be taken for granted. For example, many respondents do not label aggravated assault or rape as such when the perpetrator is a relative or spouse, or when there was only limited force or threat of force used, or when the psychological effects of such a label are too distressing. Hence, again asking "Have you ever been raped?" will result in overly conservative prevalence estimates (Essock-Vitale & McGuire, 1985; Gordon & Riger, 1989; Koss, 1993). Further, many victims are exceedingly reluctant to disclose their victimization experiences. Reasons for willful non-disclosure include: (1) fear of retribution by an assailant, particularly if the assailant is known or proximate to victim, (2) fear of stigma attached to being a victim of a particular type of crime (e.g., rape, domestic violence), (3) fear of being blamed, (4) history of negative outcomes following previous disclosure (e.g., court involvement leading to acquittal), (5) lack of encouragement to discuss victimization, and (6) fear of psychological consequences of disclosure (e.g., depression, anxiety upon re-visiting the event) (Kilpatrick, 1983; Koss, 1993; Resnick et al., 1996). It should be obvious that investigators conducting prevalence studies must not *assume* that all victimization events will be specifically and easily reported. Unfortunately, this stipulation has not always been met (e.g., Bachman, 1994; FBI UCR, 1991; Helzer, Robins, & McEvoy, 1987).

Given that the above factors will combine to reduce the likelihood that a crime event will be reported, what procedural aspects of assessment are essential to maximize sensitivity? Two components appear crucial: (1) contextually orienting, empathetic preface statements and (2) behavioral descriptions of index events that elicit closed-ended responses. Because traumatic events such as violent crime are associated with extremely aversive emotional and cognitive states, it is important, both to respondent welfare and experimental integrity, to preface criminal victimization queries in such a way as to convey acceptance, empathy, normalization, and encouragement. Obviously, victims will disclose extremely personal and frequently humiliating information only when they feel that such disclosure is worthwhile and relevant. As Resnick et al. (1996) note, simply asking a women if she has ever been physically assaulted or raped without appropriate preface statements fails to

demonstrate concern for the respondent's welfare and does little to overcome psychological defenses such as denial utilized to minimize discomfort associated with recollection of the assault. Thus, preface statements should show interviewer concern and knowledge that occurrence of assaultive violence is *not* rare (Resnick et al., 1996). Moreover, preface statements must provide contextual orientation so that the likelihood of reporting that information sought by the investigator is maximized. For example, if questions regarding sexual assault follow a crime survey in which reported crimes are investigated, and no preface statement is used to specifically direct respondents to report *all* assaults, then respondents might be biased toward disclosing only those sexual assaults that have been reported to police (Koss, 1993). Similarly, if questions regarding assault follow a psychopathology survey, then respondents might be biased toward disclosing only those assaults that are of a relatively bizarre nature (Koss, 1993). Table 3.1 presents the preface statement employed by our group at the National Crime Victims Research and Treatment Center in the National Women's Study (NWS). Note that all assaults, by any perpetrator, occurring at any time, whether reported or not, are clearly queried.

After the preface statement orients a respondent contextually (e.g., any assault by any assailant), it is absolutely essential to employ detailed, behaviorally specific, closed-ended descriptions of trauma events under investigation. Early surveys employed "gateway" screening questions characterized by very lim-

---

TABLE 3.1

Contextually-Orienting Preface Statement from the NWS

"Another type of stressful event that many women have experienced is unwanted sexual advances. Women do not always report such experiences to the police or other authorities or discuss them with family or friends. The person making the advances isn't always a stranger, but can be a friend, boyfriend, or even a family member. Such experiences can occur anytime in a woman's life—even as a child. Regardless of how long ago it happened or who made the advances..."

ited behavioral specificity. If respondents endorsed the gateway question, further questions about assault followed. Unfortunately, gateway questions do not adequately orient respondents to the type of responses the examiner is seeking (i.e., they fail to state that one is interested in all assaults, not just those reported to police or perpetrated by strangers) and are extremely subject to individual respondent's subjective interpretation of queries (i.e., definitional variance) (Koss, 1993). By contrast, behaviorally specific descriptions of assault events minimize variance associated with cultural differences, personal differences in intellect, psychological stability, general willingness to disclose, or understanding of criminal justice terminology (e.g., "rape," "aggravated assault"). These questions are highly detailed and require only "yes" "no" answers. In addition to removing definitional and cultural variance, closed-ended "yes" or "no" questions simplify the role of respondent and minimize the risk that anyone will overhear disclosure of highly personal events. Table 3.2 presents one set of behaviorally specific questions employed in the NWS:

TABLE 3.2
Behaviorally Specific, Closed-Ended Rape Screening Questions from the NWS

"**1.** Has a man or boy ever made you have sex by using force or threatening to harm you or someone close to you? Just so there is no mistake, by sex we mean putting a penis in your vagina.

2. Has anyone, male or female, ever made you have oral sex by using force or threat of harm? Just so there is no mistake, by oral sex we mean that a man or a boy put his penis in your mouth or someone, male or female, penetrated your vagina or anus with their mouth or tongue.

3. Has anyone ever made you have anal sex by using force or threat of harm? Just so there is no mistake, by anal sex we mean that a man or boy put his penis in your anus.

4. Has anyone, male or female, ever put fingers or objects in your vagina or anus against your will by using force or threats?"

Women responding affirmatively to one or more of these four questions were classified as rape victims.

INCIDENCE AND PREVALENCE ESTIMATES: CRIMINAL VIOLENCE

A commonly cited index of violent crime in this country is the Federal Bureau of Investigation's Uniform Crime Report. This report is archival in that it is based only on crimes *reported* to police departments across the country and provides information regarding cases of forcible rape, robbery, aggravated assault, and murder. Only crimes reported during each one year period are considered, and only the most serious crime is indexed for any respondent (i.e., when a respondent has been raped and robbed, only the rape is tallied). Because most crimes are not reported to police, the FBI's Uniform Crime Report is an extremely conservative and somewhat misleading measure of crime. In an attempt to address this shortcoming, the Bureau of Justice Statistics annually conducts the National Crime Victimization Survey (NCVS), in which approximately 100,000 adults aged 12 years and older and representative of the United States population are randomly contacted and queried about victimization occurring over the previous 6 months. Although the NCVS, and particularly the newly redesigned NCVS, represent improvement over simple reporting of archival police records, significant methodological weaknesses continue to exist, resulting in estimates of victimization that are lower than those observed by epidemiological researchers in the social sciences (Hanson, et al., 1995). The following is an example of an NCVS sexual assault screener:

> "2. Incidents involving forced or unwanted sexual acts are often difficult to talk about. Have you been forced or coerced to engage in unwanted sexual activity by—
> a. someone you didn't know before
> b. a casual acquaintance OR
> c. someone you know well."

(Note that the behaviors comprising "sexual activity" are not specified.)

In the August, 1994 report on the NCVS, Bachman and Saltzman noted that for women, overall *past year incidence* of rape/sexual assault was 0.46 percent. Disaggregating this number revealed that 0.16 percent were victims of completed rape, defined as "carnal knowledge through use of force or threat of force, including attempts," and 0.13 percent were victims of attempted rape. About 36 percent of sexually assaulted women suffered serious or minor injury. Physical assault of women was more frequent than sexual assault, with 0.8 percent meeting criteria for aggravated assault (assault with a weapon, or assault in which injury was experienced). Women were more than six times as likely to report violence by a partner, and were more likely to be injured if their assailant was also an intimate. Relatively less specific information regarding sexual assault was available from this report for males. The overall annual rate of rape/sexual assault in male respondents was 0.05 percent. The rate of aggravated assault of men was at least twice that of women, with 1.7 percent of surveyed males indicating that they had been physically attacked. As mentioned, although improved, the NCVS estimates of assaultive violence continue to be lower than those of other non-criminal justice surveys. Possible reasons for this discrepancy include insufficient preface statements and limited behavioral description, particularly of sexual assaults.

A frequently cited large-scale epidemiological study on assaultive violence and its effects was conducted by Helzer et al. (1987). This Epidemiological Catchment Area study employed the Diagnostic Interview Schedule (DIS) (Robins, Helzer, Cottler, & Goldring, 1988) to identify traumatic events, and suffered from most of the methodological weaknesses outlined above. Specifically, gateway-type screening questions were used to identify PTSD criterion A trauma events. No behaviorally specific, closed-ended questions followed gateway screens, and no preface statements were employed to give contextual reference to respondents. Moreover, with the exception of combat exposure and recent robbery or mugging experiences, only events that resulted in PTSD symptoms were included in traumatic event prevalence estimates, and no data exist for overall prevalence of crime. As such, reported rates are gross underestimates of actual crime prevalence and are not reviewed here.

Koss, Gidycz, and Wisniewski (1987) improved on Helzer et al.'s (1987) methodology in their national study of rape and sexual assault in college students. Although both men and women were studied, rates of victimization were available only for female respondents (males were assessed exclusively as perpetrators). Participants were 3,187 women aged 18–24 years attending colleges across the United States. Over 80 percent were unmarried and Caucasian. Participants completed a 330-item questionnaire that included 10 items specific to sexual assault occurring since age 14 (the Sexual Experiences Survey (SES)). SES questions are behaviorally specific, and measure sexual assaults over a range of intensity, from fondling to forcible rape. Rape was defined as an affirmative response to any of the three following questions:

"Have you had sexual intercourse when you didn't want to because a man gave you alcohol or drugs?"

"Have you had sexual intercourse when you didn't want to because a man threatened or used some degree of physical force (twisting your arm, holding you down, etc.) to make you?"

"Have you had sex acts (anal or oral intercourse or penetration by objects other than the penis) when you didn't want to because a man threatened or used some degree of physical force (twisting your arm, holding you down, etc.) to make you?"

(Note that sexual intercourse was defined as penetration of a woman's vagina, no matter how slight, by a man's penis).

The most serious sexual victimization experience for each subject was considered for scoring purposes. No qualitative (e.g., perceptions of life threat) or quantitative (e.g., number of perpetrators at each incident) data were reported. Although lifetime experiences were the object of study, no trauma history was reported for respondents prior to age 14. This last point is potentially problematic when one considers that at least 30 percent of sexual assault victims state that this experience occurred prior to age 15 (Burnam et al., 1988).

Overall, 15.4 percent of the sample reported that they had been raped at some point in their lives and 12.1 percent reported that they had experienced an attempted rape. Lessor forms of sexual assault were reported by 14.4 percent of the sample, and 11.9 percent indicated that they had been coerced into sex (e.g., by a supervisor or employer). Rates of victimization did not differ as a function of income, but did vary according to race, with Caucasian respondents reporting higher rates of rape than African American women. Rates of lifetime rape for ethnic subgroups were as follows: Caucasians: 16 percent; Hispanics: 12 percent; African Americans: 10 percent; Native Americans: 40 percent; and Asian Americans: 7 percent. A conservative estimate of past 6-month incidence of rape in which anal sex, penetration by objects, or use of intoxicants were not considered to be "rape" equaled 3.8 percent, a number significantly greater than that obtained by the NCVS discussed above. Although these prevalence rates were obtained from a sample of college students and are not applicable to the female population in general, the investigators point out that their results are very relevant for a significant proportion of women in this country. Indeed, fully 25 percent of 18–24 year olds are engaged in post secondary education in the United States.

Burnam et al. (1988) also conducted a large scale survey of sexual assault with a randomly selected, stratified community sample of 3,132 adults from two Los Angeles communities. Although this investigation was part of the same ECA study as Helzer et al. (1987), assessment of sexual assault was supplemented to increase detection. As with other ECA sites, the DIS was used to establish diagnoses. The sample was 53 percent female, 42 percent Caucasian, and 46 percent Hispanic with a mean age of 36 years, and an average of 14 years of education. The response rate was 68 percent. Interviews were conducted in-person, and the sex of the interviewer was not matched to that of the respondent. With regard to assault, participants were asked:

> *"In your lifetime, has anyone ever tried to pressure or force you to have sexual contact? By sexual contact I mean their touching your sexual parts, your touching their sexual parts, or sexual intercourse."*

Although not specified through preface statements, this question applied to both childhood and adult experiences, perpetrated by strangers and known assailants. While slightly more detailed than the single-question screen employed in earlier research, several aspects of this measure (e.g., *"touching sexual parts"*) lack behavioral specificity. Further, this is a very liberal definition of assault and involves a wide

range of experiences, from inappropriate touching to rape. Thus, factors serving to reduce sensitivity (lack of behavioral description, lack of orienting preface statement) are combined with factors that might falsely increase prevalence rates. Rather than offset each other, this combination of methodological weakness likely reduces validity of conclusions regarding prevalence and outcome. Indeed, the assaultive events did not even have to occur, simply pressure to have "sexual contact" was enough for respondents to endorse the item. Finally, multiple trauma experiences were not disaggregated, and physical assault was not directly assessed.

For the overall sample of men and women, the lifetime prevalence of sexual assault was 13.2 percent. Fully two-thirds of those victimized indicated that they had experienced two or more sexual assaults. More women (16.7 percent) than men (9.4 percent), and more Caucasians (19.9 percent) than Hispanics (8.1 percent) were assaulted. Sexual victimization occurred in early life for most respondents. Eighty percent of the sample indicated that they experienced their first assault between 18 and 25 years of age (32 percent indicated that they were assaulted prior to age 16 years, and 34 percent between the ages of 16 and 20). Only 6.5 percent of victimized participants experienced a first sexual assault after age 65 years.

Breslau et al. (1991) expanded the focus of victimization assessment to include physical as well as sexual assault in their study of 1,007 young adults, aged 21–30 years (median age = 26 years), who were members of a health maintenance organization (HMO) in the Detroit, Michigan area. Interviews were conducted in person and the response rate for this study was 84 percent. Women comprised 61.7 percent of the sample, 80.7 percent of participants were Caucasian, 45 percent were married, 21 percent had a high school education, 46 percent had a high school education plus some college, and 29.3 percent were college graduates. Given these demographic characteristics, and the fact that all were members of an HMO, it is apparent that some limits on generalizability of results are in order. Within these limits, however, subjects were randomly selected and appear representative of slightly more educated, young adults residing in urban locations in the

Midwest. Assessment of trauma in this study, although a significant advancement from that employed by Helzer et al. (1987), suffered from some of the pitfalls outlined above. A limited preface statement was used, but it did not specifically direct respondents to report all trauma at any age by any perpetrator, irrespective of police involvement. Further, a global traumatic event screen (i.e., including accidents, disasters) was used to the exclusion of specific screens for physical and sexual assault, and no behavioral description of traumatic events was present to control definitional variance (e.g., rape was defined as "rape.") Instead, examples of several traumatic events were listed. For example, participants were asked about:

"...being attacked or raped, being in a fire or flood or bad traffic accident, being threatened with a weapon, or watching someone being badly injured or killed."

Given these methodological shortcomings, crime estimates are likely conservative. Indeed, reported rates are lower than those obtained in other epidemiological studies. The overall lifetime rate of physical assault was 8.3 percent and rape was 1.6 percent. Since no men reported being raped, it was possible to determine that the rate of rape among women equaled 2.6 percent. Race, education, gender, and marital status-based analyses were reported for overall traumas, and were thus not specific to assaultive violence. In these analyses differences were noted on the basis of race or marital status. However, men and less educated respondents were more likely to report experiencing trauma.

Norris (1992) improved upon the methodology of previous researchers in her study of 1,000 South-East Coast residents from 4 cities following hurricane Hugo in 1989. Sampling was not random; rather a quota procedure was employed to obtain a balanced sample of Caucasians and African Americans; men and women; and younger (18–39 years), middle-aged (40–59 years), and older (60+ years) adults. Interviews were conducted in-person, and the response rate was 71 percent. The Traumatic Stress Schedule (Norris, 1990) was employed to assess occurrence of nine classes of traumatic events, including sexual and physical assault. No prefacing statements were employed to increase likelihood that all assaults (not just reported or stranger perpetrated) would be endorsed. Moreover, physical and sexual assault queries, while more direct than those employed in previous investigations, were somewhat general, and characterized by only limited behavioral specificity. In addition, subtypes of sexual assault, such as rape, were not directly assessed. Thus, as with previous investigations, prevalence estimates of violence are probably conservative. The assault-related questions were as follows:

"Did anyone ever beat you up or attack you?"

"Did anyone ever make you have sex by using force or threatening to harm you? This includes any type of unwanted sexual activity."

Rates of physical assault for the total sample were 15.0 percent (lifetime) and 2.4 percent (past-year), respectively. Similarly, lifetime and past-year rates of sexual assault were 4.4 percent and 0.4 percent, respectively. Men reported significantly greater levels of lifetime physical assault than women (18.7 percent versus 11.7 percent), whereas women reported more lifetime sexual assault than men (7.3 percent vs. 1.3 percent). Past-year rates of physical assault and sexual assault did not differ significantly between the sexes. As in several previous studies, racial differences were observed, with Caucasians reporting significantly higher rates of physical assault (18.4 percent) than African Americans (11.6 percent). Levels of lifetime sexual assault and past year rates of both physical and sexual assault were not significantly different across races. Finally, age differences in rates of reported physical assault were apparent, with younger (19.1 percent lifetime, 4.6 percent past-year) and middle-aged (16.8 percent lifetime, 2.3 percent past-year) adults reporting significantly higher levels of lifetime physical assault than older adults (8.6 percent lifetime, 0.0 percent past year). An identical pattern was observed for lifetime sexual assault. Approximately 6.6 percent of younger adults and 4.5 percent of middle-aged adults reported a lifetime sexual assault, compared to 1.9 percent of older adults. Age-specific differences in lifetime rates of victimization have been observed in several studies (Kessler et al., 1995; Kilpatrick et al.,

1992; Norris & Kaniasty, 1994) and are somewhat counter-intuitive. Although older adults are at lowest risk of new victimization, they were young adults at one time. As such, lifetime levels should be at least as high, if not higher, than lifetime levels of assault observed in younger adults, assuming that crime rates have been constant over time. The finding that lifetime rates of victimization are consistently *lower* in older adults implies that (a) this age group grew up in a less violent society, (b) this age group does not report embarrassing victimization events that did, in fact, occur at rates similar to today's levels for younger adults (perhaps due to problems with memory, or age-specific generational or cultural prohibitions against such disclosure), or (c) younger adults over-report. Unfortunately, no data exist to support any of these explanations, and additional research is needed to illuminate causes of age-based differences.

Kilpatrick et al. (1992) as well as Kilpatrick, Resnick, Saunders, and Best (in press) and Resnick et al. (1993) improved upon existing methodology even further in their National Women's Study, in which 4,008 female adults aged 18–81 years were interviewed by telephone three times over a two-year period. Men were not included in the study sample, and only data from the first interview are considered here. Participants were selected using random digit dialing methodology. Of the 4,008 women recruited, 2,008 were a national household probability sample, and the remaining 2,000 were an oversample of women aged 18–34 years, the age range for which victimization risk is greatest. Data were weighted to reflect the age and racial composition of the United States. A completion rate of 85.2 percent was achieved. The average age for participants (44.9 years) was somewhat higher than in several previous studies. Seventeen percent did not complete high school; 63.4 percent completed high school; and 20.0 percent completed college. Approximately two-thirds were married; half were employed full-time, and a fifth of the sample worked in the home. Twenty-seven percent earned less than $15,000 annually. Caucasians comprised 85.2 percent of the sample, and African Americans comprised 11.6 percent.

This study differed significantly from its predecessors in that it supplemented DIS based diagnostic procedures with contextually orienting preface statements for both physical and sexual assault. As can be seen in Table 3.1, this preface statement made clear that *all* assaults were of interest to the investigators, not just those perpetrated by strangers or reported to police. Moreover, as is evident in Table 3.2, extremely detailed, closed-ended behavioral descriptions of both physical and sexual assault were utilized, thereby diminishing definitional bias resulting from cultural, intellectual, educational, or psychological factors. Characteristics of up to three sexual assaults (first, most recent, worst) and one physical assault were obtained. Completed rape was defined by penetration of mouth, anus, or vagina through force or threat of force, occurring without the woman's consent. Fully 12.7 percent of women reported experiencing a completed rape in their lifetime, defined as an affirmative answer to any item in Table 3.2. Only 22 percent of rapes were perpetrated by strangers, and only 16 percent of cases were reported to police. Husbands and boyfriends were responsible for 19 percent of rapes, and other relatives accounted for 27 percent. Over half (58.5 percent) of the rape victims indicated that they felt their lives were in danger during the assault and over half reported serious (9.8 percent) or minor (46.3 percent) injury. Fully 29.3 percent of rapes occurred prior to age 11, and about two-thirds occurred prior to age 18.

Approximately 14 percent of the study sample indicated that they had experienced a sexual assault that did not qualify as rape, and 10.3 percent reported that they had been severely physically assaulted. Twenty-one percent of physical assault cases were perpetrated by strangers and 46 percent were reported to police. Husbands and boyfriends were responsible for 47 percent of physical assault cases, and other relatives were responsible for an additional 22 percent of cases. Three-fourths (74.8 percent) of physical assault victims reported that they perceived their lives were in danger during the assault, and over two-thirds reported suffering serious (28.7 percent) or minor (43.5 percent) injury. The relationship between physical assault and age was the opposite of that observed with rape, with risk of physical assault increasing with age. Two thirds of crime victims (including those who experienced homicide of a close friend or relative and sexual molestation) reported experiencing at least two different criminal acts.

Prevalence of rape and physical assault *were not* given individually in terms of demographic subgroups. Instead, *incidence* of new victimization (either physical assault or rape) occurring during the two years between Waves I and III of this longitudinal study were reported. When the unique effects of age, student status, employment status, marital status, race, sensation-seeking, and poverty level were examined to predict new assault, only student status, sensation-seeking, and prior history of victimization were significant, with prior assault, high sensation-seeking, and student status associated with increased risk of *new* victimization. The rate of new victimization (either rape or physical assault) in women with one prior victimization was 11.9 percent, 10.8 percent of women with two prior victimizations experienced a new victimization during the two-year follow-up, and fully 23 percent of women with three or more prior victimizations were newly victimized at follow-up. Incidence of new assault in women with high sensation-seeking scores was 5.4 percent, compared to 2.9 percent of low scorers. Finally, incidence of new victimization in women who were students (10.2 percent) was much higher than non-students (4.0 percent).

The orienting preface statements and detailed behavioral description of assault events appear to have produced a highly sensitive instrument by which to measure various forms of sexual assault. This sensitivity is evident when contrasting this study with two that did not utilize preface statements and behavioral specific descriptions. The rate of rape found by Resnick et al. was five times that reported for women by Breslau et al. (1991) (12.7 percent versus 2.6 percent), and the rate of general sexual assault was three times that observed by Norris (1992) (22.7 percent versus 7.3 percent).

The final crime prevalence investigation reviewed, the *National Comorbidity Study* was conducted by Kessler et al. (1995). Participants were 2,812 men and 3,065 women aged 15–54 years who represented a subsample of 8,098 originally interviewed individuals. Respondents were selected through randomized stratified national sampling procedures. The subsample of participants were re-interviewed in-person and completed PTSD and trauma assessment measures (the DIS) that were not part of the original interview. The overall response rate was 82.4 percent. Although this study represented an improvement over most earlier investigations, it did not include detailed preface statements or sufficiently detailed behavioral descriptions of trauma events to detect all instances of criminal victimization. Instead, participants were handed a written list of events and asked if any of these had happened to them. Illustrative items from this list relevant to this chapter are given below:

> *"You were raped (someone had sexual intercourse with you when you did not want to by threatening you or using some degree of force)."*
> *"You were sexually molested (someone touched or felt your genitals when you did not want them to)."*
> *"You were seriously physically attacked or assaulted."*
> *"You were threatened with a weapon, held captive, or kidnaped."*

Because they were of only limited behavioral specificity, these items had the potential to introduce definitional bias, and conservative estimates of criminal victimization are expected, particularly for sexual assault and rape. As was the case in previous studies, men reported experiencing significantly more physical assault and women reported experiencing significantly more sexual assault in their lifetimes. For women, lifetime rates of rape and molestation equaled 9.2 percent and 12.3 percent, respectively; and lifetime rates of physical attack and being threatened with a weapon were 6.9 percent and 6.8 percent, respectively. By contrast, men reported very low rates of lifetime rape (0.7 percent) and molestation (2.8 percent), but high rates of physical attack (11.1 percent) and being threatened with a weapon (19.0 percent). Table 3.3 summarizes criminal violence prevalence rates across these studies by demographic groups.

In general, these studies represent improvements over simple archival reporting of crime rates and early epidemiological investigations of victimization. However, in addition to verifying that a particular form of assault has occurred, social science researchers are typically interested in determining mental health outcomes of such events. In order to derive conceptual

TABLE 3.3 Prevalence and Incidence Estimates: Violent Crime and PTSD

STUDY	SEXUAL ASSAULT[1]	RAPE	ASSAULT	RAPE PTSD	ASSAULT PTSD
Bachman & Saltzman (1995) NCVS (Population)					
Male (Past Year)	—	0.05%	1.7%	—	—
Female (Past Year)	0.5%	0.2%	0.8%	—	—
Koss et al. (1987) (College Women)					
Female	14.4%	15.4%	—	—	—
Female (Past 6 Months)		3.8%	—	—	—
Caucasian		16%	—	—	—
African American		10%	—	—	—
Hispanic		12%	—	—	—
Native American		40%	—	—	—
Burnam et al. (1988) (L. A. Community)[1]					
Both Sexes	13.2%	—	—	—	—
Male	9.4%	—	—	—	—
Female	16.7%	—	—	—	—
Caucasian	19.9%	—	—	—	—
Hispanic	8.1%	—	—	—	—
Breslau et al. (1991) (HMO)					
Both Sexes	—	—	8.3%	—	22.6%
Female	—	2.6%	—	80%	—
Kilpatrick et al. (1992) NWS (Population)					
Female	14.3%	12.7%	10.3%	32.0%	38.5%
Female (Past Year)	1.6%	0.7%	1.8%	12.4%	17.8%
Kessler et al. (1995) NCS (Population)					
Male	2.8%	0.7%	11.1%	65.0%	1.8%
Female	12.3%	9.2%	6.9%	45.9%	21.3%
Norris (1992) (South-East Coast)					
Both Sexes	4.4%	—	15.0%	13.6%	13.3%
Male[2]	1.3%	—	18.7%	—	5.5%[2]
Female[2]	7.3%	—	11.7%	—	11.5%[2]
Caucasian[2]	4.2%	—	18.4%	—	7.2%[2]
African American[2]	4.6%	—	11.6%	—	10.4%[2]
Young Adult[2]	6.6%	—	19.1%	—	7.8%[2]
Middle Aged Adult[2]	4.5%	—	16.8%	—	13.6%[2]
Older Adult[2]	1.9%	—	8.6%	—	3.3%[2]

(Continued)

TABLE 3.3   Continued

STUDY	SEXUAL ASSAULT[1]	RAPE	ASSAULT	RAPE PTSD	ASSAULT PTSD
Both Sexes (Past Year)	0.4%	—	2.4%	—	—
Male (Past Year)	0.6%	—	1.7%	—	—
Female (Past Year)	0.2%	—	3.1%	—	—
Caucasian (Past Year)	0.4%	—	2.2%	—	—
African American (Past Year)	0.4%	—	2.6%	—	—
Young Adult (Past Year)	0.5%	—	4.6%	—	—
Middle-Aged Adult (Past Year)	0.6%	—	2.3%	—	—
Older Adult (Past Year)	0.0%	—	0.0%	—	—

Note: Prevalence rates are *lifetime* estimates, unless otherwise noted. "Assault" refers to physical assault.

[1]Includes molestation, and for the Burnam et al. study, includes rape.

[2]In the Norris study, rates of PTSD for these variables are in response to rape, physical assault, *or* robbery, not simply "Assault."

models that outline assault-to-psychopathology pathways, multiple aspects of trauma and traumatic response must be considered. Unfortunately, most studies of assault-related psychopathology have been somewhat limited in their assessment of variables that play a potentially important role in mental and emotional functioning. Specifically, assault events are routinely examined in isolation, with little consideration given to the differential effects of multiple versus single assault, early-childhood versus later-life assault, assault by stranger versus acquaintance assault, and so forth. This point is particularly relevant when considering that approximately 50 percent of physically and sexually assaulted individuals have prior victimization histories (e.g., Kilpatrick, 1990). Kilpatrick, Resnick, Saunders, and Best (in press) have suggested that new studies be designed in accord with the following: (1) Temporal boundaries of prevalence, rates should be widened to include all adult, or even all lifetime, events. Failure to attend to crime occurring across the lifespan (e.g., the Bureau of Justice Statistics National Crime Victimization Survey, NCVS) produces incidence, rather than prevalence, rates and inappropriately simplifies causal models of pathology; (2) Multiple or complex victimization histories for each respondent should be collected and considered in causal models of psychopathology, as opposed to focusing on one type of crime, occurring at one point in time, committed by one type of assailant (e.g., the FBI's UCR in which only the most serious victimization is included in prevalence rates); (3) Studied samples should be representative of the population of interest; (4) Both quantitative (e.g., level of physical injury experienced, number of perpetrators, presence of weapon during assault) and qualitative (e.g., perceptions of life threat during assault, fear of crime) aspects of victimization history should be obtained and studied; finally, (5) Other contextual factors that influence posttraumatic outcome, including familial and personal history of psychopathology, social and vocational adjustment, and level of social support, should be assessed.

RISK FACTORS: ASSAULTIVE VIOLENCE

It is reasonable to assume that different risk factors are relevant for different types of criminal victimization, perpetrated by different classes of individuals (Hanson et al., 1995). That is, factors associated with risk of rape may well differ from those associated with being physically attacked. Similarly, risk of assault by one's spouse is probably associated with several risk factors that do not increase likelihood of assault by a stranger, and vice versa. Because of this, studies that seek to determine prevalence and risk of assaultive violence should consider contextual factors in order to develop predictive models of and treatments for violence. Indeed, it is necessary to identify risk factors prior to developing and implementing risk-reduction strategies (Hanson et al., 1995).

Risk of assaultive violence varies with gender, age, race, socioeconomic status, prior victimization history, psychiatric history, substance use, personality characteristics, and geographic location (Adler et al., 1994; Bachman, 1994; Breslau et al., 1991; Hanson et al., 1995; Norris, 1992). Several of these risk factors (e.g., gender, age) have been outlined above. As is evident from inspection of aforementioned prevalence rates, women are at tremendously increased risk of all forms of sexual assault, while men are more likely than women to experience physical assault, particularly at the hands of strangers. Women are more likely to be physically attacked by known individuals such as husbands or ex-husbands (31 percent of assaults), boyfriends (16 percent of assaults), other relatives (27 percent of assaults) and acquaintances (9 percent of assaults) (Kilpatrick et al., in press). By contrast, men suffer violent crime from strangers at a rate 11 times that of known perpetrators (Bachman & Saltzman, 1994). Comparing the sexes directly, men are at about twice the risk of experiencing physical assault by a stranger than women (Bachman, 1994).

Age is negatively correlated with risk of sexual assault, but may be positively correlated with risk of physical assault within a limited range (Bachman & Saltzman, 1994; Bureau of Justice Statistics, 1992; Kilpatrick et al., 1992; Norris, 1992). Kilpatrick et al. noted that 62 percent of forcible rapes reported by participants in the NWS occurred prior to age 18. Considering any assault, Kilpatrick et al. (in press) noted that 23.7 percent of their sample reported victimization onset before age 17; 46.8 percent experienced assault between age 17–29; and only 26.8 percent reported their first attack occurred after age 30. Similarly, NCVS data show that respondents 12–19 years old were at

2–3 times risk of crime than those over 20 years of age (Whitaker & Bastian, 1991).

Estimates of risk associated with racial status have been mixed. Several studies have found Caucasians at increased risk: Norris (1992) found that Caucasians were more likely to be physically assaulted than African Americans, and no significant differences were observed in rates of risk of sexual assault. Cottler, Compton, Mager, Spitznagel, and Janca (1992) also noted that risk of general exposure to traumatic events was elevated for Caucasians. Burnam et al. (1988) noted that Caucasians were sexually assaulted at a higher rate than Hispanics in the Los Angeles area. Two studies have found no relationship between risk of violence and race: Breslau et al. (1991) reported that race was not associated with increased risk of exposure to trauma (these investigators did not differentiate accidents, and so on, from criminal victimization), and Bachman and Saltzman (1994) reported that rates of partner violence were not different across races. Still other studies have found African Americans at greatest risk: The FBI UCR (1991) and other epidemiological studies (Hanson et al., 1993; Kilpatrick et al., 1991) indicate that African Americans are at greater risk for violent assault than Caucasians. The NCVS (Bachman & Saltzman, 1994) found that annual rates of victimization (a composite variable including rape, sexual assault, robbery, and physical assault) were greater in African American women (4.5 percent) than Caucasians (3.5 percent). Kilpatrick et al. (1991) reported that only 19 percent of Caucasians were victims of violent crime, relative to 28 percent of African Americans and 30 percent of Hispanic Americans. Discrepancies across studies may be attributable to confounding effects of income, education, age, geographic location, and gender. However, Kilpatrick, Acierno et al. (1997) addressed this issue, in part, and found that women of minority status were at increased risk of assault after effects of age, education, assault history, and substance use were controlled. Additional research is needed in which all demographic variables are examined in multivariate analyses to in order to isolate true effects of race on victimization risk.

Income appears to be inversely related to risk of various forms of violent assault (Kilpatrick et al., in press; Reiss & Roth, 1993). Bachman and Saltzman (1994) reported that women with earning less than $10,000 annually were more likely to have been victimized by their partner. Similarly, in their longitudinal study, Kilpatrick et al. noted that women with incomes less than $10,000 were at almost twice the risk of experiencing a *new* assault in the two year follow-up period. Moreover, this effect was apparent even after impact of victimization history was controlled. However, in their Los Angeles study Hanson et al. (1993) observed that income was not as powerful a predictor of past-year assault as some other demographic factors (e.g., age, gender).

One of the most potent predictors of future victimization is past victimization (Hanson et al., 1995; Kilpatrick et al., in press; Koss & Dinero, 1989; Sorenson, Siegel, Golding, & Stein, 1991; Steketee & Foa, 1987; Zawitz, 1988). Kilpatrick, Acierno, et al. (in press) reported that risk of new assault in previously assaulted women was increased by a factor of 5, *over and above* the effects of age, race, education, and substance use. Further, this risk appears to increase at a linear rate. That is, Kilpatrick et al. (in press) noted that, compared to women who had not been assaulted, odds of experiencing a new assault over a two year period were doubled for women with one assault, increased by a factor of 5 for women with two assaults, and elevated by a factor of 13 for women with three or more prior victimizations. Importantly, this risk appears to be longstanding, and the best predictor of adult sexual assault is child sexual assault (Koss & Dinero, 1989; Wyatt, Gutherie, & Notgrass, 1992). When considering these data, one must be careful not to leap to explanations that blame the victim for their assault. As Hanson et al. (1995) point out, part of the assaultive risk associated with past victimization is probably due to residential location and crime type. That is, remaining in violent neighborhoods or being continually accessible to perpetrators (e.g., due to financial hardship, domestic violence, child abuse) will increase risk of victimization.

It is extremely difficult to isolate psychiatric status as a risk factor for assault because longitudinal studies that specify the order of onset of psychopathology and victimization are lacking. Moreover, most existing research is oriented toward conceptualizing assault as a risk factor for psychopathology, rather than the reverse. Nevertheless, the relationship between mental health problems and assaultive violence is strong. Saunders, Kilpatrick, Resnick, and Tidwell (1989) found that 72.2 percent of patients presenting to a community mental health center were victims of physical assault, sexual assault, or were the family members of homicide victims. Burnam et al. (1988) found that major depression, antisocial personality disorder, and phobias were associated with increased likelihood of reporting later sexual assault. Further, Breslau et al. (1991) reported that having family members with psychopathology nearly doubled risk that one would be exposed to traumatic events in general. It is not unreasonable to presume that mental illness increases one's vulnerability for assault. Indeed, affective disorders might result in reduced ability to perceive dangerous situations and reduced resources to escape from these situations. Similar arguments could be made for the psychoses and dementias. Moreover, individuals with mental illness might elicit aggressive or assaultive behavior from others (Hanson et al., 1995). Finally, predatory assailants might target mentally ill individuals with the supposition that they will be less likely to choose to defend themselves, less competent in defending themselves if they choose to do so, and less convincing in their accusations if perpetrators are caught.

Another powerful risk factor for assault is substance use. Several investigations offer evidence that substance use precedes, as opposed to exclusively follows, assault. Kilpatrick, Acierno et al. (1997) analyzed longitudinal data from the NWS and demonstrated that drug use in previously non-victimized women was associated with increased risk of new assault. This risk was evident over and above effects of age, race, and education. However, the reciprocal relationship was also noted. That is, a new assault in previously non-using women was associated with increased risk of substance use. Cottler et al. (1992) found that odds of being assaulted for hard drug users and marijuana users were 5.06 and 1.46 times those of non-users, respectively. Burnam et al. (1988) also reported that risk of sexual assault was increased in substance abusers. Moreover, Breslau et al. (1991) noted that odds of experiencing traumatic events in individuals with alcohol or drug use problems were 1.47 and 1.79 times those of individuals without such substance use problems, respectively. In addition, Kessler et al. (1995) reported alcohol and drug abusers were about 1.5 times as likely to experience traumatic events than non-users. Childhood experience of assault was not directly addressed in these studies, however, and the temporal pattern of onset remains unclear. This point may be moot, however, when one considers that, irrespective of childhood assault history, continued illicit drug use increases risk of *new* assault (Kilpatrick, Acierno, et al., 1997).

The personality trait of "sensation-seeking" has been posited as a risk factor for assault. As outlined by Hanson et al. (1995), sensation-seeking individuals tend to engage in risk-taking behaviors, and tend to underestimate the danger of risky situations (Zuckerman, 1979). Moreover, they approach potentially dangerous situations with less fear and anxiety than non-sensation seekers. As a result, sensation seekers may not perceive the relative risk of victimization associated with certain behaviors. Kilpatrick et al. (in press) directly studied this trait in the NWS and found that adult women with sensation seeking-scores above the median experienced higher rates of physical and sexual assault (5.4 percent) during the two-year follow-up period than women with below-median scores (2.9 percent). Moreover, increased risk was evident after controlling for poverty and prior victimization status. However, sensation-seeking is inversely related to age, more prevalent in males, and characteristic of substance abusers (Zuckerman, 1983). Because these characteristics are themselves associated with increased risk of assault, conclusions regarding independent effects of sensation-seeking are premature.

Using archival data based on police reports (i.e., the FBI's UCR), Reiss and Roth (1993) reported that violent crime levels are positively correlated with community size. For cities with populations lower than 10,000, the past 6-month *reported* violent crime rate (rape, robbery, and aggravated assault) was 0.36 percent, compared to 2.24 percent for cities with over 1,000,000 residents. Similar results are obtained when non-reported crimes are also considered. Data from the NCVS (Bureau of Justice Statistics, 1992) demonstrated that violent crime rates were lowest in rural areas, higher in suburban areas, and highest in cities. Hanson et al. (1995) note, however, that the UCR and the NCVS are more sensitive to crime perpetrated by strangers, relative to crime perpetrated by known assailants. As such, geographically based risk factors might not be relevant to risk of victimization by relatives, acquaintances, or partners.

PREVALENCE ESTIMATES: VIOLENT CRIME-RELATED PTSD

PTSD is almost unique among DSM-IV diagnostic classes in that an etiological component, exposure to a severe traumatic event, is clearly specified. Not elucidated, however, is the manner by which traumatic events such as rape or physical assault lead to PTSD and other post-traumatic psychopathology. Kilpatrick, Veronen, and Resick (1979), and Keane, Zimering, & Caddell (1985) have adapted Mowrer's (1960) two-factor model of phobic avoidance to explain post-traumatic psychopathology. According to this conceptualization, assault serves as the unconditioned stimulus that leads to the unconditioned responses characteristic of PTSD (i.e., avoidance, hyperarousal, and intrusive ideation). Initial responses typically also include symptoms of depression and panic. As with phobic fear, these responses become associated with salient stimuli present in the environment during the attack (e.g., perpetrator characteristics, location of assault) that then elicit learned fear responses in the future. Thus, when a victim is exposed to an individual who resembles the perpetrator, or finds herself in an elevator similar to the one in which she was assaulted, a conditioned response identical or very similar to the unconditioned response occurs. In order to reduce or eliminate extreme aversiveness of this learned anxiety response, individuals will escape from and subsequently avoid conditioned stimuli. This avoidance behavior naturally results in diminution of the fear response, and is thus negatively reinforced, thereby increasing the probability of future avoidance. Moreover, because repeated, extended exposure to conditioned stimuli is avoided, extinction of fear responses does not occur.

According to two-factor theory, conditioned post-traumatic anxiety responses are initially acquired through classical conditioning and maintained (in the form of avoidance) through operant conditioning. It should not be supposed on the basis of this model, however, that individual differences, cognitive behavior, cultural variables, and prior history do not play a role in the development of PTSD. Indeed, the conditioning model should be considered a potential pathway with which these other variables interact. Support for conditioning-based etiological conceptualization of PTSD, particularly as it relates to avoidance behavior, has been provided by Wirtz and Harrell (1987a, 1987b), who showed that avoidant victims experienced more psychological distress than those who exposed themselves to relevant fear-producing stimuli, irrespective of initial distress level. This finding is consistent with conditioning theory, which predicts that such avoidance would result in maintenance, rather than exposure-based extinction of the fear response. In addition, success of exposure-based treatments for PTSD (e.g., Foa, Rothbaum, Riggs, & Murdock, 1991; Foa, Hearst-Ikeda, & Perry, 1995; Fairbank & Keane, 1982) also provides indirect support for the model. Recently, the conditioning theory of post-traumatic psychopathology has been supplemented by cognitive models that emphasize the role of perceptions of controllability over past and future events, and estimates of the risk of danger associated with specific stimuli in determining outcome. In addition Keane (1985) has outlined the relevance of other individual factors to post-traumatic stress.

Prevalence estimates of crime-related PTSD are inextricably tied to the effectiveness with which surveys detect victimization. Simply put, if a traumatic event is not identified, PTSD is generally not evaluated. The aforementioned review of assessment strategies largely addresses this issue. However, other problems exist in detection and diagnosis of PTSD. For example, early studies required respondents to link their post-traumatic symptomatology to traumatic events. This level of insight might be lacking or purposefully denied by respondents, resulting in overly conservative prevalence estimates. Additionally, some studies employed non-standardized methods of assigning diagnosis, decreasing the comparability of PTSD rates across studies. It is also important that studies of PTSD prevalence in crime victims collect

data about the crime itself in order to identify risk factors for PTSD. Several risk factors (e.g., completed rape, perceived life threat, injury) associated with assault have been identified, but these account for less than 20 percent of the variance in the PTSD diagnosis, and the impact of other potential risk factors has not been outlined. Of the studies providing information about victimization prevalence reviewed above, Breslau et al. (1991), Norris (1992), Resnick et al. (1993), and Kessler et al. (1995) also provided data on PTSD prevalence.

Breslau et al. (1991) studied members of an HMO who were between the ages of 21 and 30 years, and PTSD prevalence estimates across the lifespan were precluded. As mentioned, this study employed a relatively weak method of trauma assessment, potentially yielding artificially low prevalence estimates. Although PTSD diagnoses were based on the DIS-R, a well-validated structured clinical interview, respondents were required to link PTSD symptomatology with traumatic events (up to three were considered), thereby further reducing sensitivity of the measure to PTSD. Results indicated that rape was associated with highest levels of PTSD. Fully 80 percent of women who had been raped in this sample developed PTSD at some point in their lives. Relatively fewer (22.6 percent) physical assault victims developed lifetime PTSD. Rates of PTSD following physical assault did not differ across the sexes. Sizeable differences in rates of PTSD following physical and sexual assault may be a function of the manner by which rape was assessed, in addition to differences produced by various types of assault. That is, this study used the term "rape" when assessing victimization prevalence. Koss (1993) noted that such queries pull for stereotypical interpretations of the term (e.g., stranger rape). As such, it is very likely that those women who had experienced a rape that was consistent with cultural stereotypes, or particularly violent rape, were more likely to report. Indeed, Resnick et al. noted that given the insensitive screening approach used for rape, women in this study who reported rape were most likely to be those whose assaults were most consistent with the type reported to police. Moreover, as Resnick et al. noted, this rate of PTSD is consistent with the rate observed among other populations of self-reported rape victims (e.g., Rothbaum, Foa, Riggs, Murdock, & Walsh, 1992). Such assaults are more likely to be characterized by injury and life threat, factors associated with the development of PTSD. If this was the case, it was not so much the type of assault, but the *intensity* of the assault that led to differences in PTSD rates. Support for this position is provided by studies described below, in which behaviorally specific queries were used to assess rape and physical assault. These investigations found that both forms of assault produced similar levels of PTSD.

In her study of 1,000 non-randomly selected adults, Norris (1992) derived a PTSD diagnosis on the basis of respondent's answers to standardized questionnaires, rather than on the basis of structured clinical interviews. Specifically, responses to items from the Traumatic Stress Schedule (Norris, 1990) and the Brief Symptom Inventory (Derogatis & Spencer, 1982) were combined to address each DSM-III-R diagnostic criterion for recent PTSD. Although this method of arriving at diagnostic classification is arguably less reliable, and hence less valid than that associated with structured clinical interviews, items corresponded closely with DSM specifications for PTSD. The overall rate of *current* crime-related PTSD was 8.5 percent. Among lifetime sexual assault victims, the rate of current PTSD was 13.6 percent. A similar PTSD rate of 13.3 percent was observed among victims of physical assault. Rates by demographic subgroups were available only for an aggregate crime variable defined by sexual assault, physical assault, and robbery. Crime-related PTSD was significantly higher in female crime victims (11.5 percent female victims versus 5.5 percent male victims), and significantly lower in older adult crime victims (3.3 percent older adults versus 7.8 percent younger adults and 13.6 percent middle-aged adults). The level of crime-related PTSD did not vary significantly according to race (Caucasians = 7.2 percent, African Americans = 10.4 percent).

Observed sex-based differences might be attributable to differences in type of victimization. While women suffered more sexual assault, men experienced more physical assault. Thus, sexual assault may be more predictive of PTSD. However, this conclusion is not strongly supported on the basis of this study, because sexual assault was vaguely defined

(i.e., "any type of unwanted sexual activity"). The age-based differences in PTSD are similar to those reported previously in the literature (Norris & Murrell, 1988). A possible explanation for reduced PTSD in older adults noted in this study might be due to the lifetime nature of the crime variable. That is, it is possible that older adults were victimized long ago and PTSD was initially present in them (when they were younger) at a level similar to younger adults (arguing against a cohort effect), but these symptoms then remitted over several decades. Alternatively, it may be the case that PTSD manifests itself differently in older adults, with perhaps greater somatic symptomatology and less overt hyperarousal or re-experiencing.

Kilpatrick et al. (1992) and Resnick et al. (1993) studied 4,008 adult women using the DIS-R accompanied by a sensitive traumatic event screen (the NWS PTSD module; Kilpatrick, Resnick, Saunders, & Best, 1989) to assign diagnosis. Failure to include males in the sample precluded analysis of sex-based differences. PTSD diagnosis did not require respondents to link symptomatology with traumatic events. Thirty-two percent of rape victims had lifetime PTSD, and 12.4 percent had current (past 6 months) PTSD. Rates of lifetime and current PTSD in physical assault victims were similarly high: 38.5 percent and 17.8 percent, respectively. Lifetime and current rates of PTSD observed in response to other forms of sexual assault equaled 30.8 percent and 13.0 percent, respectively. Experiencing the homicide death of a family member or friend also produced severe emotional reactions. Of women experiencing this event, 22.1 percent reported lifetime PTSD and 8.9 percent had current PTSD. Overall, crime victims had higher rates of lifetime (25.8 percent) and current (9.7 percent) PTSD than non-crime victims (9.4 percent lifetime PTSD, and 3.4 percent current PTSD).

The final study reviewed, that of Kessler et al. (1995) included males as well as females, but was limited to young and middle-aged adults. As was the case with Breslau et al. (1991) and Resnick et al. (1993), PTSD diagnoses were established using the DIS (diagnosis of other psychopathology was via the Composite International Diagnostic Interview (CIDI) World Health Organization, 1990). As mentioned, only minimal behavioral specificity characterized the trauma assessment used in this study, and PTSD was assessed for only one event (the one designated as "most upsetting") per respondent. Therefore, estimates of the rate of PTSD in response to individual crimes are potentially low. Results indicated that once exposed to any type of trauma women were more than twice as likely to develop PTSD, at any age, than men. Fully 20.4 percent of women and 8.6 percent of men who were exposed to trauma developed PTSD. Rape was most strongly associated with PTSD in both men and women. Sixty-five percent of men and 45.9 percent of women indicating that rape was the "most upsetting experienced trauma" developed PTSD. Molestation was also associated with high rates of PTSD in both men and women. Of the male respondents who endorsed molestation as their most upsetting trauma, 12.2 percent developed PTSD. This rate was significantly less than the 26.5 percent of molested women who developed PTSD. In an improvement over previous studies, rates of PTSD by sex in response to physical attack were disaggregated by Kessler et al. Only 1.8 percent of men who indicated that being physically attacked was their most upsetting trauma developed PTSD. The rate for women (21.3 percent) was more in line with those of previous studies.

In general, rates of PTSD in women following physical assault and abuse are comparable to those observed with rape. Indeed, Kilpatrick et al. (1987a) noted that lifetime rates of post-rape and post-assault PTSD in women were 57.1 percent and 36.8 percent, respectively, while Resnick et al. (1993) found rates of post-rape and post-assault PTSD of 32 percent and 38.5 percent, respectively. Although these rates vary significantly as a function of age and gender, both forms of assault are clearly detrimental to the psychological status of victims. Table 3.3 summarizes PTSD prevalence rates across these studies by demographic groups.

RISK FACTORS: VIOLENT CRIME-RELATED PTSD

Every victim of severe criminal victimization does *not* develop PTSD. Therefore, there are individual, contextual, and societal variables that determine rel-

ative risk of the disorder. Unfortunately, inadequate traumatic event screens and narrowly focused trauma assessments used in existing surveys have severely limited identification and study of risk factors associated with PTSD. That is, in instances where trauma has been identified, very little information on contextual, individual, situational, and other related factors has been gathered and reported. Thus, parameters of risk associated with crime-related PTSD remain largely unspecified, or specified on only a univariate level.

Of course, any factor that increases risk of assault may also be considered to increase the potential for PTSD. As such, the following risk factors are examined somewhat independent of their association with assault risk (discussed above). The likelihood of developing PTSD appears to vary according to quantitative crime characteristics (e.g., degree of injury experienced), qualitative crime characteristics (e.g., level of perceived life threat), and demographic characteristics (e.g., gender, age). PTSD risk was consistently elevated for women across studies in which sexes were compared (Breslau, et al., 1991; Cottler et al., 1992; Kessler et al., 1995; Norris, 1992). This finding was particularly noteworthy for physical assault, with women at about 10 times the risk following assault than men. Although rape produced equally high rates of PTSD in both sexes, the frequency of its occurrence in adult males appears to be so low as to justify no further comment.

As was the case for exposure to crime, age is inversely related to PTSD risk (Kilpatrick et al., 1989). Norris (1992) noted that the rate of current PTSD in older adult crime victims (3.3 percent) was less than half that reported by younger adult victims. However, her crime measure was somewhat vague; sex differences were not considered in terms of age, and analyses did not attempt to control for severity or type of crime. Kessler et al. (1995) also observed an age-related trend for lifetime PTSD in both men and women who had been exposed to trauma, with diminished risk associated with increased age. More conclusive statements regarding the effect of age on PTSD prevalence were precluded, however, since this sample was of restricted age range (15–54 years) and did not include any older adults.

Conclusions regarding effects of race on risk of PTSD are mixed. This is not surprising when considering that effects of race on risk of exposure to violence are also largely variable. Norris (1992) contrasted rates of crime-related PTSD in African Americans and Caucasians and observed no differences, although African Americans did report higher levels of stress in response to trauma in general. Breslau et al. (1991) assessed PTSD in persons exposed to any type of trauma, and also found no race-based differences. Kilpatrick et al. (1989) also failed to find race based differences in PTSD for crime victims. Although initially associated with increased risk, Cottler et al. (1992) controlled for age, gender, cocaine use, and depression, and found that race no longer predicted PTSD in those exposed to any type of trauma. Similarly, in their meta-analysis assessing distress in victims of interpersonal violence, Weaver and Clum (1995) found no race-based differences. By contrast, Green et al. (1990) noted that African American survivors of disaster did evince greater rates of PTSD, and Norris (1992) reported that African Americans reported more subjective distress (but not PTSD, per se) following general trauma. Therefore, race differences in PTSD might be apparent only in victims of non-criminal trauma. However, the majority of existing studies have not assessed prevalence of PTSD by race in terms of victimization type; thus, this conclusion may be premature.

In addition to increasing risk of future assault, experience of prior victimization also appears to elevate risk of PTSD upon experience of future trauma. Considering NWS data, Kilpatrick et al. (in press) noted that women who endured multiple trauma throughout their lifetime were more likely to be diagnosed with PTSD than women who experienced one or no traumas. Specifically, these investigators found that 3.2 percent of non-assaulted women had current PTSD, compared to 19.4 percent of women who were assaulted in the previous two years, and 18.3 percent of women who were assaulted both in the previous two years and in the distant past. However, 52.9 percent of women with two prior assaults who were newly assaulted had current PTSD. Thus, deleterious effects of repeated victimization are clear: Victims become sensitized rather than desensitized to traumatic crime.

Breslau et al. (1991) reported risk ratios for PTSD in individuals exposed to trauma with pre-existing psychiatric conditions. Odds of developing PTSD in response to any trauma in those scoring high on measures of neuroticism were 1.53 those of non-neurotic individuals. Similarly, risk of PTSD in trauma victims with pre-existing anxiety or depression was 2.46 times that of non-anxious or non-depressed trauma survivors. Kessler et al. (1995) also noted that the incidence of existing psychiatric conditions was high in individuals with PTSD. Cottler et al. (1992) specifically studied the risk of PTSD in drug users and found that cocaine abuse, but not marijuana use, was associated with increased risk of PTSD among trauma victims (most often assaultive violence), even after effects of depression, gender, race, and age were controlled. Psychiatric illness in family members also appears to be associated with increased risk of PTSD following general trauma. For example, Breslau et al. (1991) reported that odds of developing PTSD for trauma victims were almost tripled when their family members suffered from anxiety, and were doubled when family members evinced histories of antisocial personality disorder.

Cognitive appraisal style may also be associated with differential risk of developing PTSD. Falsetti and Resick (1990) demonstrated variation in causal attributions of positive and negative events in victims and non-victims. Specifically, victims tended to characterize causes of hypothetical negative events as more internal than non-victims, but rated causes of hypothetical positive events as more unstable. Moreover, victims described the causes of their trauma as stable. Such attributional styles have been associated with depressive outcome (Seligman, Abramson, Semmel, & von Baeyer, 1984) and might also potentiate PTSD. Unfortunately, the temporal order of onset of this attributional style and PTSD (or victimization) was not ascertained, and these attributions might be a result, rather than a contributing factor, in PTSD.

As mentioned, characteristics of assaultive violence also affect risk of developing PTSD. Crime characteristics can be divided into qualitative (i.e., perceived life threat) and quantitative (e.g., experienced injury). Weaver and Clum (1995) and Kilpatrick et al. (1989) indicated that subjective factors may be more strongly related to psychological outcome of trauma, particularly when the nature of the trauma involves interpersonal violence. Kilpatrick et al. and Resnick et al. (1993) divided female crime victims into mutually exclusive groups on the basis of perceived life threat and injury during crime and reported rates of lifetime PTSD for each. PTSD prevalence in victims who experienced life threat but not injury ranged from 20.6 percent to 26.6 percent; among those with injury only, the rate ranged form 25 percent to 30.6 percent. Finally, in victims with both life threat and injury, the rate of PTSD was 30.8 percent to 45.2 percent. By comparison, the rate of crime-related PTSD in victims with neither life threat or injury was 19.0 percent (Resnick et al., 1993). Overall, Kilpatrick et al. found that female rape victims who experienced both physical injury and perceived life threat were 8.5 times more likely to develop PTSD than crime victims not experiencing these events.

Additional factors that may be positively related to development of post-trauma psychopathology include: intensity of anxiety and distress experienced during trauma, extent of dissociation during trauma, and limited education or low socio-economic status (Breslau et al. 1991; Freedy, Resnick, Kilpatrick, Dansky, & Tidwell, 1994; Norris, 1992). By contrast, stable sources of social support appear to buffer against development of post-traumatic problems in psychological functioning (Burgess & Holstrom, 1979). As is evident from the above review, variables that increase risk of PTSD have been only preliminarily identified in narrowly focused and potentially misleading univariate analyses. To date, the interactions between trauma type and age, race, and gender on PTSD remain unknown. Moreover, very little multivariate analysis of risk factors for PTSD and crime-related PTSD exists. Such analysis is essential to discerning actual risk of PTSD associated with each factor.

COMORBIDITY: VIOLENT
CRIME-RELATED PTSD

Concurrent experience of other psychiatric disorders with PTSD is quite common in crime victims (Breslau et al., 1991; Davidson, Hughes, Blazer, & George, 1991; Helzer et al., 1987; Shore, Vollmer, & Tatum, 1989). Moreover, many of the symptoms of PTSD comprise the diagnostic criteria of major depressive or anxiety disorders. Helzer et al. (1987) and Breslau et al. (1991) noted that almost 80 percent of individuals with PTSD in their samples had experienced another psychiatric disorder, compared to 30 percent to 40 percent of those without PTSD. However, large relative risk estimates may be a function of exposure to traumatic events, rather than to PTSD per se. That is, comparisons were typically made between those who were PTSD positive and those who were PTSD negative. Comorbid psychopathology uniquely related to PTSD would logically involve comparisons between those who were victimized and were PTSD positive and similarly victimized individuals who were PTSD negative. Such analyses have not been conducted with any of the summarized data.

In the most comprehensive comorbidity study to date, Kessler et al. (1995) reported that lifetime rates of other psychological disorders in men and women with PTSD were 88.3 percent and 79.0 percent, respectively. Comorbid disorders appearing with the greatest frequency included depression, substance abuse, and phobia. Approximately 48 percent of the men and women with PTSD had a lifetime history of major depression, compared to 11.7 percent of non-PTSD men and 18.8 percent of non-PTSD women. Fully 51.9 percent of the PTSD men and 27.9 percent of PTSD women abused alcohol (rates of drug abuse were similar), compared to approximately 34.4 percent of non-PTSD men and 13.5 percent of non-PTSD women. Simple or social phobia was noted in about 30 percent of men and women with PTSD. A slightly larger proportion of women (12.6 percent) than men (7.3 percent) met criteria for panic disorder. Interestingly, agoraphobia was observed in 18 percent of men and 22.4 percent of women with PTSD, compared to 4.1 percent and 7.8 percent of non-PTSD men and women, respectively. Rates of other disorders, including generalized anxiety disorder, mania, and conduct disorder were also significantly elevated in participants diagnosed with PTSD. Note, however, that rates of comorbidity in the Kessler et al. study were not limited to crime-related PTSD. Moreover, these rates described lifetime, rather than current, comorbidity.

Comorbidity estimates provided by Breslau et al. (1991) were similar to those of Kessler et al. (1995); however, rates were not given by sex. Approximately 37 percent of those with PTSD also had a history of major depression, compared to 11% of those without PTSD. Alcohol abuse and drug abuse were also relatively more prevalent in individuals with lifetime PTSD (31.2 percent alcohol abuse; 21.5 percent drug abuse), as opposed to those without lifetime PTSD (20.5 percent alcohol abuse, 10.6 percent drug abuse). As in the Kessler et al. study, approximately 20 percent of PTSD positive individuals also had lifetime agoraphobia and 9.7 percent had lifetime panic, compared to 2–3.7 percent of PTSD negative participants. Other disorders that were significantly more prevalent in individuals with PTSD included OCD (15 percent), dysthymia (13 percent), mania (5 percent), and GAD. As with the Kessler et al. study, rates of comorbidity observed by Breslau et al. did not necessarily reflect *concurrent* conditions.

In their final summary to the National Institute of Justice for grant 84-IJ-CX-0039, Kilpatrick et al. (1987b) also reported comorbidity rates consistent with those above for PTSD and depression, panic, agoraphobia, and social phobia. Burnam et al. (1988) did not assess PTSD directly, but did report rates of disorders with onset *after* sexual assault events. As such, concurrently comorbid psychopathological states are illustrated. Results indicated that 13 percent of assaulted individuals developed major depression, 16 percent developed alcohol abuse or dependence, 18 percent began abusing drugs, 10 percent developed a phobia, 3 percent began experiencing panic, and 4 percent developed obsessive-compulsive disorder.

Recently, Irwin et al. (1996) demonstrated that crime-related PTSD is strongly associated with Irritable Bowel Syndrome (IBS). While not a psychiatric diagnosis per se, this disorder is most certainly affected by psychological processes. Fully 36 percent of their IBS patients also presented with PTSD. Along slightly different lines, Letourneau, Resnick, Kilpatrick, Saunders, and Best (1996) assessed prevalence of PTSD and trauma in female crime victims reporting a history of sexual dysfunction. This study is unique in that risk of comorbid PTSD and sexual

problems was assessed over and above effects attributable to rape alone. Women with PTSD were almost three times as likely to experience sexual dysfunction, even after effects of rape, assault-related injury, and depression were controlled.

Women participating in the NWS were also screened for bulimia nervosa. Interestingly, participants who had been physically or sexually assaulted and subsequently developed PTSD were at particularly increased risk (odds were 3.3 to 1) of developing bulimia nervosa (Dansky, Brewerton, Kilpatrick, & O'Neil, 1997). By contrast, risk of this eating disorder increased only marginally among women who had been victimized, but did not develop PTSD. It appears either that individuals who are victimized and predisposed to develop PTSD are also predisposed to engage in binge eating and purging, or that certain aspects of PTSD (e.g., its intense anxiety component) potentiate these behaviors in women. Table 3.4 contains summary comorbidity data for PTSD.

As mentioned, high rates of depression and general anxiety in individuals with PTSD may be a function of diagnostic criterion overlap between disorders. By contrast, high comorbidity of substance use disorders in individuals with PTSD may reflect inappropriate, albeit intermittently effective, stress reduction strategies (Acierno et al., in press; Kilpatrick et al., in press). Indeed, individuals with PTSD are characterized by increased hyperarousal and distress, and substances such as alcohol might reduce this arousal, while substances such as cocaine might address depressive symptomatology. The high prevalence of agoraphobia, social phobia, and specific phobia lend additional support to the conditioning theory of PTSD. That is, these disorders are very likely diagnosed in response to avoidance of cues associated with criminal victimization that now elicit conditioned fear responses. As such, they reflect severe manifestations of the PTSD avoidance component. IBS and sexual dysfunction both might be the result of increased anxiety and distress. While IBS problems are likely associated with long-standing and pervasive anxiety, sexual dysfunction is probably related to contextual stimuli that elicit conditioned fear responses, particularly in rape victims. The findings regarding PTSD and bulimia nervosa are startling,

TABLE 3.4   PTSD Lifetime Comorbidity Estimates

STUDY	PTSD + DEPRESSION	PTSD + ALCOHOL ABUSE	PTSD + DRUG ABUSE	PTSD + SOCIAL PHOBIA	PTSD + SIMPLE PHOBIA	PTSD + AGORAPHOBIA	PTSD + PANIC
Kilpatrick et al. (1987b)							
Female	31.8%	—	—	18.2%	—	18.2%	13.6%
Burnam et al. (1988)[1]							
Both Sexes	13.4%[1]	15.7%[1]	18.4%[1]	—	10.4%[1]	—	2.8%[1]
Breslau et al. (1991)							
Both Sexes	36.6	31.2	21.5	—	—	21.5	9.7
Kessler et al. (1995) NCS							
Male	47.9	51.9	34.5	27.6	31.4	16.1	7.3
Female	48.5	27.9	26.9	28.4	29.0	22.4	12.6

[1]The Burnam et al. study did not diagnose PTSD per se, and rates of other disorders are, in this case, independent of PTSD and not comparable across studies.

and additional study is necessary to illuminate the exact nature of this comorbid relationship.

CONCLUSION

In general, rates of lifetime PTSD in response to sexual assault range from 30 percent to 80 percent, depending on the type of sexual victimization; and rates of PTSD in response to physical assault range from 23 percent to 39 percent. Overall, men are physically assaulted more than women, and are sexually assaulted less than women. Women develop PTSD in response to physical or sexual assault at about the same rate, whereas men rarely develop PTSD in response to physical assault, but regularly develop PTSD in response to severe sexual assault such as rape (a much rarer occurrence for them). Given any trauma, women are at 6 times the risk of men for developing PTSD (Kessler et al., 1995). Thus, rates of PTSD are greater for women than men.

Race-based differences in prevalence of victimization and PTSD remain unresolved, with some studies, but not others, showing Caucasians at increased risk of assault and African Americans at increased risk of developing PTSD. However, these differences might be due to culturally based response biases or influence of uncontrolled confounding factors such as education or socio-economic status. Age-based differences in both victimization prevalence and PTSD seem clear: Younger people are at increased risk of victimization, and, once victimized, are more likely to develop PTSD. Further research is needed to ascertain precisely why rates of victimization are lower in older adults, and if reduced risk of PTSD is attributable to some resiliency associated with age, or if older adults simply display post-traumatic symptomatology differently (e.g., perhaps more somatically) than younger adults.

Some forms of trauma (e.g., rape) are undoubtably more distressing than others, and carry with them greater likelihood of developing PTSD. Existing research has demonstrated that completed rape, perceived life threat during assault, and injury due to assault are associated with increased risk of PTSD. Future research should continue to isolate those qual-itative and quantitative factors of assault that increase risk of PTSD, so that at-risk populations are quickly identified, and preventive interventions effectively designed to meet individual victims' specific needs.

REFERENCES

Acierno, R., Byrne, C., Resnick, H. S. & Kilpatrick, D. G. (in press). Adult victims of physical violence. In N. Singh (Ed.) *Volume 9: Applications in diverse populations.* NY: Elsevier Science.

Adler, N. E., Boyce, T., Chesney, M. A., Cohen, S., Folkman, S., Kahn, R. L., & Syme, S. L. (1994). *Socioeconomic status and health. American Psychologist, 49,* 15–24.

American Psychiatric Association (1987). *Diagnostic and statistical manual of mental disorders* (3rd. ed., Rev.). Washington DC: Author.

American Psychiatric Association (1994). *Diagnostic and statistical manual of mental disorders* (4th ed.). Washington DC: Author.

Bachman, R. (1994). *Violence against women. A national crime victimization survey report.* U.S. Department of Justice, Office of Justice Programs, Bureau of Justice Statistics.

Bachman, R. & Saltzman, L. E. (1994). *Violence against women: Estimates from the redesigned survey.* U.S. Department of Justice Special Report NCJ-154348, Office of Justice Programs, Bureau of Justice Statistics.

Breslau, N., Davis, G. C., Andreski, P., & Petersen, E. (1991). Traumatic events and posttraumatic stress disorder in an urban population of young adults. *Archives of General Psychiatry, 48,* 216–222.

Bureau of Justice Statistics. (1992). *Criminal victimization in the United States, 1990.* Washington, DC: U.S. Government Printing Office.

Burgess, A. W., & Holstrum, L. (1974). The rape trauma syndrome. *American Journal of Psychiatry, 131,* 981–986.

Burnam, M. A., Stein, J. A., Golding, J. M., Siegel, J. M., Sorenson, S. B., Forsythe, A. B, & Telles, C. A. (1988) Sexual assault and mental disorders in a community population. *Journal of Consulting and Clinical Psychology, 56,* 843–850.

Cottler, L. B., Compton, W. M., Mager, D., Spitznagel, E. L., and Janca, A. (1992). Posttraumatic stress disorder among substance users from the general population. *American Journal of Psychiatry, 149,* 664–670.

Dansky, B. S., Brewerton, T. D., Kilpatrick, D. G., & O'Neil, P. M. (1997). The National Women's Study: Relationship of victimization and posttraumatic stress disorder to bulimia nervosa. *International Journal of Eating Disorders.*

Davidson, L. M., Hughes, D., Blazer, D., & George, L. K. (1991). Post-traumatic stress disorder in the community: An epidemiological study. *Psychological Medicine, 21,* 713–721.

Derogatis, L., & Spencer, P. (1982). *The brief symptom inventory (BSI): Administration, scoring and procedures manual: 1.* Baltimore, MD: Author.

Essock-Vitale, S. M., & McGuire, M. T. (1985). Women's lives viewed from an evolutionary perspective. I. Sexual histories, reproductive success, and demographic characteristics of a random sample of American women. *Ethnology and Sociobiology, 6,* 137–154.

Fairbank, J. A., & Keane, T. M. (1982). Flooding for combat-related stress disorders: Assessment of anxiety reduction across traumatic memories. *Behavior Therapy, 13,* 499–510.

Falsetti, S. A., & Resick, P. A. (1990). *Causal attributions, self-blame, and perceived responsibility in victims of crime.* Unpublished manuscript, University of Missouri-St. Louis.

Federal Bureau of Investigation. (1991). *Uniform Crime Reports for the United States: 1990.* United States Government Printing Office.

Federal Bureau of Investigation (1995). *Uniform crime reports for the United States 1994.* United States Government Printing Office.

Foa, E. B., Hearst-Ikeda, D., & Perry, K. J. (1995). Evaluation of a brief cognitive-behavioral program for the prevention of chronic PTSD in recent assault victims. *Journal of Consulting and Clinical Psychology, 63,* 948–955.

Foa, E. B., Rothbaum, R., Riggs, D., & Murdock, T. (1991). Treatment of PTSD in rape victims: A comparison between cognitive behavioral procedures and counseling. *Journal of Consulting and Clinical Psychology, 59,* 715–723.

Freedy, J. R., Resnick, H. S., Kilpatrick, D. G., Dansky, B. S., & Tidwell, R. P. (1994). The psychological adjustment of recent crime victims in the criminal justice system. *Journal of Interpersonal Violence, 9,* 450–468.

Gordon, M. T., & Riger, S. (1989). *The female fear.* New York: Macmillan.

Green, B. L. (1990). Defining trauma: Terminology and generic stressor dimensions. *Journal of Applied and Social Psychology, 20,* 1632–1642.

Green, B. L. (1994). Psychosocial research in traumatic stress: An update. *Journal of Traumatic Stress, 7,* 341–357.

Green, B. L., Lindy, J., Grace, M., Gleser, G., Leonard, A., Korol, M., & Winget, C. (1990). Buffalo Creek survivors in the second decade: Stability of stress symptoms. *American Journal of Orthopsychiatry, 60,* 43–54.

Hanson, R., Kilpatrick, D. G., Freedy, J. R., & Saunders, B. (1993). Los Angeles County following the 1992 civil disturbances: Degree of exposure and impact on mental health. *Journal of Consulting and Clinical Psychology, 63* 87–96.

Hanson, R. F., Kilpatrick, D. G., Falsetti, S. A., & Resnick, H. S. (1995). Violent crime and mental health. In J. R. Freedy & S. E. Hobfoll (Eds.) *Traumatic stress: From theory to practice* (129–161). New York: Plenum Press.

Harlow, C. W. (1989). *Injuries from crime.* Bureau of Justice Statistics Special Report NCJ-116811. Washington, DC: U.S. Department of Justice.

Helzer, J. E., Robins, L. N., & McEvoy, L. (1987). Posttraumatic stress disorder in the general population. *New England Journal of Medicine, 317,* 1630–1634.

Higgins, S., Delaney, D., Budney, A., Bickel, W., Hughes, J., Foerg, F., & Fenwick, W. (1991). A behavioral approach to achieving initial cocaine abstinence. *American Journal of Psychiatry, 148,* 1218–1224.

Irwin, C., Falsetti, S. A., Lydiard, R. B., Ballenger, J. C., Brock, C. D., & Brener, W. (1996). Comorbidity of posttraumatic stress disorder and irritable bowel syndrome. *Journal of Clinical Psychiatry, 57,* 576–578.

Keane, T. M. (1985). Defining traumatic stress: Some comments on the current terminological confusion. *Behavior Therapy, 16,* 419–423.

Keane, T. M., Zimering, R. T., & Caddell, J. M. (1985). A behavioral formulation of posttraumatic stress disorder in Vietnam veterans. *The Behavior Therapist, 8,* 9–12.

Kessler, R. C., Sonnega, A., Bromet, E., Hughes, M., & Nelson, C. B. (1995). Posttraumatic stress disorder in the National Comorbidity Survey. *Archives of General Psychiatry, 52,* 1048–1060.

Kilpatrick, D. G. (1983). Special feature: Assessment and treatment of rape victims. *The Clinical Psychologist, 36* (4).

Kilpatrick, D. G. (1990, August). *Violence as a precursor of women's substance abuse: The rest of the drug-violence story.* Presented at Topical Mini-Convention on Substance Abuse and Violence at the 98th Annual Convention of the American Psychological Association, Boston, MA.

Kilpatrick, D. G., Acierno, R., Resnick, H., Saunders, B., & Best, C. (1997). A two-year longitudinal analysis of the relationships among assault and substance abuse in women. *Journal of Consulting and Clinical Psychology, 65,* 835–847.

Kilpatrick, D. G., & Amick, A. E. (1985). Rape trauma. In M. Hersen & C. G. Last (Eds.), *Behavior therapy casebook* (pp. 86–103). New York: Springer.

Kilpatrick, D. G., Best, C. L., Veronen, L. J., Amick, A. E., Villeponteaux, L. A., & Ruff, G. A. (1985). Mental health correlates of criminal victimization: A random community survey. *Journal of Consulting and Clinical Psychology, 53* (6), 866–873.

Kilpatrick, D. G., Edmunds, C. N., & Seymour, A. K. (1992). *Rape in America: A report to the nation.* Arlington, VA: National Victim Center & Medical University of South Carolina.

Kilpatrick, D. G., & Resnick, H. S. (1993). PTSD associated with exposure to criminal victimization in clinical and community populations. In J. R. Davidson & E. B. Foa (Eds.) *Post-traumatic stress disorder in review: Recent research and future directions* (pp. 113–143). Washington, DC: American Psychiatric Press.

Kilpatrick, D. G., Resnick, H. S., Saunders, B. E., & Best, C. L. (1989). *The National Womens Study PTSD module.* Charleston, SC: Crime Victims Research and Treatment Center, Department of Psychiatry, Medical University of South Carolina. Unpublished instrument.

Kilpatrick, D. G., Resnick, H. S., Saunders, B. E., & Best, C. L. (in press). Rape, other violence against women, and posttraumatic stress disorder: Critical issues in assessing the adversity-stress-psychopathology relationship. In B. P. Dohrenwend (Ed.), *Adversity, Stress, & Psychopathology.* Washington, DC: American Psychiatric Press.

Kilpatrick, D. G., Saunders, B. E., Amick-McMullan, A., Best, C. L., & Veronen, L. J., & Resnick, H. S. (1989). Victim and crime factors associated with the development of crime-related post-traumatic stress disorder. *Behavior Therapy, 20,* 199–214.

Kilpatrick, D. G., Saunders, B. E., Veronen, L. J., Best, C. L., & Von, J. M. (1987a). Criminal victimization: Lifetime prevalence, reporting to police, and psychological impact. *Crime and Delinquency, 33*(4), 479–489.

Kilpatrick, D. G., Seymour, A.,K, & Boyle, J. (1991). *America speaks out: Citizens' attitudes about victims' rights and violence*. Arlington, VA: National Victim Center.

Kilpatrick, D. G., Sutker, P. B., & Smith, A. D. (1976). Deviant drug and alcohol use: The role of anxiety, sensation seeking, and other personality variables. In M. Zuckerman and C. Speilberg (Eds.), *Emotions and anxiety: New concepts, methods, and applications* (pp. 247–278). New York: Lawrence Earlbaum Associates.

Kilpatrick, D. G., Veronen, L. J., & Resick, P. A. (1979). The aftermath of rape: Recent empirical findings. *American Journal of Orthopsychiatry, 49*, 658–669.

Kilpatrick, D. G., Veronen, L. J., Saunders, B. E., et al. (1987b). *The psychological impact of crime: A study of randomly surveyed crime victims. Final Report*. National Institute of Justice Grant No.: 84-IJ-CX-0039.

Koop, C. E. (1992). Violence in America: A public health emergency. *Journal of the American Medical Association, 267*, 3075–3076.

Koss, M. P. (1993). Detecting the scope of rape: A review of prevalence research methods. *Journal of Interpersonal Violence, 8*, 198–222.

Koss, M. P., & Dinero, T. E. (1989). Discrimination analysis of risk factors for sexual victimization among a national sample of college women. *Journal of Consulting and Clinical Psychology, 57*, 242, 250.

Koss, M. P., Gidycz, C., & Wisniewski, N. (1987). The scope of rape: Incidence and prevalence of sexual aggression and victimization in a national sample of higher education students. *Journal of Consulting and Clinical Psychology, 55*, 162–170.

Letourneau, E. J., Resnick, H. S., Kilpatrick, D. G., Saunders, B. E., & Best, C. L. (1996). Comorbidity of sexual problems and posttraumatic stress disorder in female crime victims. *Behavior Therapy, 27*, 321–336.

Mowrer, O. H. (1960). *Learning theory and the symbolic processes*. New York: Wiley.

Norris, F. H. (1990). Screening for traumatic stress: A scale for use in the general population. *Journal of Applied Social Psychology, 20*, 1704–1718.

Norris, F. H. (1992). Epidemiology of trauma: Frequency and impact of different potentially traumatic events on different demographic events. *Journal of Consulting and Clinical Psychology, 60*, 409–418.

Norris, F., & Kaniasty, K. (1992). A longitudinal study of the effects of various crime prevention strategies on criminal victimization, fear of crime, and psychological distress. *American Journal of Community Psychology, 20*, 625–648.

Norris, F., & Kaniasty, K. (1994). Psychological distress following criminal victimization in the general population: Cross sectional, logitudinal, and prospective analyses. *Journal of Consulting and Clinical Psychology, 62*, 111–123.

Norris, F., & Murrell, S. A. (1988). Prior experience as a moderator of disaster impact on anxiety symptoms in older adults. *American Journal of Community Psychology, 16*, 665–685.

Novello, A. C. (1992). A medical response to violence. *Journal of the American Medical Association, 267*, 3007.

Reiss, A. J., & Roth, J. A. (1993). *Understanding and preventing violence*. Washington, DC: National Academy Press.

Resnick, H. S., Falsetti, S. A., Kilpatrick, D. G., & Freedy, J. R. (1996). Assessment of rape and other civilian trauma-related PTSD: Emphasis on assessment of potentially traumatic events. In T. W. Miller (Ed.), *Theory and assessment of stressful life events*, (pp. 235–271). Madison, CT: International Universities Press.

Resnick, H. S., Kilpatrick, D. G., Dansky, B. S., Saunders, B. E., & Best, C. L. (1993). Prevalence of civilian trauma and PTSD in a representative national sample of women. *Journal of Consulting and Clinical Psychology, 61*, 984–991.

Robins, L., Helzer, J., Cottler, L., & Goldring, E. (1988). *NIMH diagnostic interview schedule, version III, revised (DIS-III-R)*. St. Louis: Washington University Press.

Rosenberg, M. L., & Fenley, M. A. (1991). *Violence in America: A public health approach*. New York: Oxford University Press.

Rothbaum, B. O., Foa, E. B., Riggs, D. S., Murdock, T., & Walsh, W. (1992). A prospective examination of posttraumatic stress disorder in rape victims. *Journal of Traumatic Stress, 5*, 455–475.

Saunders, B. E., Kilpatrick, D. G., Resnick, H. S., & Tidwell, R. P. (1989). Brief screening for lifetime history of criminal victimization at mental health intake: A preliminary study. *Journal of Interpersonal Violence, 4*, 267–277.

Seligman, M. E., Abramson, L. Y., Semmel, A., & von Baeyer, C. (1984). Depressive attributional style. *Southern Psychologist, 2*, 18–22.

Shore, J. H., Vollmer, W. M., & Tatum, E. L. (1989). Community patterns of posttraumatic stress disorders. *Journal of Nervous and Mental Disease, 177,* 681–685.

Sorenson, S. B., Siegel, J. M., Golding, J. M., & Stein, J. A. (1991). Repeated sexual victimization. *Violence and Victims, 6,* 299–308.

Steketee, G., & Foa, E. B. (1987). Rape victims. Posttraumatic stress responses and their treatment: A review of the literature. *Journal of Anxiety Disorders, 1,* 69–86.

Veronen, L. J., & Kilpatrick, D. G. (1983). Stress management for rape victims. In D. Meichenbaum & M. E. Jaremko (Eds.), *Stress reduction and prevention.* New York: Plenum.

Weaver, T. L., & Clum, G. A. (1995). Psychological distress associated with interpersonal violence: A meta-analysis. *Clinical Psychology Review, 15,* 115–140.

Wirtz, P. W., & Harrell, A. V. (1987a). Victim and crime characteristics, coping responses, and short-and long-term recovery from victimization. *Journal of Consulting and Clinical Psychology, 55,* 866–871.

Wirtz, P. W., & Harrell, A. V. (1987b). Effects of postassault exposure to attack-similar stimuli on long-term recovery of victims. *Journal of Consulting and Clinical Psychology, 55,* 10–16.

Whitaker, C. J., & Bastian, L. D. (1991). *Teenage victims: A national crime survey report (NCJ-128129).* Washington, DC: U.S. Department of Justice.

World Health Organization (1990). *Composite international diagnostic interview: Version 1.0.* Geneva, Switzerland: World Health Organization.

Wyatt, G. E., Guthrie, D., & Notgrass, C. M. (1992). Differential effects of women's child sexual abuse and subsequent sexual revictimization. *Journal of Consulting and Clinical Psychology, 3,* 561–572.

Zawitz, M. W. (Ed.). (1988). *Report to the nation on crime and justice (2nd ed.).* Washington, DC: U.S. Department of Justice.

Zuckerman, M. (1979). *Sensation seeking: Beyond the optimal level of arousal.* Hillsdale, NJ: Lawrence Earlbaum Associates.

Zuckerman, M. (1983). *Biological bases of sensation seeking, impulsivity, and anxiety.* Hillsdale, NJ: Lawrence Earlbaum Associates.

CHAPTER 4

COMBAT-RELATED POSTTRAUMATIC STRESS DISORDER: PREVALENCE, RISK FACTORS, AND COMORBIDITY

WILLIAM E. SCHLENGER, PH.D.
JOHN A. FAIRBANK, PH.D.
B. KATHLEEN JORDAN, PH.D.
JUESTA M. CADDELL, PH.D.

Mental and Behavioral Health Research Program,
Research Triangle Institute,
Research Triangle Park, NC 27709

and

Department of Psychiatry and Behavioral Sciences,
Duke University Medical Center
Durham, NC 27710

In this chapter we describe the basic epidemiology of combat-related posttraumatic stress disorder (PTSD). Epidemiology is the study of the occurrence of diseases in human populations, and includes studies of the prevalence of specific disorders (i.e., what proportion of a specified population has the disorder in a given time period), how a particular disorder relates to other disorders (i.e., comorbidities), and what kinds of characteristics and/or exposures are associated with increased probability of having the disorder (i.e., risk factors).

By "combat-related PTSD" we mean PTSD that occurs among people who are "participants"— whether as active combatants, in support roles, or as bystanders—in wars or similar activities. As a result, studies of combat-related PTSD have typically focused on veterans of the world's many wars. By focusing on war veterans, we control (to some extent) the nature of the event(s) to which the people studied were exposed, which is important because the nature of the exposure has been shown to be one of the critical determinants of PTSD (Fairbank, Schlenger, Caddell, & Woods, 1993).

It is important to study the experiences of war veterans for several reasons. First is their sheer numbers. There have been, and continue to be, so many wars and war-like events that the number of people who have been (and, unfortunately, will be) exposed to "war zone trauma" is very large. Zwi (1991) counted 127 wars and more than 20 million war-related deaths in the world since World War II.

Second, it was largely through observation and documentation of the postwar experiences of soldiers exposed to combat that the syndrome known today as PTSD came to be recognized. Although scattered accounts of the postwar problems of those exposed to combat have appeared following many of recorded history's numerous wars, the medical and scientific communities' efforts to describe and understand these problems did not achieve a critical mass until World

War I. Although many of the postexposure symptoms of WWI veterans were observed and acknowledged, the syndrome was described as "shell shock" and attributed to neurological damage resulting from proximity to exploding shells. There was, however, little systematic study of those exposed, the nature of their exposures, or the course of their subsequent symptoms.

Building on what had been learned through observation of the veterans of World War One, the postwar psychological problems of WW II veterans were studied more systematically, with follow-ups at 5 years (Brill & Beebe, 1956), 10 years (Futterman & Pumpian-Midlin, 1951), 15 years (Archibald & Tuddenham, 1965), 24 years (Keehn, Goldberg, & Beebe, 1974), 30 years (Klonoff, McDougall, Clark, Kramer, & Horgan, 1976), and 40 or more years (Sutker, Allain, & Winstead, 1993) after the war. Although these studies as a group contain important methodological limitations (e.g., all involve samples of convenience, rather than probability samples), they demonstrate that soldiers exposed to combat or other stressors of war (e.g., prisoner of war experiences) may manifest a variety of stress-related symptoms long after the exposure.

In this chapter we use the term "combat-related PTSD" to refer to PTSD that occurs in people who have been exposed to "war zone trauma." We do so in acknowledgment of the fact that in addition to what are typically thought of as traditional combat experiences (e.g., firing a weapon at someone, being fired upon), there are a variety of other "extreme events" that occur with increased frequency in war zones (e.g., exposure to death and dying, atrocities). The current usage of the term "combat-related PTSD" therefore means PTSD associated with exposure to combat and/or the other extreme events to which one is typically exposed in a war zone.

Although we focus in this chapter on the experiences of those exposed to war zone trauma, research conducted in recent years and documented well in other chapters of this book has demonstrated that the PTSD syndrome is not specific to war zone trauma, but rather can result from exposure to a variety of extreme events. These include such diverse events as criminal victimization (Kilpatrick et al., 1985), sexual assault (Nadelson, Notman, Zackson, & Gornick, 1982; Winfield, George, Swartz, & Blazer, 1990), and exposure to natural or man-made disasters (Gleser, Green, & Winget, 1981; Green et al., 1990a; MacFarlane, 1986; Shore, Tatum, & Vollmer, 1986; Smith, North, McCool, & Shea, 1990; Steinglass & Gerrity, 1990). Recent evidence (Breslau, Davis, Andreski, & Peterson, 1991) also demonstrates clearly that exposure to a variety of extreme events is much more prevalent in the general population than was previously thought. Thus although combat veterans are a large and identifiable subgroup that is at risk for development of PTSD, it is clear that they are by no means the only such subgroup.

In presenting findings about the epidemiology of combat-related PTSD, we will emphasize findings of *community* studies, rather than *clinical* studies. Community epidemiologic studies are aimed at assessing specific exposures (e.g., trauma) and/or disorders (e.g., combat-related PTSD) among a specified population (e.g., war veterans), regardless of whether individuals have sought treatment or otherwise come to the attention of the treatment system. Consequently, community studies involve the study of samples selected for reasons *other than their exposure or disorder status*. Instead, samples for such studies should be selected to *represent* the specific population or subgroup to which inference is being made (e.g., Vietnam veterans)—i.e., they should be *probability* samples of a clearly defined population or subgroup.

We emphasize findings from community studies for at least two reasons. First, although clinical studies are extremely valuable for improving our understanding of those who seek treatment for PTSD and for designing systems of care that can effectively meet their needs, such studies contain an inherent bias that limits their utility for enhancing our *scientific* understanding of the basic epidemiology of PTSD. That bias arises in part from the well-established fact (cf. Shapiro et al., 1984) that only a relatively small proportion of those who meet the diagnostic criteria for a specific psychiatric disorder actually seek treatment for it. The impact of the (pre-inclusion attrition) bias introduced by this self-selection of treatment-seeking populations cannot be definitively determined, since the bias cannot be studied in a randomized experiment. This fact limits the contribution that clinical studies can make to our understanding of the basic epidemiology of psychiatric disorders.

Second, it is also true that not everyone who seeks treatment for a given disorder actually has that disorder. With PTSD, issues of secondary gain (e.g., malingering) are thought to be important among those seeking treatment, and represent another source of potential bias. Further, although many of those exposed to trauma may experience symptoms of PTSD, not all will develop the full syndrome (Weiss et al., 1992).

We begin our description of the epidemiology of combat-related PTSD by reviewing the findings of community-based studies of the prevalence of combat-related PTSD among war veterans and related populations. We then describe some of the psychiatric and other comorbidities associated with combat-related PTSD, and finally turn to a summary of what is known about risk factors.

A. PREVALENCE OF COMBAT-RELATED PTSD

As we will demonstrate below, the epidemiology of combat-related PTSD varies with both the nature of the exposure (i.e., the experiences that people had while in the war zone) and the characteristics of the participants. Although it is tautological to say that anyone who meets the criteria for the diagnosis of PTSD has been exposed to one or more "extreme events," it is also true that not everyone who has been exposed subsequently develops PTSD. As a result, assessment of exposure is an important component of the internal validity of epidemiologic studies of combat-related PTSD. In addition, findings described below show that the nature of the exposure is an important factor in the etiology of PTSD.

Findings from recent general population epidemiologic studies suggest that exposure to "extreme events" of various kinds is more prevalent than once thought. For example, in a comprehensive review of the disaster literature, Green (1996) cited a report by the International Federation of Red Cross and Red Crescent Societies that attests to the startling worldwide frequency of, and resultant mortality and morbidity resultant from, natural and technological disasters. From 1967 to 1991, a total of 7,766 disasters were reported throughout the world, killing over seven million people and adversely affecting many

times more. Findings from the National Comorbidity Study (Kessler et al., 1995) indicate that 60.7 percent of men and 51.2 percent of women in the United States have been exposed to one or more traumatic events, with 19.7 percent of the men and 11.4 percent of the women reporting exposure to three or more such events. Similarly, Breslau et al., (1991) found that 39.1 percent of a sample of young adult (ages 21 to 30) members of a health maintenance organization in Detroit reported having been exposed to traumatic events during their lifetimes. Chu and Dill (1990) found that 66 percent of a sample of female psychiatric inpatients had a history of childhood sexual and/or physical abuse. Similarly, Bryer and colleagues (1987) found that three-quarters of a sample of female psychiatric inpatients had a lifetime history of physical and/or sexual abuse.

In their national survey of exposure to crime among adult women in the United States, Resnick, Kilpatrick, Dansky, Saunders, and Best (1993) found that 12.7 percent reported a completed rape, 14.3 percent reported molestation or attempted sexual assaults, 10.3 percent had been physically assaulted, 13.4 percent reported the death of a close friend or relative by homicide, and 35.6 percent reported that at some time in their life they had been the victim of any type of crime. Of those exposed to some type of crime, more than one half (51.8 percent) of the sample reported that they had experienced more than one type of crime or multiple episodes of the same type of crime.

Based on a review of the history of armed conflicts involving European countries since 1918, Orner (1992) listed over 60 instances of wars between countries, civil wars, episodes of terrorism, and military interventions. Orner also notes that although there exist no reliable, empirically based estimates on the prevalence of exposure to war trauma among veterans and civilians in these countries, the prevalence of exposure to war trauma in Europe alone is likely to be extremely high.

With respect to exposure to war trauma among American veterans of the Vietnam war, Kulka et al. (1990a) found that 64.2 percent of the men who served in Vietnam had been exposed during their lifetimes to one or more traumatic events, compared to

47.8 percent of men who served in the military but not in Vietnam and 44.5 percent of the men who did not serve in the military. Estimates of lifetime exposure among women were 70.8 percent of those who served in Vietnam, 49.5 percent of other women veterans, and 37.2 percent of the nonveteran women.

The point of the above is that exposure to "extreme events" is not a rare occurrence, even among the general population, and that the likelihood of such exposure is higher among those who have served in a war zone. It is important to remember, however, that the exposures of individuals within a given war zone will differ, and that the profile of exposures will differ from war zone to war zone. Although it is undoubtedly true that "war is hell," each individual's experience of a given war is different, and the nature of the war's specific "exposure profile" (i.e., how many people are exposed to which kinds of extreme events) is an important determinant of each war zone's emotional sequelae. Therefore, we present findings about the prevalence of combat-related PTSD for subsets grouped by war and by role. The PTSD prevalence findings across wars are summarized in Table 4.1.

1. PTSD among Vietnam Veterans

Although there have been wars throughout human history, PTSD was not studied intensively or systematically among war veterans until the Vietnam war. Study of PTSD among Vietnam veterans was facilitated by the publication in 1980 of DSM-III (APA, 1980), because: (1) it included PTSD as a diagnostic category defined by a specific cluster of symptoms, and (2) DSM-III's emphasis on behavioral criteria improved the chances that PTSD diagnoses could be made *reliably,* even outside of clinical settings.

In the decade following the publication of DSM-III, estimates of the prevalence of PTSD among U.S. Vietnam veterans based on several major epidemiologic studies were reported. These include findings from the National Vietnam Veterans Readjustment Study (NVVRS) (Kulka et al., 1990a, 1990b), the Centers for Disease Control's (CDC) Vietnam Experience Study (CDC, 1988), the Department of Veterans Affairs' Twin Study (Goldberg, True, Eisen, & Henderson, 1990), the St. Louis site of the National

Institute of Mental Health's Epidemiologic Catchment Area (ECA) Program (Helzer, Robins, & McEvoy, 1987), the American Legion Study (Snow, Stellman, Stellman, & Sommer, 1988) and a study conducted by the Traumatic Stress Study Center at the University of Cincinnati (Green et al., 1990a).

To date, the most comprehensive examination of the prevalence of PTSD among Vietnam veterans comes from the NVVRS (Kulka et al., 1990a, 1990b), a congressionally mandated, community epidemiologic study of the prevalence of PTSD and other postwar psychological problems among Vietnam veterans (n=1,632), other veterans of the same era (n=716), and nonveterans (n=668) matched to the Vietnam veterans on age, sex, and race/ethnicity. Cases of PTSD were identified in the NVVRS on the basis of comprehensive multimeasure assessment that included both self-report scales and structured clinical interviews (see Schlenger et al., 1992), thereby increasing the internal validity of case versus noncase comparisons. All NVVRS samples were probability samples (see Kulka et al., 1990b), and therefore yielded unbiased national estimates of parameters, assuring high external validity of the findings. For these and other reasons, the NVVRS findings are the most definitive available with respect to the postwar adjustment of Vietnam veterans.

NVVRS findings (Schlenger et al., 1992) indicated that 15.2 percent of men and 8.5 percent of women had current PTSD (i.e., met the DSM-III-R criteria during the 6 months prior to the interview) at the time the study was conducted. By contrast, the current prevalence among comparable era veterans was 2.5 percent among men and 1.1 percent among women; and for nonveterans 1.2 percent among men and 0.3 percent among women. Lifetime prevalence rates—i.e., the estimated proportion who had met the DSM-III-R criteria for PTSD *at any time in their lives,* whether or not they met the criteria *currently*— among Vietnam veterans were 30.9 percent for men and 26.9 percent for women (Weiss et al., 1992).

The NVVRS also reported PTSD prevalence estimates for selected racial/ethnic subgroups. Of the approximately 3.2 million U. S. veterans who served in the Vietnam war (Kulka et al., 1990b), about 170,000 (5 percent) were Hispanic men and about

TABLE 4.1 Summary of Combat-Related PTSD Prevalence Estimates

RESEARCH STUDY, BY CONFLICT	SAMPLE	CASE IDENTIFICATION METHOD	LIFETIME PREVALENCE	CURRENT PREVALENCE
World War II				
Pacific Theater Study (Sutker et al., 1993)	36 POW survivors and 29 combat veterans 40 years after war experience	PTSD symptom checklist administered by clinician	—	70% (former POWs); 18% (combat veterans)
40-Year Follow-Up of POWs (Kluznick et al., 1986)	188 former POWs	PTSD symptom checklist administered by clinician	67% (following imprisonment)	24% moderate residual PTSD symptoms, 8% severe symptoms
POW Study (Engdahl et al., 1991)	62 former POWs	PTSD symptom checklist based on clinical examination	—	50% (within 1 year of release from captivity); 29% (>40 years later)
POW Study (Eberly & Engdahl, 1991)	408 former POWs (343 European theater and 65 Pacific theater)	PTSD symptom checklist based on clinical interview or record review	70% (European POWs); 79% (Pacific POWs)	—
Korean War				
POW Study (Eberly & Engdahl, 1991)	18 former POWs	PTSD symptom checklist based on clinical interview or record review	53%	—
Vietnam War				
National Vietnam Veterans Readjustment Study (Kulka et al., 1990a, 1990b; Jordan et al., 1991; Schlenger et al., 1992; Weiss et al., 1992)	1,632 male and female Vietnam veterans; 716 other veterans of same era; 668 nonveterans (community epidemiologic study using probability samples)	Combination of self-report scales and structured clinical interviews	Met DSM-III-R criteria for PTSD at any time in their lives: 30.9% (men); 26.9% (women); 26.3% (men with partial PTSD); 21.2% (women with partial PTSD)	Met DSM-III-R criteria during 6 months prior to interview: 15.2% (men); 8.5% (women); 11.1% (men with partial PTSD); 7.8% (women with partial PTSD); 13.7% (white/other men); 20.6% (African American men); 27.9% (Hispanic men)
Vietnam Experience Study (CDC, 1988)	2,490 Army enlisted men with one tour of duty in Vietnam (probability sample)	Survey interview	14.7%	Past month: 2.2%

(Continued)

TABLE 4.1 Continued

RESEARCH STUDY, BY CONFLICT	SAMPLE	CASE IDENTIFICATION METHOD	LIFETIME PREVALENCE	CURRENT PREVALENCE
Department of Veterans Affairs' Twin Study (Goldberg et al., 1990)	2,092 male, monozygotic twin pairs (sample drawn from Vietnam Era Twin Registry)	Mail and telephone interviews	—	16.8%
St. Louis Site of Epidemiologic Catchment Area Program (Helzer et al., 1987; Keane & Wolfe, 1990)	64 self-identified Vietnam veterans from general population sample	Survey interview	—	3.5% for veterans not wounded, 20% for those wounded; overall, weighted estimate of 11.8%
American Legion Study (Snow et al., 1988)	2,858 American Legion members in six states	Mail survey	—	1.8% to 15% (depending on how exposure to combat was operationalized)
Cincinnati Study (Green et al., 1990a)	200 veterans recruited from a variety of sources	Structured clinical interview administered by trained clinicians	—	17% (among those not seeking treatment)
Australian Vietnam Veterans Health Study (O'Toole et al., 1994)	641 from national sample of Australian veterans of Vietnam War	Structured clinical interview	11.7% to 20.9% (depending on how exposure to trauma and PTSD were assessed)	1-month prevalence: 11.6%
Vietnamese Refugee Study (Hinton et al., 1993)	201 newly arrived refugees from Vietnam	Structured clinical interview (translated from English into Vietnamese)	—	3.5% (7.2% among ethnic Vietnamese; 0.9% among ethnic Chinese)
Israeli Conflicts				
1982 Lebanon War Study (Solomon et al., 1987)	382 frontline combat soldiers who had experienced acute stress reaction; 334 demographically matched frontline combat soldiers who did not experience acute combat stress reaction	Prospective study 1 year after war	—	1 year after war: 16% (among soldiers who had not had an acute combat stress reaction during war); 59% (among those who had experienced a combat stress reaction)

Study	Sample	Instrument		Findings
Israeli Soldier Study (Solomon et al., 1991)	659 Israeli military participants in Gulf War	Self-report symptom checklist	—	Elevated levels of distress associated with higher perceptions of threat and lower levels of self-efficacy, social support, and trust in military authorities
Elderly Israeli Holocaust Survivors Gulf War Exposure Study (Solomon & Prager, 1992)	61 elderly Holocaust survivors and 131 comparable civilians not exposed to Holocaust	Self-report symptom checklist	—	Higher levels of perceived danger and more distress symptoms in response to Gulf War events than those without Holocaust exposure
Persian Gulf War				
Reservists Study (Perconte et al., 1993)	439 activated Army, Navy, and Marine reservists deployed to Operation Desert Shield/Storm	Mississippi Scale for Combat-Related PTSD	—	15.5%
Army National Guard or Reserve Troops Study (Sutker et al., 1993)	215 activated and deployed troops	Mississippi Scale adapted for Desert Storm and PTSD Checklist—Military Version	—	16% to 19%
Fort Devens, MA, Study (Wolfe et al., 1993)	2,344 veterans returned from Operation Desert Shield/Storm	Mississippi Scale for Combat-Related PTSD	—	4% (men); 9% (women)
Active-Duty and Reservists Study (Stretch et al., 1996)	1,524 troops deployed to Operation Desert Shield/Storm	Impact of Event Scale and Brief Symptom Inventory	—	8% (active-duty troops); 9.3% (reservists)
Longitudinal Study of Reservists (Southwick et al., 1993, 1995)	62 National Guard reservists	Mississippi Scale and a PTSD symptom checklist	—	At 2-year follow-up point: 10% to 13% (increasing over the 1-, 6-, to 24-month post-deployment period)
"Peacekeeping" Missions				
Somalian Study (Litz et al., 1997)	3,461 active-duty military forces who had served in Somalia	Mississippi Scale and PTSD Checklist	—	8% (similar among men and women)

350,00 (11 percent) were African American men (Kulka et al., 1990b). NVVRS findings (Schlenger et al., 1992) indicate that there are significant differences in the prevalence of current PTSD among African American, Hispanic, and white/other male Vietnam veterans. The prevalence for white/other men was 13.7 percent (2.3 percent for white/other era veterans, 1.0 percent for white/other civilian counterparts), 20.6 percent for African American men (4.4 percent for African American era veterans, and 1.3 for African American civilian counterparts), and 27.9 percent for Hispanic men (2.1 percent for Hispanic era veterans, 3.9 percent for Hispanic civilian counterparts). The prevalence of current PTSD for Vietnam veteran women, more than 95 percent of whom were white, was 8.5 percent. These findings suggest important differences in prevalence among subgroups defined by sociodemographic characteristics.

In addition to the PTSD syndrome, the NVVRS investigators noted that many of the Vietnam veterans studied had clinically significant PTSD symptoms, but the pattern did not meet the DSM-III-R criteria. A common example of this was veterans whose symptom picture met fully the DSM-III-R A criterion (exposure to trauma), B criterion (re-experiencing symptoms), and D criterion (hyperarousal) for PTSD but not the C criterion (numbing/avoidance), and who used alcohol or drugs in ways clearly linked to their PTSD symptoms. Such sub-syndromal phenomena were described as "partial PTSD" (Weiss et al., 1992), and it was estimated that 11.1 percent of male Vietnam veterans had partial PTSD at the time of the study. When added to the current prevalence estimate (15.2 percent plus 11.1 percent), more than one in four Vietnam veterans was estimated to be experiencing clinically significant PTSD symptoms 15 or more years after their service in Vietnam.

Other epidemiologic studies of PTSD among Vietnam veterans have focused on smaller subsets of the population. For example, in the CDC Vietnam Experience Study (CDC, 1988), which was one component of a comprehensive, congressionally mandated study of the health effects of Vietnam service, researchers studied a random sample (n=2,490) of Army enlisted men who had served one tour of duty in Vietnam. Using a survey interview as the basis for identify-ing cases of PTSD, the CDC study team estimated a lifetime prevalence of combat-related PTSD of 14.7 percent and a current (past month) prevalence of 2.2 percent. Similarly, in the VA twin study (Goldberg et al., 1990), a sample of 2,092 male, monozygotic twin pairs drawn from the Vietnam Era Twin Registry was surveyed via mail and telephone interviews. The current prevalence of PTSD among the twins who served in Vietnam was 16.8 percent, compared to 5.0 percent among those who served elsewhere.

In the St. Louis site of the NIMH-ECA study, Helzer et al. (1987) studied 64 self-identified Vietnam veterans from a general population sample, with PTSD diagnoses based on survey interviews. Findings suggested a lifetime prevalence of combat-related PTSD of 6.3 percent. Keane and Wolfe (1990) have noted that Helzer later reported that the weighted prevalence rate for PTSD in Vietnam veterans in the St. Louis ECA survey was 11.8 percent. In the American Legion study (Snow et al., 1988), a sample (n=2,858) of American Legion members in six states was surveyed by mail. Results suggested a current PTSD prevalence ranging from 1.8 percent to 15 percent, depending on how exposure to combat was operationalized. In the Cincinnati study (Green et al., 1990a), a sample of Vietnam veterans (n=200) recruited from a variety of sources was assessed for PTSD by trained clinicians using a structured clinical interview. Current PTSD prevalence among those veterans who were not seeking treatment was estimated to be 17 percent.

Although much of the research on the sequelae of the Vietnam War has focused on American veterans, there have been some studies of other participants as well. O'Toole and colleagues (1994) estimated the prevalence of PTSD in a national sample (n=641) of Australian veterans of the Vietnam war. Findings indicated a lifetime PTSD prevalence ranging from 11.7 percent to 20.9 percent, depending upon how exposure to trauma and PTSD were assessed. The current (1-month) estimate of PTSD prevalence among Australian Vietnam veterans, assessed by structured clinical interviews, was 11.6 percent.

There are a number of methodological differences among these studies of Vietnam veterans that impact on their utility. First, PTSD prevalence estimates from many of these studies are based on small or nonrepresentative samples of Vietnam veterans. Second, most of the studies employed PTSD case identification procedures whose relationship to clinical diagnosis, or to any other criterion measure, is unknown.

In spite of these and other important methodological differences among the various studies of Vietnam veterans, however, a thorough review (Kulka et al., 1991) of the methods and findings of seven major epidemiologic studies of the prevalence of PTSD among Vietnam veterans demonstrated surprisingly good agreement of findings. Although the estimates of current PTSD prevalence in seven major studies ranged from 1.8 to over 25 percent, the estimates from the majority of the studies lie very nearly within the 95 percent confidence interval of the NVVRS estimates (13.0 percent to 17.4 percent). This suggests that PTSD among Vietnam veterans is an important and—sadly—*continuing* public health problem.

Finally, the PTSD literature has documented the harmful effects of noncombatants as well. For example, Hinton et al. (1993) assessed 201 newly arrived refugees from Vietnam for PTSD and other psychiatric disorders using structured clinical interviews that were translated from English into Vietnamese. These investigators reported that 3.5 percent of the sample met DSM-III-R criteria for PTSD with rates higher among ethnic Vietnamese (7.2 percent) than among ethnic Chinese (0.9 percent). Prevalence of psychiatric disorder was highest among former soldiers in the Army of the Republic of Vietnam and re-education camp survivors.

2. PTSD among Veterans of Other Wars

Although there have been, and unfortunately will probably continue to be, many other wars, until recently there have been few methodologically sound epidemiologic studies of PTSD among veterans of those wars. One important reason for this is that prior to the publication of DSM-III, there did not exist a widely agreed-upon, operationalizable definition of the disorder. In the following sections we summarize findings about the prevalence of PTSD from studies of veterans of several other wars.

a. World War II and Korean War Veterans. Although the prevalence of the PTSD syndrome as defined in DSM-III was not studied well among World War II and Korean War veterans in the years immediately following those wars (for obvious reasons), studies of PTSD among combatants and others exposed to those wars have recently been conducted. Sutker and her colleagues (Sutker, Allain, & Winstead, 1993) studied samples of World War II prisoners of war and combat veterans about 40 years after their war experience, and found current PTSD prevalence rates of 18 percent for combat veterans and 70 percent for former prisoners of war. Similarly, in a follow-up study of former prisoners of war from World War II, Kluznick, Speed, Van Valkenburg, and Magraw (1986) found that two thirds had had PTSD at some time following their imprisonment, and about 21 percent still had at least moderate residual PTSD symptoms about 40 years after the end of the war. Engdahl and his colleagues (Engdahl, Speed, Eberly, & Schwartz 1991) also studied a convenience sample of 62 former World War II prisoners of war, and found that 50 percent met criteria for PTSD within one year of their release from captivity, and 29 percent still had PTSD 40 or more years later. Similarly, Eberly & Engdahl (1991) reported findings for a larger sample of POWs, where they found lifetime PTSD prevalence rates of 70, 79, and 53 percent, respectively, among World War II POWs who served in Europe, the Pacific, or Korean War POWs. Also, Weisaeth and Eitinger (1991a, 1992b) have recently summarized findings from studies conducted in Europe.

b. Israeli War Veterans. One of the best studied combat-exposed groups other than Vietnam veterans is Israeli war veterans. Solomon and her colleagues have studied extensively the development of PTSD and its correlates in groups of participants in the 1982 Lebanon war, and more recently among those exposed to the Gulf War. Concerning the Lebanon war, Solomon, Weisenberg, Schwarzwald, and Mikulincer (1987) reported a PTSD prevalence rate of 16 percent one year after the war among soldiers who had not experienced an acute combat stress reaction during the war, a rate very comparable to findings for Vietnam veterans. The rate among soldiers who had experienced a combat stress reaction, however, was 59 percent. Solomon and her colleagues subsequently studied these veterans at two (Solomon & Mikulincer, 1988) and three (Solomon, 1989) years postwar. Concerning the Gulf War, Solomon, Margalit, Waysman, & Bleich (1991) studied 659 Israeli military participants in the Gulf War, and found that elevated levels of distress were associated with higher perceptions of threat and lower levels of self-efficacy, social support, and trust in military authorities. Relatedly, Solomon & Prager (1992) studied distress during the Gulf War among 61 elderly Holocaust survivors and 131 comparable civilians not exposed to the Holocaust. Holocaust survivors reported higher levels of perceived danger and more distress symptoms than those without Holocaust exposure.

c. Persian Gulf War Veterans.

A number of studies have appeared in the literature of PTSD among veterans who served in the Persian Gulf War (Operation Desert Shield/Storm; ODS). Perconte, Wilson, Pontius, Dietrick, and Spiro (1993) assessed a convenience sample of 591 Army, Navy, and Marine reservists including some who were deployed and served in ODS (n=439), some who were deployed to Europe (n=26), and some who were not deployed (n=126). The PTSD prevalence rate among the ODS reservists was 15.5 percent, compared to 4 percent or less for the comparison groups. Sutker, Uddo, Brailey, and Allain (1993) reported a PTSD prevalence rate of 16–19 percent (depending on case identification method) among a convenience sample of 215 Army National Guard or Reserve troops who were activated and deployed to the Persian Gulf. Wolfe, Brown, and Kelley (1993) studied 2,344 veterans who returned from ODS to Fort Devens, MA. PTSD prevalence rates based on the Mississippi Scale for Combat-Related PTSD were 4 percent for men and 9 percent for women. Stretch et al. (1996) studied convenience samples of active duty and reserve veterans who were (n=1,524) or were not (n=2,727) deployed to ODS. PTSD prevalence rates for active duty troops were 8.0 percent among those deployed versus 1.3 percent among the non-deployed, and 9.3 percent versus 2.1 percent for reservists. Thus a variety of studies have demonstrated that the rate of PTSD is higher among ODS veterans than among a variety of comparison groups.

Southwick and his colleagues (Southwick et al., 1993; Southwick et al., 1995) have conducted a longitudinal study of ODS participants, assessing a convenience sample of reservists at 1-, 6-, and 24-months following their return from the Gulf. At the two-year follow-up point, the prevalence of PTSD in the sample was 10–13 percent, depending on the case identification method used (Mississippi Scale or PTSD symptom checklist). Interestingly, the prevalence of PTSD increased in this sample over time, raising questions about the nature of the onset of combat-related PTSD. Additionally, analysis of the symptom severity data indicated that hyperarousal symptoms were rated as more severe at all three assessment points than either re-experiencing or avoidance symptoms, raising questions about the dynamics among the major PTSD symptom clusters (e.g., see Litz et al., 1997)

d. PTSD among "Peacekeepers."

Finally, the recently declared end of the Cold War appears to have resulted in a potentially important change in the role of military forces that may alter the nature of their future exposures. In recent years, U.S. (and other nations') military forces have been called upon to serve a "peacekeeping" role in a number of areas in which internal conflict became unignorable (e.g., Somalia, Bosnia). Although their task is to "keep the peace," anecdotal reports suggest that the exposures of peacekeeping forces may be quite similar to the exposures of military forces in war zones. So it is reasonable to ask: Do peacekeepers also develop PTSD?

The findings from one of the first published epidemiologic studies of the prevalence of PTSD among peacekeeping forces suggests that the answer to this question may be: yes. Litz and his colleagues (Litz, Orsillo, Friedman, Ehlich, and Batres, 1997) studied a cohort of 3,461 active duty military forces who served in Somalia soon after their return to the United States. Findings indicated that 8 percent of the cohort met criteria for PTSD, and that the prevalence did not differ between men and women soldiers. Additionally, exposure to war zone stressors was found to be strongly related to PTSD severity. Although the study did not include a non-exposed comparison group (e.g., sociodemographically comparable active duty forces *not* deployed to Somalia), the findings are nevertheless consistent with the hypothesis that "peacekeeping" is hazardous duty, and that those who serve as peacekeepers are at increased risk for PTSD.

As a group, all of the studies described above add to our understanding of the epidemiology of PTSD following exposure to war zone stress. It is interesting to note, however, the consistency with which PTSD prevalence estimates for the various war trauma exposure groups from different countries and different wars fall within the 95 percent confidence interval of the NVVRS estimates.

3. PTSD and Women in the Military

In the United States, women have been informally involved in the military since the Civil War, but it wasn't until 1943 that the Women's Army Corps was established, allowing a group of nurses to serve formally in the Army during World War II. For the next 25 years, women held "traditional" roles in the military, such as health care workers and clerks. During the 1970s and 1980s, however, a number of other occupational specialties were opened to women, as were the military academies (Army, Navy, and Air Force).

Additionally, the number of women in the U. S. military has increased dramatically in recent years. In 1995, there were about 200,000 women on active duty in the U. S. military, representing about 14 percent of all active duty personnel (Adelsberger, 1994). The proportion of incoming recruits who are women is even higher—19 percent in early 1994 (Adelsberger, 1994)—and it is expected that women will comprise 20 percent of the active duty force in the near future. The largest group of active duty women—approximately 70,000—are serving in the Army.

Some believe that women in the active duty military today are at greatly increased risk for exposure to stress and its sequelae because they have multiple characteristics that are associated with discrimination or other negative evaluation. For example, in addition to being women they are more likely than ever to be minority group members (Moore, 1991)—about 40 percent are classified as minority group members (53 percent in the Army). Also, they (and particularly African American women) are the group most likely to be single parents: 13.3 percent of African American female military personnel are single parents compared to 7.4 percent of white female personnel, 2 percent of African American male personnel, and 1.4 percent of white male personnel (Moore, 1991). Thus, women in the military may be subject to multiple life stressors to which their male counterparts are not subject, independent of those specifically related to service in the military.

In addition to serving in greater numbers, women now serve in a much broader array of positions than ever before. In 1987, all combat service support positions in the U. S. Army were opened to women, and in April 1993, the Secretary of Defense lifted the prohibitions against women flying combat aircraft. Although the Army still has a combat-exclusion policy that prohibits women from joining direct combat units in the armor, infantry, and cannon-artillery forces, it recently opened additional positions to women so that now approximately 67 percent of all positions in the Army are open to women (Adelsberger, 1994). This means that women in the military are now subject to many of the same military-related stressors to which men have been historically subjected.

Thus there are more women in the military today, and they are more likely to occupy positions that put them at risk for exposure to a broader array of stressors than ever. Given these trends, it is clear that we must improve our understanding of exposure to stressors and their impact on women in the military. Additionally, it seems clear that the kinds of stressors to which women in the military are likely to be exposed may differ substantially, both qualitatively and quantitatively, from the stressors to which men in the military are exposed. Moreover, recent and continuing changes in the roles that women fulfill in the military are likely to increase both the prevalence of exposure to extreme events and other stressors and the types of extreme events to which they are exposed.

Because historically their roles have been limited to "noncombat" assignments, the prevalence of exposure to extreme events and its sequelae have not been well studied for women in the military. The most thorough examination of the psychological impact of exposure to war zone stressors on women in the military to date is from the NVVRS (Kulka et al., 1990a), which was one of the first studies to document in detail the war zone experiences of women veterans. A multidimensional index of exposure to war zone stressors was developed that included measures of: exposure to wounded and dead; exposure to enemy fire; direct combat involvement; abusive violence; deprivation; and other potential stressors. Based on the multidimensional index, about 40 percent of the women were judged to have experienced high stressor exposure while in Vietnam (Kulka et al., 1990a).

NVVRS findings concerning PTSD prevalence indicate that 26.9 percent of the women who served in Vietnam had met the DSM-III-R criteria for PTSD at some time in their lives (Weiss et al., 1992), and that 8.5 percent were cases of PTSD at the time the study was conducted in 1987, many years after their service in Vietnam (Schlenger et al., 1992). Among those exposed to high levels of war zone stress, the current prevalence of PTSD was even higher: 17.5 percent, versus 2.5 percent for those with low/moderate exposure. The current prevalence of PTSD among women era veterans and women civilian counterparts, formulated using the same methods as the estimates for theater veterans, was 1.1 percent and 0.3 percent, respectively.

In addition, the NVVRS team estimated the prevalence of "partial PTSD"—defined as the presence of clinically significant PTSD symptoms that did not meet the full diagnostic criteria (Weiss et al., 1992)—among women Vietnam veterans. Findings indicated that 21.2 percent of women Vietnam veterans had suffered from partial PTSD at some time in their lives, and that 7.8 percent had partial PTSD at the time they were interviewed.

B. COMORBIDITY

Another important component of the epidemiology of combat-related PTSD is its pattern of *comorbidities*— i.e, do people who have PTSD also have co-occurring other disorders? Although psychiatric and substance abuse comorbidities are often emphasized, it is impor-

tant to keep a broad range of potential comorbidities in mind, since any systematic comorbidity is a potentially important clinical and etiologic consideration.

Community studies of the general population have documented high rates of comorbid psychiatric disorder among people with PTSD. In the National Comorbidity Study, Kessler et al. (1995) reported that 79 percent of the women and 88.3 percent of the men with PTSD also met criteria for another lifetime psychiatric disorder. In contrast, 46.2 percent of women and 54.8 percent of men with disorders other than PTSD were found to have co-morbid psychiatric disorders. The co-occurring disorders most prevalent for men with PTSD were alcohol abuse or dependence (51.9 percent), major depressive episode (47.9 percent), conduct disorder (43.3 percent), and drug abuse and dependence (34.5 percent). The disorders most frequently comorbid with PTSD among women were major depressive episode (48.5 percent), simple phobia (29.0 percent), social phobia (28.4 percent), and alcohol abuse/ dependence (27.9 percent).

The earliest examination of the comorbidities of combat-related PTSD were provided by clinicians who were attempting to describe their Vietnam veteran patients. For example, Sierles and his colleagues at the North Chicago VA Medical Center described comorbidities in small samples of Vietnam veterans with PTSD being treated as inpatients (Sierles, Chen, McFarland, and Taylor, 1983) and outpatients (Sierles, Chen, Messing, Besyner, & Taylor 1986). In both groups, more than 80 percent of patients were found to have one or more comorbid psychiatric disorders. Similarly, Keane and Wolfe (1990) studied patients in the Boston VA Medical Center's PTSD program and found high rates of comorbid substance abuse, major depression, dysthymic disorder, and antisocial personality disorder. An analysis of national hospital discharge data for 539,557 veterans treated on medical, surgical, psychiatric, and substance abuse treatment wards in DVA Medical Centers during 1991 indicates that 6.2 percent were identified as having co-occurring chart diagnoses of PTSD and substance abuse or dependence (Walker, Howard, Lambert, Suchinsky 1994).

The most comprehensive examination of a broad range of comorbidites of combat-related PTSD comes from the NVVRS. Kulka et al. (1990a) found that virtually all Vietnam veterans with PTSD had met the criteria for one or more other psychiatric disorders (including substance abuse; three-quarters if alcohol disorders are excluded) at some time during their lives, and half were characterized by a current comorbid disorder. In men, the most prevalent comorbid disorders were alcohol abuse or dependence (75 percent lifetime, 20 percent current), generalized anxiety disorder (44 percent lifetime, 20 percent current), and major depression (20 percent lifetime, 16 percent current). Among women veterans (Jordan et al., 1991), the most frequently occurring were major depression (42 percent lifetime, 23 percent current), generalized anxiety disorder (38 percent lifetime, 20 percent current), and dysthymic disorder (33 percent lifetime).

In addition to psychiatric comorbidity, physical health comorbidities and co-occurring life adjustment problems have also been studied. CDC (1988) studied the physical health of Vietnam theater and Vietnam-era veterans as part of its Vietnam Experience Study (VES). Although Vietnam veterans were found to rate their health more poorly and to report more physical health problems in an interview, physical examination findings showed few health differences. In the NVVRS, Kulka et al. (1990a) found no differences between Vietnam theater veterans and Vietnam-era veterans in self-evaluations of health status or number of reported health problems, but did find that Vietnam veterans with PTSD reported more health problems and rated their health more poorly than did Vietnam-era veteran or nonveteran controls. Shalev, Bleich, and Ursano (1990) similarly found that Israeli veterans with PTSD reported more somatic symptoms than did matched controls, but that the groups did not differ on laboratory test findings. This study also showed a greater frequency of adverse health practices (e.g., smoking, alcohol use) among veterans with PTSD.

The NVVRS also provided a comprehensive examination of the association of PTSD with other life adjustment problems. Although Vietnam veterans as a group were found not to differ substantially from Vietnam-era veterans or nonveteran controls in a broad range of current life adjustment domains (Kulka et al., 1990a), Vietnam veterans with PTSD

were found to have profound and pervasive problems in their daily lives. This included problems in family and other interpersonal relationships, employment, and involvement with the criminal justice system. Thus, combat-related PTSD is associated with high levels of psychological distress *and* with pervasive disruptions in life functioning.

More recently, Zatzick and his colleagues (Zatzick et al., 1997a; Zatzick et al., 1997b) have assessed the contribution of combat-related PTSD to health functioning and quality of life in Vietnam veterans. Analyzing data from the NVVRS, these investigators found that PTSD made a significant independent contribution to impaired functioning and quality of life when analyzed in a multivariate framework, adjusting for comorbid psychiatric and medical conditions. These findings demonstrate that combat-related PTSD plays an important role in veterans' functioning independent of a variety of comorbid conditions to which the impaired functioning might be attributable.

C. RISK FACTORS

Another important component of epidemiology is the study of "risk factors" associated with a given disorder. Kraemer et al. (1997) have recently provided a specific typology of "risk factor" terms that is helpful in clarifying and standardizing efforts to understand the various potential types of risk and their relationship to etiology. They make the important point that "risk factors" are a specific subset of correlates of a specific outcome—i.e., correlates that have been shown to *precede* in time the onset of the outcome under study—and also specify the additional criteria that a candidate risk factor must meet to be considered a *causal* risk factor.

The reason for interest in risk factors is clear—identification of risk factors may contribute to the development of primary or secondary prevention programs (by identifying characteristics associated with increased probability of developing the disorder), and may yield clues for hypotheses concerning the etiology of the disorder.

Examinations of potential risk factors are best conducted within the framework of existing theory (to reduce the potential for spurious results). The PTSD literature contains descriptions of a variety of conceptual approaches that have been proposed to explain the development and maintenance of psychiatric and other adjustment problems following exposure to trauma. Examples of psychological approaches include psychodynamic models (Horowitz, 1974; Horowitz & Kaltreider, 1980), conditioning and learning models (Keane, Zimering, & Caddell, 1985), and cognitive and information-processing models (Chemtob, Roitblat, Hamada, Carlson, & Twentyman, 1988; Foa, Steketee, & Rothbaum, 1989; Litz & Keane, 1989). Biological models, on the other hand, emphasize the role of neurochemical systems (Krystal et al., 1989) and genetic influences (Davidson, Smith, & Kudler, 1989).

Identification of risk factors is best conducted in samples with high internal and external validity. Problems with internal validity, such as inaccurate case identification, can result in both under and over estimates of the size of relationships between potential risk factors and the measure of caseness, as can problems with external validity, such as unrepresentative sampling (i.e., if the samples are not probability samples of the target population). The result in both cases is biased and misleading results. We therefore focus here on the findings from studies with the strongest internal and external validity.

1. Risk Factors for Vietnam Veterans

The study of combat-related PTSD with the highest external validity—because of the use of true probability samples—is the NVVRS. The conceptualization that guided the examination of risk factors in the NVVRS is the "diathesis-stress" model (Keane, 1989; Meehl, 1962; Zubin & Spring, 1977). As applied to the study of reactions to traumatic stress, the diathesis-stress model is a biopsychosocial conceptualization that describes the interpersonal variability in reactions to extreme events in terms of the interactions of internal and external factors. The model posits that extreme events may elicit crisis in almost everyone, but, depending on the intensity of the stressor and the individual's threshold for tolerating it, the trauma will either be contained homeostatically or lead to an episode of disorder (Zubin & Spring, 1977). Similarly, Lazarus and Folkman

(1984) and their colleagues have advanced the position that the patterns of adjustment after stress exposure differ because they are influenced by the variance in characteristics of both the stressor and the individual. Recently, comprehensive biopsychosocial models have been proposed that incorporate a range of variables that may act as vulnerability, protecting, or potentiating factors (Foy, Osato, Houskamp, & Neumann, 1992; Jones & Barlow, 1990).

The NVVRS findings described earlier indicate that the prevalence of PTSD is higher among African American and Hispanic Vietnam veterans than among white/others, suggesting the possibility that race/ethnicity could be a risk factor for combat-related PTSD. Why might this be the case? Biopsychosocial and diathesis-stress models suggest the answer to this question lies in an assessment of the interaction of characteristics of the person, characteristics of the exposure, and characteristics of the peri- and post-exposure environment as determinants of post-exposure adjustment. In principle, then, the observed differences among the subgroups might be due to three kinds of factors: (a) differences in characteristics or exposures that they brought with them to the war [i.e., differential "predisposition"], (b) differences in the nature and/or magnitude of their exposure to trauma during their service in Vietnam, or (c) differences in their postexposure experiences. The NVVRS data base affords the unusual opportunity to examine in a multivariate framework the relationships of a wide range of stressor characteristics, individual characteristics that may have rendered one more (or less) vulnerable to stressors, and post-exposure experiences in determining post-exposure adjustment.

Differences in Pre-Exposure Characteristics: Potential "Vulnerabilities." Many powerful social forces interacted during the Vietnam era to determine which soldiers went to Vietnam and what kinds of experiences they had while they were there. As a result, it is possible that differences in one or more kinds of "vulnerability" to PTSD existed between the race/ethnicity subgroups, and that those differences account for the observed differences in PTSD prevalence.

To examine the role of "potentially predisposing factors," the NVVRS investigators (Schlenger et al.,

1992) selected more than 80 characteristics and experiences that predate military or Vietnam experience and that might conceivably account for differences in current PTSD prevalence rates between the study groups. The kinds of characteristics included ranged from sociodemographic characteristics of the veteran's family of origin to aspects of the family's social environment to evidence of specific psychiatric disorders in the veteran before his/her service in Vietnam.

The impact of these factors was assessed via a series of multiple regression analyses that provided estimates of the difference in current prevalence for each of the race/ethnicity subgroup contrasts with the effects of the predisposing factors controlled. Potential predisposing factors became candidates for inclusion in the analyses if they were significantly related to the probability of being a current case of PTSD, and significantly related to the specific group contrast being modeled (the two conditions that define a statistical confound [Cochran, 1983]). The models were fit via a backward elimination procedure, starting with all predisposing factors that met these requirements.

The adjustment for predisposing factors had a substantial impact on the contrasts of race/ethnicity subgroups of male Vietnam veterans. The adjustment reduced the current PTSD prevalence difference between white/others and African Americans by 10 percent, the difference between white/others and Hispanics by 57 percent, and the difference between African Americans and Hispanics by 67 percent. Despite these reductions in group prevalence differentials, the adjusted current PTSD prevalence for white/others remained about six percentage points lower than for white/others than for African Americans or Hispanics. The difference in current PTSD prevalence between African American and Hispanic males became statistically nonsignificant, however, when adjusted for predisposing factors. This means that if African American and Hispanic Vietnam veterans had gone to the war with the same profile of these "predisposing" characteristics, there would be no difference in current PTSD prevalence between the two groups today.

Differences in War Zone Stress Exposure. A second factor that might contribute to differences be-

tween the subgroups in PTSD prevalence is their relative levels of exposure to war zone stress. That is, if the groups were unequally exposed to trauma and other stressors of the war zone, we could expect them to differ in PTSD prevalence.

Measurement of exposure to war zone stress was an important aspect of the NVVRS for several reasons. First, the basic hypothesis underlying the study's quasi-experimental design was that involvement in combat leads to exposure to trauma which may lead to the development of PTSD, so the contrasts of most interest involved comparing "combat veterans" to other veterans or to nonveterans. Since we know that those who served in Vietnam were not equally exposed to combat or other war zone stressors, it was important to develop a war zone stress exposure measure that would allow the Vietnam veterans to be divided into relative exposure groups, and thereby improve the internal validity of the study's comparisons.

Because prior research demonstrated that exposure to war zone stress is a multidimensional phenomenon (e.g., Laufer, Gallops, & Frey-Wouters, 1984), it was important that the overall exposure measure reflect the basic underlying dimensions. Thus, while exposure to firefights and other direct combat experiences is an important element of war zone stress, it is not the only element. Other elements that have been shown to be related to postwar adjustment include exposure to people who are wounded, dying, or dead, and exposure to (or participation in) abusive violence (Laufer et al., 1984; Egendorf, Kadushin, Laufer, Rothbart, & Sloan, 1981).

Additionally, prior research with combat veterans has shown that the various dimensions of war zone stress exposure may be differentially related to subsequent development of stress reaction symptoms, and that the impact of stress exposure may differ among subgroups of the veteran population (Laufer, Brett, & Gallops, 1985). Thus it was important that the exposure measure was sensitive to the full range of stressors to which theater veterans might have been exposed.

The NVVRS war zone stress exposure measures were developed from a set of nearly 100 survey interview items that covered eight broad stressor content areas that prior research suggested should be included in a comprehensive assessment, and used principal components analysis to derive empirically a set of specific measures of the underlying dimensions. This resulted in the identification of four war zone stress dimensions for men and six for women. Internal consistency reliabilities of the scales ranged from .70 to .94 (median = .87).

Second-order principal components analyses indicated that the specific dimensions could be combined statistically into a single overall index of exposure (separately for men and women). Doing so provided a single index that reflected the variability from all of the important dimensions of war zone stress exposure, separately for men and women veterans. These overall indices were used to define "high" and "low/moderate" stress exposure groups.

NVVRS findings (Kulka et al., 1990b) indicate that exposure to war zone stress was not equally distributed among the race/ethnicity subgroups. About 23 percent of white/other males were classified by the multidimensional index as "high exposure," but significantly higher percentages of African American and Hispanic men were so classified: 37 percent of African American men and 33 percent of Hispanic men. The difference in exposure between African American men and Hispanic men was not statistically significant.

Additionally, there was a substantial differential in the prevalence of PTSD between the high and low/moderate exposure groups. For all Vietnam veterans, the current prevalence of PTSD was 36 percent in the high exposure group, versus 9 percent for the low/moderate exposure group. Similar differentials held for the race/ethnicity subgroups. Among white/others, the differential was 34 versus 8; for African Americans, 38 versus 10; and for Hispanics, 48 versus 18.

Could these differences in exposure levels account for the remaining differences in current PTSD prevalence rates among the race/ethnicity subgroups? To clarify the role of war zone stress exposure, the war zone stress exposure index was added to the predisposition adjustment models for the male theater veteran racial/ethnic subgroup contrasts (Schlenger et al., 1992). This allowed comparison of current prevalence rates among the race/ethnicity subgroups while controlling for predisposing characteristics *and* war zone stress exposure.

With the predisposing factors and exposure to war zone stress controlled, the difference in current PTSD prevalence between white/other and African American theater veterans was reduced to statistical nonsignificance. That is, if white/other and African American Vietnam veterans had had the same background characteristics when they went to Vietnam, and had been exposed to similar levels of war zone stress, there would be no difference in the prevalence of PTSD today.

The effect on the contrasts of Hispanics with white/others and with African Americans, however, was different. The difference in current prevalence between white/other and Hispanic males was reduced slightly, from 6.1 percent (adjusted for predisposition) to 5.4 percent, but remained statistically significant. The difference for the African American versus Hispanic contrast, which had been reduced to statistical nonsignificance when only predisposing factors were controlled, was increased to a statistically significant 6.3 percent (Hispanics higher than African Americans) when war zone stress exposure was also controlled. Thus although the adjustment for both predisposition and exposure eliminated the prevalence differential between white/others and African Americans, even when both are controlled the current PTSD prevalence for Hispanics is significantly higher than for white/others or for African Americans. It remains for further research to identify the determinants of this difference, which may be accounted for at least in part by a variety of post-exposure factors (e.g., nature of the homecoming experience, post-war life experiences, etc.).

Structural Equation Modeling Approaches to Risk Factor Analysis. In addition to the work of the NVVRS research team, other investigators have used the NVVRS data to examine risk issues. In a comprehensive set of studies, the Kings and their colleagues have applied structural equation modeling techniques to examine the relationships between PTSD and a wide variety of potential causal factors. In the first of these studies, King, King, Gudanowski, & Vreven (1995) examined the relationships of war zone stressor exposure with PTSD. Four war zone stressor indexes—

labeled traditional combat, atrocities/abusive violence, perceived threat, and malevolent environment—were developed from the NVVRS Vietnam experience items on the basis of expert judgment, and were found to be reliable for both men and women. These indexes were used in a structural equations framework to test a causal model of their relationships to PTSD. Atrocities/abusive violence, perceived threat, and malevolent environment all had direct effects on PTSD, with malevolent environment having the largest. Traditional combat had an indirect effect through perceived threat, but no direct effect. Only the traditional combat-perceived threat path coefficient differed between men and women veterans.

In the second study, King, King, Foy, and Gudanowski (1996) used the NVVRS data to study the relationships among prewar factors, war zone stress, and PTSD. Four prewar factors were examined (family environment, childhood antisocial behavior, maturity at entry to Vietnam, and previous trauma history) along with the war zone stress factors developed in the first study. Results favored a model with eleven latent variables, on which scores for men and women varied for nine, so different models resulted for men and women. For both sexes, war zone stress factors were important, but prewar factors also contributed, more so for men than women. Among the prewar factors, trauma history and age at exposure had direct effects on PTSD for men, while for women only prior trauma history had a direct effect. The patterns of indirect effects of the prewar factors also varied for men and women. Findings underline the contribution of family instability during childhood and prior trauma history to the development of combat-related PTSD.

In a third study, King, King, Fairbank, Keane, and Adams (1998) used structural equation modeling to assess the contribution of potential resilience and recovery factors to PTSD. Beginning with a nine-factor measurement model (that included the four war zone stress factors, four resilience/recovery factors [hardiness, structural social support, functional social support, and stressful life events], and PTSD), they again found gender differences in the magnitudes of the loadings. Among the resilience/recovery factors, hardiness, functional social support, and stressful life events were found to have direct effects on PTSD for

both genders, as did structural social support for men. Findings demonstrate a complex pattern of direct and indirect relationships among the latent variables.

Similarly, Fontana, Rosenheck, and their colleagues have applied structural equation modeling approaches using the NVVRS data base. Based on findings from their earlier studies with treatment-seeking samples (Fontana, Rosenheck, & Brett, 1992; Fontana and Rosenheck, 1993), Fontana and Rosenheck (1994) assessed premilitary risk factors (childhood physical or sexual abuse, race/ethnicity, symptoms of conduct disorder, and family instability), war zone stress exposure factors (combat, participation in abusive violence, receiving disciplinary action, and nonmilitary trauma exposure during military service), homecoming reception (society's welcome and family support), and post-military trauma exposure. Findings indicated that homecoming experiences and war zone exposures were the most important factors, but that a variety of other factors play significant roles. The final model accounted for 48 percent of the variance in PTSD.

More recently, Fontana, Schwartz, & Rosenheck (1997) reported findings of structural equation analyses for women Vietnam veterans. The women who served in Vietnam are a much more homogeneous group than the men, in that more than 90 percent were white and nearly 90 percent were nurses (and therefore both older and better educated on average than the men). Using data from the NVVRS, Fontana, Schwartz, & Rosenheck found similar models applied to women Vietnam veterans and to a comparison group of women who served in the military during the Vietnam era but did not serve in Vietnam, and that exposure to war zone stressors and sexual or physical abuse in childhood were both important predictors of PTSD among women veterans.

Finally, in a unique and important contribution to the field, True et al. (1993) reported findings from the Twin Study aimed at assessing the genetic contribution to the post-exposure expression of PTSD symptoms among Vietnam veterans. Findings from analyses involving 4,042 mono- and di-zygotic twin pairs showed a heritable contribution to the prevalence of nearly all PTSD symptoms many years after exposure, even with combat exposure controlled. Importantly, a genetic influence on PTSD symptom expression was also found among twins who did not serve in Vietnam, suggesting that the genetic contribution is not specific to combat-related PTSD.

2. Risk Factors for Veterans of Other Wars

Risk factors for combat-related PTSD have also been studied for veterans of other wars as well. For example, Engdahl and his colleagues (Engdahl, Harkness, Eberly, Page, & Bielinski, 1993) modeled trauma response among former prisoners of war using structural equations models. Subjects were American military personnel who had been taken prisoner during World War II or the Korean War who were followed by the National Academy of Science's Institute of Medicine over a period of years, along with a comparison group of nonprisoners. Models were estimated with data from the 1967 and 1985 follow-ups, and separately for World War II and Korean War prisoners. Findings demonstrated that both exposure factors and individual resilience factors play a role in combat-related PTSD.

Solomon and her colleagues have studied extensively the contributions of exposure and post-exposure factors to the development of PTSD in Israeli veterans, focusing particularly on social cognitive variables such as self-efficacy, attributional style, and coping (Mikulincer & Solomon, 1988; Solomon, Mikulincer, & Benbenishty, 1989; Solomon, Benbenishty, & Mikulincer, 1991). Findings indicated that self-efficacy was a function of current psychiatric status, prior adjustment, and specific exposures, and that over time the influence of exposure characteristics is reduced. These and other findings guided the development of a specialized intervention aimed at treating chronic PTSD in these veterans (Solomon et al., 1992).

More recently, several investigations of risk factors for combat-related PTSD among Persian Gulf War veterans have been reported. Engel and colleagues (Engel et al., 1993) studied the relationship between pre-exposure sexual and physical abuse on combat-related PTSD among a convenience sample of 297 ODS veterans. Importantly, the investigators were able to collect measures of physical and sexual abuse in this sample before their participation in ODS. Findings of multivariate analyses showed that for women veterans, those who reported pre-ODS abuse reported higher post-ODS PTSD symptoms than those who did not, even after adjustment for pre-ODS psychiatric history and level of ODS combat exposure. This finding is consistent with prior findings of the importance of prior trauma, and suggests the possibility that exposure to trauma creates an additional vulnerability if one is subsequently exposed.

Similarly, Sutker and her colleagues (Sutker, Davis, Uddo, & Ditta, 1995) conducted a case-control study with a convenience sample of ODS veterans with and without PTSD. Multivariate analyses showed that hardiness, avoidance coping, family cohesion, and satisfaction with social support significantly discriminated the cases from the noncases. The investigators noted, however, that the study does not provide a basis for causal attribution.

Finally, Wolfe, Brown, & Bucsela (1992) report interesting findings about the impact of current wars on veterans of past wars. Studying a convenience sample of female Vietnam veterans who had been evaluated for PTSD prior to the onset of ODS, they found that post-ODS symptom levels were generally higher (suggesting a possible exacerbation related to ODS), but that those with the highest pre-ODS symptom levels were significantly more susceptible to increased symptomatology. This finding is also consistent with a model that suggests that repeated exposures may produce increased vulnerability.

D. FUTURE DIRECTIONS

The above summaries demonstrate that much progress has been made in empirical documentation of the epidemiology of combat-related PTSD since the inclusion of PTSD as a specific diagnostic category in DSM-III. The finding of increased prevalence of PTSD among those who serve in war zones has been documented across a wide variety of wars, for both military and civilian participants, and using a variety of methodologies. Additionally, the fact that PTSD often co-occurs with other psychiatric disorders (e.g., depression) and other adjustment problems (e.g., relationship difficulties) is also now well established. Although less widely established, evidence is mounting that PTSD is related to a variety of other adjustment problems *independent of its comorbidities* (i.e., that the relationship of PTSD to other outcomes is not fully explainable by the comorbidities themselves). Additionally, substantial progress has been made on the issue of PTSD assessment and case identification, with multisource–multimethod approaches becoming the "gold standard."

In spite of excellent progress, a number of issues remain. The two most important of these are the problem of retrospective measurement and the problem of causal attribution in studies attempting to establish etiology.

For a variety of reasons, retrospective measurement of exposure and other variables has been the standard approach. This is problematic for a number of reasons, the most important of which is the potential for current symptom levels to interfere with retrospective reports. For example, it is conceivable that the observed correlation between combat exposure and PTSD symptoms may be due in part to a mechanism through which those who are symptomatic today are more prone to report exposures than those not symptomatic. Similarly, it is conceivable that the assessment of pre-exposure characteristics is similarly affected by current symptomatology—e.g., those who are currently symptomatic may be more likely to report abusive childhood experiences. Although there is some evidence that retrospective reports of combat exposure are valid (e.g., Schlenger et al., 1992), prospective studies are required to address this problem definitively. As noted above, this is a direction in which the field is clearly moving.

Problems of causal attribution in the study of etiology are not unique to PTSD. Given that at present the gold standard for "definitive" causal attribution is random assignment, it is clear that definitive causal attributions about the etiology of PTSD will not be established under this gold standard—i.e., we hope that no one ever randomly assigns people to varying levels of traumatic exposure. Important developments in alternatives to random assignment are being made, however, including quasi-experimental designs that provide a stronger basis for causal inference and model-based analytic approaches such as structural equation modeling. We have described above some instances of application of these methods, and look forward to their becoming tomorrow's standards for the field.

REFERENCES

Adelberger, B. (1994, August). As job restrictions ease, female recruiting prospers. *Army Times*, p. 14.

American Psychiatric Association. (1980). *Diagnostic and statistical manual of mental disorders* (3rd ed.). Washington, DC: Author.

American Psychiatric Association. (1987). *Diagnostic and statistical manual of mental disorders* (3rd ed. Rev.). Washington, DC: Author.

Archibald, H. C., & Tuddenham, R. D. (1965). Persistent stress reaction after combat: A 20-year follow-up. *Archives of General Psychiatry, 12,* 475–481.

Breslau, N., Davis, G. C., Andreski, P., & Peterson, E. (1991). Traumatic events and post-traumatic stress disorder in an urban population of young adults. *Archives of General Psychiatry, 48,* 216–222.

Breyer, J. B., Nelson, B. A., Miller, J. B., & Krol, P. A. (1987). Childhood sexual and physical abuse as factors in adult psychiatric illness. *American Journal of Psychiatry, 144,* 1426-1430.

Brill, N., & Beebe, G. (1956). *A follow-up study of war neuroses* (VA Medical Monograph). Washington, DC: U.S. Government Printing Office.

Centers for Disease Control Vietnam Experience Study. (1988). Health status of Vietnam veterans: I. Psychosocial characteristics. *Journal of the American Medical Association, 259,* 2701–2707.

Chemtob, C., Roitblat, H. L., Hamada, R. S., Carlson, J. G., & Twentyman, C. T. (1988). A cognitive action theory of post-traumatic stress disorder. *Journal of Anxiety Disorders, 2,* 253–275.

Chu, J. A., & Dill, D. L. (1990). Dissociative symptoms in relation to childhood physical and sexual abuse. *American Journal of Psychiatry, 147,* 887–892.

Cochran, W. G. (1983). *Planning and analysis of observational studies.* New York: Wiley and Sons.

Davidson, J., Smith, R., & Kudler, H. (1989). Familial psychiatric illness in chronic posttraumatic stress disorder. *Comprehensive Psychiatry, 30,* 339–345.

Eberly, R. E., & Engdahl, B. E. (1991). Prevalence of somatic and psychiatric disorders among former prisoners of war. *Hospital and Community Psychiatry, 42,* 807–813.

Egendorf, A., Kadushin, C., Laufer, R. S., Rothbart, G., & Sloan, L. (1981). *Legacies of Vietnam: Comparative adjustment of veterans and their peers.* Washington, DC: U.S. Government Printing Office.

Engdahl, B. E., Harkness, A. R., Eberly, R. E., Page, W. F., & Bielinski, J. (1993). Structural models of captivity trauma, resilience, and trauma response among former prisoners of war 20 to 40 years after release. *Social Psychiatry and Psychiatric Epidemiology, 28,* 109–115.

Engdahl, B. E., Speed, N., Eberly, R. E., & Schwartz, J. (1991). Comorbidity of psychiatric disorders and personality profiles of American World War II prisoners of war. *Journal of Nervous and Mental Disease, 179,* 181–187.

Engel, C. C., Engel, A. L., Campbell, S. J., McFall, M. E., Russo, J., & Katon, W. (1993). Posttraumatic stress disorder symptoms and precombat sexual and physical abuse in Desert Storm veterans. *Journal of Nervous and Mental Disease, 181,* 683–688.

Fairbank, J. A., Schlenger, W. E., Caddell, J. M., & Woods, M. G. (1993) Posttraumatic stress disorder. In P. B. Sutker & H. E. Adams (Eds.), *Comprehensive handbook of psychopathology* (2nd ed., pp. 145–165). New York: Plenum Press.

Foa, E. B., Steketee, G., & Rothbaum, B. O. (1989). Behavioral/cognitive conceptualizations of post-traumatic stress disorder. *Behavior Therapy, 20,* 155–176.

Fontana, A., & Rosenheck, R. (1993). A causal model of the etiology of war-related PTSD. *Journal of Traumatic Stress, 6,* 475–500.

Fontana, A., & Rosenheck, R. (1994). Posttraumatic stress disorder among Vietnam theater veterans: A causal model of etiology in a community sample. *Journal of Nervous and Mental Disease, 182,* 677–684.

Fontana, A., Rosenheck, R., & Brett, E. (1992). War zone traumas and posttraumatic stress disorder symptomatology. *Journal of Nervous and Mental Disease, 180,* 748–755.

Fontana, A., Schwartz, L. S., & Rosenheck, R. (1997). Posttraumatic stress disorder among female Vietnam veterans: A causal model of etiology. *American Journal of Public Health, 87,* 169–175.

Foy, D. W., Osato, S. S., Houskamp, B. M., & Neumann, D. A. (1992). PTSD etiology. In P. A. Saigh (Ed.), *Post-traumatic stress disorder: A behavioral approach to assessment and treatment* (pp. 28–49). New York: Pergamon Press.

Futterman, S., & Pumpian-Midlin, E. (1951). Traumatic war neuroses five years later. *American Journal of Psychiatry, 108,* 401–408.

Gleser, G., Green, B., & Winget, C. (1981). *Prolonged psychosocial effects of disaster: A study of Buffalo Creek.* New York: Academic Press.

Goldberg, J., True, W. R., Eisen, S. A., & Henderson, W. G. (1990). A twin study of the effects of the Vietnam war on posttraumatic stress disorder. *Journal of the American Medical Association, 263,* 1227–1232.

Green, B. L. (1996). Traumatic stress and disaster: Mental health effects and factors influencing adaptation. In J. R. T. Davidson, & A. C. McFarlane (Eds), *International Review of Psychiatry.*

Green, B. L., Grace, M. C., Lindy, J. D., Gleser, G. C., & Leonard, A. (1990a). Risk factors for PTSD and other diagnoses in a general sample of Vietnam veterans. *American Journal of Psychiatry, 147,* 729–733.

Green, B. L., Lindy, J. D., Grace, M. C., Gleser, G. C., Leonard, A. C., Korol, M., & Winget, C. (1990b). Buffalo Creek survivors in the second decade: Stability of stress symptoms. *American Journal of Orthopsychiatry, 60,* 43–54.

Helzer, J. E., Robins, L. N., & McEvoy, M. A. (1987). Post-traumatic stress disorder in the general population: Findings of the Epidemiologic Catchment Area Survey. *New England Journal of Medicine, 317,* 1630–1634.

Hinton, W. L., Chen, Y. J., Du, N., Tran, C. G., Lu, F. G., & Miranda, J. (1993). DSM-III-R disorders in Vietnamese refugees: Prevalence and correlates. *Journal of Nervous and Mental Disease, 181,* 113–122.

Horowitz, M. (1974). Stress response syndromes: Character style and dynamic psychotherapy. *Archives of General Psychiatry, 31,* 768–781.

Horowitz, M. J., & Kaltreider, N. B. (1980). Brief psychotherapy of stress response syndromes. In T. B. Karasu & L. Bellak (Eds.), *Specialized techniques in individual psychotherapy.* New York: Brunner/Mazel.

Jones, J. C., & Barlow, D. H. (1990). The etiology of post-traumatic stress disorder. *Clinical Psychology Review, 10,* 299–328.

Jordan, B. K., Schlenger, W. E., Hough, R., Kulka, R. A., Weiss, D., Fairbank, J. A., & Marmar, C. R. (1991). Lifetime and current prevalence of specific psychiatric disorders among Vietnam veterans and controls. *Archives of General Psychiatry, 48,* 207–215.

Keane, T. (1989). Post-traumatic stress disorder: Current status and future directions. *Behavior Therapy, 20,* pp. 149–153.

Keane, T. M., & Wolfe, J. (1990). Comorbidity in post-traumatic stress disorder: An analysis of community and clinical studies. *Journal of Applied Psychology, 20,* 1776–1788.

Keane, T., Zimering, R., & Caddell, J. (1985). A behavioral formulation of posttraumatic stress disorder in Vietnam veterans. *Behavior Therapist, 8,* 9–12.

Keehn, R. J., Goldberg, I. E., & Beebe, G. W. (1974). Twenty-four year mortality follow-up of Army veterans with disability separations for psychoneurosis in 1944. *Psychosomatic Medicine, 32*(1).

Kessler, R. C. Sonnega, A., Bromet, E., Hughes, M., & Nelson, C. B. (1995). Posttraumatic stress disorder in the National Comorbidity Survey. *Archives of General Psychiatry, 52,* 1048–1060.

Kilpatrick, D., Best, C. Veronen, L., Amick, A., Villeponteaux, L, & Ruff, G. (1985). Mental health correlates of criminal victimization: A random community survey. *Journal of Consulting and Clinical Psychology, 53,* 866–873.

King, D. W., King, L. A., Foy, D. W., & Gudanowski, D. M. (1996). Prewar factors in combat-related posttraumatic stress disorder: Structural equation modeling with a national sample of female and male Vietnam veterans. *Journal of Consulting and Clinical Psychology, 64,* 520–531.

King, D. W., King, L. A., Gudanowski, D. M., & Vreven, D. L. (1995). Alternative representations of war zone stressors: Relationships to posttraumatic stress disorder in male and female Vietnam veterans. *Journal of Abnormal Psychology, 104,* 184–196.

King, L. A., King, D. W., Fairbank, J. A., Keane, T. M., & Adams, G. A. (1998). Resilience/recovery factors in posttraumatic stress disorder among female and male Vietnam veterans: Hardiness, postwar social support, and additional stressful life events. *Journal of Personality and Social Psychology, 74,* 420–434.

Klonoff, H., McDougall, G., Clark, C., Kramer, P., & Horgan, J. (1976). The neuropsychological, psychiatric, and physical effects of prolonged and severe stress: 30 years later. *Journal of Nervous and Mental Disease, 163,* 246–252.

Kluznick, J. C., Speed, N., VanValkenburg, C., & Magraw, R. (1986). Forty-year follow-up of United States Prisoners of War. *American Journal of Psychiatry, 143,* 1443–1446.

Kraemer, H. C., Kazdin, A. E., Offord, D. R., Kessler, R. C., Jensen, P. S., & Kupfer, D. J. (1997). Coming to terms with the terms of risk. *Archives of General Psychiatry, 54,* 337–343.

Krystal, J. H., Kosten, T. R., Southwick, S., Mason, J. W., Perry, B. D., & Giller, E. L. (1989). Neurobiological aspects of PTSD: Review of clinical and preclinical studies. *Behavior Therapy, 20,* 177–198.

Kulka, R. A., Schlenger, W. E., Fairbank, J. A., Hough, R. L., Jordan, B. K., Marmar, C. R., & Weiss, D. S. (1990a). *Trauma and the Vietnam war generation: Report of findings from the National Vietnam Veterans Readjustment Study.* New York: Brunner/Mazel.

Kulka, R. A., Schlenger, W. E., Fairbank, J. A., Hough, R. L., Jordan, B. K., Marmar, C. R., & Weiss, D. S. (1990b). The National Vietnam Veterans Readjustment Study: Tables of findings and technical appendices. New York: Brunner/Mazel.

Kulka, R. A., Schlenger, W. E., Fairbank, J. A., Hough, R. L., Jordan, B. K., Marmar, C. R., & Weiss, D. S. (1991). Assessment of PTSD in the community: Prospects and pitfalls from recent studies of Vietnam veterans. *Psychological Assessment, 3,* 547–560.

Laufer, R., Brett, E., & Gallops, M. (1985). Symptom patterns associated with posttraumatic stress disorder among Vietnam veterans exposed to war trauma. *American Journal of Psychiatry, 142,* 1304–1311.

Laufer, R. S., Gallops, M. S., & Frey-Wouters, E. (1984). War stress and trauma: The Vietnam veteran experience. *Journal of Health and Social Behavior, 25,* 65–85.

Lazarus, R., & Folkman, S. (1984). *Stress. appraisal, and coping.* New York: Springer.

Litz, B. T., & Keane, T. M. (1989). Information processing in anxiety disorders: Application to the understanding of post-traumatic stress disorder. *Clinical Psychology Review, 9,* 243–257.

Litz, B. T., Orsillo, S. M., Friedman, M., Ehlich, P., & Batres, A. (1997). Posttraumatic stress disorder associated with peacekeeping duty in Somalia for U.S. military personnel. *American Journal of Psychiatry, 154,* 178–184.

Litz, B. T., Schlenger, W. E., Weathers, F. W., Caddell, J. M., Fairbank, J. A., & LaVange, L. M. (1997). Predictors of emotional numbing in post-traumatic stress disorder. *Journal of Traumatic Stress, 10,* 607–618.

McFarlane, A. (1986). Long-term psychiatric morbidity after a natural disaster: Implications for disaster planners and emergency services. *Medical Journal of Australia, 145,* 561–563.

Meehl, P. (1962). Schizotaxia, schizotypy, schizophrenia. *American Psychologist, 17,* 827–838.

Mikulincer, M., & Solomon, Z. (1988). Attributional style and combat-related posttraumatic stress disorder. *Journal of Abnormal Psychology, 97,* 308–313.

Moore, B. L. (1991). African-American women in the U.S. military. *Armed Forces & Society, 17,* 363–384.

Nadelson, C., Notman, M., Zackson, H., & Gornick, J. (1982). A follow-up study of rape victims. *American Journal of Psychiatry, 139,* 1266–1270.

Orner, R. J. (1992). Post-traumatic stress disorders and European war veterans. *British Journal of Clinical Psychology, 31,* 387–403.

O'Toole, B. I., Marshall, R. P., Grayson, D. A., Schureck, R. J., Dobson, M., French, M., Pulvertaft, B., Meldrum, L., Bolton, J., & Vennard, J. (1994). *The Australian Vietnam Veterans Health Study: III. Psychological health of Australian Vietnam veterans and the relationship to combat.* Unpublished manuscript.

Perconte, S. T., Wilson, A. T., Pontius, E. B., Dietrick, A. L., & Spiro, K. J. (1993). Psychological and war stress symptoms among deployed and non-deployed reservists following the Persian Gulf War. *Military Medicine, 158,* 516–521.

Resnick, H. S., Kilpatrick, D. G., Dansky, B. S., Saunders, B. E., & Best, C. L. (1993). Prevalence of civilian trauma and posttraumatic stress disorder in a representative national sample of women. *Journal of Consulting and Clinical Psychology, 61,* 984–991.

Schlenger, W. E., Kulka, R. A., Fairbank, J. A., Hough, R. L., Jordan, B. K., Marmar, C. R., & Weiss, D. S. (1992). The prevalence of post-traumatic stress disorder in the Vietnam generation: A multimethod, multisource assessment of psychiatric disorder. *Journal of Traumatic Stress, 5,* 333–363.

Shalev, A., Bleich, A., & Ursano, R. J. (1990). Posttraumatic stress disorder: Somatic comorbidity and effort tolerance. *Psychosomatics, 31,* 197–203.

Shapiro, S., Skinner, E. Kessler, L., Von Korff, M., German, P., Tischler, G., Leaf, P., Benham, L., Cottler, L., & Regier, D. (1984). Utilization of health and mental health services: Three Epidemiologic Catchment Area sites. *Archives of General Psychiatry, 41,* 971–978.

Shore, J. H., Tatum, E. L., & Vollmer, W. M. (1986). Evaluation of mental effects of disaster: Mount St. Helens eruption. *American Journal of Public Health, 76* (Suppl. 3), 76–83.

Sierles, F. S., Chen, J. J., McFarland, R. E., & Taylor, M. A. (1983). Posttraumatic stress disorder and concurrent psychiatric illness: A preliminary report. *American Journal of Psychiatry, 140,* 1177–1179.

Sierles, F. S., Chen, J. J., Messing, M. L., Besyner, J. K., & Taylor, M. A. (1986). Concurrent psychiatric illness in non-Hispanic outpatients diagnosed as having post-

traumatic stress disorder. *Journal of Nervous and Mental Disease, 174,* 171–173.

Smith, E., North, C., McCool, R., & Shea, J. (1990). Acute postdisaster psychiatric disorders: Identification of persons at risk. *American Journal of Psychiatry, 147,* 202–206.

Snow, B. R., Stellman, J. M., Stellman, S. D., & Sommer, J. F. (1988). Post-traumatic stress disorder among American Legionaires in relation to combat experience in Vietnam: Associated and contributing factors. *Environmental Research, 47,* 175–192.

Solomon, Z. (1989). Psychological sequelae of war: A 3-year prospective study of Israeli combat stress reaction casualties. *Journal of Nervous and Mental Disease, 177,* 342–346.

Solomon, Z., Benbenishty, R., & Mikulincer, M. (1991). The contribution of wartime, pre-war, and post-war factors to self-efficacy: A longitudinal study of combat stress reaction. *Journal of Traumatic Stress, 4,* 345–361.

Solomon, Z., Bleich, A., Shoham, S., Nardi, C., & Kotler, M. (1992). The "Koach" project for treatment of combat-related PTSD: Rationale, aims, and methodology. *Journal of Traumatic Stress, 5,* 175–193.

Solomon, Z., Margalit, C., Waysman M., & Bleich, A. (1991). In the shadow of the Gulf war: Psychological distress, social support and coping among Israeli soldiers in a high risk area. *Israel Journal of Medical Science, 27,* 687–695.

Solomon, Z., & Mikulincer, M. (1988). Psychological sequelae of war: A 2-year follow-up study of Israeli combat stress reaction casualties. *Journal of Nervous and Mental Disease, 176,* 264–269.

Solomon, Z., Mikulincer, M., & Benbenishty, R. (1989). Locus of control and combat-related post-traumatic stress disorder: The intervening role of battle intensity, threat appraisal, and coping. *British Journal of Clinical Psychology, 28,* 131–144.

Solomon, Z., & Prager, E. (1992). Elderly Israeli Holocaust survivors during the Persian Gulf war: A study of psychological distress. *American Journal of Psychiatry, 149,* 1707–1710.

Solomon, Z., Weisenberg, M., Schwarzwald, J., & Mikulincer, M. (1987). Posttraumatic stress disorder among frontline soldiers with combat stress reaction: 1982 Israeli experience. *American Journal of Psychiatry, 144,* 448–454.

Southwick, S. M., Morgan, A., Nagy, L. M., Bremner, D., Nicolaou, A. L., Johnson, D. R., Rosenheck, R., & Charney, D. S. (1993). Trauma-related symptoms in veterans of Operation Desert Storm: A preliminary report. *American Journal of Psychiatry, 150,* 1524–1528.

Southwick, S. M., Morgan, C. A., III, Darnell, A., Bremner, D., Nicolaou, A. L., Nagy, L. M., & Charney, D. S. (1995). Trauma-related symptoms in veterans of Operation Desert Storm: A 2-year follow-up. *American Journal of Psychiatry, 152,* 1150–1155.

Steinglass, P., & Gerrity, E. (1990). Natural disasters and post-traumatic stress disorder: Short-term vs. long-term recovery in two disaster-affected communities. *Journal of Applied Social Psychology, 20,* 1746–1765.

Stretch, R. H., Marlowe, D. H., Wright, K. M., Bliese, P. D., Knudson, K. H., & Hoover, C. H. (1996). Posttraumatic stress disorder symptoms among Gulf War veterans. *Military Medicine, 161,* 407–410.

Sutker, P. B., Allain, A. N., & Winstead, D. K. (1993). Psychopathology and psychiatric diagnoses of World War II Pacific theater prisoner of war survivors and combat veterans. *American Journal of Psychiatry, 150,* 240–245.

Sutker, P. B., Davis, J. M., Uddo, M., & Ditta, S. R. (1995). War zone stress, personal resources, and PTSD in Persian Gulf War returnees. *Journal of Abnormal Psychology, 104,* 444–452.

Sutker, P. B., Uddo, M., Brailey, K., & Allain, A. N., Jr. (1993). War-zone trauma and stress related symptoms in Operation Desert Shield/Storm (ODS) returnees. *Journal of Social Issues, 49,* 33–49.

True, W. R., Rice, J., Eisen, S. A., Heath, A. C., Goldberg, J., Lyons, M. J., & Nowak, J. (1993). A twin study of genetic and environmental contributions to liability for posttraumatic stress symptoms. *Archives of General Psychiatry, 50,* 257–264.

Walker, R. D., Howard, M. O., Lambert, M. D., & Suchinsky, R. (1994). Psychiatric and medical comorbidities of veterans with substance use disorders. *Hospital and Community Psychiatry, 45,* 232–237.

Weiss, D. S., Marmar, C. R., Schlenger, W. E., Fairbank, J. A., Jordan, B. K., Hough, R. L., & Kulka, R. A.

(1992). The prevalence of lifetime and partial post-traumatic stress disorder in Vietnam theater veterans. *Journal of Traumatic Stress, 5,* 365–376.

Weisaeth, L., & Eitinger, L. (1991a). Research on PTSD and other post-traumatic reactions: European literature. *PTSD Research Quarterly, 2,* 1–7.

Weisaeth, L., & Eitinger, L. (1991b). Research on PTSD and other post-traumatic reactions: Euopean literature (Part II). *PTSD Research Quarterly, 2,* 1–8.

Winfield, I., George, L., Swartz, M., & Blazer, D. (1990). Sexual assault and psychiatric disorders among a community sample of women. *American Journal of Psychiatry, 147,* 335–341.

Wolfe, J., Brown, P. J., & Bucsela, M. L. (1992). Symptom responses of female Vietnam veterans to Operation Desert Storm. *American Journal of Psychiatry, 149,* 676–679.

Wolfe, J., Brown, P. J., & Kelley, J. M. (1993). Reassessing war stress: Exposure and the Persian Gulf War. *Journal of Social Issues, 49,* 15–31.

Zatzick, D. F., Marmar, C. R., Weiss, D., Browner, W., Metzler, T., Golding, J., Stewart, A., Schlenger, W., and Wells, K. (1997). Posttraumatic stress disorder and functioning and quality of life outcomes in female Vietnam veterans. *Military Medicine, 162,* 661–665.

Zatzick, D., Marmar, C., Weiss, D., Browner, W., Metzler, T., Golding, J., Stewart, A., Schlenger, W., and Wells, K. (1997). Posttraumatic stress disorder and functioning and quality of life outcomes in a nationally representative sample of male Vietnam veterans. *American Journal of Psychiatry, 154,* 1690–1694.

Zubin, J., & Spring, B. (1977). Vulnerability: A new view of schizophrenia. *Journal of Abnormal Psychology, 86,* 103–126.

Zwi, A. B. (1991). Militarism, militarization, health and the third world. *Medicine and War, 7,* 262–268.

CHAPTER 5

POSTTRAUMATIC STRESS DISORDER: PREVALENCE AND RISK FACTORS RELATIVE TO DISASTERS

A. C. McFARLANE, M.D.
University of Adelaide
The Queen Elizabeth Hospital

NICHOLAS POTTS, M.D.
University of Adelaide
The Queen Elizabeth Hospital

HISTORICAL BACKGROUND

Disasters, by their nature, are events that capture human attention and concern. However, the public interest in these events tends to be relatively short lived and their long-term morbidity is often underestimated by welfare and health service providers. Disaster research has highlighted the often very prolonged adverse consequences of such events. The first systematic research in the field was conducted by the Swiss psychiatrist, Edouard Stierlin (1909, 1911). He studied an earthquake that affected Messina in Italy in 1907 and a mining disaster which occurred in 1906. He found that a substantial proportion of the victims developed long-term posttraumatic symptoms. The Messina earthquake was an event of much greater magnitude than is often studied by disaster researchers, having killed 70,000 of the town's inhabitants. Stierlin found that 25 percent of the survivors experienced sleep disturbances and nightmares.

His theoretical formulations were more akin with current reasoning than those prevalent at the time. For example, Kraepelin (1899) suggested that traumatic neurosis in which fear played the dominant aetiological factor was rare and "atypical." Stierlin strongly disagreed with this view and believed the term neurosis was not a good descriptor because he believed it was a psychogenic disorder in which no psychopathological predisposition was required. He demonstrated the value of studying non-clinical populations and how these can challenge many of the perceptions that arise in clinical settings. In a setting where there was little secondary gain, he was struck by the inaccuracy of the lay perception that posttraumatic psychopathology was secondary to simulation.

The field of traumatic stress has grown up around three main groups of victims from three types of events. Namely, disasters, war veterans, and criminal victimization. Disasters are unusual events because they occur randomly and usually involve large numbers of people, and in contrast to events such as criminal assault, are all traumatized simultaneously. Thus there are particular lessons which can be learned because of the capacity to collectively investigate the reactions in the victims, as well as the associated communal processes that mitigate and aggravate the effects of these events.

DEFINITION

Although everyone knows the meaning of the word "disaster," like the word "stress," it is rarely defined. The Oxford English Dictionary (Sykes, 1987) definition of disaster is: "sudden or great misfortune; calamity; complete failure." Given this breadth of definition, it is an issue of some complexity as to how disasters are clearly separated from other types of traumatic events (Green, 1996). The original derivation of the term came from the Latin and implied the meaning "the stars are evil." In contrast to these general definitions, the early disaster researchers Kingston and Rosser (1974) suggest the term be used to describe "massive collective stress." Norris's suggestions (1992) was more focused, suggesting that these were events where there were "violent encounters with nature, technology or human kind."

This question of definition is not a trivial issue because researchers often underestimate the complexity of characterizing the experience of individuals who have experienced disasters. Van der Kolk (1996) has argued that one of the primary characteristics of traumatic experiences is that they are events that challenge an individual's capacity to create a narrative of their experience and to integrate their traumatic experience with other events. As a consequence their traumatic memories are often not coherent stories and tend to consist of intense emotions or somatosensory impressions. Thus these are events that take the capacity of language to an extreme. Hence it is easy for researchers and clinicians alike to not fully embrace the horror and the helplessness which research data and patients' stories embody. This is a critical issue for the development of adequate methodologies and instruments to describe and characterize disaster experience.

THE PROBLEMS OF MEASURING DISASTER EXPOSURE

In contrast to the effort put into the development of valid and reliable measures of adverse life events, surprisingly little attention has been given to the issue in the area of traumatic experience, and particularly disasters (McFarlane, 1996). For example, one of the only populations to rate stressful items differently on Holmes and Rahe's (1967) life events scale in a significantly different way was a group of earthquake victims; surprisingly they rated the severity of the impact of major losses as significantly less than populations unaffected by the disaster itself did (Janney, Masuda, & Holmes, 1977). This suggests that traumatized groups may have a different perspective on their experience than populations who have not confronted that particular event may have. This has the potential to create significant errors when investigators are trying to judge the severity of traumatic stresses and to determine what components of disasters are markedly distressing to most people.

This is a complex issue both from a clinical and research perspective. There are many components of disasters which include the actual impingement of the event on the individual (e.g., injury) as well as the events the individual actually witnessed. These will be influenced by the person's mental state (e.g., did he/she panic or dissociate?) and the person's perception of the risks and capacity to act adaptively. On the other hand, there will be objective measures of exposure such as seeing death and injury or actually being injured. Similarly, the duration of exposure and awareness of destruction and loss are objective issues.

In contrast, matters that may be equally important in determining the degree of traumatization include the perceptions that one survived the experience through freak circumstances or was kept safe by chance, and that one had no control over the circumstances for one's behavior. DSM-IV recognized the relative importance of these subjective components in determining the nature of the traumatic experience. To try and resolve these issues systematically, Green (1993a) has suggested eight generic dimensions of trauma that need to be taken into account. Hence, defining the exact nature of disaster and the differences between different individual's experience is a much more complex question than would appear to be the case on first examination.

THE CONTRIBUTIONS OF DISASTER RESEARCH

Since the original diagnostic criteria for posttraumatic stress disorder (PTSD) were developed in 1980 (APA, 1980), there has been considerable development in the empirical basis for the diagnostic criteria. The original criteria were influenced to a large degree by the work of Kardiner (1941) in his studies of World War I veterans with very long-standing posttraumatic disorders. Hence, the groupings of the symptoms in DSM-III were organized along the axis of the intrusive phenomena, the curtailment of resources or withdrawal, and the "physioneurosis." These diagnostic criteria provided a particular focal point for research in disaster settings following their publication. Characteristically, this work was done in much closer proximity to the event initiating the symptoms than had been the case in the veterans who Kardiner had studied. These research findings were summarized by Green (1993b) and played an important role in the reformulation of the phenomena of PTSD in DSM-IV. The current criteria relate much more closely to the acute forms of the disorder as they will be observed in disaster populations.

In general, these studies have demonstrated the similarity between different types of disasters and the significant mental health effect these events have on the survivors in comparison to people who were not exposed to similar adversity.

In contrast to studies of veterans where many issues are raised about the importance of secondary gain and problems about the general social status of returned veterans, the study of disaster survivors are thought to provide a less complex indication of the chronic effects of trauma. As with many areas of research in the traumatic stress field, research has now moved beyond the simple description of prevalence, psychological morbidity, and crude indicators of resilience or vulnerability. In general, the second wave of disaster research is now asking significantly more sophisticated questions about the nature and process of posttraumatic adaptations (Green & Solomon, 1995). Disaster studies provide an unusually useful way of beginning to look at questions such as the gradient of exposure and the longitudinal course of traumatic adaptability.

The Prevalence of Disaster

There has been a general reluctance to acknowledge just how frequently traumatic experiences befall people's lives. When PTSD was first defined in DSM-III (APA, 1980) the original stressor criterion characterized traumatic events as being outside the range of usual human experience. However, when the prevalence of such events is systematically examined it is apparent that trauma is surprisingly commonplace. Kessler, Sonnega, Bromet, and Nelson (1995) found that 63.3 percent of the male population had experienced an event that met the DSM-IV stressor criterion. Norris (1992) in a study of 1,000 adults in Southern United States, found that 69 percent of the sample had experienced a traumatic stressor in their lives and this included 21 percent in the past year alone. The report of the Red Cross highlighted the differential impact of disasters in Third World countries. In the period 1967 to 1991, an average of 17,000,000 people living in developing countries were effected by disasters each year, as compared to about 700,000 in developed countries (a striking ratio of 166 to 1!) (International Federation of Red Cross and Red Crescent Societes, 1993).

It is important to emphasize that disasters cover a range of experiences. Distinction is often drawn between natural and technological events. It is on occasions proposed that man-made disasters are more likely to be difficult for individuals to tolerate. Natural disasters possibly are able to be dismissed as acts of God. At the other end of the extreme are events involving active human design, such as assault, torture, and rape. These are premeditated acts which are on occasions purposely planned and implemented. Smith and North (1993) articulated the commonly held opinion that technological and human made disasters are likely to be more traumatic than natural disasters as they provoke a greater sense of being the deliberate victim of one's fellow human beings. On the other hand, a recent meta-analysis of the relationship between disasters and trauma-related psychopathology (Rubonis & Bickman, 1991) came to the opposite conclusion—namely, that natural disasters resulted in greater rates of disorder. Thus, the common sense of appeal of the idea that the trauma of rape, torture, and interpersonal assault would have a greater capacity to disrupt an individual's psychological assumptions than events such as hurricanes and floods does not appear to be substantiated by the objective evidence. The large body of disaster-related studies cannot be possibly covered.

CONTROLLED STUDIES

Interestingly, there are several studies which have been conducted, in which the investigators had previously collected an epidemiological data set. Canino, Bravo, Rubio-Stipec, and Woodberry (1990) studied the impact of a mud slide and flood in Puerto Rico which killed 800 people. Fortuitously, a year before they had studied this population and were able to re-evaluate 375 of their initial subjects. They have had a significant increase in the symptoms of depression and a range of somatic complaints from the pre-disaster levels but failed to demonstrate any increase in panic disorder or alcohol abuse. An increased prevalence of posttraumatic stress disorder was identified.

Smith, Robins, and Pryzbeck (1986) investigated a series of disaster events in St. Louis involving exposure to dioxin, floods, and tornados. Newly exposed individuals had high levels of new PTSD symptoms and depression symptoms. However the depressive symptoms increased only in those who had had previous depression. Pfeiffer and Norris (1989) also happened to be conducting epidemiological data in an area effected by floods. They were studying older people and found that personal loss accounted for more depression and anxiety in the three to six months after the flood when taking account of pre-disaster levels of symptomatology.

Comparing epidemiological studies is difficult for a series of reasons. Until recently, often competing diagnostic systems and systems of methodologies have been used. As well, samples are often selective and not nonrepresentative. Only the identification of operationally defined PTSD diagnostic criteria and

the refinement of assessment methodologies have made it possible to carefully investigate the epidemiology of PTSD. In addition, within traumatized populations there will be significant variations in the level of exposure and the intensity of threat experience. Therefore the prevalence of PTSD found in any study of a disaster will be partially dependent upon the level of exposure that is required before a subject can be included, given that subjects in populations with high levels of exposure are likely to have higher prevalence estimates.

Similarly, studies of clinical populations are likely to yield higher prevalence rates. A total of 15 studies have assessed the prevalence of PTSD amongst the victims of natural and technological disasters (McFarlane & de Girolamo, 1996). Nine of these were carried out in the United States and the remaining six in other countries, including developing countries (Columbia, Fiji, and Mexico). The rates vary significantly according to the sample and the type of the disaster. For example, Shore, Vollmer, and Tatum (1989) examined the impact of the Mt. St. Helen's volcanic eruption and compared the exposed population with a control group. Lifetime prevalence in the Mt. Helen group was 3.6 percent compared to 2.6 percent in the control. In contrast, McFarlane (1988) studied a representative sample of 469 volunteer firefighters exposed to a severe natural disaster in Australia. This study found a rate of 16 percent of PTSD and it appeared that half of the sufferers had gone into remission at 42 months (McFarlane, 1992).

The Buffalo Creek disaster, the collapse of a slag dam and subsequent flood that took place in 1972, is one of the most comprehensively studied disasters (Green et al., 1991; Green, Lindy, Grace, & Leonard, 1992; Grace, Green, Lindy, & Leonard, 1993; Green & Lindy, 1994). During a 14-year follow-up, they found a 59 percent lifetime rate among the survivors while 25 percent still met the criteria for a current diagnosis of PTSD. A group of subjects, who were children at the time of the disaster, were also followed up 17 years later (Green & Lindy, 1994). A lifetime rate of 32 percent was found for flood-related PTSD, while the current rate for flood-related PTSD was 7 percent.

Lima et al. (1991a) and Lima, Pai, Santacruz, and Lozano (1991b) studied the victims of the Armero eruption in Columbia living in shelters (n = 102) or attending primary care clinics and found a PTSD rate of 32 percent and 42 percent, respectively. Conyer, Sepulveda, Medina, Caraveo, and De La Fuente (1987) conducted a study of victims of a Mexican earthquake and found a similar rate of 32% percent. Madakasica and O'Brien (1987) found a rate of 59 percent amongst the victims of a tornado living in a rural community. Steinglass and Gerrity (1990) have found a rate of 15 percent at 4 months and of 21 percent at 16 months in the victims of a tornado and a flood from two communities. However, Canino et al. (1990) found a considerably lower rate of PTSD (4 percent) in flood victims, as compared to 0.7 percent in the unexposed control group, as did North, Smith, McCool, and Lightcap (1989) and Smith et al. (1986), who found prevalence rates between 2 and 5 percent among victims of natural disasters.

Holen's study of the Alexander Kieland oil rig disaster (1991) where 123 oil rig workers were killed compared their outcomes with matched employees of the oil industry. Using the Norwegian Health System data base which keeps detailed records, they were able to demonstrate that the two groups had similar base lines of both physical and psychiatric morbidity in the two-year period leading up to the disaster. Following the event, the survivors had eight times as many psychiatric diagnoses and had used twice as much sick leave. They also had significantly more somatic complaints. A variety of studies have examined the issue of prevalence. However, there are fewer controlled studies.

In summary, the prevalence rates of posttraumatic morbidity following disasters varies significantly (see Table 5.1). Norris (1992) suggested the estimate rates of PTSD in disaster-exposed individuals was approximately 6 percent. Holen's (1991) data suggested there were prevalence rates of approximately 12 percent in his follow-up of psychiatric morbidity compared with 1.5 percent in the comparison group. Canino et al.'s (1990) study showed lower rates after the Puerto Rico mud slide, suggesting a prevalence rate of 4 to 5 percent. One of the highest rates was demonstrated by Goenjian et al. (1994) following the Armenian earthquake where they demonstrated a rate of 67 percent meeting PTSD criteria 18 months after the earthquake.

This suggests that even in extreme circumstances, the development of disaster-rated morbidity is the exception rather than the rule. Hence, a range of other factors which contribute to psychiatric morbidity need to be examined. The fact that the majority of people adapt and cope does provide a quandary to service providers. The morbidity which does arise is easy to be missed and underestimated. Frequently services are provided and withdrawn prematurely once the more obvious physical signs of a disaster are contained.

It is also important to emphasize that focusing on posttraumatic stress disorder alone can miss the prevalence of a range of other significant psychological distress. Green et al. (1992) in their benchmark study of the Buffalo Creek disaster found that 95 percent of those who had a posttraumatic stress disorder also attracted some other psychiatric diagnosis. McFarlane and Papay (1992) examined this question in the firefighters exposed to the Ash Wednesday bushfire disaster. Three and a half years after that disaster, the majority had comorbid disorders, particularly major depressive disorder. This was similar to the finding of Kessler et al. (1995) in the National Comorbidity Survey. Smith, North, McCool, and Shea (1990) similarly demonstrated that PTSD occurred four times more frequently in conjunction with comorbid diagnoses than it did alone, even in close proximity to the event. Hence, studies of disasters need to consider their capacity to create a range of psychiatric morbidities.

PHENOMONOLOGY OF POST-DISASTER MORBIDITY

The study of disasters provides an opportunity to explore in some detail the question as to whether there are different patterns of symptomatic distress following different types of events. This issue was investigated in particular detail by Green (1993b). A range of important observations has been found. In particular, controlled disaster-affected populations demonstrate that the intensity of intrusive symptoms decreases significantly over the passage of time, particularly in the first two years after the disaster. Hence, intrusive symptoms were less specific to PTSD than were avoidance and disordered arousal.

TABLE 5.1 PTSD and Disasters

AUTHORS	COUNTRY	STUDIED SAMPLE	SAMPLE SIZE	PTSD PREVALENCE
Canino et al., 1990	Puerto Rico	Flood victims	321	4%
Conyer et al., 1987	Mexico	Earthquake victims	524	32%
Durham et al., 1985	USA	Apartment explosion	53	21%
Fairley et al., 1986	Fiji	Cyclone victims	75	66%
Green et al., 1992	USA	Buffalo Creek victims	193	59% (lifetime) 25% (current)
Lima et al., 1991a	Columbia	Victims of Armero eruption	500	24%
Lima et al., 1991b	Columbia	as above	102	42%
Madakasiza & O'Brien, 1987	USA	Victims of a tornado	116	59%
McFarlane, 1992	Australia	Firefighters exposed to severe natural disaster	147	22% (at 8 months) 36% (at 42 months)
North et al., 1989b	USA	Victims of tornado	42	2%
Palinkas et al., 1993	USA	People exposed to Exxon Valdez oil spill	599	9%
Realmuto et al., 1991	USA	Victims of technological disaster	24	12%
Shore et al., 1989	USA	Volcanic eruption	1016	4.5% (men) 3% (women)
Smith et al., 1986	USA	Flood victims and dioxin exposure	172	5%
Steinglass & Gerrity, 1989, 1990	USA	Victims of tornado (town a) and flood (town b)	39(a) 76(b)	15% a (4 months) 21% b (16 months)
Weisaeth, 1989	USA	Victims of industrial disaster	125	80% (high stress) 71% (medium stress)

Thus, whilst these intrusive symptoms are critical to the formulation of the nature of PTSD, it is important to take account of the fact that they exist in many individuals who did not develop a fully symptomatic condition. Green (1993b) found that there were significant variations in the absolute levels of symptoms from one study to the next. One of the problems with the comparisons between different studies is that often different instrumentation and different time periods were used. By combining various symptom clusters, she was able to show that there is some range in the relevant frequency of symptoms and that the ranking of these symptoms was not sufficiently

affected by the passage of time. The intrusive symptoms and nightmares and sleep disturbance were the most frequent difficulties. Similarly, an exaggerated startle response was somewhat more frequent than the avoidance and numbing symptoms, such as loss of interest or caring. The finding that survivor guilt was a relatively uncommon phenomena in disaster-affected populations was possibly one of the reasons why this was dropped from the DSM-IV criteria.

In general, it appears that the pattern of symptoms associated with complex PTSD (Herman, 1992) are very uncommon in the aftermath of disasters. These events do not lead to the same disruption of the victim's personal relationships and affect modulation as occurs following experiences such as child abuse.

LONGITUDINAL COURSE

Disasters have provided a useful setting for examining the longitudinal effects of catastrophic stress. In particular, Green and Solomon (1995) have demonstrated the importance of the different types of posttraumatic stress disorder. Blank (1993) has highlighted that the longitudinal course of PTSD has multiple variations—namely, acute, delayed, chronic, intermittent, residual, and reactived patterns. As well, there is a need to define posttraumatic syndromes in which full criteria are not met. People with continuing symptoms who do not reach severity sufficient to warrant diagnosis often continue to demonstrate significant morbidity.

Furthermore, disasters can have serious long-term consequences other than the onset of psychological disorders. These events can modify an individual's vulnerability to subsequent traumatic events, even in the absence of a symptomatic response. For other individuals, these experiences can become powerful sources of motivation in terms of their taking on particular social roles, for example, as a community advocate.

The impact of disasters on physical health also requires specific mention as physical morbidity is frequently the reason for help-seeking amongst disaster victims (McFarlane, Atchison, Rafalowicz, & Papay, 1994). This highlights that primary health care providers need to be educated about the possibility that posttraumatic morbidity will present with a range of somatic complaints in the aftermath of these events.

The impact of disasters on behavior of the interpersonal functioning of victims has been little investigated. This is surprising given the popular prejudice that emerged in the 1880s in relation to "railway spine" that traumatic neurosis was essentially induced by the payment of compensation (Trimble, 1981). This is an issue that not infrequently occurs in disaster settings where some third party is held to be negligent. There are now four studies which have examined the impact of compensation of PTSD in disaster settings and following accidents.

First, a study of the Buffalo Creek disaster (Grace et al., 1993) compared a group who went through the litigation process with those who accepted an uncontested payment and found few differences in outcome. Mayou, Bryant, and Duthie (1993) found that being involved in compensation did not affect the outcome of motor accident victims—a similar finding to that after the Pan American flight 103 crash over Lockerbie in Scotland (Brooks & McKinlay, 1992). Litigation also did not effect the outcome of the victims of the 1983 Ash Wednesday disaster, although they felt very traumatized by the litigation process. Thus, although trauma can have dramatic effects on ability to perform in a variety of social roles, this variation cannot substantially be attributed to the payment of compensation. However, defining the optimal payment system for compensation and maximizing victims' motivation to play a useful social role are important matters of concern. This is particularly the case following disasters because the lengthy delays in finding suitable resolution mechanisms for compensation can on occasions be more disruptive for the individual than the acute experience itself.

Gunn (1996) has highlighted how an anticipation of these issues led to an effective mechanism for dealing with some of these questions following the Zebruggen ferry disaster. This limited a number of the steps in the legal process which meant the seeking of compensation was less likely to dominate the survivors' lives and preoccupation in the aftermath of the disaster. This has much to recommend it, particularly in events where there is a single defendant who is often very well funded by their defense counsel.

One of the important issues in community samples is the apparent differences in the phenomenology compared with clinical populations. In a longitudinal follow-up of victims of disaster, McFarlane and Yehuda (1996) found that eight years after the disaster only 4 percent of those who initially attracted a PTSD diagnosis continued to do so. Whilst 60 percent continued to complain of the intrusive symptoms and disordered arousal was as common as it was at 42 months, many failed to continue to describe the symptoms of avoidance and estrangement which were the main reasons why they did not qualify for the PTSD diagnosis. Thus, in relatively well functioning groups, their withdrawal from the world does not dominate the clinical picture to the same extent. At eight years, their disordered arousal was the most prominent feature, suggesting that anxiety and depressive symptoms are an important residual of the disorder.

Clinical populations from the same event tended to demonstrate much greater stability of the intrusion and avoidance symptomatology. Thus, further investigation of these questions in disaster-affected groups is warranted. In particular, it may be the case that in the most severe forms, the symptoms of PTSD may be relatively stable with the passage of time whilst in the less intense forms, the specific trauma-related symptoms of intrusion and avoidance may decrease whilst the disordered affect and arousal may remain.

ETIOLOGICAL ISSUES AND RISK FACTORS

One of the uncomfortable facts which has emerged from the systematic investigation of disasters is that posttraumatic psychopathology emerges in a minority. This emphasizes the need to look at a range of other variables that may be contributing to the onset of symptomatic distress. Weisaeth (1996a, b) has made a major contribution to investigating the role and effects of exposure in disaster. Collective disasters provide an opportunity to look at the different components of the disaster experience that contribute to the ongoing distress. During these large-scale events the survivor is not alone, which means that there is a need to look at issues such as leadership and dependence upon others for one's own rescue. Also the magnitude of these events often means that in the immediate aftermath the inadequacy of emergency operations to contain the catastrophe means that the victim will have to look to a range of innovative solutions in containing the chaos. As well, group processes may play an important component in the longer term adaptation.

From a descriptive perspective, it is apparent that there is a link between quantitative and qualitative dimensions of trauma and that both contribute to adaptation. Green (1990) has proposed several generic dimensions of traumatic stressors which include the receipt of intentional harm or injury, exposure to grotesque sights and scenes, witnessing or learning of violence to loved ones, learning of exposure to a noxious agent, and causing death or severe harm to another.

Weisaeth's study of a factory disaster in a prospective design of the acute, sub-acute, and long-term reactions highlighted a number of these issues (Weisaeth, 1996a, b, 1989). He showed that mortality and injuries were dependent upon the distance from the explosion and this in turn correlated strongly with the later development of posttraumatic stress disorder. In the high exposure group, PTSD prevalence rates were 36 percent after seven months, 27 percent after two years, 22 percent after three years and 19 percent after four years. This contrasted to the medium exposure group where there was a decrease in the PTSD rate from 17 percent after seven months to 2 percent after four years. Thus, the intensity of the stressor not only accounted for the initial prevalence but also the possible longevity of the symptoms. Recognizing its significance as a prognostic risk factor was an important observation. He found that for employees who witnessed the event, even at a close distance, it was not a severe enough event to cause real PTSD. Whilst a minority were distressed in the initial weeks, premorbid sensitivity played an important role in the development of symptoms in this group, highlighting the inter-relationship between vulnerability factors and exposure.

Kessler et al. (1995) has highlighted the importance of examining gender issues. Green has examined this question in some detail (1996). Although it is difficult to draw conclusions, it appears that women in general may be more at risk of anxiety disorders. Solomon, Mikulincer, Freid, and Wosner (1987) made an interesting observation that mid-range levels of support availability were associated with the most favorable outcomes for women. In contrast women with high support availability did poorly. This study also found that women with excellent spouse support had worse outcomes than those with weaker spouse ties. In contrast, men tended to do better if they had a stronger spouse relationship. This suggests that for some, the strength of attachment may be a burden rather than supportive at times of extreme stress.

It is difficult to make any definitive comments about the impact of age on morbidity. Studies frequently examine age-specific groups, which make comparisons difficult. This is an area which requires further investigation. A range of other risk factors have been examined including family history, prior life events, and prior traumatization. As is the case in other traumatic situations (Weisaeth, 1996b) these vulnerability factors appear to have a general effect in disasters as in other trauma-related situations. Particularly in situations of relatively low exposure, vulnerability factors such as premorbid personality and previous psychiatric disorder have an important role to play.

In summary, vulnerability and protective factors are necessary to explain much of the probability of developing PTSD. PTSD and other trauma-related disorders represent the outcome of a biopsychosocial matrix of variables. These factors can operate along a variety of axes. The context in which the event occurs in the individual's life is the base from which the disorder emerges. The nature of the stressor and the recovery environment involve a series of complex interactions modifying the ability of the individual to quench immediate posttraumatic distress. It is in this postdisaster period that these vulnerability factors may play a critical role. In general, it appears that women are more vulnerable and that personality plays an important role except in situations of extreme exposure. On the other hand it is important to emphasize that posttraumatic stress disorder emerges in previously healthy individuals whose modest vulnerability would otherwise have little relevance.

CONCLUSION

One contribution of disaster research which has largely gone unnoticed has been the relevance of the findings to understanding the more general relationship between psychiatric disorder and life events. A major problem which had plagued researchers endeavouring to investigate the relationship between day to day adversity and psychiatric disorder was the whole question of cause and effect. Longitudinal studies of life events demonstrated that life events were as likely to have been caused by psychiatric disorder as was the reverse relationship in which the disorder had arisen as a consequence of some adversity. Disasters by their very nature are beyond individual's control, in other words, they are truly independent life events. Hence they provide a relatively methodologically sophisticated way of beginning to investigate these causal associations. However, one of the problems which occurs in most disasters is that pre-existing measures of the adjustment of population do not exist. This is an important issue because many studies have failed to take account of the existing psychological morbidity which would inevitably exist within the disaster-affected communities. The National Comorbidity Survey (Kessler et al., 1995) and the ECA study (Helzer, Robins, & McEvoy, 1987) have demonstrated the point that approximately 20 to 25 percent of the population will have a psychiatric disorder of some form at any given time. A critical question is the way in which the existing symptoms within individuals are modified by traumatic experiences, as well as the nature of the psychopathology which emerges in most people who were otherwise well adjusted at the time of the traumatic event. Hence, there is a need to differentially investigate PTSD triggered by traumatic events in those with predisposition in contrast to "true PTSD" which emerges in those who are asymptomatic at the time of the event.

REFERENCES

American Psychiatric Association (1980). *Diagnostic and statistical manual of mental disorders* (3rd ed.). Washington, DC: Author.

American Psychiatric Association (1994). *Diagnostic and statistical manual of mental disorders* (4th ed.). Washington, DC: Author.

Blank, A. S. (1993). The longitudinal course of posttraumatic stress disorder. In J. R. T. Davidson & E. B. Foa (Eds.), *Posttraumatic stress disorder: DSM-IV and beyond* (pp. 3–22). Washington, DC: American Psychiatric Press.

Brooks, N. & McKinlay, W. (1992). Mental health consequences of the Lockerbie disaster. *Journal of Traumatic Stress, 5,* 527–543.

Canino, G., Bravo, M., Rubio-Stipec, M., & Woodberry, M. (1990). The impact of disaster on mental health: Prospective and retrospective analyses. *International Journal of Mental Health, 19,* 51–69.

Conyer, R. C., Sepulveda, Amor J., Medina, Mora M. E., Caraveo, J., & De La Fuente, J. R. (1987). Prevalencia del sindrome de estres posttraumatico en la poblacion sobreviviente a un desastre natural. *Salud Publica Mexicana, 29,* 406–411.

Goenjian, A. K., Najarian, L. M., Pynoos, R. S., Steinberg, A. M., Petrosian, P., Setrakyan, S., & Fairbainks, L. A. (1994). Posttraumatic stress reactions after single and double trauma. *Acta Psychiatrica Scandinavica, 90,* 214–221.

Grace, M. C., Green, B. L., Lindy, J. D., & Leonard, A. C. (1993). The Buffalo Creek disaster: A 14-year follow-up. In J. P. Wilson & B. Raphael, (Eds.), *International handbook of traumatic stress syndromes* (pp. 441–449). New York: Plenum Press.

Green, B. L. (1990). Defining trauma: Terminology and generic stressor dimensions. *Journal of Applied Social Psychology, 20,* 1632–1642.

Green, B. L. (1993a). Identifying survivors at risk: Trauma and stressors across events. In J. P. Wilson & B. Raphael (Eds.), *International handbook of traumatic stress syndromes* (pp. 135–144). New York: Plenum Press.

Green, B. L. (1993b). Disasters and posttraumatic stress disorder. In J. R. T. Davidson & E. B. Foa (Eds.), *Posttraumatic stress disorder: DSM-IV and beyond.* Washington, DC: American Psychiatric Press.

Green, B. L. (1996). Traumatic stress and disaster: Mental health effects and factors influencing adaptation. In F. L. Mak & C. C. Nodelsen (Eds.), *International review of psychiatry,* vol. 2. Washington, DC: American Psychiatric Press.

Green, B. L., Korol, M., Grace, M. C., Vary, M. G., Leonard, A. C., Gleser, G. C., & Smitson-Cohen, S. (1991). Children and disatser: Age, gender, and parental effects on PTSD symptoms. *Journal of the American Academy of Child and Adolescent Psychiatry, 30,* 945–951.

Green, B. L., & Lindy, J. D. (1994). Posttraumatic stress disorder in victims of disasters. *Psychiatric Clinics of North America, 17* (2), 301–309.

Green, B. L., Lindy, J. D., Grace, M. C., & Leonard, A. C. (1992). Chronic posttraumatic stress disorder and diagnostic comorbidity in a disaster sample. *Journal of Nervous and Mental Disease, 180,* 760–766.

Green, B. L., & Solomon, S. (1995). The mental health impact of natural and technological disasters. In J. R. Freedy & S. E. Hobfall, (Eds.), *Traumatic stress: From theory to practice.* New York & London: Plenum Press.

Gunn, J., & Taylor, P. J. (1993). *Introduction in forensic psychiatry* (pp. 1–20). Oxford, England: Butterworth Heinemann.

Helzer, J. E., Robins, L. N., & McEvoy, L. (1987). Posttraumatic stress disorder in the general population: Findings of the Epidemiologic Catchment Area survey. *New England Journal of Medicine, 317* (26), 1630–1634.

Herman, J. L. (1992). Complex PTSD: A syndrome in survivors of prolonged and repeated trauma. *Journal of Traumatic Stress, 5,* 377–391.

Holen, A. (1991). A longitudinal study of the occurrence and persistence of post traumatic health problems in disaster. *Stress Medicine, 7,* 11–17.

Holmes, T. H. & Rahe, R. H. (1967). The social readjustment rating scale. *Journal of Psychosomatic Research, 11,* 213–218.

International Federation of Red Cross and Red Crescent Societies (1993). *World disaster report, 1993.* Dordrecht, The Netherlands. Martinus Nijhoff.

Janney, J. G., Masuda, M., & Holmes, T. H. (1977). Impact of a natural catastrophe on life events. *Journal of Human Stress, 3* (2), 22–23, 26–34.

Kardiner, A. (1941). *The traumatic neuroses of war.* New York: Hoeber.

Kessler, R., Sonnega, A., Bromet, E., & Nelson, C. B. (1995). Posttraumatic stress disorder in the National Comorbidity Survey. *Archives of General Psychiatry, 52,* 1048–1060.

Kingston, W., & Rosser, R. (1974). Disaster: Effect on medical and physical state. *Journal of Psychosomatic Research, 18,* 437–456.

Kraepelin, E. (1899). *Psychiatrie* (6th ed.). Leipzig: Verlag von Johann Ambrosius Barth.

Lima, B. R., Pai, S., Caris, L., Haro, J. M., Lima, A. M., Toledo, V., Lozano, J., & Santacruz, H. (1991a). Psychiatric disorders in primary health care clinics one year after a major Latin American disaster. *Stress Medicine, 7,* 25–32.

Lima, B. R., Pai, S., Santacruz, H., & Lozano, J. (1991b). Psychiatric disorders among poor victims following a major disaster: Armero, Columbia. *Journal of Nervous and Mental Disease, 179,* 420–427.

Madakasira, S. & O'Brien, K. F. (1987). Acute posttraumatic stress disorders in victims of a natural disaster. *Journal of Nervous and Mental Disease, 175,* 286–288.

Mayou, R., Bryant, B., & Duthie, R. (1993). Psychiatric consequences of road traffic accidents. *British Medical Journal, 307,* 647–651.

McFarlane, A. C. (1988). The phenomenology of posttraumatic stress disorders following a natural disaster. *Journal of Nervous and Mental Disease, 176* (1), 22–29.

McFarlane, A. C. (1992). Avoidance and intrusion in posttraumatic stress disorder. *Journal of Nervous and Mental Disease, 180* (7), 439–445.

McFarlane, A. C. (1996). Attitudes to victims: Issues for medicine, the law & society. In C. C. Sumner, M. Israel, M. O'Connor, & R. Sarre (Eds.), *International victimology: Selected papers from the 8th International Symposium on Victimology.* Canberra: Australian Institute of Criminology.

McFarlane, A. C., Atchison, M., Rafalowicz, E., & Papay, P. (1994). Physical symptoms in post-traumatic stress disorder. *Journal of Psychosomatic Research, 38* (7), 715–726.

McFarlane, A. C. & de Girolamo, G. (1996). The nature of traumatic stressors and the epidemiology of posttraumatic reactions. In B. van der Kolk, A. C. McFarlane & L. Weisaeth (Eds.), *Traumatic stress: The effects of overwhelming experience on mind, body and society* (pp. 129–154). New York: Guilford Press.

McFarlane, A. C. & Papay, P. (1992). Multiple diagnoses in posttraumatic stress disorder in the victims of a natural disaster. *Journal of Nervous and Mental Disease, 180* (8), 498–504.

McFarlane, A. C. & Yehuda, R. (1996). Resilience, vulnerability and the course of posttraumatic reactions. In B. van der Kolk, A. C. McFarlane & L. Weisaeth (Eds.), *Traumatic stress: The effects of overwhelming experience on mind, body and society* (pp. 155–181). New York: Guilford Press.

Norris, F. (1992) Epidemiology of trauma: Frequency and impact of different potentially traumatic events on different demographic groups. *Journal of Consulting and Clinical Psychology, 60,* 409–418.

North, C. S., Smith, E. M., McCool, R. E., & Lightcap, P. E. (1989). Acute postdisaster coping and adjustment. *Journal of Traumatic Stress, 2,* 353–360.

Pfeiffer, J. & Norris, F. (1989). Psychological symptoms in older subjects following natural disasters: Nature, timing and duration in course. *Journal of Gerentological Social Science, 44,* 207–217.

Rubonis, A. & Bickman, L. (1991). Psychological impairment in the wake of disaster: The disaster-psychopathology relationship. *Psychological Bulletin, 109,* 384–399.

Shore, J. H., Vollmer, W. M., & Tatum, E. L. (1989). Community patterns of posttraumatic stress disorders. *Journal of Nervous and Mental Disease, 177* (11), 681–685.

Smith, E. M. & North, C. S. (1993). Posttraumatic stress disorder in natural disasters and technological accidents. In J. P. Wilson & B. Raphael (Eds.), *International handbook of traumatic stress syndromes* (pp. 405–419). New York: Plenum Press.

Smith, E., North, C. S., McCool, R. E., & Shea, J. M. (1990). Acute post disaster psychiatric disorder: Identification of persons as risk. *American Journal of Psychiatry, 147,* 202–206.

Smith, E. M., Robins, L. N., & Pryzbeck, T. R. (1986). Psychosocial consequences of a disaster. In J. H. Shaw (Ed.), *Disaster studies, new methods and findings.* Washington, DC: American Psychiatric Press.

Solomon, Z., Mikulincer, M., Freid, B. & Wosner, Y. (1987). Family characteristics and posttraumatic stress disorder: A follow-up of Israeli combat stress reaction casualties. *Family Process, 3,* 383–394.

Steinglass, P. & Gerrity, E. (1990). Natural disasters and posttraumatic stress disorder: Short term versus long term recovery rates in two disaster-affected communities. *Journal of Applied and Social Psychology, 20,* 1746–1765.

Stierlin, E. (1909). *Über psychoneurophatische Folgezust ände bei den Überlebenden der Katastrophe von Courriéres am 10. Marz 1906* (On the *psychoneuropathic consequences among the survivors of the Courrierés catastrophe of* 10 March 1906). Unpublished doctoral dissertation, University of Zürich.

Stierlin, E. (1911). Nervöse und psychische Störungen nach Katastrophen (Nervous and psychic disturbances after catastrophes). *Deutsche Medizinische Wochenschrift, 37,* 2028–2035.

Sykes, J. B. (Ed.). *The Concise Oxford Dictionary,* 7th ed. (1987). Oxford: The Clarendon Press.

Trimble, M. (1981). *Post-traumatic neurosis: From railway spine to whiplash.* Chichester: John Wiley.

van der Kolk, B. A. (1996). Trauma and memory. In B. van der Kolk, A. C. McFarlane, & Weisaeth, L. (Eds.), *Traumatic stress: The effects of overwhelming experience on mind, body and society* (pp. 279–302). New York: Guilford Press.

Weisaeth, L. (1989). The stressors and the post-traumatic stress syndrome after an industrial disaster. *Acta Psychiatrica Scandinavica, 80,* 25–37.

Weisaeth, L. (1996a). PTSD: The stressor response relationship. In E. Giller & L. Weisaeth (Eds.), *Post Traumatic Stress Disorder. Bailliere's Clinical Psychiatry, International Practice and Research, 2* (2), 191–216.

Weisaeth, L. (1996b). PTSD: Vulnerability and protective factors. In E. Giller & L. Weisaeth (Eds.), *Post Traumatic Stress Disorder Disorder. Bailliere's Clinical Psychiatry, International Practice and Research, 2* (2), 217–228.

CHAPTER 6

THE NEUROBIOLOGY OF POSTTRAUMATIC STRESS DISORDER: AN INTEGRATION OF ANIMAL AND HUMAN RESEARCH

J. DOUGLAS BREMNER, M.D.
Yale University School of Medicine
Yale Psychiatric Institute
West Haven VA Medical Center and the National Center for PTSD

STEVEN M. SOUTHWICK, M.D. and DENNIS S. CHARNEY, M.D.
Yale University School of Medicine
Yale Psychiatric Institute

I. PTSD: BIOLOGY AND PHENOMENOLOGY

Posttraumatic stress disorder (PTSD) is characterized by specific symptoms which develop following exposure to a "threat to the life of oneself or others" (Diagnostic and Statistical Manual-IV). An important point of this chapter is that symptoms of PTSD and other psychiatric disorders related to stress, such as the dissociative disorders, are a behavioral manifestation of stress-induced changes in brain structure and function. Animals exposed to severe stress (such as electric shock) show acute increases in stress-related neurotransmitters and neuropeptides, the chemical messengers of the brain, including corticotropin releasing factor (CRF), norepinephrine, serotonin, dopamine, endogenous benzodiazepines, and endogenous opiates. Long-term alterations in behavior are seen in animals exposed to chronic stress, and are associated with changes in these neurotransmitters and neuropeptides. Each of these neurotransmitters and neuropeptides have specific sites, or receptors, located on neurons to which they bind in order to exert their effects, which are also affected by stress, leading to changes in receptor number or affinity (the "stickiness" of binding to neurotransmitters and neuropeptides). Alterations in neurotransmitters and neuroreceptors result in changes in neuronal function in specific brain areas which are involved in the stress response. Stress also results in changes in the structure of neurons in these regions, which can lead to changes in function. These effects combine to alter the neuronal inter-connections, which result in long-term changes in brain "circuits" involved in the stress response.

Brain regions involved in stress also play a role in memory and emotion. It has been hypothesized that the symptoms of PTSD are mediated by abnormalities in these brain regions (Bremner, Krystal, Charney, & Southwick, 1996; Bremner, Krystal, Southwick, & Charney, 1995; Pitman, 1989). These include alterations in memory and emotion, as well as

Acknowledgments: The research results presented in this review were supported by the National Center for PTSD Grant and a VA Career Development Award to Dr. Bremner.

exaggerated responsiveness of the body's physiological "stress response system" to cues of the original trauma which are in and of themselves essentially harmless.

This chapter will review findings from animal studies demonstrating alterations in brain function and structure following exposure to stress. First, the use of animal models for the study of stress will be reviewed. Then, findings from animal studies related to stress-induced alterations in norepinephrine, corticotropin releasing factor (CRF)/hypothalamic-pituitary-adrenal (HPA) axis, endogenous benzodiazepine, dopamine, endogenous opiate, and serotonin function will be examined. Evidence for the involvement of brain regions involved in memory and emotion, including hippocampus and amygdala, in the detrimental effects of stress will be reviewed. Studies which have begun to replicate these findings in human populations of PTSD patients will outlined. Extrapolations will be made from findings in biological studies to the clinical presentation of patients with PTSD.

II. ANIMAL MODELS FOR PTSD

The use of animal models is well established in the study of biological bases for psychiatric disorders. Animal models are justified based on the fact that experimental manipulations can be carried out in animal populations which are not possible in human populations. There is a long history of creating animal models for the study of depression, and more recently anxiety. Most methodologies for animal models for depression and anxiety involve exposure of the animal to extreme stress. In one of the more popular animal models, animals are exposed to repeated stress from which they cannot escape. This eventually leads to certain behaviors which are termed "learned helplessness," which correlate with specific biological changes, such as depletion of brain norepinephrine. Behavioral changes related to stress include weight loss and decreased food intake, decreased active behavior in novel environments such as "open fields," decreased competitiveness and normal aggressiveness, decreased grooming and play activity, decreased responding for rewards, and decreased self-stimulation of brain reward centers, deficits in memory and attention,

sleep disturbances, and increased defecation (indicative of "anxiety" in the rat) (Weiss, Simson, Ambrose, Webster, & Hoffman, 1985).

Animal models developed as an indirect model for depression are actually a direct model for PTSD, since exposure to extreme stress (typically uncontrollable) is required for the diagnosis of PTSD. In addition, behaviors seen in rodents exposed to stress in many ways parallel behaviors seen in humans with a history of traumatic stress. For instance, decreased exploration in open fields can be seen as avoidance, decreased grooming and play activity as being cut off from others, and decreased responding for rewards and self-stimulation as emotional numbing.

From a review of the animal literature, it is clear that not all stressors have an equal effect on behavior and biology. The most popular stress paradigm involves chronic inescapable footshock. Other stressors have been utilized, however, including forced swim in cold water and immobilization. More "ecological" stressors include "defeat stress" and being the subordinate member of a social colony, referred to hereafter as "social stress." In evaluating stressors it is important to ask specific questions, such as what was the temperature of the water? what was the length of time of immobilization? were there preceding stressors? how may applications of stress were applied? how much time passed from the application of the stressor to the measurement of the biological variable? The temporal sequence of stressors also needs to be taken into consideration. Some studies involve acute stress, or exposure to a single stressor. Other studies involve exposure to chronic stress, followed by re-exposure. Different periods of stress employed in different studies can have an important impact on the findings, as will be described below.

III. NEUROTRANSMITTER AND NEUROPEPTIDAL SYSTEMS INVOLVED IN STRESS AND PTSD NORADRENERGIC SYSTEMS

The locus coeruleus/noradrenergic system plays an important role in the stress response (Bremner, Krystal, Southwick, & Charney, 1996a, 1996b). The majority of norepinephrine cell bodies in the brain are located in a brainstem site called the locus coeruleus (dorsal pons) (reviewed in Holets, 1990), with long neurons which project to multiple brain sites for direct release of norepinephrine neurotransmitter (Figure 6.1). Norepinephrine neurons project from the locus coeruleus to cerebral cortex, cerebellum, cingulate gyrus, thalamus, hippocampus, hypothalamus, amygdala, bed nucleus of the stria terminalis, nucleus accumbens, and thoracic spinal cord (reviewed in Foote, Bloom, & Aston-Jones, 1983; Heal & Marsden, 1990). There are relatively restricted inputs to the locus coeruleus, primarily from the nucleus paragigantocellularis (PGI) and the nucleus preposi-

tus hypoglossi (Aston-Jones, Ennis, Pieribone, Nickell, & Shipley, 1985; Aston-Jones, Shipley, et al., 1991) and other sites (Cedarbaum & Aghajanian, 1978). A variety of neurotransmitters and neuropeptides involved in the stress response regulate locus coeruleus function, with stimulatory effects from corticotropin releasing factor (CRF) (Valentino, Page, & Curtis, 1991) and glutamate (Akaoka & Aston-Jones, 1991; Ennis & Aston-Jones, 1988), and inhibitory effects from norepinephrine, epinephrine, endogenous opiates, GABA (Aghajanian, Cedarbaum, & Wang, 1977; Aston-Jones et al., 1991; Cedarbaum

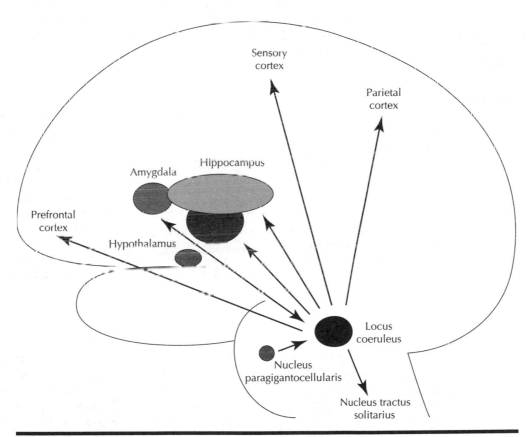

FIGURE 6.1 A functional neuroanatomy of norepinephrine, showing projection pathways from the locus coeruleus (site of the majority of the norepinephrine cell bodies in the brain) to target sites in cortical and subcortical structures. States of stress and fear result in a rapid increase in firing of neurons in the locus coeruleus, with release of norepinephrine transmitter in target sites in the brain. This results in an increase in attention and vigilance, as well as enhancement of memory recall, which can be lifesaving in threatening situations. Patients with PTSD, however, develop long-term alterations in the function of this system.

& Aghajanian, 1977; Korf, Bunney, & Aghajanian, 1974), benzodiazepines (Grant, Huang, & Redmond, 1980; Simson & Weiss, 1994), and serotonin (Akaoka & Aston-Jones, 1993; Aston-Jones, Akaoka, Charlety, & Chouvet, 1991).

The neuroanatomy of locus coeruleus is well suited to the role it plays in the stress response. The central nucleus of the amygdala, which is involved in the conditioned fear response (see section below, "The Amygdala"), has outputs to the lateral nucleus of the hypothalamus, which in turn mediates the increase in heart rate and blood pressure associated with fear. The nucleus paragigantocellularis (PGI), a major input to the locus coeruleus, also controls peripheral sympathetic activity. Stimulation of the PGI during stress could lead to parallel activation of central and sympathetic systems (Aston-Jones et al., 1985; Aston-Jones et al., 1991). The locus coeruleus responds to changes in the environment (e.g., physical sensations) or internal states (e.g., drop in blood pressure due to a loss of blood) through projections from sensory relay areas such as the nucleus tractus solitarius and the raphe to the locus coeruleus. The locus coeruleus represents a "central relay station" which responds to information from a variety of sources, and rapidly and globally activates neuronal function through simultaneous release of norepinephrine neurotransmitter throughout the brain. This release of transmitter leads to increased gene transcription and other secondary intracellular responses which are important in the stress response (Stone, 1987; Stone, John, Bing, & Zhang, 1992; Stone, Zhang, John, & Bing, 1991; Stone, Zhang, John, Filer, & Bing, 1993).

Stress results in a rapid and robust activation of the locus coeruleus/noradrenergic system. During states of rest, feeding, and grooming, locus coeruleus neurons discharge in a slow, phasic manner (Aghajanian, 1978; Aghajanian et al., 1977; Aston-Jones, 1985; Foote, Aston-Jones, & Bloom, 1980; Grant & Redmond, 1984). A variety of novel stimuli activate the locus coeruleus, including visual threats (Aston-Jones, 1985; Cedarbaum & Aghajanian, 1978; Foote, Aston-Jones, & Bloom, 1980; Grant et al., 1980; Grant & Redmond, 1984; Korf et al., 1974; Rasmussen & Jacobs, 1986). Novel stimuli-induced locus

coeruleus activation is associated with an increase in heart rate and blood pressure, and plasma norepinephrine (Abercrombie & Jacobs, 1987a; Abercrombie & Jacobs, 1987b; Grant & Redmond, 1984). Behaviors which are characteristically seen during situations of stress and fear are associated with an increase in activation of the locus coeruleus/noradrenergic system. In the cat, exposure of stressors such as a dog results in increased locus coeruleus activity associated with defensive behaviors such as arched back, piloerection, flattened ears, increased heart rate and blood pressure, and mydriasis (Levine, Litto, & Jacobs, 1990), while behaviorally activating but nonstressful stimuli, such as seeing an inaccessible rat, have no effect (Abercrombie & Jacobs, 1987a; Rasmussen, Morilak, & Jacobs, 1986). Visual threat to monkeys also activates the locus coeruleus (Grant & Redmond, 1984). Infusion of norepinephrine into the hypothalamus of cats results in defensive/aggressive behaviors such as hissing, growling, and ear retraction (Barret, Shaikh, Edinger, & Siegel, 1987), while electrical stimulation of the locus coeruleus in monkeys results in similar fear-related behaviors (Redmond, Huang, Snyder, & Maas, 1976; Redmond & Huang, 1979). Administration of the alpha2 antagonists, yohimbine and piperoxane, which result in an increase in firing of the locus coeruleus (Rasmussen & Jacobs, 1986) and increased release of norepinephrine in target brain structures, produce behaviors consistent with anxiety or fear in several animal species (Blanchard, Taukulis, Rodgers, Magee, & Blanchard, 1993; Redmond, 1979). Agents which decrease firing in the locus coeruleus, including opiates, benzodiazepines (Drugan, Ryan, Minor, & Maier, 1984; Tanaka et al., 1990), ethanol (Shirao et al., 1988), and clonidine (Aghajanian, 1978; Aghajanian & Vandermaelen, 1982) have the opposite effect. These findings led to the hypothesis that increased noradrenergic activity is involved in the pathogenesis of anxiety and the stress response (Redmond et al., 1976).

Increases in locus coeruleus activity during stress are associated with an increase in regional turnover and release of norepinephrine in brain regions which are innervated by the locus coeruleus. We have recently reviewed in more depth the effects of stress on norepinephrine metabolism and release in specific brain regions (Bremner, Krystal, Southwick, & Charney, 1996b). In summary, acute and chronic stress, including footshock, restraint, and forced swim, result in increased turnover and release of norepinephrine in several target brain regions of the locus coeruleus, including cerebral cortex, hippocampus, hypothalamus, and amygdala. Increased turnover of norepinephrine is manifested by an increased release of norepinephrine in these brain regions as measured by microdialysis, increased levels of the norepinephrine metabolite MHPG, decreased brain norepinephrine content (suggestive of increased utilization), and increased levels of the rate limiting enzyme of norepinephrine synthesis, tyrosine hydroxylase (Abercrombie, Keller, & Zigmond, 1988; Adell, Garcia-Marquez, Armario, & Gelpi, 1988; Anisman & Zacharko, 1985; Glavin et al., 1983; Irwin, Ahluwalia, & Anisman, 1986; Melia et al., 1992; Nissenbaum, Zigmond, Sved, & Abercrombie, 1991; Rossetti, Portas, Pani, Carboni, & Gessa, 1990; Shirao et al., 1988; Tanaka et al., 1982; Tanaka et al., 1983; Weiss et al., 1981; Yokoo et al., 1990). Animals with a prior history of exposure to chronic stress show an increase in norepinephrine release, MHPG, and tyrosine hydroxylase upon re-exposure to an acute stimulus, for several brain regions, including hippocampus, hypothalamus, and cortex. Re-exposure of animals with a history of prior footshock to the environment where footshock originally occurred results in an increased release of norepinephrine within the hypothalamus (Yokoo et al., 1990) and an increase in the norepinephrine metabolite, 3-methoxy-4-hydroxyphenylglycol (MHPG), in whole brain samples with associated fear-related behaviors such as increased defecation (Cassens, Roffman, Kuruc, & Schildkraut, 1980). These findings suggest that norepinephrine may be a chemical substrate for the conditioned fear responsiveness to complex spatial stimuli which is mediated by the hippocampus (described below in "The Hippocampus"). When synthesis is not able to keep up with demand, chronic stress results in a decrease in brain norepinephrine content with associated behavioral changes which have been termed "learned helplessness" (Petty, Kramer, Wilson, & Chae, 1993; Weiss, Stone, & Harrell, 1970; Weiss et al., 1981).

Chronic stress also results in an increased firing of the locus coeruleus (Korf, Aghajanian, & Roth, 1973; Pavcovich, Cancela, Volosin, Molina, & Ramirez, 1990; Simson & Weiss, 1988a; Simson & Weiss, 1988b). A decrease in density of alpha2 noradrenergic receptors specific to the hippocampus and amygdala, with an increase in affinity in the amygdala, has been associated with acute cold-restraint stress in the rat (Nukina, Glavin, & LaBella, 1987). In addition, chronic, but not acute, stress in rats blocks the reduction of locomotor activity normally associated with administration of the alpha2 agonist, clonidine, suggesting a decreased responsiveness of alpha2 receptors following chronic stress (Cancela, Volosin, & Molina, 1988). Administration of the alpha2 antagonist, idazoxan, results in increased locus coeruleus responsivity to external stimuli such as tail compression. Similarly, animals with a history of chronic stress have increased locus coeruleus responsivity to external stimuli, which has led to the idea of a "functional blockade" of alpha2 receptors with stress (Simson & Weiss, 1989; Simson & Weiss, 1994). Animals with a history of exposure to chronic stress have an increase in norepinephrine release in the hippocampus following administration of idazoxan (Nisenbaum & Abercrombie, 1993). An increase in locus coeruleus responsiveness and regional norepinephrine release with re-exposure to stressors in individuals with a prior history of stress exposure may explain clinical findings of stress sensitization in PTSD (Bremner, Southwick, Johnson, Yehuda, & Charney, 1993).

Studies in healthy human subjects are consistent with a relationship between stress and increased catecholaminergic function (reviewed in Bremner, Krystal, Southwick, & Charney, 1996b; reviewed in Weiner, 1984). Administration of catecholamines results in behaviors similar to those seen during stress. For instance, administration of norepinephrine to healthy subjects results in an increase in blood pressure, respiratory rate, and subjective sensations of anxiety, while administration of epinephrine causes increases in blood pressure, heart rate, cardiac output, respiratory rate, and subjective sensations of anxiety (Goodman & Gilman, 1985). The situation of an approaching parachute jump was associated with an increase in subjective fear and a steady increase in heart rate (Fenz & Epstein, 1967; Fenz & Jones, 1972). Experimental induction of anger and fear in healthy subjects resulted in an increase in diastolic blood pressure and heart rate. Air Force pilots had an increase in both urinary norepinephrine and epinephrine during flight in comparison to ground activity (von Euler & Lundberg, 1954). During public speaking, plasma epinephrine levels increased two-fold, while during physical exercise, plasma norepinephrine levels increased three-fold (Dimsdale & Moss, 1980). Plasma epinephrine and norepinephrine levels increased over baseline in healthy subjects during cognitive stressors (mental arithmetic), physical stressors (knee bends), pain stressors (cold pressor and venipuncture) (Ward, Mefford, & Parker, 1983), public speaking (Taggart, Carruthers, & Sommerville, 1973), and race car driving (Taggart & Carruthers, 1971). The norepinephrine metabolite, plasma MHPG, was found to increase in healthy subjects during emotional stress (Lader, 1974; Buchsbaum, Muscettola, & Goodwin, 1981). Urinary MHPG increased in naval aviators after landings of aircraft on aircraft carriers (Rubin, Miller, & Clark, 1970). Plasma MHPG was correlated with state anxiety in healthy subjects exposed to the anticipatory stress of receiving an electric shock, while there was no such correlation in the absence of the electric shock threat (Uhde et al., 1982; Uhde et al., 1984). Significant within-individual correlations between changes in urinary MHPG and changes in state anxiety have been found in healthy human subjects (Sweeney, Maas, & Heninger, 1978). These studies are consistent with a relationship between norepinephrine and stress in healthy human subjects.

Considerable interest has been focused on the relationship between norepinephrine and PTSD (Bremner, Krystal, Southwick, & Charney, 1996a; Bremner, Krystal, Southwick, & Charney, 1996b; Murberg, 1994) (Table 6.1). Kardiner noted in 1941 that veterans with psychiatric conditions related to their war experiences exhibited what appeared to be a hyperresponsiveness of the sympathetic system, manifested by increases in heart rate, blood pressure, sweatiness, irritability, palpitations, vertigo, dizziness, nausea, and syncope. Kolb hypothesized that the central disturbance of PTSD consisted of the

TABLE 6.1 Evidence for Altered Catecholaminergic Function in Posttraumatic Stress Disorder

Increased resting heart rate and blood pressure	+/-
Increased heart rate and blood pressure response to traumatic reminders	+++
Increased resting urinary NA and Epi	+
Increased resting urinary dopamine	+++
Increased resting plasma NA	-
Increased plasma NA in response to traumatic reminders	+
Increased MHPG with exercise	+
Increased orthostatic heart rate response to exercise	+
Decreased binding to platelet alpha2 receptors	+
Relative decrease in alpha2 receptors on platelets with epinephrine administration	+/-
Altered growth hormone response to desipramine (alpha2 probe)	-
Decrease in basal and stimulated activity of cAMP	+/-
Decrease in platelet MAO activity	+
Increased symptoms, heart rate, and plasma MHPG with yohimbine	+
Increased startle response with yohimbine	+
Differential brain metabolic response to yohimbine	+
Altered sleep function (suggestive of NA dysfunction)	+++
Alterations in event-related potentials (suggestive of NA dysfunction)	+

-	One or more studies did not support this finding (with no positive studies), or the majority of studies do not support this finding;
+/-	An equal number of studies supported this finding as studies that did not support this finding;
+	At least one study supports this finding with no studies not supporting the finding, or the majority of studies support the finding;
++	Two or more studies support this finding, with no studies conducted that do not support the finding;
+++	Three or more studies support this finding, with no studies that do not support the finding.

"conditioned emotional response" to the original traumatic event which resulted in a heightened physiological response, mediated through adrenergic systems, to subsequent events which were reminiscent of the original trauma (Kolb, 1984).

Since the time of Kardiner the psychophysiology technique has been used extensively to study conditioned emotional responding and sympathetic correlates of exposure to traumatic reminders in PTSD. Physiological variables which are recorded typically include heart rate, systolic and diastolic blood pressure, skin conductance, electromyographic (EMG) activity of the frontalis, corrugator, zygomaticus or orbicularis oculi muscles, and skin temperature. These variables reflect in part activity of the peripheral sympathetic nervous system. Exposure to traumatic reminders and neutral scenes utilized in the psychophysiology paradigm include slides (with or without accompanying sounds) of scenes similar to the original trauma or reading scripts which are descriptions of what actually happened during the original trauma. Comparisons are then made between exposure to trauma-related material and both the baseline and/or the neutral exposures. Wenger (1948) noted that veterans of the Second World War with stress-related symptoms had increased heart rate and skin conductance at baseline in comparison to patients with other psychiatric disorders and healthy control subjects. Dodds & Wilson (1960) first described increased heart rate and blood pressure responses in combat veterans with and without stress-related pathology who were exposed to combat slides and sounds in comparison to healthy controls. They also found increased heart rate at baseline in both the combat veterans with stress-related pathology and combat veterans without pathology in comparison to the healthy controls.

A number of investigators have utilized the psychophysiology paradigm since the time of these original studies. Conflicting results have been obtained with regard to baseline heart rate and blood pressure in patients with PTSD, which may be largely related to acclimatization to the testing environment. An increase in reactivity to traumatic reminders has been a consistent finding in patients with PTSD. An increase in heart rate in response to auditory reminders of trauma (such as tapes of the sound of gunfire) has

been found in Vietnam combat veterans with PTSD in comparison to healthy nonveteran controls (Blanchard, Kolb, Pallmeyer, & Gerardi, 1982) and Vietnam combat veterans without PTSD (Blanchard, Kolb, Gerardi, Ryan, & Pallmeyer, 1986). No increase in heart rate in response to the stressor of mental arithmetic was found in any of these studies. An increase in heart rate following exposure to combined combat slides and sounds has been found in Vietnam combat veterans with PTSD in comparison to Vietnam combat veterans without PTSD (Keane, Wolfe, & Taylor, 1987; Malloy, Fairbank, & Keane, 1983; McFall, Murburg, Ko, & Veith, 1990). Hearing scripts of the individual's traumatic experiences resulted in an increase in heart rate in Vietnam combat veterans with PTSD in comparison to Vietnam combat veterans without PTSD (Pitman, Orr, Forgue, de Jong, & Claiborn, 1987; Pitman, van der Kolk, Orr, & Greenburg, 1990). An increase in heart rate with traumatic scripts has also been found in WWII and Korean veterans with PTSD in comparison to those without PTSD (Orr, Pitman, Lasko, & Herz, 1993) and in patients with civilian trauma-related PTSD in comparison to controls (Shalev, Orr, Peri, Schreiber, & Pitman, 1992). Prins, Kaloupek, and Keane (1995) have more completely summarized scientific findings from this area and Kaloupek and Bremner (1996) have outlined methodological issues relevant to the psychophysiology study paradigm.

Alterations in sleep function may also be secondary to altered pontine function and noradrenergic dysregulation in PTSD. PTSD patients have been found to have an increase in phasic rapid eye movement (REM) activity (Ross et al., 1994), decreased total sleep time, and increased "micro-awakenings" (Mellman, Kulick-Bell, Ashlock, & Nolan, 1995) relative to controls. These abnormalities may play a role in nightmares in PTSD patients (Ross, Ball, Sullivan, & Caroff, 1989). Ross et al. (1989) have reviewed in detail the literature related to sleep dysfunction in PTSD.

Event-related potentials (ERP) have been used as a method for studying central brain processes which are felt to be reflective of noradrenergic function. A study in patients with combat-related PTSD found a delayed N2 and attenuated P3 that failed to differentiate target from distractor tones, indicating that the patients had difficulty distinguishing task stimuli of different relevance. The authors interpreted this result as consistent with an impairment in the ability of PTSD patients to attend to relevant stimuli and process information normally, which may be secondary to alterations in noradrenergic function in the hippocampal formation (McFarlane, Weber, & Clark, 1993).

Several groups have examined peripheral measures of noradrenergic function in PTSD. An increase in norepinephrine and epinephrine has been found in 24-hour urines of combat-related PTSD patients in comparison to patients with other psychiatric disorders (Kosten, Mason, Ostroff, & Harkness, 1987). An increase in the norepinephrine/cortisol ratio has been found to more specifically differentiate patients with PTSD from these patient groups (Mason, Giller, Kosten, & Harkness, 1988). Severity of PTSD symptoms in combat veterans was correlated with level of urinary norepinephrine (Yehuda, Southwick, Giller, Ma, & Mason, 1992). Women with sexual abuse-related PTSD were found to have elevated levels of urinary norepinephrine and epinephrine, which correlated with PTSD symptoms as measured with the Impact of Events (IES) Scale (but no difference in norepinephrine/cortisol ratio) relative to abused controls and normal women (Lemieux & Coe, 1995). Other investigators, however, have found no difference in urinary levels of norepinephrine, epinephrine, MHPG or cortisol in patients with combat-related PTSD in comparison to Vietnam veterans without PTSD (Pitman & Orr, 1990), or in plasma levels of norepinephrine at baseline in Vietnam veterans with PTSD in comparison to healthy controls (Blanchard, Kolb, Prins, Gates, & McCoy, 1991; McFall, Veith, & Murburg, 1992; Murberg, 1994). An increase in plasma epinephrine (McFall et al., 1990) and norepinephrine (Blanchard et al., 1991) with exposure to traumatic reminders, and increased MHPG with physical exercise (Hamner, Diamond, & Hitri, 1994) has been found in Vietnam veterans with PTSD in comparison to healthy subjects. Children with PTSD were found to have increased orthostatic heart rate response, suggesting noradrenergic dysregulation (Perry, 1994). Another study of sexually abused girls (the majority of whom did not meet criteria for PTSD) compared to healthy girls demonstrated elevated levels of catecholamine synthesis (sum of epinephrine, norepinephrine, dopamine, and their metabolites), which showed only a trend toward significance after adjusting for differences in height between the sexually abused girls and controls (p = .1) (DeBellis, Lefter, Trickett, & Putnam, 1994). Although these studies do not consistently support an increase in basal sympathetic function in PTSD, they do suggest that patients with PTSD may have an increased responsiveness of the sympathoadrenal system.

Studies of peripheral norepinephrine receptor function have had mixed results. A decrease in platelet adrenergic alpha2 receptor number as measured by total binding sites for the alpha2 antagonist [3H]rauwolscine was found in patients with combat-related PTSD (Perry, Giller, & Southwick, 1987). Some studies (Perry, Southwick, & Giller, 1991; Perry, 1994) found a significantly greater reduction in number of platelet alpha2 receptors after exposure to agonist (epinephrine) in PTSD patients in comparison to healthy controls. Other studies (Kohn, Newman, Lerer, Orr, & Pitman, 1995) did not find a difference between patients and controls in the effects of epinephrine on forskolin-stimulated adenylate cyclase activity (a probe of alpha2 receptor function), while Weizmann et al. (1994) found a trend for this parameter to be decreased in PTSD (p = .057).

Probes of the beta-adrenergic receptor-mediated cyclic adenosine 3',5'-monophosphate (cAMP) system have been developed. The beta-receptor-associated adenylate cyclase unit consists of three components: the receptor to which transmitter binds, a guanyl nucleotide binding unit, and a catalytic unit. Isoproterenol and prostaglandin (PGE-1) probes the receptor binding component, aluminum chloride plus sodium fluoride probes the guanyl nucleotide binding unit, and forskolin acts on the catalytic unit. cAMP signal transduction can therefore be tested using a combination of these probes. In an initial study, a decrease was found in lymphocyte basal, isoproterenol, and forskolin-stimulated cAMP signal transduction, and platelet basal, forskolin, PGE-1, and aluminum chloride plus sodium fluoride stimulated adenylate cyclase levels (Lerer, Ebstein, Shestatsky, Shemesh, & Greenberg, 1987). A replication study showed lower platelet basal and forskolin-stimulated activity in PTSD, but no difference in aluminum chloride plus sodium fluoride or PGE-1-stimulated adenylate cyclase activity (Lerer, Bleich, Bennett, Ebstein, & Balkin, 1990). Two replication studies did not find a difference between patients with PTSD and controls in platelet basal, PGE-1, aluminum chloride plus sodium fluoride, or forskolin-stimulated adenylate cyclase activity (Kohn et al., 1995; Weizmann et al., 1994). One study found a decrease in basal platelet monoamine oxidase (MAO) activity (Davidson, Lipper, Kilts, Mahorney, & Hammett, 1985) in patients with combat-related PTSD in comparison to controls. In summary, results are mixed regarding alterations in noradrenergic receptor function in PTSD, and findings to date do not specifically support the hypothesis of alteration in the beta-adrenergic cAMP system.

Pharmacological studies have also been performed to examine noradrenergic function in patients with PTSD. One study did not find a difference in growth hormone response to desipramine (a probe of central alpha$_2$ receptor function) between women with sexual assault-related PTSD and controls (Dinan, Barry, Yatham, Mobayed, & Brown, 1990). Administration of the alpha2 antagonist, yohimbine, which results in an increase of release of norepinephrine in the brain, results in flashbacks in 40 percent and panic attacks in 70 percent of Vietnam veterans with combat-related PTSD. PTSD patients report an increase in PTSD-specific symptomatology, including intrusive memories, emotional numbing, and hyperarousal with yohimbine. Yohimbine administration also results in increased MHPG, blood pressure, and heart rate response in patients with PTSD in comparison to normal healthy controls (Southwick et al., 1993). Administration of yohimbine resulted in an increase in the acoustic startle response in Vietnam combat veterans with PTSD relative to combat veterans without PTSD (Morgan et al., 1995). The alpha2 agonist, clonidine, which results in decreased noradrenergic activity, has been shown to be efficacious in civilians with PTSD in open trials (Kinzie & Leung, 1989).

Alterations in noradrenergic function may be associated with changes in central brain function in patients with PTSD. Preclinical studies have shown that high-dose yohimbine administration results in a decrease in brain metabolism in neocortical areas,

including temporal, parietal, prefrontal and orbitofrontal cortex, as well as caudate. Other pharmacological studies suggest that norepinephrine has a dose-response effect on neuronal activity (which is associated with metabolism), so that while high levels of norepinephrine release result in a decrease in neuronal activity, low levels of norepinephrine release are associated with an increase in neuronal activity (reviewed in Bremner, Krystal, Southwick, & Charney, 1996a). Positron emission tomography (PET) studies measuring brain glucose metabolism with [18F]2-fluoro-2-deoxyglucose (FDG) examined brain metabolic response in patients with combat-related PTSD (N = 10) and controls (N = 10) following administration of yohimbine and placebo. Yohimbine was associated with a differential effect on brain metabolism in neocortical areas, including orbitofrontal, temporal, prefrontal, and parietal cortex, with metabolism having a tendency to increase in the controls and decrease in the patients (Bremner, Innis, et al., 1997).

There are several possible explanations for our PET yohimbine findings in PTSD. Previous studies support the idea of a dose response curve for norepinephrine, where low levels of norepinephrine release result in increased metabolism, and high levels of norepinephrine release result in decreased metabolism in neocortical areas of the brain. One possibility is that yohimbine administration results in relatively greater norepinephrine release in PTSD patients than controls, leading to decreased metabolism in PTSD and increased metabolism in controls. It is also possible that differences in pre- or post-synaptic sensitivity between PTSD and controls accounts for our findings. Blockade of pre-synaptic alpha2 receptors at the level of the locus coeruleus leads to an increase in firing of noradrenergic neurons, with increased release of norepinephrine at the level of cortical neurons. This may result in a decrease in cortical neuronal activity and metabolism. On the other hand, post-synaptic alpha2 receptors have an inhibitory effect on cortical neuronal activity, which means that blockade of these receptors leads to an enhancement of neuronal activity and metabolism. Following this model, yohimbine may be having a primary effect on presynaptic alpha2 neurons in PTSD patients, and a primary effect on post-synaptic alpha2 neurons in normal controls. In summary, the findings are consistent with our previous hypotheses of alterations in noradrenergic brain function in PTSD (Bremner, Krystal, Southwick, & Charney, 1996b), and are suggestive of enhanced noradrenergic activity in these patients. Consistent with this, we recently used PET $H_2[^{15}O]$ to show increased activation during exposure to traumatic reminders in the area of the locus coeruleus in combat veterans with PTSD relative to those without PTSD (Bremner, Innis, et al., 1997).

Dopamine

The three major dopaminergic neuronal systems include the nigrostriatal, mesolimbic, and mesocortical projection systems. Nigrostriatal systems involve dopaminergic projections from the substantia nigra to the striatum, mesolimbic systems are comprised of projections from the midbrain to the nucleus accumbens, and mesocortical involve projections from midbrain to medial prefrontal cortex. Mesocortical dopaminergic systems are the most sensitive neural system to mild stressors: mild and brief stress in the form of footshock results in a selective increase in dopamine release (Abercrombie, Keefe, DiFrischia, & Zigmond, 1989; Deutch, Tam, & Roth, 1985; Imperato, Puglisi-Allegra, Casolini, & Angelucci, 1991; Inoue, Tsuchiya, & Koyama, 1994) and metabolism (Abercrombie et al., 1989; Imperato et al., 1991; Kalivas & Duffy, 1989) in the medial prefrontal cortex. Chronic stress also resulted in an increased release of dopamine (Finlay, Zigmond, & Abercombie, 1994) and dopamine metabolism (Sudha & Pradhan, 1995) in medial prefrontal cortex. Higher levels of stress can also result in increased dopamine release in nucleus accumbens (Abercrombie et al., 1989; Imperato et al., 1991; Roth, Tam, Ida, Yang, & Deutch, 1988) and striatum (Abercrombie et al., 1989; Keefe, Stricker, Zigmond, & Abercrombie, 1990) and dopamine metabolism in nucleus accumbens (Imperato et al., 1991) and striatum (Abercrombie et al., 1989; Keefe et al., 1990) as well as in medial prefrontal cortex. Following lesions of the prefrontal cortex, footshock results in significant increases in dopamine levels in the nucleus accumbens (Deutch, Clark, & Roth, 1990), suggesting

that stress results in a preferential increase in meso-prefrontal cortical dopamine release. Administration of dopamine D2 receptor agonist (pramipexole) resulted in a reversal of stress-induced behavioral deficits (Willner, Lappas, Cheeta, & Muscat, 1994).

Stress-induced increases in mesoprefrontal cortical dopamine release is susceptible to modulation by several neurotransmitter systems. N-methyl-D-aspartate (NMDA) and opiate receptor blockade in the ventral tegmental area (VTA) prevents stress-induced activation of the cortical dopamine system (Kalivas & Abhold, 1987). In addition, pre-administration of benzodiazepines prevents attenuation of stress-induced activation of dopamine neurotransmission (Roth et al., 1988).

Studies of the effects of stress on dopaminergic systems may be relevant to PTSD. Intracranial self-stimulation for mesocortical and mesolimbic dopaminergic systems has been used as a model for anhedonia, or a decreased ability to take pleasure in activities. Uncontrollable stress was shown to lead to a decrease in intracranial stimulation for mesocortical and mesolimbic systems (Zacharko, Bowers, Kokkinidis, & Anisman, 1983; Zacharko, Gilmore, MacNeil, Kasian, & Anisman, 1990). These studies suggest that symptoms of emotional numbing, decreased interest in things, and being cut off from others may be related to alterations in mesocortical and mesolimbic dopaminergic systems. Administration of cocaine and amphetamine, which both stimulate endogenous dopamine release, results in an increase in paranoid and vigilance behaviors. One could speculate that alterations in dopamine systems may also play a role in the pathophysiology of these particular symptoms in patients with PTSD.

Although little work has been done to examine dopaminergic function in PTSD, one study in patients with combat-related PTSD found elevations in urinary dopamine relative to controls, which correlated with PTSD symptom severity (Yehuda et al., 1992), while women with sexual abuse-related PTSD were found to have elevated urinary dopamine relative to controls (Lemieux & Coe, 1995). Another study in sexually abused girls (most of whom did not meet criteria for PTSD) showed elevations of the dopamine metabolite, homovanillic acid (HVA), relative to normal girls (DeBellis et al., 1994). In summary, clinical studies to date, although preliminary, are consistent with increased dopamine release and metabolism in PTSD.

Corticotropin Releasing Factor/Hypothalamic-Pituitary-Adrenal Systems

The corticotropin releasing factor (CRF)/hypothalamic-pituitary-adrenal (HPA) axis system plays an important role in the stress response. Exposure to stressful situations is associated with a marked increase in cortisol release from the adrenal. Cortisol is important in effecting many of the expressions of the stress response, such as increased gluconeogenesis, inhibition of growth and reproductive systems, and containment of inflammatory responses. Cortisol release from the adrenal is regulated by adrenocorticotropin releasing hormone (ACTH) release from the pituitary, which in turn is primarily regulated by CRF release from the paraventricular nucleus (PVN) of the hypothalamus.

CRF is distributed in several brain areas, in addition to the PVN, which have been implicated in the behavioral and physiological responses to stress, including the central nucleus of the amygdala, hippocampus, prefrontal and cingulate cortices, locus coeruleus, thalamus, periacqueductal gray, and cerebellum (reviewed in Schatzberg & Nemeroff, 1988). Intraventricular injection of CRF results in a series of physiological and behavioral responses which are adaptive during stress and which are considered to be characteristic of anxiety responses. These behaviors include increased locomotion and grooming in an open field environment, a decrease in punished responding and time spent on the open arms of an elevated plus maze. CRF injected into the central nucleus of the amygdala results in an increase in the magnitude of the startle response and significantly improves retention of the inhibitory avoidance response, a measure of learning and memory (reviewed in Dunn & Berridge, 1990).

The CRF/HPA axis and norepinephrine systems are involved in a mutually inter-regulatory network. CRF-containing neurons from the paraventricular nucleus of the hypothalamus project to the locus coer-

uleus, and noradrenergic neurons from the locus coeruleus project to the paraventricular nucleus. Increases in CRF result in an increase in discharge rate of locus coeruleus neurons (Valentino et al., 1991), and conversely, emerging evidence suggests that brain norepinephrine systems stimulate CRF release at the level of the PVN (reviewed in Dunn & Berridge, 1990).

Stressors early in life may have long-term effects on the CRF/HPA axis. Both prenatal (light and noise) (Fride, Dan, Feldon, Halevy, & Weinstock, 1986) and early maternal deprivation stress (Stanton, Gutierrez, & Levine, 1988; Levine, Weiner, & Coe, 1993) and early manipulation stress (Levine, 1962) resulted in increased glucocorticoid response to subsequent stressors. Prenatal stress was associated with a failure of habituation of glucocorticoid responsiveness to novel stimuli (Fride et al., 1986). Increased glucocorticoid responsivity to ACTH challenge in maternal deprivation stress suggested an increase in adrenocortical responsivity with early stress (Stanton et al., 1988). Daily handling within the first few weeks of life (picking up rat pups and then returning them to their mother) resulted in increased Type II glucocorticoid receptor binding which persisted throughout life. This was associated with increased feedback sensitivity to glucocorticoids, and reduced glucocorticoid-mediated hippocampal damage in later life (Meaney, Aitken, van Berkel, Bhatnager, & Sapolsky, 1988; Meaney, Aitken, Sharma, & Sarrieau, 1989) (see below, "The Hippocampus"). It is not clear, however, whether early handling in these experiments represents a form of "stress innoculation" or is a form of early stressor. These hormonal systems have profound effects on neuronal development, which means that stress-induced alterations could have profound effects on development of the brain.

Studies in human subjects have validated the important role of cortisol in the stress response. Underwater demolition team training (Rubin, Rahe, Arthur, & Clark, 1969), landing aircraft on aircraft carriers (Miller, Rubin, Clark, Crawford, & Arthur, 1970), and other highly stressful experiences (reviewed in Miller, 1968) resulted in elevations in serum cortisol relative to background levels. The exact relationship between stress and cortisol in human subjects, however, is complex, and is highly dependent on psychological factors. For instance, in one study measuring levels of urinary cortisol in helicopter ambulance medics, there was no difference between ground time and time flying on combat missions with the threat of death. Overall, the medics had lower cortisol levels than expected from normal samples. The authors noted that psychological factors, such as feelings of being in control, invulnerability, and downplaying the threat of death, probably played an important role in the findings (Bourne, Rose, & Mason, 1967). Consistent with this, combat veterans under threat of an impending attack in Vietnam showed differing levels of cortisol depending on their role. The officers and the radioman, who were actively planning the response, had elevated levels, while the enlisted men, who had no part in the preparation, had lowered levels (Bourne, Rose, & Mason, 1968). Miller (1968) summarized this literature and concluded that psychological factors, including feelings of control and competency, play an important role in the cortisol response to stress.

Several clinical studies suggest that alterations in HPA axis function may be associated with PTSD (Table 6.2). A large increase in urinary cortisol was found during the stress of bombardment in veterans of the Korean War (Howard et al., 1955). A decrease in urinary cortisol levels has been found in Vietnam veterans with chronic PTSD in comparison to controls and patieders in some studies (Mason, Giller, Kosten, Ostroff, & Podd, 1986; Yehuda, Southwick, Nussbaum, Giller, & Mason, 1991; Yehuda, Boisoneau, Mason, & Giller, 1993) but not others (Pitman & Orr, 1990), while decreased plasma cortisol was found in 24-hour sampling in patients with combat-related PTSD relative to healthy controls and patients with depression (Yehuda, Teicher, Levengood, Trestman, & Siever, 1994). On the other hand, women with a history of childhood sexual abuse-related PTSD (Lemieux & Cole, 1995) and patients with PTSD related to a natural disaster (Baum, Cohen, & Hall, 1993) had elevated levels of urinary cortisol relative to controls. Male patients with combat-related PTSD (Kosten, Wahby, & Giller, 1990; Kudler, Davidson, Meador, Lipper, & Ely, 1987; Olivera & Fero, 1990) and female patients with sexual assault-related PTSD (Dinan et al., 1990)

TABLE 6.2 Evidence for Alterations in CRF/HPA Axis Function in PTSD

Alterations in urinary cortisol	+/-*
Decreased plasma cortisol with 24-hour sampling	+
Super-suppression with DST	+
Blunted ACTH response to CRF	+
Elevated CRF in CSF	+
Increased lymphocyte glucocorticoid receptors	++

-	One or more studies did not support this finding (with no positive studies), or the majority of studies do not support this finding;
+/-	An equal number of studies supported this finding as studies that did not support this finding;
+	At least one study supports this finding with no studies not supporting the finding, or the majority of studies support the finding;
++	Two or more studies support this finding, with no studies conducted that do not support the finding;
+++	Three or more studies support this finding, with no studies that do not support the finding.

*Findings of decreased urinary cortisol in older male combat veterans and holocaust survivors, and increased cortisol in younger female abuse survivors, may be explainable by differences in gender, age, trauma type, or developmental epoch at the time of the trauma.

have been shown to suppress normally with the standard 1 mg dexamethasone suppression test (DST). Studies utilizing lower doses of DST (0.5 mg) suggest that PTSD may be associated with a super-suppression of the cortisol response in comparison to normal controls (Yehuda, Southwick, et al., 1993), which appears to be the opposite of patients with major depression who are non-suppressers with the standard 1 mg DST test. PTSD patients have also been found to have a significantly lower ("blunted") adrenocorticotropin hormone (ACTH) response to corticotropin releasing factor (CRF) than controls, suggesting an increased release of neuronal CRF (Smith et al., 1989). Consistent with this are findings of elevated levels of CRF in the cerebrospinal fluid of Vietnam combat veterans with PTSD relative to healthy subjects (Bremner, Licinio, et al., 1997). Other studies showed that patients with combat-related PTSD had an increase in lymphocyte glucocorticoid receptors in comparison to healthy subjects, nonPTSD combat veterans and patients with other psychiatric disorders (Yehuda, Lowy, Southwick, Shaffer, & Giller, 1991; Yehuda, Boisoneau, Lowy, & Giller, 1995). These studies demonstrate that alterations in cortisol and HPA axis function are associated with PTSD. One possible explanation of clinical findings to date is an increase in neuronal CRF release, with resultant blunting of ACTH response to CRF, increased central glucocorticoid receptor responsiveness, and resultant low levels of peripheral cortisol due to enhanced negative feedback. Interestingly, nonhuman primates with variable foraging mothers (a model for early-life stress) had elevated CSF CRF and decreased CSF cortisol levels in adulthood, a picture that is closer to PTSD than depression (Coplan et al., 1996).

Benzodiazepine Systems

Benzodiazepine receptors are present throughout the brain (Mohler & Okada, 1977), with the highest concentration in cortical grey matter (Hirsch, Garrett, & Beer, 1985). Benzodiazepines potentiate and prolong the synaptic actions of the inhibitory neurotransmitter gamma-aminobutyric acid (GABA). Central benzodiazepine receptors and GABAa receptors are part of the same macromolecular complex. These receptors have distinct binding sites, although they are functionally coupled and regulate each other in an allosteric manner. A correlation has also been found between the efficacy of the benzodiazepines and their potency at displacing [3H]diazepam binding, which suggests that these compounds are physiologically relevant (Mohler & Okada, 1977; Squires & Braestrup, 1977). The hypothesis that alterations in benzodiazepine receptor function play a role in the pathophysiology of stress-related psychiatric disorders such as PTSD is supported by several lines of preclinical evidence (reviewed by Guidotti, Baraldi, Leon, & Costa, 1990).

Administration of inverse agonists of benzodiazepine receptors, such as beta-carboline-3-carboxylic acid ethyl ester (beta-CCE), result in behavioral and biological effects similar to those seen in anxiety and stress, including increases in heart rate, blood pressure, plasma cortisol, and catecholamines (Braestrup, Smiechen, Neef, Nielsen, & Petersen, 1982). Administration of N-methyl-beta-carboline-3-carboxamide results in the development of an inability to learn maze escape behaviors, as is seen in the learned helplessness paradigm (Drugan, Maier, Skolnick, Paul, & Crawley, 1985). Administration of the beta-carboline FG 7142 also results in an increase in local cerebral glucose utilization in brain structures involved in memory, including lateral septal nucleus, mammillary bodies, and anterior thalamic nuclei (Ableitner & Herz, 1987). The effects of the beta-carbolines are blocked by administration of benzodiazepines (Ninan et al., 1982), or pretreatment with the benzodiazepine antagonist flumazenil (Drugan et al., 1985).

Studies using the animal model of uncontrollable stress, a model for stress-related psychiatric disorders such as PTSD, suggest alterations in benzodiazepine receptor function associated with uncontrollable stress (reviewed in Bremner, Davis, Southwick, Krystal, & Charney, 1993; Charney, Deutch, Krystal, Southwick, & Davis, 1993). Multiple studies have found that animals exposed to acute or chronic inescapable stress in the form of cold swim or footshock (but not defeat stress) (Miller et al., 1987) develop a decrease in benzodiazepine receptor binding (Bmax) (but not typically KD) in frontal cortex, but not other regions, including pons, striatum, or thalamus (Braestrup, Nielsen, Nielsen, & Lyon, 1979; Drugan et al., 1989; Medina, Novas, & De Robertis, 1983; Medina, Novas, Wolfman, De Stein, & De Robertis, 1983; Weizman et al., 1990). Some studies (Drugan, Basile, Crawley, Paul, & Skolnick, 1986; Drugan et al., 1989; Medina, Novas, & De Robertis, 1983; Medina, Novas, Wolfman, et al., 1983; Weizman et al., 1990) but not others (Braestrup et al., 1979; Havoundjian, Paul, & Skolnick, 1986; LeFur, Guilloux, Mitrani, Mizoule, & Uzan, 1979; Skerritt, Trisdikoon, & Johnston, 1981) showed decreases in cerebral cortex. Some studies showed decreases in hippocampus (Drugan et al., 1989; Weizman et al.,

1990), and hypothalamus (Drugan et al., 1989; Lippa et al., 1987), but other studies did not replicate these results (Braestrup et al., 1979; LeFur et al., 1979; Medina, Novas, & De Robertis, 1983; Skerritt et al., 1981). Differences in findings between different groups may be related to types of stressors, stressor duration, animal species strain, and ligand used to measure benzodiazepine receptor binding. Decreases in benzodiazepine receptor binding are associated with alterations in memory manifested by deficits in maze escape behaviors (Weizman et al., 1989; Drugan et al., 1989). Changes in benzodiazepine receptor function appear to be specific to uncontrollable stress, as opposed to controllable stress, and are prevented by pre-administration of benzodiazepines (Drugan et al., 1984). In addition, animals exposed to inescapable stress exhibit decreases in binding of the benzodiazepine receptor antagonist flumazenil (formerly designated Ro-15-1788) (Drugan et al., 1989), which are associated with deficits in learning, and decreased depolarization-induced release of GABA relative to controls (Petty & Sherman, 1981). These studies suggest that acute and chronic stress are associated with specific decreases in benzodiazepine receptor binding in frontal cortex.

A decrease in benzodiazepine receptor binding (Bmax) has been demonstrated in the so-called Maudsley genetically fearful strain of rat in comparison to non-fearful rats in several brain structures including the hippocampus (Robertson, Martin, & Candy, 1978).

Evidence from clinical studies performed to date suggests a possible role for alterations in benzodiazepine receptor function in PTSD. Healthy subjects exposed to the stress of war were found to have a decrease in binding of benzodiazepine receptors on peripheral mitochondria during the stressful period before and during war relative to the period after the war, which was correlated with an improvement of anxiety after the end of the war (Weizman, Laor, et al., 1994). No difference was found in anxiety response to the benzodiazepine receptor antagonist, flumazenil, between patients with combat-related PTSD and controls (Randall et al., 1995). Flumazenil, however, has no effect on the receptor per se: future studies are required with other agents, such as inverse

agonists, which have an effect on the benzodiazepine receptor. Perhaps the most convincing piece of evidence linking benzodiazepine receptor function to the pathophysiology of PTSD is the efficacy of the benzodiazepines in their treatment (reviewed in Bremner & Charney, 1994). PTSD patients specifically report an improvement in intrusive and hyperarousal symptoms with benzodiazepines (Bremner, Southwick, Darnell, & Charney, 1996).

Opiates

Endogenous opiate systems play a role in the stress response (Grossman, 1988). Exposure to stress results in an increased release of opiate peptides and the development of an analgesia to pain known as stress-induced analgesia (Helmstetter & Fanselow, 1987; Maier et al., 1981). Stress-induced analgesia can be blocked by administration of the opiate receptor antagonist naltrexone (Helmstetter & Fanselow, 1987; Maier et al., 1981). In rats with a history of inescapable stress, re-exposure to the environment where the shock took place is sufficient to reinvoke stress-induced analgesia (Hemingway & Reigle, 1987). Rats exposed to inescapable stress develop decreased binding of the mu-opiate receptor agonist DAGO in the midbrain (Stuckey, Marra, Minor, & Insel, 1989). Perhaps one of the most important functions of the endogenous opiate system is a counter-regulatory one, serving to decrease activity of other major stress axes, such as CRF and norepinephrine (Grossman, 1988). For instance, preadministration of morphine to rats exposed to inescapable stress attenuated the stress-induced release of norepinephrine in hypothalamus, hippocampus, amygdala, midbrain, and thalamus (Tanaka et al., 1983). Opiates cause a decrease in firing from the locus coeruleus; this provides an explanation for the favorable response of hyperarousal symptoms of PTSD to opiates such as heroin (Bremner, Southwick, et al., 1996).

Endogenous opiates may play an important role in responses to early stress. Stress in the first few weeks of life results in a decrease in levels of ornithine decarboxylase, a key regulator of cell growth. Administration of beta-endorphin also results in a decrease in ornithine decarboxylase, suggesting that beta-endorphin may mediate the effects of early stress on activity of this enzyme (and therefore cell growth) (Bartolome, Johnston, & Schanberg, 1994). These findings suggest that endogenous opiates are involved in the stress response at all stages of development.

Several lines of evidence suggest that alterations in endogenous opiate systems may be associated with the clinical symptomatology of patients with PTSD. Since the time of World War II, surgeons working on the battlefield have noted that wounded soldiers have a reduced need for opiate analgesic medication, suggesting that the stress of combat is associated with an increase in endogenous opiate release (Howard et al., 1955). PTSD patients have been shown to have high rates of heroin abuse and dependence (Kulka et al., 1990). In one study, PTSD patients reported an improvement in symptoms of hyperarousal and intrusive symptomatology with heroin administration. This was in contrast to other substances of abuse, such as cocaine (Bremner, Southwick, et al., 1996). Vietnam veterans with PTSD had a reduced sensitivity to pain during exposure to traumatic reminders in the form of a videotape with combat-related scenes (van der Kolk, Greenburg, Orr, & Pitman, 1989). This analgesia to pain is reversible with the opiate antagonist, naloxone, which prompted the authors to point out the parallel between their finding and the stress-induced analgesia response in animals (Pitman, van der Kolk, et al., 1990). PTSD patients have been found to have a relative increase in plasma beta-endorphin levels in response to exercise, with no difference in baseline levels, in comparison to healthy controls (Hamner & Hitri, 1992). These studies are interesting, and suggest that additional studies should be performed in this area in the future.

Serotonin

The serotonin system is involved in the stress response. Acute electric shock resulted in increased metabolism of serotonin in medial prefrontal cortex, nucleus accumbens, amygdala, and lateral hypothalamus (Inoue et al., 1994). Conditioned fear stress resulted in a preferential increase in serotonin metabolism in medial prefrontal cortex (Inoue et al., 1994). Chronic electric shock resulted in a decrease

in serotonin (5HT) release in frontal cortex which are associated with stress-induced behavioral deficits ("learned helplessness") (Petty, Kramer, & Wilson, 1992). Preadministration of benzodiazepines or tricyclic antidepressants prevents stress-induced decreases in serotonin and the acquisition of behavioral deficits (Petty et al., 1992), while injection of serotonin (5HT) into the frontal cortex after stress exposure reverses behavioral deficits (Sherman & Petty, 1982). Chronic restraint stress results in a decrease in 5HT1A binding in the hippocampus (Mendelson & McEwen, 1991; Watanabe, Sakai, McEwen, & Mendelson, 1993). Animals exposed to social stress had a decrease in binding of 5HT1A receptors in hippocampus and dentate gyrus, and a decrease in 5HT2 binding in parietal cortex (McKittrick, Blanchard, Blanchard, McEwen, & Sakai, 1995). Administration of 5HT1A agonists such as buspirone result in a reversal of stress-induced behavioral deficits (Drugan, Crawley, Paul, & Skolnick, 1987; Przegalinski, Moryl, & Papp, 1995).

There is some preliminary evidence to support alterations in serotonin reuptake site function in PTSD. Patients with combat-related PTSD had reduced paroxetine binding sites (lower Bmax and Kd) in platelets (evidence of reduced serotonin reuptake site function) (Arora, Fichtner, O'Connor, & Crayton, 1993), with decreases in Bmax significantly correlated with PTSD, anxiety, and depressive symptoms (Fichtner, O'Connor, Yeoh, Arora, & Crayton, 1995). Lower pretreatment Kd values predicted positive response to treatment with serotonin reuptake inhibitors, and there was a trend toward lower Bmax values predicting treatment response (Fichtner, Arora, O'Connor, & Crayton, 1994). Another study found no difference in platelet serotonin levels or uptake relative to controls (Mellman & Kumar, 1994). Studies of 5HT1A function have not been suggestive of abnormality. One study in women with sexual assault-related PTSD did not find a difference in prolactin response to buspirone (a probe of 5HT1A function) between women with sexual assault-related PTSD and controls (Dinan et al., 1990). A study in victims of SCUD missile attacks with PTSD did not find an effect of serotonin on forskolin-stimulated adenylate cyclase activity in platelets (a putative probe of 5HT1A) (Weizman, et al., 1994). Further research is necessary to clarify the role of serotonin dysfunction in PTSD. Perhaps the best clinical evidence for serotonergic involvement in PTSD is the responsiveness of patients with abuse-related PTSD to the serotonin reuptake inhibitor, fluoxetine, in controlled clinical trials (van der Kolk et al., 1994).

Other Neuropeptides and Neurotransmitters

Other neurotransmitter and neuropeptide systems are involved in stress (Table 6.3). Thyroid releasing hormone (TRH) released from the hypothalamus causes release of thyroid stimulating hormone (TSH) from the pituitary, which in turn stimulates thyroid hormone (thyroxine, or T4) release from the thyroid gland. TRH prevented the acquisition of stress-induced behavioral effects (Drago, Pulvirenti, Spadaro, & Pennisi, 1990). Stress is associated with an increase in plasma thyroid levels (Groscolas & LeLoup, 1989; Langer, Vigas, Kvetnansky, Foldes, & Culman, 1983). Studies in monkeys showed that stress results in a slow increase in plasma thyroid hormone, with a peak at greater than 24 hours after the stressor (Mason, Mougey, Brady, & Tolliver, 1968).

In humans, a relationship between stress and thyroid disease was first pointed out many years ago. Patients with hyperthyroidism exhibit symptoms of anxiety and hyperarousal, which has prompted many clinicians to routinely screen psychiatric patients for thyroid disorders. Recently, patients with combat-related PTSD were found to have increased baseline plasma levels of thyroid hormone compared to controls (Mason et al., 1994). PTSD patients also had a pattern of increased thyrotropin stimulating hormone (TSH) response to thyrotropin releasing hormone (TRH) relative to normal controls and patients with depression (Kosten et al., 1990).

Stress is associated with increases in acetylcholine release and metabolism in the hippocampus (Imperato et al., 1991) and glutamate release in the frontal cortex (Moghaddam, 1993). Preclinical studies show that somatostatin is involved in the stress response and modulation of corticotropin releasing factor release. Recent clinical studies in Vietnam combat veterans with PTSD showed increased somatostatin levels in cerebrospinal fluid relative to controls. Increased so-

TABLE 6.3 Evidence for Alterations in Other Neurotransmitter and Neuropeptidal Systems in PTSD

Benzodiazepine

Increased symptomatology with benzodiazepine antagonist	-

Opiate

Naloxone-reversible analgesia	+
Increased plasma beta-endorphin response to exercise	+

Serotonin

Decreased serotonin reuptake site binding in platelets	++
Decreased serotonin transmitter in platelets	-
Blunted prolactin response to buspirone (5HT1A probe)	-
Altered serotonin effect on cAMP in platelets (5HT1A probe)	-

Thyroid

Increased baseline thyroxine	+
Increased TSH response to TRH	+

Somatostatin

Increased somatostatin levels at baseline in CSF	+

-	One or more studies did not support this finding (with no positive studies), or the majority of studies do not support this finding;
+/-	An equal number of studies supported this finding as studies that did not support this finding;
+	At least one study supports this finding with no studies not supporting the finding, or the majority of studies support the finding;
++	Two or more studies support this finding, with no studies conducted that do not support the finding;
+++	Three or more studies support this finding, with no studies that do not support the finding.

matostatin levels were significantly correlated with increased CRF levels in the PTSD patients, but not the controls (Bremner, Licinio, et al., 1997).

IV. EFFECTS OF STRESS ON THE NEUROBIOLOGY OF LEARNING AND MEMORY

Recently there has been considerable interest in alterations in memory function in PTSD (Journal of Traumatic Stress, 1995, Volume 8). Memory alterations in PTSD take the form of deficits in both short-term memory as well as potentiation of recall of traumatic experiences and dissociative flashbacks (Pitman, 1989; Bremner, Krystal, et al., 1995; Bremner, Krystal, Charney, & Southwick, 1996). PTSD patients also demonstrate alterations in emotion-related learning, such as conditioned fear responses, increased startle, and failure of extinction. Studies in animals show that exposure to extreme stress results in alterations in memory function with associated long-term changes in brain regions involved in memory, including amygdala, hippocampus, parahippocampus, orbitofrontal cortex, cingulate, and thalamus. Other brain regions involved in memory and attention, such as parietal cortex and cerebellum, also probably play a role in stress-related symptoms.

Memory formation involves encoding (the initial laying down of the memory trace), storage (or consolidation), and retrieval. Consolidation occurs over several weeks or more, during which time the memory trace is susceptible to modification. A number of schema have been formulated to describe memory function. Many authors make the distinction between declarative ("explicit") and nondeclarative ("implicit" or "procedural") memory (Squire & Zola-Morgan, 1991; Schacter, 1995). Explicit memory includes free recall of facts and lists, and working memory, which is the ability to store information in a visual or verbal buffer while performing a particular operation utilizing that information. In contrast, implicit memory is demonstrated only through tasks or skills in which the knowledge is embedded. Forms of implicit memory include priming, conditioning, and tasks or skills.

Memory is mediated by several connected subcortical and cortical brain regions. The amygdala, hippocampus, and adjacent cortical areas have been shown to play an important role in memory. Other regions involved in memory include the prefrontal cortex, including what is known as the dorsolateral prefrontal cortex (middle frontal gyrus, principal sulcus region, or Area 46), orbital gyrus, anteromedial prefrontal cortex (including anterior cingulate cortex), cerebellum, and parietal association cortex. In addition, memories are stored in the primary cortical sensory and motor areas which correspond to the particular sensory modality related to the memory. These brain regions interact with one another in the mediation of memory function.

It has long been hypothesized that brain regions involved in memory also play a role in stress and the fear response. Early neuroanatomical studies showed that removal of the cerebral cortex of the cat, which left only subcortical regions including amygdala, thalamus, hippocampus, and hypothalamus, resulted in accentuated fearful responses to potentially threatening or novel stimuli, accompanied by signs of diffuse sympathetic activation such as increased blood pressure, sweating, piloerection, and increased secretion of epinephrine from the adrenal medulla (Cannon, 1927). This behavioral response became termed as "sham rage," and led to the original hypothesis that subcortical brain structures above the level of the midbrain, such as the hypothalamus, hippocampus, cingulate, entorhinal cortex, and thalamus, may be involved in emotional responses such as fear (Kluver & Bucy, 1937, 1939; Papez, 1937; reviewed in LeDoux, 1977). MacLean (1949) later added the amygdala to the "Papez Circuit" of "limbic" brain structures, so called because of their relationship to olfaction in evolution, which were hypothesized to play a role in fear and anxiety. These early neuroanatomical investigations were valuable in showing that brain regions involved in memory also play an important role both in fear-related behaviors seen naturally in the wild, and in manifestations of increased catecholaminergic activity. Below, brain regions involved in memory are outlined, with a review of normal function and stress-induced changes in function, followed by a discussion of possible correlates with PTSD (Figure 6.2).

The Hippocampus

The hippocampus plays an important role in explicit memory. Case studies such as the famous case of H.M. found a relationship between severe deficits in

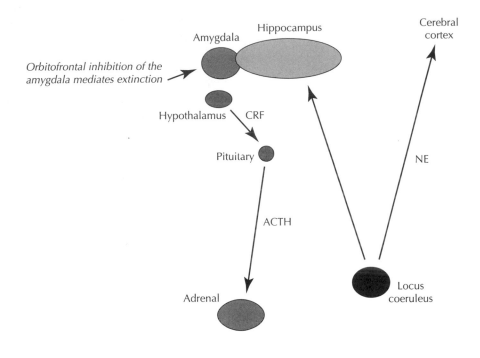

FIGURE 6.2 The Neuroanatomy of the Effects of Stress on Brain Regions Involved in Memory. Multiple brain areas mediate stress and fear responses, including amygdala, hippocampus, orbitofrontal cortex, cerebral cortex, hypothalamus, and the brain stem. These regions are functionally inter-related. Long-term changes in function and structure of these regions lead to symptoms of PTSD.

explicit memory measured with free verbal recall and lesions of the medial temporal lobes (i.e., hippocampus and adjacent structures). Lesions including the hippocampus and adjacent cortex (dentate gyrus, hippocampus proper, subicular complex, and entorhinal cortex), amygdala, and surrounding perirhinal and parahippocampal cortices in primates led to deficits in explicit memory measured with working memory tasks (Mishkin, 1978). Damage to the amygdala alone was not associated with declarative memory impairment (Zola-Morgan, Squire, & Amaral, 1989), while damage to the cortical areas adjacent to the amygdala, including perirhinal cortex and parahippocampal gyrus (which has important efferent and afferent connections with the hippocampus), was associated with pronounced explicit memory

impairment (Murray & Mishkin, 1986; Zola-Morgan, Squire, Amaral, & Suzuki, 1989). These studies demonstrated that the hippocampal region (dentate, hippocampus proper, subicular complex, and entorhinal cortex) and the adjacent perirhinal cortex and parahippocampal gyrus are involved in explicit memory. Recent positron emission tomography (PET) studies of cerebral blood flow are also consistent with a role for the hippocampus in explicit memory (Grasby, Frith, Friston, Frackowiak, & Dolan, 1993; Squire et al., 1992).

The hippocampus has long been felt to be involved in the emotions of fear and anxiety (Gray, 1982). The hippocampus is also known to play an important role in placement of memory traces in space and time (Parkinson, Murray, & Mishkin, 1988), including conditioned fear responses related to the context of a fear-inducing situation. In conditioned fear response experiments where a tone (conditioned stimulus) is paired with electric footshock (unconditioned stimulus), re-exposure of the animal to the tone will result in conditioned fear responses (increase in "freezing" responses, which is characteristic of fear), even in the absence of the shock. In addition, reintroduction to the context of the shock, or the environment where the shock took place (i.e., the testing box), even in the absence of the shock or the tone, will result in conditioned fear responses. Lesions of the amygdala before fear conditioning block fear responses to both simple stimuli (tone) and to the context of the footshock. Lesions of the hippocampus, on the other hand, do not interfere with acquisition of conditioned emotional responses to the tone in the absence of the shock, although they do interfere with acquisition of conditioned emotional responses to the context (Phillips & LeDoux, 1992). Lesions of the hippocampus one day after fear conditioning (but not as much as 28 days after fear conditioning) also abolish context-related fear responses, but not fear related to the cue (tone), while lesions of the amygdala block fear responses to both the cue and the context (Kim & Fanselow, 1992). These studies suggest that the hippocampus has a time-limited role in fear responses to complex phenomena with stimuli from multiple sensory modalities, but not to stimuli from simple sensory stimuli. The amygdala integrates information from multiple sensory modalities and effects the conditioned emotional response. The role of the hippocampus is to formulate conditioned responses to complex spatially related stimuli. It probably does this by integrating complex spatially related stimuli, and passing this information through the subiculum to the amygdala, which effects the stress response.

There is a wealth of evidence from studies in animals that stress results in long-term alterations in brain systems involved in memory (McEwen et al., 1992; Sapolsky, Uno, Rebert, & Finch, 1990). For instance, there is a considerable amount of evidence derived from research in animals which suggests that stress is associated with damage to hippocampal neurons. Monkeys who died spontaneously following exposure to severe stress were found on autopsy to have multiple gastric ulcers, consistent with exposure to chronic stress, and hyperplastic adrenal cortices, consistent with sustained glucocorticoid release. These monkeys also had damage to the CA3 subfield of the hippocampus (Uno, Tarara, Else, Suleman, & Sapolsky, 1989). Studies in a variety of animal species (Sapolsky, Packan, & Vale, 1988; Sapolsky et al., 1990) suggest that direct glucocorticoid exposure results in decreased dendritic branching in the hippocampus (Wooley, Gould, & McEwen, 1990) and a loss of neurons (Uno et al., 1989). Glucocorticoids appear to exert their effect by increasing the vulnerability of hippocampal neurons to insults such as excitatory amino acids (Sapolsky, 1986; Virgin et al., 1991). High levels of glucocorticoids seen with stress have also been associated with deficits in new learning (Luine, Villages, Martinex, & McEwen, 1994), with the magnitude of deficits in new learning behaviors correlated with the number of damaged cells in the CA3 region of the hippocampus. These studies suggested the possibility that high levels of cortisol released during stress could damage the hippocampus in humans with PTSD, leading to deficits in verbal memory function and decreased hippocampal volume.

Studies in clinical populations are consistent with deficits in verbal memory function. PTSD exhibit alterations in memory, including nightmares, flashbacks, intrusive memories, and amnesia for the traumatic event. We have reported an increase in the dissociative symptom of amnesia as measured with the SCID-D (Dissociative Disorders) in Vietnam combat veterans with PTSD in comparison to Vietnam combat veterans without PTSD (Bremner, Steinberg, Southwick, Johnson, & Charney, 1993). Episodes of amnesia in these patients took the form of gaps in memory which lasted from minutes to hours or days. Individual patients reported a range of experiences, from driving on the highway and suddenly noticing that three hours had passed, to walking down a street in Boston and then finding themselves in a motel room in Texas, with no idea of how they got there.

Evidence from other studies in traumatized patients are also consistent with abnormalities of explicit memory function. In one group of 321 Danish survivors of WWII concentration camps with high levels of psychiatric symptomatology who were seeking compensation for disability, there were complaints of memory impairment suggestive of deficits in explicit recall 10 or more years after release from internment in 87 percent of individuals. Severe intellectual impairment was also found on testing in 61 percent of cases (Thygesen, Hermann, & Willanger, 1970). Korean prisoners of war have been found to have an impairment on explicit memory tasks of free verbal recall measured with the Logical Memory component of the Wechsler Memory Scale in comparison to Korean veterans without a history of containment (Sutker, Winstead, Galina, & Allain, 1991). We found deficits in explicit verbal memory function as measured with the Wechsler Memory Scale (WMS)-Logical component and the Selective Reminding Test-verbal, in Vietnam combat veterans with PTSD (Bremner, Scott, et al., 1993) and adult survivors of childhood abuse (Bremner, Randall, Capellie, et al., 1995) without deficits in IQ as measured by the Wechsler Adult Intelligence Scale-Revised. Studies have found deficits in explicit short-term memory as assessed with the Auditory Verbal Learning Test (AVLT) in Vietnam combat veterans with PTSD in comparison to National Guard veterans without PTSD (Uddo, Vasterling, Brailey, & Sutker, 1993) and the California New Learning Test in Vietnam veterans with combat-related PTSD in comparison to controls (Yehuda, Keefer, et al., 1995). Deficits in academic performance have also been shown in Beirut adolescents with PTSD in comparison to Beirut adolescents without PTSD (Saigh, Mroueh, & Bremner, 1997).

Other aspects of cognitive function have been investigated in PTSD. Vietnam veterans with PTSD were found to have decreased IQ relative to controls, suggesting that low intelligence may be a risk factor for PTSD (McNally & Shin, 1995). Patients with combat-related PTSD were found to have deficits in autobiographical memory, characterized by an inability to retrieve specific memories, relative to controls (McNally, Lasko, Macklin, & Pitman, 1995; McNally, Litz, Prassas, Shin, & Weathers, 1994). PTSD patients showed a relative deficit in retrieval of specific autobiographical memories in response to positive cues (McNally et al., 1995), as well as a greater effect of negative emotional cues (combat slides and sounds) on decreasing specificity of retrieved auto-

biographical memories (McNally et al., 1994). Patients with combat-related PTSD have increased rates of childhood abuse (Bremner, Southwick, et al., 1993), and other studies have noted a relationship between childhood trauma and impairments in autobiographical memory (cited in McNally et al., 1994). Traumatic events during childhood may result in a disruption in development of the normal catalogue of memories which lead to a sense of identity and the "story of one's life," which explains findings of deficits in autobiographical memory in PTSD. Studies of implicit memory bias for trauma-relevant material showed no differences between PTSD patients and controls using a perceptual identification paradigm (identifying words on a computer screen) (McNally & Amir, 1996), although a significant implicit memory bias was found for combat-relevant sentences using a noise judgment task (PTSD subjects rated the volume of noise accompanying "old" trauma sentences as less loud than new sentences, whereas controls did not) (Amir, McNally, & Wiegartz, 1996).

Studies utilizing neuroimaging techniques have found that stress in humans may be associated with changes in brain structure, including the morphology of the hippocampus. Studies in concentration camp survivors from World War II seeking compensation for disability utilized pneumoencephalography and reported "[cerebral] atrophy of varying degrees" and "diffuse encephalopathy" in up to 81 percent of cases (referenced in Thygesen et al., 1970). We compared hippocampal volume measured with MRI in Vietnam combat veterans with PTSD (N = 26) and healthy subjects (N = 22) matched for factors which could affect hippocampal volume, including age, sex, race, years of education, height, weight, handedness, and years of alcohol abuse. Patients with combat-related PTSD had an 8 percent decrease in right hippocampal volume in comparison to controls (p < 0.05), but no significant decrease in volume of comparison structures including temporal lobe and caudate. Deficits in free verbal recall (explicit memory) as measured by the Wechsler Memory Scale-Logical Component, percent retention, were associated with decreased right hippocampal volume in the PTSD patients (r = 0.64; p < 0.05). There was not a significant difference between PTSD patients and controls in left hippocampal volume, or in volume of the comparison regions measured in this study, left or right caudate and temporal lobe volume (minus hippocampus) (Bremner, Randall, Scott, et al., 1995). We also found a statistically significant 12 percent decrease in left hippocampal volume in 17 patients with a history of PTSD related to severe childhood physical and sexual abuse, in relationship to 17 controls matched on a case-by-case basis with the patients (Bremner, Randall, et al., 1997) (Figure 6.3). PET $H_2[^{15}O]$ studies of PTSD during exposure to traumatic reminders in the form of combat-related slides and sounds showed activation in right posterior parahippocampus relative to non-PTSD combat veterans (Bremner, Innis, et al., 1997).

Other aspects of the alterations in memory function seen in PTSD may be mediated by the hippocampus and adjacent cortex. Electrical stimulation of the temporal lobe (including hippocampus and adjacent cortical regions, parahippocampal gyrus, amygdala, and temporal lobe neocortex) in patients with epilepsy resulted in the subjective experience of a number of symptoms which are similar to those seen in PTSD.

Eighteen out of 35 patients experienced symptoms of some kind. These included the subjective sensation of fear (7 patients), complex visual hallucinations (i.e., flashbacks) (5), memory recall (5), deja vu (4), and emotional distress (3) (Gloor, Olivier, Quesney, Andermann, & Horowitz, 1982). In another study, electrical stimulation of the hippocampus and amygdala in epileptic patients was also associated with visual and auditory hallucinations, dream-like and memory-like hallucinations which descriptively are similar to flashbacks reported by patients with PTSD (Halgren, Walter, Cherlow, & Crandall, 1978). An increase in dissociative symptomatology and disruption of delayed word recall was found in normal subjects following intravenous administration of ketamine hydrochloride, a noncompetitive antagonist of the N-methyl-D-aspartate (NMDA) receptor (Krystal et al., 1994). The NMDA receptor, which is highly concentrated in the hippocampus, probably mediates memory function at the molecular level through mechanisms such as long-term potentiation (LTP) (reviewed in Krystal, Bennett, Bremner, Southwick, & Charney, 1995).

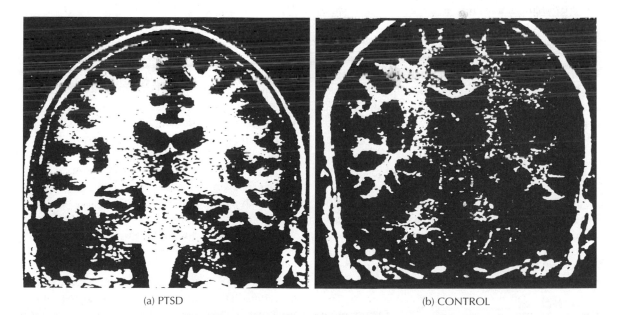

(a) PTSD   (b) CONTROL

FIGURE 6.3   Magnetic resonance scan of a patient with PTSD and a normal comparison subject. There is visible atrophy of the hippocampus in the patient with PTSD relative to the comparison subject.

We have hypothesized that stress-induced hippocampal dysfunction may mediate many of the symptoms of PTSD which are related to memory dysregulation, including both explicit memory deficits as well as memory distortions similar to those seen with hippocampal stimulation, as reviewed above (Bremner, Krystal, Southwick, & Charney, 1995; Bremner, Krystal, Charney, & Southwick, 1996). The hippocampus and adjacent cortex plays an important role in binding together information from multiple sensory cortices into a single memory at the time of retrieval, and in locating a memory trace in space and time. For instance, during an episode of sexual abuse, there is the smell of the perpetrator, the sounds involved in the abuse, the visual appearance of the perpetrator and the scene where the abuse takes place, tactile sensations, and the temporal relationship of the elements of memory to other aspects of the individual's life experiences. All of these individual features are stored in the primary sensory cortical areas to which they correspond, for instance, smell is stored in the olfactory cortex. When a similar situation recurs, the hippocampus and adjacent cortex activates cortical areas and brings together the diverse sensory elements in relevant spatiotemporal format in order to recreate the memory. Abnormalities of hippocampal function in PTSD may impair the ability of the hippocampus to recreate a normal memory. Traumatic memories may not be able to be placed in space and time, leading to fragmentation or amnesia. Traumatic memories may intrude into consciousness without any discernible reason, leading to the symptom of intrusive memories and flashbacks.

The Amygdala

The amygdala is involved in memory for the emotional valence of events. The paradigm of conditioned fear has been utilized as an animal model for stress-induced abnormalities of emotional memory (Davis, 1992). Noise bursts elicit the acoustic startle response, which is used in the measurement of the conditioned fear response. Fear conditioning (reviewed above in "The Hippocampus") results in an increase in the startle response. The neuroanatomy and neurophysiology of conditioned fear responses in animals have been well characterized (Davis, 1992). Lesions of the central nucleus of the amygdala have been shown to completely block fear-potentiated startle (Hitchcock & Davis, 1986; Hitchcock, Sananes, & Davis, 1989) while electrical stimulation of the central nucleus increases acoustic startle (Rosen & Davis, 1988). The central nucleus of the amygdala projects to a variety of brain structures via the stria terminalis and the ventral amygdalofugal pathway. One pathway is from the central nucleus to the brainstem startle reflex circuit (nucleus reticularis pontis caudalis). Lesions of this pathway at any point (caudal lateral hypothalamus-subthalamic area, substantia nigra, central tegmental field) block the development of fear-potentiated startle, while lesions of fibers which project outward from the central nucleus of the amygdala to sites other than the brainstem startle circuit have no effect (Hitchcock & Davis, 1991). The excitatory neurotransmitters play an important role in fear conditioning mediated by the amygdala, as demonstrated by the fact that antagonists of the N-methyl-D-aspartate (NMDA) receptor infused into the amygdala block the acquisition (but not the expression) of the fear-potentiated startle response (Miserendino, Sananes, Melia, & Davis, 1990). These findings demonstrate that the amygdala is involved in emotional memory, including conditioned fear responses, as well as effecting the stress response.

Pathways from the amygdala to the lateral hypothalamus effect peripheral sympathetic responses to stress (Iwata, LeDoux, Meeley, Arneric, & Reis, 1986). Electrical stimulation of the amygdala in cats resulted in peripheral signs of autonomic hyperactivity and fear-related behaviors seen in the wild when the animal is being attacked or is attacking, including alerting, chewing, salivation, piloerection, turning, facial twitching, arching of the back, hissing, and snarling (Hilton & Zbrozyna, 1963), which was associated with a depletion of norepinephrine in the brain and epinephrine and norepinephrine in the adrenal, suggesting an increase in catecholamine turnover.

Studies in human subjects support a role for the amygdala in emotion and the stress response. Studies in human subjects have demonstrated that the threat of electric shock results in an increase in startle response (Grillon, Ameli, Woods, Merikangas, & Davis,

1991). Patients with unilateral temporal lobectomy (including amygdala resection) showed impaired acquisition of fear conditioning relative to controls (La-Bar, LeDoux, Spencer, & Phelps, 1995). These subjects, however, showed no difference in recall of emotional words relative to controls (Phelps, LaBar, & Spencer, 1997), suggesting that although the amygdala probably plays an important role in the specific paradigm of conditioned fear, it may not play a unique role in all facets of emotional experience in human subjects. Electrical stimulation of the amygdala in human subjects resulted in an increase in heart rate and blood pressure, increased muscle tension, and subjective sensations of fear or anxiety (Chapman et al., 1954). Amygdala stimulation of human subjects is also accompanied by activation of the stress response system, as manifested by increases in peripheral catecholamines, in a similar fashion to that seen in animals during conditioned fear responses (Gunne & Reis, 1963). We have not found a difference in amygdala volume measured with MRI between patients with combat-related PTSD (Bremner et al., unpublished data, 1/96) or abuse-related PTSD (Bremner, Randall, et al., 1997) and matched controls.

Investigations have also addressed alterations in emotional memory as demonstrated by conditioned emotional responses in patients with PTSD. The conditioned emotional response can be studied in humans in the laboratory utilizing the psychophysiology paradigm, which is reviewed above in "Noradrenergic Systems." Lawrence Kolb (1984) noted that patients with PTSD have a heightened physiological responsiveness to reminders of the original trauma which resemble conditioned responses. These conditioned responses to cues related to the original trauma (combat films and sounds, scripts of traumatic events) are parallel to those seen with the conditioned fear paradigm in animals.

Studies have also found abnormalities of the startle response in patients with PTSD. Increased startle magnitude has been found in Vietnam combat veterans with PTSD in comparison to Vietnam combat veterans without PTSD in some studies (for 80 dB bursts of white noise) (for 95 and 100 dB noise—Butler et al., 1990) but not others (Paige, Reid, Allen, & Newton, 1990). One study showed increased baseline star-

tle in PTSD relative to controls in an experimental setting where electric shock was to be delivered at some point during the experiment. PTSD patients did not demonstrate greater increases in startle, however, when explicitly told that they were now going to receive shock (Morgan, Grillon, Southwick, Davis, & Charney, 1995). No difference in trials to habituation of startle response between PTSD and controls was demonstrated in one study (Ross, Ball, Cohen, et al., 1989). An increase in heart rate and skin conductance during the startle paradigm was reported in patients with civilian PTSD in comparison to controls (Shalev et al., 1992). One study in children with PTSD found an absent normal inhibition of acoustic startle by nonstartling acoustic prestimulation (Ornitz & Pynoos, 1989). In summary, there is evidence for abnormalities in startle response in PTSD. The heightened responsiveness to reminders of the original trauma, or conditioned emotional stimuli, and abnormalities of the startle response are probably mediated by the amygdala, in addition to other brain regions reviewed within this chapter.

Prefrontal Cortex, Anterior Cingulate, and Orbitofrontal Cortex

Considerable evidence suggests that the dorsolateral prefrontal cortex (principal sulcus, or middle frontal gyrus) is involved in the working memory type of explicit memory function (Goldman-Rakic, 1988). Working memory refers to the ability to store information in a visual or verbal buffer while performing a particular operation utilizing that information. In non-human primates, working memory is assessed by the delayed-response tasks, in which monkeys perform tasks based on previously received information after a short time delay. These tasks typically involve learning a "set of rules," which is considered an important component of the memory function mediated by the dorsolateral prefrontal cortex. Lesions of the dorsolateral prefrontal cortex result in deficits in working memory tasks, while explicit memory for features of the stimuli are unaffected. PET $H_2[^{15}O]$ studies of cerebral blood flow in normal human subjects are also consistent with a role for dorsolateral prefrontal cortex in both encoding and retrieval of explicit memory traces and attention (reviewed in McCarthy, 1995). Deficits in explicit memory function (reviewed above) could therefore be consistent with abnormalities in dorsolateral prefrontal cortex function, in addition to hippocampal dysfunction. An increase in neurological soft signs in Vietnam combat veterans with PTSD could also be explainable by abnormalities in frontal lobe function (Gurvits et al., 1993).

The anteromedial (or ventromesial) prefrontal cortex includes the anterior cingulate gyrus and is functionally and anatomically distinct from the dorsolateral prefrontal cortex. In the late nineteenth century the famous patient named Phineas Gage had a projectile metal spike pass through his frontal cortex, with damage specifically to the anterior cingulate, anteromedial prefrontal cortex, and parts of the orbitofrontal cortex. Following the accident the patient had normal memory recall and cognitive function, but his behavior deteriorated to irresponsibility, profanity, and lack of social conventions, which indicated a deficit in the planning and execution of socially suitable behavior. This case suggests that the anteromedial frontal cortex (including anterior cingulate) is responsible for socially appropriate behavior and the processing of emotionally related stimuli (Damasio, Grabowski, Frank, Galaburda, & Damasio, 1994). Symptoms such as feeling cut off from others and avoidance in PTSD patients may be related to dysfunction of anteromedial prefrontal cortex. Studies of human patients with brain lesions has shown that damage to the anterior one third of the frontal cortex (including anterior cingulate) often results in seizures in which the individual experiences intense feelings of fear or anguish as a symptom, suggesting that the anteromedial prefrontal cortex plays a role in fear-related behavior. In addition, some patients have been observed to experience visual hallucinations as well during seizures, which are reminiscent of the flashbacks seen in victims of trauma (Goldensohn, 1992). Studies in PTSD patients during exposure to reminders of their traumatic experiences have shown activation of anterior cingulate (Rauch et al., 1996) and mid-cingulate (Bremner, Innis, et al., 1997).

Abnormalities in the Stroop test, a marker of anterior cingulate function (Pardo, Pardo, Janer, & Raichle, 1990), have been associated with PTSD. Delays in color-naming with PTSD-related words such as "body-bag" are involuntary, and provide quantitative measures of the intrusive cognition which is an important part of PTSD. Vietnam combat veterans with PTSD have been found to take longer to color-name "PTSD" words than obsessive words, positive words, and neutral words, and this delay was correlated with severity of PTSD symptomatology as measured by the Mississippi Scale (McNally, Kaspi, Riemann, & Zeitlin, 1990; McNally, English, & Lipke, 1993). Stroop interference has also been shown in patients with PTSD related to the trauma of rape (Foa, Feske, Murdock, Kozak, & McCarthy, 1991; Cassiday, McNally, & Zeitlin, 1992). No difference was found when subliminal interference was compared to supraliminal interference with the Stroop task (McNally, Amir, & Lipke, 1996).

The orbitofrontal cortex is another frontal cortical area which is of importance from the standpoint of the effects of stress on memory. The orbitofrontal cortex is the primary sensory cortical area for smell. It also plays a role in the fear response, extinction, and certain types of memory. The orbitofrontal cortex may be involved in abnormalities of emotional memory which are seen in patients with PTSD. Studies of human patients with brain lesions have shown that lesions of the orbitofrontal cortex result in symptoms of intense fear during seizures. In addition, some patients have been observed to experience visual hallucinations as well during seizures (Goldensohn, 1992). Some case reports have described a relationship between damage to the orbitofrontal cortex and visual hallucinations which appear to be similar to the flashbacks which are characteristic of PTSD (Fornazzari, Farcnik, Smith, Heasman, & Ichise, 1992).

Orbitofrontal cortex is also involved in the neural mechanism of extinction. As reviewed above, in the conditioned fear paradigm, repetitive pairing of a light (conditioned stimulus) and a shock (unconditioned stimulus) will result in a conditioned fear response to the light alone. Repeated exposure to the light alone will eventually lead to the loss of conditioned responding, a phenomenon known as extinction of the conditioned fear response. Lesions of the medial orbitofrontal cortex in extinction to conditioned stimuli in this paradigm, suggesting that this region plays a role in extinction of conditioned stimuli (Morgan & LeDoux, 1994). Studies have shown that this extinction is due in fact to an inhibition by orbitofrontal cortex of subcortical brain structures (such as the amygdala) which mediate conditioned fear responding. A failure of extinction of conditioned emotional responding is a characteristic of patients with PTSD. For example, a veteran who has a conditioned fear response of becoming startled and agitated with the sound of a car backfiring, which is associated with the original aversive stimulus of gunfire in Vietnam, does not become less agitated with repeated exposures to cars backfiring. We have found the greatest differential response of cerebral metabolism measured with PET between PTSD patients and controls following administration of yohimbine in the orbitofrontal cortex, with a relative blunting of metabolism in this region with yohimbine in PTSD (Bremner, Innis, et al., 1997). Exposure of PTSD patients to traumatic cues resulted in a failure of orbitofrontal cortical activation as measured with PET H$_2$[^{15}O] relative to combat-exposed controls (Bremner, Innis, et al., 1997). These findings are consistent with orbitofrontal dysfunction in PTSD, and suggest a neural mechanism for the failure of extinction which characterizes PTSD patients.

Neocortex

Parietal cortex has been demonstrated to play an important role in spatial memory and attention. Single-cell recordings from alert monkeys have shown an activation of the parietal cortex when monkeys are required to attend to a visual location. PET H$_2$[^{15}O] studies during sustained attention showed increases in blood flow in the right prefrontal and superior parietal cortex (Posner, Peterson, Fox, & Raichle, 1988). PET H$_2$[^{15}O] in patients with combat-related PTSD showed increased activation of parietal cortex with traumatic reminders relative to non-PTSD combat veterans (Bremner, Innis, et al., 1997). Other neocortical regions besides parietal cortex are involved in memory function. Explicit memory storage takes place in sensory brain areas in which an event is first experienced. For instance, visual information

is stored in the occipital cortex, tactile information in the sensory cortex, auditory information in the middle temporal gyrus, olfactory information in the orbitofrontal cortex, and motor information in the motor cortex (precentral gyrus). The hippocampus has been hypothesized to bring together diverse memory elements in the correct spatiotemporal context at the time of memory retrieval (Zola-Morgan & Squire, 1990). PET H$_2$[^{15}O] studies showed activation in insula, medial temporal cortex, sensorimotor cortex, and visual association cortex in PTSD patients during traumatic reminders relative to a control task (Rauch et al., 1996). We have found greater activation with traumatic reminders in combat veterans with PTSD relative to those without PTSD in motor cortex, in addition to other regions described above (Bremner, Innis, et al., 1997).

Stress-Induced Neuromodulation of Memory

Neurotransmitters and neuropeptides released during stress have a modulatory effect on memory function. These include norepinephrine, epinephrine, adrenocorticotropic hormone (ACTH), glucocorticoids, corticotropin releasing factor (CRF), opioid peptides, endogenous benzodiazepines, dopamine, vasopressin, and oxytocin (De Wied & Croiset, 1991). Brain regions involved in memory are richly innervated by these neurotransmitters and neuropeptides.

Removal of the adrenal medulla, site of most of the body's epinephrine, results in impairment in new learning and memory, which is restored by administration of adequate amounts of epinephrine (Borrell, De Kloet, Versteeg, & Bohus, 1983). Posttraining administration of epinephrine after a learning task influences retention with an inverted U-shaped curve: retention is enhanced at moderate doses and impaired at high doses (Gold & van Buskirk, 1975; Liang, Juler, & McGaugh, 1986; McGaugh, Castellano, & Brioni, 1990). Low dose (0.2 microgram) injections of norepinephrine into the amygdala facilitate memory function, while higher doses (0.5 microgram) impair memory function (Liang, McGaugh, & Yao, 1990). Lesions of the dorsal noradrenergic bundle result in an impairment in the learning and memory (reviewed in Robbins, Everitt, & Cole, 1985; Cole & Robbins,

1992) and acquisition of conditioned fear responding (Selden, Robbins, & Everitt, 1990). Activation of the noradrenergic system through electrical stimulation of the locus coeruleus (Velly, Kempf, Cardo, & Velley, 1985), administration of the alpha2 antagonist, yohimbine (Goldberg & Robertson, 1983) or amphetamine (Sara, 1985), (both of which stimulate brain norepinephrine release) enhance memory acquisition and storage. Norepinephrine increases neuronal firing in the hippocampus, suggesting a possible mechanism for enhancement of memory storage (Madison & Nicoll, 1982). The acetylcholine antagonist, scopolamine, impairs memory as measured by acquisition and retention of an inhibitory avoidance task as well as place learning (Decker & McGaugh, 1989). Combined blockade of both the cholinergic and noradrenergic systems with scopolamine and propranolol, respectively, at doses which had no effect individually, when administered in combination profoundly impaired inhibitory avoidance as well as spatial learning (Decker, Gill, & McGaugh, 1990). In summary, epinephrine and norepinephrine released during stress act to enhance the formation of memory traces (McGaugh, 1989, 1990).

ACTH and glucocorticoids also affect learning and memory. Low doses of ACTH given immediately after a new learning task enhance retention, while a 10-fold higher dose has the opposite effect (Gold & van Buskirk, 1975). ACTH enhanced the acquisition of learning in a conditioned fear paradigm (see above, "The Amygdala"). ACTH also delayed extinction of the avoidance response (see above, "Orbitofrontal Cortex") (De Wied & Jolles, 1982). The effects of ACTH on learning and memory are mediated through the hippocampus and amygdala (Van Wimersma Greidanus, Croiset, Bakker, & Bouman, 1979). Glucocorticoids, in contrast, enhance extinction in the conditioned fear paradigm (De Wied & Jolles, 1982). The neuropeptide CRF, which stimulates release of ACTH from the pituitary and hence glucocorticoids from the adrenal, has anxiogenic effects when administered into the cerebral ventricles (Britton, Koob, & Vale, 1982).

Other neurotransmitters and neuropeptides released during stress have effects on learning and memory. Opiate receptor agonists when administered after training in a learning task impair retention, while opiate receptor antagonists such as naloxone enhance re-

tention (Castellano, 1975). Vasopressin injected three hours before or after a new learning paradigm increases resistance to extinction, possibly through effects on consolidation, as well as facilitating new learning, while oxytocin has the opposite effect (Gaffori & De Wied, 1986). Gamma-aminobutyric acid (GABA) antagonists such as bicuculline, which block the action of GABA, impair memory retention following administration into the amygdala, while GABA agonists have the opposite effect (Brioni, Nagahara, & McGaugh, 1989). Analogues of thyrotropin releasing hormone (TRH) also facilitate learning and memory (Drago et al., 1991).

Recent studies have begun to address the question of neuromodulation of memory function with stress in human subjects. In one recent study, the beta-adrenergic antagonist, propranolol, or placebo, was administered one hour before a neutral or an emotionally arousing (stress-related) story in healthy human subjects. Propranolol, but not placebo, interfered with recall of the emotionally arousing story, but not the neutral story, suggesting that activation of beta-adrenergic receptors in the brain enhanced the encoding of the emotionally arousing memories (Cahill, Prins, Weber, & McGaugh, 1994). The cortisol analogue, dexamethasone, impaired verbal recall in young (but not elderly) healthy subjects (Newcomer, Craft, Hershey, Askins, & Bardgett, 1994). The findings indicate that preclinical studies of neuromodulation are relevant to human subjects.

Findings related to neuromodulation of memory function are of importance for understanding the symptomatology of PTSD. Increased release of neurotransmitters and neuropeptides with modulatory actions on memory function during stress probably plays a role in deficits in encoding and retrieval, as well as the enhancement of specific traumatic memories, which is part of the clinical presentation of PTSD. Chronic abnormalities in the function of these neurotransmitter and neuropeptide systems in PTSD may contribute to the abnormalities in memory seen in these patients. For instance, vasopressin has been shown to increase electromyographic responses during personal traumatic imagery, but not during generic traumatic slides, suggesting a facilitation of traumatic remembrance (Pitman, Orr, & Lasko, 1993).

We have reviewed above how neuromodulators may be involved in the mechanisms of stress sensitization and the pathological retrieval of traumatic memories in patients with PTSD. Hopefully, an extension of preclinical findings on the effects of stress-related neuromodulators on memory function to clinical populations will enhance our understanding of memory alterations in PTSD.

Mechanisms involving state-dependent recall (Bower, 1981), which are applicable to memory alterations in PTSD, may be mediated by some of these neuromodulators described above. State-dependent recall refers to the phenomenon where a similar affective state to the time of encoding leads to a facilitation of memory retrieval. For instance, memories which were encoded during a state of sadness will have a facilitated retrieval during similar states of sadness. Similar situations can occur for other emotional states. To extend this concept to PTSD, it can be seen that particular emotions will predominate at the time of the original abuse, such as extreme fear or sadness. These emotional states occur infrequently during routine adult life which is free of stressors. The recurrence of the state of extreme fear or sadness which occurred during the original abuse during psychotherapy or with exposure to a subsequent stressor may lead to a delayed recall of the original abuse experiences. A clinical example of this would be the victim of sexual abuse who has no recall of her sexual abuse experiences until subsequent victimization by rape as an adult which leads to a recall of the original trauma.

V. CONCLUDING REMARKS

Multiple neurotransmitter and neuropeptide systems are involved in the stress response, including corticotropin releasing factor (CRF), norepinephrine, serotonin, dopamine, endogenous benzodiazepines, and endogenous opiates. These transmitters mutually regulate one another in the execution of the stress response. Chronic stress is associated with long-term alterations in these transmitters and peptides, which translate into changes in neuronal function, and structure. Preliminary clinical studies in patients with PTSD are beginning to replicate many of the findings from animal studies.

Brain regions in which there are the greatest changes with stress, including hippocampus and amygdala, are those which are involved in memory and emotion, as well as the stress response. Neurotransmitter and neuropeptidal systems involved in stress modulate behavior and memory function through direct actions on these brain regions. Chronic stress, probably through long-term alterations in these systems, can lead to long-term behavioral and memory disturbances. This may represent the mechanism for many of the symptoms of PTSD. Exposure to subsequent stressors is also associated with altered release of neuromodulators, resulting in altered memory recall in PTSD patients. Other concepts such as state-dependent memory, fear conditioning, stress sensitization, and failure of extinction are important models for understanding how changes in brain function translate into symptoms of PTSD.

Studies to date have provided only an incomplete picture of biological mechanisms in PTSD. The animal literature of stress is vast, and this chapter represents only a partial overview. This chapter was intended as a review of the current status of the topic, and to raise awareness about how the neurobiology of stress relates to PTSD, and to what extent these findings have been replicated in humans. Hopefully, increased understanding of the neurobiology of PTSD can lead to specific advances in treatment of this troubling disorder (Friedman, 1988, 1991).

REFERENCES

Abercrombie, E. D., & Jacobs, B. L. (1987a). Single-unit response of noradrenergic neurons in the locus coeruleus of freely moving cats. I. Acutely presented stressful and nonstressful stimuli. *Journal of Neuroscience, 7,* 2837–2843.

Abercrombie, E. D., & Jacobs, B. L. (1987b). Single-unit response of noradrenergic neurons in the locus coeruleus of freely moving cats. II. Adaptation to chronically presented stressful stimuli. *Journal of Neuroscience, 7,* 2844–2848.

Abercrombie, E. D., Keefe, K. A., DiFrischia, D. S., & Zigmond, M. J. (1989). Differential effect of stress on in vivo dopamine release in striatum, nucleus accumbens, and medial frontal cortex. *Journal of Neurochemistry, 52,* 1655–1658.

Abercrombie, E. D., Keller, R. W., Jr., & Zigmond, M. J. (1988). Characterization of hippocampal norepinephrine release as measured by microdialysis perfusion: Pharmacological and behavioral studies. *Neuroscience, 27,* 897–904.

Ableitner, A., & Herz, A. (1987). Changes in local cerebral glucose utilization induced by the Beta-carbolines FG 7142 and DMCM reveal brain structures involved in the control of anxiety and seizure activity. *Journal of Neuroscience, 7,* 1047–1055.

Adell, A., Garcia-Marquez, C., Armario, A., & Gelpi, E. (1988). Chronic stress increases serotonin and noradrenaline in rat brain and sensitizes their responses to further acute stress. *Journal of Neurochemistry, 50,* 1678–1681

Aghajanian, G. (1978). Tolerance of locus coeruleus neurons to morphine and suppression of withdrawal response by clonidine. *Nature, 276,* 186–188.

Aghajanian, G., Cedarbaum, J., & Wang, R. (1977). Evidence for norepinephrine-mediated collateral inhibition of locus coeruleus neurons. *Brain Research, 136,* 570–577.

Aghajanian, G. K., & VanderMaelen, C. P. (1982). Alpha2-adrenoceptor-mediated hyperpolarization of locus coeruleus neurons: Intracellular studies in vivo. *Science, 215,* 1394–1396.

Akaoka, H., & Aston-Jones, G. (1991). Opiate withdrawal-induced hyperactivity of locus coeruleus neurons is substantially mediated by augmented excitatory amino acid input. *Journal of Neuroscience, 11,* 3830–3839.

Akaoka, H., & Aston-Jones, G. (1993). Indirect serotonergic agonists attenuate neuronal opiate withdrawal. *Neuroscience, 54,* 561–565.

Amir, N., McNally, R. J., & Wiegartz, P. S. (1996). Implicit memory bias for threat in posttraumatic stress disorder. *Cognitive Therapy and Research, 20,* 625–635.

Anisman, H., & Zacharko, R. M. (1985). Behavioral and neurochemical consequences associated with stressors. *Annals of the New York Academy of Sciences,* 205–229.

Arora, R. C., Fichtner, C. G., O'Connor, F., & Crayton, J. W. (1993). Paroxetine binding in the blood platelets of post-traumatic stress disorder patients. *Life Sciences, 53,* 919–928.

Aston-Jones, G. (1985). The locus coeruleus: Behavioral function of locus coeruleus derived from cellular attributes. *Physiology and Psychology, 13,* 118–126.

Aston-Jones, G., Akaoka, H., Charlety, P., & Chouvet, G. (1991). Serotonin selectively attenuates glutamate-evoked activation of noradrenergic locus coeruleus neurons. *Journal of Neuroscience, 11,* 760–769.

Aston-Jones, G., Chiang, C., & Alexinsky, T. (1991). Discharge of noradrenergic locus coeruleus neurons in behaving rats and monkeys suggests a role in vigilance. In C. D. Barnes & O. Pomeiano, (Eds.), *Progress in brain research,* (pp. 501–519). Elsevier Science Publishers.

Aston-Jones, G., Ennis, M., Pieribone, V. A., Nickell, W. T., & Shipley, M. T. (1985). The brain nucleus locus coeruleus: Restricted afferent control of a broad efferent network. *Science, 234,* 734–737.

Aston-Jones, G., Shipley, M. T., Chovet, G., Ennis, M., van Bockstaele, E., Pieribone, V., Shiekhattar, R., Akaoka, H., Drolet, G., Astier, B., Charley, P., Valentino, R. J., & Williams, J. T. (1991). Afferent regulation of locus coeruleus neurons: anatomy, physiology and pharmacology. In C. D. Barnes & O. Pomeiano, (Eds.), *Progress in brain research,* (pp. 47–75). Elsevier Science Publishers.

Barrett, J. A., Shaikh, M. B., Edinger, H., & Siegel, A. (1987). The effects of intrahypothalamic injections of norepinephrine upon affective defense behavior in the cat. *Brain Research, 426,* 381–384.

Bartolome, J. V., Johnston, J. G., & Schanberg, S. M. (1994). Inhibition of liver ornithine decarboxylase expression in neonatal rats by maternal separation or CNS beta-endorphin is independent of the pituitary. *Life Science, 54,* 679–686.

Baum, A., Cohen, L., & Hall, M. (1993). Control and intrusive memories as possible determinants of chronic stress. *Psychosomatic Medicine, 55,* 274–286.

Blanchard, E. B., Kolb, L. C., Gerardi, R. J., Ryan, P., & Pallmeyer, T. P. (1986). Cardiac response to relevant stimuli as an adjunctive tool for diagnosing post-traumatic stress disorder in Vietnam veterans. *Behavior Therapist, 17,* 592–606.

Blanchard, E. B., Kolb, L. C., Pallmeyer, T. P., & Gerardi, R. J. (1982). A psychophysiological study of post-traumatic stress disorder in Vietnam veterans. *Psychiatric Quarterly, 54,* 220–229.

Blanchard, E. B., Kolb, L. C., Prins, A., Gates, S., & McCoy, G. C. (1991). Changes in plasma norepinephrine to combat-related stimuli among Vietnam veterans with posttraumatic stress disorder. *Journal of Nervous and Mental Disease, 179,* 371–373.

Blanchard, R. J., Taukulis, H. K., Rodgers, R. J., Magee, L. K., & Blanchard, D.C. (1993). Yohimbine potentiates active defensive responses to threatening stimuli in Swiss-Webster mice. *Pharmacology, Biochemistry, & Behavior, 44,* 673–681.

Borrell, J., De Kloet, E. R., Versteeg, D. H. G., & Bohus, B. (1983). Inhibitory avoidance deficit following short-term adrenalectomy in the rat: The role of adrenal catecholamines. *Behavioral Neurology and Biology, 39,* 241.

Bourne, P. G., Rose, R. M., & Mason, J. W. (1967). Urinary 17-OCHS levels in combat: Data on seven helicopter ambulance medics in combat. *Archives of General Psychiatry, 17,* 104–110.

Bourne, P. G., Rose, R. M., & Mason, J. W. (1968). 17-OCHS levels in combat: Special Forces "A" Team under threat of attack. *Archives of General Psychiatry, 19,* 135–140.

Bower, G. H. (1981). Mood and memory. *American Psychologist, 36,* 129–148.

Braestrup, C., Nielsen, M., Nielsen, E. B., & Lyon, M (1979). Benzodiazepine receptors in the brain as affected by different experimental stresses: The changes are small and not unidirectional. *Psychopharmacology, 65,* 273–277.

Braestrup, C., Schmiechen, R., Neef, G., Nielsen, M., & Petersen, E. N. (1982). Interaction of convulsive ligands with benzodiazepine receptors. *Science, 216,* 1241–1243.

Bremner, J. D., & Charney, D. S. (1994). The anxiety disorders. In R. E. Rakel (Ed.), *Conn's current therapies* (pp. 1103–1107). Philadelphia: W.B. Saunders Press.

Bremner, J. D., Davis, M., Southwick, S. M., Krystal, J. H., & Charney, D. S. (1993). The neurobiology of posttraumatic stress disorder. In J. M. Oldham, M. G. Riba, & A. Tasman (Eds.), *Reviews of psychiatry,* Vol. 12, (pp.182–204). Washington, DC: American Psychiatric Press.

Bremner, J. D., Innis, R. B., Ng, C. K., Staib, L., Duncan, J., Bronen, R., Zubal, G., Rich, D., Krystal, J. H., Dey, H., Soufer, R., & Charney, D. S. (1997). PET measurement of central metabolic correlates of yohimbine administration in posttraumatic stress disorder. *Archives of General Psychiatry, 54,* 146–156.

Bremner, J. D., Krystal, J. H., Charney, D. S., & Southwick, S. M. (1996). Neural mechanisms in dissociative amnesia for childhood abuse: Relevance to the current controversy surrounding the "False Memory Syndrome." *American Journal of Psychiatry, 153,* FS71–82.

Bremner, J. D., Krystal, J. H., Southwick, S. M., & Charney, D. S. (1995). Functional neuroanatomical correlates of the effects of stress on memory. *Journal of Traumatic Stress, 8,* 527–554.

Bremner, J. D., Krystal, J. H., Southwick, S. M., & Charney, D. S. (1996a). Noradrenergic mechanisms in stress and anxiety: I. Preclinical studies. *Synapse, 23,* 28–38.

Bremner, J. D., Krystal, J. H., Southwick, S. M., & Charney, D. S. (1996b). Noradrenergic mechanisms in stress and anxiety: II. Clinical studies. *Synapse, 23,* 39–51.

Bremner, J. D., Licinio, J., Darnell, A., Krystal, J. H., Nemeroff, C. B., Owens, M., & Charney, D. S. (1997). Elevated CSF corticotropin-releasing factor concentrations in posttraumatic stress disorder. *American Journal of Psychiatry, 154,* 624–629.

Bremner, J. D., Randall, P. R., Capelli, S., Scott, T., McCarthy, G., & Charney, D. S. (1995). Deficits in short-term memory in adult survivors of childhood abuse. *Psychiatry Research, 59,* 97–107.

Bremner, J. D., Randall, P., Scott, T. M., Bronen, R. A., Seibyl, J. P., Southwick, S. M., Delaney, R. C., McCarthy, G., Charney, D. S., & Innis, R. B. (1995). MRI-based measurement of hippocampal volume in combat-related posttraumatic stress disorder. *American Journal of Psychiatry, 152,* 973–981.

Bremner, J. D., Randall, P., Vermetten, E., Staib, L., Bronen, R. A., Capelli, S., Mazure, C. M, McCarthy, G., Innis, R. B., & Charney, D. S. (1997). MRI-based measurement of hippocampal volume in posttraumatic stress disorder related to childhood physical and sexual abuse: A preliminary report. *Biological Psychiatry, 41,* 23–32

Bremner, J. D., Scott, T. M., Delaney, R. C., Southwick, S. M., Mason, J. W., Johnson, D. R, Innis, R. B., McCarthy, G., & Charney, D. S. (1993). Deficits in short-term memory in post-traumatic stress disorder. *American Journal of Psychiatry, 150,* 1015–1019.

Bremner, J. D., Southwick, S. M., Darnell, A., & Charney, D. S. (1996). Chronic PTSD in Vietnam combat veterans: Course of illness and substance abuse. *American Journal of Psychiatry, 153,* 369–375.

Bremner, J. D., Southwick, S. M., Johnson, D. R., Yehuda, R., & Charney, D. S. (1993). Childhood physical abuse in combat-related posttraumatic stress disorder. *American Journal of Psychiatry, 150,* 235–239.

Bremner, J. D., Steinberg, M., Southwick, S. M., Johnson, D. R., & Charney, D. S. (1993). Use of the Structured Clinical Interview for DSMIV-Dissociative Disorders for systematic assessment of dissociative symptoms in posttraumatic stress disorder. *American Journal of Psychiatry, 150,* 1011–1014.

Brioni, J. D., Nagahara, A. H., & McGaugh, J. L. (1989). Involvement of the amygdala GABAergic system in the modulation of memory storage. *Brain Research, 487,* 105–112.

Britton, D. R., Koob, G., & Vale, W. (1982). Intraventricular corticotropin-releasing factor enhances behavioral effects of novelty. *Life Science, 31,* 363–367.

Buchsbaum, M. S., Muscettola, G., & Goodwin, F. K. (1981). Urinary MHPG, stress response, personality factors and somatosensory evoked potentials in normal subjects and patients with major affective disorders. *Neuropsychobiology, 7,* 212.

Butler, R. W., Braff, D. L., Rausch, J. L., Jenkins, M. A., Sprock, J., & Geyer, M. A. (1990). Physiological evidence of exaggerated startle response in a subgroup of Vietnam veterans with combat-related PTSD. *American Journal of Psychiatry, 147,* 1308–1312.

Cahill, L., Prins, B., Weber, M., & McGaugh, J. L. (1994). Alpha-adrenergic activation and memory for emotional events. *Nature, 371,* 702–703.

Cancela, L. M., Volosin, M., & Molina, V. A. (1988). Chronic stress attenuation of alpha-2 adrenoceptor reactivity is reversed by naltrexone. *Pharmacology, Biochemistry, and Behavior, 31,* 33–35.

Cannon, W. B. (1927). The James-Lange theory of emotions: A critical examination and an alternative theory. *American Journal of Psychology, 39,* 106–124.

Cassens, G., Roffman, M., Kuruc, A., & Schildkraut, J. J. (1980). Alterations in brain norepinephrine metabolism induced by environmental stimuli previously paired with inescapable shock. *Science, 209,* 1138–1140.

Cassiday, K. L., McNally, R. J., & Zeitlin, S. B. (1992). Cognitive processing of trauma cues in rape victims with posttraumatic stress disorder. *Cognitive Therapy and Research, 16,* 283–295.

Castellano, C. (1975). Effects of morphine and heroin on discrimination learning and consolidation in mice. *Psychopharmacology, 42,* 235–242.

Cedarbaum, J. M., & Aghajanian, G. K. (1977). Catecholamine receptors on locus coeruleus neurons: Pharmacological characterization. *European Journal of Pharmacology, 44,* 375–385.

Cedarbaum, J. M., & Aghajanian, G. K. (1978). Afferent projections to the rat locus coeruleus as determined by a retrograde tracing technique. *Journal of Comparative Neurology, 178,* 1–16.

Chapman, W. P., Schroeder, H. R., Guyer, G., Brazier, M. A. B., Fager, C., Poppen, J. L., Solomon, H. C., & Yakovlev, P. I. (1954). Physiological evidence concerning the importance of the amygdaloid nuclear region in the integration of circulating functions and emotion in man. *Science, 129,* 949–950.

Charney, D. S., Deutch, A. Y., Krystal, J. H., Southwick, S. M., & Davis, M. (1993). Psychobiologic mechanisms of posttraumatic stress disorder. *Archives of General Psychiatry, 50,* 294–299.

Cole, B. J., & Robbins, T. W. (1992). Forebrain norepinephrine: Role in controlled information processing in the rat. *Neuropsychopharmacology, 7,* 129–141.

Coplan, J. D., Andrews, M. W., Rosenblum, L. A., Owens, M. J., Friedman, S., Gorman, J. M., & Nemeroff, C. B. (1996). Persistent elevations of cerebrospinal fluid concentrations of corticotropin-releasing factor in adult nonhuman primates exposed to early-life stressors: Implications for the pathophysiology of mood and anxiety disorders. *Proceedings of the National Academy of Sciences, 93,* 1619–1623.

Damasio, H., Grabowski, T., Frank, R., Galaburda, A. M., & Damasio, A. R. (1994). The return of Phineas Gage: Clues about the brain from the skull of a famous patient. *Science, 264,* 1102–1105.

Davidson, J., Lipper, S., Kilts, C. D., Mahorney, S., & Hammett, E. (1985). Platelet MAO activity in posttraumatic stress disorder. *American Journal of Psychiatry, 142,* 1341–1343.

Davis, M. (1992). The role of the amygdala in fear and anxiety. *Annual Reviews of Neuroscience, 15,* 353–375.

DeBellis, D., Lefter, L., Trickett, P. K., & Putnam, F. W. (1994). Urinary catecholamine excretion in sexually abused girls. *Journal of the American Academy of Child and Adolescent Psychiatry, 33,* 320–327.

Decker, M. W., Gill, T. M., & McGaugh, J. L. (1990). Concurrent muscarinic and beta-adrenergic blockade in rats impairs place-learning in a water maze and retention of inhibitory avoidance. *Brain Research, 513,* 81–85.

Decker, M. W., & McGaugh, J. L. (1989). Effects of concurrent manipulations of cholinergic and noradrenergic function on learning and retention in mice. *Brain Research, 477,* 29–37.

Deutch, A. Y., Clark, W. A., & Roth, R. H. (1990). Prefrontal cortical dopamine depletion enhances the responsiveness of mesolimbic dopamine neurons to stress. *Brain Research, 521,* 311–315.

Deutch, A. Y., Tam, S. Y., & Roth, R. H. (1985). Footshock and conditioned stress increase 3,4-dihydroxyphenylacetic acid (DOPAC) in the ventral tegmental area but not substantia nigra. *Brain Research, 333,* 143–146.

De Wied, D., & Croiset, G. (1991). Stress modulation of learning and memory processes. *Methods and Achievements in Experimental Pathology, 15,* 167–199.

De Wied, D., & Jolles, J. (1982). Neuropeptides derived from pro-opiocortin: Behavioral, physiological and neurochemical effects. *Physiological Reviews, 62,* 976.

Dimsdale, J., & Moss, J. (1980). Plasma catecholamines in stress and exercise. *Journal of the American Medical Association, 243,* 340–342.

Dinan, T. G., Barry, S., Yatham, L. N., Mobayed, M., & Brown, I. (1990). A pilot study of a neuroendocrine test battery in posttraumatic stress disorder. *Biological Psychiatry, 28,* 665–672.

Dodds, D., & Wilson, W. P. (1960). Observations on persistence of war neurosis. *Diseases of the Nervous System, 21,* 40–46.

Drago, F., Grassi, M., Valerio, C., Coppi, G., Lauria, N., Nicotra, G. C., & Raffacle, R. (1991). Behavioral changes induced by the thyrotropin-releasing hormone analogue, RGH 2202. *Peptides, 12,* 1309–1313.

Drago, F., Pulvirenti, L., Spadaro, F., & Pennisi, G. (1990). Effects of TRH and prolactin in the behavioral despair (swim) model of depression in rats. *Psychoneuroendocrinology, 15,* 349–356.

Drugan, R. C., Basile, A. C., Crawley, J. N., Paul, S. M., & Skolnick, P. (1986). Inescapable shock reduces [3H]Ro 5–4864 binding to peripheral type benzodiazepine receptors in the rat. *Pharmacology, Biochemistry, and Behavior, 24,* 1673–1677.

Drugan, R. C., Crawley, J. N., Paul, S. M., & Skolnick, P. (1987). Buspirone attenuates learned helplessness behavior in rats. *Drug Development and Research, 10,* 63–67.

Drugan, R. C., Maier, S. F., Skolnick, P., Paul, S. M., & Crawley, J. N. (1985). An anxiogenic benzodiazepine receptor ligand induces learned helplessness. *European Journal of Pharmacology, 113,* 453–457.

Drugan, R. C., Morrow, A. L., Weizman, R., Weizman, A., Deutsch, S. I., Crawley, J. N., & Paul, S. M. (1989). Stress-induced behavioral depression in the rat is associated with a decrease in GABA receptor-mediated chloride ion flux and brain benzodiazepine receptor occupancy. *Brain Research, 487,* 45–51.

Drugan, R. C., Ryan, S. M., Minor, T. R., & Maier, S. F. (1984). Librium prevents the analgesia and shuttlebox escape deficit typically observed following inescapable shock. *Pharmacology, Biochemistry, and Behavior, 21,* 749–754.

Dunn, A. J., & Berridge, C. W. (1990). Physiological and behavioral responses to corticotropin-releasing factor administration: Is CRF a mediator of anxiety or stress responses? *Brain Research Reviews, 15,* 71–100.

Ennis, M., & Aston-Jones, G. (1988). Activation of locus coeruleus from nucleus paragigantocellularis: A new excitatory amino acid pathway in the brain. *Journal of Neuroscience, 8,* 3644–3657.

Fenz, W. D., & Epstein, S. (1967). Gradients of physiological arousal of experienced and novice parachutists as a function of an approaching jump. *Psychosomatic Medicine, 29,* 33–51.

Fenz, W. D., & Jones, G. B. (1972). Individual differences in physiological arousal and performance in sport parachutists. Psychosomatic *Medicine, 34,* 1–18.

Fichtner, C. G., Arora, R. C., O'Connor, F. L., & Crayton, J. W. (1994). Platelet paroxetine binding and fluoxetine pharmacotherapy in posttraumatic stress disorder: Preliminary observations on a possible predictor of clinical treatment response. *Life Sciences, 54,* 39–44.

Fichtner, C. G., O'Connor, F. L., Yeoh, H. C., Arora, R. C., & Crayton, J. W. (1995). Hypodensity of platelet serotonin uptake sites in posttraumatic stress disorder: Associated clinical features. *Life Sciences, 57,* 37–44.

Finlay, J. M., Zigmond, M. J., & Abercrombie, E. D (1994). Increased dopamine and norepinephrine release in medial prefrontal cortex induced by acute and chronic stress: Effects of diazepam. *Brain Research,* 619–627.

Foa, E. B., Feske, U., Murdock, T. B., Kozak, M. J., & McCarthy, P. R. (1991). Processing of threat related information in rape victims. *Journal of Abnormal Psychology, 100,* 156–162.

Foote, S. L., Aston-Jones, G., & Bloom, F. E. (1980). Impulse activity of locus coeruleus neurons in awake rats is a function of sensory stimulation and arousal. *Proceedings of the National Academy of Science USA, 77,* 3033–3037.

Foote, S. L., Bloom, F. E., & Aston-Jones, G. (1983). Nucleus locus coeruleus: New evidence of anatomical and physiological specificity. *Physiology Reviews, 63,* 844–914.

Fornazzari, L., Farcnik, K., Smith, I., Heasman, G. A., & Ichise, M. (1992). Violent visual hallucinations in frontal lobe dysfunction: Clinical manifestations of deep orbitofrontal foci. *Journal of Neuropsychiatry and Clinical Neuroscience, 4,* 42–44.

Fride, E., Dan, Y., Feldon, J., Halevy, G., & Weinstock, M. (1986). Effects of prenatal stress on vulnerability to stress in prepubertal and adult rats. *Physiology and Behavior, 37,* 681–687.

Friedman, M. J. (1988). Toward rational pharmacotherapy for posttraumatic stress disorder: An interim report. *American Journal of Psychiatry, 145,* 281–285.

Friedman, M. J. (1991). Biological approaches to the diagnosis and treatment of posttraumatic stress disorder. *Journal of Traumatic Stress, 4,* 67–91.

Gaffori, O., & De Wied, D. (1986). Time-related memory effects of vasopressin analogues in rats. *Pharmacology, Biochemistry and Behavior, 25,* 1125.

Glavin, G., Tanaka, M., Tsuda, A., Kohno, Y., Hoaki, Y., & Nagasaki, N. (1983). Regional rat brain noradrenaline turnover in response to restraint stress. *Pharmacology, Biochemistry and Behavior, 19,* 287–290.

Gloor, P., Olivier, A., Quesney, L. F., Andermann, R., & Horowitz, S. (1982). The role of the limbic system in experiential phenomena of temporal lobe epilepsy. *Annals of Neurology, 12,* 129–144.

Gold, P. E., & van Buskirk, R. (1975). Facilitation of time-dependent memory processes with posttrial epinephrine injections. *Behavioral Biology, 13,* 145–153.

Goldberg, M., & Robertson, D. (1983). Yohimbine: A pharmacological probe for study of the alpha-2-adrenoreceptor. *Pharmacology Reviews, 35,* 143–180.

Goldensohn, E. (1992). Structural lesions of the frontal lobe: Manifestations, classification, and prognosis. In P. Chauvel, A. V. Delgado-Escueta et al., (Eds), *Advances in Neurology,* New York: Raven Press.

Goldman-Rakic, P. S. (1988). Topography of cognition: Parallel distributed networks in primate association cortex. *Annual Reviews of Neuroscience, 11,* 137–156.

Goodman & Gilman (Eds.). (1985). *The pharmacological basis of therapeutics,* 7th ed. New York: MacMillan.

Grant, S. J., Huang, Y. H., & Redmond, D. E. (1980). Benzodiazepines attenuate single unit activity in the locus coeruleus. *Life Sciences, 27,* 2231.

Grant, S. J., & Redmond, D. E. (1984). Neuronal activity of the locus coeruleus in awake Macaca arctoides. *Experimental Neurology, 84,* 701–708.

Grasby, P. M., Frith, C. D., Friston, K. J., Frackowiak, R. S. J., & Dolan, R. J. (1993). Activation of the human hippocampal formation during auditory-verbal long-term memory function. *Neuroscience Letters, 163,* 185–188.

Gray, J. A. (1982). *The neuropsychology of anxiety.* New York: Oxford Univ. Press.

Grillon, C., Ameli, R. Woods, S. W., Merikangas, K. & Davis, M. (1991). Fear-potentiated startle in humans: Effects of anticipatory anxiety on the acoustic blink reflex. *Psychophysiology, 28,* 588–595.

Groscolas, R., & LeLoup (1989). The effect of severe starvation and captivity stress on plasma thyroxine and triiodothyronine concentrations in an Antarctic bird (Emperor Penguin). *General Comparative Endocrinology, 73,* 108–117.

Grossman, A. (1988). Opioids and stress in man. *Journal of Endocrinology, 119,* 377–381.

Guidotti, A., Baraldi, M., Leon, A., & Costa, E. (1990). Benzodiazepines: A tool to explore the biochemical and neuro-physiological basis of anxiety. *Federation Proceedings, 39,* 1039–1042.

Gunne, L. M., & Reis, D. J. (1963). Changes in brain catecholamines associated with electrical stimulation of amygdaloid nucleus. *Life Sciences, 11,* 804–809.

Gurvits, T. G., Lasko, N. B., Schacter, S. C., Kuhne, A. A., Orr, S. P., & Pitman, R. K. (1993). Neurological status of Vietnam veterans with chronic posttraumatic stress disorder. *Journal of Neuropsychiatry and Clinical Neuroscience, 5,* 183–188.

Halgren, E., Walter, R. D., Cherlow, D. G., & Crandall, P. H. (1978). Mental phenomena evoked by electrical stimulation of the human hippocampal formation and amygdala. *Brain, 101,* 83–117.

Hamner, M. B., Diamond, B. I., & Hitri, A. (1994). Plasma norepinephrine and MHPG responses to exercise stress in PTSD. In M. M. Murberg (Ed.), *Catecholamine function in posttraumatic stress disorder: Emerging concepts.* (pp. 221–232). Washington DC: American Psychiatric Press.

Hamner, M. B., & Hitri, A. (1992). Plasma beta-endorphin levels in posttraumatic stress disorder: A preliminary report on response to exercise-induced stress. *Journal of Neuropsychiatry, 4,* 59–63.

Havoundjian, H., Paul, S. M., & Skolnick, P. (1986). Rapid, stress-induced modification of the benzodiazepine receptor-coupled chloride ionophore. *Brain Research, 375,* 401–406.

Heal, D. J., & Marsden, C. A. (1990). *The pharmacology of noradrenaline in the central nervous system.* Oxford: Oxford Medical Publications.

Helmstetter, F. J., & Fanselow, M. S. (1987). Effects of naltrexone on learning and performance of conditioned fear-induce freezing and opioid analgesia. *Physiology and Behavior, 39,* 501–505.

Hemingway, R. B., & Reigle, T. G. (1987). The involvement of endogenous opiate systems in learned helplessness and stress-induced analgesia. *Psychopharmacology, 93,* 353–357.

Hilton, S. M., & Zbrozyna, A. W. (1963). Amygdaloid region for defense reactions and it efferent pathway to the brain stem. *Journal of Physiology, 165,* 160–173.

Hirsch, J. D., Garrett, K. M., & Beer, B. (1985). Heterogeneity of benzodiazepine binding sites: A review of recent research. *Pharmacology, Biochemistry and Behavior, 23,* 681–685.

Hitchcock, J. M., & Davis, M. (1986). Lesions of the amygdala, but not of the cerebellum or red nucleus, block conditioned fear as measured with the potentiated startle paradigm. *Behavioral Neuroscience, 100,* 11–22.

Hitchcock, J. M., & Davis, M. (1991). Efferent pathway of the amygdala involved in conditioned fear as measured with the fear-potentiated startle paradigm. *Behavioral Neuroscience, 105,* 826–842.

Hitchcock, J. M., Sananes, C. B., & Davis, M. (1989). Sensitization of the startle reflex by footshock: Blockade by lesions of the central nucleus of the amygdala or its efferent pathway to the brainstem. *Behavioral Neuroscience, 103,* 509–518.

Holets, V. R. (1990). The anatomy and function of noradrenaline in the mammalian brain. In D. J. Heal & C. A. Marsden (Eds.), *The Pharmacology of Noradrenaline in the Central Nervous System.* (pp. 1–27). Oxford: Oxford University Press.

Howard, J. M., Olney, J. M., Frawley, J. P., Peterson, R. E., Smith, L. H., Davis, J. H., Guerra, S., & Dibrell, W. H. (1955). Studies of adrenal function in combat and wounded soldiers. *Annals of Surgery, 141,* 314–320.

Imperato, A., Puglisi-Allegra, S., Casolini, P., & Angelucci, L. (1991). Changes in brain dopamine and acetylcholine release during and following stress are independent of the pituitary-adrenocortical axis. *Brain Research, 538,* 111–117.

Inoue, T., Tsuchiya, K., & Koyama, T. (1994). Regional changes in dopamine and serotonin activation with various intensity of physical and psychological stress in the rat brain. *Pharmacology, Biochemistry, and Behavior, 49,* 911–920.

Irwin, J., Ahluwalia, P., & Anisman, H. (1986). Sensitization of norepinephrine activity following acute and chronic footshock. *Brain Research, 379,* 98–103.

Iwata, J., LeDoux, J. E., Meeley, M. P., Arneric, S., & Reis, D. J. (1986). Intrinsic neurons in the amygdaloid field projected to by the medial geniculate body mediate emotional responses conditioned to acoustic stimuli. *Brain Research, 383,* 195–214.

Kalivas, P. W., & Abhold, R. (1987). Enkephalin release into the ventral tegmental area in response to stress: Modulation of mesocortical dopamine. *Brain Research, 414,* 339–348.

Kalivas, P. W., & Duffy, P. (1989). Similar effects of daily cocaine and stress on mesocorticolimbic dopamine neurotransmission in the rat. *Biological Psychiatry, 25,* 913–928.

Kaloupek, D., & Bremner, J. D. (1996). Psychophysiology research methods in posttraumatic stress disorder. In E. Carlson (Ed.), *Trauma research methodology.* (pp. 82–104). Sidran Press.

Kardiner, A. (1941). *The traumatic neuroses of war,* Psychosomatic Monograph II-III. Washington DC: National Research Council.

Keane, T. M., Wolfe, J., & Taylor, K. L. (1987). Post-traumatic stress disorder: Evidence for diagnostic validity and method for psychological assessment. *Journal of Clinical Psychology, 43,* 32–43.

Keefe, K. A., Stricker, E. M., Zigmond, M. J., & Abercrombie, E. D. (1990). Environmental stress increases extracellular dopamine in striatum of 6-hydroxydopamine-treated rats: In vivo microdialysis studies. *Brain Research, 527,* 350–355.

Kim, J. J., & Fanselow, M. S. (1992). Modality-specific retrograde amnesia of fear. *Science, 256,* 675–677.

Kinzie, J. D., & Leung, P. K. (1989). Clonidine in Cambodian patients with posttraumatic stress disorder. *Journal of Nervous and Mental Diseases, 177,* 546–550.

Kluver, H., & Bucy, P. C. (1937). "Psychic blindness" and other symptoms following bilateral temporal lobectomy in rhesus monkeys. *American Journal of Physiology, 119,* 352–353.

Kluver, H., & Bucy, P. C. (1939). Preliminary analysis of functions of the temporal lobes in monkeys. *Archives of Neurology and Psychiatry, 42,* 979–1000.

Kohn, Y., Newman, M. E., Lerer, B., Orr, S. P., & Pitman, R. K. (1995). Absence of reduced platelet adenylate cyclase activity in Vietnam veterans with PTSD. *Biological Psychiatry, 37,* 205–208.

Kolb, L. C. (1984). The post-traumatic stress disorder of combat: A subgroup with a conditioned emotional response. *Military Medicine, 149,* 237–243.

Korf, J., Aghajanian, G. K., & Roth, R. H. (1973). Increased turnover of norepinephrine in the rat cerebral cortex during stress: Role of the locus coeruleus. *Neuropharmacology, 12,* 933–938.

Korf, J., Bunney, B. S., & Aghajanian, G. K. (1974). Noradrenergic neurons: Morphine inhibition of spontaneous activity. *European Journal of Pharmacology, 25,* 165–169.

Kosten, T. R., Mason, J. W., Ostroff, R. B., & Harkness, L. (1987). Sustained urinary norepinephrine and epinephrine elevation in posttraumatic stress disorder. *Psychoneuroendocrinology, 12,* 13–20.

Kosten, T. R., Wahby, V., & Giller, E. (1990). The dexamethasone suppression test and TRH stimulation test in post-traumatic stress disorder. *Biological Psychiatry, 28,* 657–664.

Krystal, J. H., Bennett, A., Bremner, J. D., Southwick, S. M., & Charney, D. S. (1995). Toward a cognitive neuroscience of dissociation and altered memory functions in posttraumatic stress disorder. In M. J. Friedman, D. S. Charney, A. Y. Deutch, (Eds.), *Neurobiological and clinical consequences of stress: From normal adaptation to PTSD.* (pp. 239–269). New York: Raven Press.

Krystal, J. H., Karper, L. P., Seibyl, J. P., Freeman, G. K., Delaney, R., Bremner, J. D., Heninger, G. R., Bowers, M. B., Jr., & Charney, D. S. (1994). Subanesthetic effects of the noncompetitive NMDA antagonist, ketamine, in humans. *Archives of General Psychiatry, 51,* 199–214.

Kudler, H., Davidson, J., Meador, K., Lipper, S., & Ely, T. (1987). The DST and posttraumatic stress disorder. *American Journal of Psychiatry, 144,* 1068–1071.

Kulka, R. A., Schlenger, W. E., Fairbank, J. A., Hough, R. L., Jordan, B. K., Marmar, C. R., & Weiss, D. S. (1990). *Trauma and the Vietnam war generation. Report of findings from the National Vietnam Veterans Readjustment Study.* New York: Brunner/Mazel.

LaBar, K. S., LeDoux, J. E., Spencer, D. D., & Phelps, E. A. (1995). Impaired fear conditioning following unilateral temporal lobectomy in humans. *Journal of Neuroscience, 15,* 6846–6855.

Lader, M. (1974). The peripheral and central role of the catecholamines in the mechanisms of anxiety. *International Pharmacopsychiatry, 9,* 125–137.

Langer, P., Vigas, M., Kvetnansky, R., Foldes, O., & Culman, J. (1983). Immediate increase of thyroid hormone release during acute stress in rats: Effect of biogenic amines rather than that of TSH? *Acta Endocrinologica, 104,* 443–449.

LeDoux, J. E. (1993). Emotional memory systems in the brain. *Behavioral and Brain Research, 58,* 69–79.

LeFur, G., Guilloux, F., Mitrani, N., Mizoule, J., & Uzan, A. (1979). Relationship between plasma corticosteroids and benzodiazepines in stress. *Journal of Pharmacology and Experimental Therapeutics, 211,* 305–308.

Lemieux, A. M., & Coe, C. L. (1995), Abuse-related posttraumatic stress disorder: Evidence for chronic neuroendocrine activation in women. *Psychosomatic Medicine, 57,* 105–115.

Lerer, B., Bleich, A., Bennett, E. R., Ebstein, R. P., & Balkin, J. (1990). Platelet adenylate cyclase and phospholipase C activity in posttraumatic stress disorder. *Biological Psychiatry, 27,* 735–740.

Lerer, B., Ebstein, R. P., Shestatsky, M., Shemesh, Z., Greenberg, D. (1987). Cyclic AMP signal transduction in posttraumatic stress disorder. *American Journal of Psychiatry, 144,* 1324–1327.

Levine, E. S., Litto, W. J., & Jacobs, B. L. (1990). Activity of cat locus coeruleus noradrenergic neurons during the defense reaction. *Brain Research, 531,* 189–195.

Levine, S. (1962). Plasma-free corticosteroid response to electric shock in rats stimulated in infancy. *Science, 135,* 795–596.

Levine, S., Weiner, S. G., & Coe, C. L. (1993). Temporal and social factors influencing behavioral and hormonal responses to separation in mother and infant squirrel monkeys. *Psychoneuroendocrinology, 4,* 297–306.

Liang, K. C., Juler, R. G., & McGaugh, J. L. (1986). Modulating effects of posttraining epinephrine on memory: Involvement of the amygdala noradrenergic system. *Brain Research, 368,* 125–133.

Liang, K. C., McGaugh, J. L., & Yao, H. Y. (1990). Involvement of amygdala pathways in the influence of post-training intra-amygdala norepinephrine and peripheral epinephrine on memory storage. *Brain Research, 508,* 225–233.

Lippa, A. S., Klepner, C. A., Yunger, L., Sano, M. C., Smith, W. V., & Beer, B. (1987). Relationship between benzodiazepine receptors and experimental anxiety in rats. *Pharmacology, Biochemistry and Behavior, 9,* 853–856.

Luine, V., Villages, M., Martinex, C., & McEwen, B. S. (1994). Repeated stress causes reversible impairments of spatial memory performance. *Brain Research, 639,* 167–170.

MacLean, P. D. (1949). Psychosomatic disease and the visceral brain. Recent developments bearing on the Papez Theory of Emotion. *Psychosomatic Medicine, 11,* 338–353.

Madison, D. V. & Nicoll, R. A. (1982). Noradrenaline blocks accommodation of pyramidal cell discharge in the hippocampus. *Nature, 299,* 636–638.

Maier, S. F., Davies, S., Grau, J. W., Jackson, R. L., Morrison, D. H., Moye, T., Madden, J., & Barchas, J. D. (1981). Opiate antagonists and long-term analgesic reaction induced by inescapable shock in rats. *Journal of Comparative Physiology and Psychology, 94,* 1172–1183.

Malloy, P. F., Fairbank, J. A., & Keane, T. M. (1983). Validation of a multimethod assessment of posttraumatic stress disorders in Vietnam veterans. *Journal of Consulting and Clinical Psychology, 51,* 488–494.

Mason, J. W., Giller, E. L., Kosten, T. R., & Harkness, L. (1988). Elevation of urinary norepinephrine/cortisol ratio in posttraumatic stress disorder. *Journal of Nervous and Mental Disease, 176,* 498–502.

Mason, J. W., Giller, E. L., Kosten, T. R., Ostroff, R. B., & Podd, L. (1986). Urinary free cortisol levels in post-traumatic stress disorder patients. *Journal of Nervous and Mental Disease, 174,* 145–149.

Mason, J. W., Mougey, E. H., Brady, J. V., & Tolliver, G. A. (1968). Thyroid (plasma butanol-extractable io-dine) responses to 72-hr. avoidance sessions in the monkey. *Psychosomatic Medicine, 30,* 682–696.

Mason, J., Southwick, S., Yehuda, R., Wang, S., Riney, S., Bremner, J. D., Johnson, D., Lubin, H., Blake, D., Zhou, G., Guzman, F., & Charney, D. S. (1994). Eleva-tion of serum free triiodothyronine, total triiodothyro-nine, thyroxine-binding globulin, and total thyroxine levels in combat-related posttraumatic stress disorder. *Archives of General Psychiatry, 51,* 629–641.

McCarthy, G. (1995). Functional neuroimaging of mem-ory. *The Neuroscientist, 1,* 155–163.

McEwen, B. S., Angulo, J., Cameron, H., Chao, H. M., Daniels, D., Gannon, M. N., Gould, E., Mendelson, S., Sakai, R., Spencer, R., & Woolley, C. (1992). Par-adoxical effects of adrenal steroids on the brain: Pro-tection versus degeneration. *Biological Psychiatry, 31,* 177–199.

McFall, M. E., Murburg, M. M., Ko, G. N., & Veith, R. C. (1990). Autonomic responses to stress in Vietnam combat veterans with posttraumatic stress disorder. *Biological Psychiatry, 27,* 1165–1175.

McFall, M. E., Veith, R. C., & Murburg, M. M. (1992). Basal sympathoadrenal function in posttraumatic stress disorder. *Biological Psychiatry, 31,* 1050–1056.

McFarlane, A. C., Weber, D. L., & Clark, C. R. (1993). Abnormal stimulus processing in posttraumatic stress disorder. *Biological Psychiatry, 34,* 311–320.

McGaugh, J. L. (1989). Involvement of hormonal and neu-romodulatory systems in the regulation of memory storage: Endogenous modulation of memory storage. *Annual Reviews of Neuroscience, 12,* 255–287.

McGaugh, J. L. (1990). Significance and remembrance: The role of neuromodulatory systems. *Psychological Science, 1,* 15–25.

McGaugh, J. L., Castellano, C., & Brioni, J. (1990). Picro-toxin enhances latent extinction of conditioned fear. *Behavioral Neuroscience, 104,* 264–267.

McKittrick, C. R., Blanchard, D.C., Blanchard, R. J., McE-wen, B. S., & Sakai, R. R. (1995). Serotonin receptor binding in a colony model of chronic social stress. *Bi-ological Psychiatry,* 383–393.

McNally, R. J., & Amir, N. (1996). Perceptual implicit mem-ory for trauma-related information in posttraumatic stress disorder. *Cognition and Emotion, 10,* 551–556.

McNally, R. J., Amir, N., & Lipke, H. J. (1996). Subliminal processing of threat cues in posttraumatic stress disor-der? *Journal of Anxiety Disorders, 10,* 115–128.

McNally, R. J., English, G. E., & Lipke, H. J. (1993). As-sessment of intrusive cognition in PTSD: Use of the modified Stroop paradigm. *Journal of Traumatic Stress, 6,* 33–41.

McNally, R. J., Kaspi, S. P., Riemann, B. C., & Zeitlin, S. B. (1990). Selective processing of threat cues in posttraumatic stress disorder. *Journal of Abnormal Psychology, 99,* 398–402.

McNally, R. J., Lasko, N. B., Macklin, M. L., & Pitman, R. K. (1995). Autobiographical memory disturbance in combat-related posttraumatic stress disorder. *Be-havioral Research and Therapy, 33,* 619–630.

McNally, R. J., Litz, B. T., Prassas, A., Shin, L. M., & Weathers, F. W. (1994). Emotional priming of auto-biographical memory in posttraumatic stress disorder. *Cognition and Emotion, 8,* 351–367.

McNally, R. J., & Shin, L. M. (1995). Association of intel-ligence with severity of posttraumatic stress disorder symptoms in Vietnam combat veterans. *American Journal of Psychiatry, 152,* 936–938.

Meaney, M. J., Aitken, D. H., Sharma, S., & Sarrieau, A. (1989). Neonatal handling alters adrenocortical negative feedback sensitivity and hippocampal type II glucocor-ticoid receptor binding in the rat. *Neuroendocrinology, 50,* 597–604.

Meaney, M. J., Aitken, D. H., van Berkel, C., Bhatnagar, S., & Sapolsky, R. M. (1988). Effect of neonatal han-dling on age-related impairments associated with the hippocampus. *Science, 239,* 766–768.

Medina, J. H., Novas, M. L., & De Robertis, E. (1983). Changes in benzodiazepine receptors by acute stress: Different effect of chronic diazepam or RO 15–1788 treatment. *European Journal of Pharmacology, 96,* 181–185.

Medina, J. H., Novas, M. L., Wolfman, C. N. V., De Stein, M. L., & De Robertis, E. (1983). Benzodiazepine re-ceptors in rat cerebral cortex and hippocampus un-dergo rapid and reversible changes after acute stress. *Neuroscience, 9,* 331–335.

Melia, K. R., Rasmussen, K., Terwilliger, R. Z., Haycock, J. W., Nestler, E. J., & Duman, R. S. (1992). Coordi-nate regulation of the cyclic AMP system with firing rate and expression of tyrosine hydroxylase in the rat locus coeruleus: Effects of chronic stress and drug treatments. *Journal of Neurochemistry, 58,* 3–502.

Mellman, T. A., Kulick-Bell, R., Ashlock, L. E., & No-lan, B. (1995). Sleep events among veterans with combat-related posttraumatic stress disorder. *American Journal of Psychiatry, 152,* 110–115.

Mellman, T. A., & Kumar, A. M. (1994). Platelet serotonin measures in posttraumatic stress disorder. *Psychiatry Research, 53,* 99–101.

Mendelson, S. D., & McEwen, B. S. (1991). Autoradiographic analyses of the effects of restraint-induced stress on 5HT1A, 5HT1C and 5HT2 receptors in the dorsal hippocampus of male and female rats. *Neuroendocrinology, 54,* 454–461.

Miller, L. G., Thompson, M. L., Greenblatt, D. J., Deutsch, S. I., Shader, R. I., & Paul, S. M. (1987). Rapid increase in brain benzodiazepine receptor binding following defeat stress in mice. *Brain Research, 414,* 395–400.

Miller, R. G. (1968). Secretion of 17-hydroxycorticosteroids (17-OHCS) in military aviators as an index of response to stress: A review. *Aerospace Medicine, 39,* 498–501.

Miller, R. G., Rubin, R. T., Clark, B. R., Crawford, W. R., & Arthur, R. J. (1970). The stress of aircraft carrier landings: I. Corticosteroid responses in naval aviators. *Psychosomatic Medicine, 32,* 581–588.

Miserendino, M. J. D., Sananes, C. B., Melia, K. R., & Davis, M. (1990). Blocking of acquisition but not expression of conditioned fear-potentiated startle by NMDA antagonists in the amygdala. *Nature, 345,* 716–718.

Mishkin, M. (1978). Memory in monkeys severely impaired by combined but not separate removal of amygdala and hippocampus. *Nature, 173,* 297–298.

Moghaddam, B. (1993). Stress preferentially enhances extraneuronal levels of excitatory amino acids in the prefrontal cortex: Comparison to hippocampus and basal ganglia. *Journal of Neurochemistry, 60,* 1650–1657.

Mohler, H., & Okada, T. (1977). Benzodiazepine receptors: Demonstration in the central nervous system. *Science, 198,* 849–851.

Morgan, C. A., Grillon, C., Southwick, S. M., Davis, M., & Charney, D. S. (1995). Fear-potentiated startle in posttraumatic stress disorder. *Biological Psychiatry, 38,* 378–385.

Morgan, C. A., Grillon, C., Southwick, S. M., Nagy, L. M., Davis, M., Krystal, J. H., & Charney, D. S. (1995). Yohimbine facilitated acoustic startle in combat veterans with posttraumatic stress disorder. *Psychopharmacology, 117,* 466–471.

Morgan, M. A., & LeDoux, J. E. (1994). Medial orbital lesions increase resistance to extinction but do not affect acquisition of fear conditioning. *Proceedings of the Society for Neuroscience, 2,* 1006.

Murberg, M. M. (Ed.). (1994). *Catecholamine function in posttraumatic stress disorder: Emerging concepts.* Washington DC: American Psychiatric Press.

Murray, E. A., & Mishkin, M. (1986). Visual recognition in monkeys following rhinal cortical ablations combined with either amygdalectomy or hippocampectomy. *Journal of Neuroscience, 6,* 1991–2003.

Newcomer, J. W., Craft, S., Hershey, T., Askins, K., & Bardgett, M. E. (1994). Glucocorticoid-induced impairment in declarative memory performance in adult humans. *Journal of Neuroscience, 14,* 2047–2053.

Ninan, P. T., Insel, T. M., Cohen, R. M., Cook, J. M., Skolnick, P., & Paul, S. M. (1982). Benzodiazepine receptor-mediated experimental "anxiety" in primates. *Science, 218,* 1332–1334.

Nissenbaum, L. K., & Abercrombie, E. D. (1993). Presynaptic alterations associated with enhancement of evoked release and synthesis of norepinephrine in hippocampus of chronically cold-stressed rats. *Brain Research, 608,* 280–287.

Nissenbaum, L. K., Zigmond, M. J., Sved, A. F., & Abercrombie, E. (1991). Prior exposure to chronic stress results in enhanced synthesis and release of hippocampal norepinephrine in response to a novel stressor. *Journal of Neuroscience, 11,* 1478–1484.

Nukina, I., Glavin, G. B., & LaBella, F. S. (1987). Acute cold-restraint stress affects alpha2-adrenoreceptors in specific brain regions of the rat. *Brain Research, 401,* 30–33.

Olivera, A. A. & Fero, D. (1990). Affective disorders, DST, and treatment in PTSD patients: Clinical observations. *Journal of Traumatic Stress, 3,* 407–414.

Ornitz, E. M., & Pynoos, R. S. (1989). Startle modulation in children with posttraumatic stress disorder. *American Journal of Psychiatry, 146,* 866–870.

Orr, S. P., Pitman, R. K., Lasko, N. B., & Herz, L. R. (1993). Psychophysiological assessment of posttraumatic stress disorder imagery in World War II veterans. *Journal of Abnormal Psychology, 102,* 152–159.

Paige, S. R., Reid, G. M., Allen, M. G., & Newton, J. E. O. (1990). Psychophysiological correlates of posttraumatic stress disorder in Vietnam veterans. *Biological Psychiatry, 27,* 419–430.

Papez, J. W. (1937). A proposed mechanism of emotion. *American Medical Association Archives of Neurology and Psychiatry, 38,* 725–743.

Pardo, J. V., Pardo, P. J., Janer, K. W., & Raichle, M. E. (1990). The anterior cingulate cortex mediates processing selection in the Stroop attentional conflict paradigm. *Proceedings of the National Academy of Sciences USA, 87,* 256–259.

Parkinson, J. K., Murray, E. A., & Mishkin, M. (1988). A selective mnemonic role for the hippocampus in monkeys: Memory for the location of objects. *Journal of Neuroscience, 8,* 4159–4167.

Pavcovich, L. A., Cancela, L. M., Volosin, M., Molina, V. A., & Ramirez, O. A. (1990). Chronic stress-induced changes in locus coeruleus neuronal activity. *Brain Research Bulletin, 24,* 293–296.

Perry, B. D. (1994). Neurobiological sequelae of childhood trauma: PTSD in children. In M. M. Murberg (Ed.), *Catecholamine function in posttraumatic stress disorder: Emerging concepts,* (pp. 233–256). Washington, DC: American Psychiatric Press.

Perry, B. D., Giller, E. J., & Southwick, S. M. (1987). Altered platelet alpha-2 adrenergic binding sites in posttraumatic stress disorder (letter). *American Journal of Psychiatry, 144,* 1324–1327.

Perry, B. D., Southwick, S. M., & Giller, E. J. (1991). Adrenergic receptor regulation in posttraumatic stress disorder. In E. J. Giller (Ed.), *Biological assessment and treatment of posttraumatic stress disorder,* (pp. 87–114). Washington DC: American Psychiatric Press.

Petty, F., Kramer, G., & Wilson, L. (1992). Prevention of learned helplessness: in vivo correlation with serotonin. *Pharmacology, Biochemistry and Behavior, 43,* 361–367.

Petty, F., Kramer, G., Wilson, L., & Chae, Y. L. (1993). Learned helplessness and in vivo hippocampal norepinephrine release. *Pharmacology, Biochemistry and Behavior, 46,* 231–235.

Petty, F., & Sherman, A. D. (1981). GABAergic modulation of learned helplessness. *Pharmacology, Biochemistry and Behavior, 15,* 567–570.

Phelps, E. A., LaBar, K. S. & Spencer, D. D. (1998). Emotional memory following unilateral temporal lobectomy. *Brain and Cognition,* (in press).

Phillips, R. G., & LeDoux, J. E. (1992). Differential contribution of amygdala and hippocampus to cued and contextual fear conditioning. *Behavioral Neuroscience, 106,* 274–285.

Pitman, R. K. (1989). Posttraumatic stress disorder, hormones, and memory (editorial). *Biological Psychiatry, 26,* 221–223.

Pitman, R., & Orr, S. (1990). Twenty-four hour urinary cortisol and catecholamine excretion in combat-related posttraumatic stress disorder. *Biological Psychiatry, 27,* 245–247.

Pitman, R., Orr, S., Forgue, D., Altman, B., & deJong, J. (1990). Psychophysiologic responses to combat imagery of Vietnam veterans with posttraumatic stress disorder versus other anxiety disorders. *Journal of Abnormal Psychology, 99,* 49–54.

Pitman, R. K., Orr, S. P., Forgue, D. F., de Jong, J. B., & Claiborn, J. M. (1987). Psychophysiologic assessment of posttraumatic stress disorder imagery in Vietnam combat veterans. *Archives of General Psychiatry, 44,* 970–975.

Pitman, R. K., Orr, S. P., & Lasko, N. B. (1993). Effects of intranasal vasopressin and oxytocin on physiologic responding during personal combat imagery in Vietnam veterans with posttraumatic stress disorder. *Psychiatry Research, 48,* 107–117.

Pitman, R. K., van der Kolk, B. A., Orr, S. P., & Greenberg, M. S. (1990). Naloxone-reversible analgesic response to combat-related stimuli in posttraumatic stress disorder. *Archives of General Psychiatry, 47,* 541–544.

Posner, M. I., Petersen, S. E., Fox, P. T., & Raichle, M. E. (1988). Localization of cognitive operations in the human brain. *Science, 240,* 1627–1631.

Prins, A., Kaloupek, D. G., & Kcane, T. M. (1995). Psychophysiological evidence for autonomic arousal and startle in traumatized adult populations. In M. J. Friedman, D. S. Charney, & A. Y. Deutch (Eds.), *Neurobiological and clinical consequences of stress: From normal adaptation to PTSD.* (pp. 291–314). New York: Raven Press.

Przegalinski, E., Moryl, E., & Papp, M. (1995). The effect of 5HT1A receptor ligands in a chronic mild stress model of depression. *Behavioral Research,* 1305–1310.

Rainey, J. M., Aleem, A., Ortiz, A., Yeragani, V., Pohl, R., & Berchou, R. (1987). A laboratory procedure for the induction of flashbacks. *American Journal of Psychiatry, 144,* 1317–1319.

Randall, P. K., Bremner, J. D., Krystal, J. H., Nagy, L. M., Heninger, G. R., Nicolaou, A. L., & Charney, D. S. (1995). Effects of the benzodiazepine receptor antagonist flumazenil in PTSD. *Biological Psychiatry, 38,* 319–324.

Rasmussen, K., & Jacobs, B. L. (1986). Single unit activity of locus coeruleus neurons in the freely moving cat. II. Conditioning and pharmacological studies. *Brain Research, 371,* 335–344.

Rasmussen, K., Morilak, D. A., & Jacobs, B. L. (1986). Single-unit activity of locus coeruleus neurons in the freely moving cat. I. During naturalistic behaviors and in response to simple and complex stimuli. *Brain Research, 371,* 324.

Rauch, S. L., van der Kolk, B. A., Fisler, R. E., Alpert, N. A., Orr, S. P., Savage, C. R., Fischman, A. J., Jenike, M. A., & Pitman, R. K. (1996). A symptom provocation study of posttraumatic stress disorder using positron emission tomography and script-driven imagery. *Archives of General Psychiatry, 53,* 380–387.

Redmond, D. E., Jr. (1987). Studies of the nucleus locus coeruleus in monkeys and hypotheses for neuropsychopharmacology. In H. Y. Melzer (Ed.), *Psychopharmacology: The Third Generation of Progress.* (pp. 967–975). New York: Raven Press.

Redmond, D., & Huang, Y. (1979). New evidence for a locus coeruleus-norepinephrine connection with anxiety. *Life Sciences, 25,* 2149–2162.

Redmond, D. E. Jr., Huang, Y. H., Snyder, D. R., & Maas, J. W. (1976). Behavioral effects of stimulation of the nucleus locus coeruleus in the stump-tailed monkey (macaca arctoides). *Brain Research, 116,* 502–510.

Robbins, T. W., Everitt, B. J., & Cole, B. J. (1985). Functional hypotheses of the coeruleocortical noradrenergic projection: A review of recent experimentation and theory. *Physiology and Psychology, 13,* 127–150.

Robertson, H. A., Martin, I. L., & Candy, J. M. (1978). Differences in benzodiazepine receptor binding in Maudsley-reactive and nonreactive rats. *European Journal of Pharmacology, 50,* 455–457.

Rosen, J. B., & Davis, M. (1988). Enhancement of acoustic startle by electrical stimulation of the amygdala. *Behavioral Neuroscience, 102,* 195–202.

Rosen, J. B., Hitchcock, J. M., Sananes, C. B., Miserendino, M. J., & Davis, M. (1991). A direct projection from the central nucleus of the amygdala to the acoustic startle pathway: Anterograde and retrograde tracing studies. *Behavioral Neuroscience, 105,* 817–825.

Ross, R. J., Ball, W. A., Cohen, M. E., Silver, S. M., Morrison, A. R., & Dinges, D. F. (1989). Habituation of the startle reflex in posttraumatic stress disorder. *Journal of Neuropsychiatry, 1,* 305–307.

Ross, R. J., Ball, W. A., Dinges, D. F., Kribbs, N. B., Morrison, A. R., Silver, S. M., & Mulvaney, F. D. (1994). Rapid eye movement sleep disturbance in posttraumatic stress disorder. *Biological Psychiatry, 35,* 195–202.

Ross, R. J., Ball, W. A., Sullivan, K. A., & Caroff, S. N. (1989). Sleep disturbance as the hallmark of posttraumatic stress disorder. *American Journal of Psychiatry, 146,* 697–707.

Rossetti, Z. L., Portas, C., Pani, L., Carboni, S., & Gessa, G. L. (1990). Stress increases noradrenaline release in the rat frontal cortex: Prevention by diazepam. *European Journal of Pharmacology, 176,* 229–231.

Roth, R. H., Tam, S. Y., Ida, Y., Yang, J. X., & Deutch, A. Y. (1988). Stress and the mesocorticolimbic dopamine systems. *Annals of the New York Academy of Sciences, 537,* 138–147.

Rubin, R. T., Miller, R. G., & Clark, B. R. (1970). The stress of aircraft carrier landings: II. 3-methoxy-4-hydroxyphenylglycol excretion in naval aviators. *Psychosomatic Medicine, 32,* 589–596.

Rubin, R. T., Rahe, R. H., Arthur, R. J., & Clark, B. R. (1969). Adrenal cortical activity changes during underwater demolition team training. *Psychosomatic Medicine, 31,* 553–564.

Saigh, P. A., Mroueh, M., & Bremner, J. D. (1997). Scholastic impairments among traumatized adolescents. *Behaviour Research and Therapy, 35,* 429–436.

Sapolsky, R. (1986). Glucocorticoid toxicity in the hippocampus: Synergy with an excitotoxin. *Neuroendocrinology, 43,* 440–446.

Sapolsky, R. M., Packan, D. R., & Vale, W. W. (1988). Glucocorticoid toxicity in the hippocampus: In vitro demonstration. *Brain Research, 453,* 367–371.

Sapolsky, R. M., Uno, H., Rebert, C. S., & Finch, C. E. (1990). Hippocampal damage associated with prolonged glucocorticoid exposure in primates. *Journal of Neuroscience, 10,* 2897–2902.

Sara, S. J. (1985). Noradrenergic modulation of selective attention: Its role in memory retrieval. *Annals of the New York Academy of Science, 444,* 178–193.

Schacter, D. L. (1995). Implicit memory: A new frontier for cognitive neuroscience. In M. S. Gazzaniga (Ed.), *The Cognitive Neurosciences.* Cambridge, MA: MIT Press.

Schatzberg, A. F., & Nemeroff, C. B. (Eds.). (1988). *The hypothalamic-pituitary-adrenal axis: Physiology, pathophysiology, and psychiatric implications.* New York: Raven Press.

Selden, N. R. W., Robbins, T. W., & Everitt, B. J. (1990). Enhanced behavioral conditioning to context and impaired behavioral and neuroendocrine responses to conditioned stimuli following ceruleocortical noradrenergic lesions: Support for an attentional hypothesis of central noradrenergic function. *Journal of Neuroscience, 10,* 531–539.

Shalev, A. Y., Orr, S. P., Peri, T., Schreiber, S., & Pitman, R. K. (1992). Physiologic responses to loud tones in Israeli patients with posttraumatic stress disorder. *Archives of General Psychiatry, 49,* 870–874.

Sherman, A. D., & Petty, F. (1982). Additivity of neurochemical changes in learned helplessness and imipramine. *Behavioral Neurology and Biology, 35,* 344–353.

Shirao, I., Tsuda, A., Ida, Y., Tsujimani, S., Satoh, H., Oguchi, M., Tanaka, M., & Inanega, K. (1988). Effect of acute ethanol administration on norepinephrine metabolism in brain regions of stressed and non-stressed rats. *Pharmacology, Biochemistry, and Behavior, 30,* 769–773.

Simson, P. E., & Weiss, J. M. (1988a). Altered activity of the locus coeruleus in an animal model of depression. *Neuropsychopharmacology, 1,* 287–295.

Simson, P. E., & Weiss, J. M. (1988b). Responsiveness of locus coeruleus neurons to excitatory stimulation is uniquely regulated by alpha-2 receptors. *Psychopharmacology Bulletin, 24,* 349–354.

Simson, P. E., & Weiss, J. M. (1989). Blockade of alpha2-adrenergic receptors, but not blockade of gamma-aminobutyric acid, serotonin, or opiate receptors, augments responsiveness of locus coeruleus neurons to excitatory stimulation. *Neuropharmacology, 28,* 651–660.

Simson, P. E., & Weiss, J. M. (1994). Altered electrophysiology of the locus coeruleus following uncontrollable stress: Relationship to anxiety and anxiolytic action. In M. M. Murberg, (Ed.), *Catecholamine function in posttraumatic stress disorder. Emerging concepts.* (pp. 63–86). Washington DC: American Psychiatric Press.

Skerritt, J. H., Trisdikoon, P., & Johnston, G. A. R. (1981). Increased GABA binding in mouse brain following acute swim stress. *Brain Research,* 398–403.

Smith, M. A., Davidson, J., Ritchie, J. C., Kudler, H., Lipper, S., Chappell, P., & Nemeroff, C. B. (1989). The corticotropin-releasing hormone test in patients with posttraumatic stress disorder. *Biological Psychiatry, 26,* 349–355.

Southwick, S. M., Krystal, J. H., Morgan, C. A., Johnson, D., Nagy, L. M., Nicolaou, A., Heninger, G. R., & Charney, D. S. (1993). Abnormal noradrenergic function in posttraumatic stress disorder. *Archives of General Psychiatry, 50,* 266–274.

Squire, L. R., Ojemann, J. G., Miezin, F. M., Petersen, S. E., Videen, T. O., & Raichle, M. E. (1992). Activation of the hippocampus in normal humans: A functional anatomical study of memory. *Proceedings of the National Academy of Science, 89,* 1837–1841.

Squire, L. R., & Zola-Morgan, S. (1991). The medial temporal lobe memory system. *Science, 253,* 1380–1386.

Squires, R. F., & Braestrup, C. (1977). Benzodiazepine receptors in rat brain. *Nature, 266,* 732–734.

Stanton, M. E., Gutierrez, Y. R., & Levine, S. (1988). Maternal deprivation potentiates pituitary-adrenal stress responses in infant rats. *Behavioral Neuroscience, 102,* 692–700.

Stone, E. A. (1987). Central cyclic-AMP-linked noradrenergic receptors: New findings on properties as related to the actions of stress. *Neuroscience and Biobehavioral Reviews, 11,* 391–398.

Stone, E. A., John, S. M., Bing, G., & Zhang, Y. (1992). Studies on the cellular localization of biochemical responses to catecholamines in the brain. *Brain Research Bulletin, 29,* 285–288.

Stone, E. A., Zhang, Y., John, M., & Bing, G. (1991). C-fos response to administration of catecholamines into brain by microdialysis. *Neuroscience Letters, 133,* 33–35.

Stone, E. A., Zhang, Y., John, S., Filer, D., & Bing, G. (1993). Effect of locus coeruleus lesion on c-fos expression in the cerebral cortex caused by yohimbine injection or stress. *Brain Research, 603,* 181–185.

Stuckey, J., Marra, S., Minor, T., & Insel, T. R. (1989). Changes in mu opiate receptors following inescapable shock. *Brain Research, 476,* 167–169.

Sudha, S., & Pradhan, N. (1995). Stress-induced changes in regional monoamine metabolism and behavior in rats. *Physiology and Behavior, 57,* 1061–1066.

Sutker, P. B., Winstead, D. K., Galina, Z. H., & Allain, A. N. (1991). Cognitive deficits and psychopathology among former prisoners of war and combat veterans of the Korean conflict. *American Journal of Psychiatry, 148,* 67–72.

Sweeney, D. R., Maas, J. W., & Heninger, G. R. (1978). State anxiety, physical activity, and urinary 3-methoxy 4-hydroxyphenethylene glucol excretion. *Archives of General Psychiatry, 35,* 1418–1423.

Taggart, P., & Carruthers, M. (1971). Endogenous hyperlipidemia induced by emotional stress of racing driving. *Lancet, 1,* 363–366.

Taggart, P., Carruthers, M., & Sommerville, W. (1973). Electrocardiogram, plasma catecholamines, and lipids, and their modification by oxprenolol when speaking before an audience. *Lancet, 2,* 341–346.

Tanaka, M., Kohno, Y., Nakagawa, R., Ida, Y., Takeda, S., & Nagasaki, N. (1982). Time-related differences in noradrenaline turnover in rat brain regions by stress. *Pharmacology, Biochemistry and Behavior, 16,* 315–319.

Tanaka, M., Kohno, Y., Tsuda, A., Nakagawa, R., Ida, Y., Iimori, K., Hoaki, Y., & Nagasaki, N. (1983). Differential effects of morphine on noradrenaline release in brain regions of stressed and non-stressed rats. *Brain Research, 275,* 105–115.

Tanaka, M., Tsuda, A., Yokoo, H., Yoshida, M., Ida, Y., & Nishimura, H. (1990). Involvement of the brain noradrenaline system in emotional changes caused by stress in rats. *Annals of the New York Academy of Science, 159–174*.

Thygesen, P., Hermann, K., & Willanger, R. (1970). Concentration camp survivors in Denmark: Persecution, disease, disability, compensation. *Danish Medical Bulletin, 17*, 65–108.

Uddo, M., Vasterling, J. T., Brailey, K., & Sutker, P. B. (1993). Memory and attention in posttraumatic stress disorder. *Journal of Psychopathology and Behavioral Assessment, 15*, 43–52.

Uhde, T. W., Boulenger, J.-P., Post, R. M., Siever, L. J., Vittone, B. J., Jimerson, D.C., & Roy-Byrne, P. P. (1984). Fear and anxiety: Relationship to noradrenergic function. *Psychopathology, 17(suppl 3)*, 8–23.

Uhde, T. W., Siever, L. J., Post, R. M., Jimerson, D.C., Boulenger, J.-P., & Buchsbaum, M. S. (1982). The relationship of plasma-free MHPG to anxiety and psychophysical pain in normal volunteers. *Psychopharmacology Bulletin, 18*, 129–132.

Uno, H., Tarara, R., Else, J. G., Suleman, M. A., & Sapolsky, R. M. (1989). Hippocampal damage associated with prolonged and fatal stress in primates. *Journal of Neuroscience, 9*, 1705–1711.

Valentino, R. J., Page, M. E., & Curtis, A. L. (1991). Activation of noradrenergic locus coeruleus neurons by hemodynamic stress is due to local release of corticotropin-releasing factor. *Brain Research, 555*, 25–34.

van der Kolk, B. A., Dreyfuss, D., Michaels, M., Shera, D., Berkowitz, R., Fisher, R., & Saxe, G. (1994). Fluoxetine in posttraumatic stress disorder. *Journal of Clinical Psychiatry, 146*, 517–222.

van der Kolk, B. A., Greenberg, M. S., Orr, S. P., & Pitman, R. K. (1989). Endogenous opiates, stress induced analgesia, and posttraumatic stress disorder. *Psychopharmacology Bulletin, 25*, 417–421.

Van Wimersma Greidanus, T. J. B., Croiset, G., Bakker, B., & Bouman, H. (1979). Amygdaloid lesions block the effect of neuropeptides (vasopressin, ACTH (4–10)) on avoidance behavior. *Brain Research Bulletin, 3*, 227.

Velly, J., Kempf, E., Cardo, B., & Velley, L. (1985). Long-term modulation of learning following locus coeruleus stimulation: Behavioral and neurochemical data. *Physiology and Psychology, 13*, 163–171.

Virgin, C. E., Taryn, P. T. H., Packan, D. R., Tombaugh, G. C., Yang, S. H., Horner, H. C., & Sapolsky, R. M. (1991). Glucocorticoids inhibit glucose transport and glutamate uptake in hippocampal astrocytes: Implications for glucocorticoid neurotoxicity. *Journal of Neurochemistry, 57*, 1422–1428.

von Euler, U.S., & Lundberg, U. (1954). Effect of flying on epinephrine excretion in Air Force personnel. *Journal of Applied Physiology, 6*, 551.

Ward, M. M., Mefford, I. N., & Parker, S. D. (1983). Epinephrine and norepinephrine responses in continuously collected plasma to a series of stressors. *Psychosomatic Medicine, 45*, 471–486.

Watanabe, Y., Sakai, R. R., McEwen, B. S., & Mendelson, S. (1993). Stress and antidepressant effects on hippocampal and cortical 5HT1A and 5HT2 receptors and transport sites for serotonin. *Brain Research, 615*, 87–94.

Weiner, H. (1984). The psychobiology of anxiety and fear. In *Diagnosis and treatment of anxiety disorders*, (pp. 33–62). Washington DC: American Psychiatric Press.

Weiss, J. M., Goodman, P. A., Losito, B. G., Corrigan, S., Charry, J. M., & Bailey, W. (1981). Behavioral depression produced by an uncontrollable stressor: Relationship to norepinephrine, dopamine, and serotonin levels in various regions of rat brain. *Brain Research Reviews, 3*, 167–205.

Weiss, J. M., Simson, P. G., Ambrose, M. J., Webster, A., & Hoffman, L. J. (1985). Neurochemical basis of behavioral depression. *Advances in Behavioral Medicine, 1*, 233–275.

Weiss, J. M., Stone, E. A., & Harrell, N. (1970). Coping behavior and brain norepinephrine levels in rats. *Journal of Comparative Physiology and Psychology, 72*, 153–160.

Weizman, A., Weizman, R., Kook, K. A., Vocci, F., Deutsch, S. I., & Paul, S. M. (1990). Adrenalectomy prevents the stress-induced decrease in in vivo [3H]Ro 15–1788 binding to GABAA benzodiazepine receptors in the mouse. *Brain Research, 519*, 347–350.

Weizman, R., Gur, E., Laor, N., Reiss, A., Yoresh, A., Lerer, B., & Newman, M. E. (1994). Platelet adenylate cyclase activity in Israeli victims of Iraqi Scud missile attacks with posttraumatic stress disorder. *Psychopharmacology*, 509–512.

Weizman, R., Laor, N., Karp, L., Dagan, E., Reiss, A., Dar, D. E., Wolmer, L., & Gavish, M. (1994). Alteration of platelet benzodiazepine receptors by stress of war. *American Journal of Psychiatry, 151*, 766–767.

Weizman, R., Weizman, A., Kook, K. A., Vocci, F., Deutsch, S. I., & Paul, S. M. (1989). Repeated swim stress alters brain benzodiazepine receptors measured in vivo. *Journal of Pharmacology and Experimental Therapeutics, 249,* 701–707.

Wenger, M. A. (1948). Studies of autonomic balance in Army Air Force personnel. *Comparative Psychology Monographs 19, 101,* 1–11.

Willner, P., Lappas, S., Cheeta, S., & Muscat, R. (1994). Reversal of stress-induced anhedonia by the dopamine receptor agonist, pramipexole. *Psychopharmacology,* 454–462.

Wooley, C. S., Gould, E., & McEwen, B. S. (1990). Exposure to excess glucocorticoids alters dendritic morphology of adult hippocampal pyramidal neurons. *Brain Research, 531,* 225–231.

Yehuda, R., Boisoneau, D., Lowy, M. T., & Giller, E. L. (1995). Dose-response changes in plasma cortisol and lymphocyte glucocorticoid receptors following dexamethasone administration in combat veterans with and without posttraumatic stress disorder. *Archives of General Psychiatry, 52,* 583–593.

Yehuda, R., Boisoneau, D., Mason, J. W., & Giller, E. L. (1993). Glucocorticoid receptor number and cortisol excretion in mood, anxiety and psychotic disorders. *Biological Psychiatry, 34,* 18–25.

Yehuda, R., Keefer, R. S. E., Harvey, P. D., Levengood, R. A., Gerber, D. K., Geni, J., & Siever, L. J. (1995). Learning and memory in combat veterans with posttraumatic stress disorder. *American Journal of Psychiatry, 152,* 137–139.

Yehuda, R., Lowy, M. T., Southwick, S. M., Shaffer, S., & Giller, E. L. (1991). Increased number of glucocorticoid receptor number in posttraumatic stress disorder. *American Journal of Psychiatry, 149,* 499–504.

Yehuda, R., Southwick, S. M., Giller, E. L., Ma, X., & Mason, J. W. (1992). Urinary catecholamine excretion and severity of PTSD symptoms in Vietnam combat veterans. *Journal of Nervous and Mental Disease, 180,* 321–325.

Yehuda, R., Southwick, S. M., Krystal, J. H., Bremner, J. D., Charney, D. S., & Mason, J. W. (1993). Enhanced suppression of cortisol with low dose dexamethasone in posttraumatic stress disorder. *American Journal of Psychiatry, 150,* 83–86.

Yehuda, R., Southwick, S. M., Nussbaum, E. L., Giller, E. L., & Mason, J. W. (1991). Low urinary cortisol in PTSD. *Journal of Nervous and Mental Disease, 178,* 366–369.

Yehuda, R., Teicher, M. H., Levengood, R. A., Trestman, R. L., & Siever, L. J. (1994). Circadian regulation of basal cortisol levels in posttraumatic stress disorder. *Annals of the New York Academy of Science,* 378–380.

Yokoo, H., Tanaka, M., Yoshida, M., Tsuda, A., Tanaka, T., & Mizoguchi, K. (1990). Direct evidence of conditioned fear-elicited enhancement of noradrenaline release in the rat hypothalamus assessed by intracranial microdialysis. *Brain Research, 536,* 305–308.

Zacharko, R. M., Bowers, W. J., Kokkinidis, L., & Anisman, H. (1983). Region-specific reductions of intracranial self-stimulation after uncontrollable stress: Possible effects on reward processes. *Behavioral Brain Research, 9,* 129–141.

Zacharko, R. M., Gilmore, W., MacNeil, G., Kasian, M., & Anisman, H. (1990). Stressor-induced variations of intracranial self-stimulation from the mesocortex in several strains of mice. *Brain Research, 533,* 353–357.

Zola-Morgan, S. M., & Squire, L. R. (1990). The primate hippocampal formation: Evidence for a time-limited role in memory storage. *Science, 250,* 288–290.

Zola-Morgan, S., Squire, L. R., & Amaral, D. G. (1989). Lesions of the amygdala that spare adjacent cortical regions do not impair memory or exacerbate the impairment following lesions of the hippocampal formation. *Journal of Neuroscience, 9,* 1922–36.

Zola-Morgan, S., Squire, L. R., Amaral, D. G., & Suzuki, W. A. (1989). Lesions of perirhinal and parahippocampal cortex that spare the amygdala and hippocampal formation produce severe memory impairment. *Journal of Neuroscience, 9,* 4355–4370.

CHAPTER 7

GENETICS AND POSTTRAUMATIC STRESS DISORDER

WILLIAM R. TRUE, PH.D., M.P.H.
Saint Louis University of Public Health
and
Research Service
Department of Veterans Administration Medical Center

ROGER PITMAN, M.D.
Harvard Medical School
and
Rescarch Service
Department of Veterans Administration Medical Center

To suggest that genetic factors are important in the causation of PTSD perhaps flies in the face of intuition. After all, PTSD is the prototypical environmentally caused disorder, because it only arises in the aftermath of disaster or trauma. The argument of this chapter is not so polarized as the oversimplified approach of genes verses the environment or nature verses nurture. Instead, we will demonstrate that neither the individual nor the trauma alone explains the development of PTSD. We will examine the available literature to determine whether or not there is evidence for genetic factors in the etiology of the disorder. This determination is best made as part of a brief review of extant epidemiological findings which clearly demonstrate traumatic exposures are associated with the development of PTSD, but also show not all persons exposed to trauma become affected. In fact, epidemiological studies have consistently found the number of persons experiencing trauma who become affected are a minority, forcing us to address the question of what factors influence both vulnerability and resilience.

Next, we will focus on our present understanding of the environmental and genetic contributions to the individual profile of vulnerability as far as present knowledge may permit. Finally, the hope is to understand further the mechanisms whereby genetic factors, with the stimulus of a trauma, alter important psychophysiological attributes of the individual. Thereby the relationship of individual to trauma may be understood not as involving immutable environmental insult, but rather as the interaction of personal endowments and tendencies with the "slings and arrows of outrageous [environmental] fortune." In the quantitative and analytical style of the scientist, no doubt inferior to the voice of the poet, we will try to better understand why one's path through life is a complex emotional, intellectual, and physiological conversation between the organism and its setting.

EPIDEMIOLOGICAL EVIDENCE
OF WAR TRAUMA

The topic of epidemiology is addressed thoroughly in other chapters, but here our question is more specific: What do we know about the epidemiology of PTSD which suggests that consideration of genetic factors is in order? How might the genetic perspective contribute to our knowledge of individual differences in susceptibility for PTSD which is apparent from epidemiologic research? Early stages of epidemiologic findings often involve an alert clinician who reports a case or set of cases that call attention to a problem, which may yet be without a diagnostic label. In PTSD research, an example of such an early report is that of clinician and advocate Sarah Haley (1974), who reported the unique difficulties associated with psychotherapy among Vietnam veterans presenting PTSD like symptoms. At about the time of Haley's paper, Shatan (1973) also described PTSD symptoms in self-identified cases among members of a Vietnam veteran support group. Other case studies among volunteers in treatment appeared in reports by Nace, Meyers, O'Brien, Ream, and Mintz (1977) and Wilson and Krauss (1985). These early reports serve a vital function as an impetus for later sophisticated research and suggested symptoms and attributes which were incorporated as part of the PTSD diagnosis in DSM-III (American Psychiatric Association [APA], 1980). Later, case series (Huffman, 1970; Nace et al., 1977), similar to case reports, built upon cumulative experiences as a sequence of patients filled out the descriptive material useful for suggesting symptoms of a formal disorder. These studies mentioned so far provide the kind of evidence which psychiatric epidemiological researchers used to develop candidate lists of symptoms, suggested how they might group, and initiated etiological hypotheses.

Following these case reports PTSD was investigated in large cross-sectional samples. The first epidemiological surveys conducted with peer-reviewed scientific rigor can be characterized as identifying representative samples with the goal of addressing the issue of generalizability (Egendorf, Radushin, Laufer, Rothbart, & Sloan, 1981; Card, 1983). More formal studies were to come, including the major population based PTSD cross-sectional surveys discussed below. What is particularly striking about the evolution of PTSD as a diagnosis is that these early major surveys about the syndrome were published after the PTSD diagnosis was officially formulated in 1980 (APA, 1980). While the revision in 1987 (APA, 1987) did have the benefit of the first wave of population studies, the disorder was first defined in terms of the clinical presentations of largely self-defined patients who were presented to the literature in terms of case reports, volunteers, and case series descriptions.

The second phase of PTSD research addressed more systematically the question of whether traumatic life events such as military combat could produce the psychopathology first referred to as PTSD in the 1980 publication of DSM-III. The association between exposure and sequelae could be directly assessed because of the care and precision in identifying samples, and the thoroughness of the assessment batteries. This phase culminated in the National Vietnam Veterans Readjustment Study (NVVRS) (Kulka et al., 1988). The NVVRS found that 15.2 percent of Vietnam theater veterans suffered from current PTSD, as opposed to only 2.5 percent of comparable Vietnam era veterans (who did not serve in Vietnam). An additional 15.7 percent of Vietnam theater veterans were found to have suffered from PTSD sometime in the past. As part of a large-scale twin study of the effects of service in Vietnam, Goldberg, True, Eisen, and Henderson (1990) utilized data from monozygotic (MZ) twins from the Vietnam Era Twin (VET) Registry who were discordant for service in Vietnam to show a differential prevalence of presumptive current PTSD in Vietnam theater (16.8 percent) versus era (5.0 percent) veterans. In contrast, the exhaustive Centers for Disease Control (CDC) Vietnam Experience Study (1988) found much lower estimates of PTSD (15 percent lifetime, and 2.2 percent in the last month). As reviewed in Goldberg, Eisen, True, and Henderson (1992), the difference between the CDC study and the other PTSD studies was primarily the "objective" measure of combat exposure used by the CDC, where only the Military Occupational Speciality classification of "tactical" as opposed to "non-tactical" denoted combat exposure. Although varying in prevalence estimates, the studies listed here, and others, support an etiologic role for combat exposure in PTSD. This role was clear in terms of the monotonic relationships found across studies where the highest levels of traumatic exposure were associated with more evidence of the presence of the PTSD disorder. Goldberg et al. (1990) found that at the highest level of combat, there was a 9.2-fold increase in risk for having a presumptive diagnosis of PTSD (95 percent CI 4.8–17.6). The highest level of combat was also associated with increased risk for 5 of the 13 symptoms of PTSD. These five highly combat-correlated symptoms ranged from "had times when feelings or actions became stronger..." with an odds ratio of 7.2 (95 percent CI 4.4–11.6) to "persistent avoidance of stimuli associated with the trauma ..." with an odds ratio of 13.4 (95 percent CI 7.1–25.0).

PTSD PREDISPOSITION

From the epidemiological evidence it is apparent that even at the highest levels of combat exposure, only a minority report significant symptoms. The next phase of PTSD research must address the question: If traumatic life events such as combat are capable of producing PTSD, why do only some, rather than all, persons exposed to such events develop this disorder? This is arguably the single question most often posed to PTSD experts by laymen. In fact, the NVVRS (Kulka et al., 1988) devotes a full chapter to the issue, identifying those variables postulated as predisposing.

The NVVRS approach was to control for a number of factors, including childhood and family demographic and social variables as well as a series of variables including childhood behavior problems, mental health status, adult mental health status, and even war stress exposure measures in Vietnam. This "conservative approach" controlled for mental health problems and exposure to trauma, both of which are influenced by genes (Kendler, 1993; Lyons et al., 1993) and may well be indicators of vulnerability dimensions. Thus, the NVVRS took only a glancing look at the issue of predisposition, treating predisposing factors to PTSD as confounding its pursuit of establishing whether military combat causes PTSD. However, other studies focusing on the issue of predis-

position have found factors such as family history of anxiety (Davidson, Swartz, Storck, Krishnan, & Hammett 1985; Davidson, Smith, & Kudler, 1989); personal history of behavioral problems (Helzer, Robins, & McEvoy, 1987); neuroticism and history of treatment for a psychological disorder (McFarlane, 1989); lower arithmetic aptitude and more self-reported school difficulties (Pitman, Orr, Lowenhagen, Macklin, & Altman, 1991); and history of early separation from caretakers, pre-existing anxiety and depressive disorders, neuroticism, and family history of anxiety and antisocial behavior (Breslau, Davis, Andreski, & Peterson, 1991) significantly predict the development of PTSD after exposure to a stressor.

The fact that disorders which are co-morbid with PTSD, (e.g., other anxiety disorders) are known to have genetic contributions suggests that shared genetic factors might contribute to vulnerability to PTSD. The NVVRS estimates that 8 percent of male Vietnam theater veterans with PTSD also have panic disorder (PD), a 15-fold increase over theater veterans without PTSD. In family studies there is evidence that relatives of firefighters affected by PTSD have an increased incidence of anxiety disorders including PTSD (McFarlane, 1989). Davidson et al. (1985) and Davidson, Smith and Kudler (1989) have shown that the relatives of PTSD probands have higher rates of anxiety disorders than either combat or depressed controls. Two studies found increased rates of alcoholism in relatives of PTSD probands (Davidson et al., 1985; Speed, Engdahl, Schwartz, & Eberly, 1989), suggesting shared factors, including genetic contributions, in the etiology of the two disorders. These comorbidity findings suggest a plausible rationale for a familial predisposition to PTSD in that disorders associated with PTSD such as alcoholism are known to "run" in families.

The best way to study vulnerability to combat-related PTSD would be to evaluate individuals longitudinally, i.e., before and after combat exposure. However, because no one knows exactly where, when, or even whether any of our armed forces will go to war, such a study would require screening thousands of recruits to generate an exposed sample sufficient for analysis. The power of prospective designs is that at the outset no one is affected by the disorder, but some are or will be exposed to a potential etiological variable. To illustrate the design dilemma, we may imagine a Vietnam veteran in the office of a therapist being treated for PTSD. As the story unfolds, the patient may try to separate the sources of distress as being part of, or distinct from, the military experience. The patient may say, "I'd like to know what I would have been like if I'd never gone to war." Anecdotally, this hypothetical patient is expressing an ideal research design, where the individual could be compared to him- or herself, after being exposed to different life courses. Such a situation also suggests the theoretically best approach for separating the issues of predisposition from the etiological role of combat exposure. With such an approach, it would *not* be necessary to take the path that the scientists of the NVVRS did, i.e., of controlling for what may be either variables in the causal chain, effect modifiers or confounding variables.

APPLICABILITY OF THE TWIN RESEARCH TECHNIQUE

The above example is only partly hypothetical, because there is in nature the biological reality of twinning, in which one's genetic replicate (identical twin) may have taken a different course on life's road, and given sufficient numbers of twin pairs, such comparisons as the patient wanted to make can be accomplished. While the utility of the twin approach for the research problem delineated is apparent, it is important to note that it is only one of several research designs which are informative about the genetic contributions to causation.

Genesigns include family studies, adoption studies, and twin studies. Family studies consist of systematic history and data gathering from each member of families of interest. There are several types of adoption studies. One involves comparing adopted offspring whose biological parents have a disorder to adopted offspring of parents without the disorder. A second approach compares adopted persons whose biological parents did not have a disorder, but whose adoptive parents did, to adoptive persons without a disorder in either biologic or adoptive parents. A third common adoption study identifies adopted children

with a disorder and proceeds to examine the degree to which the disorder is present in the biologic and adoptive families. Like twin and family studies, adoption studies may provide insight into the impact of genes and environment on a given disorder.

The third genetically informative study is the twin design. The characteristics of a twin design are based upon the assumption that twins have two sources of influence which tend to make them similar, and one source of influence which tends to make them different. First, we know that monozygotic (MZ) or identical twins share all of their genes by definition, while dizygotic (DZ) or fraternal twins share half their genes, just as is true for any other siblings. Therefore, MZ twins are twice as alike genetically as DZ twins. Further, because both kinds of twins are raised in a household and are educated, play, and circulate in the same worlds, particularly as children, both MZ and DZ twins have shared environmental experiences. Examples of shared environment include having parents who are both high school graduates, living in the same neighborhood, and going to common schools. Genes and shared or family environment are the two sources which promote similarity within twin pairs. The third influence is unique environmental influences, which denote those life circumstances which are experienced by one, but not both, members of the twin pair. Obviously this is the factor that determines dissimilarity within identical twin pairs. So identical twins are similar for two reasons: they share all of their genes and their family environment. They are dissimilar to the degree they live different lives and have different unique environmental experiences. In contrast, DZ twin pairs share approximately half of their genes just as any siblings do, and they, like MZ twins, share all of the common environment. DZ twins have more dissimilarities than MZ twins because they experience unique environments but share only 50 percent of their genes. Because MZ twins are twice as alike genetically as DZ twins, we expect to find MZ twin pairs more phenotypically correlated than DZ twin pairs in genetically influenced traits. Indeed, in the case of a simple additive genetic effect, we would find that the MZ correlation is approximately twice that of the DZ twin correlation. Therefore we are presented with the obvious methodological implication that the unit of analysis in twin studies is the twin pair, not the individual respondent. The primary observations of a twin study are the MZ twin correlation and the DZ twin correlation, computed over the total number of pairs of each zygosity under study. In a twin study of substantial complexity, involving thousands of twin pairs, some are surprised that the summary data for analysis of an observation comes down to two numbers: an MZ and a DZ correlation coefficient.

VIETNAM ERA TWIN (VET) REGISTRY

Having described the approach, it is necessary to review the particulars of the Department of Veterans Affairs Vietnam Era Twin Registry, a unique resource for twin studies and particularly informative for topics related to combat exposure and PTSD. The VET Registry was created in the early 1980s. Details regarding the development and characteristics of the Registry have previously been published (Eisen, True, Goldberg, Henderson, & Robinette, 1987; Eisen, Neuman, Goldberg, Rice, & True, 1989; Goldberg, True, Eisen, Henderson, & Robinette 1987; Henderson et al., 1990). The Registry contains 7,375 male-male twin pairs born between 1939 and 1957 where both siblings served on active military duty during the Vietnam era (May 1965–August 1975). The Registry was assembled by applying an algorithm that matched same last name, different first name, same date of birth, and similar Social Security numbers contained in a Department of Defense computer data base of approximately 5.5 million servicemen. Military records of possible twin pairs were then examined to confirm twinship. Baseline information was also extracted from components of the military record, including enlistment records, aptitude test scores, military assignments, and discharge circumstances. The VET Registry was originally developed as part of a Department of Veterans Affairs effort to investigate the effects of service in the Vietnam war and particularly the influence of combat exposure on the health of veterans.

According to a questionnaire and blood group typing methodology which correctly assesses zygosity in over 97 percent of cases, 2,556 (53.5 percent) pairs of Registry members were identified as MZ and 2,092 pairs (43.8 percent) as DZ. For the remaining

126 pairs (2.7 percent) zygosity could not be identified and these members were excluded from further consideration. The VET Registry contains representatives from all ethnic groups. It does not, however, contain women, who during the Vietnam era served in too few numbers to produce a twin data base large enough for research purposes. Seventy-five percent of Registry members were currently married at the time of the 1987 Survey of Health, 11 percent were never married, and 77 percent had fathered at least one child. More than 95 percent had completed high school, and 91 percent were employed full-time. Registry members were equally employed in blue-collar (45 percent) and in white-collar occupations (45 percent) (10 percent undetermined occupation). Registry members were mostly middle income earners (83 percent greater than $20,000 annually, 35 percent greater than $40,000 annually in 1987). Registry members are representative of all twins who served in the military during the Vietnam War on a variety of sociodemographic and other variables (Goldberg et al., 1987).

Data for the twin design employed in the PTSD analyses described here are based upon the Survey of Health which was conducted as a mailed survey in 1987. For 1 percent of respondents, the survey was conducted by telephone. Areas covered by the 75-item questionnaire included occupation, education, employment, income, family life, health status, alcohol and tobacco use, military service, and mental health status, including posttraumatic stress symptomatology. Of the total VET Registry, 4,774 twin pairs responded to the 1987 Survey of Health. The overall case-wise response rate was 74.4 percent, and the pair-wise response rate was 64.4 percent. Reasons for non-response included: refused, 9.5 percent; death, 2.7 percent; ineligible, 0.4 percent; unavailable for study (either outside the United States or too ill to respond), 0.5 percent; and no response to repeated mailings or telephone calls, 12.4 percent.

COMBAT EXPOSURE AND PTSD

To illustrate different approaches using the genetically informative twin design, we refer to two published projects concerning PTSD which were derived from analysis of VET Registry data (Goldberg et al., 1990; True et al., 1993). The first study was a co-twin control analysis, where the identical twin serves as a perfect familial control for his twin brother. We utilized the co-twin control design to ask: "What is the relationship of the *environmental* variables, service in Southeast Asia, and level of combat exposure, to the occurrence of PTSD?" The basic approach is no different in principle than the methodology found in any of thousands of case-control studies published with controls selected who may be matched on the standard "age, sex, ethnicity" or some other permutation of control variables. The difference is that identical twins are perfect familial controls, matched with thousands upon thousands of variables, conceived of or not, extending to the entire genome of each twin. By controlling so completely, the role of genetics is *removed* from consideration.

In this epidemiologic investigation, Goldberg et al., (1990) identified 715 MZ twin pairs from the VET Registry who were discordant for military service in Southeast Asia and for whom military records included complete service-related data. As part of the 1987 Survey of Health, combat exposure was measured by asking each veteran whether he had engaged in 19 specific combat activities. A global index of combat exposure was constructed by summing over all positive responses; this index was strongly correlated with combat medal awards in military records (Janes, Goldberg, Eisen, & True, 1991). PTSD symptoms were identified on the basis of 15 Survey of Health items that closely resembled the DSM-III-R PTSD criteria. The respondent was asked to rate the frequency of experiencing each item during the past six months, and by applying the DSM-III-R PTSD diagnostic algorithm to the responses, we were able to derive a presumptive diagnosis of PTSD. The presumptive PTSD prevalence was 16.8 percent in twins who had served in Vietnam versus 5.0 percent in co-twins who had not. There was a ninefold increase in the prevalence of PTSD comparing twins exposed to high levels of combat with their unexposed co-twins. Thus the environmental role of traumatic exposures in the development of PTSD was demonstrated while accounting for potential genetic vulnerability. The specific contribution of the MZ co-twin control ap-

proach was to establish both the direction and magnitude of influence of combat exposures to PTSD. In this twin study, Goldberg et al (1990) overcame a number of weaknesses common to PTSD research. By utilizing the co-twin control design, a suitable control group was identified. Since the identical twin brothers share all of their genes and have a common childhood family life, a host of potential unmeasurable confounding variables were controlled. Thus the observation that there is an increasing risk for PTSD as a function of combat exposure can be made with the confidence that the association is not due to mitigating factors such as dysfunctional childhood family environments or *solely* due to a genetic liability.

GENETICS OF PTSD SYMPTOMS

The second twin design employed a completely different research approach using genetic modeling techniques. In this case, it is not the co-twin control aspect of the twin model which is of interest, but rather the fact that among all twins, fraternal and identical, exposed to trauma and unexposed, there exist patterns which describe the degree to which one member of a twin pair is similar to the other. Therefore, all twin pairs of both zygosities are informative, whether one or both or neither served in Southeast Asia. The full twin model allows one to ask the question: "What are the environmental and genetic contributions to the susceptibility to experiencing PTSD symptoms?" Compared to the inquiry posed by the co-twin design, this question is much more inclusive in terms of etiology, because of its broader scope. The full genetic model is able to determine the magnitude of environmental and genetic exposures, but does not specify which particular exposure, or which gene or genes might be implicated.

The statistical methods involved are complex, and best explicated in a recent volume (Neale & Cardon, 1992); however, an illustration of some basic assumptions of the genetic model can be seen in Figure 7.1. Figure 7.1 is a liability threshold curve where the categories of PTSD affection status, i.e. none, mild, and severe, comprise the classes of the phenotype (the observable characteristic). Genetic and environmental influences are estimated under a multifactorial

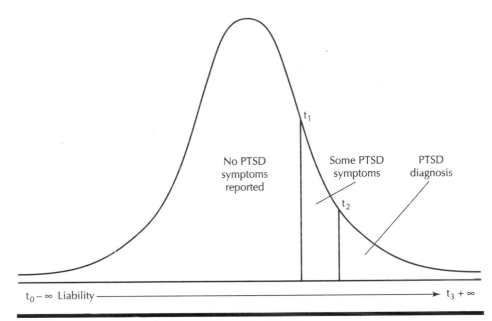

No PTSD
symptoms
reported

Some PTSD
symptoms

PTSD
diagnosis

t_1

t_2

$t_0 - \infty$ Liability

$t_3 + \infty$

FIGURE 7.1 Liability Threshold Model for Risk of PTSD

threshold model in which multiple unmeasured genetic and environmental risk factors determine an underlying continuous liability distribution with a threshold determining expression of a given phenotype, in this case PTSD symptoms. Above a given threshold the phenotype is expressed and the individual displays the characteristic. Below the threshold, the individual does not show the characteristic. As portrayed in Figure 7.1, the liability threshold model assumes that there is a single normally distributed dimension of liability with abrupt thresholds (t_0, t_1...t_3) superimposed, with the two thresholds t_1 and t_2 corresponding to the levels of severity. These thresholds determine whether symptoms of PTSD will be expressed (t_1) and whether criteria of diagnosis of full-blown PTSD will be met (t_2). The probability of developing PTSD increases directly as the severity and number of traumatic experiences increases as indicated by the thresholds (Heath, 1990; Heath & Martin, 1993).

Operating under the assumptions of the liability threshold model, True et al. (1993) performed genetic analyses on 15 PTSD-symptom items reported in the Survey of Health by 2,224 MZ and 1,818 DZ VET Registry twin pairs. Adjusting for genetic influences on combat exposure, the investigators found that genetic factors accounted for 13 percent–30 percent of the variance in liability to current PTSD symptoms in the reexperiencing cluster, 30 percent–34 percent in the avoidance cluster, and 28 percent–32 percent in the arousal cluster. For 13 of the 15 PTSD symptoms evaluated, the data supported an additive polygenic model; for two, adding dominance to the model provided the best fit. Interestingly, the shared familial environment did not contribute to susceptibility to PTSD symptoms. In other words, variables such as the individual's childhood family life (i.e., parenting styles, shared experiences with siblings), educational experiences, and economic background did not contribute to vulnerability for PTSD symptoms in this analysis. Therefore, in this study, "familial" was synonymous with "inherited." Of course genes alone do not account for PTSD since the remaining variance in liability was due to unique environmental experiences. These experiences include a host of unmeasured variables, including other potential sources of trauma. Despite this gap in knowledge, we can attest that some persons are more likely than others to develop PTSD because of their genetic composition. With continued work researchers may define a characteristic profile for individuals with a high, genetically influenced liability for PTSD. A profile of genetically predisposed persons will likely demonstrate differences in vulnerability to the physiological abnormalities associated with PTSD. Although there is a substantial literature identifying the biological characteristics of PTSD, there has been little research investigating the heritability of PTSD physiology. We now turn attention to proposed research for investigating the genetic influence on PTSD psychophysiology. Successful research examining the hypotheses discussed below should shed light on the mechanisms by which genes influence the risk for this disorder.

Genetic Research on PTSD—a Clinical Approach

In the above study, combat exposure was found to be a strong predictor of the reexperiencing PTSD symptom cluster, of a single aspect of the avoidance cluster, but not of the arousal cluster. Because PTSD only results from exposure to a severely stressful event, such as military combat, the PTSD must influence the biology associated with the individual's vulnerability to develop PTSD after such an event. Clinical research over the past decade, mostly in Vietnam combat veterans, has identified a number of biologic markers for the PTSD condition. The term "biologic marker" as used here simply refers to a biologic or physiologic dependent variable that has been shown to differ significantly between subjects with and without PTSD.

Biologic markers may be pre-existing or result as a consequence of exposure to trauma. The marker may only have come into existence subsequent to the combat exposure or may be acquired as a consequence of combat exposure per se, regardless of the development of PTSD. Alternately, a marker may be acquired only concomitantly with the PTSD. A biologic PTSD marker may also have existed beforehand and come to be associated with PTSD because its presence placed the individual at higher risk. Such a marker may place an individual at risk for PTSD

either because it increases the likelihood of the individual's being exposed to combat, or because it increases the likelihood of the individual's developing PTSD following combat exposure.

A biologic marker that increases an individual's risk for developing PTSD following combat exposure represents what we will term here a "vulnerability" marker. A vulnerability marker may either be inherited or develop as a consequence of an individual's pre-combat environment. However, this would also be expected to be true for a marker that developed as a consequence of the pre-combat, family environment that is shared by twins. A twin study employing exclusively MZ subjects is capable of identifying a vulnerability marker for PTSD that is based on heredity and/or shared family environment, referred to here as a "familial vulnerability" marker. As used here, "familial" refers to a marker influenced by either genes shared in the family and/or environment shared in the family. A vulnerability marker could arise as the result of unshared, or unique, pre-combat environment, in which case it would not be expected to differ among MZ and DZ twins with PTSD. In addition, a given biologic PTSD marker need not have a single origin, i.e., two or more of the above possibilities may combine to account for a biologic PTSD marker.

In order to identify the familial nature of PTSD markers, MZ and DZ twins, with and without PTSD, will have to be compared on a number of known physiologic measures associated with PTSD. We now examine the rationale for such research currently being conducted by the authors and colleagues. The PTSD markers discussed next, startle response, event-related potentials, and hypothalamic-pituitary-adrenocortical axis probes, all differ systematically between persons with PTSD verses controls. Thus, these measures are ideal phenotypes for identifying the mechanisms by which genes and or shared environmental factors may influence symptomology.

Startle represents an unconditioned phasic reactivity mediated by simple brainstem neural circuitry (Davis, 1984) but modulated by higher influences, including conditioned emotional responses. Startle is characterized by a predictable pattern of muscular activity. Sudden, intense stimuli can also produce changes in autonomic reactivity, including heart rate

(HR) acceleration, increased skin conductance (SC) response (R) magnitude, and a slower rate of SCR decline over repeated stimulus presentations (Boucsein, Baltissen, & Euler, 1984; Dimberg, 1990; Roth, Dorato & Kopell, 1984). Individual differences such as current emotional state or the presence of clinical anxiety can influence muscular and autonomic startle response magnitude and habituation.

Findings in identical twins indicate that HR (Boomsma & Gabrielli, 1985; Carroll, Hewitt, Last, Turner, & Sims, 1985; Ditto, 1993; Kotchoubei, 1987) and electrodermal (Kotchoubei, 1987; Lykken, Iacono, Haroian, McGue, & Bouchard, 1988) response magnitude and habituation have strong genetic determinants. Lykken et al (1988) found that genetic contributions explained 70 percent of the variance in SCR habituation, as measured by response slope across trial presentations, 59 percent of the variance in mean SCR magnitude across trials, and 41 percent of the variance in a SCR trials-to-criterion measure. MZ twin correlations for these respective measures were: .72, .62, and .42. Kotchoubei (1987) reported 45 percent heritability for HR response magnitude to high intensity tone presentations, with an MZ twin correlation of .41. Similar heritabilities have been reported for HR reactivity while playing a video game: 48 percent, MZ twin correlation .56 (Carroll et al., 1985), and doing mental arithmetic: 62 percent, MZ twin correlation .63 (Ditto, 1993).

Studies of physiologic responses to sudden, loud tone stimuli in PTSD have provided evidence of both larger magnitude physiologic responses and slower habituation. Orr, Lasko, Shalev, and Pitman (1995) recently reported significantly larger accelerative HRRs to sudden, loud (i.e., startling) tones in Vietnam veterans with PTSD compared with non-PTSD combat control subjects. Paige, Reid, Allen, and Newton (1990) previously reported the same finding. In work from a third, independent laboratory, Shalev, Orr, Peri, Schreiber, and Pitman (1992) reported the same finding in mixed civilian/veteran PTSD subjects compared with patients with other anxiety disorders, mentally healthy subjects with past traumatic experiences, and mentally healthy subjects with no trauma history. Shalev et al. (1992) also found significantly larger SCRs in PTSD versus non-PTSD subjects. Recently obtained

data reveal that physiologic responses to sudden, loud tones in PTSD remain unchanged with alprazolam treatment despite symptomatic improvement (Shalev, et al., 1994), suggesting that these responses represent trait, rather than state, markers for PTSD.

In light of the studies cited above suggesting genetic bases for SC and HR reactivity and habituation, it is possible that the greater HR reactivity and slower decline of SCRs to repeated presentations of a sudden, loud tone stimulus found in PTSD subjects, which are consistent with a "defensive" response pattern (Turpin, 1983), reflect one or more inherited vulnerability factors for the emergence of PTSD upon exposure to a requisite stressor, as has previously been proposed by Orr, Lasko, Shalev and Pitman (1995).

Another promising physiological measure for detecting heritable markers for PTSD includes event-related potentials (ERPs). ERPs are stimulus-evoked EEG changes recorded at the scalp. Defined peaks in the ERP waveform reliably distinguish cerebral events triggered by the physical (exogenous) or informational (endogenous) properties of the eliciting stimulus. ERPs are by convention labeled as "P" for positive and "N" for negative deflections, followed by a number approximating the deflection's latency from the eliciting stimulus' onset in milliseconds, e.g., P300 (or simply P3). Peak latencies reflect the time course of processing stages, whereas amplitudes presumably index the intensity of the associated operations. Twin studies have generally supported a strong genetic basis for the various ERP components (Friedman, 1990; Polich, 1989), and animal studies have revealed genetic effects on ERP amplitude/intensity slope (Siegel, Sisson & Driscoll 1993).

In the first study of ERPs performed in PTSD, Paige et al. (1990) found significant differences in the slope of the linear function relating intensity of the eliciting auditory stimulus to P2 amplitude. PTSD subjects showed a mean negative (i.e., reducing) P2 slope, whereas non-PTSD subjects showed a mean positive (i.e., augmenting) P2 slope. In Pavlovian theory, the relationship between stimulus intensity and response magnitude is considered to reflect "strength" of the nervous system (Gray, 1964). This concept originally derived from experiments involving conditioning, reaction time, and attention, in which response magnitude was found to increase as a function of the intensity of the eliciting stimulus, but only up to a limiting value, termed "the threshold of transmarginal inhibition." Beyond this threshold, further increases in stimulus intensity were found to lead to a decrease in the magnitude of the elicited response (Razran, 1957). Individuals with so-called Pavlovian weak nervous systems hypothetically reach the threshold of transmarginal inhibition at a lower level of stimulus intensity, suggesting a need to attenuate the effects of extreme stimuli in order to render them more tolerable. In the stimulus intensity modulation paradigm employed by Paige et al. (1990), P2 reduction in PTSD subjects may be interpreted as a manifestation of an overly sensitive nervous system. Sensitive individuals might be more vulnerable to develop PTSD upon exposure to stress, so that reduced P2 slope could conform to the pattern for a familial, possibly inherited, vulnerability factor.

The reliability with which endogenous ERP components reflect specific aspects of task processing associated with the allocation of attention has been well established (Hillyard & Kutas, 1983). For example, latency and amplitude of the centroparietally distributed P3 reflects the timing and attentional capacity involved in stimulus evaluation (Desmedt, Nguyen, & Bourguet, 1987). Twin and family studies provide compelling evidence for genetic influences on P3 (Eischen & Polich, 1994; O'Connor, Morzorati, Christian, & Li, 1994; Polich & Burns, 1987; Steinhauer, Hill, & Zubin, 1987; Surwillo, 1980). Two studies have specifically demonstrated heritability of the P3 response in target discrimination tasks in normal subjects. O'Connor et al. (1994) found that genetic contributions explained 49 percent of the variance in P3 amplitude, with an observed MZ twin correlation of .55. Rogers and Deary (1991) did not specify the percentage of variance accounted for by inheritance but reported an MZ twin correlation of .50.

Abnormalities in P3 amplitude have been observed in several psychiatric disorders, including alcoholism (Porjesz, Begleiter, & Samuelly, 1980), depression (Diner, Holcomb, & Dykman, 1985), schizophrenia (Mirsky & Duncan, 1986; Pfefferbaum, Wenegrat, Ford, Roth, & Kopell, 1984), and recently PTSD (see below). Researchers have also

recognized the potential utility of endogenous ERPs as vulnerability markers for psychopathology (Cloninger, 1990; Ebmeier et al., 1990; Friedman, 1990). Support for ERPs as vulnerability markers derives from the observation that they appear to reflect trait as opposed to state factors (Blackwood et al., 1987). For instance, several studies have reported reduced P3 amplitude in individuals genetically at risk for alcoholism (reviewed in Polich, Pollock, & Bloom, 1994), schizophrenia (Herman, Mirsky, Ricks, & Gallant, 1977; Saletu, Saletu, Marasa, Mednick, & Schulsinger, 1975), and psychopathology in general (Cloninger, 1990; Friedman, 1990).

McFarlane, Weber, and Clark (1993) investigated the P3 component in PTSD subjects using the Pfefferbaum et al. (1984) auditory target discrimination task. ERPs were obtained from 18 mixed-trauma, PTSD and 20 normal, non-PTSD subjects. Subjects were instructed to press a button in response to infrequent target tones against a background sequence of frequent and infrequent distractor tones. P3s to both types of infrequent stimuli were attenuated in the PTSD subjects, indicating abnormal processing under conditions of stimulus change. PTSD subjects also showed a significantly longer N2 latency to both types of infrequent stimuli and longer reaction times to the target stimulus.

The above endogenous ERP findings suggest that PTSD patients suffer from a general impairment in the organization of perceptual experience. In terms of symptomatology, these findings may reflect a biologic index of the disturbed concentration observed in PTSD. However, there is a dearth of systematically collected data on disturbed concentration, or other PTSD arousal symptoms, prior to the occurrence of the traumatic event. It is conceivable that pre-existing perceptual information processing abnormalities could adversely affect the encoding of a traumatic event in persons who go on to persistently reexperience that event. In challenging sensory environments, disturbance in selective attention, as indicated by diminished P3 in a target discrimination task, has the capacity to generate excessive arousal, as the individual struggles to resolve cognitive confusion. It is also possible that information processing abnormalities that existed in PTSD patients prior to the traumatic event may impair attention to present environmental stimuli and facilitate the intrusion of traumatic memories. In either of these cases, attenuated P3s to infrequent stimuli might be expected to represent a pre-existing familial, possibly inherited, vulnerability factor.

The hypothalamic-pituitary-adrenocortical (HPA) axis represents another promising area in which to identify heritable physiological markers of PTSD. It is well established that the HPA axis response to stress is initiated by environmental causes. Indeed, the severity of the stressor has often been defined by the strength of the HPA response. However, individual response differences under constant stressor conditions have led to the realization that HPA response is also determined by factors other than the objective nature of the stressor (Hellhammer & Wade, 1993), including gender, prior stress history, social and cognitive factors, and inheritance. Hellhammer and Wade (1993) subjected twins to a number of HPA probes, including corticotropin releasing factor and physical and psychological stress. Average baseline and stimulated MZ pair cortisol correlations were 0.83. The authors noted that in none of their numerous investigations of stress reactivity could so much of the variance in cortisol response be explained as by genetic factors; they concluded that inheritance is a significant determinant of HPA axis reactivity.

A common HPA axis probe is the dexamethasone (DEX) suppression test (DST) (Carroll et al., 1981). The synthetic glucocorticoid DEX mimics the effects of cortisol by acting directly on feedback sites in the hypothalamus and pituitary with the ultimate effect of inhibiting release of cortisol from the adrenals. Failure of this suppression, indicative of an overactive HPA axis, is often shown by patients with major depressive disorder (MDD).

Four studies (cited in Yehuda et al., 1993) of cortisol response to the standard 1 mg oral dose of DEX have failed to find cortisol nonsuppression in PTSD subjects, even those with comorbid depression. However, findings of increased lymphocyte glucocorticoid receptors (Yehuda, Lowy, Southwick, Shaffer, & Giller, 1991) and lower urinary cortisol excretion (Yehuda et al., 1990) in PTSD suggest the opposite phenomenon, i.e., supersuppression, or *more* effective feedback inhibition of cortisol release. This has been confirmed in a study employing a lower dose of DEX. Yehuda et al. (1993) gave 0.5 mg oral DEX to 21 Vietnam veterans with PTSD and 12 normal subjects. After correcting for differences in plasma DEX levels, PTSD subjects showed significantly lower plasma cortisol levels both 9 and 17 hours later.

In general, the HPA axis abnormalities in PTSD are counterintuitive, in that they seem to be opposite to the physiologic stress response. The reason for this, and the origin of cortisol hypersuppression in PTSD, remain obscure. It is possible that intense hormonal effects induced by exposure to an extremely traumatic, environmental event may induce lasting changes in HPA axis function. However, the possibility must also be entertained that the prior existence of an atypical HPA response predilection, characterized by a net diminution in functionally available cortisol due to overactive inhibitory feedback, confers a vulnerability upon exposure to extreme stress. Theoretical support for this possibility derives from the consideration that, although cortisol is commonly regarded as a "stress hormone," it may also be viewed as an "anti-stress hormone," operating to terminate the physiologic stress state induced by catecholamines, corticotropin, and other neuropeptides.

It is not necessary that two or more identified vulnerability markers for PTSD bear any tight relationship to each other. A number of factors may make independent contributions to vulnerability. Some degree of phenotypic independence of vulnerability factors is supported by the finding that an additive, polygenic, rather than single-gene dominance, model best fits the data in PTSD (True et al., 1993). However, it is possible that separately identified vulnerability markers may, at least in part, either derive from a common origin and/or exert their effects through a final common pathway. The association of these proposed markers in the vulnerability to PTSD will become clearer following current research endeavors. An investigation of the genetic and environmental contributions to PTSD markers is currently being conducted with members of the VET Registry. Over the next few years, psychophysiological data from VET Registry twins should begin to answer the questions posed herein.

A wealth of theoretical considerations (Keane, Fairbank, Caddell, Zimering, & Bender, 1985; Kolb

& Multalipassi, 1982; Pitman, 1988) and psychophysiologic evidence (reviewed in Orr, 1994) points to conditioning as one of the mechanisms linking the symptoms of PTSD to the precipitating trauma. Under the conditioning model, cues associated with the traumatic unconditioned stimulus become classically conditioned stimuli for the trauma, evoking conditioned responses in the form of cognitive and physiologic PTSD symptoms. The focus of interpretation of these findings has been on the impact of the trauma on the individual. The possible contribution of pre-existing individual differences in capacity to form conditioned responses, i.e., conditionability, has received little attention. Human experimental evidence has indicated that individuals who are more autonomically arousable (Eysenck, 1979; Hugdahl, Fredrikson, & Ohman, 1977), and who more poorly habituate this arousal (Ohman & Bohlin, 1973), are more conditionable (Hugdahl et al., 1977). The concept of heightened arousability in vulnerable individuals may potentially serve to integrate the biologic marker findings in PTSD. It is plausible that individuals who on a constitutional, possibly inherited, basis are more emotionally arousable, terminate this arousal more poorly, habituate more slowly, and condition more readily will be vulnerable to developing PTSD upon exposure to extremely stressful events. On the other hand, according to the DSM-IV, PTSD entails "persistent symptoms of increased arousal [that were] not present before the trauma" (APA, 1994). Thus, it is also plausible that individuals who have acquired a state of hyperarousal because of exposure to a traumatic event will show the same findings. These considerations illustrate the impossibility of resolving the origin of biologic markers for PTSD on inferential grounds. Data from a study of PTSD markers in twins are capable of resolving the competing possibilities and shedding light on these important aspects of PTSD's pathogenesis.

It is foreseeable that biologic vulnerability markers for PTSD could be utilized to screen persons at risk for exposure to extremely stressful life events, e.g., firefighters, policemen, or soldiers in combat-related military occupational specialties or deployed to a war zone. Those found to possess high vulnerability for the development of PTSD could be advised to avoid such exposure or be considered for other assignments (primary prevention), or targeted for early intervention after exposure occurred (secondary prevention). In order to optimally diagnose and treat PTSD, it is vital to recognize the specific signs and symptoms of the disorder, as distinguished from nonspecific, pre-existing, vulnerability factors, or from mental disorders that would have developed regardless of the traumatic exposure. In other words, it is best to avoid mistaking the thinness of a patient's skin for the depth of his wounds.

ACKNOWLEDGMENTS

This work was supported by the Department of Veterans Affairs Health Services Research and Development Service (Study 256). Partial support was provided by the NIDA (Bethesda, MD) grant 1 R01 DAO 4604–01; NIAAA grant 1 R01 AA10339–01, NIMH grant 1 R01 MH54636, Great Lakes Veterans Affairs Health Services Research and Development Program, Ann Arbor, MI, LIP 41–065; Public Health Service grants MH-37685 and MH-31302; and NIDA training grant DAO72261–01 awarded to Washington University, St. Louis, MO.

The following organizations provided invaluable support in the conduct of this study: The staff of the Vietnam Era Twin Registry, Hines VA Medical Center, Hines, IL., Department of Defense; National Personnel Records Center, National Archives and Records Administration; the Internal Revenue Service; National Opinion Research Center; National Research Council, National Academy of Sciences; the Institute for Survey Research, Temple University. Editorial support was provided by Jeffrey Scherrer, M. A., School of Public Health, St. Louis University Health Sciences Center.

Most importantly, the authors gratefully acknowledge the continued cooperation and participation of the members of the Vietnam Era Twin Registry. Without their contribution this research would not have been possible.

REFERENCES

American Psychiatric Association. (1980). *Diagnostic and statistical manual of mental disorders* (3rd ed. Rev.). Washington, DC: Author.

American Psychiatric Association. (1987). *Diagnostic and statistical manual of mental disorders* (3rd ed. Rev.). Washington, DC: Author.

American Psychiatric Association. (1994). *Diagnostic and statistical manual of mental disorders* (4th ed. Rev.). Washington, DC: Author.

Blackwood, D. H. R., Whalley, L. J., Christie, J. E., Blackburn, I. M., St Clair, D. M., & McInnes, A. (1987). Changes in auditory P3 event-related potential in schizophrenia and depression. *British Journal of Psychiatry, 150,* 154–160.

Boomsma, D. I., & Gabrielli, W. F., Jr. (1985). Behavioral genetic approaches to psychophysiological data. *Psychophysiology, 22,* 249–260.

Boucsein, W., Baltissen, R., & Euler, W. (1984). Dependence of skin conductance reactions and skin resistance reactions on previous level. *Psychophysiology, 21,* 212–218.

Breslau, N., Davis, G. C., Andreski, P., & Peterson, E. (1991). Traumatic events and posttraumatic stress disorder in an urban population of young adults. *Archives of General Psychiatry, 48,* 216–222.

Card, J. J. (1983). *Lives after Vietnam: The personal impact of military service.* Lexington, MA: D.C. Heath & Company.

Carroll, B. J., Feinberg, M., Greden, J. F., Tarika, J., Albala, A. A., Haskett, R. F., James, N. M., Kronfol, Z., Lohr, N., Steiner, M., de Vigne, J. P., & Young, E. (1981). A specific laboratory test for the diagnosis of melancholia. *Archives of General Psychiatry, 38,* 15–22.

Carroll, D., Hewitt, J. K., Last, K. A., Turner, J. R., & Sims, J. (1985). A twin study of cardiac reactivity and its relationship to parental blood pressure. *Physiology and Behavior, 34,* 103–106.

Cloninger, C. R. (1990). Event-related potentials in populations at genetic risk: Genetic principles and research strategies. In J. W. R. Rohrbaugh, R. Parasuraman, & R. Johnson, Jr. (Eds.), *Event-related brain potentials: Basic issues and applications* (pp. 333–342). New York: Oxford University Press.

Davidson, J., Smith, R., & Kudler, H. (1989). Familial psychiatric illness in chronic posttraumatic stress disorder. *Comprehensive Psychiatry, 30,* 339–345.

Davidson, J., Swartz, M., Storck, M., Krishnan, R. R., & Hammett, E. (1985). A diagnostic and family study of posttraumatic stress disorder. *American Journal of Psychiatry, 142,* 90–93.

Davis, M. (1984). The mammalian startle response. In R. C. Eaton (Eds.), *Neural Mechanisms of Startle Behavior.* (285–351). New York: Plenum Press.

Desmedt, J. E., Nguyen, T. H., & Bourguet, M. (1987). Bit-mapped colour imaging of human evoked potentials with reference to the N20, P22, P27 and N30 somatosensory responses. *Electroencephalography and Clinical Neurophysiology, 68,* 1–19.

Dimberg, U. (1990). Facial electromyographic reactions and autonomic activity to auditory stimuli. *Biological Psychology, 31,* 137–147.

Diner, B. C., Holcomb, P. J., & Dykman, R. A. (1985). P300 in major depressive disorder. *Psychiatry Research, 15,* 175–184.

Ditto, B. (1993). Familial influences on heart rate, blood pressure, & self-report anxiety responses to stress: Results from 100 twin pairs. *Psychophysiology, 30,* 635–645.

Ebmeier, K. P., Potter, D. D., Cochrane, R. H. B., Mackenzie, A. R., McAllister, H., Besson, J. A. O., & Salzen, E. A. (1990). P300 and smooth eye pursuit: Concordance of abnormalities and relation to clinical features in DSM-III schizophrenia. *Acta Psychiatrica Scandinavica, 82,* 283–288.

Egendorf, A., Radushin, C., Laufer, R. S., Rothbart, G., & Sloan, L. (1981). *Legacies of Vietnam: Comparative adjustment of veterans and their peers.* New York, NY: The Center for Policy Research Inc.

Eischen, S. E., & Polich, J. (1994). P300 from families. *Electroencephalography and Clinical Neurophysiology, 92,* 369–372.

Eisen, S., Neuman, R., Goldberg, J., Rice, J., & True, W. (1989). Determining zygosity in the Vietnam Era Twin Registry: An approach using questionnaires. *Clinical Genetics, 35,* 423–432.

Eisen, S. A., True, W. R., Goldberg, J., Henderson, W., & Robinette, C. D. (1987). The Vietnam Era Twin (VET) Registry: Method of construction. *Acta Geneticae Medicae et Gemellologiae (Roma), 36,* 61–66.

Eysenck, H. J. (1979). The conditioning model of neurosis. *Behavioral and Brain Sciences, 2,* 155–199.

Friedman, D. (1990). Event-related potentials in populations at genetic risk: A methodological review. In J. W. Rohrbaugh, R. Parasuraman, & R. Johnson, Jr. (Eds.), *Event-related brain potentials: Basic issues and applications* (pp. 310–332). New York, NY: Oxford University Press.

Goldberg, J., Eisen, S. A., True, W. R., & Henderson, W. G. (1992). Health effects of military service: Lessons learned from the Vietnam experience. *Annals of Epidemiology, 2,* 841–853.

Goldberg, J., True, W. R., Eisen, S. A., & Henderson, W. G. (1990). A twin study of the effects of the Vietnam War on posttraumatic stress disorder. *Journal of the American Medical Association, 263,* 1227–1232.

Goldberg, J., True, W., Eisen, S., Henderson, W., & Robinette, C. D. (1987). The Vietnam Era Twin (VET) Registry: Ascertainment bias. *Acta Genet Med Gemellol, 36,* 67–78.

Gray, J. A. (1964). *Pavlov's typology.* New York: MacMillan.

Halcy, S. A. (1974). When the patient reports atrocities. *Archives of General Psychiatry, 30,* 91–94.

Heath, A. C. (1990). Persist or quit? Testing for a genetic contribution to smoking persistence. *Acta Genet Med Gemellol (Roma), 39,* 447–458.

Heath, A. C., & Martin, N. G. (1993) Genetic models for the natural history of smoking: Evidence for a genetic influence on smoking persistence. *Addictive Behavior, 18,* 19–34.

Hellhammer, D. H., & Wade, S. (1993). Endocrine correlates of stress vulnerability. *Psychotherapy and Psychosomatics, 60,* 8–17.

Helzer, J. E., Robins, L. N., & McEvoy, L. (1987). Posttraumatic stress disorder in the general population: Findings of the Epidemiologic Catchment Area study. *The New England Journal of Medicine, 317,* 1630–1634.

Henderson, W. G., Eisen, S., Goldberg, J., True, W. R., Barnes, J. E., & Vitek, M. E. (1990) The Vietnam Era Twin Registry: A resource for medical research. *Public Health Reports, 105,* 368–373.

Herman, J., Mirsky, A. F., Ricks, N. L., & Gallant, D. (1977). Behavioral and electrographic measures of attention in children at risk for schizophrenia. *Journal of Abnormal Psychology, 86,* 27–33.

Hillyard, S. A., & Kutas, M. (1983). Electrophysiology of cognitive processing. *Annual Review of Psychology, 34,* 33–61.

Huffman, R. E. (1970). Which soldiers break down: A survey of 610 psychiatric patients in Vietnam. *Bulletin of the Menninger Clinic, 34,* 343–351.

Hugdahl, K., Fredrikson, M., & Ohman, A. (1977). "Preparedness" and "arousability" as determinants of electrodermal conditioning. *Behaviour Research and Therapy, 15,* 345–353.

Janes, G. R., Goldberg, J., Eisen, S. A., & True, W. R. (1991). Reliability and validity of a combat exposure index for Vietnam era veterans. *Journal of Clinical Psychology, 47,* 80–86.

Keane, T. M., Fairbank, J. A., Caddell, J. M, Zimering, R. T., & Bender, M. E. (1985). A behavioral approach to assessing and treating post-traumatic stress disorders in Vietnam veterans. In C. R. Figley (Ed.), *Trauma and its wake: The assessment of treatment of post-traumatic stress disorders* (pp. 257–294). New York: Brunner/Mazel.

Kendler, D. S. (1993). Twin studies of psychiatric illness: Current status and future directions. *Archives of General Psychiatry, 50,* 905–915.

Kolb, L. C., & Multalipassi, L. R. (1982). The conditioned emotional response: A sub-class of the chronic and delayed post-traumatic stress disorder. *Psychiatric Annals, 12,* 979–987.

Kotchoubei, B. I. (1987). Human orienting reaction: The role of genetic and environmental factors in the variability of evoked potentials and autonomic components. *Activitas Nervosa Superior, 29,* 103–108.

Kulka, R. A., Schlenger, W. E., Fairbank, J. A., Hough, R. L., Jordan, B. K., Marmar, C. R., & Weiss, D. S. (1988). *Contractual report of findings from the National Vietnam Veterans Readjustment Study.* Research Triangle Park, NC: Research Triangle Institute.

Lykken, D. T., Iacono, W. G., Haroian, K., McGue, M., & Bouchard, T. J. (1988). Habituation of the skin conductance responses to strong stimuli: A twin study. *Psychophysiology, 25,* 4–15.

Lyons, M. J., Goldberg, J., Eisen, S. A., True, W., Tsuang, M. T., Meyer, J. M., & Henderson, W. G. (1993). Do genes influence exposure to trauma? A twin study of combat. *American Journal of Medical Genetics (Neuropsychiatric Genetics), 48,* 22–27.

McFarlane, A. C. (1989). The aetiology of post-traumatic morbidity: Predisposing, precipitating and perpetuating factors. *British Journal of Psychiatry, 154,* 221–228.

McFarlane, A. C., Weber, D. L., & Clark, C. R. (1993). Abnormal stimulus processing in posttraumatic stress disorder. *Biological Psychiatry, 34,* 311–320.

Mirsky, A. F., & Duncan, C. C. (1986). Etiology and expression of schizophrenia: Neurobiological and psychosocial factors. *Annual Review of Psychology, 37,* 291–319.

Nace, E. P., Meyers, A. L., O'Brien, C. P., Ream, N., & Mintz, J. (1977). Depression in veterans two years after Viet Nam. *American Journal of Psychiatry, 134,* 167–170.

Neale, M. C., & Cardon, L. R. (1992). *Methodology for genetic studies of twins and families.* Dordrecht, The Netherlands: Kluwer Academic Publishers.

O'Connor, S., Morzorati, S., Christian, J. C., & Li, T. K. (1994). Heritable features of the auditory oddball event-related potential: Peaks, latencies, morphology and topography. *Electroencephalography and Clinical Neurophysiology, 92,* 115–125.

Ohman, A., & Bohlin, G. (1973). Magnitude and habituation of the orienting reaction as predictors of discriminative electrodermal conditioning. *Journal of Experimental Research in Personality, 6,* 293–299.

Orr, S. P. (1994). An overview of psychophysiological studies of PTSD. *PTSD Quarterly, 5,* 1–7.

Orr, S. P., Lasko, N. B., Shalev, A. Y., & Pitman, R. K. (1995). Physiologic responses to loud tones in Vietnam veterans with post-traumatic stress disorder. *Journal of Abnormal Psychology, 104:* 75–82.

Paige, S. R., Reid, G. M., Allen, M. G., & Newton, J. E. O. (1990). Psychophysiological correlates of posttraumatic stress disorder in Vietnam veterans. *Biological Psychiatry, 27,* 419–430.

Pfefferbaum, A., Wenegrat, B. G., Ford, J. M., Roth, W. T., & Kopell, B. S. (1984). Clinical application of the P3 component of event-related potentials: II. Dementia, depression and schizophrenia. *Electroencephalography and Clinical Neurophysiology, 59,* 104–124.

Pitman, R. K. (1988). Post-traumatic stress disorder, conditioning, and network theory. *Psychiatric Annals, 18,* 182–189.

Pitman, R. K., Orr, S. P., Lowenhagen, M. J., Macklin, M. L., & Altman, B. (1991). Pre-Vietnam contents of posttraumatic stress disorder veterans' service medical and personnel records. *Comprehensive Psychiatry, 32,* 416–422.

Polich, J. (1989). Neuroanatomical contributions to individual differences in P300 morphology. In E. Basar, T. H. Bullock (Eds.), *Springer series in brain dynamics 2* (pp. 331–338). Berlin: Springer.

Polich, J., & Burns, T. (1987). P300 from identical twins. *Neuropsychologia, 25,* 299–304.

Polich, J., Pollock, V. E., & Bloom, F. E. (1994). Meta-analysis of P300 amplitude from males at risk for alcoholism. *Psychological Bulletin, 115,* 55–73.

Porjesz, B., Begleiter, H., & Samuelly, I. (1980). Cognitive deficits in chronic alcoholics and elderly subjects assessed by evoked brain potentials. *Acta Psychiatrica Scandinavica Suppl 286, 62,* 15–29.

Razran, G. (1957). The dominance-contiguity theory of the acquisition of classical conditioning. *Psychological Bulletin, 54,* 1–46.

Rogers, T. D., & Deary, I. (1991). The P300 component of the auditory event-related potential in monozygotic and dizygotic twins. *Acta Psychiatrica Scandinavica, 83,* 412–416.

Roth, W. T., Dorato, K. H., & Kopell, B. S. (1984). Intensity and task effects on evoked physiological responses to noise bursts. *Psychophysiology, 21,* 466–481

Saletu, B., Saletu, M., Marasa, J., Mednick, S., & Schulsinger, F. (1975). Acoustic evoked potentials in offsprings of schizophrenic mothers ("high risk" children for schizophrenia). *Clinical Electroencephalography, 6,* 92–102.

Shalev, A. Y., Orr, S. P., Peri, P., Schreiber, S., & Pitman, R. K. (1992). Physiologic responses to loud tones in Israeli post-traumatic stress disorder patients. *Archives of General Psychiatry, 49,* 870–975.

Shalev, A. Y., Peri, T., Gelpin, G., Gur, E., Oumanski, L., & Bloch, M. (1994). Startle and alprazolam in PTSD and panic disorder. *American Psychiatric Association 1994 Annual Meeting New Research Program and Abstracts,* p. 212.

Shatan, C. F. (1973). The grief of soldiers: Vietnam combat veterans' self-help movement. *American Journal of Orthopsychiatry, 43,* 640–653.

Siegel, J., Sisson, D. F., & Driscoll, P. (1993). Augmenting and reducing of visual evoked potentials in roman high- and low-avoidance rats. *Physiology and Behavior, 54,* 707–711.

Speed, N., Engdahl, B., Schwartz, J., & Eberly, R. (1989). Posttraumatic stress disorder as a consequence of the POW experience. *Journal of Nervous and Mental Disorder, 177,* 147–153.

Steinhauer, S. R., Hill, S. Y., & Zubin, J. (1987). Event-related potentials in alcoholics and their first-degree relatives. *Alcohol, 4,* 307–314.

Surwillo, W. W. (1980). Cortical evoked potentials in monozygotic twins and unrelated subjects: Comparisons of exogenous and endogenous components. *Behavior Genetics, 10,* 201–209.

True, W. R., Rice, J., Eisen, S. A., Heath, A. C., Goldberg, J., Lyons, M. J., & Nowak, J. (1993). A twin study of genetic and environmental contributions to liability for posttraumatic stress symptoms. *Archives of General Psychiatry, 50,* 257–264.

Turpin, G. (1983). Unconditioned reflexes and the autonomic nervous system. In D. Siddle (Ed.), *Orienting and habituation: Perspectives in human research,* (pp. 1–70). New York: John Wiley & Sons.

Wilson, J. P., & Krauss, G. E. (1985). Predicting post-traumatic stress disorders among Vietnam veterans. In W. E. Kelly (Ed.), *Post-traumatic stress disorder and the war veteran patient* (pp. 102–147). New York: Brunner/Mazel.

Yehuda, R., Lowy, M. T., Southwick, S. M., Shaffer, S., & Giller, E. L. (1991). Lymphocyte glucocorticoid receptor number in posttraumatic stress disorder. *American Journal of Psychiatry, 149,* 499–504.

Yehuda, R., Southwick, S. M., Krystal, J. H., Bremner, D., Charney, D. S., & Mason, J. W. (1993). Enhanced suppression of cortisol following dexamethasone administration in posttraumatic stress disorder. *American Journal of Psychiatry, 150,* 83–86.

Yehuda, R., Southwick, S. M., Nussbaum, G., Wahby, V., Giller, E. L., Jr., & Mason, J. W. (1990). Low urinary cortisol excretion in PTSD. *Journal of Nervous and Mental Disease, 178,* 366–369.

CHAPTER 8

GENDER AND POSTTRAUMATIC STRESS DISORDER

GLENN SAXE, M.D.,
Chairman, Dept of Child and Adolescent Psychiatry
Boston University School of Medicine

and

JESSICA WOLFE, PH.D., DIRECTOR
Women's Health Sciences Division, National Center for PTSD

Gender powerfully influences the way people think about themselves and others. It may be the first quality that a person notices in others (Cross & Markus, 1993) and is one of the earliest social constructs that children apprehend (Kohlberg, 1966; Kohlberg & Ullian, 1974). Most children have a clear sense of their gender identity by the time they are two or three years old (Slaby & Frey, 1975; Thompson, 1975). Once this identity is developed, it profoundly influences subsequent thought, feelings, and behavior (Sherif, 1982). Given the power of gender to affect the way in which events are processed, it is expected that notions of gender would influence the processing of extreme events. This chapter focuses upon how gender influences the processing of these extreme events. Specifically, we review how gender, traumatic events, and posttraumatic stress disorder (PTSD) are related.

The most well documented psychopathological response to extreme events is PTSD. Attention has recently been devoted to differential prevalence rates of PTSD in traumatized men and women. A number of large epidemiological studies have concluded that women are more at risk for PTSD than men (Breslau, Davis, Andreski, & Peterson, 1991; Breslau & Davis, 1992; Cottler, Compton, Mager, & Spitznagel, 1992; Kessler, Sonnega, Bromet, Hughes, & Nelson, 1995; Norris, 1992). These studies have found that women have up to twice the rate of PTSD as men (e.g.,

Kessler et al., 1995), findings which are consistent with sex differences reported for rates of major depression and for other anxiety disorders (Robins & Regier, 1991; Robins et al., 1984). The present chapter is concerned with understanding the meaning of these data. These critical findings on the higher prevalence of PTSD in women may be spurious, as systematic biases can enter any gender-related research. Alternatively, these findings may indicate important differences in vulnerabilities to traumatic events between women and men. In order to fully understand how gender, trauma, and PTSD are related, this chapter will begin with a review of these epidemiological studies. We will then review controversies with these studies and use multiple perspectives in order to understand their meaning. Specifically, we will review biological, psychodynamic, and social-cognition perspectives on gender in order to understand whether women are more vulnerable than men to traumatic events, and how systematic biases can enter into research on gender. We use a multi-perspective approach because the construct of gender is so complex, controversial, and powerful that no one perspective appears to capture the totality of it's influence.

There are numerous studies exploring the nature of PTSD and the nature of gender, respectively. Unfortunately, there are very few empirical studies examining how gender and PTSD are related. Thus far, the literature on this topic is largely descriptive and primarily documents different prevalence rates of PTSD. A possible reason why this critical literature has not advanced is that the study of the relationship between gender, trauma, and PTSD is laden with difficult methodological and conceptual issues. For example, men and women tend to experience different types of traumatic events across the life span. Women are much more likely to experience interpersonal violence, particularly sexual violence, than men (e.g., Norris, 1992; Kessler et al., 1995). Women are also more likely to seek help for distress than men (e.g., Phillips & Segal, 1969). These methodological issues potentially confound any estimation of the differential effects of trauma on men and women. A major conceptual issue within the area of gender studies involves the concept that gender is not a binary variable. The construct of gender is multiply determined and influenced by genetics, hormonal environments, and socialization. Concepts such as gender identity and gender roles color the variable of gender into much finer hues than simply "male" or "female." Moreover the topic of gender and PTSD is laden with social and political controversy. For example, any notion of women being more "at risk" for PTSD, despite lower rates of exposure to trauma (e.g., Kessler et al., 1995), is reminiscent of the notion of women as the "weaker sex," which has deleterious political implications.

In the absence of any comprehensive or sophisticated empirical literature on the relationship between gender and PTSD, this chapter should be viewed as an exploration of the possible relationships between these two constructs and, particularly, about why data appears to conclude that women are more vulnerable to traumatic events than men. In concluding, we specifically outline areas of study that can lead to the development of further empirical study of the relationship between gender and PTSD.

PREVALENCE OF PTSD IN MEN AND WOMEN

In order to derive a preliminary understanding of how gender, trauma, and PTSD are related, it is important to understand differences in the rates of PTSD between traumatized females and males. The current section reviews a series of large community studies on the rates of PTSD in adults and children. After the data from community samples are reviewed, findings from a series of studies on PTSD following natural disasters are considered.

In one of the earlier studies, Breslau and colleagues (Breslau et al., 1991; Breslau & Davis, 1992) used the Diagnostic Interview Schedule (Spitzer, 1981; Robins, Helzer, Croughan, & Radcliffe, 1981) to study a large urban sample (n = 1,007) of male and female health membership organization (HMO) members and found that 39 percent (n = 394) of the combined sample described exposure to an event consistent with the definition of a traumatic stressor. Of individuals who reported trauma, nearly 24 percent met Diagnostic and Statistical Manual of Mental Disorders, third edition-revised (DSM III-R; American Psychiatric Association, 1987) criteria for PTSD, yielding a lifetime sample prevalence of 9.2 percent. Moreover, nearly 57 percent (n = 53) of those with the disorder were classified as "chronic," defined as being symptomatic for more than one year. These two studies together highlighted an important finding: The PTSD diagnosis was linked to certain respondent characteristics, notably female gender. In fact, results showed that female respondents were *four* times more likely than men to develop chronic forms of PTSD following exposure to a traumatic event. In addition to gender, study results identified other PTSD "risk" factors including early separation from parents, a family history of anxiety disorders or antisocial personality, pre-existing anxiety or depression in the proband, and "neurotic style," variables which are often widely represented in women. Apart from the sequelae of rape, in which the PTSD diagnosis was exceedingly high, negligible gender outcome differences were found following other forms of traumatic exposure. Thus initial findings of greater PTSD in women were not readily explained.

Subsequently, Cottler et al. (1992), using the St. Louis area sample from the National Institute of Mental Health's Epidemiological Catchment Area (ECA) study, explored PTSD rates and their relationship to substance abuse in men and women utilizing the Diagnostic Interview Schedule. Relying on a relatively ethnically diverse sample of young and middle-aged men and women, their results indicated that female gender and cocaine or opiate use were the two strongest predictors of both exposure to a traumatic stressor and the subsequent development of PTSD. Although significant first-order correlations were found for younger age, Caucasian race, antisocial personality (ASP) diagnosis, and depression, there were no gender interactions among these outcomes. Similar to the work by Breslau et al. (1991, 1992), Cottler et al. (1992) based PTSD prevalence estimates on a model incorporating the most common traumatic life events, a method that potentially limits knowledge about the broader variety of stressor events. In addition, neither rape nor sexual assault—typically very strong predictors of PTSD in women—were distinctively classified, possibly influencing results based on the prevalence of the specific events and their sequelae.

Norris (1992) employed more rigorous diagnostic and stressor definitions to characterize traumatic exposure and PTSD in a large sample (n = 1,000) of men and women, classifying a spectrum of stressors into categories encompassing violent, hazard/natural disaster, and accidental occurrences. Also, the author obtained continuous measures of global distress and PTSD symptomatology using the Perceived Stress Scale (Cohen, Kamarck, & Mermelstein, 1983) and the Traumatic Stress Schedule (Norris, 1990), as opposed to earlier studies that relied exclusively on dichotomous classifications of these variables. These findings again showed the emergence of certain gender differences: Women were more likely to have suffered sexual assault while men evidenced increased risk for motor vehicle accidents, physical assault, and combat exposure, experiences producing higher overall exposure rates for males. In addition, a number of significant interactions pertaining to gender, event typology, and distress emerged. First, rape yielded the highest rates of PTSD although stated rates (14 percent) were lower than those found in other studies. Second, although the finding failed to reach statistical significance, women demonstrated a trend for higher rates of PTSD in general. Third, among participants who had been *criminally* victimized, women were significantly more likely to meet PTSD criteria than men. Thus, these data preliminarily suggest a differential gender risk for stressor exposure as well as for the subsequent development of PTSD when exposure is roughly comparable.

More recently, Kessler et al. (1995) studied the prevalence of PTSD in a nationally representative sample of 5,877 individuals between the ages of 15 and 54 as part of the National Comorbidity Survey using the Composite International Diagnostic Interview (Robins, Wing, Wittchen, & Helzer, 1988). In this study, 60.7 percent of men and 51.2 percent of women reported at least one traumatic event. Men were more likely than women to report witnessing someone being injured or killed, being involved in a fire, flood, or natural disaster, being involved in a life threatening accident, being physically attacked, and combat exposure. Women were more likely to report rape, sexual molestation, childhood parental neglect, and childhood physical abuse. Similar to previous studies, certain types of traumatic events were more likely to cause PTSD than others. For example, rape was the event most likely to lead to PTSD.

These authors reported that although men were more likely to experience a traumatic event than women, women were more likely to develop PTSD. As 20.4 percent of the women and 8.2 percent of the men developed PTSD, the investigators concluded that women exposed to a traumatic event were more than twice as likely to develop PTSD.

The National Vietnam Veterans Readjustment Study (NVVRS) offers some of the most comprehensive data on the long-term functioning of male and female veterans following war exposure (Kulka et al., 1988; 1990). Secondary analyses by Weiss et al. (1992) found surprisingly few differences in PTSD lifetime prevalence between men and women: Male Vietnam theater veterans demonstrated a lifetime PTSD rate of 30.9 percent while the rate among female theater counterparts was 26 percent. Lifetime rates for partial PTSD were also highly comparable: Just over 22 percent of men met partial PTSD criteria compared to 21.2 percent of women. Thus, although current diagnostic rates for male and female veterans were more disparate (e.g., 15.2 percent men, 8.7 percent women), the likelihood of having had the disorder at some point following the war was similar. Still, these analyses do not consider possible differences in PTSD base rates nor potential interactions of gender by stressor type (Wolfe, Brown, Furey, & Levin, 1993).

Using a sample of young adults, Fischer (1992) evaluated college students and determined that among child abuse victims, females were significantly more likely than males to have suffered incest; also, heterosexual forms of abuse were significantly more common in girls than boys. Importantly, the attributions of females about the childhood event were substantially less likely to evidence blame for the perpetrator. These findings suggest that both exposure and event-related attributions vary by gender. Finally, childhood sexual abuse was a significant predictor of subsequent teenage or adult sexual abuse for women, suggesting that traumatic exposure is a factor leading to adult women's subsequent traumatic exposure and adverse psychological outcomes. Walker (1980) reported that boys experience significantly more physical abuse from their mother, a finding that, again, suggests a complex interaction between gender and exposure to trauma.

Unlike interpersonal violence, the relevance of gender as a factor in outcome following natural or technological disasters is equivocal, although some authors have shown an association between female gender and poorer recovery (e.g., Burger, 1992; Steinglass & Gerrity, 1990). Realmuto, Wagner, and Bartholow (1991) evaluated a community 13 months after its exposure to a technological disaster and found that PTSD was significantly more common among women overall. Positively diagnosed individuals also were more likely to be older and to have histories of prior psychiatric problems. Steinglass and Gerrity (1990), in another study involving two communities exposed to a severe natural disaster, found that female gender was again associated with higher rates of PTSD (although PTSD for the total sample decreased over time at four and 16 month follow-ups). Thus, there is preliminary information suggesting poorer post-disaster recovery in females in community samples when event characteristics are relatively stable. Still, the broad lack of event comparability makes these analyses difficult.

IS GENDER A "RISK-FACTOR" FOR PTSD?

The majority of the aforementioned studies appear to support the conclusion that women are more at risk for PTSD then men. A number of the reviewed studies find that males are more likely to be exposed to a traumatic event but females are more likely to develop PTSD after a given trauma. This conclusion—that female sex is a "risk-factor" for PTSD—must be critically evaluated. Accepting such a notion, as previously mentioned, has enormous social and political consequences and must be reviewed with particular scrutiny. The following section reviews a number of methodological difficulties with this literature.

1) The Nature of the Stressor. The types of traumatic events men and women experience may differ markedly. Women are more likely to be exposed to rape, sexual molestation, and childhood parental neglect. With the exception of physical attacks, men are more likely to be exposed to impersonal stressors including life threatening accidents, fires, floods, natural disasters, combat, and witnessing the injury or death of another (Kessler et al., 1995). As numerous investigators have reported, sexual trauma is associated with high rates of PTSD. The literature also suggests that women are significantly more likely to be exposed to sexual stressors. Although some studies have controlled for differences in exposure and found higher rates of PTSD in women (Kessler et al., 1995), these studies have not collected important details about the traumatic event. For example, analyses of the different events that women and men experience reveal that women are more likely to experience events that occur repeatedly (childhood sexual and physical abuse and neglect, perhaps rape) and in childhood. No study of sex differences in the prevalence rates of PTSD has systematically studied dimensions of the traumatic experience factors such as the chronicity of the event or the age at which the event occurred, that could conceivably influence rates of PTSD. In a recent review of this issue, Wolfe and Kimerling (1996) suggest that the following domains of the traumatic event must be assessed in order to fully evaluate apparent differences in rates of PTSD between men and women: "a) the total number of traumatic events, b) the duration of exposure (e.g., episodic or chronic), and c)the severity of exposure across dimensions (e.g., life threatening vs. non-life threatening; moderate vs. severe)" (p. 217). They add that it is particularly important to assess "role-related, social/contextual, and symbolic or connotative factors associated with particular stressors" (Wolfe & Kimerling, p. 217) in order to understand the differential effect of these stressors on men and women.

2) Reporting Styles.   Extensive research shows that women and men have different reporting styles (Phillips & Segal, 1969; Russo & Olmedo, 1983; Russo & Sobel, 1981). These differences may affect the degree to which women and men disclose experiences of traumatic events and symptoms of PTSD. Women endorse more symptoms of physical illness and emotional distress than men. Further, they tend to report a greater severity of symptoms overall (Verbrugge, 1983, 1985). These findings may mean that women truly have a greater frequency and degree of symptoms than men. Alternatively, they could also suggest that women either have a bias to over-report or men to under-report symptoms. Such reporting biases may affect estimates of PTSD prevalence rates between men and women.

3) Diagnostic Biases.   There is evidence that healthcare practitioners have diagnostic biases about gender. For example, studies of depression have found that women are more likely to be diagnosed with depression independent of whether they actually have that disorder (Loring & Powell, 1988). The higher rates of PTSD among females may have been influenced by similar diagnostic biases.

4) Gender or Sex Differences.   As the aforementioned studies involved sex differences in prevalence of PTSD, they are indirectly related to the influence of gender on PTSD. It is important to distinguish sex from gender as gender is a much more powerful and important construct. As previously described, men and women vary in the degree to which they identify with their biological sex and conform to traditional notions of sex roles. Lott and Maluso (1993), making the distinction between sex and gender, write,

> *Whereas sex denotes a limited set of innate structural and physiological characteristics related to reproduction, and divides the animal species into female and male, gender is specific to humans and connotes all the complex attributes ascribed by culture(s) to human females and males, respectively (p. 99).*

These "complex attributes" about what it means to be a woman or man, girl or boy, amplify and re-amplify biological differences between males and females. Powerful messages from family, community, and culture further structure these attributes. Although gender involves the subtle variables of identity, roles, and relationships, sex is defined as a binary variable. To date, no empirical study of PTSD has measured the construct of gender and associated correlates, yet all the studies reviewed in this chapter have examined sex differences in PTSD rates. One can thus only indirectly surmise the effect of gender on PTSD from their results.

PERSPECTIVES ON GENDER

The literature involving PTSD prevalence variations by gender cannot fully be understood without a grounding in basic conceptions of gender. We review three perspectives on gender: biological, feminist/psychodynamic, and social-cognition. Each of these perspectives has a distinct, but not mutually exclusive, way of understanding gender. We review how each of these perspectives can be used to understand the literature reporting the different prevalence rates of PTSD that were observed between men and women. Although the biological, psychodynamic, and social-cognition perspectives on gender are rather well developed, to our knowledge, no attempts have been made to link these theoretical perspectives to an understanding of how individuals respond to traumatic events. We attempt to make this link because we believe this information can greatly enrich our understanding of the trauma response.

1. Biological Perspective

The biological perspective looks at structural and physiological differences between men and women in order to determine whether any of these known differences can account for the observed differences in outcome. An important caveat is that, to date, almost all biological studies of PTSD have been conducted with male subjects. No biological studies, to our knowledge, have directly compared males and females, and only a very limited number of studies have examined the relationship between PTSD and a sex steroid (e.g., testosterone; Mason, Giller, Kosten, & Wahby, 1990). Therefore any discussion regarding the biology of gender differences and their relation to PTSD should be considered preliminary. In the following section we review a number of important psychobiological differences between men and women and their possible relationship to PTSD. Since there are large literatures on the biologies of sex differences and of PTSD, respectively, we present findings that could be most relevant to understanding gender differences in PTSD.

a) Hippocampal Damage. The hippocampus is potentially one of the most critical structures implicated in the processing of traumatic experience through its role as supplier of contextual information in memory. Recently, three studies using magnetic resonance imaging (MRI) have shown reduced hippocampal volumes in subjects with PTSD. Bremner et al. (1995) and Gurvitz, Shenton, and Pitman (1995) found reductions in hippocampal volume in male combat veterans with PTSD. Similarly, Stein and colleagues (1994) found that women with PTSD who experienced childhood sexual abuse had smaller hippocampal volumes.

These studies suggest that a hippocampal volumetric reduction might be related to PTSD in males and females. Since no study has directly compared females and males with PTSD, it is undetermined whether there are any systematic differences in hippocampal volume between men and women that could explain some of the reported greater PTSD prevalence rates among females. Despite the lack of data on this issue, there is evidence that there are sex differences in the response of the hippocampus to the environment. The hippocampus has been found to be more plastic in female rats (Juraska, 1991). Females responded to enriched environments with greater sprouting of dendritic trees than males. This difference stemmed from a suppression of plasticity by testosterone (Juraska, 1991). This pre-clinical finding

(i.e., the hippocampus of females are more responsive to enriched environments) potentially suggests that this critical brain structure might be highly susceptible to damage by noxious environments. A recent study using magnetic resonance imaging (MRI) and positron emission tomography (PET) found that aging diminishes the size and activity of the hippocampus to a greater degree in women than men (Murphy et al., 1996). This study found that although there was more brain atrophy over time in men than women, certain brain structures (particularly the hippocampus) diminished more in women. These data preliminarily suggest that females could be more vulnerable to hippocampal damage than males, suggesting one possible mechanism in the higher prevalence of PTSD in women.

b) Hemispheric Lateralization. A recent study using PET in patients with PTSD found that there are important hemispheric differences in the processing of intrusive memories (Rauch et al., 1996). This study measured regional cerebral blood flow changes in 8 patients (6 females, 2 males) with PTSD who were induced to reexperience their trauma with script-driven imagery. The investigators reported increased blood flow on the right limbic, paralimbic, and visual areas and decreased blood flow on the left inferior frontal and middle temporal cortex. This study is limited by a small number of subjects and the absence of a comparison group that did not have PTSD. Nevertheless, the findings suggest the possibility of important hemispheric differences in the processing of traumatic memories; specifically, the increased activation of the right limbic system and the decreased activity of the left inferior frontal system (responsible for speech production). As numerous studies have described important sex differences in the lateralization of the brain (LeVay, 1993), this study may be useful for understanding sex differences in rates of PTSD.

Females have a larger corpus callosum and anterior commissure relative to brain size then males (Allen, Richey, Chai, & Gorski, 1991; de Lacoste, Adesanya, & Woodward, 1990). Consistent with these differences, females have reduced hemispheric asymmetry compared to males (LeVay, 1993). This difference is particularly pronounced in the area of speech production. A study using functional magnetic resonance imaging found that during speech production women used both the left and right inferior frontal lobe whereas men used only the left inferior frontal lobe (Shaywitz et al., 1995). This finding may give females a protective advantage in PTSD since the aforementioned study found that the activity of the inferior frontal lobe was only diminished on the left during an intrusive memory provocation. No study, however, has directly compared men and women with PTSD in terms of the activity of the inferior frontal lobe. Speech production could be implicated in the development of PTSD since the ability to conceptualize and verbalize feelings has been described as an important protective factor in this disorder (Krystal, 1988).

While the findings reported by Rauch et al. (1996) suggest that a greater use of both hemispheres for language (Shaywitz et al., 1995) may offer a protective advantage in PTSD, there is some evidence that limbic processing in females could constitute an additional vulnerability. A study using PET that measured regional metabolism during induced feelings of sadness found that when women felt sad, they had increased bilateral activity of the limbic system compared to men (George et al., 1995; George, Ketter, Parekh, Herscovitch, & Post, 1996). As described above, there was increased limbic system activation during intrusive memories in subjects with PTSD on the right hemisphere. Females' heightened limbic responsiveness to basic emotional stimuli in general could represent a vulnerability to the development of PTSD.

c) Norepinepherine Function.

Norepinepherine (NE) is a neurotransmitter that is primarily stored in the locus coeruleus and released diffusely in the brain. This neurotransmitter is instrumental in influencing levels of arousal and attention (Zigmond, Finlay, & Sved, 1995). A number of studies of Vietnam veterans with PTSD have found it to be related to PTSD. Vietnam veterans with PTSD have been found to have elevated 24-hour urinary norepinepherine levels (Kosten, Mason, Giller, Ostroff, & Harkness, 1987) and augmented MHPG response to yohimbine administration (an agent that stimulates the locus coeruleus) (Southwick et al., 1993), as well as a decrease in platelet alpha$_2$-adrenergic receptors compared to a non-PTSD control group (Perry, Giller, & Southwick, 1987). Yohimbine administration also induces flashbacks and panic attacks in veterans with PTSD (Southwick et al., 1993). These studies support the role of a dysregulated norepinepherine system in individuals with PTSD. Specifically, individuals with PTSD have higher norepinepherine output and subsequent down-regulation of norepinepherine receptors than controls. Norepinepherine has been exclusively studied in men with PTSD, making it difficult to infer any role for this neurotransmitter in the differential rate of PTSD between men and women. Nevertheless, important sex differences have been found in norepinepherine function. Thus this system may be implicated in the difference in prevalence rates and PTSD.

Estrogen administration, *in vitro,* increases central norepinepherine availability (Paul, Axelrod, & Saavendra, 1979). Chronic estrogen treatment reduces B-adrenergic receptors in the rat cortex (Wagner, Crutcher, & Davis, 1979). In humans, estrogen alters platelet alpha$_2$-adrenergic binding with variations in the levels of these receptors throughout the menstrual cycle (Best, Rees, Barlow, & Cowen, 1992). Jones and colleagues (1983) found an increase in platelet alpha$_2$-adrenergic receptors in women just after menstruation. Studies comparing females and males for norepinepherine activity found that neonate and adult females have greater NE output than males (Claustre, Peyrin, Fitoussi, & Mornex, 1980; Cuche, Kuchel, Barbeau, & Genest, 1975; Dalmaz & Peyrin, 1982). Norepinepherine levels have also been found to fluctuate across phases of the menstrual cycle and are highest during the luteal phase (Goldstein, Levinson, & Kaiser, 1983; Zuspan & Zuspan, 1973; Jones et al., 1983). These findings, however, have not been replicated in some studies (Frankenhauser, Dunne, & Lundberg, 1976; Patkai, Johansson, & Post, 1974). If they are accurate, they represent one possible mechanism implicated in higher rates of PTSD in females.

Fluctuations of NE throughout the menstrual cycle are intriguing as this suggests that symptoms of

PTSD would be highest during phases of high NE output (luteal phase). No study to our knowledge has assessed fluctuations in PTSD symptoms throughout the menstrual cycle but such studies can yield useful information. As NE influences basic systems of arousal and attention and is implicated in the processing of traumatic events, it is possible that women would be more vulnerable to traumatic events during specific phases of the menstrual cycle.

d) Hypothalamic-Pituitary-Adrenal (HPA) Axis.

The HPA axis has been broadly implicated in the pathogenesis of PTSD. Subjects as diverse as Vietnam combat veterans (Mason et al., 1990) and Holocaust survivors (Yehuda, Kahane, et al., 1995) with PTSD have been found to have low urinary cortisol levels compared to non-PTSD control subjects. Combat veterans with PTSD have been found to have an increase in lymphocytes glucocorticoid receptors (Yehuda, Boisoneau, Lowy, & Giller, 1995; Yehuda, Lowry, Southwick, Shatter, & Giller, 1991) and an increased suppression of cortisol in response to dexamethasone (Yehuda et al., 1993). The number of glucocorticoid receptors is a particularly interesting index as it has been found to be correlated with the severity of PTSD. A recent study of female rape victims found that those with the lowest levels of salivary cortisol measured shortly after the rape were more likely to acquire PTSD measured six months later (Resnick, Yehuda, Pitman, & Foy, 1995). The findings of low cortisol and subsequent up-regulation of glucocorticoid receptors are important for understanding the pathogenesis of PTSD, as the glucocorticoid release has been called a "containing" or "counter-regulating" response (McEwen, 1995). That is, the release of glucocorticoids are thought to prevent the stress response from becoming too excessive. Given the critical role of the HPA axis in the pathogenesis of PTSD, it is possible that intrinsic differences in this system between women and men constitute a mechanism for the increased vulnerability of women to PTSD.

Although no studies have compared HPA axis function in men and women with actual PTSD, one study has compared men and women exposed to extreme stress. A study of individuals living near the Three Mile Island nuclear power plant at the time of the nuclear accident found that men who lived close to the power plant had higher urinary cortisol levels than women. Importantly, no differences in cortisol levels were found between men and women who lived a prescribed distance from the plant (Schaeffer & Baum, 1984). Consistent with this finding, a study of neonates found that when males were exposed to the mild stress of a behavioral assessment they had higher salivary cortisol responses than females, although females had higher heart rate increases to the same stress (Davis & Emory, 1995). A study of adolescents and adults under mildly stressful conditions (public speaking and performing mental arithmetic in public) found that males had 1.5 to 2-fold higher cortisol levels than females (Kirschbaum, Wust, & Hellhammer, 1992). Further, males had increased cortisol levels in anticipation of these stressors than females who remained unchanged or even showed decreased cortisol levels while anticipating a stressful event (Kirschbaum et al., 1992). This finding of higher cortisol responses to stress in males than females has also been documented in animal studies (Weinberg & Wong, 1986). A number of studies, however, have not found greater release of cortisol in males (Gallucci et al., 1993; Scallet, Suomi, & Bowman, 1981).

The findings that males tend to have higher glucocorticoid responses to stress then females has important implications for understanding sex differences and PTSD. If the release of cortisol is an important method for "counter-regulating" stress, then the increased release of this steroid offers males an advantage over females in responding to stressful conditions. The finding that low cortisol after rape predicts PTSD symptoms, and that individuals with PTSD have lower cortisol levels and up-regulation of glucocorticoid receptors, are consistent with this hypothesis.

Other studies have implicated sex steroids in the attenuated cortisol response to stress in females. One study found that females taking oral contraception pills containing sex steroids had lower cortisol responses during stress (Kirschbaum, Pirke, & Hellhammer, 1995). Cortisol release also fluctuates routinely during the menstrual cycle. Specifically, women had lower cortisol responses to stress in the follicular than in the luteal phase (Tersman, Collins, & Eneroth,

1991). Similar to the data on norepinepherine response, the fact that glucocorticoid responses to stress fluctuate systematically in the menstrual cycle suggests that perhaps symptoms of PTSD fluctuate in a similar way. Such data also raise the possibility that women might be more vulnerable to traumatization if exposed during certain phases of the menstrual cycle. Although this hypothesis is speculative, studies of women's stress-related symptoms across the menstrual cycle are clearly needed.

e) Behavioral Sensitization.   Several investigators have speculated that the phenomena of behavioral sensitization or kindling may be an important pathogenic factor contributing to the development of PTSD (Charney, Deutch, Krystal, Southwick, & Davis, 1993; van der Kolk, 1994; Post, Weiss, & Smith, 1995). Sensitization or kindling refers to the phenomenon of increased response magnitude following exposure to a given stimulus. Repeated presentations of the stimulus create a situation of perpetually increasing magnitudes of response. Sensitization and kindling are mechanisms well known for their link to cocaine dependence (Post, Weiss, Pert, & Uhde, 1987) and seizures (Goddard, McIntyre, & Leech, 1969). They have also been used as models for understanding bipolar disorder (Post, Rubinow, & Ballenger, 1986) and have recently been used to explain the symptoms of PTSD (Charney et al., 1993; van der Kolk, 1994; Post et al., 1995). These processes are useful in explaining the increasing responsiveness to stressful events that are known to occur in individuals with PTSD. They help explain the chronicity and treatment refractory nature of PTSD and are consistent with what is known about the neurobiology of PTSD (Charney et al., 1993; van der Kolk, 1994; Post et al., 1995).

There is evidence suggesting that females are more vulnerable to sensitization than males. Studies in animal populations have demonstrated that female rats have significantly greater behavioral response magnitudes to repeated administrations of amphetamines, often twice as high as males (Robinson, Becker, & Presty, 1982). This increase in sensitization was found in both normal and ovarectomized females but not in genetic males with testes. Such

results suggest that the decrease in sensitization to amphetamine in males is due in large part to the presence of testosterone (Robinson et al., 1982; Camp & Robinson, 1988a, 1988b). There is also evidence that estrogen, but not testosterone, can lower seizure thresholds (Newmark & Penry, 1980). Such data, on the increased behavioral sensitization in females and the reduced seizure thresholds caused by estrogen, could support a sensitization or kindling explanation for the increased prevalence of PTSD in women.

This section reviewed sex differences in a number of neurobiological systems and the evidence supporting the idea that these differences may be instrumental in understanding the documented higher prevalence of PTSD in females. Although the data reviewed are far from conclusive, and some data are contradictory, there is emerging evidence that the female hippocampus is more vulnerable to damage, that the female limbic system has an increased responsivity to emotional signals (at least negative ones, e.g., sadness), that there is increased noradrenergic and decreased glucocorticoid activity to stress in females, and that the female brain is more vulnerable to mechanisms of sensitization. Each of these neurobiological responses has in some way been linked to PTSD. Thus, there is a literature suggestive of neurobiological vulnerability in females (or resiliency in males) although, to date, no study has directly compared traumatized men or women or men and women with PTSD. Thus, there is a great need for studies of sex differences in brain structure and function in individuals with PTSD. The compelling literature on the neuroendocrinology of PTSD must be expanded to include gender. At the very least, females should be included as subjects in neurobiological studies. In the absence of such studies, any conclusions regarding gender-related neurobiological vulnerabilities to PTSD remain speculative.

Future studies must also account for the relationship between the menstrual cycle and neurobiological changes in PTSD. The literature on changes in noradrenergic and glucocorticoid differences across the menstrual cycle is preliminarily compelling. It is important to study the possible consequent changes in posttraumatic symptoms across the menstrual cycle, and whether women are more vulnerable to PTSD if traumatized at certain phases of the menstrual cycle.

2. Feminist/Psychodynamic Perspective

Psychodynamic and psychoanalytic perspectives of gender have experienced a tremendous degree of up-heaval in recent years due to feminist challenges to Freud's earlier notions about gender differences (Freud, 1931). Although details of this debate are beyond the scope of this chapter, they have resulted in a "self-in-relation" theory about women and men which, although still controversial, has received a large degree of acceptance (Jordan & Surrey, 1986; Miller, 1986). This theory describes separate lines of development between men and women, particularly around the nature of relationships.

The self-in-relation theory suggests a special status of relationships for women. According to this model, a woman's sense of herself is very closely related to relationships with others and, particularly, to the reciprocal caring in relationships. Miller (1986, p. 597) suggests that women's sense of themselves is defined by "the ongoing intrinsic inner awareness and responsiveness to the continuous existence of other or others and the expectation of mutuality in this regard." This sense is "...very much organized around being able to make and then to maintain affiliation and relationships" (Miller, 1986, p. 597). A woman's self-esteem is thus highly related to the quality of her relationships and is based on the sense that she is "a part of relationships and is taking care of relationships" (Jordan & Surrey, 1986, p. 597). Although relationships are, of course, important to most men, men define themselves less by relationships. Theories on the nature of these differences concern early attachments and identifications primarily based on the mother–child relationship. Chadorow (1978) proposes that mothers and daughters experience a sense of similarity and continuity with each other that is not experienced in a mother–son relationship. When daughters think about issues related to who they are, they have a ready reference point—"I am like my mother." According to Chadorow, a son must answer "I am not like my mother." Because boys must change their identifications early in development, they can more easily see themselves as separate and distinct than can girls and are less focused on relationships than are girls. Girls' development,

in contrast, is marked by a stronger sense of connection.

From an interpersonal point of view, women and men thus have very different ways of thinking about themselves and others. Gilligan (1982) extends this theory into other domains when she writes about differences in moral judgments between women and men. The female approach is based on attachment and caring while the male approach is based on separation and individuality. Thus, women tend to base judgments in larger part on the preservation of relationships while men tend to make judgments more strongly on rules of justice and fairness. Numerous studies have found that females are more empathic than males (e.g., Eisenberg & Lennon, 1983; Hoffman, 1977). In an extensive review of the literature, Hall (1978) reported that females were better than males at decoding and interpreting visual and auditory cues about others' affective states.

The self-in-relation perspective to gender differences offers one possible explanation for why women may be more vulnerable to traumatic events than men. Using this perspective, women could be more vulnerable to interpersonal traumatic events because relationships are more closely tied to personal identity and sense of self. If a woman's sense of herself and her self-esteem is closely tied to "...being able to make and then to maintain affiliation and relationships" (Miller, 1986), then she would be particularly vulnerable to the violation of these relationships by others. In this way, the experience of assault by another person, particularly in a close trusting relationship, may lead to strong tendencies to restore the relationship or to blame herself for losing the relationship or causing the assault.

Studies reviewed in this chapter have reported that women are more likely to experience interpersonal trauma then men (Norris, 1992; Kessler et al., 1995). They are more likely to be traumatized by someone they know, and are much more likely to experience sexual trauma. Using a self-in-relation perspective, one can surmise that these are precisely the types of traumatic events to which women would have the most difficulty coping. Thus women may have higher prevalence rates of PTSD than men because the types of trauma that they tend to experience are the types of traumas to which they are most vulnerable. The types of traumas that women are more likely to be exposed to—domestic violence, rape, childhood sexual abuse—are so laden with relational meanings that they would lead to profound reappraisals of "connections" with others. Such connections are a critical factor in women's development and are integrally linked to a woman's sense of identity and self (Jordan and Surrey, 1986; Miller, 1986). Further, as interconnections are so important for women, the impact of disclosing the traumatic experiences in interpersonal relationships are particularly salient for women. Disclosure of trauma, particularly rape, may have devastating effects on one's relationships with others (Herman, 1992). No study has examined sex differences in rates of disclosure after a traumatic experience, but one would expect that the experience of disclosing an interpersonal trauma would be different for women for the reasons outlined above. As the propensity to disclose and share one's experience is generally an important protective factor after a traumatic event (Pennebacker & Sussman, 1988), this difficulty could contribute to the observed vulnerability of women to traumatic events.

Traumatic events are alienating experiences. Victims frequently feel totally alone. As Herman (1992) has written

> Traumatic events call into question basic relationships. They breach the attachments of family, friendship, love, and community. They shatter the construction of the self that is formed and sustained in relation to others.... The damage to relational life is not a secondary effect of trauma, as originally thought. Traumatic events have primary effects not only on the psychological structures of the self but also on the systems of attachment and meaning that link individual and community (p. 51).

This experience of disconnection is very difficult for women. It is fueled by the consistent finding that the types of traumatic events that women tend to experience are private (sexual trauma, domestic violence) and, at times, cannot be shared without severing relations with one's community. The experience of support and belonging that individuals acquire through membership in community is a critically important factor for recovery after trauma (Harvey, 1996).

A particular manner in which interpersonal traumas may leave women increasingly vulnerable, and would be expected from a self-in-relation perspective, concerns the way in which women tend to attribute responsibility for these events. Studies have demonstrated that females are more likely to attribute blame for events to themselves than to others (Fischer, 1992). Traumatic events in particular are more likely to lead to self-blame among female than male victims. Fischer (1992) found that female child abuse victims were more likely to blame themselves for the abuse and to display confusion about what behaviors constituted abuse and assault than male victims. Males were more likely to attribute blame to the perpetrator. Such differences in attributional styles have significant implications for outcome after a traumatic event. Gidycz and Koss (1991) found that college age females who blamed themselves for a traumatic event had significantly poorer outcomes than those who did not blame themselves. There are many possible explanations for such differences in attributional style. A self-in-relation perspective would explain such differences through women's greater need to maintain, restore, and repair relationships.

The self-in-relation perspective focuses on social and developmental differences between women and men and offers important ways to understand why women could have greater vulnerability to traumatization. Specifically, as women's development is integrally related to connections with others, women may be vulnerable to the types of trauma they encounter, to the degree that these are relationship-based. This perspective offers ways of understanding why women may blame themselves after a trauma and fail to disclose the trauma. Although the self-in-relation perspective offers many ways to understand gender-related differences in response to interpersonal trauma, it is limited by the fact that no studies have directly compared the impact of relationships on traumatized women and men. These ideas are testable and require studies on how traumatized men and women experience relationships and the impact of this experience on posttraumatic sequelae. Further, studies can evaluate variables such as how traumatized women and men attempt to maintain and restore relationships and how they make decisions about disclosing the trauma.

3. Social-Cognition Perspective. Social-cognition theories describe gender as a "social category" (Ashmore, 1990; Cross & Markus, 1993; Deaux, 1984). According to this perspective, an individual's gender identity is partially determined by the meanings of being a male and female in the social environment in which an individual grows up and lives. Social-cognition theorists describe gender as a central organizing construct by which individuals develop a self-concept and the way in which this self-concept is constructed is strongly influenced by the social meanings of being a male or female in a given environment. In a comprehensive review of these ideas, Ashmore (1990) describes the factors that lead to the development of gender identity as (1) the influence of culture, (2) relationships with specific men and women, and (3) self-guided activities (activities that children engage in have a self-perpetuating influence on gender identity). According to this view, biology has an important place in the development of gender identity, in that identity begins with the awareness of physical difference, but this identity is impacted more by social environment.

Cross and Markus (1993) describe gender as a basic dimension used to divide the universe "perhaps second only to what is part of the self and what is not part of the self" (p. 58). Gender is one of the first social categories acquired by children (Slaby & Frey, 1975; Spence, 1985). This category is powerfully used by children to understand themselves and others and, once developed, determines a great deal of subsequent behavior (Sherif, 1982). Cross & Markus (1993) describe the influence of gender as so pervasive that "...referring to it as a role or a category, while useful in detailing its precise behavioral consequences, runs the risk of trivializing the importance of gender identity in human experience" (p. 59).

In order to fully understand the meaning of the different prevalence rates of PTSD between men and women, it is critical to understand how gender is constructed as a social category and the power of this category to influence the thoughts, feelings, and beliefs of traumatized individuals. Such an understanding requires research which directly compares the thoughts and beliefs of traumatized women and men, and examines the effect of these cognitions on symptoms

and behavior. In order to definitively understand the influence of the social categorization of gender, such studies must directly measure gender identity and cognitions about gender. In the absence of such studies, notions about the influence of the social categorization of gender are preliminary. Nevertheless, given the power of this category, it is critical that PTSD researchers and clinicians consider the possible influences of gender on their subjects and patients. With these caveats, we offer the following hypotheses about the influence of the social categorization of gender on the development of PTSD.

In many social environments, boys and girls learn that men are active, aggressive, and instrumental while women are passive, relational, and emotional (Ashmore, 1981; Ashmore, Del Boca, & Wohlers, 1986; Eagly, 1987). Although such notions of gender are changing somewhat as women enter the work force, there is evidence that they have changed little in the past twenty-five years (Bergen & Williams, 1991; Heilman, Block, Martell, & Simon, 1989). These notions of the meanings of gender are repeatedly reinforced by family, school, community, and culture (Hoffman & Hurst, 1990; Hyde, Krajnik, & Skuldt-Niederberger, 1991). These notions are remarkably similar across cultures (Kenrick & Trost, 1993). For a great many reasons, individuals are motivated to conform to these shared social notions about gender. Social environments, of course, vary in the degree to which the above gender meanings are accepted and expressed. Individuals also vary in terms of the degree to which (1) gender as a social category is integrated into self-concept and (2) the above notions of gender are a part of that self-concept (Ashmore, 1990). Nevertheless, most studies of men and women, at least in western culture, have found a high degree of acceptance of the above notions of gender (Ashmore, 1981; Ashmore et al., 1986; Eagly, 1987).

Using a social-cognition perspective, one can surmise the differential impact of trauma on women and men by understanding how the meanings of the traumatic event relate to the shared meanings of being a woman or man in a given social environment. Traumatic events lead to profound feelings of passivity, helplessness, and powerlessness (Herman, 1992). The event is usually unexpected, and, frequently, victims feel that their life is in jeopardy. During the event, the victim feels out of control and terrified. Later, if individuals are stricken with intrusive memories of the trauma, the feelings of passivity, helplessness, and terror are repeatedly relived. We believe this experience of passivity and helplessness is different for women and men. First, this experience is likely to be more dissonant with the social construction of masculinity than femininity. In most cultures, men have few frames of reference for the role of victim: They are not viewed as passive or helpless. In addition, the shared social notion of masculinity is as active, in control, and aggressive. The shared social notion of femininity, in contrast, is more passive and vulnerable (Ashmore, 1981; Ashmore et al., 1986; Eagly, 1987).

If it is true that cognitions related to traumatic events are more dissonant to male than female gender identity, the impact of this dissonance on traumatized individuals must be considered. Festinger (1957) proposed that cognitive dissonance is distressing and that individuals will be motivated to reduce this dissonance. Typically, cognitive dissonance can be reduced by altering cognitions or behavior. Traumatized men who experience a dissonance between their cognitions related to their gender (e.g., active, strong, in control) and their cognitions related to trauma (e.g., passive, weak, and helpless) may be motivated to change their thoughts and behavior in very meaningful ways. Men may be motivated to alter their cognitions about their gender identity in less adaptive (e.g., "I am not a 'real' man") or more adaptive ways (e.g., "Men are not always strong"). Men may also be motivated to alter their thoughts and beliefs about the trauma (e.g., "what trauma?", "it was no big deal," "life goes on…don't dwell on the past"). Men whose beliefs about their gender arc particularly threatened may change their behavior in destructive ways in order to reduce cognitive dissonance. Aggressive behaviors and perpetration of trauma are well described in traumatized males (e.g., Groth & Burgess, 1980; Lewis, 1992) and may be motivated by this need to reduce dissonance ("I really am a man if I can assault you"). We thus hypothesize that the cognitive dissonance between constructs of masculinity and trauma create strong motivation in men to alter their thoughts and behavior in order to reduce the experienced impact of

the trauma. To the degree that women experience less cognitive dissonance, they may be less motivated (for this reason at least) to minimize the impact of trauma. As described in the previous section, there are other reasons why females may be motivated to minimize the impact of trauma.

It is important to consider how shared social constructions of gender may influence clinicians and researchers in their assessments of traumatized individuals. There is very little empirical data on this topic. It should be stated at the outset that clinicians and researchers have historically not acknowledged the impact of sexual trauma on women (Herman, 1992). One can speculate, however, using a social-cognition perspective that clinicians and researchers may be less likely to acknowledge the impact of trauma on men because they share a social construct of gender. In other words, as clinicians and researchers have shared social constructs of men as active, instrumental, and aggressive; and women as passive, dependent, and emotional, they may similarly experience cognitive dissonance while assessing male trauma. As, we suspect, a primary means of reducing such cognitive dissonance is altering cognitions to minimize the impact of trauma, this could occur while assessing traumatized men and may be a reason that the prevalence rate of PTSD is higher in women. Consistent with this notion are findings that clinicians are more likely to diagnose women than men as depressed, independent of the degree of symptoms (Loring & Powell, 1988). Studies have also found that observers have important gender-related biases about the emotional state of others. For example, a well-known study had subjects observing a videotape of a baby playing with a jack-in-the-box toy and were told that the baby was either male or female. The baby cried at one point in the videotape when the jack-in-the-box opened. Subjects who were told that the baby was a girl were more likely to label the emotion as "fear." Subjects who were told that the baby was a boy were more likely to label the emotion as "anger." Although the total mechanisms for such judgments are not fully understood, this study suggests that observers judge the emotional state of others in ways that are at least partly consonant with their own beliefs about gender (Condry & Condry, 1976).

Using a social-cognition perspective, we hypothesize a cognitive dissonance in males between gender-related cognitions and trauma-related cognitions that is not experienced by females. We hypothesize that this dissonance influences men to minimize the impact of trauma and may be a reason for the difference in prevalence rates of PTSD between men and women. This dissonance may also contribute to changes in gender-related cognitions and to aggressive behavior in traumatized men. Women may be more likely to report posttraumatic symptoms because they can more easily acknowledge these symptoms than men. Clinicians and researchers may falsely elevate estimations of the prevalence rates of PTSD in women because of shared social biases about men and women. These ideas are, of course, preliminary but are testable and require the assessment of trauma and gender-related cognitions in comparably traumatized women and men.

SUMMARY AND CONCLUSIONS

Accumulating evidence supports a higher prevalence rate of PTSD in women than men. Well-designed epidemiological studies have found that women have approximately twice the rate of PTSD despite the fact that they are less likely to be exposed to traumatic stressors (Norris, 1992; Kessler et al., 1995). These data are compelling, but, as we have reviewed, the relationship between gender and trauma is multidimensional and complex. Differences between men and women on numerous variables, including types of trauma, reporting styles, and observer biases about gender, limit the interpretations of data related to definitive gender differences and PTSD. Further, the lack of studies which directly compare traumatized males and females on all but the most rudimentary descriptive indices makes any conclusions about gender and PTSD preliminary.

This chapter has filtered data from many sources through the lenses of three different psychological perspectives on gender. We have identified a number of important vulnerability factors for women. We have also found a number of different ways in which estimations of the higher prevalence of PTSD in women may be distorted. In our review of the literature, we have found evidence of differences in brain morphology and function that could lead to certain forms of vulnerability in women. Evidence of increased female vulnerability to trauma was also identified in a number of neurotransmitter systems. Review of the psychodynamic literature suggests that women may have a particular vulnerability to traumatic stressors that they encounter frequently. The social-cognition literature suggests a mechanism by which men may minimize the impact of trauma to themselves and to others. Such social interpretations could also be shared by clinicians and researchers, and lead them to minimize the impact of trauma on men.

We are aware that, in the absence of studies that directly compare traumatized men and women or that measure the construct of gender, such conclusions make important and unsubstantiated assumptions. At the very least, we hope that readers will find our review of these three perspectives on gender useful in their own struggle to understand their patients and to make sense of the existing data on sex differences and PTSD.

The future offers a number of important research directions. First, there are opportunities to study gender differences and PTSD across a range of neurobiological systems. To date, women have largely been excluded from neurobiological studies of PTSD. As we reviewed, there may be important gender-related biological differences between PTSD in women and men. There is also reason to believe that there are important neurobiological differences in women across the life span and across the menstrual cycle. As women may have particular developmental vulnerabilities to interpersonal traumas, there are important opportunities to study the meanings of relationships in traumatized women and men, and to discover the degree to which this relates to outcomes. There are also opportunities to study traumatized women and men within the context of relationships and to determine dynamic differences in emotional responsivity. We have suggested a number of important cognitive differences between traumatized men and women. Although we have hypothesized cognitive dissonance as one mechanism explaining differences between traumatized men and women, there are many other testable ideas about the effect of trauma on cognition. We also strongly believe that, in order to fully understand the relationship between gender and PTSD, studies must actually measure a variety of gender correlates and not simply sex as a binary variable.

We are aware that there are a great many other responses to trauma than PTSD. For clarity and focus, we decided to primarily examine the relationship between gender and PTSD. There are many known sex differences in other disorders that are commonly described in traumatized individuals, such as: dissociative disorders (Saxe et al., 1993), somatoform disorders (Cloninger, Martin, Guze, & Clayton, 1986; Pribor, Yutzey, Dean, & Wetzel, 1993; Saxe et al., 1994), personality disorders (Gunderson, Zanarini, & Kisiel, 1991), mood disorders and other anxiety disorders (e.g., Robins & Regier, 1991; Robins et al., 1984). There is a need to understand the gender-related differences in these responses to trauma. Also, the high comorbidity of PTSD with these disorders raises other questions. The well-known difference between internalizing and externalizing symptoms between males and females, respectively, must be understood. We have alluded to some answers in this chapter, but, clearly, there is a great need to study these issues.

Gender continues to be a powerful construct that is highly influential in diverse contexts. Thus far, clinicians and researchers interested in trauma and PTSD have little empirical data to guide their practice and studies. We hope that the ideas presented in this chapter add to an ongoing effort to understand how gender and trauma are related, and contribute to the development of a new gender-based research agenda in PTSD.

REFERENCES

Allen, L. A., Richey, M. F., Chai, Y. M., & Gorski, R. (1991). Sex differences in the corpus callosum of the living human being. *Journal of Neuroscience, 11,* 933–942.

Ashmore, R. D. (1981). Sex stereotypes and implicit personality theory. In D. L. Hamilton (Ed.), *Cognitive processes in stereotyping and intergroup behavior* (pp. 1–36). Hillsdale, NJ: Erlbaum.

Ashmore, R. D. (1990). Sex, gender, and the individual. In L. A. Pervin (Ed.), *Handbook of personality: Theory and research* (pp. 486–525). New York: Guilford Press.

Ashmore, R. D., Del Boca, F. K., & Wohlers, A. J. (1986). Gender stereotypes. In R. D. Ashmore & F. K. Del Boca (Eds.), *The social psychology of female-male relations: A critical analysis and central concepts* (pp. 69–119).

Bergen, D. J., & Williams, J. E. (1991). Sex stereotypes in the United States revisited: 1972–1988. *Sex Roles, 24,* 413–423.

Best, N. R., Rees, M. P., Barlow, D. H. & Cowen, P. (1992). Effect of estradiol implant on noradrenergic function and mood in menopausal subjects. *Psychoneuroendocrinology, 17,* 87–93.

Bremner, J. D., Randall, P., Scott, T. M., Bronen, R., Seibyl, J. P., Southwick, S. M., Delaney, R. C., McCarthy, G., Charney, D. S., & Innis, R. B. (1995). MRI-based measures of hippocampal volume in patients with PTSD. *American Journal of Psychiatry, 152,* 973–981.

Breslau, N., & Davis, G. C. (1992). Posttraumatic stress disorder in an urban population of young adults: Risk factors for chronicity. *American Journal of Psychiatry, 149,* 671–675.

Breslau, N., Davis, G. C., Andreski, P., & Peterson, E. (1991). Traumatic events and posttraumatic stress disorder in an urban population of young adults. *Archives of General Psychiatry, 48,* 216–222.

Burger, L. (1992). *Coping with repetitive natural disasters: A study of the Ladysmith floods.* (Tech. Rep. No. 26). University of South Africa, Psychology Department.

Camp, D. M., & Robinson, T. E. (1988a). Susceptibility to sensitization, I: Sex differences in the enduring effects of chronic D-amphetamine treatment on locomotion, stereotyped behavior and brain monoamines. *Behavioral Brain Research, 30,* 55–68.

Camp, D. M., & Robinson, T. E. (1988b). Susceptibility to sensitization, II: The influence of gonadal hormones on enduring changes in brain monoamines and behavior produced by the repeated administration of D-amphetamine on restraint stress. *Behavioral Brain Research, 30,* 69–88.

Chadorow, N. (1978). *The reproduction of mothering: Psychoanalysis and the sociology of gender.* Berkeley, CA: University of California Press.

Charney, D. C., Deutch, A. Y., Krystal, J., Southwick, S. & Davis, M. (1993). Psychobiological mechanisms of posttraumatic stress disorder. *Archives of General Psychiatry, 50,* 294–305.

Claustre, J., Peyrin, L., Fitoussi, R., & Mornex, R. (1980). Sex differences in the adrenal response to hypoglycemic stress in human. *Psychopharmacology, 67,* 147–153.

Cloninger, C. R., Martin, R. L., Guze, S. B., & Clayton, P. J. (1986). A prospective follow-up and family study of somatization in men and women. *American Journal of Psychiatry, 143,* 873–878.

Cohen, S., Kamarck, T., & Mermelstein, R. (1983). A global measure of perceived stress. *Journal of Health and Social Behavior, 24,* 385–396.

Condry, J. C., & Condry, S. (1976). Sex differences: A study of the eye of the beholder. *Child Development, 47,* 812–819.

Cottler, L. B., Compton, W. M., Mager, D., & Spitznagel, E. (1992). Posttraumatic stress disorder among substance abuse users from the general population. *American Journal of Psychiatry, 149,* 664–670.

Cross, S. E., & Markus, H. R. (1993). Gender in thought, belief, and action: A cognitive approach. In A. E. Beall & R. J. Sternberg (Eds.), *The psychology of gender* (pp. 54–98). New York: Guilford.

Cuche, J. L., Kuchel, O., Barbeau, A., & Genest, J. (1975). Sex differences in urinary catecholamines. *Endocrine Research Communications, 2,* 549–559.

Dalmaz, Y., & Peyrin, L. (1982). Sex differences in catecholamine metabolites in human urine during development and at adulthood. *Journal of Neural Transmission, 54,* 193–207.

Davis, M., & Emory, E. (1995). Sex differences in neonatal stress reactivity. *Child Development, 66,* 14–27.

Deaux, K. (1984). From individual differences to social categories. Analysis of a decade's research on gender. *American Psychologist, 39,* 105–116.

de Lacoste, M. C., Adesanya, T., & Woodward, D. J. (1990). Measures of gender differences in the human brain and their relationship to brain weight. *Biological Psychiatry, 28,* 931–942.

Durkin, K. (1985a). Television and sex role acquisition 1: Content. *British Journal of Social Psychology, 24,* 101–113.

Durkin, K. (1985b). Television and sex role acquisition 1: Content. *British Journal of Social Psychology, 24,* 191–210.

Eagly, A. H. (1987). *Sex differences in social behavior: A social-role interpretation.* Hillsdale, NJ: Erlbaum.

Eisenberg, N., & Lennon, R. (1983). Sex differences in empathy and related capacities. *Psychological Bulletin, 94,* 100–131.

Festinger, L. (1957). *A theory of cognitive dissonance.* Evanston, IL: Row, Peterson.

Fischer, G. J. (1992). Gender differences in college student sexual abuse victims and their offenders. *Annals of Sex Research, 5,* 215–226.

Frankenhauser, M., Dunne, E., & Lundberg, U. (1976). Sex differences in sympathetic-adrenal medullary reactions induced by different stressors. *Psychopharmacology, 47,* 1–5.

Freud, S. (1931/1961). Female sexuality. In J. Strachey (Ed.), *The standard edition of the complete psychological works of Sigmund Freud* (Volume 21; pp. 225–243). London: Hogarth Press.

Gallucci, W. T., Baum, A., Laua, L., Rabin, R. S., Chrousos, G. P., Gold, P. W., & Kling, M. A. (1993). Sex differences in sensitivity to the hypothalamic-pituitary-adrenal axis. *Health Psychology, 12,* 420–425.

George, M. S., Ketter, T. A., Parekh, P. I., Herscovitch, P., & Post, R. M. (1996). Gender differences in rCBF during transient self induced sadness and happiness. *Biological Psychiatry, 40,* 859–871.

George, M. S., Ketter, T. A., Parekh, P. I., Horowitz, B., Herscovitch, P., & Post, R. M. (1995). Brain activity during transient sadness and happiness in healthy women. *American Journal of Psychiatry, 152,* 341–351.

Gidycz, C. A., & Koss, M. P. (1991). Predictors of long-term sexual assault trauma among a national sample of victimized college women. *Violence and Victims, 6,* 175–190.

Gilligan, C. (1982). *In a different voice: Psychological theory and woman's development.* Cambridge, MA: Harvard University Press.

Goddard, G. V., McIntyre, D. C., & Leech, C. K. (1969). A permanent change in brain function resulting from daily electrical stimulation. *Experimental Neurology, 25,* 295–330.

Goldstein, D. S., Levinson, P. & Keiser, H. R. (1983). Plasma and urinary catecholamines during the human ovulatory cycle. *American Journal of Obstetrics, 146,* 824–829.

Groth, A. N., & Burgess, A. W. (1980). Male rape: Offenders and victims. *American Journal of Psychiatry, 137,* 806–810.

Gunderson, J. G., Zanarini, M. C., & Kisiel, C. L. (1991). Borderline personality disorder: A review of the data on DSM III-R descriptions. *Journal of Personality Disorders, 5,* 967–975.

Gurvitz, T. V., Shenton, M. E., & Pitman, R. K. (1995). *Reduced hippocampal volume on magnetic resonance imaging in chronic posttraumatic stress disorder.* Paper presented at the annual meeting of the International Society of Traumatic Stress Studies, Miami, FL.

Hall, J. A. (1978). Gender effects in decoding nonverbal cues. *Psychological Bulletin, 85,* 845–858.

Harvey, M. R. (1996). An ecological view of psychological trauma. *Journal of Traumatic Stress, 9,* 3–23.

Heilman, M. E., Block, C. J., Martell, R. F., & Simon, M. C. (1989). Has anything changed? Current characterizations of men, women, and managers. *Journal of Applied Psychology, 74,* 935–942.

Herman, J. L. (1992). *Trauma and recovery: The aftermath of violence—from domestic abuse to political terror.* New York, NY: Basic Books.

Hoffman, C., & Hurst, N. (1990). Gender stereotypes: Perception or rationalization? *Journal of Personality and Social Psychology, 58,* 197–208.

Hoffman, M. L. (1977). Sex differences in empathy and related behaviors. *Psychological Bulletin, 54,* 712–722.

Hyde,, J., Krajnik, M., & Skuldt-Niederberger, K. (1991). Androgyny across the life span: A replication and longitudinal follow-up. *Developmental Psychology, 27*(3) 516–519.

Jones, S. B., Bylund, D. B., Rieser, C. A., Shekim, W. O., Byer, J. A., & Carr, G. W. (1983). Alpha$_2$-adrenergic receptor binding in human platelets: Alterations during the menstrual cycle. *Clinical Pharmacological Therapy, 34,* 90–96.

Jordan, J. V., & Surrey, J. L. (1986). The self-in-relation: Empathy and the mother daughter relationship. In T. Bernay & D. W. Cantor (Eds.), *The psychology of today's women.* Cambridge, MA: Harvard University Press.

Juraska, J. M. (1991). Sex differences in cognitive regions of the brain. *Psychoneuroendocrinology, 16,* 105–119.

Kenrick, D. T., & Trost, M. R. (1993). The evolutionary perspective. In A. E. Beall & R. J. Sternberg (Eds.), *The psychology of gender* (pp. 149–172). New York, NY: Guilford.

Kessler, R. C., Sonnega, A., Bromet, E., Hughes, M., & Nelson, C. B. (1995). Posttraumatic stress disorder in the National Comorbidity Survey. *Archives of General Psychiatry, 52,* 1048–1060.

Kirshbaum, C., Pirke, K. M., & Hellhammer, D. H. (1995). Preliminary evidence for reduced cortisol responsivity to psychological stress in women using oral contraceptive medication. *Psychoneuroendocrinology, 20,* 509–514.

Kirschbaum, C., Wust, S., & Hellhammer, D. (1992). Consistent sex differences in cortisol responses to psychological stress. *Psychosomatic Medicine, 54,* 648–657.

Kohlberg, L. (1966). A cognitive developmental analysis of children's sex role concepts and attitudes. In E. Maccoby (Ed.), *The development of sex differences* (pp. 82–172). Stanford, CA: Stanford University Press.

Kohlberg, L., & Ullian, D. Z. (1974). Stages in the development of psychosexual concepts and attitudes. In R. C. Friedman, R. M. Richard, & R. L. Van der Weile (Eds.), *Sex differences in behavior* (pp. 209–222). New York, NY: Wiley Press.

Kosten, T. R., Mason, J. W., Giller, E. L., Ostroff R. B., & Harkness, L. (1987). Sustained urinary norepinepherine and epinepherine elevation in PTSD. *Psychoneuroendocrinology, 12,* 13–20.

Krystal, H. (1988). *Integration and self healing: Affect, trauma, and alexithymia.* Hillsdale, NJ: Analytic Press.

Kulka, R. A., Schlenger, W. E., Fairbank, J. A., Hough, R. L., Jordon, B. K., Marmarc, C. R., & Weiss, D. S. (1988). *National Vietnam Veterans Readjustment Study (NVVRS).* NC: Research Triangle Institute.

Kulka, R. A., Schlenger, W. E., Fairbank, J. A., Hough, R. L., Jordon, B. K., Marmarc, C. R., & Weiss, D. S. (1990). *Trauma and the Vietnam War Generation.* New York, NY: Brunner/Mazel.

LeVay, S. (1993). *The sexual brain.* Cambridge, MA: MIT Press.

Lewis, D. O. (1992). From abuse to violence: Psychophysiological consequences of maltreatment. *Journal of the American Academy of Child and Adolescent Psychiatry, 31,* 383–391.

Loring, M., & Powell, B. (1988). Gender, race, and DSM-III: A study of the objectivity of psychiatric diagnostic behavior. *Journal of Health and Social Behavior, 29,* 1–22.

Lott, B., & Maluso D. (1993). The social learning of gender. In A. E. Beall & R. J. Sternberg (Eds.), *The psychology of gender* (pp. 99–123). New York, NY: Guilford Press.

Mason, J. W., Giller, E. L., Kosten, T. R., & Wahby, V. S. (1990). Serum testosterone levels in posttraumatic stress disorder patients. *Journal of Traumatic Stress, 3,* 449–457.

McEwen, B. S. (1995). Adrenal steroid actions on the brain: Dissecting the fine line between protection and damage. In M. J. Friedman, D. S. Charney, & A. Y. Deutch (Eds.), *Neurobiological and clinical consequences of stress: From normal adaptation to post-*

traumatic stress disorder (pp. 135–147). Philadelphia, PA: Lippincott-Raven.

Miller, J. B. (1986). *Toward a new psychology of women* (2nd ed.). Boston, MA: Beacon Press.

Murphy, D. G., DeCarli, C., McIntosh, A. R., Daly, E., Mentis, M. J., Pietrini, P., Szczepanik, J., Schapiro, M. B., Grady, C. L., Horwitz, B., & Rapoport, S. (1996). Sex differences in human brain morphometry and metabolism: An in vivo quantitative magnetic resonance imaging and positron emmission tomography study on the effects of aging. *Archives of General Psychiatry, 53,* 385–394.

Newmark, M. E., & Penry, J. K. (1980). Catamenial epilepsy: A review. *Epilepsia, 21,* 281–300.

Norris, F. (1990). Screening for traumatic stress: A scale for use in the general population. *Journal of Applied Social Psychology, 20,* 1704–1718.

Norris, F. H. (1992). Epidemiology of trauma: Frequency and impact of different potentially traumatic events on different demographic groups. *Journal of Consulting and Clinical Psychology, 60,* 409–418.

Patkai, P., Johansson, G., & Post, B. (1974). Mood alertness and sympathetic-adrenal medullary activity during the menstrual cycle. *Psychosomatic Medicine, 36,* 503–512.

Paul, S. M., Axelrod, J., & Saavendra, J. M. (1979). Estrogen-induced efflux of endogenous catecholamines from the hypothalamus in vitro. *Brain Research, 178,* 479–505.

Pennebacker, J. W., & Sussman, J. R. (1988). Disclosure of traumas and psychosomatic processes. *Social Science and Medicine, 26,* 327–332.

Perry, B. D., Giller E. L., & Southwick, S. M. (1987). Altered plasma alpha-2 adrenergic receptor affinity in PTSD. *American Journal of Psychiatry, 144,* 1511–1512.

Phillips, D., & Segal, B. (1969). Sexual status and psychiatric symptoms. *American Sociological Review, 34,* 58–72.

Post, R. M., Rubinow, D. R., & Ballenger, J. C. (1986). Conditioning and sensitization in the longitudinal course of affective illness. *British Journal of Psychiatry, 149,* 191–202.

Post, R. M., Weiss, S. R. B., & Smith, M. A. (1995). Sensitization and kindling: Implications for the evolving neural substrates of post-traumatic stress disorder. In M. J. Friedman, D. S. Charney, & A. Y. Deutch (Eds.), *Neurobiological and clinical consequences of stress: From normal adaptation to post-traumatic stress disorder* (203–224). Philadelphia, PA: Lippincott-Raven.

Pribor, E. F., Yutzy, J., & Wetzel, R. (1993). Briquet's syndrome, dissociation, and abuse. *American Journal of Psychiatry, 150,* 1507–1511.

Rauch, S. L., van der Kolk, B. A., Fisler, R. E., Alpert, N. M., Orr, S. P., Savage, C. R., Fischman, A. J., Jenike, M. A., & Pitman, R. K. (1996). A symptom provocation study of post-traumatic stress disorder using positron emission tomography and script-driven imagery. *Archives of General Psychiatry, 53,* 380–387.

Realmuto, G. M., Wagner, N., & Bartholow, J. (1991). The Williams pipeline disaster: A controlled study of a technological accident. *Journal of Traumatic Stress, 4,* 469–479.

Resnick, H. S., Kilpatrick, D. G., Best, C. L., & Kramer, T. L. (1992). Vulnerability-stress factors in development of posttraumatic stress disorder. *Journal of Nervous and Mental Disease, 180,* 424–430.

Resnick, H., Yehuda, R., Pitman, R. K., & Foy, D. W. (1995). Effect of previous trauma on acute plasma cortisol level following rape. *American Journal of Psychiatry, 152,* 1675–1677.

Robins, L. N., Helzer, J. E., Croughan, J. L., & Radcliffe, K. S. (1981). National Institute of Mental Health diagnostic interview schedule: Its history, characteristics, and validity. *Archives of General Psychiatry, 38,* 381–389.

Robins L. N., Helzer J. E., Weissman, M. M., Gravaschel, H., Gruenberg, E., Burke, J. D., Jr., & Reiger, D. A. (1984). Lifetime prevalence of specific psychiatric disorders in three sites. *Archives of General Psychiatry, 41,* 949–958.

Robins, L. N., & Regier, D. A. (1991). *Psychiatric disorders in America: The Epidemiologic Catchment Area Study.* New York, NY: Free Press.

Robins, L. N., Wing, J., Wittchen, H. U., & Helzer, J. E. (1988). The Composite International Diagnostic Interview: An epidemiological instrument suitable for use in conjunction with different diagnostic systems and in different cultures. *Archives of General Psychiatry, 45,* 1069–1077.

Robinson, T. E., Becker, J. B., & Presty, S. K. (1982). Long term facilitation of amphetamine-induced rotational behavior and striatal dopamine release produced by a single exposure to amphetamine: Sex differences. *Brain Research, 253,* 231–241.

Russo, N. F., & Olmedo, E. L. (1983). Women's utilization of outpatient psychiatric services: Some emerging priorities for rehabilitation psychologists. *Rehabilitation Psychology, 28,* 141–155.

Russo, N. F., & Sobel, S. B. (1981). Sex differences in the utilization of mental health facilities. *Professional Psychologist, 12,* 7–19.

Saxe, G. N., Chinman, G., Berkowitz, R., Hall, K., Lieberg, G., Schwartz, J., & van der Kolk, B. A. (1994). Somatization in patients with dissociative disorders. *American Journal of Psychiatry, 151,* 1329–1334.

Saxe, G. N., van der Kolk, B. A., Berkowitz, R., Chinman, G., Hall, K., Lieberg, G., & Schwartz, J. (1993). Dissociative disorders in psychiatric inpatients. *American Journal of Psychiatry, 150,* 1037–1042.

Scallet, A. C., Suomi, S. J., & Bowman, R. E. (1981). Sex differences in adrenocortical response to controlled agonistic encounters in rhesus monkeys. *Physiology and Behavior, 26,* 385–390.

Schaeffer, M. A., & Baum, A. (1984). Adrenal cortical response to stress at Three Mile Island. *Psychosomatic Medicine, 46,* 227–237.

Shaywitz, B., Shaywitz, S. G., Pugh, K. R., Constable, R. T., Skudlanksi, P., Fullbright, R. K., Bronen, R. A, Fletcher, J. M., Shankweiler, D. P., & Katz, L. (1995). Sex differences in the functional organization of the brain for language. *Nature, 373,* 607–609.

Sherif, C. (1982). Needed concepts in the study of gender identity. *Psychology of Women Quarterly, 6,* 375–398.

Slaby, R. G., & Frey, K. S. (1975). Development of gender constancy and selective attention to same-sex models. *Child Development, 46,* 849–856.

Southwick, S. M., Krystal, J. H., Morgan, A., Johnson, D., Nagy, L. M., Nicolaou, A., Heniger, G. R., & Charney, D. S. (1993). Abnormal noradrenergic function in posttraumatic stress disorder. *Archives of General Psychiatry, 50,* 266–274.

Spence, J. T. (1985). Gender identity and its implications for concepts of masculinity and femininity. In T. B. Sonderegger (Ed.), Nebraska symposium on motivation: Psychology of gender (pp. 59–95). Lincoln, NB: University of Nebraska Press.

Spitzer, R. (1981). *NIMH Diagnostic Interview Schedule, Version 3.* Rockville, MD: National Institute of Mental Health. Public Health Service.

Stein, M. B., Hannah, C., Koverola, C., et al. (1994). *Neuroanatomical and neuroendocrine correlates in adulthood of severe sexual abuse in childhood.* Paper presented at the 33rd Annual Meeting of the American College of Neuropsychopharmacology, San Juan, PR.

Steinglass, P., & Gerrity, E. (1990). Natural disasters and post-traumatic stress disorder: Short-term versus long-term recovery in two disaster-affected communities. Special Issue: Traumatic stress: New perspectives in theory, measurement, and research: II. Research findings. *Journal of Applied Social Psychology, 20,* 1746–1765.

Tersman, Z, Collins, A., & Eneroth, P. (1991). Cardiovascular responses to psychological and physiological stressors during the menstrual cycle. *Psychosomatic Medicine, 53,* 185–197.

Thompson, S. K. (1975). Gender labels and early sex-role development. *Child Development, 46,* 339–347.

van der Kolk, B. A. (1994). The body keeps the score: Memory and the evolving psychobiology of PTSD. *Harvard Review of Psychiatry, 1,* 253–265.

Verbrugge, L. M. (1983). Multiple roles and physical health of women and men. *Journal of Health and Social Behavior, 24,* 16–30.

Verbrugge, L. M. (1985). Gender and health: An update on hypotheses and evidence. *Journal of Health and Social Behavior, 26,* 156–182.

Wagner, H. R., Crutcher, K. A., & Davis, J. N. (1979). Chronic estrogen treatment decreases beta-adrenergic responses in rat cerebral cortex. *Brain Research, 71,* 147–151.

Walker, C. (1980). *The physically and sexually abused child.* New York, NY: Pergamon Press.

Weinberg, J., & Wong, R. (1986). Adrenocortical responsiveness to novelty in the hamster. *Physiology and Behavior, 37,* 669–672.

Weiss, D. S., Marmar, C. R., Schlenger, W. E., Fairbank, J. A., Jordan, B. K., & Kulka, R. A. (1992). The prevalence of lifetime and partial post-traumatic stress disorder in Vietnam theater veterans. *Journal of Traumatic Stress, 5,* 365–376.

Wolfe, J., Brown, P. J., Furey, J., & Levin, K. (1993). Development of a war-time stressor scale for women (WMSS). *Psychological Assessment: A Journal of Consulting and Clinical Psychology, 5,* 330–335.

Wolfe, J., & Kimerling, R. (1996). Gender issues in the assessment of PTSD. In J. P. Wilson & T. M. Keane (Eds.), *Assessing psychological trauma and PTSD: A handbook for practitioners.* New York, NY: Guilford.

Yehuda, R., Boisoneau, D., Lowy, M. T., & Giller, E. L. (1995). Dose response changes in plasma cortisol and lymphocyte glucocorticoid receptors following dexamethasone administration in combat veterans with and without PTSD. *Archives of General Psychiatry 1995, 52,* 583–593.

Yehuda R., Kahana B., Binder-Byrnes, K., Southwick, S. M., Mason, J. W., & Giller, E. L. (1995). Low urinary cortisol excretion in Holocaust survivors with posttraumatic stress disorder. *American Journal of Psychiatry 152*(7), 982–986.

Yehuda, R., Lowy, M. T., Southwick, S. M., Shaffer, S., & Giller, E. L. (1991). Lymphocyte glucocorticoid receptor number in PTSD. *American Journal of Psychiatry, 149,* 499–504.

Yehuda, R., Southwick, S. M., Krystal, J. H., Bremner, D., Charney, D. S., & Mason, J. W. (1993). Enhanced suppression of cortisol following a low dose of dexamethasone in combat veterans with posttraumatic stress disorder. *American Journal of Psychiatry, 150,* 83–96.

Yehuda, R., Southwick, S. M., Nussbaum, G., Wahby, V., Giller, E. L., Jr., & Mason, J. W. (1990). Low urinary cortisol excretion in patients with posttraumatic stress disorder. *Journal of Nervous and Mental Disease, 178,* 366–369.

Zigmond, M. J., Finlay, J. M., & Sved, A. F. (1995). Neurochemical studies of central noradrenergic responses to acute and chronic stress: Implications for normal and abnormal behavior. In M. J. Friedman, D. S. Charney, & A. Y. Deutch (Eds.), *Neurobiological and clinical consequences of stress: From normal adaptation to post-traumatic stress disorder* (pp. 45–61). Philadelphia, PA: Lippincott-Raven.

Zuspan, F. P., & Zuspan, K. J. (1973). Ovulatory plasma amine (epinepherine and norepinepherine) surge in the woman. *American Journal of Obstetrics and Gynecology, 117,* 654–660.

CHAPTER 9

SOCIOECONOMIC CONSEQUENCES OF TRAUMATIC STRESS*

JOHN A. FAIRBANK, PH.D.
Duke University Medical Center

LORI EBERT, M.A.
Research Triangle Institute

GARY A. ZARKIN, PH.D.
Research Triangle Institute

Research on the long-term effects of traumatic stress, from combat to childhood sexual abuse, has focused largely on mental health outcomes, with little attention to broader social and economic repercussions. For example, a search of the listings of titles, key words, and abstracts of more than 11,500 journal articles, books, and book chapters comprising the traumatic stress literature contained in the National Center for PTSD Pilots data base in May 1997 identified fewer than a score of citations that focus on labor market outcomes, such as employment, work hours, and wages. An electronic search of the Journal of Economic Literature (American Economic Association, 1997) failed to yield a single study of the labor force that considered the potential impact of exposure to traumatic events of any type, or accounted for the influence of trauma on mental health.

In as much as investigators have looked beyond the mental health effects of traumatic stress, the focus has largely been on outcomes or processes related to interpersonal functioning. Recent research on the association between exposure to trauma and characteristics of an individual's interpersonal relations, such as intimacy, social conflict, and social support, has increased understanding of some of the functional consequences of such exposure (Barrett, Resnick, Foy, Dansky, Flanders, & Stroup, 1996; Kazak et al., 1997). However, this literature is still quite modest in scope in comparison to the number of studies on the psychological and biological aspects of exposure to traumatic stress (cf. Friedman, Charney, & Deutch, 1995; Saigh, 1992). Moreover, this work does not speak to the economic consequences of traumatic stress for individuals or society.

Health economists have tried to estimate the costs of various medical diseases (e.g., cardiovascular disease), psychiatric disorders (e.g., affective disorders) or addictive behaviors (e.g., smoking or alcohol abuse) on society. Estimating the costs of any specific disease or disorder includes the direct treatment costs and indirect social costs, such as loss of work and productivity resulting from sickness, and time costs related to obtaining care (Wells, Sturm, Sherbourne, & Meredith, 1996). Recent research on the total costs of affective disorders, for example, places the total direct treatment costs and indirect social costs at a staggering $44 billion annually (Greenberg, Stiglin, Finkelstein, & Berndt, 1993). In their review of findings from Greenberg et al. (1993) and other studies,

*The authors gratefully acknowledge the support of the National Institute of Mental Health (NIMH) through research grant 1 R01 MH56256-01.

Wells et al. (1996) noted a consistent pattern in which the indirect costs of affective disorders, including reduced productivity of the depressed person and increased burden on family members, far exceed the direct costs of treatment.

The indirect costs of psychiatric disorder associated with losses in earnings alone are substantial. Findings from the National Comorbidity Survey (NCS) show that psychiatric disorder reduces annual income among men by 13 percent and among women by 18 percent (Ettner, Frank, & Kessler, 1997). Given that wages, salaries, and other forms of employee compensation comprise about 75 percent of national income in the United States (Statistical Abstract, 1996), the indirect costs to our society of mental illness associated with lost earnings of this magnitude are nontrivial.

The impact of trauma history on productivity and performance in the workplace is little understood from an empirical perspective and has largely been overlooked in theoretical conceptualizations of the effects of traumatic stress. We were able to locate fewer than two dozen studies presenting data on the relationship between traumatic stress exposure or PTSD and labor market outcomes. Many of these studies were not designed primarily with this purpose in mind and therefore include only a limited assessment and analysis of labor market outcomes. Additionally, this relatively small body of research attempts to address the economic consequences of traumatic stressors as diverse as concentration camp internment, childhood sexual abuse, and combat exposure. Nonetheless, what data do exist provide evidence for some connection between a history of trauma, PTSD, and such labor market outcomes as employment status, occupational stability, and earnings.

One purpose of this chapter is to provide an introduction to research on mental health and labor market outcomes and to communicate the relevance of this topic to researchers in the field of traumatic stress. A primary goal is to provide an analytic review of the existing research on relationships between traumatic stress exposure, mental health, and labor market outcomes. Given the limited scope of research in this area, another key aim is to guide and inform future research on the economic outcomes of exposure to traumatic stress.

With these goals in mind, the chapter is structured as follows. First, we introduce the labor market outcome variables and analytic approaches that are standard practice in economics research. Next, we review the major general population studies that use such approaches to examine associations between mental health and labor market outcomes. We then provide a detailed review of studies which have specifically examined relationships between traumatic stress exposure and labor market outcomes. In reviewing this research we offer a framework that emphasizes the manner in which traumatic stress exposure is measured and the extent to which relevant sociodemographic variables and mental health indicators are utilized in evaluating associations between trauma and labor market outcomes

STUDYING LABOR MARKET OUTCOME VARIABLES: A PERSPECTIVE FROM THE ECONOMICS LITERATURE

Our primary task in this paper is to review literature pertinent to evaluating the relationship between traumatic stress and subsequent labor market outcomes. The labor market variables used in these studies fall into two categories: outcome variables that reflect labor market status at a point in time (e.g., employment status, wages), and outcome variables that reflect an individual's labor market history (e.g., number of different jobs or employers, number of periods of unemployment).

Measuring Labor Market Outcomes

Point in Time Labor Market Variables. Most of the literature we review below will analyze one or more point in time variables. In economics research, current employment status is generally captured by a set of indicator variables. Individuals are classified as *employed* if they are working at the time of the study, or if they have a job but are not at work due to sickness, vacation, labor dispute, bad weather, or other temporary layoff. Individuals are *unemployed* if they do not have a job and are looking for work. Individuals who are going to school, keeping house, retired, disabled, or institutionalized are typically not considered to be in the labor force and therefore excluded from analyses of employment and unemployment. A number of investigators have examined relationships between traumatic stress exposure and current employment status. However, not all have adhered to this standard in determining employment status.

Hours of work reflect the time spent at the job working for pay. Because hours may vary widely from week to week, individuals may be asked their usual hours worked at the job. *Wages* reflect the amount of money a person is paid per unit time. Typically, self-reported wages are pre-tax wages, and they do not include the value of any fringe benefits. To compare individuals with different payment schedules, analysts must convert the wages of all individuals to a common unit of time. For example, an estimated hourly wage for individuals paid on a monthly basis can be computed by dividing their monthly salary by the usual hours worked in the last month at the job. In the trauma literature, the most commonly used point in time labor market outcome variables are employment status and personal income. Obviously personal income can come from a variety of sources other than paid work. Thus, presently little is known about the relationship between traumatic stress exposure and work-related earnings per se. Where examined, associations between trauma and hours worked are typically evaluated by contrasting individuals who work full-time with those working part-time.

Occupational status is often used as a dependent measure in studies of the trauma-labor market outcome relationship. The construct of occupational status is related to that of occupational prestige, the notion that occupations vary in the degree of prestige or status they are accorded in a given culture. Measures of occupational status vary widely in the studies reviewed here. Some authors (e.g., McCarren et al., 1995) simply classify occupations into categories based on the codes used by the Bureau of the Census. Other investigators develop more elaborate measures of occupational status (e.g., Weinfeld, Sigal, & Eaton, 1981; Kulka et al., 1990). For example, one measure is based on an index of socioeconomic status developed by Duncan (1961) and calibrated to the 1980 Census occupational scheme by Stevens and Cho (1985). This socioeconomic index (SEI) is based on predicted prestige scores of occupations obtained in a regression of prestige (based on individuals' evaluation of the relative merits of occupations) on levels of income and education (Kulka et al., 1990). Scores on the SEI range from 0 to 100.

Labor Market History Variables. Some analysts will evaluate the relationship between psychological distress and labor market variables that reflect individuals' labor market attachment or stability. Some of the most commonly used labor market history variables include the number of different employers or periods of unemployment since high school (or over some period of time, such as over the last five years), the number of different jobs over some period of time, or the longest period of time spent with the same employer. Trauma researchers have analyzed these variables separately and used them in combination to develop scales to measure constructs related to occupational stability (e.g., Kulka et al., 1990).

Sociodemographic Covariates of Labor Market Outcomes

At a minimum, four sociodemographic control variables should be considered in analyses of labor market variables. These standard sociodemographic variables are educational attainment, age, gender, and race/ethnicity. Other variables often included in such models are marital status, years of work experience, years of tenure at the present employer, physical health status, and geographic region of residence. More educated individuals are more likely to work (Pencavel, 1986), earn more money (Mincer, 1974), and work longer hours (Pencavel, 1986). Age has an important independent effect on wages, hours, and the propensity to be employed and unemployed (Weiss, 1986). Typically, younger and older workers have lower wages, all else equal, compared to prime age workers. Similarly, younger and older individuals are less likely to be in the labor force and employed, as they are more likely to be in school or retired, respectively. Gender and race/ethnicity effects may also be important as women generally have lower wages, work fewer hours, and are less likely to be employed than men (Mroz, 1987); similarly, Black men in the United States have lower wages and are more likely to be unemployed compared to White men.

As to the other sociodemographic covariates, married men generally have higher wages than single men, and more experienced workers and workers with more tenure at a particular employer are paid more than individuals with less experience and tenure. Grossman (1972) stressed the importance of health status as a determinant of labor market participation. He showed that poor physical health was associated with lower wages, fewer hours of work, and a lower probability of being employed. Similarly, one might expect that individuals with mental health problems associated with exposure to trauma would have lower wages, work fewer hours, and be less likely to be employed. The availability of jobs and the wage level may be affected by the region of the country and size of the city in which an individual lives (Hanoch, 1980; Treiman & Hartmann, 1981).

A number of studies that have examined associations between traumatic stress exposure and labor market outcomes have relied solely on univariate statistics. In reviewing these findings it is important to recognize that they do not take into account the known effects on employment and earnings of the sociodemographic variables detailed above.

Additionally, it is worth noting that while certain of these standard sociodemographic covariates are stable characteristics of the individual (e.g., gender, race/ethnicity), others such as education and physical health status may also be influenced by traumatic stress. Therefore in modeling the effects of trauma on labor market outcomes sociodemographic measures may sometimes be utilized as mediating rather than control variables.

MENTAL HEALTH AND LABOR MARKET OUTCOMES

Relative to the prevalence of mental illness in the United States and the costs of psychiatric disorder to individuals, their families, and society, there have been few studies examining the relationship between mental health status and labor market variables. Although few in number, we review several of the key

extant studies in this literature here in recognition of their potential to inform nascent work on the relationship between traumatic stress, PTSD, and labor market outcomes. What follows is not an exhaustive review of the literature, but an overview of some of the main findings from four large studies spanning different eras: The longitudinal NAS-NRC twins study of the 1950s to early to mid 1970s, the NIMH ECA program from the early 1980s, the MWHS from the late 1980s, and the NCS from the early to mid 1990s. The proper names for study acronyms are defined in the following paragraphs.

Findings from the NAS-NRC Twins Study. Bartel and Taubman (1979) were among the first to examine the relationship between mental health and labor market behavior. They explored associations between several diseases (including mental disorders) and individual earnings, wages, weekly hours worked, the probability of being out of the labor force, and the probability of being unemployed. They used longitudinal data from a panel of 2,500 white male twin pairs maintained by the National Academy of Science-National Research Council (NAS-NRC). These investigators found that men who were diagnosed as either psychotic or neurotic had lower earnings and wages, worked fewer hours per week, and had a greater probability of being out of the labor force. With respect to individual earnings, Bartel and Taubman reported a reduction in 1974 earnings of approximately 27 percent for men who received a psychiatric diagnosis during the preceding five years (1968–1973). The aggregate earnings losses associated with this effect were then estimated by multiplying the percentage loss in earnings, mean annual earnings of workers, the incidence rates of the diseases, and the number of individuals employed in 1974. Bartel and Taubman estimated mental health problems produced an aggregate national loss of $1,685 million in 1974 earnings. In a subsequent study, Bartel and Taubman (1986) found that although both psychoses and neuroses were negatively related to earnings, the estimated impact of psychoses was nearly three times larger than that of typically less severe neuroses.

Because women and racial minorities were excluded from the NAS-NRC sample, limitations on the generalizability of these findings to the present work-force are nontrivial. Nonetheless, Bartel and Taubman's work provided initial evidence that, by deleteriously affecting earnings and employment, mental illness has economic costs both to the individual and society as a whole.

Findings from the NIMH ECA.   Frank and Gertler (1991) used data from the National Institute of Mental Health (NIMH) Epidemiological Catchment Area (ECA) Program (Eaton & Kessler, 1985) to explore the relationship between mental health and earnings among men age 18 to 64. The design of the ECA improved on that of the earlier NAS-NRC twins study by including representative samples of racial and ethnic minorities of men and women. Additionally, the ECA study employed structured diagnostic interviews, while the NAS-NRC mental health measures were based on service utilization (i.e., respondents only knew and could report their diagnoses if they had consulted professionals). Using these population-based interview data, Frank and Gertler found that the presence of a mental disorder reduced earnings by about 21 percent, an effect comparable in magnitude to that found using utilization-based measures.

Mullahy and Sindelar (1990) also used the NIMH ECA data to explore the labor force participation of both men and women. The probability of being employed was hypothesized to be a function of socio-economic and demographic characteristics (e.g., age, education, nonlabor income), physical health, and self-reported as well as diagnosed mental health variables. These diagnosed mental health measures included six categorical variables indicating whether the individual met criteria for substance abuse, depression, manic-depressive disorder, obsessive-compulsive disorder, schizophrenia, or antisocial personality disorder. Although coefficient estimates for many of the specific psychiatric diagnoses were not significant, the set of diagnoses were jointly significant for both men and women. Overall, Mullahy and Sindelar's results provide some evidence in support of the hypothesis that mental illness decreases labor force participation.

Findings from the MWHS.   Using data from the New England Research Institute's Massachusetts

Womens' Health Study (MWHS), Ruhm (1992) examined the effects of depression and a variety of physical health problems (e.g., hypertension, arthritis, cardiovascular disease) on labor force participation and employment among a community sample of 2,500 women who were between the ages of 45 and 57. Depression was assessed using a multimethod, multisource approach that included scores on the Center for Epidemiological Studies-Depression (CESD) scale, and information on usage of antidepressant medications and related medications for psychological distress (e.g., sleeping pills). Ruhm found that women regularly using antidepressive medications or having high depression scores were less likely to work or participate in the labor force than women who did not use such medications or who had lower CESD scores. In a series of analyses that considered the effects of education, occupation, and physical health problems, depression was nonetheless found to have a strong negative influence on individual participation in the labor force.

Findings from the NCS.   Ettner et al. (1997) used data from the National Comorbidity Survey (NCS) to examine the impact of psychiatric disorders on current employment status, usual weekly work hours, and personal income during the previous year. The sampling design of the NCS differed from prior studies, such as the ECA and MWHS, in that it collected information from a national sample of the non-institutionalized adult population living in the coterminus 48 states of the United States. Prior studies had relied on samples recruited from a state or several metropolitan areas. In the NCS, psychiatric disorder was assessed using a modified version of the Composite International Diagnostic Interview (CIDI) that permitted DSM-III-R diagnosis of a number of psychiatric disorders, including major depression, dysthymia, mania, generalized anxiety disorder, panic disorder, simple phobia, social phobia, agoraphobia, alcohol abuse, alcohol dependence, drug abuse, and drug dependence.

Analyses were conducted separately for men and for women. The predictors of primary interest were indicators of psychiatric disorder with respect to each psychiatric disorder during the past 12 months. Marital status, race/ethnicity, rural residence, education, foreign birth, and other standard sociodemographic variables were included as controls in the analysis. A robust finding was that psychiatric disorders significantly reduced employment among both men and women. Specifically, the probability of employment was reduced by about 11 percentage points, from 83 percent to 72 percent for women, and from 94 percent to 83 percent for men.

For employed men, psychiatric disorders had a small but measurable impact on work hours, while for women and for men the presence of one or more psychiatric disorders was related to a significant drop in earnings. Annual income declined 18 percent for women and 13 percent for men. The authors noted, however, that findings on earnings and work hours were sensitive to estimation methods and specification of the analysis models.

Summary of Findings

Overall, the studies reviewed above consistently found a relationship between mental health and labor market outcomes, although the magnitude of the reported effects vary from study to study. More recent studies, such as the ECA and NCS, have used representative samples, structured diagnostic interviews, and multivariate models that include the key sociodemograhic control variables used in analyzing labor market outcomes. In contrast, as the subsequent literature review will show, relatively few studies have specifically examined the relationship between traumatic stress exposure, mental health, and labor market outcomes. To date, only studies of combat exposure have used structured diagnostic interviews and specifically examined relationships between PTSD and labor market outcomes.

TRAUMA, PTSD, AND LABOR MARKET OUTCOMES

Next, we review studies in the literature on trauma, PTSD, and labor market outcomes organized by type of trauma. Four types of traumatic stress exposure are addressed in this literature: trauma related to the Holocaust; sexual and physical abuse in childhood; combat exposure and other stressors associated with

providing military service in a war zone; and refugee experiences. We limit our review to those empirical studies which include a control or comparison group and in which exposure to trauma and/or symptoms of posttraumatic stress are specifically assessed. Studies are discussed in terms of the multidimensionality and breadth of trauma assessments, the extent to which economic control variables are considered in the analysis, and approaches used to determine the effect of mental health factors, especially PTSD, on the trauma-labor market outcome relationship.

Studies of Survivors of Concentration Camps and the Holocaust

Findings from Eitinger. Eitinger (1973) conducted the first controlled study of labor market participation in a population exposed to a specific type of trauma—Norwegian civilians who were interred in Nazi prison camps during World War II. Exposure to the index trauma, concentration camp internment, was documented through official government records. Within the context of a retrospective archival study of psychosocial stress, he examined survivors' occupational stability and occupational status through the mid-1960s. Labor market measures available in the records included number of professions, number of different jobs, and change in occupational status. A description of the measure used to evaluate changes in occupational status is not provided in the study methods.

For purposes of this study, the case-control design excluded from the survivors sampling frame two subgroups of ex-prisoners whose files appeared in the central registry. The first of these was composed of university students arrested by the Nazis, and the second was composed of Norwegian military personnel who were prisoners of war (POWs). These groups were excluded because it was believed that their level of exposure to brutality and inhumane treatment was less consistently severe than that of the concentration camp survivors. The final sample of survivors consisted of 498 former prisoners whose files were randomly selected from the registry.

The records data also included an indicator of the duration of imprisonment, but information on other dimensions of the traumatic event, such as frequency and severity of exposure to specific aspects of internment (e.g., witnessing other prisoners injured or killed), was not available. Specific traumatic stress symptoms or disorders also were not assessed as the study predated the inclusion of PTSD in official diagnostic nomenclatures, such as the DSM.

A control group, matched for sex, age, socioeconomic status, and occupational category, was selected from national health insurance records. Some information on neuroses and psychoses in ex-prisoner and control samples was provided, but this information was not particularly informative for present purposes.

Ex-prisoners evidenced less occupational stability than controls in that they were more likely to have had more than one profession and a greater number of jobs during the evaluation period. Former prisoners were also more likely than controls to undergo an "obvious decline" in occupational status. Eitinger (1973) interprets these results as suggesting that quality of life or "adjustment" was compromised in Norwegian concentration camp survivors as compared to individuals of similar age and status who did not experience this trauma.

Findings from Weinfeld, Sigal, and Eaton. Weinfeld et al. (1981) examined current family income, current occupational status, and changes in occupational status in a community sample of Jewish Holocaust survivors. The sample consisted of respondents to a survey of heads of Jewish households in Montreal, Canada. The investigators classified respondents as exposed to the Holocaust if they reported that they were in Europe during World War II in a capacity other than "service in the Allied Armed forces." From a total sample of 657 respondents to the survey, 135 indicated that they met such exposure criteria. Of these, 56 indicated that their primary experience involved internment—39 in a concentration camp and 17 in a labor camp. Others reported that their primary experience involved hiding (25 respondents) and armed resistance or service in a regular army (13 respondents). A sizable minority of those who indicated that they were in Europe during World War II (41 respondents) did not specify the nature of their experiences.

To control for the effects of immigration and of exposure to the Holocaust, two comparison groups were derived from the sample. The first was composed of 120 respondents who were not in Europe during World War II and who were born outside of Canada. The second comparison group was composed of 196 native-born Canadians (non-immigrants) who did not experience the Holocaust as defined in the study. Three indicators of "economic achievement" were utilized in this study: (1) family income; (2) occupational status as measured by the Blishen index, a measure derived from average levels of education and income associated with different occupations in Canada and survey-based prestige rankings; and (3) changes in occupational status, defined as the difference in occupational status scores of the respondent's first full time job in Canada and his current last/usual job. Regression analyses revealed that the family incomes and occupational status of Holocaust survivors were negatively and significantly affected by their experience compared to other immigrants and to respondents born in Canada. No statistically significant between-group differences were found for changes in occupational status.

The Eitinger (1973) and Weinfeld et al. (1981) studies provide consistent evidence that Holocaust survivors experienced less achievement and stability in the labor market relative to their counterparts who did not experience this type of trauma. Survivors reported lower family incomes and less occupational stability, that is, a greater numbers of jobs and more vocational and professional changes. The effect of the Holocaust on patterns of occupational status is unclear, however. One controlled study detected a decline among survivors while another found no decline and no statistically significant differences between survivors and controls. We speculate that variations in findings on occupational status are due to a variety of methodologic differences between studies, such as variations in characteristics of the study samples (e.g., differing selection criteria for Holocaust and control samples), in methods of data collection (e.g., record abstraction versus survey), and in the manner in which occupational status and changes therein were measured and analyzed. Additionally, differences in economic climates in time and place could also lead to variations in findings. Eitinger's research was conducted in Norway in the 1960s while Weinfeld et al.'s sample was living in Montreal in the 1970s.

In the Weinfeld et al. (1981) study, exposure is largely inferred from group status, that is, respondents were classified according to their activities and/or location during World War II. In the absence of a more complete assessment of exposure to the dimensions of the Holocaust that one would expect to be traumatic, the "false positive" and "false negative" classification rates are unknown and unknowable. Other investigators have expressed similar concerns with regard to inferring exposure to war stress from veteran status (Schlenger, Jordan, & Fairbank, 1993).

Different analytic approaches may also contribute to variations in labor market findings across studies. Eitinger's findings were based on bivariate analyses, while Weinfeld conducted multivariate analyses that included some of the sociodemographic control variables, such as education, that economists have found to affect labor market outcomes. Still, Eitinger was the first study of exposure and labor market outcomes to include a comparison group. Moreover, Eitinger's sample may have been relatively homogeneous with respect to gender, race, and age.

Studies of Sexual and Physical Abuse in Childhood

Findings from Russell. In 1978, Russell (1986) interviewed 930 women residents of San Francisco about their experiences with incestuous abuse and other forms of sexual exploitation. This was one of the first studies of childhood sexual abuse (CSA) that was methodologically rigorous with respect to both sampling and measurement. Russell used a multiethnic probability sample of women who ranged in age from 18 to over 85. Data were gathered in face-to-face interviews that included 39 screening questions to assist respondents in identifying potentially traumatic sexual experiences. These questions focused on behaviors or sexual acts. Terms such as "rape," "incest," and "molest" were largely avoided with the understanding that not all women would label even clearly exploitive sexual experiences in these ways. Using this approach, 16 percent of the women in Russell's sample reported one or more incidents of incestuous abuse before age 18; 31 percent of these women indicated that they had been sexually abused by a nonrelative during this time period. These prevalence rates are for incidents of "contact" abuse (i.e., abuse involving contact with the breasts or genitals). The Russell (1986) study was designed to be a broad study of the prevalence and experience of incest and extrafamilial CSA. However, some data are presented on the relationship between incestuous abuse and respondents' economic circumstances including occupational functioning.

Russell (1986) found a significant relationship between incest victimization and employment status, with twice as many incest victims as nonvictims being unemployed at the time of the interview. There were no other associations between incest victimization per se and later socioeconomic outcomes. However, respondents' subjective ratings of the degree of trauma associated with the abuse were related to labor market outcomes. For these analyses Russell derived a "degree of trauma" measure from two multiple-choice questions on the impact of the abuse. The first question asked the respondent to rate how upset she was by the experience; the second asked her to consider, from her current perspective, how much of an effect the abuse had on her life. Occupational status was measured by classifying the respondent's current occupation as upper middle, middle, or lower class based on Census Bureau categories and job prestige as measured by a scale developed by the National Opinion Research Center. Among women reporting one or more incidents of incestuous abuse, those who perceived their abuse to have been extremely traumatic evidenced a consistent pattern of more negative socioeconomic outcomes. Compared with women who reported lesser degrees of trauma (i.e., considerable, some, or no trauma resulting from the abuse), women in the extreme trauma group were less likely to have attended college, held positions of lower occupational status during their adult lives, and had lower household incomes for the year prior to the study.

One possibility is that these findings are an artifact of survey research methods such that women who were functioning more poorly at the time of the interview recalled their earlier abuse experiences as more traumatic. Abuse severity was, however, the strongest determinant of the degree of subjective trauma reported. Moreover, further analyses revealed that the severity of the abuse experienced (in terms of the sexual activities involved) was significantly related to indices of poverty and downward social mobility. Poverty was defined as a household income below $7,500 at the time of the interview in 1978. Downward social mobility was indicated by the respondent having a lower occupational status and/or educational attainment than her mother.

A major strength of the Russell (1986) study was the inclusion of a detailed state-of-the-art exposure measure. Over 35 questions were used to screen for experiences of sexual trauma with a series of follow-up questions administered for each abuse incident identified during screening. Moreover, sexual trauma was not treated solely as a dichotomous variable in examining labor market outcomes. Specifically, characteristics of the women's abuse experiences and subjective ratings of the impact of the abuse were considered and found to affect labor market outcomes in several analyses.

The Russell (1986) study was not primarily a study of the relationship between sexual trauma and labor market outcomes; thus one might anticipate that the study would have some limitations in this regard. Most notably, Russell's findings on the relationship between exposure, specifically incestuous abuse in childhood, and labor market outcomes rely solely on bivariate analyses. Therefore these results do not control for demographic variables commonly considered in economic modeling of labor market outcomes (e.g., age, race/ethnicity) nor do they consider the influence of possible correlates of incestuous abuse such as other forms of family disruption and dysfunction. Given that an aim of this chapter is to review findings on mental health factors that affect the trauma-labor market outcome relationship, we also note that Russell (1986) does not provide data on respondents' psychological functioning. Thus, the extent to which reported associations between incestuous abuse and labor market outcomes are mediated by the effects of such abuse on respondents' mental health cannot be determined. Such data are needed to answer the question of whether PTSD or other psychiatric dis-

orders are important mechanisms through which incestuous abuse influences labor market outcomes.

Findings from Mullen and Colleagues.   In a study conducted in New Zealand, Mullen, Martin, Anderson, Romans, and Herbison (1994) mailed a health questionnaire to 2,250 women randomly selected from lists of voters in a city of 130,000 people. The questionnaire contained items that screened for childhood sexual abuse (CSA), operationally defined as "unwanted sexual advances before the age of 16 years." All women who reported CSA in the mail survey were recruited for a more in-depth personal interview. A comparable number of women who reported no physical or sexual abuse, either as an adult or in childhood, were randomly selected to serve as a comparison group. The final interview consisted of 492 women, 248 of whom reported a history of CSA (before age 16).

The prevalence of any CSA before age 16 in this New Zealand sample of adult women was 32 percent. Categorized by abuse severity, 3.8 percent reported CSA involving penetration, 15.9 percent reported being touched in the genital area or being coerced into touching the perpetrator's genitals, and 12.3 percent reported non-genital fondling or non-contact forms of abuse. The rates of CSA in Mullen et al.'s (1994) sample are somewhat lower than those reported by Russell (1986). However, the definitions of CSA vary between the two studies, and Mullen et al.'s rates are not outside the ranges reported in other North American samples (Finkelhor, 1979; Finkelhor, 1984; Wyatt, 1985). Key findings from the Mullen et al. (1994) study were that women reporting a history of CSA were more likely to (a) have employment histories that placed them in the lowest socioeconomic status (SES) categories, (b) be engaged in "unskilled" labor despite comparable educational attainment, and (c) evidence a decline in SES from their family of origin to their current circumstances. There were no group differences with respect to current employment status. SES "was estimated from [the respondent's] current occupation and, where relevant, that of her partner" (Mullen et al., 1994, p. 37)

Mullen et al. (1994) extended Russell's (1986) work by presenting multivariate analyses examining relationships between childhood sexual abuse and labor market outcomes. These analyses consider the role of risk factors for CSA such as poor parental mental health and physical or emotional maltreatment in childhood which may also deleteriously affect functional outcomes. Characteristics of the abuse or dimensions of exposure, specifically, abuse severity, are also considered. Across all analyses, labor market outcomes were most strongly affected in women who had experienced more invasive forms of abuse (i.e., abuse involving genital fondling or intercourse). Three factors were found to be risk factors for both CSA and negative labor market outcomes in this sample: frequent parental discord, and physical and emotional maltreatment in childhood. Even after adjusting for the affects of these risk factors using logistic regression, women who reported CSA involving intercourse were more than 4 times as likely to experience a decline in SES than non-abused controls. Thus, consistent with Russell (1986), the results of this study suggest that a history of childhood sexual abuse can have deleterious affects on women's economic welfare and that such affects are strongest for women who experienced more severe forms of abuse.

Findings from Hyman. Hyman (1993), in an unpublished doctoral dissertation, used data from the National Lesbian Health Care Survey (Bradford & Ryan, 1988) to systematically examine the relationship between a history of sexual victimization in childhood and women's economic welfare as adults. Hyman hypothesized that "the experience of child sexual abuse adversely affects the economic welfare of adult women by shaping their physical and mental health and by interfering with the acquisition of the skills necessary to perform successfully in the world of work" (1993, p. 2). To evaluate this hypothesis, Hyman used a series of regression models to examine associations between childhood sexual abuse, health, mental health, and a variety of labor market outcomes.

The National Lesbian Health Care Survey, conducted in 1984 and 1985, was intended as a broad assessment of the "physical, social, and mental health" (Hyman, 1993, p. 62) of lesbian women in the United States. The study was publicized by a variety of organizations including the American Psychological As-

sociation, the American Public Health Association, and the Office of Gay and Lesbian Health in New York. Outreach efforts were made in order to involve lesbians from a wide range of geographic and age groups, as well as women who did not actively participate in the gay and lesbian community. Questionnaires were distributed to 4,000 women, and 1,925 women completed the survey.

Respondents were identified as having experienced childhood sexual abuse if they responded affirmatively to either of the following questions: "Did any of your relatives have sex with you while growing up?" or "Were you ever raped or sexually attacked while growing up?" Respondents' abuse experiences were categorized into one of four categories—intrafamilial abuse without coercion, intrafamilial abuse with coercion, extrafamilial abuse by a known perpetrator, extrafamilial abuse by an unknown perpetrator. Coercion appears to have been inferred on the basis of a respondent indicating that she was "raped or sexually attacked." As a comprehensive measure of childhood sexual victimization, this assessment has a number of limitations. Most notably, questions that ask about abuse experiences are less precise than recent research and clinical convention suggests is necessary to develop a sensitive and specific measure that maximizes identification of true positive and true negative abuse histories (cf. Solomon et al., 1996; Russell, 1986; Wyatt & Peters, 1986). In order to reliably assess CSA it is considered preferable to ask about specific sexual behaviors rather than using value-laden or ambiguous terms such as "rape," "sexual attack," and "have sex with." Additionally, the respondent's age at the time of the abuse is unspecified. Unwanted sexual experiences while "growing up" could include childhood abuse as well as dating violence.

Hyman indicates that she chose to use the National Lesbian Health Care Survey data despite these limitations because no other available data set included information on CSA, health, mental health, and the *individual* woman's earnings (i.e., as opposed to *household* earnings). Moreover, in discussing the validity and reliability of these data, Hyman points out that the prevalence of CSA in this sample of lesbian women was comparable to rates found in representative samples of women in the general population

(Finkelhor et al., 1990; Russell, 1983). That is, approximately one-third of the respondents reported that they were sexually victimized while growing up.

Economic welfare in this study was defined in terms of a full range of point in time labor market outcomes. These were the respondent's employment status and, if employed, whether she worked full- or part-time, the status of her occupation (as described in Arnott and Matthaei, 1991), and her annual earnings. Hyman first examined the bivariate associations between CSA and labor market outcomes. She then conducted a series of multivariate analyses in which a broad range of sociodemographic factors previously found to affect women's economic welfare (e.g., age, race, education) were included in the model along with variables coding the type of abuse experienced. The mental and physical health indices created for this study were included in these models as well. (These indices reflected the total number of psychological or health problems reported by the respondent.) Finally both the direct and indirect effect of CSA on earnings was evaluated in each of the four abuse subgroups.

A history of childhood sexual abuse was associated with reduced labor market outcomes. Based on bivariate analyses, abuse survivors were less likely to work full-time and more likely to be unemployed than nonabused respondents. Hyman, as did Russell (1986), found that almost twice as many survivors as nonabused women were currently unemployed at the time of the study (10.2 percent and 5.5 percent respectively). In multivariate analyses, only intrafamilial abuse was a significant predictor of hours worked, with women reporting intrafamilial abuse "without coercion" *more* likely to work full time, while those reporting intrafamilial abuse "with coercion" *less* likely to work full-time. Those abuse survivors who were employed were less likely to be working as professionals and managers and more likely to be engaged in clerical or service work. Rates of CSA among laborers and service workers were upwards of 50 percent.

The women in this sample earned almost double what the average American woman earned in 1985 with over 70 percent of the respondents holding professional or managerial positions. Still, women reporting a history of childhood sexual abuse earned significantly less than their nonabused counterparts. In the full multivariate model, two forms of abuse had direct effects of annual earnings. Women who reported that they had been "raped or sexually attacked" by a relative or unknown perpetrator earned 12 to 16 percent less than nonabused respondents. Using a series of equations, Hyman also estimated the total effect of CSA on respondents' earnings, defined as the sum of direct effects of CSA on earnings as well as any indirect effects through health, mental health, and educational attainment. When both direct and indirect effects of CSA are taken into account, respondents who experienced either form of intrafamilial CSA and those who were sexually victimized by a stranger all evidenced a significant reduction in annual earnings compared to their nonabused counterparts. A positive association between CSA and total number of mental health problems was found in all three groups. These analyses indicated that, except for women reporting intrafamilial abuse "wit coercion," physical health problems, and reduced educational attainment also played a role in mediating the CSA-earnings relationship.

Hyman's findings, along with those from Russell (1986) and Mullen et al. (1994), strongly suggest childhood sexual abuse affects adult women's economic welfare. Moreover, Hyman provides initial evidence that these affects of CSA on labor market outcomes are in part mediated by reduced educational attainment and increased mental and physical health problems. Although each of the studies reviewed used a different measure of CSA, in all three, the magnitude of the affects of CSA on labor market outcomes was influenced by the nature of the abuse experienced. These results argue against using a measurement or analysis approach that simply categorizes individuals as abused or nonabused.

Findings from Lisak and Luster. The majority of research on the effects of childhood sexual abuse have focused on girls and women. However, a 1994 publication by Lisak and Luster does provide some data on aspects of occupational stability among men reporting histories of childhood sexual and physical abuse. In this study, a self-report questionnaire was administered to 90 men recruited at a booth located on a college campus in a metropolitan area of the northeastern United States. The questionnaire inquired about 17 different types of sexual experiences, as well as about physical assaults involving being hit, slapped, or otherwise physically injured by others. All incidents reported were to have occurred before the age of 16. Responses were coded for CSA and for physical abuse using criteria specified by Wyatt (1985) and by Finkelhor (1979). Forty-one percent of this volunteer sample (n = 37) reported no sexual or physical abuse during childhood, 17.8 percent (n = 16) reported sexual abuse only, 24.4 percent (n = 22) reported physical abuse only, and 16.7 percent (n = 15) reported both physical and sexual abuse in childhood. Of 31 cases of CSA reported, 77.4 percent involved physical contact. Occupational stability was assessed in terms of the number, nature, and duration of jobs previously held and reasons for leaving job (e.g., promotion, relocation, conflict with supervisors, being laid off, etc.). For analysis purposes, three occupational variables were created from these questionnaire items: Negative Reasons for Leaving Jobs, Negative Reasons for Unemployment, and Total Number of Jobs.

Lisak and Luster (1994) reported some differences between effects of CSA and physical abuse on these measures of occupational stability. Specifically, men who reported CSA only reported a significantly greater number of jobs and more negative reasons for leaving jobs than respondents who experienced no abuse or physical abuse only. Surprisingly, however, the subset of men who experienced both CSA and physical abuse did not report significantly more occupational difficulties than nonabused men.

The interpretation and generalizability of the findings of this study are constrained by several aspects of the research design. These include a small convenience sample of men, and an approach to data analysis that did not make use of information obtained on characteristics and severity of reported CSA known to affect long-term outcomes. Nevertheless, the results of this study are generally consistent with findings on the relationship of CSA to labor market outcomes for women, and provide some insight into the association of CSA to occupational stability

among young men (i.e., university students) who do not have extensive histories of involvement in the labor market.

Studies of Military Veterans

Findings from Anderson and Mitchell. Anderson and Mitchell (1992) published one of the first papers specifically evaluating links between military service, psychiatric disorder, and labor market outcomes. Using data from the NIMH Epidemiologic Catchment Area (ECA) program, Anderson and Mitchell (1992) examined the relationship between veteran status (veteran versus nonveteran) and DSM-III (APA, 1980) diagnoses on labor market outcomes. They found that the veteran status variables were insignificant but that DSM-III diagnoses (including substance abuse, but excluding depression) were negatively related to the probability of working. Anderson and Mitchell (1992) concluded that military service has an indirect effect via mental health on the likelihood of being employed. "Veterans had worse mental health than nonveterans, and this negative impact on mental health lowers the employment of veterans relative to nonveterans" (Anderson & Mitchell, 1992, p. 562).

However, as a cautionary note, Schlenger, Jordan, and Fairbank (1993) underscored the limitations of the ECA data for studying exposure to trauma as a determinant of labor market outcomes among veterans. The ECA survey instrument asked only whether individuals had served in the military and did not ask about military service in a war zone or exposure to specific dimensions of war zone stress. This concern highlights that, particularly for certain types of potentially traumatic events (e.g., disasters, providing military service in a war zone), it is important, if not critical, to assess each individual's type and degree of exposure rather than assume all those of a particular classification status (e.g., veteran, prison camp survivor) had comparable degrees of exposure.

Findings from Vincent, Long, and Chamberlain. Questionnaire data from a mail survey of Vietnam veterans in New Zealand was used to explore associations between military service variables (e.g., military specialization unit), combat exposure, PTSD, and current demographic and labor market outcome variables, such as education, employment status, and income (Vincent, Long, & Chamberlain, 1994). PTSD was assessed using the Mississippi Scale for Combat-Related PTSD (Keane et al., 1989). Bivariate analyses indicated that respondents identified as PTSD cases on the basis of elevated scores on the Mississippi Scale had significantly lower incomes than those who scored below the cut-off point of 94. The PTSD subgroup also had lower educational attainment and was almost twice as likely to be currently unemployed.

Findings from McCarren and Colleagues.

McCarren et al. (1995) examined the associations between participation in combat, PTSD, and labor market outcomes in a sample of 2,210 monozygotic twin pairs of American veterans of the Vietnam war using multivariate models. Participants were selected from the Vietnam Era Twin registry, a national listing of male twin pairs who served in the military during the Vietnam era. Labor market outcomes assessed included current employment status, occupational category (occupations grouped into seven categories), length of time in years at current position, and family income. Demographic variables relevant to economic modeling of labor market outcomes (e.g., age and education at enlistment, length of service in the military, highest education level) were also appraised. Combat exposure was evaluated with 18 questions about combat roles and experiences. From these data a five-level ordinal index of combat exposure was developed. A "presumptive diagnosis" of PTSD was made based on responses to 12 items in the survey that tapped information similar to DSM-III-R (APA, 1987) symptoms for PTSD.

In the complete sample, PTSD was associated with greater unemployment and differences in occupational classifications, household income, and educational attainment. However, after "adjusting for familial factors" by restricting analyses to twins discordant for PTSD and including premilitary and military service characteristics as covariates in multivariate analyses, only the likelihood of being unemployed related significantly to PTSD. Moreover in twin pairs

negative for PTSD, there were no significant associations between combat exposure and labor market outcomes with adjustment for premilitary and military characteristics. Thus, these authors assert that in the absence of PTSD, exposure to combat has no longer-term effects on occupational functioning and that the impact of PTSD on labor market outcomes is restricted to employment status.

These results are consistent with Anderson and Mitchell's (1992) conclusion that the effects of military service on employment are mediated by psychological disorder. However, specific findings should be interpreted with caution. Prior research suggests some degree of selection or ascertainment bias in the Vietnam Era Twin Registry (Goldberg, True, Eisen, Henderson, & Robinette, 1987), as well as nontrivial attrition problems (65 percent response rate) affecting the 1987 survey of the registry that provided the data for McCarren et al.'s (1995) study. Thus, the possibility that response bias affected the results remains a consideration. In addition, PTSD diagnoses in McCarren et al. (1995) were based solely on responses to 12 items in the 1987 survey; no validity data for this measure are reported.

Findings from the National Vietnam Veterans Readjustment Study.

The National Vietnam Veterans Readjustment Study (NVVRS; Kulka et al., 1990) investigated the prevalence of and risk factors for a range of psychosocial problems among war veterans. The NVVRS included three primary groups of respondents: (1) 1,632 male and female veterans who served in Southeast Asia during the war; (2) 716 other male and female veterans of the era; and (3) 668 nonveterans of matching age, gender, and other characteristics. Cases of PTSD were identified on the basis of comprehensive multimeasure assessment that included information from structured clinical and survey interviews, self-report scales, and clinician rating scales.

Exposure to potentially traumatic war events was assessed with 97 items that King, King, Gudanowski, and Vreven (1995) found to cluster into four dimensions of exposure: (a) stereotypical war-zone events, such as firing a weapon or receiving fire; (b) war-zone events considered deviant (e.g., participating in atrocities or exceptionally abusive acts); (c) perceived threats from a harsh and malevolent environment; and (d) day-to-day discomforts. Indicators of occupational outcomes included a measure of current employment status, and a measure of occupational or career instability. The occupational instability variable was derived from several items assessing work history: (1) number of different employers; (2) number of different kinds of jobs; and (3) number of periods of unemployment.

Bivariate analyses of NVVRS data conducted by Kulka et al. (1990) indicated that male Vietnam veterans with PTSD were more than five times more likely to be unemployed than veterans without PTSD (13.3 versus 2.5 percent). Among both men and women, those with PTSD reported significantly higher levels of occupational instability than their counterparts without PTSD (Kulka et al., 1990). Expanding upon these analyses, Zatzick and colleagues (Zatzick, Marmar, Weiss et al., 1995; Zatzick, Weiss, Marmar et al., 1997) used NVVRS data to examine the PTSD-unemployment relationship from a multivariate framework. For women, these investigators examined the impact of PTSD upon unemployment using logistic regression models that controlled for the effects of several of the standard sociodemographic covariates (age, marital status, and educational attainment) and for potentially confounding psychiatric disorders that have been shown in prior research to be frequently comorbid with PTSD (major depression, alcohol abuse and dependence, and panic disorder). After adjusting for the effects of these sociodemographic variables and comorbid psychiatric disorders, women with PTSD were 10.4 times more likely to be unemployed that their veteran counterparts without PTSD (Zatzick et al., 1997).

The regression models for men varied slightly from the models for women. In addition to the sociodemographic variables and psychiatric disorders included in the models for women, models for men controlled for chronic medical conditions, drug abuse and dependence, race/ethnicity, and region of the country in which the respondent resided at time of induction into the military. Adjusting for these effects, men were found to be 3.3 times more likely to be unemployed than their male counterparts without PTSD.

Despite large variations in methodology among the studies of combat veterans reviewed above, including substantial differences in the measurement of both PTSD and labor market outcomes, PTSD is consistently found to be associated with diminished labor market outcomes. In point of fact, PTSD remains a significant predictor of labor market outcomes for veterans even after the effects of standard sociodemographic variables, pre-exposure vulnerabilities, and comorbid psychiatric disorders are taken into account through multivariate statistical procedures. So far, attempts to determine the extent to which associations between exposure to trauma and labor market outcomes are mediated by the effects of such trauma on PTSD have been limited to studies involving veterans of war. For example, although strong conceptual arguments may be advanced that PTSD is likely to be one of the mechanisms through which CSA affects labor market outcomes, data are not yet available to test such a hypothesis empirically. To move the field toward greater understanding of the nature of the relationships among various types of traumatic events and labor market outcomes, future studies with specific risk groups (e.g., physical and sexual violence) should include a comprehensive assessment of PTSD.

Studies of Southeast Asian Refugees

Findings from Uba and Chung. In a study of a random household sample of 590 adult Cambodian refugees living in California, Uba and Chung (1991) examined the multivariate relationships between labor market outcomes and exposure to trauma, standard sociodemographic variables (e.g, age, gender), and psychological functioning. Labor market outcomes were assessed with two point in time variables: current employment status and current annual family income. Trauma was assessed in terms of three variables: a dichotomous measure (yes/no) of exposure to "trauma in Cambodia that continued to affect them," a measure of the frequency of such exposures, and a measure of amount of time spent in refugee camps (in years). Psychological functioning was assessed using the Health Opinion Survey (HOS; Leighton et al., 1963), a measure of psychological functioning that was found to be comprised of four factors (general psychopathology, psychosocial dysfunction, anxiety, and depression) identified through principal components analysis.

Application of a discriminant function analysis that included age, gender, and psychological functioning as control variables revealed a significant relationship between the trauma variables and employment status. The authors interpreted the findings as indicating that "respondents who had experienced a trauma that still disturbed them, had experienced more traumas, or spent more years in refugee camps were more likely to be unemployed (page 220)" even when controlling for the effects of psychological distress in the analysis. Multiple regression was then used to test the impact of past trauma on current family income, with psychological distress, age, gender, and number of family members employed entered into the analysis as control variables.

Findings on the impact of trauma on family income were more mixed. Reporting a trauma that still distressed the respondent at the time of the survey was related to higher annual family income, while frequency of exposure was associated with lower family income. The authors offer several possible explanations in terms of ethnocultural and personal factors that might moderate the effect of past exposure on family income among relocated refugees. Variations in findings are also potentially attributable to methodologic aspects of the study. In the studies reviewed thus far, where assessed, mental health was viewed as a mediator of the effects of trauma on labor market outcomes. In contrast, Uba and Chung (1991) control for the respondents' psychological functioning in examining the trauma-labor market outcome relationship. This includes controlling for the degree to which respondents perceive that psychological distress "impedes their ability to work." Additionally, exposure was assessed dichotomously rather than multidimensionally and family income rather than personal income was used to index the individual's earnings.

Findings from Hauf and Vaglum.

Other studies have examined the relationships either of war trauma to labor force participation or of PTSD to labor market outcomes in samples of Southeast Asian refugees.

Hauf and Vaglum (1993) interviewed 145 Vietnamese refugees on arrival and after three years in Norway. Multivariate analysis that included controls for age, gender, and mental health found that refugees who reported "witnessing other people being wounded and/or killed" were significantly more likely to be employed than their counterparts who did not experience such events. As in Uba and Chung, the analysis approach considers the effects of exposure on employment only after the effects of mental health—including the effects of trauma on mental health—are removed. Additionally, these findings need to be considered in the context of potential differences in immigration and resettlement policies and economic conditions across cultures.

Findings from Sack et al.

Sack and colleagues (1995) examined the relationship between PTSD and labor market outcomes in a community sample of Khmer/Cambodian adolescents and young adults (13–25 years of age) and their parents or legal guardians. PTSD was assessed using structured diagnostic interviews. The labor market outcomes measured were current employment for youth and annual income and receipt of public assistance (i.e., Welfare status) for parent/guardians. Bivariate analyses revealed no significant differences in labor market participation for Cambodian youth with PTSD and their counterparts with no diagnosis or with diagnoses in other categories (partial PTSD or depression). Approximately two thirds of the youth in each of four diagnostic categories were employed at the time of the study. Adult respondents with PTSD, as well as those with PTSD and comorbid depression, reported lower annual incomes than Cambodian refugee parents with no diagnosis. Refugee parents with PTSD were also more likely to be receiving public assistance.

SUMMARY AND SYNTHESIS

In this chapter we reviewed the extent empirical literature that has examined associations between traumatic stress exposure and labor market outcomes. Compared to an ever growing literature on the mental and physical health effects of traumatic stress, research on the economic consequences of trauma is still at an early stage of development with fewer than two dozen published studies on the topic. Nonetheless, one significant conclusion can be drawn from our review: Traumatic experiences not only compromise mental and physical health but can have deleterious economic consequences as well.

To date the literature has examined associations between four types of exposure and labor market outcomes: trauma related to the Holocaust; sexual and physical abuse in childhood; combat exposure; and trauma experienced by Southeast Asian refugees. We were able to locate two studies which compared labor market outcomes for Holocaust survivors with those of individuals who did not directly experience the Holocaust. In both studies Holocaust survivors evidenced less occupational stability. In addition, Weinfeld et al. (1981) reported depressed family incomes among Holocaust survivors in Canada. Findings for occupational mobility among Holocaust survivors were inconsistent. Eitinger (1973) found a significant decline in occupational status in his Norwegian survivor sample while no such decline was found in Weinfeld et al's Canadian sample.

Overall the available data also indicate that sexual abuse in childhood can adversely affect women's economic welfare. In both a probability sample of women living in San Francisco (Russell, 1986) and a national sample of lesbian women (Hyman, 1993), current rates of unemployment among respondents reporting a history of CSA were approximately twice those of nonabused women. Additionally, among working lesbians, CSA was associated with an average reduction in annual earnings of about 11 percent (Hyman, 1993). (Extrafamilial abuse by a known perpetrator was not associated with reduced earnings in this sample.) Finally, Russell (1986) and Mullen et al. (1994) in New Zealand reported significant declines in socioecomic status among women experiencing more severe forms of CSA. Little is known about the effects of childhood abuse on men's performance and participation in the labor market. However, one study found that CSA was associated with relatively unstable work histories among male university students (Lisak and Luster, 1994).

The role of mental health in the trauma-labor market outcome relationship has been most widely studied in individuals who have experienced combat and other forms of war stress. The most consistent finding in this domain is a relationship between current PTSD and reduced labor market participation in Vietnam veterans. In two large samples of Vietnam veterans in the United States and a third sample in New Zealand, veterans receiving a diagnosis of current PTSD were more likely to be unemployed than those without the disorder (Kulka et al., 1990; McCarren et al., 1995; Vincent et al., 1994; Zatzick et al., 1995; Zatzick et al., 1997). Additionally, PTSD has been found to be associated with greater occupational instabilty among Vietnam veterans (Kulka et al., 1990). However, the relationship between PTSD and income in combat veterans is equivocal with one study reporting positive results (Vincent et al., 1994) while a more methodologically sophisticated study reported no effect of PTSD on income (McCarren et al., 1995).

In studies of Vietnam veterans PTSD has largely been conceptualized as a mediator of the effects of war stress on labor market outcomes. However, Uba and Chung (1991) and Hauf and Vaglum (1993) both controlled for individual differences in psychological functioning in studying relationships between war stress and labor market outcomes in Southeast Asian refugees. Uba and Chung found that refugees who reported higher levels of trauma were more likely to be unemployed while Hauf and Vaglum found *higher* rates of employment among refugees who reported more severe trauma histories. In neither sample was war stress found to be associated with income. In contrast, Sack et al. (1995) reported lower annual incomes and greater dependence on public assistance among Cambodian refugee parents with PTSD than among those with no diagnosis.

Looking across the studies reviewed, one finds a reasonably consistent pattern of results such that traumatic stress is associated with reduced labor market outcomes. Some data also indicate that the relationship between trauma and labor market outcomes may in part be mediated by PTSD. It is tempting to draw specific conclusions from these findings. For example, generalizing from Hyman (1993), one might infer that women sexually abused as children earn 10 to 20 percent less than their nonabused counterparts. Yet, we found that the patterns and magnitude of specific trauma-income associations varied considerably among the studies reviewed. Confidence in drawing conclusions at this level of specificity is additionally diminished by the limited number of studies conducted to date and the fact that the effects of certain types of trauma have yet to be examined. Similarly, at present, definitive conclusions about the role of PTSD in the trauma-labor market outcome relationship would appear premature. The potential mediating effect of PTSD has only been examined with respect to war stress. Moreover, trauma-labor market outcome relationships have yet to be extensively evaluated in the context of other factors that may place individuals at increased risk for both exposure to traumatic stress and negative labor market outcomes (e.g., family disruptions, poor parental mental health).

With an eye toward the future, we conclude that the research reviewed here clearly suggests that trauma-labor market outcome relationships merit further investigation. Future studies should examine the economic consequences of other types of trauma, such as physical and sexual violence experienced in adulthood. Perhaps most importantly, more methodologically sophisticated research is needed.

Three key methodological/substantive issues guided this review. First, given a substantial body of research demonstrating that the characteristics and dimensions of traumatic events differentially affect mental health outcomes, we considered the approaches used in the reviewed studies to assess exposure to trauma. Findings suggest that not only do the effects on labor market outcomes vary by type of exposure, but dimensions of exposure within any given class of traumatic events can influence effects on labor market outcomes. Future research on the trauma-labor market outcome relationship should take this into account, and wherever possible, avoid simple classification of people into dichotomous categories such as exposed and nonexposed. In determining the aspects of exposure to assess in a given study, researchers may want to consider empirical data where available (e.g., data indicating that type and severity of CSA affects labor market outcomes) and what differences might mean substantively in terms of labor market outcomes. For example, certain types of exposure might be posited to affect employment status, but not necessarily earnings among individuals who are employed.

Second, researchers in the area of traumatic stress should build upon prior work in the economics literature on factors affecting labor market outcomes. The economics literature indicates the need for multivariate models that include sociodemographic variables known to strongly affect labor market outcomes, such as gender, age, educational level, and physical health. As social scientists and trauma researchers, we must also keep in mind that there may be situations where potential mediating effects of variables such as education and physical health should be considered as well.

Third, there is a need for further empirical and conceptual work exploring factors that potentially mediate the trauma-labor market outcome relationship. Thus far, the potential mediating role of psychiatric disorder—PTSD in particular—has only been examined in studies of combat veterans and Southeast Asian refugees. Inquiries into the possible mediating effects of PTSD should be extended to other types of traumatic stress. We also need more comprehensive conceptual models that specify other possible determinants of the trauma-labor market outcome relationship. Furthermore, analyses that test competing etiologic models, such as the relative influence of educational attainment versus current symptomatology on labor market outcomes among sexual abuse survivors, would have important implications for the development of interventions and for the establishment of informed policy. If such an analysis determined current symptomatology was a significant mediator of the trauma-labor market outcome relationship, subsequent analyses might attempt to learn whether the key mediating factors are overall distress, or specific PTSD symptoms, for example, concentration difficulties, interpersonal problems related to increased anger, or feelings of alienation.

In conclusion, a review and synthesis of findings on the trauma-labor market outcome relationship appears timely with respect to current concerns about costs of treating psychiatric disorder. Given that studies of other psychiatric disorders have shown that the indirect costs of psychiatric disorder are actually greater than direct costs of treatment, future research may be able to demonstrate that targeted treatment of, for example, certain PTSD symptoms is "justified" on economic as well as humanitarian grounds.

American Economic Association. (1997). *Journal of Economic Literature Database* [CD ROM], 1990–1997. Nashville, TN: American Economic Association [Producer and Distributor].

American Psychiatric Association. (1980). *Diagnostic and statistical manual of mental disorders* (3rd ed.). Washington, DC: Author.

American Psychiatric Association. (1987). *Diagnostic and statistical manual of mental disorders* (3rd ed. Rev.). Washington, DC: Author.

Anderson, K., & Mitchell, J. (1992). Effects of military experience on mental health problems and work behavior. *Medical Care, 30,* 554–563.

Arnott, T. L., & Matthaei, J. A. (1991). *Race, gender, and work: A multicultural economic history of women in the United States.* Boston: South End Press.

Barrett, D. H., Resnick, H. S., Foy, D. W., Dansky, B. S., Flanders, W. D., & Stroup, N. E. (1996). Combat exposure and adult psychosocial adjustment among U.S. Army Veterans serving in Vietnam, 1965–1971, *Journal of Abnormal Psychology, 105,* 575–581.

Bartel, A., & Taubman, P. (1979). Health and labor market success: The role of various diseases. *Review of Economics and Statistics, 61,* 1–8.

Bartel, A., & Taubman, P. (1986). Some economic and demographic consequences of mental illness. *Journal of Labor Economics, 21,* 243–256.

Bradford, J., & Ryan, C. (1988). *The National Lesbian Health Care Survey: Final report.* Washington, DC: National Lesbian and Gay Health Foundation.

Duncan, O. D. (1961). A socioeconomic index for all occupations. In A. J. Reiss, Jr. (Ed.), *Occupations and social status.* New York: Free Press.

Eaton, W. W., & Kessler, L. G. (Eds.). (1985). *Epidemiologic field methods in psychiatry. The NIMH Epidemiologic Catchment Area Program.* Orlando, FL: Academic Press.

Eitinger, L. (1973). A follow-up study of the Norwegian Concentration Camp Survivors' Mortality and Morbidity. *Israel Annals of Psychiatry and Related Disciplines, 11,* 199–209.

Ettner, S. L., Frank, R. G., & Kessler, R. C. (1997). The impact of psychiatric disorders on labor market outcomes. *National Bureau of Economic Research, Inc.,* Working Paper: 5989. Available: http://www.nber.org.

Finkelhor, D. (1979). *Sexually victimized children.* New York: Free Press.

Finkelhor, D. (1984). *Child sexual abuse: New theory and research.* New York: Free Press.

Finkelhor, D., Hotaling, G., Lewis, I. A., & Smith, C. (1990). Sexual abuse in a national survey of adult men and women: prevalence, characteristics, and risk factors. *Child Abuse and Neglect, v. 14,* 19–28.

Fleisher, B. M., & Kniesner, T. J. (1984). *Labor economics: Theory, evidence, and policy.* Englewood Cliffs, NJ: Prentice-Hall.

Frank, R. G., & Gertler, P. (1991). An assessment of measurement error bias for estimating the effect of mental distress on income. *Journal of Human Resources, 26,* 154–164.

Friedman, M. J., Charney, D. S., & Deutch, A. Y. (Eds.). (1995). *Neurobiological and clinical consequences of stress: From normal adaptation to post-traumatic stress disorder.* Philadelphia: Lippincott-Raven.

Goldberg, J., True, W. R., Eisen, S. A., Henderson, W. G., & Robinette, C. D. (1987). The Vietnam Era Twin Registry: Ascertainment bias. *Acta Geneticae Medicae et Gemellologiae, 36,* 61–66.

Greenberg, P. E., Stiglin, L. E., Finkelstein, S. N., & Berndt, E. R. (1993). The economic burden of depression in 1990. *Journal of Clinical Psychiatry, 54,* 405–418.

Grossman, M. (1972). *The demand for health: A theoretical and empirical investigation.* New York: Columbia University Press.

Hanoch, G. (1980). A multivariate model of labor supply: Methodology and estimation. In J. P. Smith (Ed.), *Female labor supply: Theory and estimation* (pp. 249–317) Princeton, NJ: Princeton University Press.

Hauff, E., & Vaughn, P. (1993). Integration of Vietnamese refugees into the Norwegian labor market: The impact of war and trauma. *International Migration Review, 27,* 388–405.

Hyman, B. (1993). The economic consequences of child sexual abuse in women (Doctoral dissertation, Brandeis University, 1993). *UMI Dissertation Services,* Order Number 9408865.

Kazak, A. E., Barakat, L. P., Meeske, K., Christakis, D., Meadows, A. T., Casey, R., Penati, B., & Stuber, M. L. (1997). Posttraumatic stress, family functioning, and social support in survivors of childhood leukemia and their mothers and fathers. *Journal of Consulting and Clinical Psychology, 65,* 120–129.

Keane, T. M., Fairbank, J. A., Caddell, J. M., et al. (1989). Clinical evaluation of a measure to assess combat exposure. *Psychology Assessment Journal of Consultation Clinical Psychology, 1,* 53–55.

King, D. W., King, L. A., Gudanowski, D. M., & Vreven, D. L. (1995). Alternative representations of war zone stressors: Relationships to posttraumatic stress disorder in male and female Vietnam veterans. *Journal of Abnormal Psychology, 104,* 184–196.

Kulka, R. A., Schlenger, W. E., Fairbank, J. A., Hough, R. L., Jordan, B. K., Marmar, C. R., & Weiss, D. S., (1990). *Trauma and the Vietnam war generation: Report of findings from the National Vietnam Veterans Readjustment Study.* New York: Brunner/Mazel.

Leighton, D. C., Harding, J. S., Mecklin, D. B., MacMillan, A., & Leighton, A. H. (1963). *The character of danger.* New York: Basic Books.

Lisak, D., & Luster, L. (1994). Educational, occupational, and relationship histories of men who were sexually and/or physically abused as children. *Journal of Traumatic Stress, 7,* 507–523.

McCarren, M., Janes, G. R., Goldberg, J., Eisen, S., True, W. R., & Henderson, W. G. (1995). A twin study of the association of post-traumatic stress disorder and combat exposure with long-term socioeconomic status in Vietnam veterans. *Journal of Traumatic Stress, 8,* 111–124.

Mincer, J. (1974). *Schooling, experience, and earnings.* New York: Columbia University Press, National Bureau of Economic Research.

Mroz, T. (1987). The sensitivity of an empirical model of married women's hours of work to economic and statistical assumptions. *Econometrica, 55,* 765–800.

Mullahy, J , & Sindelar, J. L. (1990). Gender differences in the effects of mental health on labor force participation. In I. Sirageldin (Ed.), *Research in human capital and development: Female labor force participation.* Greenwich, CT: JAI Press.

Mullen, P. E., Martin, J. L., Anderson, J. C., Romans, S. E., & Herbison, G. P. (1994). The effect of child sexual abuse on social, interpersonal, and sexual function in adult life. *British Journal of Psychiatry, 165,* 35–47.

Pencavel, J. (1986). Labor supply of men: A survey. In O. Ashenfelter & R. Layard (Eds.), *Handbook of labor economics* (pp. 1–102). Amsterdam: North-Holland.

PILOTS bibliographical database [On-line database]. (May, 1997). White River Junction, VT: National Center for Post-traumatic Stress Disorder [Producer].

Ruhm, C. J. (1992). The effects of physical and mental health on female labor supply. In Frank & Manning, Jr. (Eds.), *Economics and mental health* (pp. 152–181). Baltimore: Johns Hopkins University Press.

Russell, D. E. H. (1986). *The secret trauma: Incest in the lives of girls and women.* New York: Basic Books.

Russell, D. E. H. (1983). The incidence and prevalence of intrafamilial and extrafamilial sexual abuse of female children. *Child Abuse and Neglect, 7,* 133–146.

Sack, W. H., Clarke, G. N., Kinney, R., Belestos, G., Chanrithy, H., & Seeley, J. (1995). The Khmer Adolescent Project II: Functional capacities in two generations of Cambodian refugees, *Journal of Nervous and Mental Disease, 183,* 177–181.

Saigh, P. A. (1992). *Posttraumatic stress disorder: A behavioral approach to assessment and treatment.* Boston: Allyn and Bacon.

Schlenger, W. E., Jordan, B. K., & Fairbank, J. A. (1993). Comment on Anderson & Mitchell [Letter to editor]. *Medical Care, 31,* 470–472.

Solomon, S., Cottrol, C., Fairbank, J., Friedman, M., Green, B., King, L., Norris, F., Southwick, S., Ursano, R., & Weisaeth, L. (1996, November). *Recommendations of stressor assessment group from the NIMH-National Center for PTSD Joint Conference on Diagnosis and Assessment in PTSD Research.* NIMH-National Center for PTSD Joint Conference on Diagnosis and Assessment in PTSD Research, Boston, MA.

Stevens, G., & Cho, J. H. (1985). Socioeconomic indexes and the new 1980 Census Occupational Classification Scheme. *Social Sciences Research, 14,* 142–168.

Treiman, D. J., & Hartmann, H. I. (1981). *Women, work, and wages: Equal pay for jobs of equal value.* Washington, DC: National Academy Press.

Uba, L., & Chung, R. (1991). The relationship between trauma and financial and physical well-being among Cambodians in the United States. *Journal of General Psychology, 118,* 215–225.

U.S. Bureau of the Census. (1996). *Statistical abstracts of the United States* (166th ed.). Washington, DC.

Vincent, C., Long, N., & Chamberlain, K. (1994). Relation of military service variables to posttraumatic stress disorder in New Zealand War Veterans. *Military Medicine, 159,* 322–326.

Weinfeld, M., Sigal, J. J., & Eaton, W. W. (1981). Long-term effects of the Holocaust on selected social attitudes and behaviors of survivors: A cautionary note. *Social Forces, 60,* 1–19.

Weiss, Y. (1986). The determination of life-cycle earnings: A survey. In O. Ashenfelter & R. Layard (Eds.), *Handbook of labor economics* (pp. 603–640). Amsterdam: North-Holland.

Wells, K. B., Sturm, R., Sherbourne, C. D., & Meredith, L. S. (1996). *Caring for depression.* Cambridge, MA: Harvard University Press.

Wyatt, G. E. (1985). The sexual abuse of Afro-American and white-American women in childhood. *Child Abuse and Neglect, 9,* 507–519.

Wyatt, G. E., & Peters, S. D. (1986). Methodological considerations in research on the prevalence of child sexual abuse. *Child Abuse & Neglect, 10,* 241–251.

Zatzick, D. F., Marmar, C. R., Weiss, D. S., Browner, W., Metzler, T. J., Golding, J. M., Stewart, A., Schlenger, W. E., & Wells, K. B. (1995, November). *Posttraumatic stress disorder, and functioning and quality of life outcomes in a nationally representative sample of male Vietnam veterans.* Paper presented at the Robert Wood Johnson Clinical Scholars National Meeting.

Zatzick, D. F., Weiss, D. S., Marmar, C. R., Metzler, T. J., Wells, K., Golding, J. M., Stewart, A., Schlenger, W. E., & Browner, W. S. (1997). Posttraumatic stress disorder and functioning and quality of life outcomes in female Vietnam veterans. *Military Medicine, 162,* 661–665.

CHAPTER 10

ASSESSMENT OF PEDIATRIC POSTTRAUMATIC STRESS DISORDER

JOHN S. MARCH, M.D., M.P.H
Associate Professor and Director,
Program in Childhood and Adolescent Anxiety Disorders
Duke University Medical Center
Durham, North Carolina

Since posttraumatic stress disorder (PTSD) entered the psychiatric lexicon with DSM-III (American Psychiatric Association, 1980), a panoply of investigations have concluded that exposure to life-threatening events leads to serious and often debilitating PTSD in youth (March & Amaya-Jackson, 1994; Pynoos, Nader, et al., 1993) as in adults (March, 1993). Concomitantly, child psychiatrists and psychologists have come to appreciate the extent to which children are exposed to potentially traumatic situations, the severity of their acute distress, and the potential serious long-term psychiatric sequelae, and to embed the empirical investigation of traumatic events and their posttraumatic sequelae within a sound developmental framework (Pynoos, 1994; Pynoos, Steinberg, & Wraith, 1995). Despite the fact that psychological trauma enters into the differential diagnosis of most if not all the childhood-onset mental disorders (Amaya-Jackson & March, 1995), psychometrically valid instruments for assessing PTSD in youth above the age of 8 are just now becoming available (March & Albano, 1996).

Ideally, assessment tools targeting pediatric PTSD should: (1) provide reliable and valid ascertainment of symptoms across multiple domains; (2) identify objective and subjective responses to divergent traumatic events; (3) evaluate symptom severity; (4) incorporate and reconcile multiple observations, such as parent and child ratings; and (5) be sensitive to treatment-induced change in symptoms. With the increasing emphasis on multi-disciplinary approaches to assessment and treatment, assessment tools also must facilitate communication, not only among clinicians, but between clinicians and regulatory bodies, such as utilization review committees with managed care environments, and with schools (Saigh, 1996). Other factors influencing instrument selection include the reasons for the assessment, e.g., screening, diagnosis or monitoring treatment outcome, as well as time required for administration, level of training necessary to administer and/or interpret the instrument, reading level, and cost. While no currently available instrument is optimized for each of these goals (McNally, 1996), a complex matrix of assessment tools is available, potentially making the choice of instruments for evaluating a particular child or adolescent seem daunting (March & Albano, 1996).

In this chapter, we review the assessment of PTSD in children and adolescents, paying attention to both psychometric challenges facing the researcher and pragmatic concerns facing the practitioner. We begin with a general discussion of contextual issues that frame the assessment of PTSD in young persons, consider specific conundrums in the assessment of pediatric PTSD, describe published instruments for the categorical and dimensional assessment of PTSD, and conclude with a brief overview of assessment from a clinical vantage point. Readers interested in more general topics may wish to peruse one or more of the following recent reviews: overview of pediatric PTSD (March, Amaya-Jackson, & Pynoos, 1996; March & Amaya-Jackson, 1994; Saigh, Green, & Korol, 1996); developmental approaches to PTSD (Pynoos, 1994; Pynoos, Steinberg, & Wraith, 1995); diagnosis and comorbidity (Amaya-Jackson & March, 1995; March & Amaya-Jackson, 1994); PTSD and schools (Pynoos & Nader, 1988; Saigh, 1996); and treatment (Deblinger, McLeer, & Henry, 1990; Pynoos & Nader, 1993; Saigh, Yule, & Inamdar, 1996; Yule & Canterbury, 1994).

CONTEXTUAL ISSUES

Assessment Taken Broadly

Not all responses to a traumatic event fall within the orbit of PTSD, and many factors besides PTSD are relevant to establishing a treatment plan for a traumatized child, or to conducting research on PTSD itself, and must be adequately assessed if treatment is to show maximum benefit. At a recent NIMH consensus conference on the assessment of PTSD, the workgroup on Pediatric PTSD (John March, Chair), adopted a set of guidelines for the assessment of PTSD and corollary domains. While it is beyond the scope of this chapter to address each individually, Table 10.1 summarizes the more important domains of assessment classified by study type. Within each domain, multiple sub-domains often are critical to both research and treatment. These are presented in Table 10.2. Taken together, Tables 10.1 and 10.2 provide a broad overview of the assessment of PTSD with respect to the important domains that may predict the onset and maintenance of PTSD symptoms in clinical and clinical research settings.

Keeping a Developmental Perspective

The assessment of PTSD in children and adolescents must of necessity be embedded within a theoretically

TABLE 10.1   Variables*

DOMAIN/ SUBGROUP	POPULATION	CLINICAL	TREATMENT OUTCOME
Criterion A	E	E	E
Core PTSD symptoms	E	E	E
Functioning	E	E	E
Loss/grief	R	R	R
Life events	R	R	O
Child intrinsic variables	E/R	E/R	E/R
Comorbidity	E/R	E/R	E/R
Social context	O	R	O
Parent psychopath	O	E/R	O
Social cognition	O	E/R	O
Social skills	O	E/R	O
Biological	O	E/R	O
Outcome	NR	NR	E

*E = essential; R = recommended; O = optional

sound understanding of the developmental and social matrices within which the trauma took place and PTSD eventuated. To some extent, this renders the DSM-IV framework, which underemphasizes developmental differences and social contextual factors, less than adequate for evaluating childhood-onset PTSD. For example, some aspects of the PTSD symptom complex may be best reported by the affected child, others by parents, and still others by teachers or other observers, varying with the developmental stage of the child. Notwithstanding the fact that the child's social matrix—neighborhood, family, peer, and school environments—may strongly condition the risk, characteristics, and course of PTSD and corollary symptoms, variables like loss, secondary adversities, family functioning, and attachment-related symptoms, such as separation anxiety, receive short shrift in the DSM-IV conceptualization of pediatric PTSD.

TABLE 10.2 Assessment

DOMAIN	SUB-DOMAINS
Diagnosis	*DSM-IV*
Criterion A1: Objective	Multiple events Stressor dimensions
Criterion A2: Subjective	Emotions, e.g., feeling terrified Appraisal, e.g., life threat Attribution, e.g., helplessness Beliefs, e.g., can't be happening to me Peri-dissociation, e.g., temporal or spatial distortions Parental response
Life events	Pre-event Post-event Secondary adversities
Traumatic reminders	Mapped from stressor
PTSD symptoms	Cluster B,C,D
PTSD corollary symptoms	Guilt Anger Event-specific new fears
Functioning	Global Academic (behavioral and pedagogic arenas) Family Peer
Loss/grief	Loss/grief
Comorbidity	Affective Anxiety Disruptive behavior disorders Anger/aggression Substance abuse Dissociation Somatization Learning disorders/problems Eating disorders Sleep disorders Enuresis
Child intrinsic factors	Demographics IQ Medical history Family genetic history Temperament Psychiatric history Attachment

DOMAIN	SUB-DOMAINS
Diagnosis	*DSM-IV*
Coping behaviors	Generic To traumatic reminders
Social support	SES Parenting style Family functioning Expressed emotion Marital function Relationship with siblings School environment Peers Neighborhood
Parent psychopathology	PTSD Grief Other
Social cognition	Self-efficacy Locus of control Trauma-specific attributions
Social skills	General Peers Trauma specific
Services	Psychiatric Medical/other

Similarly, developmentally sensitive methods for assessing the objective and subjective characteristics of Criterion A events remain both critical and problematic. Posttraumatic sequelae vary with the nature of the stressor—witness the division in the field between abuse and sudden trauma research studies (Terr, 1991)—and many children experience multiple events in both categories, with exposure risk varying to some extent with age and gender (Reiss, Richters, Radke-Yarrow, & Scharrf, 1993). For example, females are more at risk for sexual abuse; males are perhaps more at risk for accidents (Saigh, Green, & Korol, 1996). Thus, the ability to map the event or events onto important domains of outcome within a developmental framework depends on improved characterization of the stressor and accompanying secondary adversities (Davidson & Foa, 1991).

Developmental themes also influence children's appraisals of threat, attribution of meaning, emotional and cognitive means of coping, toleration of their reactions, expectations about recovery, and effectiveness in addressing secondary life changes (Pynoos, 1994; Pynoos, Steinberg, & Wraith, 1995). Thus it is imperative that clinicians and researchers frame current knowledge about child and adolescent exposure to traumatic stress within a developmental framework that recognizes the intricate matrix of a changing child and environment, evolving familial and societal expectations, and an essential linkage between disrupted and normal development (Horowitz, 1996).

While relying primarily on theory rather than empirical findings, Pynoos and colleagues have taken just such an approach. They assign a prominent role to trauma-related expectations as these are expressed in the thought, emotions, and behavior of the developing child, including skewed expectations about the world, the safety and security of interpersonal life, and the child's sense of personal integrity (Pynoos, 1994; Pynoos, Steinberg, & Wraith, 1995). In this sense, traumatic experiences often unfavorably alter a child's inner plans of the world, and catastrophically shape concepts of self and others and forecasts about the future that have a powerful influence on current and future behavior. After traumatic exposure(s), these altered expectations place the child at risk for proximal and distal developmental disturbances. Such a developmental approach applies to the whole spectrum of child and adolescent traumatic stress, including: the risk of exposure; the subjective experience of traumatic situations; the nature of, and response to, acute distress; the construction and evolution of traumatic memory and narrative; the neurobiology of traumatic stress; the nature, severity, and course of trauma-related psychopathology; the influence of child intrinsic factors on resistance, resilience, and adjustment; the mediation of traumatic stress through parental function, peer relationships, and school milieu; and strategies of prevention and intervention.

Accounting for Comorbidity

Traumatized children frequently exhibit symptoms of disorders other than PTSD, and children with other disorders not uncommonly have PTSD as an intercurrent diagnosis (Famularo, Kinscherff, & Fenton, 1992; Goldman, D'Angelo, DeMaso, & Mezza-

cappa, 1992; Pynoos, Nader, Frederick, Gonda, & Stuber, 1987). Comorbid symptoms may be due to the stressor independent of concurrent PTSD or may be associated with PTSD itself. For example, March, Amaya-Jackson, Terry, and Constanzo (1998), investigating the aftermath of an industrial fire, recently demonstrated that: (1) both PTSD and collateral internalizing and externalizing symptoms rise in direct proportion to degree of exposure; (2) gender and race show variable effects on risk for PTSD and collateral symptoms; and (3) collateral symptoms are positively correlated with PTSD and may represent primary outcomes of traumatic exposure in their own right. Thus the assessment of PTSD, like other anxiety disorders of childhood (Curry & Murphy, 1995), requires a systematic search for accompanying comorbidities.

Besides true comorbidity, PTSD symptoms are often confounded by spurious comorbidity resulting from overlap between criteria sets (for example, affective constriction in PTSD overlaps anhedonia in depression) as well as confounding of other diagnoses by PTSD (for example, the child who looks depressed and inattentive because of lack of sleep). Careful questioning, not only of parents and teachers but especially of the child vis-à-vis his or her internal experiences, is often necessary to clarify the diagnostic picture. Hence, because of the high prevalence of dimensional and transitional symptomatology—real or spurious—in children with PTSD, it is crucial to include non-PTSD outcomes as targets for treatment and as predictors of treatment response in treatment outcome studies. Conversely, while multiple diagnoses should be made (where appropriate) in order to facilitate treatment planning, it is important to keep the focus on the traumatic event when considering the overall symptom picture.

Traumatic experiences have an inherent potential to induce a panoply of anxiety symptoms (Lonigan, Shannon, Taylor, Finch, & Sallee, 1994; March et al., 1998). For example, many children experience increased attachment behaviors, such as worries about the safety of family or friends, following traumatic events. Some may have been constitutionally prone to separation anxiety; others may have been separation anxious because of prior threats to important attachment bonds. Most, however, will be responding directly to activation of attachment behaviors by the traumatic event (Pynoos, Frederick, et al., 1987). While a diagnosis of separation anxiety disorder is warranted when symptoms of separation anxiety interfere with the child's daily life, it is important to remember the reasonableness of the originating threat. Thus reconstituting a safe environment must always precede otherwise premature attempts to enforce or encourage separation. Children not meeting full criteria for PTSD often manifest symptoms of generalized anxiety disorder. It is important to keep the traumatic origin of the child's anxiety in mind when designing a treatment plan for such children who may otherwise be at risk for delayed-onset PTSD. Other children display somatic symptoms as a kind of traumatic reenactment (Nader & Fairbanks, 1994). These symptoms can resemble limited-symptom panic attacks and may progress to panic disorder or to PTSD without adequate treatment. When panic disorder is present, specific panic treatments are warranted (Black, 1995). Traumatic simple phobias are relatively easy to distinguish from PTSD in that they lack tonic arousal, do not readily generalize to new situations, and so result in less psychosocial dysfunction than PTSD.

As noted below, intrusive thoughts, urges, and images—not all of them pathological (Terr, 1983)—are found in other childhood psychiatric disorders besides PTSD. For the most part, intrusive phenomenon following a traumatic event can be distinguished from non-traumatic intrusions by the presence of trauma specific contents, because the child makes a subjective link with the trauma, or because of contextual features. For example, schizophrenia, the delusional disorders, and brief reactive psychoses are readily distinguished from PTSD based on dissimilarities between psychotic intrusive thoughts and PTSD reexperiencing, and the presence of otherwise intact reality testing in PTSD.

Depressive-spectrum conditions, ranging from simple demoralization through melancholic major depression, are among the most common secondary comorbidities in PTSD, and often comprise an important treatment focus (Yule, 1992; Yule & Canterbury, 1994). Depression can sometimes be distinguished from PTSD by the self-punitive nature of the child's thoughts, by a more pervasive anhedonia than that

usually seen with phobically driven affective constriction, or by the presence of bereavement or other life adversities. A full depressive syndrome is frequently a normal reaction to the loss of a loved one (Pynoos, Nader, et al., 1987). Yet the trauma response often interferes significantly with the normal grief process. For example, reminiscing, an essential part of the bereavement process, can be drastically inhibited because the intrusive recollections of the traumatic event interferes with the child's effort to recall pleasant memories of the deceased (Pynoos, Nader, et al., 1987). Children appear to be especially vulnerable to the dual demands of trauma mastery and grief work (Eth & Pynoos, 1994). Therefore, the struggle with the child's traumatic responses must be addressed so that the process of mourning may be passed through, unencumbered by PTSD symptoms.

Obsessive-compulsive disorder (OCD) is readily distinguished from PTSD in that OCD usually lacks a PTSD-magnitude precipitant and trauma specific intrusions. Rarely, OCD may develop in the context of PTSD by secondary generalization. For example, children who have been sexually assaulted not uncommonly develop obsessional thoughts of contamination and may handle the anxiety associated with these thoughts through washing rituals. Checking rituals in response to obsessional concerns about safety issues also occur.

Self-mutilation, sexual or aggressive play, and suicidal behaviors may represent traumatic reenactments in children who have experienced sexual or physical abuse, and these symptoms should always prompt a search for traumatic antecedents (Albach & Everaerd, 1992). When children who have experienced repeated victimization demonstrate contradictory behaviors across different contexts, the diagnosis of multiple personality or other dissociative disorder should be entertained.

A wide variety of social behaviors have been reported to be abnormal in traumatized children, with problematic social behaviors serving both as a risk factor for and an outcome of traumatic experiences (Conaway & Hansen, 1989). Not surprisingly, trauma can exacerbate, and PTSD can mimic, the disruptive behavior disorders (March et al., 1998). In an epidemiological study of pediatric PTSD after an industrial fire, exposure lead to disruptive behavior disorders (DRBs) independently of PTSD itself (March et al., 1998). Similar results were noted after Hurricane Hugo (Lonigan et al., 1994; Shannon, Lonigan, Finch, & Taylor, 1994) and in children suffering chronic maltreatment (Famularo et al., 1992). Research comparing the children and adolescents with PTSD to test phobic and non-clinical controls demonstrated that PTSD subjects evidenced significantly higher scores on the Conners Teacher Rating Scale than their phobic and non-clinical counterparts (Saigh, 1989a; 1989b). Traumatic events can also exaggerate pre-existing learning disorders, rendering it harder for the child to process traumatic experiences. Reciprocal exacerbation may be especially characteristic of youth who use drugs as a maladaptive coping strategy. Before diagnosing oppositional-defiant disorder, conduct disorder, or attention-deficit hyperactivity disorder in a child who has experienced a life-threatening event, however, the clinician must rule out PTSD as the cause of the child's deteriorating school performance, inattention, irritability, or aggression.

Finally, it is important to recognize that not all reactions to traumatic events necessarily lead to the development of PTSD, especially during the initial weeks following a traumatic event (March, 1991) (Famularo, Kinscherff, & Fenton, 1990). When the stressor is modest in severity, partial PTSD is present, or when symptoms interfere with the child's daily functioning, an adjustment disorder diagnosis is appropriate (Forster, 1992). In children with sub-syndromal PTSD symptoms lasting longer than six months, the diagnosis becomes depressive or anxiety disorder not otherwise specified (NOS), depending on the clinician's preference. The more important point is that clinicians should not overlook the traumatic nature of sub-syndromal symptoms when formulating a treatment plan.

ASSESSMENT CONUNDRUMS

Despite substantial progress in understanding the etiopathogenesis, phenomenology, and course of PTSD in youth, several themes in the assessment of pediatric PTSD pose particular problems for the researcher and clinician alike.

The Stressor

A wide variety of stressors have been associated with PTSD in the pediatric population, some of which are more common to children, e.g., kidnapping, serious animal bites, or severe injury due to burns, accidental shootings or hit and run accidents (chapter 2, this volume; see also March, 1993; March & Amaya-Jackson, 1994). Children are also at special risk of witnessing violence to a family member, e.g., rape or murder, suicide behavior, and spousal or sibling abuse (Reiss et al., 1993), so that, as Saigh (1991) points out, PTSD can result from direct, witnessed, or verbal exposure.

Although the variety of environmental events capable of producing PTSD varies somewhat with age and life circumstances as do the reactions of children to these events (Garbarino, Kostelny, & Dubrow, 1991), the most recent empirical literature suggests that the objective magnitude of the stressor is directly proportional to the risk of developing PTSD (March, 1993; McNally, 1993; Saigh, Yasik, Sack, & Koplewicz, 1999). For example, in their studies of the aftermath of a school yard sniper attack, Pynoos and colleagues showed that exposure (proximity) was linearly related to the risk for PTSD symptoms (Pynoos, Frederick, et al., 1987), and that children's memory disturbances, indicating distorted cognitive processing during the event, closely followed exposure (Pynoos & Nader, 1989). Thus, when working with severely traumatized children and adolescents, it is important to remember that the PTSD symptom picture is most easily understood in the context of a molecular understanding of the traumatic event itself.

Objectively, PTSD stressors are characterized by threat to life, potential for physical injury, and an element of grotesqueness or horror that demarcates these events from lesser magnitude experiences, such as the expected death of a loved one from a serious illness. Not surprisingly then, children and adolescents for the most part react acutely to these events with surprise, terror, and a sense of helplessness, which phenomenon define the subjective features of the DSM-IV PTSD stressor criteria (March, 1993). On the other hand, aspects of the PTSD symptom picture vary with stressor-specific factors (Famularo et al., 1990;

Kendall-Tackett, Williams, & Finkelhor, 1993; Nader, Stuber, & Pynoos, 1991), making careful attention to the nature of the stressor mandatory. Parenthetically, while many sexually abused children do not meet diagnostic criteria for PTSD (Kendall-Tackett et al., 1993), clinicians must not underestimate the level of psychological impairment in this population as the effects of sexual abuse on symptom level and long-term personality functioning are often profound (Cahill, Llewelyn, & Pearson, 1991).

Unfortunately, currently published rating scales do not adequately inventory a range of PTSD-qualifying stressors or focus specifically on their objective magnitude (Criterion A1) nor do they assess a victim's subjective responses (Criterion A2), thus rendering improved assessment of DSM-IV criterion A a high priority in the field (McNally, 1996).

Secondary Adversities

Secondary adversities, such as relocation, attendance at a new school, separation from siblings, involuntary unemployment of a parent, and increased financial difficulties, commonly precede, coexist or follow PTSD (Goenjian et al., 1994). For example, there may be continued medical procedures and rehabilitation for physical injuries and disability and a difficult reintegration back into school. Children exposed to war atrocities may also suffer malnutrition, deprivation, family disruption, loss, immigration, and resettlement. When the violence or disaster results in the death of a family member or friend, there is an important interplay between traumatic and grief reactions, including continued preoccupation with the circumstances of the death and psychological dissynchrony among family members with different degrees of exposure (Pynoos, Nader, et al., 1987). Societal conditions also influence the types of traumatic events to which children are likely to be exposed and also maintenance of PTSD once exposed (Garbarino et al., 1991). For example, changing family patterns contribute to rates of intrafamilial sexual molestation. Occurrences around the world lead to significant exposures of children and adolescents to extra-familial violence; inner city violence; civil war atrocities; torture; or state terrorism. The impact of

disasters varies, not only by the severity of, for example, an earthquake or hurricane, but by building standards, advanced communication and evacuation, or disaster recovery efforts. In this context, assessment of secondary adversities is a critical piece in the understanding of the risk for and maintenance of PTSD.

Memory

The extent to which children and adolescents are capable of accurately remembering and reporting what happened and current symptoms depends to a large extent on memory functioning (Siegel, 1995). Although initial clinical attention suggested a relative absence of major amnesia in children, evidence from fields as diverse as cognitive science, child development, and trauma now suggest that PTSD involves a variety of memory disturbances (Siegel, 1995). Adult patients with combat-related PTSD and childhood sexual abuse show deficits in short-term verbal memory (Bremner, Krystal, Southwick, & Charney, 1995), which may both influence and change with treatment (Foa, Molnar, & Cashman, 1995). Dissociative memory disturbances may also occur, especially in response to physical coercion, molestation or abuse (Putnam & Trickett, 1993). Clinically, children often omit moments of extreme life threat (at times, screened by detailed recounting of other fearful moments), may distort proximity, duration or sequencing, may introduce premonitions, and may in other ways minimize their life threat. Not surprisingly, memory disturbances to some extent confound the accurate assessment of PTSD, making this an active and as yet unresolved area of investigation and, unfortunately, dubious speculation (Nash, 1994).

Traumatic Reminders

Traumatic reminders—which may be defined as conditioned stimuli directly or indirectly related to the traumatic event that provoke conditioned responses—include the external circumstances of the event and the internal emotional and physical reactions of the child. The treatment of PTSD relies heavily on identifying traumatic reminders for two reasons: (1) they shed light on the child's experience of the stressor and (2) they predict current PTSD symptoms and coping behaviors. For example, the unexpected nature of reminders may re-evoke a sense of unpreparedness and lack of control. Common reminders include the following: circumstances (e.g., location, time, preceding activity, clothes worn); precipitating conditions (e.g., high winds after a tornado, arguing); other signs of danger (e.g., staring eyes); unwanted results (e.g., fixed and dilated eyes, blood); endangering objects (e.g., trees, broken glass, weapons); and a sense of helplessness (e.g., cries for help, crying, fast heart beat, a sinking feeling, ineffectualness or moments of aloneness). Normal school procedures and academic exercises may serve as reminders. For example, a fire drill may re-evoke a sense of prior emergency or a civics class discussion of judicial proceedings may kindle fear and rage over the trial of a father's assassin.

Children with PTSD frequently avoid specific thoughts, locations, concrete items, and persons or interactions with people that remind them of the incident. They may discontinue pleasurable activities in order to avoid excitement or fear. Traumatic avoidance may selectively restrict daily activity or generalize to more phobic behavior. Diminished activity may represent a preoccupation with intrusive phenomena, a depressive reaction, an avoidance of affect laden states or of traumatic reminders, or an effort to reduce the risk of further trauma. Active behaviors, such as disruptions in the classroom, may be attempts to distract from intrusive thoughts or anxieties (e.g., yelling out bad words when there are high winds after a tornado). Since exposure to traumatic material comprises a key element of treatment (Foa, Steketee, & Rothbaum, 1989), it is not surprising that itemizing and reversing avoidance behaviors (where possible) is an important part of the therapeutic endeavor.

Psychophysiology

Sleep disturbances, irritability, difficulty concentrating, hypervigilance, exaggerated startle responses, and outbursts of aggression are evidence that the traumatized child is in a state of increased physiological arousal (Perry, 1994; Perry & Pate, 1994). Somatic symptoms of autonomic hyperactivity may be both tonic or phasic in nature, with the latter occurring more often when the child encounters traumatic reminders (Nader & Fairbanks, 1994). Symptoms of increased arousal reflect both tonic and phasic physiological activity, and they tend to reinforce the disorder. The child is "on alert," ready to respond to any environmental threat (Ornitz & Pynoos, 1989). Especially in school-age children, physiological reactivity may include somatic symptoms as a form of reexperiencing. Sleep disturbance may be severe and persistent; changes seen in sleep architecture have been noted in adult studies (Pitman, 1992). Sleep walking and night terrors are not uncommon. These sleep problems can further decrease the child's ability to concentrate and attend to important tasks and thus may also adversely impact learning and behavior in school. Hypervigilance and exaggerated startle responses may alter a child's usual behavior by leading to chronic efforts to ensure personal security or the safety of others (Ornitz & Pynoos, 1989). Lastly, temporary or chronic difficulty in modulating aggression can make children act more irritable and easy to anger, resulting in a reduced tolerance of the normal behaviors, demands, and slights of peers and family members, in unusual acts of aggression or social withdrawal (Yule & Canterbury, 1994). While direct psychophysiologial assessment is usually performed only in research settings (Ornitz & Pynoos, 1989), the clinical interview of necessity focuses on these psychophysiological disturbances, and the interoceptive and exteroceptive cues that produce them, since they comprise important treatment targets.

INSTRUMENTS FOR ASSESSING PEDIATRIC PTSD

Overview

For the most part, published instruments assessing PTSD have focused on the behavioral/symptomatic sequelae of severe catastrophic events, often in an event-specific fashion, without reflecting the DSM criteria or paying sufficient attention to psychometric validation (McNally, 1996). Additionally, little emphasis has been placed on objective measurement of exposure types, and there are no published instruments assessing the subjective symptoms of terror, horror, and helplessness that were introduced as part of the stressor (A) criteria in DSM-IV (March, 1993). Broadly applicable assessment tools designed specifically to address PTSD in children and adolescents are essential for several reasons (March & Albano, 1996). First, PTSD magnitude stressors likely differ between children and adults, for example, sexual abuse or witnessing the violent death of a parent (March et al., 1996). Second, PTSD symptoms vary with the developmental stage of the child, for example, traumatic play in early and middle childhood (Pynoos, 1994). Third, the day to day environments of young persons differ from those most typically experienced by adults, so that the presentation of PTSD also differs, as in the reciprocal interactions between the child's and parental PTSD symptoms (Pynoos, Steinberg, & Wraith, 1995). Fourth, to differentiate PTSD from normative reactions to traumatic events, gender, race, and age norms are necessary. Finally, some fears may best be viewed as adaptive protective mechanisms (Silverman, La Greca, & Wasserstein, 1995). Only when anxiety is excessive or the context developmentally inappropriate does posttraumatic anxiety become clinically significant (Marks, 1987). Thus clinicians and researchers interested in childhood-onset PTSD face the challenging task of devising assessment instruments that can differentiate pathological anxiety from fears occurring as a part of normal developmental processes (March & Albano, 1996). Within this context, the NIMH consensus panel on the assessment of pediatric PTSD reached the following conclusions:

- Multi-method multi-informant assessment of multiple domains is preferable, with assessment density from screening to exhaustive dependent on the specific purposes to which the assessment points.
- Instruments should be developmentally sensitive.
- Rigorous psychometric testing should be completed or underway.
- Age, gender, and race norms are highly desirable.
- Multi-informant forms permitting concurrent adult assessment using the same instruments are desirable.

- Instruments should be readily available (free or nominal charge for research purposes) and supported by investigator.
- Instruments should be cross culturally sensitive and translatable into different languages.
- Instruments should be capable of repeated administration.
- Both dimensional and categorical ratings are desirable, with the former calibrated against the latter within a specific event where possible.

Categorical Measures

Fears are ubiquitous among young persons. Some are adaptive, others not, and many if not most lack traumatic antecedents (Silverman et al., 1995). Thus, clinicians and researchers are faced with the prospect of differentiating normal fears from pathological anxiety. DSM-III-R addressed this nosological conundrum by introducing a subclass of anxiety disorders of childhood and adolescence (American Psychiatric Association, 1987). DSM-IV both refines these constructs and establishes a greater degree of continuity—developmental and nosological—with the adult anxiety disorders (American Psychiatric Association, 1994). Hence the DSM taxonomy reflects expert consensus regarding the clustering of symptoms in pediatric as well as adult anxiety disorders (Shaffer, Campbell, Cantwell, & Bradley, 1989), but empirical support in some cases is questionable (Beidel, 1991). In the search for methods beyond the clinical interview for establishing a diagnosis of PTSD, researchers have developed dimensional and categorical measures, the most widely recognized of which are inventoried below.

The Reaction Index (PTSD-RI).   Among published instruments, the Pynoos-Nader version of the Stress-Reaction Index (PTSD-RI) is perhaps the oldest and most widely used instrument for assessing pediatric PTSD. A variety of studies suggest that it shows modest empirical support as a semi-structured interview for making a categorical diagnosis of PTSD (see, for example, Goenjian et al., 1994). Used both dimensionally and/or categorically, various versions of the PTSD-RI have been used in studies of natural disasters (Pynoos, Goenjian, et al., 1993), criminal assault (Pynoos, Frederick, et al., 1987; Pynoos & Nader, 1990), and war zone trauma (Nader, Pynoos, Fairbanks, & Al-Ajeel, 1993). Factor analyses document that the PTSD-RI captures the major domains of PTSD: reexperiencing, avoidance/numbing, and hyperarousal (Pynoos, Frederick, et al., 1987). In the primary demonstration of construct validity for the PTSD-RI, Pynoos and Nader showed that exposure (proximity) to sniper fire on a school playground was linearly related to the risk for PTSD symptoms (Pynoos, Frederick, et al., 1987), and that children's memory disturbances, indicating distorted cognitive processing during the event, closely followed exposure (Pynoos & Nader, 1989). Ten highly exposed children were reinterviewed one week later (Pynoos, Frederick, et al., 1987) using the PTSD-RI; Cohen's *kappa* was .878, indicating excellent test-retest reliability. In an unrelated study of children exposed to an Armenian earthquake, Pynoos et al. report test-retest reliability for a backward translated version (English to Armenian to English) of the PTSD-RI of *kappa* = .98 (Pynoos, Goenjian, et al., 1993).

Childrens PTSD Inventory. The current form of the Children's PTSD Inventory (Saigh et al., unpublished manuscript) was developed to reflect the DSM-IV criteria for PTSD. Given the robust psychometric properties of the DSM-III version of the instrument (Saigh, 1988a; 1989b), the DSM-IV version adopted a similar semi-structured format. In construction of the instrument, particular emphasis was placed on using language that could be easily understood by young children. The instrument was initially field tested with a sample of 50 South African female adolescent rape victims. Using an interrater reliability format, agreement was observed in 45 of 50 cases (*kappa* = .8). A number of items were subsequently added, deleted or reworded based on clinical feedback, estimates of internal consistency, and feedback from psychiatrists and psychologists expert in pediatric PTSD.

The current instrument consists of five subtests, each of which is scored on a dichotomous basis. Following a preface that provides examples of traumatic incidents that youth may encounter, the first subtest presents 15 questions involving potential exposure to traumatic stressors. The second subtest consists of 11 questions that denote the presence or absence of reexperiencing symptoms. The third subtest lists 16 questions involving avoidance and numbing symptoms. The fourth subtest presents seven questions denoting increased arousal, and the final subtest involves five questions ascertaining whether PTSD causes significant distress. The instrument yields the following diagnoses: acute PTSD, chronic PTSD, delayed-onset PTSD, and PTSD negative.

A preliminary assessment of interrater reliability in an outpatient sample of 25 consecutively referred children and adolescents with documented exposure to sexual or physical assault generated 100 percent interrater agreement (*kappa* = 1.0) (Saigh et al., unpublished manuscript). Preliminary data indicate a kappa coefficient of .92 between clinician derived diagnoses and diagnoses that were obtained utilizing the Children's PTSD inventory. Sensitivity in this populations was 100 percent, specificity was 92 percent, and diagnostic efficiency was 96 percent. A positive predictive power of .93 and a negative predictive power of 1.0 were also noted. Additional data collection involving incarcerated juveniles, war victims, and special educational referrals is in progress.

Other PTSD Inventories. Several other structured and semi-structured PTSD inventories are available, but all are somewhat less well-developed than the previously described measures. Nader and colleagues developed the Clinician-Administered PTSD Scale-Child and Adolescent Version (CAPS-C) (Nader, Blake, Kriegler, & Pynoos, 1994) with the support of the National Center for PTSD. Modeled after the adult CAPS (Blake et al., 1990), the CAPS-C provides scalar and categorical assessment of PTSD and PTSD-related psychopathology, such as hostility or school problems. In the NIMH community violence project, Richters and Martinez developed an exposure index assessing urban violence entitled *Things I Have Seen and Heard* (Richters & Martinez, 1993). In a community (school) sample of 21 children, age 6–12, this instrument demonstrated reasonable one week test-retest reliability (r = .81).

Similarly, a cartoon posttraumatic symptom scale keyed to urban violence, entitled *Levon,* also showed reasonable one week test-retest reliability (r = .81) (Martinez & Richters, 1993).

Broad-Spectrum Interviews Including PTSD.
Using a version of the K-SADS-E with a newly developed PTSD module, McLeer and colleagues interviewed 22 clinic referred sexually abused children and adolescents. They reported interrater (parent–child) agreement of 87.5 percent for this instrument, but did not examine test-retest reliability (McLeer, Deblinger, Henry, & Orvaschel, 1992). Similarly, Silverman has evaluated test-retest reliability for PTSD as part of a wider evaluation of the reliability of the Anxiety Disorders Interview for Children (ADIS) (Silverman, 1991; Silverman & Eisen, 1992). Although only 2 of 96 children presenting to an outpatient anxiety disorders program met DSM-III-R diagnostic criteria for PTSD, they reported fair to poor test-retest reliability for PTSD: Cohen's *kappa* = .43 for the child and *kappa* = .25 for the parent interview, respectively. Fisher and colleagues (1993), using the Diagnostic Interview Schedule for Children 2.3, found fair agreement between parent and child for PTSD stressors, and somewhat higher agreement for PTSD symptoms, but did not test the statistical significance of these relationships. Finally, the Diagnostic Interview Schedule for Children and Adolescents (DICA) (Earls, Smith, Reich, & Jung, 1988) also includes a PTSD module, but test-retest and interrater reliabilities are as yet unavailable.

Dimensional Measures

Some anxiety symptoms, such as refusing to attend school in the patient with panic disorder and agoraphobia, are readily observable; other symptoms are open only to child introspection and thus to child self-report. For this and other reasons, self-report measures of anxiety, which provide an opportunity for the child to reveal his internal or "hidden" experience, have found wide application in both clinical and research settings (March & Albano, 1996). Typically, self-report measures use a Likert scale format

in which a child is asked to rate each questionnaire item in an ordinal format anchored to frequency or intensity or a combination of the two. For example, a child might be asked to rate "I feel tense" on a four point frequency dimension that ranges from almost never to often. Self-report measures are easy to administer, require a minimum of clinician time, and economically capture a wide range of important anxiety dimensions from the child's point of view. Taken together these features make self-report measures ideally suited to gathering data prior to the initial evaluation, since self-report measures used in this fashion increase clinician efficiency by facilitating accurate assessment of the prior probability that a particular child will or will not have symptoms within a specific symptom domain.

Self-Report Versions of the Friedrich/Pynoos Reaction Index.   In addition to its use as a structured interview, the PTSD-RI has been the most common scalar measure for assessing PTSD used as a self-report measure in epidemiological studies, including studies of hurricanes (Lonigan et al., 1994; Shannon et al., 1994; Shaw, Applegate, Tanner, & Perez, 1995); earthquake (Bradburn, 1991; Goenjian et al., 1995), and war zone exposure (Nader et al., 1993). However, careful psychometric studies have not been completed of the RI used as a self-report measure. It should also be noted that the PTSD-RI does not include a stressor inventory and that within and between stressor norms are unavailable.

Kiddie-Post-Traumatic Symptomatology.   As part of a series of epidemiological and treatment development studies (March et al., 1998), March and Amaya-Jackson developed a self-report PTSD measure termed the Kiddie-Post-Traumatic Symptomatology scale modeled on the Multidimensional Anxiety Scale for Children (MASC) (March, Parker, Sullivan, Stallings, & Conners, 1997) and the DSM-IV PTSD criteria set (American Psychiatric Association, 1994). Exploration of the factor structure and psychometric validation of the K-PTS symptom scale was accomplished using a sequential analytic strategy combining features of both confirmatory factor analysis (CFA) and item response theory (IRT) (King & King, 1994). Consistent with previous studies of pediatric PTSD, factor analytic analyses supported a three factor solution consisting of reexperiencing, avoidance, and hyperarousal. An expected fourth factor, numbing, proved to be highly correlated with reexperiencing.

With an approximate solution to the dimensional structure of the K-PTS in hand, these authors then submitted the three scales to an IRT-model analysis to generate "scale scores" for use in subsequent analyses. King and King recently commented on the major advantage of using IRT-generated factor scores in PTSD research, namely that each of the contributing items is optimally weighted to reflect informational content with respect to the "factor" of interest (King & King, 1994). Hence IRT factor scores exhibit less measurement error than simple unweighted scores. Importantly, the K-PTS factor scores for each scale reflected the normative T-distributions for those factors. Thus, while the K-PTS cannot make a clinical diagnosis of PTSD—ergo the term PTS—the upper and lower ends of the K-PTS T-score distribution represent significant deviance from the population mean. Subsequent versions of the K-PTS, administered as part of an NIMH-funded treatment development grant, have repeatedly confirmed the validity of the initial factor structure of the PTSD symptom component of the K-PTS, while adding sections on secondary adversities and PTSD magnitude stressors. The K-PTS symptom scale is highly correlated with the CAPS; both proved to be change sensitive when used as dependent variables in a study of the efficacy of cognitive-behavioral psychotherapy (John March, personal communication). Further psychometric studies of the K-PTS, including test-retest reliability and an ROC study are in progress.

Other Published Instruments.   Yule and Udwin (1991) used a child version of the Impact of Events Scale to examine the aftermath of a ship sinking, but psychometric studies have not been reported. Wolfe and colleagues developed the Children's Impact of Traumatic Events Scale (CITES) to assess the impact of sexual abuse from the child's perspective (Wolfe, Gentile, Michienzi, Sas, & Wolfe, 1991). The CITES ascertains four dimensions: PTSD (Intrusive Thoughts, Avoidance, Hyperarousal, and Sexual Anxiety); So-

cial Reactions (Negative Reactions from Others and Social Support); Abuse Attributions (Self-Blame and Guilt, Empowerment, Vulnerability, and Dangerous World); and Eroticism. Convergent and discriminant validity are reported to be satisfactory. This group also developed an empirically derived 20 item subscale of the Child-Behavior Checklist (CBCL) (Achenbach, 1986), which shows adequate internal consistency (Wolfe, Gentile, & Wolfe, 1989) and perhaps convergent validity (Ken Fletcher, personal communication). Parenthetically, it is important to note that these measures do not yield PTSD diagnoses.

Unpublished Instruments.   Attesting to the vigor with which researchers are pursuing new assessment tools, a variety of as yet unpublished instruments have been developed to assess PTSD in youth. These include the Child Stress Reaction Checklist specifically targeting burned children (Glen Saxe, personal communication); a child and parent screening PTSD interview, the Traumatic Events Screening Interview (TESI), developed by the Dartmouth Child Trauma Research Group and the National Center for PTSD (Julian Ford, personal communication); and the Kauai Recover Index (KRI), a 24 item variation on the Reaction Index keyed to natural disasters (Roger Hamada, personal communication). Additionally, Kenneth Fletcher (personal communication) has developed a series of child and parent report measures assessing both events and PTSD symptoms. The Dimensions of Stressful Events Scale (DOSE) covers elements of the child's reaction to the stressor(s) as inventoried on the When Bad Things Happen stressor inventory. Similarly, parent ratings of events (the Upsetting Times Checklist) and PTSD symptoms (parent PTSD interview) provide a parent check on child-reported symptoms on an accompanying child PTSD interview. Internal consistency and convergent validity are reported to be in the satisfactory to excellent range for all four scales.

CLINICAL ASSESSMENT

As in all psychiatric disorders, the first step in setting up a program of treatment for PTSD is a careful stressor-specific assessment (Nader et al., 1991).

With the caveat that parents in general are better at evaluating children's externalizing than internalizing symptoms (Costello, 1989), a multi-method multi-trait evaluation is preferable, including information from multiple sources (Amaya-Jackson, 1995; March et al., 1996). Furthermore, as pointed out earlier, children and adolescents with PTSD vary widely regarding the nature and impact of the disorder. In many if not most youth with PTSD, comorbid psychiatric illnesses, such as separation anxiety disorder, depression or disruptive behavior disorders present complex problems in differential diagnosis and therapeutics. Thus an accurate assessment of the pediatric patient with PTSD, including a careful search for complicating comorbidities, is essential to skillful clinical treatment of these patients (March & Albano, 1996). Having completed such an evaluation, it is likewise important to monitor the process and outcome of treatment using measures that sample specific symptom domains, such as reexperiencing, functional domains, such as home or school, and symptomatic distress during therapeutic exposure to traumatic reminders, such as subjective units of discomfort (SUDS). In this section, we describe procedures for the initial evaluation used in the Program for Child and Adolescent Anxiety Disorders at Duke University Medical Center.

Purpose of the Initial Evaluation

The task of differential therapeutics—defined as establishing treatments that are appropriate to divergent treatment targets—can be seen as something like a game of pick up sticks. One has to correctly identify the targets of treatment (the sticks), pair them with target-specific treatments— say, exposure-based interventions or pharmacotherapy—and sequence the interventions appropriately (pick up the sticks in the proper order) to help the patient get better. Stated even more prosaically, the hammers have to match the nails in order for treatment to be successful.

How does the process of making a diagnosis of PTSD fit this picture? Given a PTSD symptom—say, avoidance of traumatic reminders, as the presenting complaint—the clinician's first task is to confirm PTSD as the primary diagnosis. The second task is to rule out comorbid diagnoses, such as depression or panic disorder, that share features with PTSD and may account for or partially overlap with the presenting complaint. The process is directly analogous to that used by a cardiologist seeing a patient with chest pain in the emergency room. The primary hypothesis in this instance is myocardial infarction or unstable angina, an impending heart attack. To rule out other sources of cardiac pain, such as chest wall pain, gallbladder disease, and other medical conditions, and not incidentally, panic disorder, the cardiologist systematically reviews the symptoms of these disorders. Having established the diagnosis of an acute MI, the cardiologist then devises a tailored treatment plan that is specific to the needs of his or her patient. Likewise, the treating mental health provider, having established a primary diagnosis of PTSD and having documented complicating comorbidities, moves on to develop a specific treatment plan that targets those PTSD and collateral symptoms that are unique to the particular patient. To reiterate, this process moves from establishing a likely but still hypothetical diagnosis, through a systematic assessment of each DSM-IV diagnostic category, until ultimately, the clinician reaches a molecular understanding of the patient's PTSD symptoms, and how the patient has skillfully or perhaps not so skillfully coped with them. In this sense, the process of establishing a set of DSM-IV diagnoses merely serves to systematically group clusters of symptoms into those that are more or less likely to be targets of treatment whether for PTSD or for complicating comorbidities. It is this latter step—moving from the present complaint through DSM-IV—that consumes the initial evaluation. Obtaining an idotypic understanding of the patient's various PTSD symptoms, and corresponding tailored treatment for those symptoms, follows—for example, setting up a stimulus hierarchy in cognitive-behavioral psychotherapy—as treatment gets underway.

Pre-Evaluation

To speed and concentrate the evaluation process, it is helpful to gather a sizable amount of data prior to the patient's initial visit. In addition to requesting psychiatric/psychological, neuropsychological, hospitalization, and school records, we ask patients and family members to complete a packet of materials designed to assess important domains of psychopathology in the context of the patient's presenting concerns. Table 10.3 summarizes the information obtained in the Conners/March Developmental Questionnaire (Conners & March, 1996). Table 10.4 lists the rating scales we typically obtain from child and/or parent. Some scales, such as the Multidimensional Anxiety Scale for Children (MASC) (March, 1998; March et al., 1997), Children's Depression Inventory (Kovacs, 1985), and Conners Parent and Teacher Rating Scales (Conners, 1995), are available commercially; others, such as the K-PTS, are research scales that will soon be released for clinical and research use. By gathering data in advance of seeing the patient, we adjust the assessing clinician's "prior probabilities" relative to a diagnosis of PTSD, and estimate the likelihood of complicating comorbidities. By focusing on the primary and consequent differential diagnosis, we instantiate a "medical model" in which patients are seen as "OK" and a neuropsychiatric illness is framed as the object of treatment.

First Appointment

Each patient first receives an extensive evaluation (lasting one and one half hours) by a child psychia-

TABLE 10.3   Developmental Questionnaire

Demographics

History of presenting problem

Previous treatment providers

Medication history

Birth and pregnancy history

Early developmental history

School history/learning problems

Peer relationships

Family psychiatric history

Family medical history

Patient medical history

TABLE 10.4   Rating Scales

Kiddie Post-Traumatic Symptomatology

Multidimensional Anxiety Scale for Children (MASC)

Children's Depression Inventory

Conners Parent Rating Scale

Conners Teacher Rating Scale

trist or psychologist. This initial visit includes a clinical interview of the child and his or her parents covering Axis I through V of DSM-IV that is informed by a careful consideration of the rating scale data, Conners/March Developmental Questionnaire, school records, and previous mental health treatment records. A formal mental status examination is always included; in some cases, a specialized neurodevelopmental evaluation is also performed. Patients with PTSD are evaluated using the symptom checklist from the CAPS (Nader et al., 1994).

Ideally, a structured interview, such as the Anxiety Disorders Interview Schedule for Children (ADIS) (Silverman & Eisen, 1992), should be part of every diagnostic assessment. Unfortunately, we currently lack the staffing resources to complete an ADIS, which requires lengthy separate interviews of the child and one parent. Since we routinely use the ADIS with children enrolled in formal research protocols, however, we feel fairly confident that we cover all the major domains of psychopathology in the clinical interview, especially since information from the clinical interview is vetted through the rating scale data.

Feedback and Treatment Planning

Toward the close of this initial visit, the patient and his or her parent(s) discuss the results of the evaluation and decide on a treatment plan. During this "feedback" portion of the visit, the child's presenting problems are summarized in terms of DSM-IV diagnoses, which are linked to a neurodevelopmental model of PTSD and to reinforcing environmental factors. The overall goal is to move from the presenting complaint through a DSM-IV five axis diagnosis to an ideographic portrayal of the problems besetting the patient. Following a careful discussion of our diagnostic impression, we then make recommendations in each of the following categories: (1) additional assessment procedures, when required; (2) cognitive-behavioral psychotherapies; (3) pharmacotherapies; and (4) behavioral and/or pedagogic academic interventions, when necessary. A typical evaluation end product for a fourteen-year-old girl with PTSD (complicated by panic disorder and major depression) might look like this:

- Assessment: To exclude medical causes of panic or depression, obtain laboratory studies. To evaluate academic performance in the context of possible cognitive processing deficits versus effects of PTSD on learning, refer for a neuropsychological evaluation.
- Psychotherapy: To treat PTSD, cognitive-behavioral treatment using our protocol (March & Amaya-Jackson, unpublished); to treat panic, incorporate a developmentally sensitive implementation of the social phobia/panic protocol from Barlow and collengues (Barlow & Craske, 1989) within the framework of our PTSD protocol. To treat depression, adapt the grief module from Interpersonal Psychotherapy (IPT; Mufson, Moreau, Weissman, & Wickramaratne, 1994) to the Cognitive Behavioral Treatment program of Lewinsohn (CBT; Lewinsohn, Steinmetz, Antonuccio, & Teri, 1984), again in the context of the treatment of PTSD.
- Pharmacotherapy: If CBT shows no or little benefit after six weeks, begin an ascending dose titration trial of a selective serotonin reuptake inhibitor, such as fluvoxamine or sertraline (Davidson & March, 1996). If anxiety comprises a significant barrier to successful E/RP, consider adding a low-dose anxiolytic, such as clonazepam, paying careful attention to the difficulty of withdrawing benzodiazepines in PTSD patients.
- Academic: Include school-based behavioral interventions for PTSD as necessary. To help with informing school personnel about PTSD, provide parents an information packet, including working with PTSD in the school setting.

Treatment often flounders because of an insufficient appreciation of the clinical verity that "The most important leg of a three legged stool is the one that's missing." Clinically, it is crucial that the treatment of pediatric PTSD be predicated on component interventions that present a logically consistent and compelling relationship between disorder-specific targets, the treatment, and the specified outcome. While the details of each treatment rest within the implementation of that treatment, this method of developing and specifying a program of treatment carries sufficient specificity that it is unlikely that a major treatment target has been omitted.

Anticipating Treatment

Finally, the initial assessment of PTSD grades directly into clinical treatment in part through establishing a hierarchy of traumatic reminders. The explication of traumatic reminders during a "debriefing interview" points directly to the child's thoughts, feelings, and behaviors at the time of the trauma. In turn, a moment-by-moment review of the event often explicates current traumatic reminders. Traumatic reminders also provide clues to crucial PTSD maintaining factors, especially escape/avoidance behaviors. Consequently, traumatic reminders are an important clue in establishing targets for cognitive-behavioral treatment interventions, where they land on a stimulus hierarchy as putative targets for exposure-based interventions (see chapter 18, this volume).

In linking traumatic reminders to the stressor itself, many trauma therapists typically conduct a moment-by-moment replay of the traumatic event, using the metaphor of a pretend videotape of the child's experiences at the time of the trauma. Under the direction of the therapist, the child reviews what happened, including thoughts, feelings, and bodily feelings at successive moments during the trauma. The posture of the clinician is one of allowing and encouraging detailed description of the traumatic event, never one of forcing disclosure. It is important that the child understand that PTSD "uses" these details to remind the child of the trauma in the present and thereby to cause all sorts of unpleasant feelings and thoughts.

A heuristically useful device is to use a long sheet of paper with a timeline drawn down the middle. The line represents the events before the trauma, leading up to it, the trauma itself, and what happened afterwards. The timeline scale varies from days to hours to minutes to seconds, depending on the level of data needed at particular moments of the trauma. On the left side of the line, notes regarding the details of the event can be written. On the right side of the line the clinician can write thoughts, emotions, and physical sensations relating to the events. Tell the child that you are going to pretend that there is an imaginary video screen on the table and that it will show the traumatic event as he/she remembers it. Tell the child that you will be taking notes about exactly what happened and show him/her the paper. Explain that on one side of the line are going to be notes about what happened and on the other side notes about thoughts, physical sensations, and feelings. Remind the child (and yourself) that he/she needn't reexperience the event, or become upset; rather, just to describe it relatively unemotionally. Work through the event in as much detail as possible. Ask the child to go frame by frame over parts that are hurried; these often contain important material fueling current escape/avoidance symptoms. Make connections between current traumatic reminders and specific elements of the traumatic event itself. Be especially attentive to cognitive and spatial-temporal distortions, which can be corrected as the clinician and the child move through the event. Pay special attention to identifying "intervention" or "revenge" fantasies that often precede the "worst moment," namely the moment during the trauma where the child had the greatest fear and felt the most helpless. Having completed this exercise, it is relatively straightforward to set up a stimulus hierarchy for subsequent use in cognitive and exposure-based interventions.

CONCLUSION

Despite thirty years of research, assessment tools for pediatric PTSD leaves a lot to be desired with respect to breadth of symptom coverage, developmental sensitivity, ability to inventory the stressor as well as PTSD symptoms, and basic psychometric properties. Fortunately, instruments currently in development will, over the next five years, provide multi-informant self-report and interviewer-administered diagnostic and treatment outcome measures that are reliable and valid for their intended purposes, which will themselves depend on the type of research or clinical setting within which the instrument will be utilized.

REFERENCES

Achenbach, T. M. (1986). How is a parent rating scale used in the diagnosis of attention deficit disorder? *Journal of Children in Contemporary Society, 19*(1–2), 19–31.

Albach, F., & Everaerd, W. (1992). Posttraumatic stress symptoms in victims of childhood incest. *Psychotherapy & Psychosomatics, 57*(4), 143–151.

Amaya-Jackson, L. (1995). Post-traumatic stress disorder in adolescents. *Adolescent Medicine, 6*(2), 251–270.

Amaya-Jackson, L., & March, J. (1995). Posttraumatic stress disorder. In J. March (Ed.), *Anxiety disorders in children and adolescents* (pp. 276–300). New York: Guilford.

American Psychiatric Association. (1980). *Diagnostic and statistical manual of mental disorders* (3rd. ed.). Washington DC: Author.

American Psychiatric Association. (1987). *Diagnostic and statistical manual of mental disorders* (3rd ed. Rev.). Washington DC: Author.

American Psychiatric Association. (1994). *Diagnostic and statistical manual of mental disorders* (4th ed.). Washington DC: Author.

Barlow, D., & Craske, M. (1989). *Mastery of your anxiety and panic.* Albany: Graywind.

Beidel, D. C. (1991). Social phobia and overanxious disorder in school-age children. *Journal of the American Academy of Child & Adolescent Psychiatry, 30*(4), 545–552.

Black, B. (1995). Separation Anxiety Disorder and Panic Disorder. In J. March (Ed.), *Anxiety disorders in children and adolescents* (pp. 212–234). New York: Guilford Press.

Blake, D., Weathers, F., Nagy, L., Kaloupek, D., Laumiinzer, G., Charney, D., & Keane, T. (1990). A clinician rating scale for assessing current and lifetime PTSD: The CAPS-1. *Behavior Therapist, 13,* 187–188.

Bradburn, I. S. (1991). After the earth shook: Children's stress symptoms 6–8 months after a disaster. *Advances in Behaviour Research & Therapy, 13*(3), 173–179.

Bremner, J. D., Krystal, J. H., Southwick, S. M., & Charney, D. S. (1995). Functional neuroanatomical correlates of the effects of stress on memory. *Journal of Traumatic Stress, 8*(4), 527–553.

Cahill, C., Llewelyn, S. P., & Pearson, C. (1991). Long-term effects of sexual abuse which occurred in childhood: A review. *British Journal of Clinical Psychology, 30,* 117–130.

Conaway, L. P., & Hansen, D. J. (1989). Social behavior of physically abused and neglected children: A critical review. *Clinical Psychology Review, 9*(5), 627–652.

Conners, C. (1995). *Conners' rating scales.* Toronto, CA: Multi-Health Systems.

Conners, C., & March, J. (1996). *Conners/March developmental questionnaire.* Toronto: Multi-Health Systems.

Costello, E. (1989). Developments in child psychiatric epidemiology. *Journal of the American Academy of Child & Adolescent Psychiatry, 28,* 836–841.

Curry, J., & Murphy, L. (1995). Comorbidity of anxiety disorders. In J. March (Ed.), *Anxiety disorders in children and adolescents* (pp. 301 317). New York: Guilford Press.

Davidson, J. R., & Foa, E. B. (1991). Diagnostic issues in posttraumatic stress disorder: Considerations for the DSM-IV. *Journal of Abnormal Psychology, 100*(3), 346–355.

Davidson, J., & March, J. (1996). Traumatic stress disorders. In A. Tasman, J. Kay, & J. Lieberman (Eds.), *Psychiatry,* Vol. 2 (pp. 1085–1098). Philadelphia: Saunders.

Deblinger, E., McLeer, S. V., & Henry, D. (1990). Cognitive behavioral treatment for sexually abused children suffering post-traumatic stress: Preliminary findings. *Journal of the American Academy of Child & Adolescent Psychiatry, 29*(5), 747–752.

Earls, F., Smith, E. M., Reich, W., & Jung, K. G. (1988). Investigating psychopathological consequences of a disaster in children: A pilot study incorporating a structured diagnostic interview. *Journal of the American Academy of Child & Adolescent Psychiatry, 27*(1), 90–95.

Eth, S., & Pynoos, R. S. (1994). Children who witness the homicide of a parent. *Psychiatry, 57*(4), 287–306.

Famularo, R., Kinscherff, R., & Fenton, T. (1990). Symptom differences in acute and chronic presentation of childhood post-traumatic stress disorder. *Child Abuse & Neglect, 14*(3), 439–444.

Famularo, R., Kinscherff, R., & Fenton, T. (1992). Psychiatric diagnoses of maltreated children: Preliminary findings. *Journal of the American Academy of Child & Adolescent Psychiatry, 31*(5), 863–867.

Fisher, P., Hoven, C., Moore, R., Bird, H., Chiang, P., Lichtman, J., & Schwab-Stone, M. (1993). *Evaluation of a method to assess post-traumatic stress disorder in children and adolescents.* Paper presented at the American Public Health Association Annual Meeting, San Francisco, CA.

Foa, E. B., Molnar, C., & Cashman, L. (1995). Change in rape narratives during exposure therapy for posttraumatic stress disorder. Special Issue: Research on traumatic memory. *Journal of Traumatic Stress, 8*(4), 675–690.

Foa, E. B., Steketee, G., & Rothbaum, B. O. (1989). Behavioral/cognitive conceptualizations of posttraumatic stress disorder. *Behavior Therapy, 20*(2), 155–176.

Forster, P. (1992). *Nature and treatment of acute stress reactions.* Washington: American Psychiatric Press.

Garbarino, J., Kostelny, K., & Dubrow, N. (1991). What children can tell us about living in danger. *American Psychologist, 46*(4), 376–383.

Goenjian, A. K., Najarian, L. M., Pynoos, R. S., Steinberg, A. M., Manoukian, G., Tavosian, A., & Fairbanks, L. A. (1994). Posttraumatic stress disorder in elderly and younger adults after the 1988 earthquake in Armenia. *American Journal of Psychiatry, 151*(6), 895–901.

Goenjian, A. K., Pynoos, R. S., Steinberg, A. M., Najarian, L. M., Asarnow, J. R., Karayan, I., Ghurabi, M., & Fairbanks, L. A. (1995). Psychiatric comorbidity in children after the 1988 earthquake in Armenia. *Journal of the American Academy of Child & Adolescent Psychiatry, 34*(9), 1174–1184.

Goldman, S. J., D'Angelo, E. J., DeMaso, D. R., & Mezzacappa, E. (1992). Physical and sexual abuse histories among children with borderline personality disorder. *American Journal of Psychiatry, 149*(12), 1723–1726.

Horowitz, F. D. (1996). Developmental perspectives on child and adolescent posttraumatic stress disorder. *Journal of School Psychology, 34*(2), 189–191.

Kendall-Tackett, K. A., Williams, L. M., & Finkelhor, D. (1993). Impact of sexual abuse on children: A review and synthesis of recent empirical studies. *Psychological Bulletin, 113*(1), 164–180.

King, L., & King, D. (1994). Item response theory and PTSD assessment. *PTSD Research Quarterly, 5*(2), 6–8.

Kovacs, M. (1985). The Children's Depression Inventory (CDI). *Psychopharmecology Bulletin, 21,* 995–998.

Lewinsohn, P. M., Steinmetz, J. L., Antonuccio, D., & Teri, L. (1984). Group therapy for depression: The Coping with Depression course. *International Journal of Mental Health, 13*(3–4), 8–33.

Lonigan, C. J., Shannon, M. P., Taylor, C. M., Finch, A. J., & Sallee, F. R. (1994). Children exposed to disaster: II. Risk factors for the development of post-traumatic symptomatology. *Journal of the American Academy of Child & Adolescent Psychiatry, 33*(1), 94–105.

March, J. (1991). Post-traumatic stress in the emergency setting. *Emergency Care Quarterly, 7*(1), 74–81.

March, J. (1993). What constitutes a stressor? The "Criterion A" issue. In J. Davidson & E. Foa (Eds.), *Posttraumatic stress disorder: DSM-IV and beyond* (pp. 37–54). Washington DC: American Psychiatric Press.

March, J. (in press). *Manual for the Multidimensional Anxiety Scale for Children (MASC).* Toronto: Multi-Health Systems.

March, J., & Albano, A. (1996). Assessment of anxiety in children and adolescents. In L. Dickstein, M. Riba, & M. Oldham (Eds.), *Review of psychiatry XV,* Vol. XV (pp. 405–427). Washington: American Psychiatric Press.

March, J., & Amaya-Jackson, L. (1994). Post-traumatic stress disorder in children and adolescents. *PTSD Research Quarterly, 4*(4), 1–7.

March, J., & Amaya-Jackson, L. (unpublished). *Multimodality trauma treatment: A guide to cognitive-behavioral psychotherapy for children and adolescents.*

March, J., Amaya-Jackson, L., & Pynoos, R. (1996). Pediatric post-traumatic stress disorder. In J. Weiner (Ed.), *Textbook of child and adolescent psychiatry* (2nd ed.). Washington: American Psychiatric Press.

March, J., Amaya-Jackson, L., Terry, R., & Costanzo, P. (1998). Post-traumatic symptomology children and adolescents after an industrial fire. *Journal of the American Academy of Child & Adolescent Psychiatry, 36,* 1080–1088.

March, J., Parker, J., Sullivan, K., Stallings, P., & Conners, C. (1997). The Multidimensional Anxiety Scale for Children (MASC): Factor structure, reliability and validity. *Journal of the American Academy of Child & Adolescent Psychiatry, 36*(4), 554–565.

Marks, I. (1987). *Fears, phobias, and rituals.* New York: Oxford University Press.

Martinez, P., & Richters, J. (1993). The NIMH community violence project: II. Children's distress symptoms associated with violence exposure. *Psychiatry, 56,* 22–35.

McLeer, S., Deblinger, E., Henry, D., & Orvaschel, H. (1992). Sexually abused children at high risk for posttraumatic stress disorder. *Journal of the American Academy of Child & Adolescent Psychiatry, 31*(5), 876–879.

McNally, R. J. (1993). Stressors that produce posttraumatic stress disorder in children. In J. R. T. Davidson & E. B. Foa (Eds.), *Posttraumatic stress disorder: DSM-IV and beyond* (pp. 57–74). Washington: American Psychiatric Press.

McNally, R. J. (1996). Assessment of posttraumatic stress disorder in children and adolescents. *Journal of School Psychology, 34*(2), 147–161.

Mufson, L., Moreau, D., Weissman, M. M., & Wickramaratne, P. (1994). Modification of interpersonal psychotherapy with depressed adolescents (IPT-A): Phase I and II studies. *Journal of the American Academy of Child & Adolescent Psychiatry, 33*(5), 695–705.

Nader, K., Blake, D., Kriegler, J., & Pynoos, R. (1994). *Clinician Administered PTSD Scale for Children (CAPS-C), Current and Lifetime Diagnosis version, and instruction manual.* UCLA Neuropsychiatric Institute and National Center for PTSD.

Nader, K. O., & Fairbanks, L. A. (1994). The suppression of reexperiencing: Impulse control and somatic symptoms in children following traumatic exposure. Special Issue: War and stress in the Middle East. *Anxiety, Stress & Coping: An International Journal, 7*(3), 229–239.

Nader, K. O., Pynoos, R. S., Fairbanks, L. A., & Al-Ajeel, M. (1993). A preliminary study of PTSD and grief among the children of Kuwait following the Gulf crisis. *British Journal of Clinical Psychology, 32*(4), 407–416.

Nader, K., Stuber, M., & Pynoos, R. S. (1991). Posttraumatic stress reactions in preschool children with catastrophic illness: Assessment needs. *Comprehensive Mental Health Care, 1*(3), 223–239.

Nash, M. R. (1994). Memory distortion and sexual trauma: The problem of false negatives and false positives. *International Journal of Clinical and Experimental Hypnosis, 42*(4), 346–362.

Ornitz, E. M., & Pynoos, R. S. (1989). Startle modulation in children with posttraumatic stress disorder. *American Journal of Psychiatry, 146*(7), 866–870.

Perry, B. D. (1994). Neurobiological sequelae of childhood trauma: PTSD in children. *American Psychiatric Press, Inc, Washington, DC, US(42)*, 233–255.

Perry, B. D., & Pate, J. E. (1994). Neurodevelopment and the psychobiological roots of post-traumatic stress disorder. *Charles C Thomas, Publisher, Springfield, IL, US, 326.*

Pitman, R. (1992). Biological findings in posttraumatic stress disorder: Implications for DSM-IV classification. In J. Davidson & E. Foa (Eds.), *Posttraumatic stress disorder: DSM-IV and beyond* (pp. 173–189). Washington DC: American Psychiatric Press.

Putnam, F. W., & Trickett, P. K. (1993). Child sexual abuse: A model of chronic trauma. *Psychiatry, 56*(1), 82–95.

Pynoos, R. S. (1994). Traumatic stress and developmental psychopathology in children and adolescents. *Sidran Press, Lutherville, MD, US, 171,* 65–98.

Pynoos, R. S., Frederick, C. J., Nader, K., Arroyo, W., Steinberg, A., Eth, S., Nunez, F., & Fairbanks, I. (1987). Life threat and posttraumatic stress in school-age children. *Archives of General Psychiatry, 44*(12), 1057–1063.

Pynoos, R. S., Goenjian, A., Tashjian, M., Karakashian, M., Manjikian, R., Manoukian, G., Steinberg, A. M., & Fairbanks, L. A. (1993). Post-traumatic stress reactions in children after the 1988 Armenian earthquake. *British Journal of Psychiatry, 163,* 239–247.

Pynoos, R. S., & Nader, K. (1988). Psychological first aid and treatment approach to children exposed to community violence. Research implications. *Journal of Traumatic Stress, 1*(4), 445–473.

Pynoos, R. S., & Nader, K. (1989). Children's memory and proximity to violence. *Journal of the American Academy of Child & Adolescent Psychiatry, 28*(2), 236–241.

Pynoos, R. S., & Nader, K. (1990). Children who witness the sexual assaults of their mothers. *Brunner/Mazel, Inc, New York, NY, US, 560,* 165–178.

Pynoos, R. S., & Nader, K. (1993). Issues in the treatment of posttraumatic stress in children and adolescents. In J. P. Wilson & B. Raphael (Eds.), *International handbook of traumatic stress syndromes* (pp. 535–549). New York: Plenum Press.

Pynoos, R. S., Nader, K., Black, D., Kaplan, T., Hendriks, J. H., Gordon, R., Wraith, R., Green, A., & Herman, J. L. (1993). The impact of trauma on children and adolescents. *Plenum Press, New York, NY, US, 1011,* 535–657.

Pynoos, R. S., Nader, K., Frederick, C. J., Gonda, L., & Stuber, M. (1987). Grief reactions in school age children following a sniper attack at school. *Israel Journal of Psychiatry and Related Sciences, 24*(1–2), 53–63.

Pynoos, R. S., Steinberg, A. M., & Wraith, R. (1995). A developmental model of childhood traumatic stress. *John Wiley & Sons, New York, NY, US, 2,* 72–95.

Reiss, D., Richters, J., Radke-Yarrow, M., & Scharrf, D. (1993). *Children and violence.* New York: Guilford Press.

Richters, J., & Martinez, P. (1993). The NIMH Community Violence Project: I. Children as victims and witnesses to violence. *Psychiatry, 56,* 7–21.

Saigh, P. A. (1988). The validity of the DSM-III posttraumatic stress disorder classification as applied to adolescents. *Professional School Psychology, 3*(4), 283–290.

Saigh, P. A. (1989a). A comparative analysis of the affective and behavioral symptomology of traumatized and nontraumatized children. *Journal of School Psychology, 27*(3), 247–255.

Saigh, P. A. (1989b). The validity of the DSM-III posttraumatic stress disorder classification as applied to children. *Journal of Abnormal Psychology, 98*(2), 189–192.

Saigh, P. A. (1991). The development of posttraumatic stress disorder following four different types of traumatization. *Behaviour Research & Therapy, 29*(3), 213–216.

Saigh, P. A. (1996). Posttraumatic stress disorder among children and adolescents: An introduction. *Journal of School Psychology, 34*(2), 103–105.

Saigh, P. A., Green, B. L., & Korol, M. (1996). The history and prevalence of posttraumatic stress disorder with special reference to children and adolescents. *Journal of School Psychology, 34*(2), 107–131.

Saigh, P. A., Yasik, A. E., Oberfield, R., Inamdar, S., Rubenstein, H., & Nester, J. (unpublished manuscript). The development and validation of the DSM-IV version of the Children's Posttraumatic Stress Disorder Inventory.

Saigh, P. A., Yasik, A. E., Sack, W., & Koplewicz, H. (1999). Child-adolescent posttraumatic stress disorder: Prevalence, risk and comorbidity. In P. Saigh & J. Bremner (Eds.), *Posttraumatic stress disorder: A comprehensive approach to assessment and treatment.* Boston, MA: Allyn and Bacon.

Saigh, P. A., Yule, W., & Inamdar, S. C. (1996). Imaginal flooding of traumatized children and adolescents. *Journal of School Psychology, 34*(2), 163–183.

Shaffer, D., Campbell, M., Cantwell, D., & Bradley, S. (1989). Child and adolescent psychiatric disorders in

DSM-IV: Issues facing the work group. *Journal of the American Academy of Child & Adolescent Psychiatry, 28*(6), 830–835.

Shannon, M. P., Lonigan, C. J., Finch, A. J., & Taylor, C. M. (1994). Children exposed to disaster: I. Epidemiology of post-traumatic symptoms and symptom profiles. *Journal of the American Academy of Child & Adolescent Psychiatry, 33*(1), 80–93.

Shaw, J. A., Applegate, B., Tanner, S., & Perez, D. (1995). Psychological effects of Hurricane Andrew on an elementary school population. *Journal of the American Academy of Child & Adolescent Psychiatry, 34*(9), 1185–1192.

Siegel, D. J. (1995). Memory, trauma, and psychotherapy: A cognitive science view. *Journal of Psychotherapy Practice & Research, 4*(2), 93–122.

Silverman, W. K. (1991). Diagnostic reliability of anxiety disorders in children using structured interviews. Special Issue: Assessment of childhood anxiety disorders. *Journal of Anxiety Disorders, 5*(2), 105–124.

Silverman, W. K., & Eisen, A. R. (1992). Age differences in the reliability of parent and child reports of child anxious symptomatology using a structured interview. *Journal of the American Academy of Child & Adolescent Psychiatry, 31*(1), 117–124.

Silverman, W. K., La Greca, A. M., & Wasserstein, S. (1995). What do children worry about? Worries and their relation to anxiety. *Child Development, 66*(3), 671–686.

Terr, L. C. (1983). Life attitudes, dreams, and psychic trauma in a group of "normal" children. *Journal of the American Academy of Child Psychiatry, 22*(3), 221–230.

Terr, L. C. (1991). Childhood traumas: An outline and overview. *American Journal of Psychiatry, 148*(1), 10–20.

Wolfe, V. V., Gentile, C., Michienzi, T., Sas, L., & Wolfe, D. A. (1991). The Children's Impact of Traumatic Events Scale: A measure of post-sexual-abuse PTSD symptoms. *Behavioral Assessment, 13*(4), 359–383.

Wolfe, V. V., Gentile, C., & Wolfe, D. A. (1989). The impact of sexual abuse on children: A PTSD formulation. *Behavior Therapy, 20*(2), 215–228.

Yule, W. (1992). Post-traumatic stress disorder in child survivors of shipping disasters: The sinking of the *Jupiter. Psychotherapy & Psychosomatics, 57*(4), 200–205.

Yule, W., & Canterbury, R. (1994). The treatment of post traumatic stress disorder in children and adolescents. *International Review of Psychiatry, 6*(2–3), 141–151.

Yule, W., & Udwin, O. (1991). Screening child survivors for post-traumatic stress disorders: Experiences from the *Jupiter* sinking. *British Journal of Clinical Psychology.*

CHAPTER 11

PSYCHOLOGICAL ASSESSMENT OF TRAUMATIZED ADULTS

FRANK W. WEATHERS, PH.D.
Auburn University

TERENCE M. KEANE, PH.D.
Boston Department of Veterans Affairs Medical Center
and Boston University School of Medicine

Over the last ten years, the development and psychometric evaluation of assessment tools for posttraumatic stress disorder (PTSD) has been one of the most productive areas of investigation in the field of traumatic stress. The remarkable progress that has been achieved can be illustrated by considering that in the mid-1980s, when investigators for the National Vietnam Veterans Readjustment Study (NVVRS) undertook their landmark epidemiological study of PTSD in Vietnam veterans, they were unable to identify a single measure that had been shown to be valid for distinguishing PTSD cases from non-cases (Kulka et al., 1991). Consequently, they conducted a preliminary validation study to identify appropriate measures of PTSD for use in the main study. Today, however, due to the pioneering work in the NVVRS and subsequent efforts by numerous other trauma researchers, there is an abundance of instruments to assess PTSD. More than two dozen well-validated measures are currently available, including structured interviews, questionnaires, and psychophysiological protocols, several of which, such as the Impact of Event Scale (IES; Horowitz, Wilner, & Alvarez, 1979) and the Mississippi Scale for Combat-Related PTSD (Mississippi Scale; Keane, Caddell, & Taylor, 1988), can be considered psychometrically mature on the basis of the extensive empirical literature they have inspired.

This rapid increase in the number of PTSD assessment tools has clearly had a positive impact on the field of traumatic stress. The availability of standardized measures has greatly facilitated the rapidly accumulating empirical literature regarding the clinical features, etiology, course, and treatment of PTSD, and has provided clinicians the means for evaluating the presence and severity of posttraumatic symptoms in their patients. Despite the gains that have been made, however, several problems remain. First, as we discuss later in the chapter, the assessment of trauma and PTSD raises many complex conceptual and methodological issues that have yet to be resolved or in some cases even fully articulated. Second, the assessment of PTSD has not yet become routine outside of trauma research centers, and continued outreach and education is needed to encourage more investigators and clinicians to add measures of trauma and PTSD to their assessment batteries.

Third, and somewhat paradoxically given the second point, there is a growing concern that the proliferation of PTSD assessment instruments is leading to fragmentation in the field. Instead of too few measures, as was the case a decade ago, today there simply may be too many. Despite the already large number of existing instruments, articles describing new measures of trauma, PTSD, or closely related constructs continue to appear regularly in the literature. While a few measures have been used successfully across different labs and trauma populations, most have not been widely adopted outside the original setting in which they were developed, and there is no clear consensus about which measures should be included in a core PTSD assessment battery. The unfortunate result is that disparities in instrumentation across studies are more the rule than the exception in PTSD research. This hinders direct comparisons of findings across studies and undermines efforts to identify commonalities among survivors of different types of traumatic events.

To document the extent of this problem, we searched the PILOTS database (Lerner, 1994), examining entries for all empirical articles published in 1996 on PTSD in adults. This informal review led to several conclusions, which obviously are bounded by the information available in the PILOTS citations:

1. Encouragingly, the use of standard PTSD assessment instruments has become the norm, though articles based on non-standardized assessment procedures (e.g., unstructured interviews, study-specific measures, chart reviews) continue to be published. Of 189 articles that fit our search criteria, 157 (83 percent) used at least one standardized measure of PTSD.

2. There is considerable variability in the measures used to assess PTSD. We identified 31 different measures in our review, and this does not take into account multiple versions of established measures, measures that existed before 1996 but were not used in the studies we reviewed, measures that are too new to have appeared in the literature, or study-specific measures. The IES and the Mississippi Scale were the most commonly used measures overall, with 68 (36 percent) and 49 (26 percent) citations respectively, and the Clinician-Administered PTSD Scale (CAPS; Blake et al., 1990; Blake et al., 1995) was the most commonly used diagnostic interview, with 37 (20 percent) citations. Overall these findings reveal some degree of overlap in PTSD assessment batteries, but indicate that the field is far from consensus.

3. Too many investigators rely exclusively on self-report measures. Only 90 (48 percent) studies used a structured interview in their assessment battery, and this may be an overestimate since it was not always possible to determine if the PTSD module of a comprehensive interview such as the Structured Clinical Interview for DSM-III-R (SCID; Spitzer, Williams, Gibbon, & First, 1990) was administered. Although

there are circumstances in which reliance on self-report measures may be the only feasible approach, a structured interview, preferably by an experienced clinician, is the foundation of any thorough assessment of PTSD.

4. Too few investigators use multiple measures, a practice that has often been advocated in the assessment of PTSD (e.g., Keane, Wolfe, & Taylor, 1987; Kulka et al., 1991). Only 75 studies (40 percent) used more than one standard measure, and only 29 (15 percent) used three or more.

5. Ironically, there is more uniformity in the assessment of comorbid problems, with the SCID, the Beck Depression Inventory (BDI; Beck, Ward, Mendelson, Mock, & Erbaugh, 1961), the State-Trait Anxiety Inventory (STAI; Spielberger, Gorsuch, & Luschene, 1970), and the Symptom Checklist-90 Revised (SCL-90-R; Derogatis, 1983) among the most commonly used instruments.

The shortcomings in the assessment of PTSD identified in our brief review are attributable to several factors. In some studies the data were collected prior to the widespread availability of well-validated measures, as in the case of secondary analyses of archival data sets. In other studies the investigators simply may not have been aware of high-quality measures that were available. In still other studies PTSD appeared to be peripheral to the primary research question, so little attention was given to assessing it.

All of these circumstances are understandable in a relatively new field and are easily addressed as the field progresses and new investigations are undertaken. What is of greater concern is that some investigators, perhaps feeling compelled by novel aspects of their research question or target population, continue to develop new PTSD instruments or to alter existing ones to create an assessment battery that will satisfy the unique demands of their study. The advantage of this decision is that the investigators have a measure that, at least in a face-valid way, is tailored to their specific assessment question and population. The disadvantages, however, are that the psychometric properties of the new measure are unknown and that the comparability with other relevant studies is compromised due to a lack of a common reference point. A better approach, if a study-specific measure were considered essential, would be to include one or more standard measures in the assessment battery in order to maintain some direct link with other research. Given the variety of well-validated PTSD measures currently available, however, the use of non-standard measures is increasingly difficult to justify.

To address these and other concerns, a group of 45 leading trauma researchers, funded in a collaborative effort by the National Center for PTSD and the National Institutes for Mental Health, gathered in the fall of 1995 for a consensus conference on the assessment of PTSD. This meeting was similar in scope and intent to a consensus conference on panic, in which leading panic researchers defined key terms and identified acceptable instruments for assessing panic disorder (Shear & Maser, 1994). Five major areas were considered, including adult PTSD, childhood PTSD, traumatic stressors, comorbidity, and functional status. The intent of the conference was not to advance a set of rigid dictates, but rather to develop flexible, pragmatic guidelines that would promote the standardization of assessment in the field of traumatic stress, thereby enhancing comparability of research findings across different trauma populations and different settings. The conclusions from this conference, which will be summarized in a forthcoming manuscript and which we cite throughout the chapter, are an important first step toward much needed uniformity in the assessment of trauma and PTSD.

In the remaining sections of this chapter we draw on the existing literature, on our own experiences developing and evaluating PTSD measures, and on recommendations from the consensus conference to describe the current status of PTSD assessment and challenges for the future. First, we discuss some of the central conceptual and methodological issues in the assessment of PTSD. Second, we outline the psychometric considerations involved in evaluating psychological tests. Third, we provide an overview of some of the most widely used PTSD interviews and self-report measures. Finally, we briefly describe different assessment scenarios that we have encountered in our work, outlining the assessment batteries used and the diagnostic decision-making involved in answering the assessment questions. This last section is intended as a cookbook which other investigators and clinicians can use to inform their own assessment practices. To the extent that a scenario fits a reader's specific assessment needs, the guidelines we provide can be adopted directly. But even in the case of a novel assessment question that does not correspond well to any of the scenarios we present, the examples in this section may provide a useful starting point toward a satisfactory solution.

No single chapter could summarize the vast literature on the assessment of PTSD; accordingly, this chapter has several limitations. First, we focus specifically on the assessment of PTSD and not on other stress-related syndromes such as acute stress disorder or complex PTSD (e.g., Herman, 1992). Second, we focus on PTSD symptoms, touching only briefly on the assessment of traumatic life events. Third, we focus on adults, since the assessment of PTSD in children is covered elsewhere in this volume (see chapter 10). Fourth, we focus on PTSD interviews and self-report measures. Information on other assessment approaches such as psychophysiological and other biological measures, neuropsychological tests, and projective tests can be found in a comprehensive new volume devoted to the assessment of PTSD (Wilson & Keane, 1997).

Finally, we focus on the diagnostic function of the assessment instruments we describe. It is important to note, however, that diagnosis is just one part of assessment, albeit a central part. As we have described elsewhere (e.g., Keane et al., 1987; Litz & Weathers, 1994), the assessment of trauma and PTSD is a complex process that unfolds in a rich interpersonal context. When properly conducted it can be both educational and therapeutic for the traumatized individual being assessed. The goals for different types of assessment vary, but in most clinical applications they would include looking beyond diagnosis to understand the impact of trauma on an individual's life, identifying and prioritizing specific targets for change, and offering clear feedback to the client.

CONCEPTUAL AND METHODOLOGICAL ISSUES IN THE ASSESSMENT OF PTSD

In this section we discuss some of the central issues regarding the assessment of PTSD in traumatized adults. Many of these issues overlap, and distinctions among them are somewhat arbitrary, but we consider them separately to highlight the unique challenges that each poses. Though some involve more purely theoretical considerations, all have significant practical implications for the actual conduct of PTSD assessments in any clinical or research context. This is by no means an exhaustive list, but the issues described below are the ones we feel bear most directly on the development and utilization of standardized PTSD assessment tools.

Evolution of the PTSD Diagnostic Criteria

Since PTSD was first introduced as a formal diagnostic entity in the DSM-III in 1980, the diagnostic criteria have evolved considerably (see Saigh & Bremner, 1998; Wilson, 1995). Most of the changes occurred between the DSM-III and the DSM-III-R, including (a) expanding the number of symptoms from 12 to 17; (b) recasting symptoms into the three clusters of reexperiencing, avoidance and numbing, and hyperarousal; (c) revising and further explicating several criteria; and (d) dropping guilt as a criterion. More modest changes for the DSM-IV included (a) an extensive reworking of Criterion A (see next section); (b) moving cued physiological reactivity from the hyperarousal cluster to the reexperiencing cluster; (c) adding the requirement that symptoms must cause marked subjective distress or functional impairment; and (d) rewording and clarifying of some symptoms.

These changes in the diagnostic criteria reflect ongoing controversy and ambiguity regarding the core phenomenology of PTSD, which again is both legitimate and understandable in a newly emerging field. The problem is that changes have occurred so rapidly that there simply has not been enough time to fully explore one definition before the next is introduced. Combined with the proliferation of PTSD assessment instruments, the evolution of the PTSD criteria has hindered the accumulation of the data needed to address the most pressing questions empirically.

Fortunately, the diagnostic criteria for PTSD appear to have stabilized. Apart from the revised definition of what constitutes a traumatic event, there appears to be little substantive difference between the PTSD criteria in the DSM-III-R and the DSM-IV. To the extent that the new definition of a trauma is more explicit and therefore possibly more stringent, some individuals may not receive a PTSD diagnosis according to the DSM-IV because they fail to meet Criterion A. But given that an unequivocal traumatic event has occurred, the DSM-III-R and the DSM-IV yield virtually identical diagnostic results. A recent investigation from our lab suggests that only a very small fraction of individuals would be classified differently under DSM-III-R versus DSM-IV criteria (Weathers, Meron, & Keane, 1997).

From a practical assessment perspective, our view is that clinicians and investigators should always adopt the most current PTSD diagnostic criteria as soon as feasible. This means that new investigations should utilize measures that accurately reflect the DSM-IV criteria. Moreover, DSM-III-R diagnoses from investigations initiated prior to 1994 can be converted to DSM-IV diagnoses in most instances, allowing researchers to explore the implications of using different definitions of PTSD. The use of the DSM-III criteria, however, is now less than optimal and is only appropriate if the investigation involves a reanalysis of an archival data set, or if information regarding the DSM-IV criteria is also collected.

Despite the emerging consensus and stability in the PTSD diagnostic criteria, a remaining concern is whether these criteria are interpreted and utilized similarly by different clinicians and investigators. Although many criteria are clearly defined and relatively straightforward to assess, we and our colleagues have struggled to reach consensus regarding the parameters of more equivocal symptoms such as flashbacks, amnesia, and foreshortened future. Also, we are well aware that other clinicians and investigators wrestle with this issue, often developing idiosyncratic meanings for problematic criteria.

Ambiguity in the PTSD diagnostic criteria makes it difficult to inquire about symptoms and to clarify them for respondents, and contributes to unreliability in ratings of symptom severity. The text of the DSM-IV provides little explication of individual PTSD symptoms, and the resources that are available (e.g., Weiss, 1997) do not resolve all of the connotative issues. In developing the CAPS we tried to anticipate typical points of confusion that occur during symptom inquiry and to provide standard follow-up prompts to address them. Nonetheless, whenever we provide consultation or training on PTSD assessment we are invariably struck by how much discussion and consensus building is needed regarding the definition of the diagnostic criteria, especially early in the implementation of a new assessment protocol.

The Criterion A Problem

One of the most vexing issues in the field of traumatic stress, and a focal point for much heated debate, is the so-called Criterion A problem, a broad label for several crucial questions regarding the proper role of traumatic events in the diagnosis of PTSD. Initially the Criterion A problem centered on questions such as how to define a traumatic event and whether experiencing a traumatic event should be a requirement for a PTSD diagnosis. These questions are still unresolved, but there appears to be a growing consensus that traumatic events can be distinguished from ordinary stressors (albeit with some inevitable imprecision and ambiguity) and that they serve a useful gatekeeping function that preserves the meaningfulness of the disorder as a distinct diagnostic entity and prevents trivialization of the suffering of survivors of overwhelming stressors. Concerns regarding Criterion A continue to focus on how to define a trauma, but have also shifted to other questions about how to measure traumatic events and whether to require a link between PTSD symptoms and a specific stressor (for more extensive discussion of the Criterion A problem, see Davidson & Foa, 1991; Kilpatrick & Resnick, 1993; Resnick, Kilpatrick, & Lipovsky, 1991; and Solomon & Canino, 1990).

Defining Traumatic Events. Some of the most marked changes in the PTSD diagnostic criteria have been in the definition of Criterion A, the requirement that an individual must have experienced a traumatic life event in order to qualify for a PTSD diagnosis. The definitions offered in the DSM-III and the DSM-III-R focused on the phrase "outside the range of usual human experience." As many observers have noted, however, this definition is unsatisfactory, in

part because traumatic events are actually fairly common and in part because it misses the essential characteristic that all traumatic events have in common. As Herman (1992) has argued:

> *Traumatic events are extraordinary, not because they occur rarely, but rather because they overwhelm the ordinary human adaptations to life. Unlike commonplace misfortunes, traumatic events generally involve threats to life or bodily integrity, or a close personal encounter with violence and death. They confront human beings with the extremities of helplessness and terror, and evoke the responses of catastrophe (p. 33).*

That traumatic events are relatively common has been well-documented in a number of recent investigations (e.g., Breslau, Davis, Andreski, & Peterson, 1991; Norris, 1992; Kessler, Sonnega, Bromet, Highes, & Nelson, 1995; Resnick, Kilpatrick, Dansky, Saunders, & Best, 1993; Vrana & Lauterbach, 1994). In the National Comorbidity Study, for example, Kessler et al. (1995) found that 60.7 percent of men and 51.2 percent of women experienced at least one traumatic event in their lives, and that 34.2 percent of men and 24.9 percent of women experienced two or more such events.

In response to these concerns, a two-part definition for Criterion A was developed for the DSM-IV, representing a sharp departure from previous definitions. The first part of the new Criterion A, which requires that "the person experienced, witnessed, or was confronted with an event or events that involved actual or threatened death or serious injury, or a threat to the physical integrity of self or others," addresses the core aspect distinguishing traumatic events from ordinary stressors. The second part, which requires that "the person's response involved intense fear, helplessness, or horror," recognizes that an individual's subjective response to an event is an important dimension to consider in defining a traumatic event.

Given its seemingly greater explicitness, the DSM-IV version of Criterion A can be seen as a more conservative definition of a trauma that should result in fewer experiences being classified as traumatic. However, this definition contains ambiguities that permit considerable interpretive flexibility. For example, while the words "experienced" and "witnessed" in the first part of the definition seem clear, the phrase "confronted with" could be construed quite broadly. Similarly, the words "death" and "serious injury" seem clear, but the phrase "threat to physical integrity" is quite ambiguous.

The practical assessment problem, then, is how to determine whether or not someone experienced at least one traumatic event that would make them eligible for a PTSD diagnosis. In extreme cases, there is little ambiguity and the decision is straightforward. Prototypical events such as rape, combat, and natural disasters are obviously catastrophic and engender nearly universal fear and horror. But many events are less clear-cut, and for these events the way in which "traumatic" is defined becomes crucial.

For example, a stressor that has received an increasing amount of attention in the last few years is chronic illness, especially cancer (see Green, Epstein, Krupnick, & Rowland, 1997). In the DSM-III, chronic illness was offered as an explicit example of a common stressor that would *not* be considered traumatic. In the DSM-IV, though, at least some chronic illnesses (those considered to be life-threatening) qualify as potentially traumatic stressors. Nonetheless, as Green et al. (1997) have observed, even life-threatening illness is not necessarily a good fit to the DSM-IV definition of a trauma, and this category of stressors remains somewhat of a gray area. Our view is that until more research is available, the most reasonable approach at this time is to attempt to apply Criterion A as it is defined in the DSM-IV, recognizing that some latitude will be needed in order to appropriately classify events that are not prototypical traumatic stressors.

Measuring Traumatic Events.   Apart from the difficulties involved in defining traumatic events, there are also problems with assessing them. Until recently, far less attention has been paid to the assessment of trauma than to the assessment of PTSD symptoms (see Krinsley & Weathers, 1995). As a result, there is a paucity of well-validated, standardized measures of trauma, but an abundance of study-specific measures, some of them inadequately conceived and poorly constructed. Very few trauma measures have been used in more than a handful of

investigations, and even the best measures have only limited psychometric data supporting their use. Currently, the most well-validated measures are those designed to assess exposure to a single type of stressor, such as combat or rape, but many of these measures are not designed to assess the two-part DSM-IV definition of Criterion A.

There are several practical considerations in assessing traumatic events. First, any PTSD assessment requires some means of establishing that the respondent experienced at least one Criterion A event, whether it be a standardized trauma measure, unstructured interview, or some other approach. If the assessment is focused on a single index event or single type of stressor, it may be sufficient to inquire about the index event to determine whether it meets both parts of Criterion A. In addition, severity of exposure to the index event can be quantified by administering a focused trauma scale. Second, there is a growing recognition that traumatic events are multidimensional and that certain event characteristics (e.g., perceived life threat, degree of actual physical harm, age at onset, chronicity, whether the trauma was interpersonal in nature) may be especially predictive of PTSD symptom severity (see Green, 1993; Resnick et al., 1991). Thus, to merely establish that a traumatic event occurred is to ignore potentially valuable information that could lead to a richer understanding of an individual's unique adaptation to that event.

Third, trauma measures vary widely in scope and format, ranging from self-report checklists assessing the presence or absence of a limited range of potentially traumatic events to comprehensive protocols assessing a wide range of stressors through both self-report and interview. Although the use of checklists and questionnaires is widespread, we are not sanguine that traumatic events can be validly determined solely on the basis of self-report. In our research and clinical assessments we use both checklist and interview formats and often find considerable divergence between them. Discrepancies occur in both directions. Sometimes respondents endorse items on a checklist that an interviewer then judges to be relatively trivial, but other times an interviewer elicits reports of unmistakably traumatic events that were not endorsed on a checklist. Although trauma interviews are typically more time-consuming and place a greater burden on both respondents and interviewers, they provide the best means for determining that reported events meet the Criterion A definition of a trauma.

In our own work, we use several different trauma measures depending on the nature of the assessment task. For quantifying degree of combat exposure, we use the Combat Exposure Scale (CES; Keane et al., 1989), a 7-item self-report measure. When screening for potential traumatic events to serve as the basis of a PTSD symptom inquiry, we use the Life Events Checklist (LEC), a self-report screening measure that accompanies the DSM-IV version of the CAPS. Positively endorsed items on the LEC, which assesses 17 different stressor categories, are followed by an interview before beginning the PTSD symptom inquiry, which is based on as many as three different traumas. When a history of trauma across the life span is the focus of an assessment, we use the Evaluation of Lifetime Stressors (ELS; Krinsley, 1996), a comprehensive protocol for assessing lifetime trauma that consists of a screening questionnaire and a follow-up interview.

Linking PTSD Symptoms to Specific Traumatic Events.

Another issue closely related to the definition and measurement of traumatic events is establishing that PTSD symptoms are attributable to a specific event. Since it was first officially recognized, PTSD has been conceptualized as an essentially unitary syndrome representing an unequivocal change from a previous level of functioning In the prototypical scenario of a single, relatively circumscribed traumatic event in an adult with no previous history of trauma or psychopathology, it is relatively straightforward to link symptoms to the trauma. But if any aspect of this scenario is changed, the picture becomes muddied. If the clinical presentation involves multiple traumatic events, childhood onset of trauma, prior psychopathology, or an underlying but previously unexpressed vulnerability to psychopathology, the task of linking symptoms to a specific event is greatly complicated.

In the DSM-IV, the first eight PTSD symptoms—including the five reexperiencing symptoms, the two effortful avoidance symptoms, and the amnesia symptom—are inherently linked to the trauma. If a person is having nightmares or intrusive thoughts, what is the content of these intrusions? If they are avoiding internal or external triggers, what event do these triggers remind them of? On the other hand, the remaining symptoms, including the emotional numbing and hyperarousal symptoms, are not explicitly linked to a trauma and therefore require clinical judgment to determine whether they can be attributed to a specific event. The consensus conference recommended that assessors should try to link these remaining symptoms to a specific event if possible, but should count symptoms toward a PTSD diagnosis if they clearly fit phenomenologically, even if they cannot be unequivocally linked to a specific trauma.

To address this issue in our own clinical and research assessments, we have included a *trauma-related* rating on the DSM-IV version of the CAPS for the numbing and hyperarousal symptoms, whereby the link between a symptom and a specific traumatic event is rated as *definite, probable,* or *unlikely.* If a symptom meets the diagnostic criterion phenomenologically, the interviewer asks about the onset of the problem. If there is an unequivocal change from a previous level of functioning following a specific traumatic event, the symptom is coded as definitely trauma-related. If the link is not explicit, but there is compelling evidence that the symptom is functionally related in some way to a traumatic event, it is coded as probably trauma-related.

An example of a *probable* rating is a woman with a history of chronic sexual abuse in childhood who complains of detachment or estrangement from others and reports that she has "always been that way." Another example is a combat veteran who can't state when his restricted range of affect began, but reports that it worsens around the anniversary of a traumatic experience in combat. Here the inference is that the restricted range of affect is functionally related to heightened reexperiencing, and thus to the trauma itself. Symptoms that are coded as either definitely or probably trauma-related are counted toward a PTSD diagnosis. Only when a symptom is clearly attributable to some other cause, with no apparent connection to a specific trauma, would it not be counted toward a diagnosis.

Handling Multiple Traumas.   The problem of linking PTSD symptoms to specific events is compounded when individuals report experiencing multiple traumatic events over their lives. A discussion of the cumulative effect of repeated trauma is beyond the scope of this chapter, but its potential complicating effect on the assessment task can be illustrated by considering some of the numerous possible outcomes of experiencing two traumatic events:

1. An initial trauma leads to no PTSD, subthreshold PTSD, or full-blown PTSD.
2. The person remains asymptomatic, recovers fully, recovers partially, remains symptomatic, or experiences a delayed onset of symptoms.
3. Then the person experiences a second trauma which (a) initiates a new PTSD syndrome that would have developed even in the absence of the first event, (b) initiates a new syndrome potentiated by the earlier trauma although no PTSD developed previously, (c) reactivates an old syndrome, (d) exacerbates a current subthreshold syndrome into a full-blown syndrome, or (e) exacerbates a current syndrome into a more severe one.

These possible pathways to a current PTSD symptom picture expand exponentially as the number of traumas increases, making the attribution of symptoms to specific traumas extraordinarily difficult. Given the high prevalence of exposure to multiple traumas that was noted earlier, confronting this issue is more the exception than the rule in the assessment of PTSD. In the hundreds of clinical and research assessments conducted in our lab, the modal presentation is a complicated clinical picture involving multiple traumas across the life span, interacting in complex ways with constitutional factors, personality factors, social learning factors, and environmental factors (see Green, Wilson, & Lindy, 1985). To ask which trauma caused the PTSD symptoms may be reductionistic and inappropriate given this multivariate, nonlinear perspective.

Comorbidity

One of the best-replicated findings regarding the descriptive psychopathology of PTSD is its association with high rates of comorbid disorders, especially depression, substance abuse, and other anxiety disorders

(see Keane & Kaloupek, 1997, for a recent review). From a conceptual perspective, this comorbidity is so prevalent that it challenges the notion of PTSD as a distinct diagnostic entity and raises questions about the functional relationships among PTSD, other disorders, and traumatic events. It is unclear if comorbid disorders are best conceptualized as independent psychopathological processes, as integral and normative aspects of the posttraumatic response, or as consequences of chronic PTSD. Comorbidity also may reflect a more general vulnerability to psychopathology that renders some individuals more susceptible to developing a variety of disorders, including PTSD.

From a practical assessment perspective, comorbid disorders complicate differential diagnosis and treatment planning. Diagnostically the task is to elicit information about all of the symptoms with which an individual presents, attribute them as accurately as possible to distinct if overlapping syndromes, and to determine, if possible, which syndrome is primary. The greater the comorbidity, the greater the number of symptoms and the more difficult the task becomes, particularly when there is direct overlap in the criteria for two syndromes. For example, PTSD and depression share anhedonia, sleep disturbance, and impaired concentration as core diagnostic criteria and also arguably overlap in terms of restricted range of affect, impairment in interpersonal functioning, and guilt. Interestingly, although the PTSD section in the DSM-IV discusses differential diagnosis, there are no explicit exclusion criteria for PTSD as there are for other Axis I disorders, including the close counterpart of PTSD, acute stress disorder.

In treatment planning, the task is to identify targets for change in therapy and to develop a strategy for tackling multiple targets hierarchically. The presence of comorbid psychopathology means that a person is presenting with a variety of clinically significant problems, each representing an important target for intervention. Considering the entire clinical picture and weighing all potential benefits and risks, a clinician must decide which problems to address first, and with which interventions. For example, an individual with PTSD who has an extensive history of alcohol and drug abuse, and who is recently sober and struggling against relapse, is a poor candidate for a trauma-focused intervention such as flooding, since the painful affects that emerge may lead the individual to resort to alcohol or drugs to alleviate their distress.

Closely related to the issue of comorbidity is the growing recognition that certain types of traumatic stress may have a far more pervasive and damaging impact on affected individuals than the current diagnostic criteria for PTSD would suggest. Investigators who have focused on chronic, interpersonal trauma, especially with a childhood onset such as incest, physical abuse, and severe emotional abuse and neglect, argue that the characteristic responses to such stressors involve a much broader range of symptoms, known as complex PTSD (Herman, 1992) or Disorder of Extreme Stress Not Otherwise Specified (DESNOS; see Herman, 1992). According to Herman (1992), the prominent symptoms of this syndrome include affect dysregulation, dissociation, characteristic distortions of personality, markedly impaired interpersonal relationships, and alterations of meaning.

Increasing evidence of variability in posttraumatic syndromes has led some to argue that PTSD is just one of a group of stress-related disorders that includes adjustment disorders, acute stress disorder, PTSD, and complex PTSD (see Brett, 1993; Davidson & Foa, 1991). Such a category exists in the International Classification of Diseases and Related Health Problems (ICD-10; World Health Organization, 1990). In the DSM-IV, however, PTSD and acute stress disorder are classified as anxiety disorders, and the symptoms of complex PTSD are listed as associated features of PTSD.

In sum, traumatized individuals typically present with a variety of clinically significant problems that extend well beyond the diagnostic criteria for PTSD. Therefore, in most assessment contexts a thorough assessment of comorbid psychopathology is essential. Those who assess victims of chronic interpersonal trauma need to be particularly aware that the modal presentation may include many problems other than the core symptoms of PTSD.

Assessing Response Bias

A potentially significant threat to the psychological assessment of PTSD is the problem of response bias, which refers broadly to test-taking behaviors that threaten the validity of inferences made on the basis of test scores. Response bias can take a number of forms, including socially desirable responding or "faking good," malingering or "faking bad," yea-saying, nay-saying, or careless or random responding. In the assessment of PTSD the concern most often centers on malingering or faking bad. Although it is not unique among psychiatric disorders in this regard, PTSD may be particularly susceptible to symptom exaggeration. It is a highly compensable disorder, not only for combat veterans but also in civilian litigation. In addition, it has been used as the basis of an insanity defense and as a mitigating factor in criminal proceedings (see Resnick, 1997).

Unfortunately, most PTSD measures are quite face-valid, meaning that the intent of their items is transparent to anyone, including respondents. Therefore, if someone were motivated to shape their answers to create a desired impression, it would be relatively easy to do so. This is particularly true for self-report measures of PTSD, most of which include no means for detecting response bias. It is less of a problem for structured interviews since clinicians can obtain additional information by making behavioral observations during the interview and requiring respondents to supply compelling descriptions of symptoms, and since final ratings are based on clinical judgment and not just on a respondent's report (see chapter 12 for further discussion of response bias).

Although the issue of response bias is of greatest concern in contexts when there is obvious incentive to exaggerate symptoms, some effort should be made to measure it whenever possible. There are several effective strategies that can be followed to help reduce response bias or to detect it when it occurs.

1. Use multiple sources of information to substantiate the real-world impact of reported symptoms, including job history, legal history, treatment history, and the reports of one or more family members, friends, or co-workers. Whenever possible, corroborate the occurrence of the trauma. For combat veterans this would involve at a minimum an inspection of their discharge papers, and preferably an examination of their full military record if available.

2. As noted earlier, if an interview is used to assess PTSD symptoms, interviewers should make careful behavioral observations to note if any of the reported problems are manifested during the assessment. Aspects of the syndrome that may reasonably be expected to appear include overt signs of emotional distress, dissociation, avoidance of painful topics, irritability, lapses in concentration, hypervigilance, and exaggerated startle. Also, interviewers should evaluate the extent to which respondents volunteer information or merely endorse symptoms after questions are posed. If they don't do so spontaneously, respondents should be urged to elaborate on their symptoms and to supply concrete behavioral examples. If respondents are unable to elaborate, or if their responses seem unnatural or contrived, the validity of their symptom endorsement is undermined.

3. Administer instruments that contain indicators of response bias. The most widely used measure containing such indicators is the Minnesota Multiphasic Personality Inventory-2 (MMPI-2; Butcher, Dahlstrom, Graham, Tellegen, & Kaemmer, 1989), which provides detailed information about several different types of response bias, including random responding, symptom exaggeration, and defensive responding. Surprisingly, only one trauma-specific measure, the Trauma Symptom Inventory (TSI; Briere, 1995), contains built-in scales to detect response bias.

4. Administer an instrument specifically designed to detect malingering, such as the Structured Interview of Reported Symptoms (SIRS; Rogers Bagby, Dickens, 1992). The SIRS is fairly simple to administer and score and its use is supported by an extensive body of research. One potential drawback is that the SIRS was developed to detect malingering of psychopathology in general and was not specifically designed to detect feigned PTSD, so little is known about its use for that purpose. We are currently administering the SIRS in several research projects to determine its utility for identifying exaggerated or malingered PTSD symptoms. Even if the SIRS does not work well with PTSD, the strategies it employs are excellent and could easily be generalized to content more appropriate for detecting the malingering of PTSD specifically.

Using Multiple Measures

The use of multiple measures has been strongly advocated in the assessment of PTSD (e.g., Keane et al., 1987; Kulka et al., 1991). The basic argument in favor of this approach is that all measures are fallible to some degree, so that combining information from multiple measures, ideally based on multiple methods, should help reduce diagnostic errors. In principle this argument is compelling, but it raises two key questions: What measures should be included in a PTSD battery, and how should they be combined in order to reach the most valid diagnostic decisions?

In her seminal work on test evaluation, Kraemer (1992) provides an extensive discussion of the complex issues involved in answering these questions and delineates statistical techniques for combining measures and constructing optimal test batteries. According to Kraemer, any legitimate test, defined as a test shown to be significantly associated with a clinical diagnosis based on a widely accepted procedure, is appropriate for inclusion in a test battery. She demonstrates how tests can be combined by using "and/or" rules or by summing weighted scores in a prediction equation.

In general, "and" rules (e.g., respondents receive a positive test if they exceed the cutoff on Test 1 *and* Test 2 *and* Test 3) are more restrictive, resulting in fewer false positives but more false negatives. In contrast, "or" rules (e.g., respondents receive a positive test if they exceed the cutoff on Test 1 *or* Test 2 *or* Test 3) are more inclusive, resulting in fewer false negatives but more false positives. The use of and/or rules permits multiple tests to be administered in sequence, which means that only the minimum number of tests needed to satisfy the rule are administered. The use of weighted scores, however, requires that all tests in a battery be administered, which can be much more time-consuming and costly.

Another approach to combining information from multiple sources is to rely on the consensus of a group of experts who meet to discuss each piece of data and determine PTSD diagnostic status on a case-by-case basis. This is a flexible, idiographic approach that is especially useful for clinical decision-making regarding highly ambiguous or complex cases, and we follow it in our own clinical case conferences. The problem with this approach is that it does not yield an empirically derived, well-defined decision rule that can be applied outside of its unique context. Although not appropriate for every assessment problem, other solutions for dealing with multiple measures include (a) excluding respondents from a study when there is discordance among measures in a battery, (b) assigning differential weights to the various measures, giving precedence to certain measures such as structured interviews, and (c) designating respondents with discordant measures as subthreshold.

To date, very little research has been conducted on the validity of combining multiple PTSD measures. The NVVRS (Kulka et al., 1990) provides perhaps the best and certainly the most extensive example, combining the use of and/or rules, prediction equations, and clinical decision-making based on expert consensus. Additional studies are sorely needed on this vital issue in order to determine which measures, in which combinations, and for which populations, best predict a PTSD diagnosis.

Clarifying Operational Definitions of PTSD Assessment Procedures

The issues discussed so far reflect various aspects of a broader concern, which is the need for much greater specificity in operational definitions of PTSD assessment procedures. Method sections of journal articles too often contain inadequate information regarding the selection, administration, and scoring of PTSD assessment measures. In general, when PTSD diagnostic status appears as a variable in a study, the method section should explicitly describe: (a) which diagnostic criteria were used (e.g., DSM-IV); (b) which instrument, and which version, was administered; (c) who administered the instrument, including credentials, experience assessing PTSD, training and experience with the specific instrument; (d) conditions under which the instrument was administered, including mode of administration (e.g., phone versus in-person, computer versus paper-and-pencil), setting (e.g., take-home versus lab, individual versus group administration), and when in the overall assessment the instrument was administered; (e) how the instrument was scored, and whether alternative scoring rules were explored; (f) how trauma was assessed, including how an index trauma was identified, how multiple traumatic events were handled,

and how symptom-event linking was handled; and (g) the inclusion and exclusion criteria for participation (e.g., male, treatment-seeking Vietnam combat veterans with no lifetime psychotic disorder and no current substance use disorder).

One area in particular that we feel needs much more attention from investigators is the specification and justification of scoring rules for converting dimensional scores to dichotomous diagnoses. Increasingly, the trend in PTSD assessment is toward measures that yield a range of scores for each symptom, indicating gradations of severity of a symptom rather than simply its presence or absence. The dimensional scores that result are ideal for many applications, but when a PTSD diagnosis is needed these dimensional measures must somehow be converted to a dichotomous decision for each individual being assessed.

There are a great many ways in which dimensional PTSD measures could be scored to yield a diagnosis. For most such measures, however, only a single, rationally derived scoring rule has been explored, typically with little empirical evidence supporting its use over alternate rules. This is unfortunate because the choice of a scoring rule can significantly influence the prevalence or base rate of PTSD in a sample. Scoring rules can range from lenient, whereby many individuals receive a diagnosis, to stringent, whereby few individuals receive a diagnosis. In our work with the CAPS, for example, we have developed and evaluated a number of different scoring rules, including rationally and empirically derived rules (Weathers, Meron, & Keane, 1997). We and others (Blanchard et al., 1995) have found that the original CAPS scoring rule, whereby symptoms are coded *present* if CAPS items are rated as *1* or higher for frequency and *2* or higher for intensity (on 4-point scales), is a relatively liberal rule that may "overdiagnose" in some circumstances. For some applications a more conservative rule may be better suited.

Given the lack of empirical evidence to-date on this crucial topic, we feel that it is incumbent upon developers of dimensional PTSD instruments to propose alternative scoring rules and conduct research comparing their diagnostic utility. Those who use these measures should, at a minimum, report which rule they employed in a given context and justify their choice. Further, when appropriate, they should use several different scoring rules and describe their relative impact on the results of the study.

PSYCHOMETRIC CONSIDERATIONS

In this section we provide a brief overview of the psychometric concepts, procedures, and issues involved in developing and evaluating new questionnaires or interviews (for a full treatment of this topic, see Weathers, Keane, King, & King, 1997). Psychological assessment instruments are evaluated in terms of their reliability and validity. Reliability is the degree to which test scores are free of measurement error, whereas validity is the degree to which test scores actually reflect the characteristic the test is thought to assess. In general, a reliable test yields consistent scores over repeated administrations and is relatively unaffected by potential sources of error, such as items and testing occasions. For PTSD instruments, as with other measures of psychopathology, the types of reliability that are of greatest concern are *internal consistency*, which refers to consistency over items on a test; *test-retest reliability*, which refers to consistency over repeated administrations of a test; and *interrater reliability*, which refers to consistency in test scores over different raters.

Internal consistency can be evaluated following a single administration of a test. It is typically quantified and reported as an alpha coefficient, an index that ranges from 0.00 to 1.00, with scores closer to 1.00 indicating greater intercorrelation of items. It is often accompanied by a report of the correlations between individual items and the total score for the remaining items (*item-scale total correlations*), which indicate how well individual items fit the other items on the scale. Test-retest reliability is determined by administering an instrument on two occasions and calculating the correlation between the two scores. One complication in a test-retest design is the length of the interval between administrations. If too brief a period is used (say, an hour), respondents' memory for how they answered previously may influence the second administration, so memory may be confounded with consistency of responding. On the other hand, if too long an interval is used (say, a month), genuine

change in clinical status may occur, confounding clinical change with consistency of responding.

For interviews, another pertinent type of reliability is interrater reliability, which involves two additional sources of error: differences in how interviewers elicit information and differences in how they score responses. In a simple interrater study, two or more raters observe the same interview and make simultaneous ratings. Alternatively, the interview can be audiotaped or videotaped and rated at a later time. This answers the question of whether different raters can make comparable ratings when they are exposed to the same information. A more stringent test of reliability is to have two raters conduct separate interviews on different occasions and make independent ratings. Like the simple interrater design, this "second opinion" design considers errors due to the way different raters use the scale, but also considers errors due to the way that different raters elicit information. For instruments yielding dimensional scores, interrater reliability is reported as a correlation coefficient or an intraclass correlation coefficient. For instruments yielding dichotomous (present/absent) decisions, reliability is reported as a kappa coefficient, a measure of agreement that is corrected for chance agreement between raters. A kappa of 0.00 indicates only chance agreement between two raters, whereas a kappa of 1.00 indicates perfect agreement.

Reliable instruments, though, are not necessarily valid. Validity refers to the accumulation of evidence supporting the inferences, interpretations, or conclusions that are made on the basis of test results. Three types of validity are considered. *Content validity* refers to evidence that items on an instrument adequately reflect the domain of interest. The evaluation of content validity is a complex, multistage process that typically includes such steps as specifying the main purposes of the instrument, carefully defining the construct, determining item format, generating a pool of items, and reviewing and revising items (see Haynes, Richard, & Kubany, 1995). Expert judgment plays a crucial role throughout the content validation process, particularly in the initial stages in which the instrument is conceived and items are created and revised. Content validation is essential for rationally developed instruments, such as the Mississippi Scale, which are developed in accordance with *a priori* theoretical conceptualizations. It is much less of a consideration for empirically developed measures, such as the PK scale of the MMPI and MMPI-2 (Keane, Malloy, & Fairbank, 1984; Lyons & Keane, 1992), which consist of items selected solely on the basis of their ability to discriminate individuals with and without a disorder.

Criterion-related validity refers to evidence that the test predicts some variable of interest, such as an outcome, behavior, or diagnosis. When the test and the criterion are measured at approximately the same time, this is known as *concurrent validity.* If the criterion is measured at some point after the test, this is known as *predictive validity.* A frequently evaluated form of concurrent validity for PTSD instruments is *diagnostic utility,* which is the extent to which an instrument predicts a PTSD diagnosis. Indices of diagnostic utility include *sensitivity* (the proportion of those with a positive diagnosis who have a positive test), *specificity* (the proportion of those with a negative diagnosis who have a negative test), and *efficiency* (the proportion of overall agreement between test and diagnosis). For PTSD measures that yield continuous scores, the diagnostic utility of a range of cutoff scores can be determined, and different cutoffs can be employed for different assessment purposes. In general, there is a tradeoff between sensitivity and specificity. Lenient cutoffs have greater sensitivity (but lower specificity) and are appropriate for screening, stringent cutoffs have greater specificity (but lower sensitivity) and are appropriate for confirming a diagnosis, and moderate cutoffs balance sensitivity and specificity and are appropriate for differential diagnosis.

Construct validity is the broadest form of validity and can be seen as subsuming the other types of validity. It refers to evidence that a test is primarily a measure of the construct of interest and not of other constructs. One of the most common approaches to establishing construct validity is to examine the pattern of correlations in a multitrait-multimethod correlation matrix (Campbell & Fiske, 1959), in which multiple measures of the construct of interest are compared to multiple measures of other conceptually distinct constructs. The construct validity of a measure is demonstrated by showing that it correlates strongly with other measures of the same construct (*convergent validity*) and correlates weakly with measures of other constructs (*discriminant validity*).

A final consideration regarding validity is what is known as *face validity.* Despite its name, this is not a true form of validity in the same sense as the other three types previously described. Rather, it refers to the degree to which the intent of a test and the content of its items are obvious to anyone who reads it, including test takers. As noted earlier, face validity renders many PTSD assessment instruments susceptible to symptom exaggeration or other types of response bias. Nonetheless, face validity may be unavoidable for rationally derived instruments and may even be desirable. When content validation procedures are carefully implemented, test items *should* reflect the domain of interest, and thus their content and intent will be obvious even to untrained observers. Another factor to consider in this regard is consumer satisfaction. Individuals undergoing an assessment for PTSD may feel puzzled or annoyed if test items appear to be irrelevant, even if the test is valid for assessing PTSD.

PTSD ASSESSMENT INSTRUMENTS

In this section we briefly review a number of structured interviews and self-report instruments for assessing PTSD, including well-established and widely used measures as well as several promising, newly published measures (for further description and contact information regarding these and other measures, see Stamm, 1996). When selecting a PTSD instrument clinicians or investigators must first address the fundamental validity question: What task is the instrument intended to accomplish and what evidence supports its use for that purpose? All of the conceptual, methodological, and psychometric issues discussed earlier are relevant to this question and will shape an appropriate answer. The next step is to address a number of practical considerations, including the amount of time available for the assessment, whether interviewers are available, and whether the format and content of the instrument are appropriate for the assessment task (see Weathers, Keane et al., 1997).

PTSD measures vary widely in format, most importantly in terms of (a) the method of administration (i.e., interview, paper and pencil, computer); (b) the wording of items or prompt questions; (c) the nature of the rating scale, including both the number of points on the scale and the way in which symptom severity is defined in the rating scale anchors (e.g, in terms of frequency of symptoms or subjective distress); and (d) the time frame assessed (e.g., past week, past month). In terms of content, all structured interviews are based directly on the DSM diagnostic criteria. However, the PTSD consensus conference divided the self-report measures of PTSD into three categories: those corresponding exactly to the DSM criteria, those tapping the core and associated features of PTSD but not corresponding exactly to the DSM criteria, and those derived empirically from existing instruments.

The consensus conference recommended that a structured interview be used to assess PTSD whenever feasible. It further recommended that a structured interview, administered by an experienced clinician and yielding both continuous and dichotomous scores, be required when an in-depth assessment of PTSD is the focus of an investigation. According to the consensus conference, DSM-correspondent self-report measures are appropriate for screening, for survey research where interviewing is not possible, or as adjuncts to a structured interview. In contrast, measures that are PTSD-focused but not DSM-correspondent should be administered only in conjunction with a structured interview or a DSM-correspondent self-report measure whenever possible. Empirically derived instruments should also be administered in conjunction with other measures, and should only be used as the sole measure of PTSD when no other measures are available, as in the case of archival data sets.

Interviews

Structured Clinical Interview for DSM-III-R (SCID). The SCID (Spitzer et al., 1990) is a comprehensive structured interview that assesses all of the major Axis I disorders. Although the published version of the SCID for the DSM-III-R did not contain a PTSD module, one was created for use in the NVVRS (Kulka et al., 1990) and has since become one of the most widely used PTSD interviews. A revised PTSD module will be included in the DSM-IV version of the SCID. As with other modules of the SCID, the PTSD module follows the DSM diagnostic criteria exactly. A standard prompt question is provided for each of the 17 PTSD symptoms, and interviewers rate each symptom as *? = inadequate information, 1 = absent, 2 = subthreshold,* or *3 = threshold.* Interviewers are encouraged to ask additional questions or to clarify as needed in order to obtain accurate information.

The SCID PTSD module appears to have adequate reliability and validity. In the NVVRS, Kulka et al. (1991) found a kappa of .93 when audiotaped SCID interviews were independently scored by a second clinician. In a more stringent test of reliability, Keane et al. (1997) found a kappa of .68 when the SCID PTSD module was administered twice by independent clinicians. Also, in the NVVRS the SCID was positively associated with other measures of PTSD, including the Mississippi Scale (kappa = .53), and the PK scale of the MMPI (kappa = .48), and had excellent sensitivity (.81) and specificity (.98) against a composite PTSD diagnosis (Kulka et al., 1991; Schlenger et al., 1992). The primary limitation of the SCID is that it yields essentially dichotomous data at the item and syndrome levels and thus is not well-suited for quantifying or detecting changes in symptom severity.

Diagnostic Interview Schedule (DIS). The DIS is a highly structured, comprehensive interview designed for use by lay interviewers in the context of epidemiological research. Variants of the DIS PTSD module have been used in all of the recent major epidemiological investigations of PTSD (Breslau, Davis, Andreski, & Peterson, 1991; Centers for Disease Control, 1988; Helzer, Robins, & McEvoy, 1987; Kessler et al., 1995; Kulka et al., 1990; Resnick et al., 1993). Like the SCID, the DIS provides a standard prompt question for each of the 17 PTSD symptoms, but interviewers are discouraged from clarifying any of the standard questions or making additional inquiries. Each symptom is scored dichotomously to indicate its presence or absence.

Although the DIS has been widely used, serious concerns have been raised about its diagnostic utility. In the preliminary validation study of the NVVRS, the DIS was found to be one of the best predictors of a clinical diagnosis of PTSD, with a sensitivity of .87, a specificity of .73, an efficiency of .84, and a kappa of .64. However, in the clinical examination component, when tested against a SCID-based PTSD diagnosis, specificity was quite high (.98), but sensitivity (.22) and kappa (.26) were poor (Kulka et al., 1991). Other investigators have subsequently made a number of modifications to the DIS module to improve its diagnostic utility, and these efforts appear to have been reasonably successful (e.g., Kessler et al., 1995; Resnick et al., 1993).

PTSD Symptom Scale—Interview (PSS I). The PSS-I (Foa, Riggs, Dancu, & Rothbaum, 1993) is a structured interview specifically designed to assess DSM-III-R PTSD symptoms. It contains 17 items, each consisting of a single prompt question corresponding to one of the 17 diagnostic criteria for PTSD. Interviewers rate the severity of each symptom over the past two weeks as *0 = not at all, 1 = a little bit, 2 = somewhat,* or *3 = very much.* A total severity score is obtained by summing ratings over all 17 items. A PTSD diagnosis is obtained by considering symptom ratings of *1* or higher as *present,* then following the DSM-III-R diagnostic algorithm.

The PSS I appears to have excellent psychometric properties. Foa et al. (1993) reported an alpha coefficient of .85 for all 17 items and an average item-scale total correlation of .45. Test-retest reliability for the total severity score was .80, and the kappa coefficient for a diagnosis of PTSD was .91. Against a SCID-based PTSD diagnosis, the PSS-I had a sensitivity of .88, a specificity of .96, and an efficiency of .94. The PSS-I also correlated strongly with the IES and the Rape Aftermath Symptom Test (RAST; Kilpatrick, 1988), as well as the BDI and STAI.

The advantages of the PSS-I are that it yields continuous and dichotomous scores, is easy to administer, and has good reliability and validity for assessing PTSD. The disadvantages are that it includes only a single prompt question for each item, its rating anchors are not explicitly defined, it assesses symptoms over a two-week rather than the one-month period required in the DSM-IV PTSD criteria, and it does not address lifetime diagnostic status. Also, the proposed scoring rule was rationally rather than empirically derived, and alternative rules have not been explored.

Structured Interview for PTSD (SI-PTSD). The SI-PTSD (Davidson, Smith, & Kudler, 1989) is a structured interview originally designed to assess both DSM-III and DSM-III-R criteria for PTSD. Items consist of initial prompt questions and follow-up questions that clarify the initial question with concrete behavioral examples. The severity of each symptom is rated on a 5-point scale, both for the past month and for the worst period since the trauma. Rating scale anchors vary across items, but generally follow the pattern of *0 = none, 1 = mild, 2 = moderate, 3 = severe, 4 = extremely severe.* Descriptors are provided for rating scale anchors to clarify what is meant by a given rating. A total severity score is obtained by summing ratings over all 17 symptoms, and symptoms are counted toward a PTSD diagnosis when they are rated as 2 or higher.

The SI-PTSD appears to be psychometrically sound. Davidson et al. (1989) reported an overall alpha of .94, test-retest reliability of .71, and remarkably strong interrater reliability, with intraclass correlations ranging from .97 to .99 and 100 percent diagnostic agreement. Against a SCID diagnosis of PTSD, the SI-PTSD had a sensitivity of .96, a specificity of .80, and a kappa of .79.

The advantages of the SI-PTSD are that it yields both continuous and dichotomous scores, it provides follow-up prompts and descriptors for rating scale anchors, and it has documented reliability and validity. The disadvantages are that it relies on a single, rationally derived scoring rule, and that it uses a "worst ever" convention for assessing lifetime ratings for individual symptoms, making it difficult to establish that lifetime symptoms occurred as part of a syndrome.

PTSD Interview (PTSD-I). The PTSD-I (Watson, Juba, Manifold, Kucala, & Anderson, 1991) is a structured interview for assessing the DSM-III-R criteria for PTSD. Individual PTSD symptoms are inquired with a single prompt question, and severity ratings are made on a 7-point scale ranging from *1 = No/Never* to *7 = Extremely/Always.* A total severity score is computed by summing ratings over the 17 symptoms, and symptoms are considered present if they are rated as *4 = Somewhat/Commonly* or higher. Lifetime diagnostic status is established through several questions about chronology that follow symptom inquiry.

Watson et al. (1991) reported strong reliability and validity for the PTSD-I. The alpha coefficient over all 17 items was .92. Test-retest reliability over a 1-week interval was .95, with 87 percent diagnostic agreement between the two administrations. Against a PTSD diagnosis based on the DIS, the PTSD-I had a sensitivity of .89, a specificity of .94, an efficiency of .92, and a kappa of .84.

The PTSD-I yields both continuous and dichotomous scores and appears to have desirable psychometric properties. A major limitation, however, is the recommended format for administration. Interviewers are instructed to give respondents a copy of the rating scale, read the questions aloud, and ask respondents to rate themselves. Like the DIS, little or no clinical judgment is involved in the assessment of PTSD symptoms. Although the PTSD-I could be implemented in other ways, the current format is more like a questionnaire than a structured interview.

Clinician-Administered PTSD Scale (CAPS). The CAPS (Blake et al., 1990; Blake et al., 1995) is a comprehensive structured interview for PTSD developed at the National Center for PTSD. Intended for use by clinicians experienced with PTSD and structured interviewing, the CAPS has several features that were designed to address some of the limitations of other PTSD interviews. First, the CAPS assesses the 17 core symptoms of PTSD, as well as associated symptoms, response validity, overall symptom severity, and the impact of symptoms on social and occupational functioning. Second, the CAPS assesses the frequency and intensity of each symptom on separate 5-point rating scales, yielding continuous and dichotomous scores for each symptom and across all 17 symptoms. Third, the CAPS contains behaviorally anchored prompt questions and rating scales to help

increase the reliability of symptom inquiry and severity ratings. Fourth, the CAPS provides specific guidelines for assessing lifetime PTSD diagnostic status, ensuring that a respondent experienced symptoms as part of a syndrome lasting at least one month. Finally, several rationally and empirically derived scoring rules have been developed for converting continuous frequency and intensity scores into dichotomous scores (Weathers, Meron, & Keane, 1997).

As with most of the other interviews described in this section, the CAPS has very strong reliability and validity. Weathers, Blake et al. (1997) found an alpha coefficient of .94 for the 17 core PTSD symptoms, and test-retest reliability coefficients ranging from .90 to .98 for total severity. Using the optimal empirically derived scoring rule, the test-retest reliability for a PTSD diagnosis was .89. Against a PTSD diagnosis based on the SCID, this same scoring rule had a sensitivity of .91, a specificity of .86, an efficiency of .89, and a kappa of .77. With respect to convergent and discriminant validity, the CAPS correlated strongly with other measures of PTSD, including the Mississippi Scale and the PK scale, and correlated moderately with measures of anxiety and depression, but correlated only weakly with measures of antisocial personality disorder.

The CAPS was recently revised for the DSM-IV. Notable changes include (a) adding a protocol to assess Criterion A, including a screening questionnaire and follow-up prompts administered by the interviewer; (b) adding a *trauma-related* convention that requires interviewers to rate the link between a symptom and a specific trauma as *definite, probable,* or *unlikely;* (c) replacing several associated features with items assessing the dissociative symptoms that are included in the criteria for acute stress disorder; (d) clarifying the rating scale anchors to enhance consistency of ratings across items. Also, to avoid confusion about the two forms of the CAPS, the current and lifetime diagnostic version, previously known as the CAPS-1, is now called the CAPS-DX, and the one-week symptom status version, previously known as the CAPS-2, is now called the CAPS-SX. Although the CAPS has many strengths, its major limitation is that it typically takes longer than other PTSD interviews to administer.

Self-Report Measures

DSM-Correspondent Measures.

PTSD Checklist (PCL).   The PCL (Weathers, Litz, Herman, Huska, & Keane, 1993; Weathers, Litz et al., 1997) is a 17-item PTSD scale developed in 1990 at the National Center for PTSD for use in establishing the construct validity of the CAPS. Originally based on DSM-III-R PTSD criteria, it was revised in 1994 to correspond to the DSM-IV PTSD criteria. Using a 5-point scale ranging from *1 = not at all* to *5 = extremely,* respondents rate how much they were bothered by each PTSD symptom over the past month. There are three versions of the PCL, which differ only in the target event specified in the reexperiencing and effortful avoidance items. The civilian version (PCL-C) refers broadly to *a stressful experience from the past,* the military version (PCL-M) refers to *a stressful military experience,* and the specific version (PCL-S) refers to a specific stressor identified by the respondent. The PCL-C and the PCL-M are appropriate when a specific trauma has not been identified, and the PCL-S is appropriate when a trauma history has been taken and a stressor has been targeted for symptom inquiry.

Weathers, Litz et al. (1997) reported excellent psychometric properties for the PCL across four different samples of male and female veterans. In the original validation sample of 123 male Vietnam veterans, test-retest reliability was .96 and alpha over all 17 items was .97. The PCL correlated strongly with other measures of PTSD, including the Mississippi Scale, the PK scale, and the IES, and correlated moderately with level of combat exposure. Against a PTSD diagnosis based on the SCID, a cutoff score of 50 on the PCL yielded a sensitivity of .82, a specificity of .83, and a kappa of .64. The PCL has been used successfully in other traumatized populations as well, including motor vehicle accident victims (Blanchard, Jones-Alexander, Buckley, & Forneris, 1996) and breast cancer survivors (Cordova et al., 1995).

PTSD Symptom Scale-Self-Report (PSS-SR).   The PSS-SR (Foa et al., 1993) is the self-report counterpart to the PSS-I. With the exception of six reworded items, the PSS-SR is identical to the PSS-I in item content, rating scale, and scoring. Like the PSS-I, the PSS-SR has solid reliability and validity. According to Foa et al. (1993), test-retest reliability for total severity over a 1-month interval was .74, and alpha for the 17 items was .91. with respect to validity, the PSS-SR correlated strongly with the RAST, the IES, the BDI, and the STAI. It also had a sensitivity of .62, a specificity of 1.00, and an efficiency of .86 against a SCID-based PTSD diagnosis. Regarding diagnostic agreement between the PSS-SR and the PSS-I, Foa et al. found a kappa of .73, indicating good correspondence between the two formats.

Falsetti, Resnick, Resick, and Kilpatrick (1993) revised the PSS-SR, slightly rewording six items and adding a 4-point rating scale to assess the frequency of each PTSD symptom. The resulting measure, known as the Modified PTSD Symptom Scale-Self-Report (MPSS-SR), yields both continuous and dichotomous scores and appears to have good psychometric properties. Like the other versions of the PSS, however, the MPSS-SR assesses symptoms over the past two weeks and does not assess lifetime symptom status.

Purdue PTSD Scale-Revised (PPTSD-R).   The PPTSD-R (Lauterbach & Vrana, 1996) is a 17-item measure corresponding to the DSM-III-R PTSD criteria. Items are rated on a 5-point scale, from *1 = not at all* to *5 = often,* indicating the frequency of symptoms over the past month. Lauterbach and Vrana (1996) reported excellent psychometric properties for the PPTSD-R in three samples of college students. Test-retest reliability for total severity over a 2-week interval was .72, and alpha over all 17 items was .91. Further, the PPTSD-R correlated strongly with the IES and the civilian version of the Mississippi Scale, and correlated moderately with the STAI and the BDI. Finally, PPTSD-R scores were significantly higher in participants reporting more severe traumatic events, and also were higher in those seeking treatment for trauma-related difficulties relative to those seeking treatment for other reasons as well as non-treatment-seeking participants. The PPTSD-R has promise as a self-report measure of PTSD, although more research is needed with other populations. Research is also needed to determine its diagnostic utility against a PTSD diagnosis based on a structured interview.

Posttraumatic Stress Diagnostic Scale (PDS). The PDS (Foa, 1995) is a newly published self-report measure of PTSD that has the distinction of being the only self-report measure to assess all six (A-F) criteria for PTSD in the DSM-IV. Part 1 of the PDS is a 13-item checklist of potential traumatic events. Part 2 consists of eight items that help determine if an event meets the DSM-IV definition of Criterion A. Part 3 assesses the frequency over the past month of the 17 PTSD symptoms, using a 4-point scale ranging from *0 = Not at all or only one time* to *3 = 5 or more times a week/almost always.* Part 4 assesses the impact of symptoms on various aspects of social and occupational functioning. The PDS yields both a dichotomous diagnostic score and a continuous symptom severity score. An individual PTSD symptom is counted as *present* if the corresponding PDS item is endorsed as a *1* or higher.

The PDS manual describes desirable psychometric properties for the scale in a normative sample of 248 adults assessed in a variety of clinical and research settings. Over an interval of approximately two weeks, test-retest reliability for symptom severity was .83, with a kappa of .74 for diagnostic agreement between the two administrations. The PDS had reasonable diagnostic utility against a PTSD diagnosis based on the SCID, with a sensitivity of .82, a specificity of .77, an efficiency of .79, and a kappa of .59. Convergent validity was demonstrated through strong correlations with the IES, the STAI, and the BDI. Although these results require confirmation in other studies, the PDS appears to have considerable promise as a measure of the DSM-IV PTSD criteria.

Davidson Trauma Scale (DTS). The DTS (Davidson, 1996) is another recently published self-report measure of PTSD, consisting of 17 items corresponding to the DSM-IV PTSD symptoms. Respondents first identify a traumatic event that is most disturbing to them, then rate the frequency and severity of each symptom over the past week on separate 5-point rating scales. Frequency ratings range from *0 = Not at all* to *4 = Every day* and severity ratings range from *0 = Not at all distressing* to *4 = Extremely distressing.* The DTS appears to be designed primarily to yield continuous scores of PTSD symptom severity. The manual provides a novel table for converting total DTS scores into a PTSD diagnosis, based on the ratio of PTSD cases to non-cases at each cutoff score as well as on the expected base rate of PTSD in the target population. However, no scoring rules are provided for converting frequency and severity ratings for individual symptoms into dichotomous scores.

Based on data from four different samples described in the manual, the DTS appears to be psychometrically sound. Test-retest reliability for total DTS scores over a 1-week interval was .86, and alpha coefficients for frequency, severity, and total scores were all greater than .90. The DTS also showed good convergent validity, correlating strongly with the CAPS, the IES, and several other measures of trauma-related psychopathology. Further, the DTS was found to be sensitive both to differences in clinical severity of PTSD and to improvement in symptoms as a result of treatment. Finally, the manual provides diagnostic utility data for several cutoff scores on the DTS. A cutoff of 40, for example, had a sensitivity of .69, a specificity of .95, and an efficiency of 83.

Like the PDS, the DTS shows promise as a self-report measure of PTSD. The one-week time frame is at odds with the DSM-IV requirement of a one-month duration for PTSD symptoms, but it might be effective for tracking treatment progress when multiple assessments over brief intervals are desired. Also, it may be useful to devise and evaluate different scoring rules for the DTS, especially for converting frequency and severity scores to dichotomous scores.

PTSD-Focused, Non-DSM-Correspondent Measures.

Impact of Event Scale (IES). The IES (Horowitz et al., 1979) was the first standardized measure of posttraumatic symptomatology to appear and is also one of the most widely used. Based on Horowitz's (1976) conceptual model of responses to stressful life events, the IES consists of 15 items, including 7 items assessing intrusive symptoms and 8 items assessing avoidance. Respondents first specify a stressful event, then rate the frequency of each symptom over the past week on a 4-point scale, with anchors of *Not at all, Rarely, Sometimes,* and *Often.* Horowitz et al. (1979) reported strong test-retest reliability (.87 for intrusion and .79 for avoidance) and internal consistency (alphas of .79 for intrusion and .82 for avoidance). Horowitz et al. also found a correlation of .42 between the two subscales, suggesting that intrusion and avoidance are related but distinct responses to significant stressors. These psychometric findings were confirmed by Zilberg, Weiss, and Horowitz (1982), and the distinction between intrusion and avoidance has been supported through several factor analyses (e.g., Schwarzwald, Solomon, Weisenberg, & Mikulincer, 1987; Zilberg et al, 1982).

Although the IES taps two key dimensions of PTSD, it does not correspond completely to the PTSD diagnostic criteria. The IES was recently revised to more directly assess the PTSD symptoms in the DSM-III-R and DSM-IV (Weiss & Marmar, 1997). The most significant change was the addition of six items assessing hyperarousal and one item assessing dissociative reexperiencing. These new items bring the IES closer to the current diagnostic criteria, although the fit is still not as close as it is for the DSM-correspondent measures described in the previous section. The IES does not assess some PTSD diagnostic criteria at all (e.g., diminished interest, foreshortened future), and assesses others only indirectly or ambiguously (e.g., restricted range of affect, inability to recall the trauma).

Other important revisions to the IES include two changes to the rating scale. First, rather than rating symptom frequency, respondents are now instructed to rate the degree of distress associated with each symptom. Second, symptoms are now rated on a 5-point scale, ranging from *0 = Not at all* to *4 = Extremely,* instead of the original 4-point scale. These changes should not preclude reasonable comparability with previous research employing the original IES, but given the confusion over scoring of the original IES (see Green, 1991), test users will need to carefully specify which version of the IES they used and how it was scored.

Mississippi Scale for Combat-Related PTSD (Mississippi Scale).   The Mississippi Scale (Keane et al., 1988) is the most widely used measure of combat-

related PTSD and has been the subject of extensive, sophisticated psychometric analysis. It consists of 35 items selected from an initial item pool of 200 items based on the DSM-III PTSD criteria and associated features. Items are rated on a 5-point scale, with anchors that vary according to item content (e.g., *1 = Never* to *5 = Very Frequently, 1 = Never True* to *5 = Always True*).

The Mississippi Scale has demonstrated consistently strong psychometric properties across a growing number of investigations. In the NVVRS, it was chosen as one of the primary PTSD indicators based on its excellent performance in the preliminary validation study and the clinical examination component (Kulka et al., 1991). Keane et al. (1988) found an alpha of .94 over all 35 items, and a one-week test-retest reliability of .97. They also found that a cutoff of 107 had a sensitivity of .93, a specificity of .89, and an efficiency of .90 against a consensus clinical diagnosis of PTSD. These results were replicated and extended by McFall et al., (1990), who found moderate to strong correlations between the Mississippi Scale and measures of combat exposure, PTSD, and anger. Recent research has focused on intensive examination of the psychometric properties of individual items (King, King, Fairbank, Schlenger, & Surface, 1993) and on the scale's underlying factor structure (King & King, 1994).

A civilian version of the Mississippi Scale, developed for assessing civilian PTSD in the NVVRS, is also available. The main modification involved rephrasing items containing references to the military. The latest version includes four items added to provide better coverage of the DSM-III-R criteria for PTSD. An initial investigation of its psychometric properties indicated that it performs well but may benefit from some revision (Vreven, Gudanowski, King, & King, 1995).

Penn Inventory for Posttraumatic Stress Disorder (Penn Inventory).   The Penn Inventory (Hammarberg, 1992) is a 26-item scale based on the DSM-III and DSM-III-R PTSD criteria. Its item format differs from the other self-report measures described in this section. Modeled after the BDI, items on the Penn consist of four statements, scored 0 to 3, reflecting increasing symptom severity. In terms of item content, coverage of the DSM-III-R criteria is not complete (e.g., no items explicitly for hypervigilance, physiological reactivity, effortful avoidance), and many items tap symptoms that are not part of the core criteria for PTSD (e.g., alienation, alterations in self-perception, disruptions in goal-directed behavior, grief), although a case could be made that they are important associated features.

In three samples including combat veterans and civilian trauma survivors, Hammarberg reported excellent psychometric properties for the Penn Inventory. In the first sample, across all participants and items alpha was .94 and test-retest reliability was .96. An overall alpha of .94 was replicated in the second sample. A cutoff of 35 yielded a sensitivity of .90, a specificity of 1.00, and an efficiency of .94, although these figures are likely partially attributable to the sampling scheme used to create the study groups. This high level of diagnostic accuracy was also replicated in the second sample. The Penn Inventory correlated strongly with the IES and the Mississippi Scale, as well with the BDI, BAI, and STAI, and correlated moderately with level of combat exposure.

Empirically Derived Measures.

PK Scale of the MMPI and MMPI-2.   The original PK scale (Keane et al., 1984) consists of 49 items on the MMPI that were found to statistically discriminate Vietnam combat veterans with and without PTSD. Keane et al. (1984) found that a cutoff score of 30 correctly classified 82 percent of veterans in both a validation and a cross-validation sample. Subsequent investigations of the PK scale have generally confirmed its diagnostic utility, although results have varied considerably across studies, probably largely due to differences in sample characteristics and diagnostic procedures. Also, mean scores and optimal cutoff scores have typically been lower than those reported by Keane et al.

Watson, Kucala, and Manifold (1986), for example, found a sensitivity of .87 and a specificity of .74 when distinguishing between combat veterans with PTSD and normal controls, but a sensitivity of .73 and a specificity of .53 for distinguishing between

PTSD patients and patients with other psychiatric disorders. Cannon, Bell, Andrews, and Finkelstein (1987) found a sensitivity of .76 and a specificity of .64 for distinguishing between veteran psychiatric inpatients with and without PTSD. The PK scale has also been used successfully with civilian trauma victims. Koretzky and Peck (1990) found that a cutoff score of 19 correctly classified 87 percent and 88 percent of participants in two different samples.

When the revised version of the MMPI, the MMPI-2, was published, two minor modifications were made to the PK scale, including dropping three repeated items and rewording one item (see Lyons & Keane, 1992). In the normative samples for the MMPI-2, the 46-item PK scale had good internal consistency, with alphas of .85 for males and .87 for females, and good test-retest reliability, with correlations of .86 for males and .89 for females.

The utility of the PK scale in a stand-alone format has also been explored. Lyons and Scotti (1994) found that 94 percent of the veterans in their sample were classified similarly on the PK scale of the MMPI when it was administered both in the context of the full MMPI and as a separate instrument. Herman, Weathers, Litz, & Keane (1996) conducted an comprehensive evaluation of the PK scale of the MMPI-2 as a stand-alone measure. They found a correlation of .90 between the stand-alone and embedded versions of the PK scale. For the stand-alone version, alpha was .96 and test-retest reliability over 2–3 days was .95. A cutoff of 24 on the stand-alone version yielded a sensitivity of .82, a specificity of .76, and a kappa of .59 against a SCID-based PTSD diagnosis. The stand-alone version also correlated strongly with the Mississippi Scale, the IES, the PCL, and the CAPS, and correlated moderately with combat exposure.

Symptom Checklist-90-R (SCL-90-R) PTSD Scales. The SCL-90-R (Derogatis, 1983) has been widely used in PTSD assessment batteries and several investigators have attempted to derive PTSD subscales from its items. For example, Saunders, Arata, and Kilpatrick (1990) identified 28 SCL-90-R items that discriminated female crime victims with and without PTSD. This subscale, the Crime-Related PTSD scale

(CR-PTSD), had an alpha of .93 and correctly classified 89 percent of the sample. Using a similar approach, Weathers et al. (1996) identified 25 items that discriminated combat veterans with and without PTSD. This subscale, the War-Zone-Related PTSD scale (WZ-PTSD), which shares fewer than half its items with the CR-PTSD scale, had an alpha of .97. A cutoff score of 1.3 had a sensitivity of .90, a specificity of .65, and a kappa of .58. This put it second only behind the Mississippi Scale in terms of diagnostic utility, and higher than the Global Severity Index (GSI), although not to a statistically significant degree. These results were replicated in a cross-validation sample. Green (1991) has argued that while the SCL-90-R may be useful in the assessment of PTSD, PTSD subscales are not likely to improve significantly on what can be achieved with the GSI.

ASSESSMENT SCENARIOS

In this section we present a number of assessment scenarios that typify many of our clinical and research endeavors. Reflecting a variety of assessment questions, these scenarios illustrate our solutions to many of the issues raised throughout this chapter. These solutions are intended to be descriptive rather than prescriptive. With respect to the selection of specific measures, we use the instruments with which we are most familiar, either those we have developed in our lab or those we feel are best suited to our needs. As can be seen from the previous section, there are multiple measures in each category that would perform adequately, so our main goal is to encourage others to adopt standardized measures for each of the essential tasks, not to insist that certain measures be used over others. Each assessment situation poses unique challenges requiring tailor-made solutions. However, to the extent that these scenarios generalize to those faced by other clinicians and investigators, they may provide a helpful starting point.

Scenario 1: Brief Clinical Assessment

Our clinical assessments vary according to the referral question, ranging from a relatively brief (1–2 hour) inpatient consultation to a comprehensive (8–10 hour) outpatient evaluation. A typical brief consultation, for which the goal is usually to simply determine if the respondent has a diagnosis of PTSD, consists of the following components:

1. A history of the present illness, including a review of previous episodes, previous treatment, and precipitants of current episode; screening for current and past psychopathology; and a brief review of social history. The overview section of the SCID is a very useful guide for this portion of the evaluation.

2. A CAPS to assess current and lifetime PTSD. This includes the Life Events Checklist (LEC) to screen for lifetime trauma, which is completed by the respondent and followed up by the clinician. Symptom inquiry focuses primarily on the identified trauma, which in our clinic is usually war-zone trauma, but also may focus on other traumas identified by the LEC. To reach a categorical diagnostic decision we use the original, rationally derived scoring rule whereby an item rated with a frequency of "1" or higher and an intensity of "2" or higher counts as a symptom toward a PTSD diagnosis. We then follow the DSM-IV diagnostic algorithm, which calls for at least one reexperiencing symptom, three avoidance and numbing symptoms, and two hyperarousal symptoms, plus the requirements regarding duration and subjective distress or functional impairment. We view this as a minimum threshold, since the "1–2" rule, with the minimum number of symptoms in each cluster, is the most lenient cutoff at which we would still feel comfortable diagnosing PTSD. Most clients in our clinic score well above this minimum threshold and clearly meet diagnostic criteria, but if someone scored below this level we would also feel confident in stating that they did not meet the DSM-IV diagnostic criteria for PTSD.

3. A Mississippi Scale. On occasion, the time available for a consultation is quite limited, and the referral question may simply be whether a patient should be referred for a more extensive evaluation. In this case, the assessment might consist of asking a patient to complete a PCL with respect to an index trauma, then briefly reviewing their answers with them.

Scenario 2: Comprehensive Clinical Assessment

Comprehensive assessments involve a more extensive evaluation of the areas noted above, with the goal of not only reaching a diagnosis of PTSD but of developing a rich case conceptualization. Additional components include:

1. A more detailed social history, with a more thorough exploration of traumatic events and other stressors across the life span. This is accomplished with a semi-structured clinical interview, along with the Evaluation of Lifetime Stressors (ELS; Krinsley, 1996), which consists of a screening questionnaire and a follow-up structured interview.

2. An MMPI-2, which provides information about PTSD (e.g., PK scale, F-2-8 profile) and other psychopathology, and which, most importantly, is the only instrument in our clinical battery with scales designed to formally assess response style (e.g., symptom exaggeration or minimization).

3. A more comprehensive assessment of comorbid psychopathology, by means of questionnaires and structured interviews. In terms of interviews, this component involves a SCID to assess mood, anxiety, psychotic, and substance use disorders, and, if warranted, a SCID-II to assess personality disorders. Questionnaires include the Beck Depression Inventory (BDI), the Beck Anxiety Inventory (BAI; Beck, Epstein, Brown, & Steer, 1988), the State-Trait Anger Expression Inventory (STAXI; Spielberger, Reheiser, & Sydeman, 1995), and the Symptom Checklist-90-Revised (SCL-90-R).

4. A psychophysiological evaluation, using either standard trauma-related stimuli, or standard stimuli plus idiographic stimuli based on the patient's unique trauma history.

Scenario 3: Survey with a Self-Report Instrument

In survey research the emphasis is typically on determining PTSD caseness in order to estimate prevalence rates and identify risk factors. Ideally, survey designs involve two stages: the survey stage, in which the survey instruments are administered to the full sample, and the validation stage, wherein a subset of respondents are also administered a diagnostic interview in order to calibrate the survey instruments for the sample. If the second stage is not feasible, it may still be possible to estimate prevalence in the survey sample by adopting scoring algorithms from a similar sample for which solid validity data are available. If neither of these approaches is possible, a rationally derived scoring algorithm may be used to estimate prevalence (e.g., scores of 2 or greater on a 5-point scale count as symptoms toward a diagnosis). However, this is much less satisfactory since it is not empirically justified for the specific sample.

For survey instruments consisting only of self-report measures, a thorny issue is how best to assess trauma. As discussed earlier, the questions are how to determine without an interview whether a respondent has experienced an event that would satisfy Criterion A and how to identify an event or events to serve as the focus for PTSD symptom inquiry. This is not a problem when a survey addresses the impact of a specific trauma or type of trauma, such as combat, rape, or disaster. But when a survey is designed to assess PTSD arising from any type of traumatic event, and respondents endorse multiple events on a self-report trauma checklist, they must be instructed as to which event to keep in mind as they rate their PTSD symptoms. Some possible approaches are:

1. Use PTSD measures that refer to a nonspecific traumatic event and don't try to link PTSD symptoms to a specific event, even if the survey includes a self-report measure of traumatic events. We would use the PCL, since it directly corresponds to the DSM-IV diagnostic criteria for PTSD and yields both a diagnosis and a dimensional severity score, and the Mississippi Scale, since it assesses associated features and has consistently emerged as the most valid self-report measure of PTSD. Depending on the target population, we would use either the civilian or military versions of these scales, and if feasible would calibrate them for the target population by administering a CAPS to a subsample of respondents.

2. Focus on a specific trauma population, such as combat veterans, rape victims, or disaster survivors, and instruct respondents to respond to items assessing PTSD symptoms with this index event in mind. In this case, we would use the specific version of the PCL and ask respondents to write in the event they experienced. Again, depending on the target population, we would also use either the civilian or military version of the Mississippi Scale, and would calibrate it if possible against the CAPS.

3. Use a self-report trauma checklist, instructing respondents to choose the event they consider the worst and respond to items assessing PTSD symptoms with that event in mind. To assess trauma exposure, we would use an extended version of the LEC that assesses both parts of the DSM-IV definition of Criterion A, as well as the chronology, frequency, and type of exposure, for a broad range of traumatic events. For a study of war-zone trauma, we would also use the Combat Exposure Scale (CES). To assess PTSD symptoms, we would use the specific version of the PCL and the civilian version of the Mississippi Scale. The recently published PDS also appears promising for this application, as it is the only self-report PTSD measure that assesses all DSM-IV diagnostic criteria for PTSD, including Criterion A.

Scenario 4: Survey with an Interview-Based Instrument

Most of the considerations described in the previous scenario also apply when a survey is administered by an interviewer. The key differences are that the interviewer can (a) judge whether stressful events that the respondent describes meet Criterion A, (b) help the respondent select one or more events for symptom inquiry, and (c) determine if reported symptoms are attributable to a specific event.

In survey research the time allotted for an assessment is usually quite limited. Also, due to the expense of interviewing large samples, lay interviewers are typically used instead of trained clinicians. For these reasons, measures such as the DIS were designed for use in large-scale epidemiological investigations. The DIS is highly structured, with little if any follow-up or clarification permitted. As noted earlier, the DIS has been used in a number of survey studies of PTSD, and has proven useful for this application. However, one of its limitations is that symptoms are rated only as present or absent. We see no reason why, for at least some applications, lay interviewers couldn't be

trained to administer interviews such as the PSS-I instead, which would yield both dichotomous ratings for symptoms and the PTSD diagnosis as well as dimensional scores reflecting PTSD symptom severity.

Scenario 5: Correlational Study

In some sense, any study involving PTSD and at least one other construct could be considered to be a correlational design. What we are referring to here, though, are studies comparing one or more measures of PTSD to measures of other constructs in an explicit correlational framework such as a multitrait-multimethod correlation matrix, a multiple regression equation, or a structural equation model. Our recommendations for this type of study are to use a structured interview for PTSD that yields dimensional severity scores for each symptom, and to use multiple measures of PTSD and all other constructs involved in the study. Self-report PTSD measures might include a DSM-correspondent scale and one or more PTSD-focused but non-DSM-correspondent scales. As a minimum battery for PTSD we would use the CAPS, the appropriate PCL, and the combat or civilian version of the Mississippi Scale. For large-scale assessment studies we would add the MMPI-2, since it would provide the PK scale as well as measures of other constructs and measures of response bias. We might also add the TSI, since it assesses a broad range of trauma-related outcomes and provides additional information about response bias.

Scenario 6: Case-Control Study

In case-control research the investigator assembles relatively homogeneous groups of participants and compares their characteristics or performance on some experimental task. Critical to this approach is the specification of explicit inclusion and exclusion criteria for the groups to be compared. In PTSD research, the PTSD group consists of participants who, at a minimum, unambiguously meet all of the DSM-IV diagnostic criteria for the disorder. There is also at least one control or comparison group composed of participants who unambiguously do *not* meet diagnostic criteria for PTSD. Other specifications might involve type of trauma (e.g., rape victims, any childhood physical or sexual abuse, any Criterion A event), comorbid disorders (e.g., no current Axis I or II disorders, no current or lifetime psychotic disorder), demographic characteristics (e.g., females between ages 18 and 45), or abilities (e.g., reads at an eighth-grade level, not color-blind). Final decisions regarding inclusion and exclusion criteria are influenced not only by conceptual considerations, but also by the resources available for conducting the research, including the number of potential participants, the amount of clinician time involved, and the overall cost of the project. If there are restrictions on any of these resources, the criteria may need to be relaxed in order to obtain a sufficiently large sample.

In case-control research it is essential to conduct a structured diagnostic interview for PTSD. In addition, we strongly recommend administering a structured interview for other lifetime and current Axis I, and possibly Axis II, disorders. PTSD interviews that yield continuous severity scores are especially useful, since the threshold for inclusion can easily be adjusted based on the needs of the study, creating a more stringent or liberal threshold for a PTSD diagnosis. Including additional PTSD measures in the assessment battery allows the creation of very "clean" groups, by requiring that participants in the PTSD group exceed recommended cutoffs on all measures, while controls score below all cutoffs. This approach can be costly, however, as it will almost certainly render some potential participants ineligible for the study due to discordant PTSD indicators.

A recent study in our lab involving a simple two-group design illustrates some of the key considerations. All participants in the study were male Vietnam theater veterans with no history of psychotic disorders, all of whom were able to read the stimulus materials and had a mental status sufficient to complete an extensive assessment and experimental protocol. Participants in the PTSD group met diagnostic criteria for current PTSD on the CAPS according to the most stringent scoring rule, whereas controls fell below the diagnostic threshold according to the original, more liberal scoring rule. In addition, PTSD participants exceeded recommended cutoff scores on the PCL and the Mississippi Scale, whereas controls

were below cutoffs on these measures. Finally, controls had no lifetime history of PTSD, either as a result of combat or a civilian trauma.

In terms of comorbidity, PTSD participants were included regardless of additional diagnoses (except for psychotic disorders), since we felt that a group of veterans with PTSD but no comorbid disorders would be unrepresentative. Controls were excluded if they had any current Axis I diagnosis, but no restrictions other than psychosis were put on lifetime disorders. To reduce the number of potential participants that were excluded from the study, a member of the research team conducted phone screens to determine probable eligibility. As a result of these inclusion and exclusion criteria, we created two groups that were quite similar in terms of demographic variables and level of combat exposure, but distinctly different in terms of PTSD symptoms.

Scenario 7: Treatment Study

In a treatment study, most of the diagnostic considerations discussed in the previous scenarios are applicable, including the need for a structured diagnostic interview, the need for explicit inclusion and exclusion criteria, and the use of multiple measures. An additional consideration is that multiple assessments are typically conducted, often over time intervals as brief as one or two weeks. This calls for a measure that can be administered quickly with minimal burden to clinician and respondent and that reflects the appropriate time frame (e.g., past week, past two weeks). Self-report measures are ideal for this purpose, especially DSM-correspondent measures, although some would require modification of the time frame to suit the specific assessment need. Interviews could be used, but are obviously more time-consuming and costly.

We would use a CAPS-DX to establish a PTSD diagnosis, using the original scoring rule. Although this rule may be too liberal for case-control research, it is still indicative of clinically significant PTSD symptomatology, and therefore is sufficient for inclusion in a treatment protocol. For brief assessment intervals over the course of treatment, we would use the CAPS-SX as the follow-up instrument, since it was designed to assess PTSD symptom severity over the past week. Alternatively, if multiple interviews were not feasible for some reason, we might administer the CAPS-DX initially, then use the PCL over the course of treatment, conducting another CAPS-DX at the end of the study and at follow-up. Additional PTSD measures could also be administered at baseline and at follow-up.

SUMMARY AND CONCLUSIONS

As we hope this chapter has made clear, considerable progress has been achieved in the development and psychometric evaluation of standardized measures to assess trauma and PTSD. Clinicians and investigators can now choose from a broad array of PTSD measures, including self-report measures, structured interviews, and psychophysiological protocols. However, there is still room for improvement. One step that can be taken immediately is to adopt standardized, well-validated measures in every setting in which the assessment of traumatized individuals is conducted. There is no longer a compelling rationale for the use of nonstandardized approaches that do not yield quantifiable indicators of symptom severity. Nor should investigators create and use new measures of trauma and PTSD unless they identify a specific assessment need that is not addressed by an existing measure.

A second step, which will take many years to fully accomplish, is to conduct additional psychometric investigations of existing instruments to enhance the precision of measurement and generalization of findings across different settings and populations. More research on individual PTSD measures is needed to: (a) replicate and extend previous psychometric findings; (b) establish norms on a variety of populations; (c) identify the possible influence of gender, ethnicity, and cross-cultural differences on test scores; and (d) develop optimal scoring rules for addressing different assessment questions. Such research is particularly important to conduct when instruments are translated into languages other than the one in which they were developed. Investigators should not simply assume that translations are psychometrically equivalent to the original instruments, but should document this empirically. Studies are also needed in which multiple measures are administered to the same sample to identify the best measure for diagnosing PTSD in a given context and to determine how best to combine different measures into an optimal PTSD assessment battery.

These steps are essential for identifying the most reliable and valid measures and for enhancing the uniformity of PTSD assessment, but improved assessment is only a means to an end. The ultimate goals are to understand how traumatic events affect those who experience them and to develop better methods of treating PTSD and other posttraumatic sequelae. Advances in PTSD assessment over the past ten years have greatly facilitated progress toward these goals, and we are confident that the increasingly rich and mature assessment literature will continue to make a significant contribution to the scientific study of traumatic stress.

REFERENCES

American Psychiatric Association. (1994). *Diagnostic and statistical manual of mental disorders* (4th ed.). Washington, DC: Author.

Beck, A. T., Epstein, N., Brown, G., & Steer, R. A. (1988). An inventory for measuring clinical anxiety: Psychometric properties. *Journal of Consulting and Clinical Psychology, 56,* 893–897.

Beck, A. T., Ward, C. H., Mendelson, M., Mock, J. E., & Erbaugh, J. K. (1961). An inventory for measuring depression. *Archives of General Psychiatry, 4,* 561–571.

Blake, D. D., Weathers, F. W., Nagy, L. M., Kaloupek, D. G., Gusman, F. D., Charney, D. S., & Keane, T. M. (1995). The development of a clinician-administered PTSD scale. *Journal of Traumatic Stress, 8,* 75–90.

Blake, D. D., Weathers, F. W., Nagy, L. M., Kaloupek, D. G., Klauminzer, G., Charney, D. S., & Keane, T. M. (1990). A clinician rating scale for assessing current and lifetime PTSD: The CAPS-1. *Behavior Therapist, 13,* 187–188.

Blanchard, E. B., Hickling, E. J., Taylor, A. E., Forneris, C. A., Loos, W., & Jaccard, J. (1995). Effects of varying scoring rules of the Clinician-Administered PTSD Scale (CAPS) for the diagnosis of post-traumatic stress disorder in motor vehicle accident victims. *Behavior Research Therapy, 33,* 471–475.

Blanchard, E. B., Jones-Alexander, J., Buckley, T. C., & Forneris, C. A. (1996). Psychometric properties of the PTSD Checklist (PCL). *Behaviour Research and Therapy, 34,* 669–673.

Breslau, N., Davis, G. C., Andreski, P., & Peterson, E. (1991). Traumatic events and posttraumatic stress disorder in an urban population of young adults. *Archives of General Psychiatry, 48,* 216–222.

Brett, B. (1993). Psychoanalytic contributions to a theory of traumatic stress. In J. P. Wilson & B. Raphael (Eds.), *International handbook of traumatic stress syndromes.* New York: Plenum Press.

Briere, J. (1995). *Trauma Symptom Inventory (TSI) professional manual.* Odessa, FL: Psychological Assessment Resources.

Butcher, J. N., Dahlstrom, W. G., Graham, J. R., Tellegen, A., & Kaemmer, B. (1989). *Minnesota Multiphasic Personality Inventory-2 (MMPI-2): Manual for administration and scoring.* Minneapolis: University of Minnesota Press.

Campbell, D. T., & Fiske, D. W. (1959). Convergent and discriminant validation by the multitrait-multimethod matrix. *Psychological Bulletin, 56,* 81–105.

Cannon, D. S., Bell, W. E., Andrews, R. H., & Finkelstein, A. S. (1987). Correspondence between MMPI PTSD measures and clinical diagnosis. *Journal of Personality Assessment, 51,* 517–521.

Centers for Disease Control. (1988). Health status of Vietnam veterans: I. Psychosocial characteristics. *Journal of the American Medical Association, 259,* 2701–2707.

Cordova, M. J., Andrykowski, M. A., Kenady, D. E., McGrath, P. C., Sloan, D. A., & Redd, W. H. (1995). Frequency and correlates of posttraumatic-stress-disorder-like symptoms after treatment for breast cancer. *Journal of Consulting and Clinical Psychology, 63,* 981–986.

Davidson, J. (1996). *Davidson Trauma Scale* [Manual]. Ontario, Canada: Multi-Health Systems.

Davidson, J. R., & Foa, E. B. (1991). Diagnostic issues in posttraumatic stress disorder: Considerations for the DSM-IV. *Journal of Abnormal Psychology, 100,* 346–355.

Davidson, J. R. T., Smith, R. D., & Kudler, H. S. (1989). Validity and reliability of the DSM-III criteria for post-traumatic stress disorder: Experience with a structured interview. *Journal of Nervous and Mental Disease, 177,* 336–341.

Derogatis, L. R. (1983). *SCL-90-R: Administration, scoring, & procedures manual-II.* Towson, MD: Clinical Psychometric Research.

Falsetti, S. A., Resnick. H. S., Resick, P. A., & Kilpatrick, D. G. (1993). The Modified PTSD Symptom Scale: A brief self-report measure of posttraumatic stress disorder. *Behavioral Assessment Review,* 161–162.

Foa, E. B. (1995). *Posttraumatic Stress Diagnostic Scale* [Manual]. Minneapolis, MN: National Computer Systems.

Foa, E. B., Riggs, D. S., Dancu, C. V., & Rothbaum, B. O. (1993). Reliability and validity of a brief instrument for assessing post-traumatic stress disorder. *Journal of Traumatic Stress, 6,* 459–473.

Green, B. L. (1991). Evaluating the effects of disasters. *Psychological Assessment, 3,* 538–546.

Green, B. L. (1993). Identifying survivors at risk: Trauma and stressors across events. In J. P. Wilson & B. Raphael (Eds.), *International handbook of traumatic stress syndromes* (pp. 135–144). New York: Plenum Press.

Green, B. L., Epstein, S. A., Krupnick, J. L., & Rowland, J. H. (1997). Trauma and medical illness: Assessing trauma-related disorders in medical settings. In J. P. Wilson & T. M. Keane (Eds.), *Assessing psychological trauma and PTSD.* New York: Guilford Press.

Green, B. L., Wilson, J. P., & Lindy, J. D. (1985). Conceptualizing PTSD: A psychosocial framework. In C. R. Figley (Ed.), *Trauma and its wake.* New York: Brunner/Mazel.

Hammarberg, M. (1992). Penn Inventory for posttraumatic stress disorder: Psychometric properties. *Psychological Assessment, 4,* 67–76.

Haynes, S. N., Richard, D. C. S., & Kubany, E. S. (1995). Content validity in psychological assessment: A functional approach to concepts and methods. *Psychological Assessment, 7,* 238–247.

Helzer, J. E., Robins, L. N., & McEvoy, M. A. (1987). Post-traumatic stress disorder in the general population. *New England Journal of Medicine, 317,* 956–960.

Herman, D. S., Weathers, F. W., Litz, B. T., & Keane, T. M. (1996). Psychometric properties of the embedded and stand-alone versions of the MMPI-2 Keane PTSD Scale. *Assessment, 3,* 437–442.

Herman, J. L. (1992). *Trauma and recovery.* New York: Basic Books.

Horowitz, M. J. (1976). *Stress response syndromes.* New York: Jason Aronson.

Horowitz, M. J., Wilner, N., & Alvarez, W. (1979). Impact of Event Scale: A measure of subjective stress. *Psychosomatic Medicine, 41,* 209–218.

Keane, T. M., Caddell, J. M., & Taylor, K. L. (1988). Mississippi Scale for combat-related posttraumatic stress disorder: Three studies in reliability and validity. *Journal of Consulting and Clinical Psychology, 56,* 85–90.

Keane, T. M., Fairbank, J. A., Caddell, J. M., Zimering, R. T., Taylor, K. L., & Mora, C. A. (1989). Clinical evaluation of a measure to assess combat exposure. *Psychological Assessment, 1,* 53–55.

Keane, T. M., & Kaloupek, D. G. (1997). Comorbid psychiatric disorders in PTSD: Implications for research. In R. Yehuda & A. McFarlane (Eds.), *Psychobiology of posttraumatic stress disorder.* New York: Annals of the New York Academy of Science.

Keane, T. M., Kolb, L. C., Kaloupek, D. G., Orrm S. P., Blanchard, E. B., Thomas, R. G., Hsieh, F. Y., & Lavori, P. W. (1997). *Psychophysiological measurement in the diagnosis of post-traumatic stress disorder: Results from a Department of Veterans Affairs cooperative study.* Manuscript submitted for publication.

Keane, T. M., Malloy, P. F., & Fairbank, J. A. (1984). Empirical development of an MMPI subscale for the assessment of combat-related posttraumatic stress disorder. *Journal of Consulting and Clinical Psychology, 52,* 888–891.

Keane, T. M., Wolfe, J., & Taylor, K. L. (1987). Posttraumatic stress disorder: Evidence for diagnostic validity and methods of psychological assessment. *Journal of Clinical Psychology, 43,* 32–43.

Kessler, R. C., Sonnega, A., Bromet, E., Hughes, M., & Nelson, C. B. (1995). Posttraumatic stress disorder in the National Comorbidity Survey. *Archives of General Psychiatry, 52,* 1048–1060.

Kilpatrick, D. G. (1988). Rape Aftermath Symptom Test. In M. Hersen & A. S. Bellack (Eds.), *Dictionary of behavioral assessment techniques.* Oxford: Pergamon Press.

Kilpatrick, D. G., & Resnick, H. S. (1993). PTSD associated with exposure to criminal victimization in clinical and community populations. In J. R. T. Davidson & E. B. Foa (Eds.), *PSTD in review: Recent research and future directions.* Washington, DC: American Psychiatric Press.

King, D. W., King, L. A., Fairbank, J. A., Schlenger, W. E., & Surface, C. R. (1993). Enhancing the precision of the Mississippi Scale for Combat-Related Posttraumatic Stress Disorder: An application of item response theory. *Psychological Assessment, 5,* 457–471.

King, L. A., & King, D. W. (1994). Latent structure of the Mississippi Scale for Combat-Related Post-traumatic Stress Disorder: Exploratory and higher-order confirmatory factor analyses. *Assessment, 1,* 275–291.

Koretzky, M. B., & Peck, A. H. (1990). Validation and cross-validation of the PTSD Subscale of the MMPI with civilian trauma victims. *Journal of Clinical Psychology, 46,* 296–300.

Kraemer, H. C. (1992). *Evaluating medical tests: Objective and quantitative guidelines.* Newbury Park, CA: Sage Publications.

Krinsley, K. E. (1996). Psychometric review of The Evaluation of Lifetime Stressors (ELS) Questionnaire & Interview. In B. H. Stamm (Ed.), *Measurement of stress, trauma, and adaptation.* Lutherville, MD: Sidran Press.

Krinsley, K. E., & Weathers, F. W. (1995). The assessment of trauma in adults. *PSTD Research Quarterly, 6,* 1–3.

Kulka, R. A., Schlenger, W. E., Fairbank, J. A., Hough, R. L., Jordan, B. K., Marmar, C. R., & Weiss, D. S. (1990). *Trauma and the Vietnam War generation: Report on the findings from the National Vietnam Veterans Readjustment Study.* New York: Brunner/Mazel.

Kulka, R. A., Schlenger, W. E., Fairbank, J. A., Hough, R. L., Jordan, B. K., Marmar, C. R., & Weiss, D. S. (1991). Assessment of posttraumatic stress disorder in the community: Prospects and pitfalls from recent studies of Vietnam veterans. *Psychological Assessment, 3,* 547–560.

Lauterbach, D., & Vrana, S. (1996). Three studies on the reliability and validity of a self-report measure of posttraumatic stress disorder. *Assessment, 3,* 17–25.

Lerner, F. (1994). *PILOTS database: User's guide* (2nd ed.). White River Junction, VT: National Center for Post-Traumatic Stress Disorder.

Levin, P., & Reis, B. (1997). Use of the Rorschach in assessing trauma. In J. P. Wilson & T. M. Keane (Eds.), *Assessing psychological trauma and PTSD.* New York: Guilford Press.

Litz, B. T., & Weathers, F. W. (1994). The diagnosis and assessment of post-traumatic stress disorder in adults. In M. B. Williams & J. F. Sommer, Jr. (Eds.), *Handbook of post-traumatic therapy.* Westport, CT: Greenwood Press.

Lyons, J. A., & Keane, T. M. (1992). Keane PTSD Scale: MMPI and MMPI-2 update. *Journal of Traumatic Stress, 5,* 111–117.

Lyons, J. A., & Scotti, J. R. (1994). Comparability of two administration formats of the Keane Posttraumatic Stress Disorder Scale. *Psychological Assessment, 6,* 209–211.

McFall, M. E., Smith, D. E., Mackay, P. W., & Tarver, D. J. (1990). Reliability and validity of Mississippi Scale for Combat-Related Posttraumatic Stress Disorder. *Psychological Assessment, 2,* 114–121.

Norris, F. (1992). Epidemiology of trauma: Frequency and impact of different potentially traumatic events on different demographic groups. *Journal of Consulting and Clinical Psychology, 60,* 409–418.

Resnick, H. S., Kilpatrick, D. G., Dansky, B. S., Saunders, B. E., & Best, C. L. (1993). Prevalence of civilian trauma and posttraumatic stress disorder in a representative national sample of women. *Journal of Consulting and Clinical Psychology, 61,* 984–991.

Resnick, H. S., Kilpatrick, D. G., & Lipovsky, J. A. (1991). Assessment of rape-related posttraumatic stress disorder: Stressor and symptom dimensions. *Journal of Consulting and Clinical Psychology, 3,* 561–572.

Resnick, P. H. (1997). Malingering of posttraumatic disorders. In R. Rogers (Ed.), *Clinical assessment of malingering and deception* (2nd ed.). New York: Guilford Press.

Rogers, R., Bagby, R. M., & Dickens, S. E. (1992). *Structured Interview of Reported Symptoms (SIRS) and professional manual.* Odessa, FL: Psychological Assessment Resources.

Saigh, P. A., & Bremner, J. D. (1998). The history of posttraumatic stress disorder. In P. A. Saigh & D. J. Bremner (Eds.). *Posttraumatic stress disorder: A comprehensive textbook..* Boston, MA: Allyn & Bacon.

Saunders, B. E., Arata, C. M., & Kilpatrick, D. G. (1990). Development of a crime-related posttraumatic stress disorder scale for women within the Symptom Checklist-90-Revised. *Journal of Traumatic Stress, 3,* 439–448.

Schlenger, W. E., Kulka, R. A., Fairbank, J. A., Hough, R. L., Jordan, B. K., Marmar, C. R., & Weiss, D. S. (1992). The prevalence of post-traumatic stress disorder in the Vietnam generation: A multimethod, multisource assessment of psychiatric disorder. *Journal of Traumatic Stress, 5,* 333–363.

Schwarzwald, J., Solomon, Z., Weisenberg, M., & Mikulincer, M. (1987). Validation of the Impact of Event Scale for psychological sequelae of combat. *Journal of Consulting and Clinical Psychology, 55,* 251–256.

Shear, M. K., & Maser, J. D. (1994). Standardized assessment for panic disorder research. *Archives of General Psychiatry, 51,* 346–354.

Solomon, S. D., & Canino, G. J. (1990). Appropriateness of DSM-III-R criteria for posttraumatic stress disorder. *Comprehensive Psychiatry, 31,* 1–11.

Spielberger, C. D., Gorsuch, R. L., & Luschene, E. (1970). *Manual for the State-Trait Anxiety Interview (self-evaluation questionnaire).* Palo Alto, CA: Consulting Psychologists Press.

Spielberger, C. D., Reheiser, E. C., & Sydeman, S. J. (1995). Measuring the experience, expression, and control of anger. In H. Kassinove (Ed.) *Anger disorders: Definition, diagnosis, and treatment.* Washington, DC: Taylor & Francis.

Spitzer, R. L., Williams, J. B. W., Gibbon, M., & First, M. B. (1990). *Structured Clinical Interview for DSM-III-R.* Washington, DC: American Psychiatric Press.

Stamm, B. H. (Ed.). (1996). *Measurement of stress, trauma, and adaptation.* Lutherville, MD: Sidran Press.

Vrana, S., & Lauterbach, D. (1994). Prevalence of traumatic events and post-traumatic psychological symptoms in a nonclinical sample of college students. *Journal of Traumatic Stress, 7,* 289–302.

Vreven, D. L., Gudanowski, D. M., King, L. A., & King, D. W. (1995). The civilian version of the Mississippi PTSD Scale: A psychometric evaluation. *Journal of Traumatic Stress, 8,* 91–109.

Watson, C. G., Juba, M. P., Manifold, V., Kucala, T., & Anderson, P. E. D. (1991). The PTSD Interview: Rationale, description, reliability, and concurrent validity of a DSM-III-based technique. *Journal of Clinical Psychology, 47,* 179–188.

Watson, C. G., Kucala, T., & Manifold, V. (1986). A cross-validation of the Keane and Penk MMPI Scales as measures of post-traumatic stress disorder. *Journal of Clinical Psychology, 42,* 727–732.

Weathers, F. W., Blake, D. D., Krinsley, K. E., Haddad, W., Huska, J. A., & Keane, T. M. (1997). *Reliability and validity of the Clinician-Administered PTSD Scale.* Manuscript submitted for publication.

Weathers, F. W., Keane, T. M., King, L. A., & King, D. W. (1997). Psychometric theory in the development of posttraumatic stress disorder assessment tools. In J. P. Wilson & T. M. Keane (Eds.), *Assessing psychological trauma and PTSD.* New York: Guilford Press.

Weathers, F. W., Litz, B. T., Herman, D. S., Huska, J. A., & Keane, T. M. (1993, October). *The PTSD Checklist (PCL): Reliability, validity, and diagnostic utility.* Paper presented at the annual meeting of the International Society for Traumatic Stress Studies, San Antonio, CA.

Weathers, F. W., Litz, B. T., Herman, D. S., Keane, T. M., Steinberg, H. R., Huska, J. A., & Kraemer, H. C. (1996). The utility of the SCL-90-R for the diagnosis of war-zone-related PTSD. *Journal of Traumatic Stress, 9,* 111–128.

Weathers, F. W., Litz, B. T., Herman, D. S., King, D. W., King, L. A., Keane, T. M., & Huska, J. A. (1997). *Three studies on the psychometric properties of the PTSD Checklist (PCL).* Manuscript submitted for publication.

Weathers, F. W., Meron, A., & Keane, T. M. (1997). *Psychometric properties of five scoring rules for the Clinician-Administered PTSD Scale (CAPS).* Poster submitted to the 13th Annual Meeting of the International Society for Traumatic Stress Studies.

Weiss, D. S. (1997). Structured clinical interview techniques. In J. P. Wilson & T. M. Keane (Eds.), *Assessing psychological trauma and PTSD.* New York: Guilford Press.

Weiss, D. S., & Marmar, C. R. (1997). The Impact of Event Scale-Revised. In J. P. Wilson & T. M. Keane (Eds.), *Assessing psychological trauma and PTSD.* New York: Guilford Press.

Wilson, J. P. (1995). The historical evolution of PTSD diagnostic criteria: From Freud to DSM-IV. In G. S. Everly, Jr. & J. M. Lating (Eds.), *Psychotraumatology.* New York: Plenum Press.

Wilson, J. P., & Keane, T. M. (Eds.). (1997). *Assessing psychological trauma and PTSD.* New York: The Guilford Press.

World Health Organization (1990). *International classification of diseases and related health problems* (10th ed.). Geneva, Switzerland: World Health Organization.

Zilberg, N. J., Weiss, D. S., & Horowitz, M. J. (1982). Impact of Event Scale: A cross-validation study and some empirical evidence supporting a conceptual model of stress response syndromes. *Journal of Consulting and Clinical Psychology, 50,* 407–414.

CHAPTER 12

PSYCHOPHYSIOLOGICAL ASSESSMENT OF POSTTRAUMATIC STRESS DISORDER*

EDWARD B. BLANCHARD, PH.D., AND TODD C. BUCKLEY, B.S.
Center for Stress and Anxiety Disorders
University at Albany-SUNY

With the reintroduction of posttraumatic stress disorder (PTSD) into psychiatric nosology by DSM-III (American Psychiatric Association, 1980), steadily growing attention has been paid to the possible role of psychophysiological measures in the assessment of the disorder. This attention to psychophysiology was based in part on the formal definitions of PTSD. Thus, DSM-III called attention (p. 236) to "symptoms of excessive autonomic arousal" but did not specifically include increased physiological responding in the formal diagnostic criteria. DSM-III-R (American Psychiatric Association, 1987) formally included increased physiological responding as one of 17 symptoms which define PTSD: "physiologic reactivity upon exposure to events that symbolize or resemble an aspect of the traumatic event" (p. 250). More recently, DSM-IV (American Psychiatric Association, 1994) retained the symptom, "physiological reactivity on exposure to internal or external cues that symbolize or resemble an aspect of the traumatic event" (p. 428), but classified it to a reexperiencing symptom instead of a hyperarousal symptom in DSM-III-R.

DOBBS AND WILSON (1960)

Empirical study of this phenomenon or symptom began prior to the publication of DSM-III (or even DSM-II [American Psychiatric Association, 1968])

with the pioneering study of Dobbs and Wilson (1960). Their study, which served as a prototype for much of the subsequent research, involved two groups of World War II (n = 19) and Korean War (n = 2) veterans: a group of 8 male combat veterans who were described as "decompensated" and suffering from "combat neurosis" and a group of 13 male veterans of approximately the same age who had had combat experience but were described as "compensated." A comparison group of 10 university students who had no combat experience and who were all younger than any of the veterans was also included. Cardiac rate (heart rate: HR), respiration rate (RR), and EEG were recorded continuously during the assessment. Subjects first lay quietly for 5 to 7 minutes during a resting baseline; this was followed by 8 minutes of exposure to combat related sounds (artillery bombardment, small arms fire, and aerial bombardment). Finally, flashing lights (to depict explosions) were added to the last 4 minutes.

Interestingly, the "decompensated" veterans (who probably had severe PTSD) were so aroused and upset by the auditory and visual stimuli that no psychophysiological data were recorded from them. Comparisons of the "compensated" veterans to the university students showed the former to have higher baseline HR and RR than the students and also to show greater within session change to the provocative stimulus (6 beats per minute [bpm] versus 2 bpm, respectively, in HR; see Table 12.1 below). One might suspect from the psychophysiological data that the

*Preparation of this chapter was supported in part by a grant from NIMH MH-48476.

"compensated" veterans had, at the very least, some lingering PTSD symptoms.

THE DATA BASE

In summarizing the literature on the use of psychophysiological assessment with PTSD, we were able to locate 31 reports. We have included both published reports and papers presented at meetings for which copies of the paper or a detailed abstract were available. We have not included numerous reports on other aspects of the psychobiology of PTSD. Instead, we have limited our coverage to reports in which non-invasive measures, that is, physiologic responses measured with surface sensors, were taken on patients with PTSD under at least two conditions: at least one condition reminiscent of the trauma and one other comparison (non-trauma-related) condition (e.g., resting baseline, non-trauma-related stimulus, etc.). (We have also included three studies of baseline measures only on participants with PTSD and a comparison group without PTSD.) Many studies like the three mentioned above have also included comparison groups of subjects (e.g., normal controls, individuals exposed to the trauma who did not develop PTSD, individuals with other psychiatric disorders, etc.).

Important methodological details and experimental findings from these reports are summarized in Tables 12.1 and 12.2. In Table 12.1 are summarized the reports for which the traumatic event was exposure to combat. They are arranged chronologically in order of date of publication. In Table 12.2 are summarized the reports in which the participants had been exposed to traumatic events other than combat. These latter reports are organized around type of trauma, motor vehicle accidents, rape, or mixed civilian trauma and then presented chronologically.

Most of the remainder of this chapter is a discussion and conclusions one can draw from the data in Tables 12.1 and 12.2, organized around rhetorical questions.

WHO HAS BEEN STUDIED?

Examining the two tables, several dominant research themes emerge. Two-thirds (21/31) of the reports in-

volve individuals for whom the traumatic event was exposure to combat, and 18 of these involve Vietnam veterans. Thus, over half of the published research on the psychophysiological assessment of PTSD involves Vietnam veterans who were, at the time they were studied, from about 11 to 25 years on average, post-trauma.

Given the findings of the National Vietnam Veterans Readjustment Study (Kulka et al., 1990), which estimated that, in the late 1980s, approximately 15 percent of those who served in southeast Asia still met the criteria for PTSD, or approximately 300,000 individuals, it is not surprising that this group has been a focal point of the research. Two other historical factors probably contributed to this focus: Kardiner (1941) in discussing the traumatic neuroses of war described a "physioneurosis" with most of the currently accepted symptoms of PTSD. Thus, those dealing with veterans had been sensitized to the issue for a long time. Second, the predecessor to the Department of Veterans Affairs, the Veterans Administration, officially (Gronvall, 1986) recognized the role of psychophysiological testing in diagnosing PTSD among veterans as early as 1986.

Two other traumatized groups have been the focus of limited psychophysiological research. There have been four reports on sexual assault survivors (SASs) and four reports on motor vehicle accident (MVA) survivors. Looking at epidemiologic studies focusing on PTSD (Norris, 1992; Kessler, Sonnega, Bromet, Hughes, and Nelson (1995), there are probably many more individuals with PTSD secondary to these two traumas than to combat.

WHAT HAS BEEN MEASURED?

Several different physiological responses have been measured, including heart rate (HR), blood pressure (BP), electrodermal activity (EDA) (either skin resistance or skin conductance), muscle activity (electromyogram [EMG]), peripheral temperature (surface temperature or sublingual temperature), and electroencephalogram (EEG). By far the most common response utilized is HR (29 of 31 studies), followed closely by EDA (18 studies) and EMG (16 studies), and finally BP (both systolic BP and diastolic BP).

TABLE 12.1   Studies of Psychophysiological Responding in War Time Trauma Populations

AUTHORS	POPULATIONS	YRS. POST TRAUMA	PROVOCATIVE STIMULI	RESPONSES
Dobbs & Wilson (1960)	Decompensated WWII vets (8) Compensated WWI, WWII, & Korean vets (13) Non-combat controls (10)	13 Years	Eight minute standardized audiotape of combat sounds accompanied by light flashes.	HR, EEG, RR
Blanchard et al. (1982)	Vietnam PTSD vets (11) Age matched non-vets (11)	11 Years	Five, 30-second, standardized audiotapes of combat sounds, alternated with 30-second trials of music. Decibel levels: 42, 52, 62, 72, 82.	HR, SBP, DBP, EMG, SC, PT
Malloy et al. (1983)	Vietnam PTSD vets (10) Vietnam Non-PTSD vets (10) Inpatient Non-PTSD Axis I (10)	14 Years	Sixty-second standardized videotaped presentations of 9 neutral scenes & 9 combat scenes with accompanying audio.	HR, SC
Blanchard et al. (1986)	Vietnam PTSD vets (57) Non-PTSD vets with similar exposure to combat (34)	15 Years	Five, 30-second standardized audiotapes of combat sounds, alternated with 30-second trials of music. Decibel levels: 40, 50, 60, 70, 80.	HR
Pallmeyer et al. (1986)	Vietnam PTSD vets (12) Non-PTSD Vietnam vets (10) Vietnam vets with Axis I (5) Era vets no disorder (5) Non-vets with anxiety disorder (8)	15 Years	Five, 30-second standardized audiotapes of combat sounds, alternated with 30-second trials of music. Decibel levels: 40, 50, 60, 70, 80.	HR, SBP, DBP, EMG, SC
Pitman et al. (1987)	Vietnam PTSD vets (18) Non-psychiatric Vietnam vets (15)	16 Years	Two, 30-second personal imagery audiotapes of traumatic war experience, with 1 standardized combat tape. Five personal imagery tapes of neutral, positive, action, & fear experiences.	HR, SC, EMG
Blanchard et al. (1989)	Vietnam PTSD vets (59) Non-PTSD vets with similar exposure to combat (12)	18 Years	Five, 30-second standardized audiotapes of combat sounds, alternated with 30-second trials of music. Decibel levels: 40, 50, 60, 70, 80.	HR
Gerardi et al. (1989)	PTSD Vietnam vets (18) Non-PTSD Vietnam vets (18)	18 Years	Five, 30-second standardized audiotapes of combat sounds, alternated with 30-second trials of music. Decibel levels: 40, 50, 60, 70, 80.	HR, SBP, DBP, PT, EMG, SC
Boudewyns & Hyer (1990)	Inpatient Vietnam vets PTSD (51)	19 Years	Three exposures to five-minute personal imagery audiotapes.	HR, EMG, SC
Pitman & Orr (1990)	Vietnam PTSD vets (7) Vietnam non-PTSD vets with another anxiety disorder (7)	19 Years	Two, 30-second personal imagery audiotapes of traumatic war experience, with 1 standardized combat tape. Five personal imagery tapes of neutral, positive, action, & fear experiences.	HR, SC, EMG
Blanchard, Kolb, Prins, et al. (1991)	Vietnam PTSD vets (15) Vietnam Non-PTSD vets (6)	20 Years	Three-minute standardized audiotape of combat sounds.	HR, Norepin

AGE/ GENDER MATCHED	RESULTS	BASELINE DIFFERENCES	SENSITIVITY/ SPECIFICITY (METHOD OF CLASSIFICATION)
Age-No Gender-Yes	Decompensated vets. terminated procedures. Data available only for compensated vets and controls. Compensated vets > Controls on HR, RR, EEG.	Both groups of Vets > Controls on HR; Decomp. > Comp. > Controls on RR; Comp > Decomp. > Controls on EEG	None reported
Yes	PTSD > Controls on HR, SBP, EMG in response to provocative stimuli.	PTSD > Controls on HR (8 BPM)	91% vs. 100% (PDA using HR data)
Yes	PTSD > both control groups on HR reactivity to combat stimuli. Discriminant function analysis using 4 measures correctly classifies 80% of the sample.	None	80% vs. 80% (PDA)
Yes	PTSD > Controls on HR at every phase & greater reactivity to standardized combat stimuli	PTSD > Controls on HR (12.6 BPM)	70% vs. 88% (Single cutoff score: the highest HR response to combat sounds)
No	PTSD > than all other control groups on baseline HR & responding to combat sounds.	PTSD vets higher than all other controls groups on HR	67% vs. 86% (PDA using HR responses)
Yes	PTSD > Controls on SC & EMG responses to personal traumatic imagery.	PTSD > Controls on resting HR (75 BPM vs. 66 BPM) Eta^2 = .16)[a]	100% vs. 61% (A discriminant function using all 3 responses)
Yes	PTSD > Controls on HR at every phase & greater reactivity to standardized combat stimuli.	PTSD > Controls on HR (10 BPM)	75% vs. 78% (Cutoff score of -1.0 for HR reactivity to combat stimuli minus HR reactivity to MA)
Age-No Gender-Yes	PTSD group was unable to suppress their physiological responses when asked to do so. Non-PTSD (n = 9) was able to fake physiological arousal.	None	70% vs. 88% (Using the single largest HR reactivity score)
N/A	Subjects showed increased arousal to audiotapes on all 3 physiological measures.	N/A	N/A
Yes	PTSD > Controls on SC & EMG responses to personal traumatic imagery.	Anxiety do > PTSD on EMG (Eta^2 = .31)	71% vs. 100% (Using PDA derived by Pitman et al., 1987)
Yes	PTSD > Controls on HR reactivity to combat stimuli. PTSD group showed 30% increase in Norepin upon exposure to traumatic cue.	None	Not reported

(Continued)

TABLE 12.1 (Continued)

AUTHORS	POPULATIONS	YRS. POST TRAUMA	PROVOCATIVE STIMULI	RESPONSES

Blanchard, Kolb & Prins (1991)	Vietnam PTSD vets (121)
	  Derivation (69)
	  Validation (52)
	
	Vietnam Non-PTSD vets (79)
	  Derivation (35)
	  Validation (44)
		20 Years	Five, 30-second standardized audiotapes of combat sounds, alternated with 30-second trials of music. Decibel levels: 40, 50, 60, 70, 80.	HR, SBP, DBP, EMG

McCaffrey et al. (1993)	Vietnam PTSD vets (5) Vietnam Non-PTSD vets (5)	21 Years	Six standardized odors: orange, Peppermint, garlic, diesel fuel, burnt hair, decaying flesh.	EEG
McFall et al. (1992)	Vietnam PTSD vets (11) Vietnam non-PTSD vets (11)	21 Years	Baseline measurements only.	HR, SBP, DBP, Epin., Norepin
Orr et al. (1993)	WWI & Korean PTSD vets (8) Non-PTSD vets (12)	42 Years	Two, 30-second personal imagery audiotapes of traumatic war experience, with 1 standardized combat tape. Five personal imagery tapes of neutral, positive, action, & fear experiences.	HR, SC, EMG
Gerardi et al. (1994)	Vietnam PTSD vets (32) Era vets/no combat exposure (26)	23 Years	In Vivo assessment in an outpatient setting.	HR, SBP, DBP, RR, SL
Orr et al. (1995)	Vietnam PTSD vets (37) Vietnam Non-PTSD vets (19)	24 Years	Fifteen 95dB, 500-millisecond tones delivered via earphones.	HR, SC, (O)EMG
Davis et al. (1996)	Persian Gulf PTSD vets (14) Persian Gulf Non-PTSD vets (15)	3 Years	Two, thirty-second personal imagery scripts.	HR, EMG
Keane et al. (Under Review)	Vietnam veterans Current PTSD vets (C) (778) Lifetime PTSD (L) (181) Never PTSD vets (N) (369)	25 Years	Twelve, standardized still images (6 combat & 6 neutral) with soundtrack of combat sounds. Two, thirty-second personal imagery audiotapes of trauma & 2 neutral tapes.	HR, SC, EMG, SBP, DBP
Muruoka et al. (Unpublished Dissertation)	Vietnam era PTSD vets (11) Vietnam era non-PTSD vets (7)	25 Years	Twenty-four hour ambulatory monitoring.	HR, SBP, DBP

AGE/ GENDER MATCHED	RESULTS	BASELINE DIFFERENCES	SENSITIVITY/ SPECIFICITY (METHOD OF CLASSIFICATION)
Yes	A predictive discriminant function derived from HR measures correctly identified 75% of the derivation sample & 80% of the validation sample.	Derivation PTSD HR 74.8 BPM NON HR 67.1 BPM Validation PTSD HR 76.9 BPM NON HR 67.7 BPM	Derivation 84% vs. 57% Validation 85% vs. 82% (PDA using HR measures)
Yes	PTSD showed a marked increase in left hemisphere activity relative to Controls upon exposure to burnt hair stimuli.	Not reported	Not reported
Yes	No statistically significant differences on any measure across the 4 baseline measurements.	None	Not reported
Yes	PTSD > Controls on HR & SC responses to personal traumatic imagery.	None	88% vs. 100% (Using discriminant function derived by Pitman, Orr, Forgue, et al., 1990)
Yes	PTSD > Controls on resting HR, SBP, & DBP.	PTSD > Controls on resting HR, SBP, & DBP	Not reported
Yes	PTSD vets showed greater (O)EMG & HR responses to stimuli & less diminution of SC across phases.	None	Not reported
Age-Yes Gender-Yes	Statistical trends for the PTSD group to be more responsive than controls on both EMG & HR.	PTSD HR = 73.2 BPM Control HR = 67.7 BPM Eta^2 = .11	Not reported
Age-No Gender-Yes	Audiovisual C > I, N on HR response C > L, N on SC C > N on DBP Imagery Scripts C, L > N on HR C > N on SC C, L > N on EMG Logistic Regression using psychophysical measures correctly classifies 69% in the derivation sample & 64% in the validation sample.	C > I, N on HR C > L on SC	Derivation 83% vs. 42% Validation 81% vs. 31% (Logistic Regression)
Age-No Gender-Yes	PTSD > non-PTSD vets on overall HR & DBP measures.	Differences were seen during waking & sleeping hours	Not reported

Note. PTSD = Posttraumatic Stress Disorder; HR = Heart Rate; SBP = Systolic Blood Pressure; DBP = Diastolic Blood Pressure; SC = Skin Conductance; EMG = Frontalis Electromyogram; (O)EMG = Orbicularis Electromyogram; PT = Peripheral Temperature; RR = Respiration Rate; Norepin. = Norepinephrine; SL = Sublingual Temperature; Epin = Epinephrine; PDA = Predictive Discriminant Analysis; MVA = Motor Vehicle Accident; BPM = Beats Per Minute; MA = Mental Arithmetic

[a]Eta^2 is an effect size measure that is a proportion of variance accounted for. Thus, multiplying by 100 would give the percentage of variance accounted for by independent variables.

TABLE 12.2 Studies of Psychophysiological Responding in Civilian Trauma Populations

AUTHORS	POPULATIONS (N)	YRS. POST TRAUMA	STIMULI	RESPONSES
Blanchard, Hickling et al. (1991)	MVA related PTSD (4)	7.5 Months	Two, 3-minute personal imagery audiotapes of MVA.	HR, SBP, DBP, SC
Blanchard et al. (1994)	MVA victims (50) PTSD (23) Sub-PTSD (10) Non-PTSD (17) Non-MVA controls (40)	2.5 Months	Two, 3-minute personal imagery audiotapes of MVA. One, standardized, 2-minute video of MVAs.	HR, SBP, DBP, EMG, SC
Bryant et al. (1995)	MBA related PTSD (10) Non-MVA normals (10)	3.25 Years	Stroop Threat word.	SC
Blanchard et al. (1996)	MVA victims (105) PTSD (38) Sub-PTSD (35) Non-PTSD (32) Non-MVA controls (54)	2.5 Months	Two, 3-minute personal imagery audiotaped descriptions of MVA. One, standardized, 2-minute video of MVAs.	HR, SBP, DBP, EMG
Kilpatrick et al. (1984)	Tx.-seeking rape victims (27)	1.25 Years	Five 1-minute personal imagery audiotapes: 1-neutral scene, 1-positive scene, 3 fear-evoking rape-related scenes.	HR, SC
Kozak et al. (1988)	PTSD rape victims (12) No rape controls (12)	Range 6 Weeks–2 Years	Standard neutral scene Standard rape scene in 30-second audiotaped format	HR, SC
Griffin et al. (1994)	Recent rape victims (90) (Sample broken down into High-Medium-Low dissociators which served as Independent Variables)	2 Weeks	Five-minute netural discussion with therapist and 5-minute trauma discussion.	HR, SC
Forneris et al. (1996)	Rape victims (13) PTSD (3) Sub-PTSD (3) Non-PTSD (7) Non-rape controls (13)	Not Reported	Two-minute personal imagery audiotapes.	HR, EMG, SBP, DPT, SC
Shalev, Orr, Peri, et al. (1992)	Civilian trauma PTSD (14) Anxiety DO (14) Normals previous trauma (15) Normals w/o previous trauma (19)	5.75 Years	Fifteen 95dB, 500-millisecond tones delivered via earphones.	HR, SC, (O)EMG
Shalev et al. (1993)	Israeli civilian trauma PTSD (13) Non-PTSD trauma civilians (13)	4.6 Years	Two, 30-second personal imagery audiotapes of traumatic war experience, with 1 standardized combat tape. Five personal imagery tapes of neutral, positive, action, & fear experiences.	HR, SC, EMG

AGE/ GENDER MATCHED	RESULTS	BASELINE DIFFERENCES	SENSITIVITY/SPECIFICITY (METHOD OF CLASSIFICATION)
N/A	Increases over baseline levels on HR for 3 of 4 (9.2 BPM) also for SBP (4 of 4) & 2 of 4 for EDA.	All were within the normal HR range at baseline except 1.	Not applicable
Yes	MVA-PTSD group was more responsive on HR measure upon presentation of idiosyncratic audiotapes relative to non-PTSD MVA victims & controls.	None	74% vs. 76% (Single cutoff score of 2 BPM when responding to personal imagery)
Yes	PTSD > Controls on responses to neutral & threat words.	None	Not reported
Yes	MVA-PTSD group was more responsive on HR measure upon presentation of idiosyncratic audiotapes relative to non-PTSD MVA victims & controls. Strong initial HR response predicted poor clinical outcome 1 year later for PTSDs.	None	69% vs. 78% (Single Cutoff score of 2 BPM Increase to Personal imagery)
N/A	HR and SC responding was greater relative to baseline for most conditions. Pleasant scene was just as effective as fear-evoking scenes in eliciting a response.	As a group, baseline hyperarousal was not evident.	Not reported
Yes	Trends for greater responding of PTSD group on both HR & SC measures. Failed to reach statistical significance.	Not reported	Not reported
N/A	High dissociators respond with lower SC responses that low or medium dissociators. No group effects on HR data.	Not Reported	Not reported
Yes	No significant differences between PTSD and non-PTSD groups.	None	Not reported
Age-Yes Gender-No	PTSD group showed larger HR & SC responses relative to the other groups. They were the only group that failed to habituate across trials.	None	Not reported
No	PTSD > Controls on HR & EMG responses to personal traumatic imagery.	Non > PTSD on SC	69% / 77% (Using PDA derived by Pitman et al. 1987)

Note. PTSD = Posttraumatic Stress Disorder; HR = Hear Rate; SBP = Systolic Blood Pressure; DBP = Diastolic Blood Pressure; SC = Skin Conductance; EMG = Frontalis Electromyogram; (O)EMG = Orbicularis Electromyogram; PT = Peripheral Temperature; Norepin. = Norepinephrine; SL = Sublingual Temperature; Epin = Epinephrine; PDA = Predictive Discriminant Analysis; MVA = Motor Vehicle Accident; BPM = Beats Per Minute

The two most commonly used responses, HR and EDA, are good indicators of sympathetic nervous system involvement (although HR is controlled jointly by sympathetic and parasympathetic input). Exploring the sympathetic nervous system underpinnings a bit further, Blanchard, Kolb, and Prins (1991) found increases in plasma norepinephrine (accompanied by elevated HR) among Vietnam veterans with PTSD compared to similar combat veterans without PTSD, following exposure to an audiotape with combat sounds. This tonic change in the biochemical substrate was consistent with Mason, Giller, Kosten, Ostroff, and Podd (1986) findings of higher 24-hour urinary levels of norepinephrine and cortisol in Vietnam veterans with PTSD. Pitman and Orr (1990), however, failed to replicate Mason et al.'s findings. One would expect to see BP responses follow a similar pattern to those found for HR.

The EMG responses were primarily from a frontal (forehead) or frontalis placement but two studies involved EMG measures of obicularis oris associated with orienting and startle responses. These skeletal muscle responses show that arousal goes beyond the autonomic nervous system.

WHAT IS THE BEST RESPONSE TO USE?

This question addresses both the research summary issue and a very practical issue. Taking a box score approach, when HR and EDA have both been used in the same study (n = 17), HR has apparently yielded · significant results in 12 instances when EDA did not, while EDA has yielded significant findings on three occasions when HR was not significant. On two occasions both yielded significant results. (One can also address this question more precisely with the results in Table 12.3, a summarization of the values for variance accounted for by the different measures in different studies. See below.)

Overall, of the 29 studies which have utilized HR, 21 (72.4 percent) found significant results. For the 18 studies using EDA, 8 (44.4 percent) found significant results. Finally, for the 16 studies using EMG, 8 (50 percent) found significant results.

Clinical Hint

Our own experience has been that EMG, especially frontal EMG, is not very useful. We recommend dropping it from psychophysiological assessments unless one has an especially compelling reason to include it. Again, from our experience, we would choose HR over EDA if one is forced to use a single physiological channel. Our preference would be to use *both HR and EDA*.

Temperature is a very slow response and does not appear useful. Blood pressure is certainly a very important health parameter and should be added, if possible, especially with a middle-aged or older male population.

WHAT FORMS OF STIMULUS PRESENTATION HAVE BEEN USED AND WHICH ARE PREFERABLE?

The overwhelming favorite for stimulus modality is auditory with 24 reports having an audio stimulus of one fashion or another, while three used solely visual stimuli, and three an audiovisual combination. One reason so many investigators may have chosen auditory stimuli is that it is difficult for the research participant to voluntarily shut off the stimulus presentation when it is auditory (one can close one's eyes to a visual stimulus but one cannot close one's ears).

Two reports (Blanchard et al., 1996; Keane et al., 1996) have compared auditory and visual traumatic stimulus presentations. One intriguing report (McCaffrey, Lorig, Pendrey, McCutcheon, & Garrett, 1993) used olfactory stimuli. We suspect using cues in the chemical senses (olfactory or gustatory) may be very powerful because these sensory channels are very old phylogenetically and make almost direct connections with the midbrain. Anecdotally, we continue to hear from patients how powerful chemical sense reminders can be for those with PTSD. More research is clearly needed on this topic.

Interestingly, very little work has been done comparing one stimulus modality to another. The three comparisons (Keane et al., 1996; Blanchard, Hickling, Taylor, Loos, & Gerardi, 1994; Blanchard

TABLE 12.3   Effect Sizes (Eta^2)[a] of Psychophysiological Responding in Trauma Populations

AUTHORS	POPULATIONS (N)	ETA² REACTIVITY SCORES TO PROVOCATIVE STIMULI	ETA² BETWEEN-GROUPS COLLAPSED ACROSS ALL EXPERIMENTAL PHASES
Blanchard et al. (1982)	Vietnam PTSD Vets (11) Age matched non-Vets (11)	Not reported	HR = .16 SBP = .23 DBP = .15 SC = .15 EMG = .00 PT = .00
Blanchard et al. (1986)	Vietnam PTSD vets (57) Non-PTSD vets with similar exposure to combat (34)	HR = .25 (Heart rate response to 60db combat sounds)	
Blanchard et al. (1989)	Vietnam PTSD vets (59) Non-PTSD vest with similar exposure to combat (12)		HR = .63[b]
Blanchard et al. (1994)	MVA victims (50) PTSD (23) Sub PTSD (10) Non-PTSD (17) Non-MVA controls (40)	HR = .19	
Blanchard et al. (1996)	MVA victims (105) PTSD (38) Sub-PTSD (35) Non-PTSD (32) Non-MVA controls (54)	HR = .11 SBP = .02	
Davis et al. (1996)	Persian Gulf PTSD vets (14) Persian Gulf Non-PTSD vets (15)	HR = .11 EMG = .02	
Gerardi et al. (1989)	PTSD Vietnam vets (18) Non-PTSD Vietnam vets (18)		HR = .16 DBP = .29
Gerardi et al. (1994)	Vietnam PTSD vets (32) Era vets/no combat exposure (26)	HR = .13 SBP = .08 DBP = .12 SL = .01 RR = .04 (Baseline Only)	
Griffin et al. (1994)	Recent rape victims (90) (Sample broken down into High-Medium-Low dissociators which served as Independent Variables)	SC = .08	
Keane et al. (Under Review)	Vietnam veterans Current PTSD vets (C) (778) Lifetime PTSD (L) (181) Never PTSD vets (N) (369)	*Audio* HR = .03 SC = .03 SBP = .01 DBP = .01 EMG = .01	

(Continued)

TABLE 12.3   Continued

AUTHORS	POPULATIONS (N)	*ETA*^{2} REACTIVITY SCORES TO PROVOCATIVE STIMULI	*ETA*^{2} BETWEEN-GROUPS COLLAPSED ACROSS ALL EXPERIMENTAL PHASES
		Video HR = .02 SC = .02 SBP = .01 DBP = .01 EMG = .02	
Muroaka et al. (Unpublished Dissertation)	Vietnam era PTSD vets (11) Vietnam era Non-PTSD vets (7)	HR = .20 DBP = .28 SBP = .05 (24-hour amubulatory measures only)	
Orr et al. (1993)	WWII & Korean PTSD vets (8) Non-PTSD vets (12)	HR = .45 SC = .40 EMG = .25	
Orr et al. (1995)	Vietnam PTSD vets (37) Vietnam Non-PTSD vets (19)		(O)EMG = .10 SC = .01 HR = .14
Pallmeyer et al. (1986)	Vietnam PTSD vets (12) Non-PTSD Vietnam vets (10) Vietnam vets with Axis I (5) Era vets no disorder (5) Non vets with anxiety disorder (8)		HR = .24 SBP = .28 DBP = .03 SC = .18 EMG = .20
Pitman et al. (1987)	Vietnam PTSD vets (18) Non-psychiatric Vietnam vets (15)	SC = .27 EMG = .14 HR = .08	
Pitman et al. (1990)	Vietnam PTSD vets (7) Vietnam Non-PTSD vets with another anxiety disorder (7)	EMG = .32 SC = .27 HR = .12	
Shalev et al. (1992)	Civilian trauma PTSD (14) Anxiety DO (14) Normals previous trauma (15) Normals w/o previous trauma (19)		(O)EMG = .03 HR = .28 SC = .44
Shalev, Orr, Peri, et al. (1993)	Israeli Civilian trauma PTSD (13) Non-PTSD trauma civilians (13)	HR = .33 EMG = .25 SC = .08	

Note. PTSD = Posttraumatic Stress Disorder; HR = Heart Rate; SBP = Systolic Blood Pressure; DBP = Diastolic Blood Pressure; SC = Skin Conductance; EMG = Frontalis Electromyogram; (O)EMG = Orbicularis Electromyogram; RR = Respiration Rate, MVA = Motor Vehicle Accident

[a]Eta^2 is an effect size measure that is a proportion of variance accounted for. Thus, multiplying by 100 would give the percentage of variance accounted for by independent variables.

[b]The data used to calculate the effect size measure for Blanchard et al., 1989, is based on statistics that utilized the combined sample of Blanchard et al., 1986 & 1989.

et al., 1996) all confounded stimulus modality with the standard stimulus versus idiosyncratic stimulus difference.

There is another dimension to stimulus presentation which has been addressed in this research: whether to use a standardized (or generic) stimulus, that is, the same stimulus is presented to all individuals in the research (with the assumption that the generic stimulus captures some part of each participant's experience of the trauma) or to use an idiosyncratically tailored stimulus for each participant (with the stipulation of the rules for creating these individualized stimuli). The former approach was used by Blanchard, Kolb, and their associates in their studies with Vietnam veterans with PTSD. An audiotape (taken from the sound track of *Apocalypse Now*) was played at progressively louder sound intensities (roughly 40, 50, 60, 70, and 80 decibels) for 30-second intervals. Sounds included AK-47 fire, mortars, helicopters, and screams of the wounded.

A variation of this was used by Malloy, Fairbank, and Keane (1983) who combined still pictures showing progressively more hazardous combat engagement with a sound track of accompanying combat sounds played at progressively louder volumes. Again, the same stimuli were used for all participants. Blanchard and colleagues (Blanchard et al., 1994; Blanchard et al., 1996) used a standardized videotape of car crashes, including scenes shot from inside the vehicle as a crash was occurring, in their work with motor vehicle accident survivors. Finally, Kozak, Foa, Olasov-Rothbaum, and Murdock (1988) used standardized 30-second audiotape descriptions of rape in their work.

Other stimulus modalities (such as Stroop words related to MVAs [Bryant, Harvey, Gordon, & Barry, 1995]) have had only a single paper reporting their usage.

The idiosyncratic approach was pioneered by Pitman and Orr (Pitman, Orr, Forgue, de Jong, & Claiborn, 1987), who used 30-second audiotaped descriptions of idiosyncratic trauma experiences. They acknowledged an intellectual debt to Peter Lang and his work on stimulus propositions and response propositions in fear arousing imagery (Lang, 1979). The versatility of this approach was shown in Israeli studies by Shalev, Orr, and Pitman (1993) in a study of victims of varying traumatic experiences (motor vehicle accidents, sexual assaults, physical assaults, terrorist attacks, and witnessing violence). Pitman and Orr have also included a standard audio description in several of their studies.

A box score approach reveals 14 reports have used standardized stimulus presentations, almost all of which were with Vietnam combat veterans, versus 14 reports which have used idiosyncratic presentations. Three reports (Blanchard et al., 1994; Blanchard et al., 1996; Keane et al., 1996) have used both idiosyncratic presentations and standardized stimuli with MVA survivors, MVA survivors, and Vietnam veterans, respectively. Both of Blanchard's MVA studies found idiosyncratic audiotapes more arousing (and thus better able to discriminate participants with PTSD from comparison groups) than standardized videotapes of car crashes. Keane et al. (1996) found the standardized audio-visual stimulus and the idiosyncratic audiotapes equally provocative with Vietnam combat veterans.

Although one of us (EBB) clearly showed a preference for the standardized stimulus early on, he has come to favor the idiosyncratic audiotape stimulus because of its flexibility and its ability to be readily adapted to subtle personal nuances of trauma experience in the individual case. As Tables 12.1 and 12.2 point out, there are reports of successful use of idiosyncratic audio stimuli with various combat veteran groups from World War II, Korean War, and Vietnam War, up to Operation Desert Storm, as well as sexual assault and rape victims, other assault victims, and motor vehicle accidents. In all of these groups of victims of diverse trauma, the idiosyncratic audiotape has proved itself.

Length of description has varied from the very precise 30-second tapes of Pitman and Orr to 2 to 3 minute descriptions used by Blanchard and colleagues with MVA survivors and by Forneris (1996) with sexual assault victims to 5 minute discussions of trauma with rape victims used by Griffin, Resick, and Mechanic, (1994) and 5-minute descriptions of combat scenes by Boudewyns and Hyer (1990).

BASELINE DIFFERENCES AND AMBULATORY PSYCHOPHYSIOLOGICAL MEASUREMENT

One can note that both Table 12.1 and Table 12.2 have columns for comments devoted to possible baseline differences in psychophysiological measures between participants with PTSD and the comparison groups. One of us (EBB) (Blanchard, 1990) called attention several years ago to the apparent baseline differences in cardiovascular responses (HR, SBP, and DBP) among Vietnam veteran groups of comparable age who either met criteria for PTSD or did not. In that report, the average difference in resting HR was 10.3 bpm while the average differences in both SBP and DBP were about 7 mm of mercury.

Subsequent reports on combat veterans, including Keane et al.'s (1996) large study of Vietnam veterans and Davis, Adams, Uddo, Vasterling, and Sutker's (1996) report on Operation Desert Storm veterans, have continued to report significant baseline differences on HR of about the same magnitude. There have also been a few reports of differences in resting EDA (Keane et al., 1996; Malloy et al., 1983).

In other traumatized populations (Table 12.2), the general rule has been an absence of baseline differences between trauma survivors with PTSD and comparison groups. Shalev et al. (1993), in the assessment of victims of various traumas, found significant resting baseline differences in skin conductance *with the stress exposed PTSD negative group having a higher skin conductance than the PTSD group*. This would seem to indicate more basal sympathetic arousal in the non-PTSDs.

Blanchard (1990) speculated on two possible explanations for the basal cardiovascular differences among combat veterans: (1) It could be the case that those with PTSD could be in a relatively permanent state of "sympathetic overdrive" and thus the baseline difference represents a true difference. (2) Alternatively, it could be that those with PTSD, having some foreknowledge of the nature of the assessment, i.e., exposure to combat stimuli (due to the necessity for informed consent), were aroused in anticipation of the psychophysiological assess-

ment and the adaptation and baseline conditions were not sufficiently long to allow this arousal to dissipate. In other words, the difference was an "experimental artifact."[1]

The first attempt to examine this issue was the study by McFall, Veith, and Murburg (1992), which took extended baseline (no provocative combat-related stimulation) measures of HR, SBP, DBP, plasma norepinephrine, and epinephrine on 11 Vietnam veterans with PTSD and 11 matched veterans without PTSD. They found no significant differences on any measure, lending some credence to the "experimental artifact" explanation.

Gerardi, Keane, Cahoon, and Klauminzer (1994) examined the medical records of 32 Vietnam veterans with PTSD and 26 Vietnam era veterans who never served in Southeast Asia. Both groups were seeking services, medical or psychological, at a VA hospital. HR, BP, and RR were taken by the triage nurse as part of admission, and recorded in the patients' charts. Comparisons revealed significantly higher resting HR (89 versus 78 bpm), SBP (133 versus 124 mm Hg), and DBP (88 versus 79 mm Hg) but no difference in respiration rate. These veterans were not assessed as part of a formal psychophysiological assessment; thus the experimental expectation was absent. Despite this situation, the basal differences were present.

Finally, in a very elegant study, Muruoka, Carlson, and Chemtob (1995) assessed 11 Vietnam veterans with PTSD and 7 comparable veterans without PTSD using 24-hour ambulatory monitoring. Across the 24 hours, the veterans with PTSD had higher average HR (81 versus 72 bpm) and DBP (80 versus 72 mm mercury). Moreover, HR during sleep was significantly greater for veterans with PTSD (71 bpm versus 63 bpm). These results seem to confirm that, at least among veterans with PTSD, there is a significant elevation in cardiovascular responses and that these patients are more aroused all of the time than veterans without PTSD.

---

[1]The NIMH in its wisdom never supported Blanchard and Kolb efforts to explore this issue. Fortunately, others have done so.

IS ONE PHYSIOLOGICAL RESPONSE SYSTEM MORE SENSITIVE THAN OTHERS?

Earlier, we summarized the preferences of various research groups for one physiological response over another in terms of frequency of use, *a relatively qualitative analysis, and counted instances of significant* results. One can see from Tables 12.1 and 12.2, that physiological responding to cues reminiscent of trauma is evident across a multitude of survivor populations. Moreover, the number of independent sites that have replicated the effects is quite impressive. To further understand how well these measures distinguish PTSD populations from non-PTSD populations, we have calculated effect sizes (*eta squared*, eta^2) for all published reports that provided adequate statistical information to do so and summarized them in Table 12.3. Eta^2 is an effect size measure that is a proportion of variance accounted for by independent variables. Thus, multiplying the values in the table by 100 would give one the percentage of variance accounted for by those independent variables (which, in this case, is diagnostic group membership).

For the sake of brevity, we have not arranged the studies into separate tables by trauma type. Rather, we organized the experimental studies (previously described in Tables 12.1 and 12.2) in Table 12.3 alphabetically by first author, and chronologically within author.

The effect size that is of greatest interest is the between-group effect size of physiological responding to provocative stimuli that are reminiscent of one's trauma. This effect size most adequately captures the essence of symptom number five, "physiological reactivity on exposure to internal or external cues that symbolize or resemble an aspect of the traumatic event," of the DSM-IV (APA, 1994) diagnostic criteria for PTSD. This effect size appears in column three. However, in some reports, this effect size could not be computed. In some of these cases, statistics were only available to compute eta^2 on the group mean differences across all phases of the psychophysiological assessment (i.e., baseline, neutral stimuli phases, and provocative stimuli). Thus, in these cases, eta^2 represents the proportion of variance accounted

for by the independent variables of group membership (PTSD versus controls) across all phases, not just the reactivity scores to provocative stimuli. These values are presented in column four.

We mentioned previously in this paper that several published reports have opted for standardized stimulus presentations, while others have utilized an idiosyncratic or personalized imagery approach. Of particular interest to us, was whether or not effect sizes differed as a function of stimulus presentation. For the six studies that utilized standardized auditory stimuli (one study used loud tones), the mean eta^2 value for HR was .33 as opposed to .17 for those studies employing personalized imagery scripts. For EMG, the standardized auditory stimuli approach yielded a mean eta^2 value of .10, while the personal imagery approach yielded a mean value of .16. For studies that measured EDA, the standardized approach yielded a mean eta^2 value of .26, while the personal imagery approach yielded a value of .16 (unfortunately, there were not enough studies across the two types of presentations to make comparisons on the other physiological channels). Based on these values, one might tenuously conclude that the type of stimulus presentation affects physiological channels in different ways. However, this statement should be approached with caution given the nature of the calculations. First, not all studies reported adequate information for the computation of eta^2, thereby reducing the accuracy of the conclusions drawn from these data. Moreover, some of the eta^2 values used were not on reactivity scores to provocative stimuli, but on group effects across all experimental phases. Finally, these data were collapsed across trauma type. Different conclusions may be drawn if effect sizes are compared within trauma populations. Finally, it could be the case that time since trauma (and thus, time with PTSD) may be linked to effect sizes. As suggested by Kolb (1987), those with chronic PTSD of many years may actually develop disordered sympathetic nervous systems. If this is the case, one would expect acute populations to respond differently than chronic populations. Thus, we suggest that the personal versus standardized approach is an interesting area for future research. *Based on personal experience we would endorse the use of idiosyncratic audiotapes as the preferred stimulus presentation method.*

Another interesting question one could ask is whether or not the modality of stimulus presentation matters. For example, are the effect sizes larger or smaller for video presentations of stimuli or audio presentations? Unfortunately, there are only three studies that have used both methods; however, all three confounded stimulus modality with personal versus standardized imagery. Of course, the use of visual presentation of stimuli is somewhat limiting in the sense that all stimuli have to be standardized by definition. It would be very difficult to create "personalized" video stimuli reminiscent of an individual's trauma. Again, we suggest this might be an interesting question to be answered by future research that employs standardized stimuli.

One study in Table 12.3 stands out for the relatively low values of eta^2, that of Keane et al., 1996.

THE VA COOPERATIVE STUDY (KEANE ET AL., 1996)

By far the most ambitious study of the role of psychophysiological assessment in PTSD is that of Keane et al. (1996). This paper reported on VA Cooperative Studies Project No. 334 by Kolb and Keane (1988) (Psychophysiology Study of Chronic Post-Traumatic Disorder). In this project detailed diagnostic data and psychophysiologic assessment data were gathered on 1,328 veterans who served in Southeast Asia during the Vietnam War era 1963–1973. They were carefully characterized, based upon multiple measures, into 3 groups: 778 who *currently* met criteria for PTSD, 181 who had been positive for PTSD at some point in their past lifetime, but who currently were not positive for PTSD, and 369 who never met the criteria for PTSD. Five psychophysiological responses were measured. Both the Pitman-Orr idiosyncratic audiotapes were used as was the audio-visual combination stimulus of Malloy et al. (1983).

Results showed significant discrimination between current PTSDs and the other two groups with the standardized audio-visual stimulus and HR and skin conductance. There was significant discrimination between the current PTSD and never PTSD with

the standardized audio-visual stimulus and DBP and with idiosyncratic audiotapes and skin resistance. The level of sensitivity and specificity were significant but relatively low.

An important part of this paper was that the non-PTSDs and current PTSDs were selected from the same population, treatment-seeking veterans from the VA. As such, they were more similar on many dimensions than comparable groups in other studies. In almost all other studies, the non-PTSD combat veterans were selected from volunteer, usually non-VA, populations.

Unfortunately, the degree of identification in this study at the level of the individual subject is such that the clinical utility of psychophysiological measures is somewhat called into question. At a practical level, this paper seems to show that HR and skin conductance responses to a standardized audio-visual presentation may be best for assessing Vietnam veterans.

FOR WHAT IS PSYCHOPHYSIOLOGICAL ASSESSMENT USEFUL?

At this point, psychophysiological assessment's main role in the assessment of PTSD seem to be one of *confirmatory adjunct*. All of the research to date relies upon some form of interview, structured or otherwise, as the "gold standard" to determine definitively whether a subject has PTSD. Most of the research has been designed (1) to see whether PTSDs are more responsive than those without current PTSD at the level of group mean differences (the answer is usually "yes") or (2) to see how well some single variable or set of variables can discriminate those with PTSD from comparison groups. Separation has ranged from 100 percent correctly classified, Malloy et al. (1983), to 65 percent correctly classified. At the high end, psychophysiological testing could begin to substitute for the structured clinical interview. At the low end, the accuracy is such that one would be uncomfortable making clinical decisions on its basis alone. Even with relatively poor discrimination, however, the psychophysiological assessment data serves as a *useful adjunct* in the overall assessment of PTSD, a point made over ten years ago by the VA (Gronvall, 1986).

"Truth Detection" and Dissimulation

A hope held by many in this field was that psycho-physiological testing might serve as a non-verbal "truth detector." It is fairly easy for a motivated individual to learn the symptomatic criteria for PTSD. If such an individual has the appropriate history of exposure to trauma, it is readily possible for that individual to feign PTSD. Psychophysiological testing might help detect the dissemblers, but probably not with the accuracy one would hope to take to court or a disability rating board.

Gerardi, Blanchard, and Kolb (1989) assessed 18 Vietnam combat veterans with PTSD and 18 comparable Vietnam combat veterans without PTSD using the standardized audiotape of combat sounds (30-second exposures at progressively higher sound levels) while measuring HR, SBP, DBP, forehead EMG, and EDA (as skin resistance level). The initial assessment yielded the usual results with good discrimination between PTSD and non-PTSD groups. Again, HR was the single best response, correctly identifying 80.6 percent of the sample ($p = .0001$).

Next, half of the randomly selected veterans without PTSD were given a description of the typical pattern of responses of those with PTSD and were asked, in a second assessment a few minutes later, to try to simulate the responding of someone with PTSD. They were given explicit information on how responses should change (e.g., increased HR). Comparisons of the simulators to those with PTSD, also assessed a second time, revealed that only DBP reactivity scores discriminated between the two groups ($p < .01$). Discriminant functions were still significant for HR, DBP, SBP, and frontal EMG, but not EDA. The best overall discrimination of veterans with PTSD from veterans without PTSD who were attempting to fake the response comes from a combination of baseline HR and maximum HR response to combat sounds. This correctly identified 89 percent of veterans with PTSD and 67 percent of those attempting to simulate PTSD.

Orr and Pitman (1993) assessed 25 Vietnam combat veterans with PTSD and 18 comparable veterans without PTSD using their 30-second idiosyncratic audiotape stimuli and HR, EDA (as skin conductance), and three different facial EMG measures. Seven weeks later the non-PTSDs were reas-

sessed and asked to produce responses like someone with PTSD by "getting yourself emotionally 'worked up.'" Thus, the instructions were less explicit and the interval considerably longer.

At the initial session a discriminant function using skin conductance and corrugator EMG correctly identified 18 of 25 PTSDs and 16 of 16 non-PTSDs. When this discriminant function was applied to the second (simulation) session data of those without PTSD, 4 subjects were identified as PTSD positives and 12 were identified as non-PTSD. In effect, 75 percent were correctly identified.

Clearly, more research is needed on this important topic. There appear to be possible instruction and practice effects which one would want to tease out.

Prediction of Future Clinical Status

An obvious question to address with psychophysiological assessment results is whether they predict future clinical status, with or without intervening treatment. One study has addressed this issue explicitly: Blanchard et al. (1996) identified 48 motor vehicle accident survivors who met the criteria for PTSD 1 to 4 months post-accident. At an assessment 12 months later 16 (33 percent) had not remitted whereas 32 had remitted totally or in part. The HR response of these 48 individuals to idiosyncratic audiotapes of their accidents had been recorded at the initial assessment. These data correctly identified 37 (of 48) individuals as still having PTSD (11/16) or as remitting (26/32) 12 months later. Other work on the prediction of remission or response to treatment is clearly needed. However, we are impressed by this level of prediction from a single variable.

Within-Treatment Session
Psychophysiological Data

In addition to pre-treatment physiological measures being used to predict long-term clinical outcome, physiological measures taken during treatment phases may be useful in assessing the adequacy of behavioral strategies used to target specific symptoms of PTSD. It has been suggested by Foa and Kozak (1986) that in order for exposure based therapies of anxiety disorders to work, therapist's need to tailor exposure exercises such that they are effectively tapping into the patients "fear network." Theoretically, when an individual's fear network is tapped, there should be a strong anxiety response that can be directly measured through physiological responses. If one fails to elicit this response, exposure will presumably not be successful. Thus, Foa and Kozak suggest that exposure exercises should be set up to achieve maximum physiological arousal in order for them to be successful. In general, one should see within-session decreases in physiological responses (habituation) during treatment if exposure is working effectively. In addition, one should also see between-session decrements in physiological responding if the exposure based therapy is working effectively. Thus, the theory proposed by Foa and Kozak is elegant in the way that it readily lends itself to being tested through the use of the physiological measures that have been shown in this chapter to readily distinguish PTSD positives and negatives (for a detailed account of propositional network theory and processing of fearful stimuli, see Foa & Kozak, 1986).

In fact, four treatment studies of PTSD addressed the issue of whether physiological responding is linked to treatment outcome. Shalev, Orr, and Pitman (1992), treated 3 cases of civilian related PTSD. Elevated physiological responses to traumatic imagery prior to treatment were treated with systematic desensitization. Physiological responding to these images was diminished at post-treatment. All patients showed improvement in overall PTSD symptoms. However, traumatic stimuli that were not used as exposure based exercises during treatment still elicited elevated physiological arousal at post-treatment.

Fairbank and Keane (1982) successfully treated a case of combat related PTSD with an exposure based therapy. Heart rate and skin conductance data taken at each session showed that responding decreased within each session after exposure. In addition, between-session decrements in overall responding were also apparent. One other case study of successful treatment of combat related PTSD (Keane & Kaloupek, 1982) provided data that showed pre- to post-treatment decrements in physiological responding (within-session data was not obtained). Boudewyns and Hyer (1990) treated 51 cases of combat related PTSD with either an exposure based therapy or conventional one-on-one counseling. As a whole, both groups showed significant physiological responding at both pre- and post-treatment. However, at an individual level, subjects who showed decreased physiological arousal at post-treatment improved at three-month follow-up when compared to those subjects who did not show decreased responding at follow-up.

These case studies and the results provided by Boudewyns and Hyer (1990) provide data that are consistent with the theory put forth by Foa and Kozak (1986). Given the current state of affairs in the health care system, with a focus of designing effective treatments that are readily translated into good outcome measures, psychophysiological correlates of treatment outcome appear to present a fruitful area of PTSD treatment outcome research.

CONCLUSIONS

Psychophysiological assessment, especially heart rate and to a lesser degree, electrodermal activity responses, measured to idiosyncratic audiotapes reminding the participant of his or her traumatic experience, appears to be useful with combat veterans and motor vehicle accident survivors, and to those with mixed trauma. It is apparently less useful in the assessment of sexual assault survivors. In the main, psychophysiological assessment can serve as a useful adjunct to standardized clinical interviews by helping to confirm PTSD diagnoses. Psychophysiological assessment may also have a very valuable role to play both in the prediction of long-term outcome to stress exposure and also in evaluating short-term outcome of treatments for PTSD.

REFERENCES

American Psychiatric Association. (1968). *Diagnostic and statistical manual of mental disorders* (2nd ed.). Washington, DC.

American Psychiatric Association. (1980). *Diagnostic and statistical manual of mental disorders* (3rd ed.). Washington, DC.

American Psychiatric Association. (1987). *Diagnostic and statistical manual of mental disorders* (3rd ed. Rev.). Washington, DC.

American Psychiatric Association. (1994). *Diagnostic and statistical manual of mental disorders* (4th ed.). Washington, DC.

Blanchard, E. B. (1990). Elevated basal levels of cardiovascular responses in Vietnam veterans with PTSD: A health problem in the making? *Journal of Anxiety Disorders, 4*, 233–237.

Blanchard, E. B., Hickling, E. J., Buckley, T. C., Taylor, A. E., Vollmer, A. J., & Loos, W. R. (1996). The psychophysiology of motor vehicle accident related posttraumatic stress disorder: Replication and extension. *Journal of Consulting and Clinical Psychology, 64*, 742–751.

Blanchard, E. B., Hickling, E. J., & Taylor, A. E. (1991). The psychophysiology of motor vehicle accident related posttraumatic stress disorder. *Biofeedback and Self-Regulation, 16*, 449–458.

Blanchard, E. B., Hickling, E. J., Taylor, A. E., Loos, W. R., & Gerardi, R. J. (1994). The psychophysiology of motor vehicle accident related posttraumatic stress disorder. *Behavior Therapy, 25*, 453–467.

Blanchard, E. B., Kolb, L. C., Gerardi, R. J., Ryan, P., & Pallmeyer, T. P. (1986). Cardiac response to relevant stimuli as an adjunctive tool for diagnosing posttraumatic stress disorder in Vietnam veterans. *Behavior Therapy, 17*, 592–606.

Blanchard, E. B., Kolb, L. C., Pallmeyer, T. P., & Gerardi, R. J. (1982). A psychophysiological study of post traumatic stress disorder in Vietnam veterans. *Psychiatric Quarterly, 54*, 220–229.

Blanchard, E. B., Kolb, L. C., & Prins, A. (1991). Psychophysiological responses in the diagnosis of posttraumatic stress disorder in Vietnam veterans. *The Journal of Nervous and Mental Disease, 179*, 99–103.

Blanchard, E. B., Kolb, L. C., Prins, A., Gates, S., & McCoy, G. C. (1991). Changes in plasma norepinephrine to combat-related stimuli among Vietnam veterans with posttraumatic stress disorder. *Journal of Nervous and Mental Disease, 179*, 371–373.

Blanchard, E. B., Kolb, L. C., Taylor, A. E., & Wittrock, D. A. (1989). Cardiac response to relevant stimuli as an adjunct in diagnosing post-traumatic stress disorder: Replication and extension. *Behavior Therapy, 20*, 535–543.

Boudewyns, P. A., & Hyer, L. (1990). Physiological responses to combat memories and preliminary treatment outcome in Vietnam veteran PTSD patients treated with direct therapeutic exposure. *Behavior Therapy, 21*, 63–87.

Bryant, R. A., Harvey, A. G., Gordon, E., & Barry, R. J. (1995). Eye movement and electrodermal responses to threat stimuli in post-traumatic stress disorder. *International Journal of Psychophysiology, 20*, 209–213.

Davis, J. M., Adams, H. E., Uddo, M., Vasterling, J. J., & Sutker, P. B. (1996). Physiological arousal and attention in veterans with post-traumatic stress disorder. *Journal of Psychopathology and Behavioral Assessment, 18*, 1–20.

Dobbs, D., & Wilson, W. P. (1960). Observations on persistence of war neurosis. *Diseases of the Nervous System, 21*, 1–6.

Fairbank, J. A., & Keane, T. M. (1982). Flooding for combat-related stress disorders: Assessment of anxiety reduction across traumatic memories. *Behavior Therapy, 13*, 499–510.

Foa, E. B., & Kozak, M. J. (1986). Emotional processing of fear: Exposure to corrective information. *Psychological Bulletin, 99*, 20–35.

Forneris, C. A., Blanchard, E. B., & Jonay, T. Y. (1996, March). Psychophysiological sequelae of sexual assault. *Proceedings of the 27th Annual Meeting of the Association for Applied Psychophysiology and Biofeedback* (pp. 38–39). Albuquerque, NM. Association for Applied Psychophysiology and Biofeedback.

Gerardi, R. J., Blanchard, E. B., & Kolb, L. C. (1989). Ability of Vietnam veterans to dissimulate a psychophysiological assessment for post-traumatic stress disorder. *Behavior Therapy, 20*, 229–243.

Gerardi, R. J., Keane, T. M., Cahoon, B. J., & Klauminzer, G. W. (1994). An in vivo assessment of physiological arousal in posttraumatic stress disorder. *Journal of Abnormal Psychology, 103*, 825–827.

Griffin, M. G., Resick, P. A., & Mechanic, M. B. (1994, November). *Psychophysiological & nonverbal assessment of peritraumatic dissociation in rape victims*. Paper presented at the 10th Annual Meeting of the International Society for Traumatic Stress Studies, Chicago, IL.

Gronvall, J. A. (1986). Supplement No. 1, IB-56, *Physician's Guide, Chapter 20*. Psychiatric Sequelae of Military Duty in a War Zone. Department of Medicine and Surgery, Veterans Administration, Washington, DC 20420.

Kardiner, A. (1941). *The traumatic neuroses of war*. NY: Harper & Row Publishers Inc.

Keane, T. M., & Kaloupek, D. G. (1982). Imaginal flooding in the treatment of a posttraumatic stress disorder. *Journal of Consulting and Clinical Psychology, 50*, 138–140.

Keane, T. M., et al. (1996, February). Results of a multi-site clinical trial on the psychophysiological assessment of post-traumatic stress disorder. Unpublished manuscript, National Center for PTSD (Boston Branch): Boston VAMC, Boston, MA.

Kessler, R. C., Sonnega, A., Bromet, E., Hughes, M., & Nelson, C. B. (1995). Post-traumatic stress disorder in the National Comorbidity Survey. *Archives of General Psychiatry, 52,* 1048–1060.

Kilpatrick, D. G., Best, C. L., Ruff, M. H., & Veronen, L. J. (1984, November). *Psychophysiological assessment in the treatment of rape-induced anxiety.* Paper presented at the annual meeting for the Association for the Advancement of Behavior Therapy, Washington, DC.

Kolb, L. C. (1987). A neuropsychological hypothesis explaining post-traumatic stress disorders. *American Journal of Psychiatry, 144,* 989–995.

Kolb, L. C., & Keane, T. (1988). Cooperative Studies Program No. 334, "Physiology study of chronic post-traumatic stress disorder." Veterans Administration, Washington, DC.

Kozak, M. J., Foa, E. B., Olasov-Rothbaum, B., & Murdock, T. (1988). *Psychophysiological response of rape victims during imagery of rape and neutral scenes.* Paper presented at Meetings of the World Congress on Behavior Therapy, Edinburgh, Scotland.

Kulka, R., Schlenger, W., Fairbank, J., Hough, R., Jordan, B., Marmar, C., & Weis, D. (1990). *Trauma in the Vietnam War generation.* NY: Brunner/Mazel.

Lang, P. (1979). A bio-informational theory of emotional imagery. *Psychophysiology, 16,* 495–512.

Malloy, P. F., Fairbank, J. A., & Keane, T. M. (1983). Validation of a multimethod assessment of posttraumatic stress disorders in Vietnam veterans. *Journal of Consulting and Clinical Psychology, 51,* 488–494.

Mason, J. W. Giller, E. L., Kosten, T. R., Ostroff, R. B., & Podd, L. (1986). Urinary free-cortisol level in post-traumatic stress disorder patients. *Journal of Nervous and Mental Disease, 174,* 145–149.

McCaffrey, R. J., Lorig, T. S., Pendrey, D. L., McCutcheon, N. B., & Garret, J. C. (1993). Odor-induced EEG changes in PTSD Vietnam veterans. *Journal of Traumatic Stress, 6,* 213–224.

McFall, M. E., Veith, R. C., & Murburg, M. M. (1992). Basal sympathoadrenal function in posttraumatic stress disorder. *Biological Psychiatry, 31,* 1050–1056.

Muruoka, M., Carlson, J. G., & Chemtob, C. M. (1995). *Twenty-four hour ambulatory blood pressure and heart rate monitoring in combat related posttraumatic stress disorder.* Unpublished doctoral dissertation, University of Hawaii.

Norris, F. H. (1992). Epidemiology of trauma: Frequency and impact of different potentially traumatic events on different demographic groups. *Journal of Consulting and Clinical Psychology, 60,* 409–418.

Orr, S. P., Lasko, N. B., Shalev, A. Y., & Pitman, R. K. (1995). Physiologic responses to loud tones in Vietnam veterans with posttraumatic stress disorder. *Journal of Abnormal Psychology, 104,* 001–008.

Orr, S. P., & Pitman, R. K. (1993). Psychophysiological assessment of attempts to simulate posttraumatic stress disorder. *Biological Psychiatry, 33,* 127–129.

Orr, S. P., Pitman, R. K., Lasko, N. B., & Herz, L. R. (1993). Psychophysiological assessment of posttraumatic stress disorder imagery in World War II and Korean combat veterans. *Journal of Abnormal Psychology, 102,* 152–159.

Pallmeyer, T. P., Blanchard, E. B., & Kolb, L. C. (1986). The psychophysiology of combat-induced post-traumatic stress disorder in Vietnam veterans. *Behaviour Research and Therapy, 24,* 645–652.

Pitman, R. K., & Orr, S. P. (1990). Twenty-four hour urinary cortisol and catecholamine excretion in combat-related posttraumatic stress disorder. *Biological Psychiatry, 27,* 245–247.

Pitman, R. K., Orr, S. P., Forgue, D. F., Altman, B., de Jong, J. B., & Herz, L. R. (1990). Psychophysiologic responses to combat imagery of Vietnam veterans with posttraumatic stress disorder versus other anxiety disorders. *Journal of Abnormal Psychology, 99,* 1–6.

Pitman, R. K., Orr, S. P., Forgue, D. F., de Jong, J. B., & Claiborn, J. M. (1987). Psychophysiologic assessment of posttraumatic disorder imagery in Vietnam combat veterans. *Archives of General Psychiatry, 44,* 970–975.

Shalev, A. Y., Orr, S. P., Peri, T., Schreiber, S., & Pitman, R. K. (1992). Physiologic responses to loud tones in Israeli patients with posttraumatic stress disorder. *Archives of General Psychiatry, 49,* 870–875.

Shalev, A. Y., Orr, S. P., & Pitman, R. K. (1992). Psychophysiologic response during script-driven imagery as an outcome measure in posttraumatic stress disorder. *Journal of Clinical Psychiatry, 53,* 324–326.

Shalev, A. Y., Orr, S. P., & Pitman, R. K. (1993). Psychophysiologic assessment of traumatic imagery in Israeli civilian patients with posttraumatic stress disorder. *American Journal of Psychiatry, 150,* 620–624.

CHAPTER 13

LEGAL ISSUES IN THE FORENSIC ASSESSMENT OF TRAUMATIZED YOUTH

DANIEL W. SHUMAN, J.D.
Southern Methodist University School of Law

DANIEL J. MADDEN, J.D.
Thornton, Summers, Bicchlin, Dunham, & Brown

While a variety of acts may cause trauma to a child, one cause of trauma that both the mental health and legal professions have increasingly addressed in recent years is trauma arising out of claims of physical or sexual abuse. Forensic assessment of these claims presents a special set of concerns that are the focus of this chapter. Not all of the issues that arise in the assessment of claims of physically or sexually traumatized youth occur in cases claiming other causes of trauma to youth. However, these cases vividly illustrate most issues that occur in all legal assessments of traumatized youth, and they present the cutting edge issues in the forensic assessment of traumatized youth with which the mental health and legal professions now wrestle. Thus, for heuristic purposes, trauma arising out of physical or sexual abuse is used throughout this chapter to explain and illustrate legal issues that arise in forensic assessment of youth who have been negligently as well as intentionally traumatized.

Allegations of childhood trauma may lead to both criminal charges and civil liability claims. Negligently or carelessly caused childhood trauma (e.g., automobile accidents), however, other than that resulting from recklessness or gross negligence, as contrasted with trauma resulting from physical or sexual abuse, is likely to lead only to civil liability claims. Moreover, it is now increasingly possible to bring both criminal charges and civil liability claims for childhood abuse long after the abuse is alleged to have occurred. In addition, in the case of negligently caused trauma to a child, it is more likely to be clear at the outset of the therapist–patient relationship that the patient is seeking care for harm that could result in litigation. All therapists should inform patients who contemplate litigation of the accompanying limitations on confidentiality and privilege for the patient-litigant, and therapists who seek to avoid involvement in the judicial process should be able to identify that risk in most cases of accidentally caused traumatic injury to a child. However, unlike treatment of most other cases of trauma, even mental health professionals who treat patients who do not initially complain about child abuse and mental health professionals who seek to avoid the legal process may affect their patient's legal claims or may be drawn into a criminal prosecution or civil liability claim as a fact or expert witness in the case of abuse. Thus, it is important that all mental health professionals understand the legal issues raised in assessments of traumatized youth, particularly where the trauma alleged constitutes abuse.

Allegations of trauma resulting from child abuse, like all childhood trauma claims, may arise both during and after the claimant's youth. However, claims arising out of abuse are not only more likely to result in criminal prosecution but as well are more likely to present specialized exceptions to the legal rules governing the timeliness of such cases. In cases in which these allegations of abuse are made while the claimant is still a child, the government may, without the consent of or consultation with the child or the child's parents or guardians, institute a prosecution of the alleged abuser charging recent acts of physical or sexual abuse, as it may for any criminal act resulting in trauma to a child. While the willingness of prosecutors to institute such cases may have increased, the problems of successfully prosecuting such cases endures. An example of one such case is the McMartin Preschool prosecutions. Reflecting the problems of objectively interviewing children about abuse and presenting their testimony, the jury returned a verdict of acquittal (Eberle & Eberle, 1993).

Because children lack the legal capacity to institute a civil claim on their own behalf, a civil damage claim during the claimant's minority (typically below the age of 18 for these purposes) for trauma resulting from abuse, or any other civil claim on behalf of a child during the child's minority, must be instituted by the child's parents or, where appropriate, the child's legal guardian. An example of such a claim would be a civil damage claim by the parents or guardians of the McMartin Preschool children, on behalf of their children or wards, against the owners and employees, alleging that they intentionally caused or negligently failed to prevent abuse. In both criminal and civil actions, evaluating the believability of the child and deciding what expert testimony to admit to assist in this evaluation have troubled the courts. These issues are discussed in the section entitled "Legal Proceedings during Youth."

Allegations of abuse, like all other allegations of trauma during youth, made after the claimant has reached majority, may also result in both criminal charges and civil liability claims, depending on the statute of limitations, which governs the time within which a claim may be brought. For example, in *California v. Franklin* (1995), George Franklin was convicted in 1990 for the murder of an eight-year-old girl, Susan Nason, in September, 1969. The prosecution could be brought 21 years later because there is no statute of limitations for murder, as there is for most other crimes. Franklin's conviction was based largely on the testimony of his adult daughter, Eileen Franklin-Lipsker, who stated that she witnessed her father kill Susan Nason, but had no adult recollection of it until her memories were triggered by a glance from her own daughter 20 years later. Reflecting the difficulties of such prosecutions long after the event in question, the conviction was overturned on federal *habeas corpus* review based on procedural errors at

trial. Similarly, in *State v. Hungerford* (1995) and *State v. Morahan* (1995), in an unsuccessful attempt to impose criminal liability, one woman accused her father of assaulting her from age 5–23 years and another woman accused her teacher of abusing her one time when she was 13. Although prosecution of these charges was not barred by the statute of limitations, the court excluded the victims' testimony in those cases reasoning that evidence that memories are repressed did not meet the applicable scientific threshold.

A statute of limitations also filters civil claims for injury sustained through tortious conduct occurring during minority, but not filed until after the claimant reaches majority. In personal injury claims, the controlling state statutes of limitation generally require that the claim be filed or waived from one to three years after the alleged tortious event. Because the statute of limitations does not run during minority, if the claim is filed within the applicable period after reaching the age of majority, there is no statute of limitations problem. Cases arising out of child abuse filed after the applicable period present a specialized exception to the general limitations rule that fall into two categories.

The first (Type 1) involves people who claim to remember the abusive events continuously but only conceptualize them as abusive after they have reached adulthood. Such a claimant might allege that she had always remembered being fondled by a parent, but that she only recently realized that it was inappropriate and had caused her psychological problems. While these cases seem to raise fewer psychology of memory problems, they raise perplexing statute of limitations problems. Because claimants are less likely to assert that they experienced difficulty conceptualizing wrongful conduct or its consequences in other types of cases of trauma to a child that might give rise to litigation, such as injury from automobile accidents and defective products, mental health professional assessments of the appropriate application of Type I exceptions tend to be restricted to childhood physical and sexual abuse claims asserted by adults.

The second (Type 2) involves people who claim to have recovered previously unavailable memories of child abuse. An example of such a claim was Stephen Cook's accusation (subsequently recanted and withdrawn) that Cardinal Joseph Bernadin sexually molested him during his childhood and that he long repressed and only recently recovered his memories of this event (McCarthy, 1993). Claimants in Type 2 cases often allege that their repressed memories of childhood abuse were only recovered in therapy, through the use of hypnosis or other memory recovery techniques. While these cases raise greater psychology of memory problems, they present fewer statute of limitations problems. The archetype for this statute of limitations exception is medical malpractice claims for surgical errors that were only discovered years later in a subsequent surgery. Because claimants are less likely to invoke this exception, asserting that they only recently recovered previously unavailable memories of wrongful conduct in other cases of trauma to a child that might give rise to litigation which are public and often well-documented events, such as injuries resulting from automobile accidents and defective products, mental health professional assessments of the appropriate application of Type II exceptions tend to be restricted to childhood physical and sexual abuse claims asserted by adults. These issues are discussed below in the section entitled "Legal Proceedings Arising after Youth."

I. LEGAL PROCEEDINGS DURING YOUTH

The testimony of the child claimant and mental health professionals who have treated or assessed the child are often pivotal to assess a claim of abuse, as well as other legal claims of trauma to a child. In both civil and criminal proceedings the child claimant's testimony may be necessary both to establish that the trauma occurred and the harm it has caused. In both civil and criminal proceedings a mental health professional's testimony may be necessary to assist in assessing the child's claims. And, in civil proceedings, where courts have traditionally been hesitant to permit the award of damages for non-physical harm like pain and suffering, the testimony of mental health professionals is often central in determining the extent of the harm and its causal nexus to the defendant's tortious conduct. To offer such testimony, both the child and the expert witness must first meet certain threshold requirements of compe-

tence and then testify in a manner which is credible to the fact finder.

A. The Child Witness

Whether because of increasing instances of trauma involving children and/or the increasing willingness of the legal system to address this trauma, the number of children called as witnesses has increased dramatically in the latter part of the twentieth century (Pepper, 1984). The testimony of the child victim in cases in which trauma to a child is alleged is often a vital component of the case. At minimum, to offer such testimony, the child witness must perceive a relevant event, remember that event when testifying, and testify to that memory sincerely in language shared by the witness, judge, and jury (DeLipsey & Shuman, 1991).

Memory is generally believed to be a constructive rather than a reproductive exercise (Bartlett, 1932; Ceci & Bruck, 1995). Memories are not simply recorded by our senses and then stored in the brain in their natural form preserving their initial quality. "The likelihood that we can remember an event from our past depends on the skill with which we execute a complex set of processes, initially during the event in question, then later at the time of its retrieval" (Ceci & Bruck, 1995, p. 41). Human memory experts usually describe the memory process in terms of a flow of information from one stage of the memory system to another. The three main stages of the system are encoding, storage, and retrieval.

Encoding refers to the process by which an individual's experience becomes registered in memory. Not everything that a person experiences is remembered. This is due, in part, to the limited attention capacity of individuals; we cannot attend to everything happening around us at one time and selectively encode some information at the cost of not encoding other information. Consequently, certain aspects of an event are attended to and others are ignored. These limitations of the human cognitive system prevent us from encoding all experienced information (Ceci & Bruck, 1995).

A variety of factors may influence the quality of encoding. These include the amount of prior knowledge about an event that may assist in the development of a schema to encode it, the interest value or salience of an event, the duration and repetition of the original event, and the stress level at the time of encoding the original event (Ceci & Bruck, 1995).

In the second phase of the memory system, encoded events enter a short-term memory store. Due to the limited memory capacity, not all memories survive the short-term memory store. Those that do survive enter a long-term memory store. While in the long-term memory store, the encoded information can be transformed, fortified, or lost (Brainerd, Regina, Howe, & Kingman, 1990). The passage of time, the number of times the event has been reexperienced, and the number and types of intervening experiences, can have a strong impact on the strength and organization of the stored information (Ceci & Bruck, 1995).

The third and final step in the memory process is the retrieval of stored information. Not all of the contents of the memory system are retrievable. A variety of cognitive as well as social factors influence the extent to which memories can be recalled. These include the condition of the original memory and whether it has undergone decay, whether cues are given by an interviewer, the extent to which an event conforms to our expectations and beliefs about the event, and the desire of the individual to retrieve the old memory (Ceci & Bruck, 1995).

Children possess impressive memory capacity, but very young children have not yet acquired a complete framework for understanding the world around them that is connected to personal experience. While an experience may be observed and stored, the presence or absence of contextual cues determines the capacity to retrieve memories of personal information experienced as a child (Fivush & Hammond, 1990). Thus, for example, it is not likely that people can gain access to verbal memories before the age of two (Loftus, 1993). However, people may have memories of salient personal events from an earlier age than previously thought. For example, an individual may remember being hospitalized or the birth of a sibling as early as age two and the death of a family member or a family move as early as age three (Usher & Neisser, 1993). In addition, the "social context and the extent to which adults can help children structure their experiences…may account for individual differences in memories for early childhood trauma" (Memon & Young, 1997, p. 5).

1. Relevant Legal Rules and Procedures. Courts apply two levels of scrutiny, competence and credibility, to the perception, memory, and sincerity of all witnesses. The first level of scrutiny, competence, is a question of law determined solely by the judge. Competence is addressed to minimum threshold requirements for testifying. If a witness is not found competent, the witness will not be permitted to testify. The second level of scrutiny, credibility, is a question of fact determined by the jury if one is being used, or by the judge acting as the trier of fact. Credibility is considered only if the witness is determined to be competent to testify. Credibility describes the weight or believability that the fact finder should give to the testimony (DeLipsey & Shuman, 1991).

2. Competence of the Child Witness. The requirement that the judge first find the child witness competent to testify addresses the child's ability to satisfy a minimum threshold of perception, memory, and sincerity. The courts are concerned that the child witness possess the capacity to testify sincerely about his or her memory of relevant events and comprehend the importance of being truthful while testifying (DeLipsey & Shuman, 1991).

There is no fixed bright line age below which a child is not regarded as competent to testify. The common practice is for the judge to talk with the child in the courtroom or in the judge's chambers to determine whether the child understands the difference between a lie and the truth, the importance of telling the truth in court, and the consequences of lying (although many have questioned the validity of this approach) (Goodman, Golding, & Haith, 1984; Melton, 1981). In most states, children ten years and older are routinely found competent to testify. Decisions regarding children under ten are made on an individual basis and relegated to the judge's discretion. In some cases, three-year-old children have been found competent to testify (*DLN v. State,* 1979). Expert testimony may be offered to challenge the competence of the child witness and, in certain circumstances, may also be admitted to challenge the credibility of the child witness before the jury (DeLipsey & Shuman, 1991).

In practice, courts are typically interested in receiving the testimony of the child witness and err in favor of finding the child competent. This trend in favor of finding the child competent to testify by adopting a low threshold for competence has resulted in more difficult questions being placed before the fact finder about the weight to give the child's testimony as well as the expert testimony that should be admitted to assist in this determination (DeLipsey & Shuman, 1991).

3. Credibility of the Child Witness.

If the judge determines that the child is competent to testify and the child testifies, the fact finder must assess the weight or credibility of the child's testimony. While there are no rules that describe how the fact finder should assess a witness' credibility, there are rules about how parties may attack or bolster a witness' credibility. The child's credibility may be attacked (impeached) through cross-examination of the child or the presentation of other witnesses (both lay and expert) to challenge the child's story. After it is attacked, the child's story may be bolstered (rehabilitated) through redirect examination of the child or the presentation of other witnesses (both lay and expert) to support the child's testimony (DeLipsey & Shuman, 1991). Mental health professionals are often offered as expert witnesses to assist the fact finder in assessing a child's credibility.

B. Expert Testimony Regarding Competence and Credibility of Children

Witnesses who possess scientific, technical, or other specialized knowledge that will assist the judge or jury to understand the evidence may be qualified to testify as experts. In some states, expert testimony of a mental health professional may be used to challenge the competence of a witness. For example, in Texas a child or adult is not competent to testify if he or she is "insane" when offered as a witness, or was "insane" while perceiving the event to which the witness is called to testify (DeLipsey & Shuman, 1991). However, courts are reluctant to prevent the introduction of relevant lay or fact testimony and therefore

generally err on the side of allowing the testimony and exclude fact witnesses from testifying as "insane persons" in only the most serious cases (*Saucier v. State,* 1951).

In addition, parties challenging testimony may argue that evidence of mental disorders suffered by a particular eyewitness is relevant and admissible. Limits on the ability of a witness to testify accurately have implications both for the admissibility of the testimony (testimonial competence) and the weight of the testimony (testimonial credibility) (Shuman, 1995b). Expert testimony bearing on the mental disability of an individual witness that affects perception, memory, sincerity, or narration may provide important information that is highly relevant in determining the competence and credibility of a witness. Whether this type of testimony is admitted is generally left to the discretion of the trial judge. This decision usually turns on the degree of the disability and its effect on testimonial credibility. Evidence of a major mental illness that may have an impact on perception of a relevant event and expert testimony explaining its effects is generally admissible to challenge the credibility of the witness (*United States v. Partin,* 1974). Conversely, evidence concerning mental disorders not likely to affect perception or memory has generally excluded (*United States v. Butt,* 1992). The question in each individual case is whether the disorder is merely an aberration in behavior or of a degree and nature that may affect the witness' ability to perceive, remember, or narrate accurately and sincerely (Shuman, 1995b). Although trial court judges are generally accorded the discretion to order a psychiatric or psychological examination of a witness' competence to testify, they are generally reluctant to do so solely to assess credibility.

A mental health professional called as an expert witness can assume a variety of roles, however not all of them are acceptable (Lorenzen, 1988). For example, while it is acceptable to provide a context to assist the fact finder to understand how children may respond to trauma, expert testimony directly addressing the child's veracity is generally not acceptable. An expert operating in this latter role is purporting to determine which witness should be believed. That is a task in American jurisprudence reserved exclusively for the fact finder.

A mental health professional who has evaluated a child may generally testify about the child's symptoms and behavior patterns, diagnosis, and whether the child's behavior and patterns are consistent with the occurrence of a particular event. The same is true for a clinician who did not examine the child, but testifies as to general clinical patterns observed in sexually abused children, and responds to hypothetical questions incorporating the facts of the case at hand. A third acceptable role is that of an expert who is qualified based upon familiarity with the scientific study of behavior. The role of such an expert is to provide the trier of fact with information that will assist it in evaluating the child's behavior patterns. A final acceptable role is that of preserving perishable and fragile testimony. The time between an incident of abuse and the date of the abuser's trial may span years. A large delay, measured as relative to the amount of life experiences (which in small children may equal a fifty percent or more increase), may result in errors in recall. Thus, subject to rules on hearsay and privilege, mental health professionals may be called upon to corroborate or clarify essential aspects of the child's statements that they heard at an earlier time either in therapy or a forensic assessment.

C. General Legal Rules about the Admissibility of Expert Testimony

Generally, although not exclusively, mental health professionals do not testify in cases involving trauma to youth as fact witnesses to inform the fact finder about relevant information that they have gained as an eyewitness to some important event in the case, but rather as expert witnesses applying their profession's knowledge to interpret or explain information presented by others. There are three legal categories of the bases for factual information about the case to which a mental health professional might offer to apply his or her expertise—personal knowledge, hypothetical questions, and extrajudicial sources of information. First, the expert might offer to rest an opinion on personal knowledge, for example, a treating therapist or a court ordered examiner's observations of a patient/litigant. In the case of a treating therapist, a written waiver of the therapist–patient privilege and confi-

dentiality should precede the use of this source of information to support an opinion. Because, ordinarily, a minor lacks the legal capacity to effectuate a valid waiver, the therapist should additionally require a written waiver of privilege and confidentiality by the minor's parents or legal guardian. In the case of a court ordered examination or independent medical examination, full disclosure about the purpose and intended use of the results of the examination and the litigant's consent to participate should precede the examination, as well as notice to and the agreement of the minor's attorney. Although these out of court statements present hearsay issues, either the admission or statement for purposes of medical diagnoses or treatment exceptions to the hearsay rule generally result in the statement of the party being excluded from the bar if the hearsay rule.

Another source of information upon which an expert might base an opinion is the use of the hypothetical question, which asks the witness to apply his or her expertise to a series of facts described in the question and supported by the evidence. While there are still some instances in which the hypothetical question is useful, as, for example, where a party has exercised the privilege against self-incrimination and refused to speak with a mental health professional, the confusion that long hypothetical questions and the lawyers' debate that they often engender over their grounding in the facts, as well as availability of alternative methods of presenting the basis for the opinion, has resulted in a decline in their use. A third source of information on which a mental health professional might base an opinion is extrajudicial or out of court sources of information, such as the reports of other health care professionals, police reports, or medical records. In some instances, these sources of information may be introduced into evidence, in others they may not be admitted and they may not be inadmissible. However, modern legal practice is that when these sources are regularly and reasonably used by experts outside the judicial setting, their use as the basis for an expert's opinion is not barred by the hearsay rule.

Even where it rests on an acceptable basis, not all expert testimony that is offered is admissible. Like all witnesses, proposed expert witnesses must be found competent to testify. Because an expert is permitted to offer opinions and conclusions that a lay witness is not permitted to offer, a special set of rules govern the competence of experts. While different courts apply a variety of tests of competence, they all entail an inquiry into the expert's qualifications in his or her claimed area of expertise and an inquiry into the body of knowledge possessed by members of that trade, profession, or calling. The inquiry into qualifications in the claimed area of expertise is generally similar from jurisdiction to jurisdiction and concerns satisfaction of the appropriate education, training, and experience to make a threshold claim as a well informed member of a relevant trade, calling, or profession. Thus, in the case of an expert who offers to testify about trauma to a child, the question of qualifications will turn on the expert's education, training, and experience to diagnose, treat, or research this type of trauma in children. Courts expect to receive the assessments of learned experts, applying professionally recognized methods and procedures. Viewed in this context, Quinn (1995) devised a set of guidelines for the evaluation of traumatized youth. Although committed to the discretion of the trial judge, there is a similarity in the functional approach applied by most trial judges. A proposed expert must convince the trial judge of his or her credentials in the relevant field and, that his or her education and training are sufficient to provide expertise or special knowledge such that the expert's opinions will be of assistance to the jury in its fact finding responsibilities. Most of the variations from jurisdiction to jurisdiction in the scrutiny of experts concern the standard used to assess the knowledge possessed by members of that trade, profession, or calling.

In federal court, and increasingly in many state courts, the relevant standard for this inquiry is set out in the United State's Supreme Court's decision in *Daubert v. Merrell Dow Pharmaceuticals* (1993) which requires the trial judge to engage in "a preliminary assessment of whether the reasoning or methodology underlying the testimony is scientifically valid and of whether that reasoning properly can be applied to the facts at issue" (p. 590). In making this determination, the judge should consider the underlying theory and whether it has been tested, its scrutiny by others in the field through peer review and publica-

tion, the error rate and standards for controlling it, and the degree of acceptance within the relevant scientific community. The application of *Daubert,* as well as its predecessors and competitors such as the general acceptance within the relevant professional community test (*Frye v. United States,* 1923), to psychiatric and psychological testimony has varied widely. Some courts considering psychiatric and psychological evidence have engaged in demanding scrutiny of the science that underlies psychiatric and psychological methods and procedures, while others have failed to appreciate or address these issues. Generally, rigorous judicial scrutiny is more likely when the expert testimony explicitly invokes the mantle of science by seeking to ground the testimony in a particular psychological test or diagnosis, for example, than when the use of science is implicit as in clinical opinion testimony (Sales, Shuman, & O'Connor, 1994). This distinction raises important and unresolved questions about the scientific grounding of clinical opinions and their ability to meet rigorous scientific standards. The most extensive body of case law applying this standard to mental health professionals testifying about traumatized youth has been in the recovered repressed memory cases discussed below in the section "The Recovered Repressed Memory Debate."

II. LEGAL PROCEEDINGS ARISING AFTER YOUTH

Both criminal and civil actions arising out of trauma to a youth can also arise long after the claimant has reached the age of majority. In addition to problems of evaluating the competence and credibility of lay and expert witnesses to provide useful information about trauma to a child that occurred long ago, a preliminary legal issue in these cases is often whether they have been timely filed. Both sets of issues may involve mental health professional's assessments of current and past (i.e.,childhood) mental condition and functioning.

A. Statute of Limitations

As noted in the introduction, where these cases brought long after the claimant has reached the age of majority involve claims of physical or sexual abuse, claimants typically assert either that they remembered the abuse continuously but only later discovered that it was wrongful or caused harm, or that the memories of abuse were previously repressed but were later recovered. Both assertions present distinct legal issues.

1. Civil.

a. Claims of Continuously Remembered Abuse.
Allegations of abuse made by adults who claim to have continuously remembered the acts of child abuse are the least controversial in terms of the psychology of memory. However, these claims present intractable statute of limitations problems. If the statute of limitations has run, the defendant may successfully move that the case be summarily dismissed, without regard to whether the abuse actually occurred.

Generally, depending on the state, a claimant has one, two, or three years from the time of the conduct complained of to bring a civil personal injury damage claim. This limitation is placed on the claimant to "increase the likelihood that courts will resolve factual questions fairly and accurately" by preventing the bringing of stale claims that involve less evidence and less reliable evidence, as well as permitting the defendant to plan for the future without the uncertainty of potential liability (*Tyson v. Tyson,* 1986, p. 75). However, if a claimant has a disability at the time of the event that is the subject of the cause of action, the statute of limitations does not begin to run until the disability is removed. Disabilities include incapacity and minority. Therefore, the statute of limitations does not begin to run in most states until the claimant reaches the age of majority.

Plaintiffs in cases in which the relevant period after reaching the age of majority has passed have attempted to apply an exception to the general rule known as the *discovery rule.* The discovery rule first emerged in medical malpractice cases where the defendant's own wrongful conduct prevented the plaintiff from learning of the injury (e.g., foreign object left in the patient following surgery) (*Gaddis v. Smith,* 1967). In these cases, courts often allow the extension of the statute of limitations by finding that the cause

of action took place, or accrued, at the time the plaintiff knew or should have known of the injury. Consequently, the statute of limitations begins to run at the time the plaintiff discovered or should have discovered the injury, rather than the time of the actual injury. In sexual abuse cases, plaintiffs have attempted to apply the discovery rule arguing that the defendant's wrongful conduct was responsible for the repression of memories that prevented the plaintiff from bringing the claim in a timely fashion.

"Type 1" recovered memory cases, in which the plaintiff claims to have always remembered the abuse but only recently realized that it was wrongful or produced injury, have not been accorded favorable discovery rule treatment. Courts are reluctant to apply this exception when the plaintiff knew or should have known well before the limitations cut off date that the defendant's alleged misconduct had caused injury and that he or she had a potential cause of action. Their reluctance is based on the absence of any impediment which might have precluded the plaintiff from bringing the cause of action in a timely manner (*Doe v. First United Methodist Church,* 1994; *Martinez-Sandoval v. Kirsch,* 1994; *Weathers v. Fulgenzi,* 1994). However, in cases that involve some compelling circumstances, such as threats by an abusive father to harm the claimant if the abuse was revealed (*Hammer v. Hammer,* 1987), courts are generally more willing to allow the action to proceed.

b. Claims of Recovered Repressed Memories of Abuse.
Although more controversial in terms of the psychology of memory, courts have been more willing to apply the discovery rule in "Type 2" cases in which the plaintiff claims to have repressed all memories of abuse until recently (Taub, 1996). However, in cases involving "Type 2" claims, many courts require corroboration by objective, verifiable evidence to apply the extension of the statute of limitations when the sufficiency of the claim has been challenged (*Mary D. v. John D.,* 1990; *S.V. v. R.V.,* 1996; *Tyson v. Tyson,* 1986). While mental health professionals may provide valuable assistance to the courts in assessing the validity of these claims of repression, in cases in which courts require corroboration to apply this exception to the statute of limitations,

mental health professional testimony has not been regarded as sufficient to meet this requirement.

Numerous state legislatures have recently extended the statute of limitations for child sexual abuse claims (Taub, 1996). Some state statutes provide that the statute of limitations does not begin to run until the abuse is discovered, if the abuse is discovered within a specific time period after the victim reaches the age of majority. These statutes place an outer limit on the time in which civil actions may be brought which varies from state to state. For example, in Connecticut, the plaintiff can bring an action for child sexual abuse if the abuse is discovered within 17 years after the victim reaches the age of majority, but in Idaho, the claimant only has 5 years after reaching the age of majority to bring an action for child sexual abuse (Connecticut; Idaho).

Other state statutes provide that an adult victim may bring suit within a specific number of years from the date the plaintiff recovered memories of the abuse. That number can be anywhere from 2 to 10 years depending on the state (e.g., California is 3 years; Maine is 6 years; Nevada is 10 years). These statutes place essentially no limit on the time in which a plaintiff can bring an action for child sexual abuse. For instance, a 65-year-old woman could potentially bring an action for child abuse against her 90-year-old parents.

Still other statutes provide that a plaintiff who was a victim of a series of acts of child sexual abuse need not establish which act of the series of acts caused the injury. The statute of limitations runs from the last act in the series (Colorado; Oklahoma; Vermont).

2. Criminal Statutes of Limitations.

Criminal statutes of limitations for child sexual abuse differ from state to state and vary greatly from states, like South Carolina and Wyoming, which have no statute of limitations for any criminal offense, to Hawaii, which has a three year statute of limitations for rape of a child. Most state statute of limitations are more like Hawaii's and allow charges to be filed only during a fixed time after the actual criminal event. Murder, however, generally has no statute of limitations (LaFave & Israel, 1992).

Courts are typically less willing to find creative solutions to statute of limitations problems in criminal actions than in civil actions. For example, the discovery rule does not apply in criminal actions because of constitutionally mandated concerns with the rights of the criminal defendant. Given the consequences of a criminal conviction, courts want cases heard while the evidence is fresh and when they have the greatest chance of reaching the correct verdict. Thus, in most cases, criminal statutes of limitation are strictly enforced.

Some courts, however, have fashioned exceptions to the general rule that extend, or toll, the statute of limitations in criminal cases. The theories that are most often are the "continuing crime" and the "concealment" theories. The continuing crime theory posits that a crime is not complete as long as the defendant continues to engage in the criminal conduct, and as long as the crime is not complete, the statute of limitations does not begin to run. For example, prosecutors have successfully used this theory in abuse cases to argue that an element of the crime is the exertion of authority over the victim and therefore the crime continued until that exertion of authority ceased, even though the abuse had ended long before (*State v. Danielski*, 1984).

The concealment argument is based upon statutory provisions in a number of states that allow for the tolling of the statute of limitations if the perpetrator conceals his crime. While this theory has met with limited success in abuse cases, there are instances in which courts have held that threats of physical violence against the victim could constitute concealment (*Crider v. State*, 1988), and the methods used to perpetrate and hide the crime of child sex abuse resulted in concealment of that crime and served to toll the statute of limitations (*Walstrom v. State*, 1988).

The success of these arguments to toll the running of the statute of limitations in criminal prosecutions for child abuse, however, is very limited. There are few cases in which either of these theories has successfully tolled the statute of limitations. However, advocates seeking to extend statute of limitations have been more successful in convincing legislatures that change is needed.

Most states have extended their statute of limitations for prosecution of child sexual abuse. Only four states remain with no extension provisions for child sexual abuse cases (Connecticut; Delaware; Hawaii; Texas). The legislative responses to the problem are varied. A number of states have simply extended the statute of limitations for prosecution in cases of child sexual abuse. For example, in Colorado if the victim of abuse is under the age of 15, the statute of limitations on criminal prosecution increases from three years to ten years. In Iowa, if the victim is under 12, the statute of limitations on criminal prosecution is extended to the victim's eighteenth birthday plus six months (Iowa).

Most states, responding to the problem of a minor victim being unable or unwilling to come forward, have enacted tolling statutes. Typically the statute of limitations is tolled until the victim reaches a certain age, usually that state's age of majority. In Idaho, for example, the statute of limitations starts to run when the victim reaches 18 years of age.

B. The Recovered Repressed Memory Debate

A core premise underlying the use of child sexual abuse-oriented memory work in psychotherapy, tolling the statute of limitations for recovered memory child abuse claims, admitting expert testimony about recovered memory supporting these claims, as well as permitting the fact finder to assess these claims, is the assumption that a substantial percentage of psychotherapy clients have abuse histories of which they are unaware (Lindsay & Read, 1995). Yet, a large body of research suggests that most traumatized people retain the memory of the traumatic event (Lindsay & Read, 1995). The problem for the legal system is how to respond to the increasing numbers of allegations of those who claim to have repressed all memory of these traumatic events and then to have recovered these memories.

Although the first generation of cases involving delayed claims of abuse failed to address the complexities of the recovered repressed memory debate or scrutinize this aspect of abuse claims, increasingly the legal system has addressed the debate and carefully scrutinized this aspect of abuse claims (Shuman, 1995b). Based on the doubts within the mental health community about the authenticity of repression and

later retrieval of memory, many courts have been reluctant to accept the validity of recovered repressed memory claims (Shuman, 1995b). Relying on the work of experimental psychologists who question the legitimacy of these recovered memory claims and argue that "there is no compelling biological or social science evidence to support the view that once-viable memories of traumatic experiences can be submerged and then recovered after intervals that extend many years" (Ornstein, Ceci, & Loftus, 1996, p. 107), many courts have become skeptical of both lay and expert testimony in support of recovered memory child abuse claims. Those who question the validity of recovered repressed memories claim the existence of this phenomenon is substantiated only by a number of clinical cases in which people, often undergoing therapy, recall a memory of a previous traumatic event (Ersdorff & Loftus, 1993). Occasionally, these memories are claimed to be corroborated from other sources, enhancing their credibility (Herman & Schatzow, 1987). But until experimental proof is available to demonstrate the phenomenon of repressed memories, which presents perplexing methodological problems, experimental psychologists and the lawyers and judges who rely on their work will likely remain skeptical of these claims (Ersdorff & Loftus, 1993).

Other courts relying on the work of clinicians who posit that the occurrence of memory repression is often more reliable than experimental psychologists conclude continue to view such claims credibly. They argue that dissociation is the most likely explanation of loss of access to, and then retrieval of, memories of severe trauma, including childhood abuse (Albert, Brown, & Courtois, 1996). They point out that the connection between trauma and dissociation, and problems of memory storage, encoding, and retrieval is currently widely accepted (Albert, Brown, & Courtois, 1996). They maintain that trauma suffered by a youth necessitates a defensive strategy for management of this overwhelming material. These strategies include dissociation and numbing that can interfere with the memory process. They suggest that something in the current environment (a retrieval cue or trigger of some sort) may reduce the use of numbing strategies thereby allowing for access to stored memories. The reduction of numbing may be gradual or abrupt, but in either case it may improve the recall of previously weak memory traces, including the event of childhood sexual abuse (Albert et al., 1996).

Those who doubt the validity of repressed memories respond that memory is fallible and can be biased by agents such as psychotherapists leading to recovery of false memories. However, clinicians who view such claims credibly respond that while the occurrence of false memory may in fact occur in some situations, that does not rule out the validity of all recovered memories (Briere, 1995). Therefore, they contend that "memory experts" should not automatically attribute claims of recovered memories to suggestion on the part of the therapist, but should treat them as a common and expectable situation that arises in all forms of psychotherapy (Courtois, 1995).

1. Legal Implications of the Recovered Memory Debate.

The legal implications of this debate effect statute of limitations and expert testimony determinations, as well as color the overall receptivity of the legal system to recovered memory claims. As discussed above, in the absence of a special statute of limitations for child sexual abuse, in most states it is possible to avoid dismissal of an abuse claim brought after the relevant one to three year personal injury limitations period following the age of majority, if the judge concludes that the claimant repressed memory of the abuse until recently. However, if the judge in a Type 2 case shares the view of experimental psychologists who do not acknowledge that the retrieval of repressed memory of child abuse occurs, the judge is less likely to accept the tolling based on a rejection of its factual predicate. Relatedly, appellate judges' and legislators' willingness to create special rules for child sexual abuse cases turn on their beliefs about the recovered repressed memory debate.

Likewise, the debate about the validity of recovered repressed memories raises issues about the admissibility of expert testimony on this subject. This debate is usually framed by the clinical/research dichotomy and whether clinically based testimony to support such claims can and/or should be required to satisfy *Daubert* like rigorous scientific scrutiny. Supporters of the admissibility of expert testimony to sustain a claim of recovered memories of child abuse point to research that they claim has validated the process of recovery. In some cases, they have had success in arguing its validity to courts (*Shahzade v. Gregory,* 1996). However, they also argue that a rigorous scientific threshold for clinical/behavioral science expert testimony is neither possible or desirable, nor done elsewhere in other areas of the law such as child custody or the insanity defense. They posit that a competent clinician's use of therapeutic techniques accepted by a respectable minority of the profession, and their resulting opinions formed by treating patients who suffer from real harm, is sufficiently helpful to satisfy standards for admissibility of expert testimony that are applied across the legal system.

Those who advocate in favor of limiting the admissibility of expert testimony to research based opinions posit that all expert testimony that invokes the mantle of science necessitates rigorous screening due to the risk of decision making errors (heuristics). This is especially true in cases of repressed memories which surveys indicate a substantial number of therapists believe to be common (Poole, Lindsay, Memon, & Bull, 1995).

> Operating on this belief, these therapists dig systematically for the presumed memories in clients who have no previous recollection of abuse. Using a variety of questionable techniques such as direct suggestion, guided visualization, hypnotic age regression, sexualized dream interpretation, and body memory analysis, a hunt for the buried memories is initiated, and any mental products that are recovered are uncritically assumed to be accurate (Ornstein et al., 1996, p. 106).

These heuristic errors cause us to give undue regard to anecdotal, clinical information that is likely to be wrong, and from which professionals are not immune. In addition, researchers find no scientific proof of repression and recovery of repressed memories as claimed. Thus, those who advocate in favor of rigorous scientific scrutiny argue that there is no scientific basis to consider therapists' testimony about these memories reliable or helpful and therefore, argue that non-experimental, clinically based testimony about recovered memories should be excluded.

2. The Case Law to Date.

a. Statute of limitations and issues of scientific validity.   The overarching question of the scientific validity of recovered repressed memory has, for the most part, not prevented plaintiffs from bringing actions after the statute of limitations has run. While some courts have dismissed Type 2 actions as time barred notwithstanding allegations of repressed memory for a variety of reasons (*Tyson v. Tyson,* 1986) (prevention of stale claims); (*Baily v. Lewis,* 1991) (judge believed that state supreme court would not allow the extension of the statute of limitations); (*Shippen v. Parrott,* 1993) (state legislature had specifically rejected the tolling of the statute in these cases), the vast majority of courts have held that allegations that a claimant has repressed memories of childhood sexual abuse tolls the applicable statute of limitations until the date that the plaintiff recovered his or her memory (*Evans v. Eckelman,* 1990; *Farris v. Compton,* 1994; *Hammer v. Hammer,* 1987; *Johnson v. Johnson,* 1988; *Mary D. v. John D.,* 1990; *Olsen v. Hooley,* 1993). Ironically, these courts do not purport to decide the validity of the theories regarding repression and recovered memories, but instead leave this matter to the trier of fact.

b. Testimony Regarding Recovered Repressed Memories.   Testimony regarding recovered repressed memories has faced greater challenges in the courts. Increasingly, the impact of the debate regarding the validity of the process of repression and recovery has caused difficulties for plaintiffs trying to introduce evidence of recovered repressed memories. For example, in *State v. Hungerford* (1995) and *State v. Morahan* (1995), discussed in the introduction, in which one woman accused her father of assaulting her from age 5 to 23 and another woman accused her teacher of abusing her one time when she was 13, the judge excluded the victim's testimony of recovered repressed memories of abuse finding that "the phenomenon of memory repression and the process of therapy used in these cases to recover the memories have not gained general acceptance in the field of psychology and are not scientifically reliable" (*State v. Morahan,* 1995, p. 378571)

Courts have been particularly concerned with admission of hypnotically refreshed repressed memo-

ries and have taken a number of approaches in determining the admissibility of this evidence (*Borawick v. Shay,* 1995). Some courts treat all such testimony as per se admissible and rely on the trier of fact to assess the witness' credibility. Other courts treat it as per se inadmissible because the testimony is open to distortion and therefore questions its reliability. Still other courts require adherence to a strict set of safeguards intended to ensure the reliability of hypnotically refreshed testimony. But the approach most frequently taken is the totality of the circumstances approach.

This approach requires the court to decide the admissibility of the testimony based on all the circumstances surrounding the gathering of the information that is the subject of the testimony. In conducting this analysis, the court will consider some of the following factors: (1) Whether the purpose of the hypnosis was to refresh a witness' memory of an accident or crime or whether is was conducted as part of therapy. In the former instance, the subject may feel pressured to remember the events in question, while if the subject has undergone therapy to discover the source of his or her psychological ailments, he or she may be less inclined to confabulate a story.

Courts will consider the possibility that the subject may have received subtle suggestions from his or her therapist that abuse may be at the root of the subject's problems; (2) Whether the witness received any suggestion from the hypnotist or therapist prior to or during hypnosis such as a theory of the cause of the subject's ailments or key information relevant to the investigation for which the subject underwent hypnosis; (3) Related to (2), the presence or absence of a permanent record, which can help the court ascertain whether suggestive procedures were used. Ideally, a videotape or audiotape would be used; (4) Whether the hypnotist was appropriately qualified by training in psychology or psychiatry; (5) Whether corroborating evidence exists to support the reliability of the hypnotically refreshed memories; (6) Whether the subject was highly hypnotizable, as such a person would be more likely to confabulate and would be more susceptible to suggestion; (7) Any expert evidence offered by the parties as to the reliability of the procedures used in the cases; (8) The court should also conduct a pretrial hearing to enable the parties to present expert evidence and to test credibility through cross-examination (*Borawick v. Shay,* 1995).

c. Expert Testimony Regarding Recovered Repressed Memories.   The admissibility of expert testimony regarding recovered repressed memories is subject to the same *Daubert* or equivalent considerations as all other expert testimony. Courts are charged with assessing the methodology underlying the expert's opinions, as well as the expert's qualifications. Just as the mental health community is divided over the validity of recovered repressed memories, so courts are divided in their assessment of the methodology underlying testimony supporting such claims. Some courts have not allowed experts to testify about the allegedly recovered memories because of doubts about the expert's methods and procedures (*Gier v. Educational Services,* 1995). Other courts have allowed experts to testify about the recovery of repressed memories finding that testimony grounded in valid scientific principles (*Isely v. Capuchin Province,* 1995; *State v. Alberico,* 1993). While not explicit in these opinions, informed speculation points to differing judicial understandings of science, child sexual abuse, and the role of judge and jury, to explain these divergent results.

III. PRACTICE POINTERS

A. Compliance with Existing Practice Guidelines and Professional Standards

Numerous professional organizations have promulgated standards or guidelines for their members' treating or assessing individuals who may have been victims of child sexual abuse (American Medical Association, 1994; American Psychiatric Association, 1993; American Psychological Association, 1995; Australian Psychological Society, 1994; British Psychological Society, 1995). While it is beyond the scope of this chapter to address the implications of these standards and guidelines for clinical practice, it is important for mental health professionals to understand their legal relevance. These standards and guidelines serve as red flags for the courts to raise fundamental problems with the validity and reliabil-

ity of a professional's methods and procedures (Shuman, 1998). Under both *Daubert* and *Frye,* professional scrutiny of the methods and procedures used in an evaluation process is fundamental to the admissibility determination. These professional standards and guidelines are at the heart of both *Daubert* and *Frye's* test for admissibility. Thus, a mental health professional's failure to comply with an applicable treatment or assessment standard or guideline should result in exclusion of any resulting testimony.

B. Avoiding Therapeutic/Forensic Role Conflicts

In most jurisdictions, a properly qualified therapist may testify as a fact witness about information learned firsthand in therapy, and as an expert witness for some purposes about mental disorder that a lay person would not be permitted to offer. However, this dual role of therapist and forensic evaluator may cause role conflicts that can harm the patient and limit the effectiveness of the expert (Greenberg & Shuman, 1996).

The conflict arises due to the differing nature of the roles of a therapist and a forensic evaluator. In most instances, therapy is based on information from the person being treated. This information may be somewhat incomplete, grossly biased, or honestly mis-perceived. But, in most instances, it is not realistic, nor advisable for the therapist to be an investigator to validate the historical truth of what a patient discusses in therapy. Trying to investigate by contacting family members, friends or co-workers and by requesting corroborating documentation may frustrate therapy even if the patient has signed a release of information. The more important question for most types of therapy is how a patient perceives or feels about the world—what is real to that patient—not factual or historical truth (Wesson, 1985).

In contrast, the role of the forensic examiner is, among other things, to offer opinions regarding the historical truth and the validity of the psychological aspects of a litigant's claim. A competent forensic evaluation almost always includes verification of the litigant's accuracy against other information sources about the events in question. This can include interviews with co-workers, neighbors, family members, and others (Greenberg & Shuman, 1997).

In addition, the risk of iatrogenic injury is heightened by therapists who testify as experts. The success of therapy depends in large part on the positive alliance of the therapist and patient (Horvath & Luborsky, 1993). To develop a positive therapist–patient alliance, a therapist must suspend judgment of the patient so that the therapist can enter and understand the private perceptual world of the patient without doing anything that would substantially threaten the relationship.

The role of the forensic examiner, on the other hand, is to assess, to judge, and to report that finding to a third party (i.e., attorney, judge, or jury) who will use that information in an adversarial setting. To assess, a forensic examiner must be detached, maybe even skeptical, and must carefully question what the litigant presents. Since a forensic psychologist or psychiatrist has not engaged in a helping relationship with the litigant, it is less likely that his or her judgement-laden testimony would cause serious or lasting emotional harm to the litigant (Greenberg & Shuman, 1997). However, it is evident that if these two roles are merged, the risks of injury to the patient are multiplied.

Thus, it is appropriate (subject to the rules on privilege, confidentiality, and qualifications) for therapists to testify as treating experts about the history the patient provides; the patient's mental status; the patient's clinical diagnosis; the care the therapist provided and the response to it; the patient's prognosis; the patient's mood, cognition, or behavior; and relevant statements that the patient made in treatment. Presented in the manner of descriptive "occurrences" and not psycho legal opinions, these do not raise issues of judgment, foundation, or historical truth. However, therapists do not ordinarily have a sufficient data base to testify appropriately about psycho legal issues of causation (i.e., the relationship of a specific act to claimant's current condition) or capacity (i.e., the relationship of diagnosis or mental status to legally defined standards of functional capacity). These issues raise questions of judgment, foundation, and historical truth which are problematic for treating experts.

C. Methods and Procedures That Invoke Heightened Scrutiny

While evidence of recovered repressed memory claims generally raise complex scientific and legal issues, certain therapeutic practices are particularly troubling. In general, there seem to be fewer concerns with memories of abuse that arise spontaneously than with those that arise as the result of memory recovery techniques (Lindsay & Read, 1995). For example, evidence of sexual abuse obtained after a therapist told his or her client who reported no child sexual abuse that their symptoms are indicative of repressed memories of child sexual abuse and that failure to remember is common to child sexual abuse survivors, and that healing depends on remembering the incidents of abuse, are particularly troubling, and should be expected to meet with heightened legal scrutiny.

In addition, use of memory recovery techniques such as hypnosis, age regression, guided imagery, sodium amytal, and instructions to work at remembering the child sexual abuse should also be expected to receive heightened legal scrutiny. A few courts continue to admit unconditionally hypnotically refreshed memory, reasoning that the fact of hypnosis should go to the weight and credibility of the evidence (Murray, 1995). However, a substantial number of courts hold that to admit testimony that has been hypnotically refreshed, the proponent must show by clear and convincing evidence that the hypnosis was a reasonably reliable means of restoring memory, that there was no suggestive or coercive conduct during the hypnotic session, and that certain safeguards were followed. These include having the hypnosis performed by a psychologist or psychiatrist that is not only experienced in the use of hypnosis, but who is independent of both parties, recording a detailed description of the facts as they are remembered prior to hypnosis, and recording all contact between the subject and the hypnotist. When any of these procedures are not followed, the testimony is unlikely to be admitted (*Borawick v. Shay,* 1995).

IV. CONCLUSION

Diagnostic nomenclature purporting to reflect a professional consensus about an aspect of mental disorder has had a profound impact on the law (Shuman, 1995a). For example, the decision to recognize post-traumatic stress disorder in the Diagnostic and Statistical Manual of Mental Disorders dramatically altered the recognition of legal claims and defenses and the role of mental health professional within the legal system. The unresolved deep divisions within the mental health community over the recovered memory debate leave the courts to sort out these questions on a case by case basis with only partisan guidance. In the absence of a purported professional consensus like that expressed in the DSM about post-traumatic stress disorder, courts will continue to struggle and reach inconsistent and unpredictable results in recovered memory cases (Shuman, 1989).

That uncertainty places a special responsibility on mental health professionals involved in the assessment of traumatized youth. While patients and therapists are generally free to agree to structure therapy in a manner acceptable to them, particularly in the forensic setting, the impact of these agreements on third parties who do not participate in these agreements may be profound. Thus, given the legal implications of assessments of traumatized youth, compliance with accepted, scientifically grounded professional norms is imperative. Failure to do so may result in the courthouse being closed to all such claimants, deserving or not.

REFERENCES

Albert, J. L., Brown, L. S., and Courtois, C. A. (1996). Symptomatic clients and memories of childhood sexual abuse: What the trauma and child sexual abuse literature tells us. *American Psychological Association, Final Report, Working Group on Investigation of Memories of Childhood Abuse.*

American Medical Association. (1994). Report of the council of scientific affairs: Memories of childhood abuse (CAS Report 5-A 94). Chicago, IL: Author.

American Psychiatric Association. (1993). Statement on memories of sexual abuse. Washington, DC: Author.

American Psychological Association. (1995). Questions and answers about memories of childhood abuse. Washington, DC: Author.

Australian Psychological Society. (1994). Guidelines relating to the reporting of recovered memories. Sydney, Australia: Author.

Baily v. Lewis, 763 F. Supp. 802 (E. D. Pa. 1991).

Bartlett, F. C. (1932). *Remembering: A study in experimental and social psychology.* Cambridge: Cambridge University Press.

Bassile v. Covenant House, 575 N.Y.S.2d 233 (Sup. Ct. N.Y. County 1991).

Borawick v. Shay, 68 F.2d 597 (2nd Cir. 1995).

Brainerd, C., Regina, V. F., Howe, M. L., & Kingman, J. (1990). The development of forgetting and reminiscence. *Monographs of the Society for Research on Child Development, 55* (3–4 Serial No. 222).

Briere, J. (1995). Science versus politics in the delayed memory debate. *The Counseling Psychologist, 23,* 291–293.

British Psychological Society.(1995). Recovered memories: The report of the working party of the British Psychological Society. Leicester, England: Author.

Cal. Civ Code §340.1 (West Supp. 1992).

California v. Franklin, reversed by Franklin v. Duncan, 884 F. Supp. 1435 (N.D. Cal. 1995).

Ceci, S. & Bruck, M. (1995). *Jeopardy in the courtroom: A scientific analysis of children's testimony.* Washington, DC: American Psychological Association.

Colo. Rev. Stat. Ann. §13-80-103.7 (West Supp. 1992) (Civil).

Colo. Rev. Stat. Ann. §16-5-401(7) (Supp. 1993) (Criminal).

Conn. Gen. Stat. Ann. §52-577(d) (West 1991). (Civil).

Conn. Gen. Stat. Ann. §34-193(a) (West Supp. 1993). (Criminal).

Courtois, C. (1995). Scientist-practitioners and the delayed memory controversy: Scientific standards and the need for collaboration. *The Counseling Psychologist, 23,* 295–299.

Crider v. State, 531 N.E.2d 1151 (Ind. 1988).

Daubert v. Merrell Dow Pharmaceuticals, Inc. 509 U.S. 579 (1993).

Del. Code Ann. Tit. 11, §205(e) (Supp. 1992).

DeLipsey, J. M. & Shuman, D. W., (1991). The child witness. In R. M. Costello & S. L. Schneider (Eds.), *Forensic psychology for the journeyman clinician.* (pp. 41–58) San Antonio: Texas Psychological Association.

DLN v. State, 590 S. W.2d 820 (Tx. Civ. App. 1979).

Doe v. First United Methodist Church, 629 N. W.2d 402 (Ohio 1994).

Doe v. LaBrosse, 588 A.2d 605 (R. I. 1991).

Eberle, P. & Eberle, S. (1993). *The abuse of innocence: The McMartin Preschool trial.* Buffalo: Prometheus Books.

Ersdorff, G. M. & Loftus, E. F. (1993). Let sleeping memories lie? Words of caution about tolling the statute of limitations in cases of memory repression. *Journal of Criminal Law, 84,* 129–174.

Evans v. Eckelman, 216 Cal. App. 3d 1609 (1990).

Farris v. Compton, 652 A.2d 49 (D.C. 1994).

Fivush, R. & Hammond, N. (1990). Autobiographical memory across the preschool years: Toward reconceptualizing childhood amnesia. In R. Fivus & J. A. Hammond (Eds.), *Knowing and remembering in young children* (pp. 223–248). New York: Cambridge University Press.

Frye v. United States, 293 F. 1013 (D.C. Cir. 1923).

Gaddis v. Smith, 417 S. W.2d 557 (Tex. 1967).

Gier v. Educational Services, 66 F.3d 940 (8th Cir. 1995).

Goodman, G. S., Golding, J. M., & Haith, M. M. (1984). Juror's reaction to child witnesses. *Journal of Social Issues, 40(2),* 139–156.

Greenberg, S. A. & Shuman, D. W., (1997). Irreconcilable conflict between therapeutic and forensic roles. *Professional Psychology· Research and Practice, 28,* 50–57.

Hammer v. Hammer, 418 N.W.2d 23 (Wis. Ct. App. 1987).

Haw. Rev. Stat. §701–108 (Supp. 1992).

Herald v. Hood, 1993 WL 277541 (Ohio App. 9 Dist. 1993).

Herman, J. & Schatzow, E. (1987). Recovery and verification of memories of childhood sexual trauma. *Psychoanalytic Psychology, 4,* 1–10.

Horvath, A. O. and Luborsky, L. (1993). The role of the therapeutic alliance in psychotherapy. *Journal of Consulting and Clinical Psychology, 61,* 561–573.

Idaho Code §6–1704 (1989). (Civil).

Idaho Code §19–402 (Supp. 1992). (Criminal).

Iowa Code Ann. §802.2 (West Supp. 1993).

Isely v. Capuchin Province, 877 F. Supp. 1055 (E.D. Mich. 1995).

Johnson v. Johnson, 701 F. Supp. 1363 (N. D. Ill. 1988).

Kan. Stat. Ann. §60–523 (Supp. 1992).

LaFave, W. R. and Israel, J. H. (1992). *Criminal Procedure,* §18.5 St. Paul, Minn: West.

Lazo, J. (1995). Comment: True or false: Expert testimony on repressed memory. *Loyola Law Review, 28,* 1345–1414.

Lindabury v. Lindabury, 522 So.2d 1117 (Fla. Dist. Ct. App. 1989).

Lindsay, D. S. and Read, J. D. (1995). "Memory Work" and recovered memories of childhood sexual abuse: Scientific evidence and public, professional and personal issues. *Psychology, Public Policy and Law, 1,* 846–908.

Loftus, E. (1993). The reality of repressed memories. *American Psychologist, 48,* 518–537.

Lorenzen, D. (1988). The admissibility of expert psychological testimony in cases involving the sexual misuse of a child. *University of Miami Law Review 42,* 1033–1072.

McCarthy, C. (1993) The Bishops Don't Have a Prayer. *The Washington Post,* November 20, 1993, Saturday, Final Edition, p. A23.

Me. Rev. Stat. Ann. Tit. 14 §752-C (West Supp. 1992).

Martinez-Sandoval v. Kirsch, 884 P.2d 507 (N. M. Ct. App. 1994).

Mary D. v. John D., 264 Cal.. Reptr. 633, remanded, 800 P.2d 858 (1990).

Melton, G. (1981). Children's competency to testify. *Law Human Behavior, 5,* 73–84.

Memon, A. & Young, M. (1997). Desperately seeking evidence: The recovered memory debate. *Legal and Criminological Psychology, 2,* 1–24.

Murray, J. M. (1995). Repression, memory and suggestibility: A call for limitations on the admissibility of repressed memory testimony in sexual abuse trials. *University of Colorado Law Review, 66,* 477–522.

Nev. Rev. Stat. §11.215 (Supp. 1993).

Okla. Stat. Ann. tit. 12 §95 (1994).

Olsen v. Hooley, 865 P.2d 1345 (Utah 1993).

Ornstein, P. A., Ceci, S. J., & Loftus, E. F. (1996). Reply to the Alpert, Brown & Courtois document: The science of memory and the practice of psychotherapy. *American Psychological Association, Final Report, Working Group on Investigation of Memories of Childhood Abuse.*

Pepper, J. N. (1984). The child witness. *Criminal Law Quarterly, 26,* 354–384.

Poole, D. A., Lindsay, D. S., Memon, A.& Bull, R.(1995). Psychotherapy and the recovery of memories of childhood sexual abuse: U.S. and British Practitioners' opinion, practices and experiences. *Journal of Consulting and Clinical Psychology, 63,* 426–437.

Quinn, K. M. (1995). Guidelines for the psychiatric examination of posttraumatic stress disorder in children and adolescents. In R. Simon (Ed.), *Posttraumatic stress disorder in litigation: Guidelines for forensic assessment* (pp. 85–98) Washington, DC: American Psychiatric Press.

Sales, B. D., Shuman, D. W., & O'Connor, M. (1994). In a dim light: Admissibility of child sexual abuse memories. *Applied Cognitive Psychology, 8,* 399–406.

Saucier v. State, 903 S.W.2d 903 (Tex. Crim. App. 1951).

Shahzade v. Gregory, 1996 U.S. Dist. LEXIS 6463 (D. Mass. 1996).

Shippen v. Parrott, 506 N.W.2d 82 (S.D. 1993).

Shuman, D. W. (1989). The diagnostic and statistical manual of mental disorders in the courts. *Bulletin of the American Academy of Psychiatry and Law, 17,* 25–32.

Shuman, D. W. (1995a). Persistent reexperiences in psychiatry and the law. In R. Simon (Ed.), *Posttraumatic stress disorder in litigation: Guidelines for forensic assessment* (pp. 1–11). Washington, DC: American Psychiatric Press.

Shuman, D. W. (1995b). *Psychiatric and psychological evidence.* (2nd ed.). Colorado Springs: Shepard's/McGraw Hill.

Shuman, D. W. (1998). The role of ethical norms in the admissibility of expert testimony. *American Bar Association Judges Journal, 37* 4–43.

State v. Alberico, 861 P.2d 192 (N. M. 1993).

State v. Danielski, 348 N. W.2d 352 (Minn. Ct. App. 1984).

State v. Hungerford, 1995 WL 378571 (N. H. Super).

State v. Morahan, 1995 WL 378571 (N. H. Super).

S.V. v. R.V., 1996 Tex. Lexis 30 (Tex 1996).

Taub, S. (1996). The legal treatment of recovered memories of child sexual abuse. *Journal of Legal Med., 17,* 183–214.

Tex. Code. Crim. Proc. Ann., art. 12.01 (West Supp. 1993).

Tyson v. Tyson, 727 P.2d 226 (Wash. 1986).

U.S. v. Butt, 955 F.2d 77 (1st Cir. 1992).

U.S. v. Partin, 493 F.2d 750 (5th Cir. 1974) cert denied, 434 U.S. 903 (1977).

Usher, J. A. & Neisser, U. (1993). Childhood amnesia and the beginnings of memory for four early life events. *Journal of Experimental Psychology: General, 122,* 155–165.

Vt. Stat. Ann. tit. 12, §522 (Supp. 1992).

Walstram v. State, 752 P.2d 225 (Nev. 1988).

Weathers v. Fulgenzi, 884 P.2d 538 (Okla. 1994).

Wesson, M. (1995). Historic truth, narrative truth, and expert testimony. *Washington Law Review, 60,* 331–354.

CHAPTER 14

FORENSIC ASSESSMENT OF TRAUMATIZED ADULTS[*]

LANDY F. SPARR, M.D.
Acting Clinical Director, Mental Health Division,
Portland VA Medical Center and
Associate Professor of Psychiatry, School of Medicine,
Oregon Health Science University, Portland, Oregon

ROGER K. PITMAN, M.D.
Coordinator for Research and Development,
Manchester, NH VA Medical Center and
Associate Professor of Psychiatry,
Harvard Medical School, Boston, Massachusetts

Recent research indicates that, on the average, about 25 percent of individuals who are exposed to a DSM-IV Criterion A traumatic event go on to develop full-blown posttraumatic stress disorder (PTSD) (Green, 1995). Unfortunately, approximately four of every ten Americans are expected to be exposed to a major traumatic event by age 30 (Davidson, 1991). No wonder one observer remarked that if mental illnesses were rated on the New York Stock Exchange, PTSD would be a growth stock worth watching (Lees-Haley, 1986). Although initial use of the PTSD term was essentially confined to post-combat trauma, the diagnosis quickly spread to encompass a host of other types of traumata, including natural disasters, criminal victimization, family violence, work-related trauma, and other cataclysmic events.

Forensic psychiatrists encouraged the listing of PTSD in the psychiatric Diagnostic and Statistical Manual (DSM). Since then, trauma victims' attorneys have increasingly used the formulation in civil and criminal cases. As expert witnesses, psychiatrists have embraced PTSD both to explain the psychological sequela of trauma in personal injury cases and to formulate opinions regarding criminal responsibility. In tort litigation, Slovenko (1994) says, PTSD is a favorite diagnosis in cases of emotional distress because it is incident specific, easy to understand, and tends to rule out other factors central to causation determination. Through PTSD, plaintiffs attempt to establish that their psychological problems issue from an alleged traumatic event and not from a myriad of other life sources. A diagnosis of depression, in contrast, may open the causation issue to many considerations (Slovenko, 1994).

While it was not long before PTSD populated the forensic landscape, it has not always received a warm reception. Faust and Ziskin (1988, 1989), in particular, have critically assailed the forensic use of PTSD because they claim the disorder lacks proven diagnostic reliability and validity. They opined that PTSD symptoms may have many alternate explanations and that exaggeration and malingering were ever possible

---

[*]The views and recommendations expressed in this article are those of the author and do not necessarily reflect official Department of Veterans Affairs policy.

The author wishes to thank Ms. Jackie Lockwood for her valuable assistance in manuscript preparation.

and even probable. Faust and Ziskin were joined by skeptics in the scientific and forensic communities, and by the public at large (Neal, 1994; Schornhorst, 1988). Public skepticism was mostly stimulated by frivolous and sometimes well-publicized workers' compensation claims (Sparr, 1995). PTSD was seen as a threat to the workers' compensation, criminal justice, and personal injury litigation systems.

Recently, one investigator asked whether fears about misuse of PTSD have come true (Rosen et al., 1995). This is a simple question with a complex answer. In the criminal arena, Appelbaum et al. (1993) have eloquently illustrated that despite early fears, the PTSD insanity defense is raised infrequently, and, like other insanity pleas, is not often successful when it is raised. It appears, however, that the primary thrust of a PTSD criminal defense has not been an insanity plea, but instead as a factor in diminished capacity considerations, pre-trial plea bargaining agreements, or sentencing determinations. Lately, PTSD has garnered legal currency in cases involving rape trauma syndrome and battered woman syndrome.

One difficulty with a blanket PTSD indictment is that it is a double-edged sword. While there are undoubtedly examples of fraud and malingering, there are also those who have legitimate claims but, for one reason or the other, are prevented from obtaining legal redress. It is well known that many injury victims have learned to distance themselves from the traumatic event to avoid discussing symptoms such as recurrent obtrusive or obsessive thoughts, nightmares, and hypervigilance. They may not be able to describe highly personal experiences in public or may intentionally mask feelings because they believe it is the right thing to do (Kiev, 1993). VA disability examiners are familiar with the silent claimant (Atkinson et al., 1982). In criminal trials, evidence regarding PTSD symptomatology both in rape trials and in self-defense claims has at times been thrown out of courts due to the putative prejudicial impact of the testimony or due to the court's interpretation of a subjective lack of imminent danger, but at other times it has been admitted as highly relevant.

In tort litigation, PTSD has followed a trend that began two decades ago when, for example, the number of personal injury lawsuit filings between private parties and federal courts rose more than 50 percent between 1980 and 1987 (Olson, 1991). Jury awards to the plaintiff escalated dramatically during the same time period. This has coincided with psychological injury becoming more widely recognized, and courts becoming increasingly willing to compensate for emotional distress in the absence of physical injury or impact (Sparr, 1990).

In the area of occupational mental stress claims (workers' compensation), the empirical data is clear. By 1985, 15 percent of all occupational disease claims were stress related. United States Chamber of Commerce statistics show that the number of mental stress claims recorded by employees jumped nearly 800 percent between 1979 and 1990, making stress related disorders the nation's fastest growing disease category (deCarteret, 1994). In a study of more than 700,000 claims filed in 11 states, the National Council on Compensation Insurance (NCCI) reported that the costs of stress claims average about 52 percent more than traumatic injury claims (Calise, 1993). In one state, workers' compensation insurance rates, among the highest in the nation, were in part blamed for the lack of economic development and diversification, and, as a result, the state instituted a workers' compensation reform act (Trethewy, 1996).

Consequently, the majority of evidence supports the concept that stress claims are (rightly or wrongly) a growth industry. This chapter provides an overview and discussion of civil and criminal legal issues in PTSD including sections on forensic psychiatric evaluation and testimony. We will emphasize the five major uses of PTSD in the legal system: diminished capacity, syndrome evidence, self-defense defense, workers' compensation, and personal injury (tort) claims.

CRIMINAL

Diminished Capacity

In the American criminal justice system, individuals are considered responsible and thus accountable or culpable for their behavior if there are two necessary ingredients: (1) a criminal act (*actus reas*); and (2) criminal intent (*mens rea*). If serious mental illness eliminates *mens rea* or "culpable mind," only the *actus reas* is left, and the individual may be deemed not criminally responsible (Sadoff, 1992). A defendant who is mentally ill may plead not guilty by reason of insanity (NGRI) but also may consider other *mens rea* defenses such as diminished capacity. In about one-half the states, evidence of abnormal mental condition is admissible on the question of whether the defendant had (or was capable of having) the requisite mental state pertinent to the crime charged. The doctrine by which this evidence is admitted is known by various names: diminished responsibility, partial responsibility, partial capacity, diminished capacity, and even partial insanity (Morris, 1975; *People v. Wells,* 1949).

In a successful PTSD criminal defense, it must be established by clear and convincing evidence that PTSD existed at the time of the violent crime and did not stem from it. In other words, the defense must establish a legal relevancy between criminal behavior, and prior and current PTSD. The trier-of-fact must be able to understand PTSD-induced criminal behavior almost like the now discredited "irresistible impulse" defense (Hall & Hall, 1987). In fact, because of the increasing recognition given to problems faced by Vietnam veterans and their related stress disorders, one state (California) mandates consideration of military service in Vietnam when judges make sentencing determinations (Shulze, 1987).

The insanity defense focuses on the defendant's responsibility for his criminal act and, if successful, involves a policy decision not to seek punishment. In contrast, a diminished capacity defense is admissible for the sole purpose of determining which crime was committed. For example, in a first-degree murder charge, many states allow the defendant to introduce evidence that he did not have the mental capacity to premeditate the act and, for that reason, only second-degree murder could have been committed. A few states admit evidence of an abnormal mental condition for the purpose of mitigating punishment after a guilty verdict. Overall, the diminished capacity rule is used mainly in cases in which the defendant is charged with first-degree murder but has been used in lesser offenses and may be used to mitigate punishment (Morris, 1975). The concept of diminished capacity has broad international acceptance, particularly in European and British legal systems where it is used more often than in the United States (Hermann, 1986). Most formulations of the diminished capacity doctrine allow psychiatric testimony to show that the defendant was not capable of either premeditating or deliberating. Since insanity defense standards have been tightened, the use of PTSD in criminal proceedings has more applicability to diminished capacity, and, in fact, has been used more often in that role. Unlike NGRI, a claim of diminished capacity does not result in commitment to a hospital.

Evidence of the defendant's mental status is admissible in Tennessee to negate elements of specific intent, including premeditation and deliberation, in first-degree murder cases (Falk, 1995). In 1994, a Tennessee appeals court reversed a first-degree murder conviction because the jury was not instructed that PTSD evidence could be considered in deciding whether specific intent or diminished capacity had been shown (*Tennessee v. Phipps,* 1994). Four experts had testified that the defendant, Phipps, had major depression and PTSD, most of them agreeing that these conditions significantly affected his behavior at the time of the crime. The court, however, had erroneously refused to instruct the jury on the defense theory that Phipps had been unable to formulate the specific intent for first-degree murder and instead issued an instruction that PTSD was not to be considered as mitigation to the charge.

The 1984 Federal Comprehensive Crime Control Act amended the US Federal Rules of Evidence to only allow psychiatric expert opinion on a complete insanity defense (Pub. L. No. 98–596, 1984). Also, new Federal sentencing guidelines and mandatory minimum sentences and their counterpart in various states have given a lesser role to the concept of diminished responsibility in the post-trial phase of a prosecution. Reduced Federal sentences (or downward departures) for diminished capacity are only allowed for "non-violent crimes." Recently the Ninth Circuit held that PTSD is one type of mental disorder that can support a reduced sentence (*US v. Cantu,* 1993). The exercise of discretion in considering mental state or mental capacity now occurs mostly in the pre-trial and trial stages. In the pre-trial stage, the diminished capacity concept may influence prosecutorial judgment and play a role in charges brought against the defendant.

Slovenko (1992) says that at trial the diminished capacity defense, variably allowed to begin with, has been more important for its symbolism than its numbers. Nevertheless, it has sometimes been argued that certain behavioral sequelae in defendants with PTSD could mitigate criminal liability (Sparr et al., 1987). For example: (1) Sensation seeking (*US v. Tindall,* 1980) (defendant is addicted to risk-taking, secondary to chronic PTSD—probable physiologic correlates—crime is committed while attempting to recreate excitement); (2) Guilt and self-punishment (Maremaa, 1981; Nordheimer, 1971) (PTSD-based guilt about real or imagined moral transgressions—crime is committed in an effort to seek punishment); (3) Substance abuse (*Cotton v. Alabama,* 1993; Grant & Coons, 1983; *Norris v. State,* 1986; *People v. Wood,* 1982) (defendant's attempt to numb PTSD-based psychic pain—disinhibited actions lead to criminal behavior); (4) Dissociative state (*Commonwealth v. Mulcahy,* 1978; *State v. Heads,* 1981) (altered state of consciousness [e.g., PTSD flashback]—defendant commits a crime while unaware of actions).

Syndrome Evidence

PTSD syndromes consist of descriptions of particular physical or emotional conditions that manifest themselves in response to specific traumatic situations. Use of the term "PTSD" in expert testimony may have advantages over a term such as "rape trauma syndrome" because it is not event specific. Many labels have been attached to survivors of traumatic events. Rape trauma syndrome describes reaction to rape; battered woman syndrome describes reactions to wife abuse; post-Vietnam syndrome describes reactions to combat in Vietnam. Recently, it has been recognized that all these reactions share common features; and, in fact, the PTSD label has been applied to victims of each of these traumatic stressors (Burge, 1988).

These syndromes were not included in DSM-III in 1980 because they were thought to be subsumed by PTSD. Furthermore, feminists did not press for inclusion of rape trauma syndrome or battered woman syn-

drome because they objected to victimization being considered a mental disorder (Buchele & Buchele, 1985). Most of these syndromes were described prior to 1980. For example, as defined by Burgess and Holmstrom (1974), rape trauma syndrome consists of behavioral, somatic, and psychological reactions that occur as a result of forcible rape. Breslau et al. (1991) compared PTSD prevalence by type of event. Women who reported being raped had a significantly higher rate of PTSD (80 percent) than those exposed to other typical PTSD stressors. Within the population studied, the majority of men acquired PTSD through combat experience or civilian assault. Most women developed PTSD symptoms following sexual assault or victimization.

In 1988, the Department of Justice reported that the annual incidence of sexual assault was 80 per 100,000 women, accounting for 7 percent of all violent crimes (Federal Bureau of Investigation, 1988). When Bownes et al. (1991) looked at 51 rape victims, 70 percent had PTSD defined by DSM-III criteria. The incidence of rape by strangers, physical force being used, weapons being displayed, or injuries being sustained were higher in the group of women who had PTSD.

The National Victims Center and Crime Victims Research Treatment Center (1992) has indicated that 12.9 percent (about twelve million) women have been raped at least once during their lifetime. Somewhat higher rates (15.4 percent) were found in representative samples of college students (Koss et al., 1987). In studies of PTSD prevalence in rape victims, the incidence ranged from 11 percent to 94 percent largely dependent upon the length of time that had elapsed after the assault. One good predictor of the severity of depression and anxiety one year after the rape was the degree to which the victim experienced psychological problems before the assault. Several studies found that rape victims with a victimization history experienced more general psychopathology following the assault than those without such a history. Other studies have reported that psychological symptoms following rape are related to the victim's perception of life threat during the assault (Foa & Riggs, 1994).

Of the many studies that have been done, none has found an absence of rape trauma syndrome in rape victims. This is strong evidence for the virtually universal presence of the reaction, since these studies were done by a series of independent teams, in disparate parts of the United States, with various populations derived from a variety of sources. The congruity of results speaks most strongly for the scientific reliability of the rape trauma syndrome phenomenon (Cling, 1988).

In 1983, the Canadian federal government moved the crime of rape into the general assault category, thus recognizing the violent rather than sexual nature of the crime (Moscarello, 1991). In the past, the legal definition of rape was forcible intercourse with a woman against her will. While not written into statute, this was interpreted to mean that the woman had to show signs of resistance. Originally, this meant "utmost" resistance, e.g., presumably to fight to near death. This requirement was lessened to "reasonable resistance under the circumstance" (although not in all states). Finally, in the 1970's, the resistance standard was dropped in most states, and a consent standard adopted (Cling, 1988).

A central issue for courts is the admission of rape trauma syndrome evidence as proof of nonconsent. Three objections have been offered. One is that rape trauma syndrome data is scientifically unreliable because it is too subjective. The second is that, even if the syndrome can be reliably assessed, it may be caused by stressors other than rape, and thus not be rape trauma syndrome. The third is that, even if it is accepted within the scientific community, its reliability has to do with its value in rape treatment, not its probative value on the consent issue. The first objection, while not totally discredited, has become of less concern to courts as more data has been amassed. The last two objections, however, have raised major impediments to the acceptance of rape trauma syndrome as legal evidence of nonconsent (Cling, 1988).

Courts have allowed PTSD testimony in civil rape cases, where the testimony is entered not to show that the rape occurred but to assess damage once a rape has been proven. In criminal rape trials, however, where testimony is entered to demonstrate that a rape occurred, rape trauma syndrome has received a mixed reception. In a rape case in which a defendant claims his victim consented to sexual conduct, prosecutors may try to rebut that claim by introducing evidence that the victim suffers from PTSD. State courts have been slow to accept its admissibility, finding it too prejudicial to the defendant and not sufficiently reliable. Although California, Minnesota, and Missouri courts have taken this approach, at least three state high courts have decided otherwise including Kansas, Montana, and Arizona (Karpay, 1986).

In a New York decision involving rape trauma syndrome (*People v. Taylor, 1988*), the court sustained the conviction and made the following points:

1. All rape victims do not react the same way. Shame, guilt, and fear of public embarrassment can be present and make the reaction unique and different from other forms of violent assault.

2. The reaction to rape may be so complex as to warrant scientific investigation, and the understanding of those reactions is not within the common experience of persons who characteristically sit on a jury (Kelner & Kelner, 1989).

Courts that allow PTSD testimony view the evidence as potentially helpful in explaining to the jury the victim's reaction to rape. The rationale is twofold. First, this evidence is most often used in rape trials where the defendant admits that sexual intercourse occurred but claims that the complainant was a willing participant (consent defense). In this situation there is usually no corroborating evidence and it is the defendant's word against the complainant's. Thus, the testimony would serve to corroborate the complainant's version of the facts. Second, it is assumed that jurors are not familiar with typical rape victims' reactions and that their decision-making could be assisted by expert testimony. Research on juror misconceptions regarding rape victims is consistent with this assumption (Frazier & Borgida, 1985; 1988).

Traditionally, courts have allowed any testimony intending to show victim consent or failure to resist physically, including evidence of the victim's prior sexual history. This practice caused rape trauma trials to revolve around the victim's personal behavior. The majority of early decisions either banned PTSD testimony outright or severely limited its scope (Trosch, 1991). At least one court has argued that allowing an expert to indicate, either expressly or implicitly, that a victim suffers from PTSD invades the jury's fact-finding province (*State v. Black*, 1987). While the admission of rape trauma syndrome testimony may prejudice the jury by bolstering the credibility of the complainant, it also may, in certain respects, be prejudicial to the victim because the evidence may "open the door" to questioning regarding details of her personal life (Frazier & Borgida, 1985).

In the case of *State v. Allewalt* (1985), the prosecution, seeking to rebut the defendant's claim of consensual sex, solicited the opinion of a psychiatrist that the alleged rape victim suffered from PTSD. The psychiatrist described PTSD as a "condition recognized in psychiatry as the emotional reaction to a traumatic event." Moreover, the psychiatrist stated that, based upon the information provided to him by the alleged victim, the traumatic event that caused the PTSD was rape. The Allewalt court articulated several reasons why the expert testimony regarding PTSD was not unduly prejudicial. First, the expert clearly informed the jury that his opinion was based on history provided by the alleged victim. Second, the expert stressed that rape was only one of many types of severe trauma that could trigger PTSD. Third, the expert's testimony was given on rebuttal regarding the issue of consent. The court concluded that "by requiring a full explanation on direct, by allowing liberal cross-examination, and by proper jury instructions—the trial court can prevent any impression that the psychiatric opinion is like a chemical reaction."

In contrast, in *Hutton v. State* (1995), the Maryland Court of Appeals held that expert testimony that an alleged sexual abuse victim suffered from PTSD was inadmissible for the purpose of proving that the abuse occurred. In reaching this conclusion, the court determined that expert testimony regarding PTSD implies the alleged victim is credible and, hence, invades the fact-finding province of the jury. In so holding, the court applied the reasoning of *Bohnert v. State* (1988), and determined that PTSD testimony goes beyond the proper scope of expert opinion because it amounts to a comment on the alleged victim's credibility. The court based its decision on several grounds. First, the unique diagnostic criteria requires an expert to rely upon the alleged victim's story in order to make a PTSD diagnosis. Second, expert testimony regarding PTSD may usurp the jury's function of determining witness credibility. The court found that this danger exists with PTSD testimony because a jury will likely give excessive weight to the expert's opinion without realizing that its validity depends on the alleged victim's veracity. Third, the responsibility of assessing the witness credibility is traditionally entrusted to the jury, which is a matter outside the expert's unique knowledge (Peterson, 1996).

The prejudicial impact question is closely tied to whether or not testimony is helpful to the trier-of-fact. Rape trauma syndrome evidence is generally deemed to be prejudicial when an expert witness bolsters a complainant's credibility by falsely creating an "aura of special reliability and trustworthiness" (*State v. Saldana*, 1982). Determination of prejudice is also affected by the way the evidence is presented. Testimony is least prejudicial if it merely describes the victim's behavior, more prejudicial if this behavior is causally linked to the alleged rape, and still more prejudicial if the expert testifies that he/she believes the complainant's assertion that a rape actually occurred (Frazier & Borgida, 1985). One court held that even the term "rape trauma syndrome" implied that a rape occurred and is therefore prejudicial (*State v. Taylor*, 1984). Courts that find the testimony generally acceptable invariably find that its probative value outweighs its prejudicial effect.

In *State v. Black* (1987), the Washington Supreme Court faced the question of whether the state should be allowed to offer expert testimony on rape trauma syndrome. After examining some of the relevant scientific literature, case law, and standards governing admissibility of expert testimony, the court held that expert testimony on rape trauma syndrome was inadmissible. The court based its decision on findings that rape trauma syndrome testimony lacks scientific reliability, and that it unfairly prejudices the defendant accused of rape. The Black court concluded that because rape trauma syndrome was developed as a therapeutic tool, it is not scientifically reliable. In part, this criticism assumes that false rape claims are common. Statistics strongly suggest that the percentage of actual false rape reports may be as low or lower than false reports for most other crimes (Dwyer, 1988).

The *State v. Saldana* (1982), *State v. McGee* (1982), and *State v. Taylor* (1984) decisions also found rape trauma syndrome evidence to be unreliable, prejudicial, and/or unhelpful to the jury. The *People v. Bledsoe* (1984) decision ruled that evidence could be admitted to educate the jury but not to prove that rape had occurred. *State v. Marks* (1982), *Delia S. v. Torres*, (1982) *State v. Allewalt* (1986), *Terrio v. McDonough* (1983), *State v. Liddell* (1984), *State v. Ogle* (1984), and *People v. Reid* (1984) upheld the admissibility of rape trauma syndrome evidence. In both Marks and Reid, which relied on the Frye standard (*Frye v. US*, 1923—see below) for expert witness testimony, the courts concluded that the rape trauma syndrome was generally accepted in the scientific community (Frazier & Borgida, 1985). The Allewalt court joined the majority view in holding that PTSD testimony is generally accepted, but, of greater significance, held that an expert may state that a complainant's PTSD symptoms were caused by rape (Sanders, 1986). Even the Taylor court, which rejected the testimony, did not question its scientific status. In Bledsoe and Saldana, the courts noted that rape trauma syndrome was generally accepted for treatment purposes but was unacceptable in a court of law because it cannot accurately and reliably determine whether a rape occurred. In *State v. Saldana* (1982), the court argued that the testimony is unreliable because not every victim exhibits rape trauma syndrome and that victims differ in the amount and type of symptoms they manifest in response to rape (Frazier & Borgida, 1985). To allow PTSD testimony would inevitably lead to a battle of experts that would add confusion rather than clarity. The Saldana court feared that instead of assisting the jury, PTSD testimony would only waste valuable time. An even larger problem introduced by "a battle of experts" is the potential to reawaken the traditional focus on the victim.

In response to growing pressures for a solution to imbalance in rape trials, virtually all states have enacted rape shield statutes that limit exploration into the victim's past. Some courts, however, have maintained that the defendant cannot escape rape shield laws once PTSD testimony enters the case (*State v. McQuillen*, 1984; Trosch, 1991). Nevertheless, courts have been urged to place boundaries on what defendants' attorneys can explore as they try to discredit the notion that the rape rather than some other trauma caused the victim's PTSD. Closely related to the danger of a defendant using cross-examination to uncover skeletons from the victim's past is the question of mandatory psychological examination. A defendant might some day attempt to use PTSD to prove consent. For example, the defendant might demand an expert examination of the victim and, if he/she exhibits insufficient PTSD symptoms, contend that rape did not occur (Trosch, 1991). Another potential difficulty occurs when the prosecution wishes to introduce the testimony of a mental health expert who has examined the victim. Because the defense is afforded the same right, the victim may be subjected to at least two psychiatric evaluations, and examination by the defendant's expert may be particularly stressful (Buchele & Buchele, 1985). In *Illinois v. Wheeler* (1992), the Illinois supreme court held that the state cannot introduce expert testimony that an alleged sexual assault victim suffers from any form of PTSD unless the victim allows a defense expert to examine her.

Overall, courts consider testimony content and have held that expert testimony of rape trauma syndrome is admissible as evidence of: (1) lack of consent; (2) damage amount in civil suits; (3) a defense to culpable behavior; and (4) an explanation for victim behavior that is inconsistent with a rape claim (Block, 1990). If the expert merely states that the complainant exhibits PTSD symptoms, the testimony usually passes the general acceptance test, its probative value outweighs its prejudicial effect, and it is admitted into evidence. Also, there are a variety of built-in safeguards. The defendant can cross-examine the prosecution's expert witness, call his own opposing experts, and request limiting jury instruction that PTSD symptoms are only circumstantial evidence, not definitive proof of rape. Courts can also require that the expert use the more generic term PTSD rather than rape trauma syndrome, thereby avoiding the impression that the complainant's symptoms could have been only caused by rape (Sanders, 1986). Finally, the expert could be presented a hypothetical question incorporating the complainant's symptomatology, and then asked to express an opinion whether or not the symptoms are consistent with those of a person with

PTSD. This procedure meets requirements of what appears to be an emerging majority rule drawn from Marks, Liddell, Ogle, Bledsoe, and Reid and eliminates the expert's rendering an opinion on the victim's credibility (Buchele & Buchele, 1985). In the final analysis the psychological and legal issues associated with the use of syndrome evidence reflect ongoing debate over the admission of any expert psychiatric testimony in court.

Self-Defense Defense

Another possible legal theory to which PTSD is relevant is self-defense. The Modern Penal Code allows the defendant to demonstrate that his/her responses were subjectively reasonable (e.g., that he/she believed the use of force was necessary). The use of PTSD in this context is usually found when "battered woman syndrome" is employed to explain a female defendant's violent acts toward her spouse. Studies have documented high rates of PTSD among battered women (Astin et al., 1993; Dutton & Goodman, 1994; Kemp et al., 1995). In these circumstances, the existence of PTSD would make the whole of the defendant's life relevant to show her state of mind at the time of the crime (Erlinder, 1984). The battered woman syndrome is not a diagnosis unto itself but, rather, cuts across a spectrum of underlying diagnostic categories (Goodstein & Page, 1981). Nevertheless, it is seen as a PTSD variation and draws upon the social science research of Lenore Walker (1980), among others. These theories help explain why more women simply do not leave their abusers (Lustberg et al., 1992). More than 50 percent of all women who are killed in the United States are murdered by previously violent husbands, usually when they attempt to terminate the relationship (Walker, 1993).

When battered women syndrome was first introduced to courts in the late 1970's, it was often excluded (Murphy, 1992). In truth, battered woman syndrome is properly used to explain the justification for self-defense, not as a defense in and of itself. In 1993, Texas became one of only three states to have legislation specifically applicable to defendants who have been victims of domestic violence. In the Texas case, *Fielder v. State* (1988), the jury convicted the defendant of voluntary manslaughter for killing her husband. The court of appeals affirmed her conviction, but the court of criminal appeals reversed. The court found that the testimony of an expert witness in this case would be extremely beneficial to the trier-of-fact because the average lay person has no basis for understanding the conduct of a woman who endures an abusive relationship.

There are basically two standards of self-defense: objective and subjective. A subjective standard centers on what a woman honestly believes was necessary to protect herself. She is thus justified in using deadly force to defend herself against a threat of imminent bodily harm. Because her justification is subjective, her belief does not necessarily have to be reasonable. Expert testimony regarding her fear of the victim may be admissible to allow a jury to understand what the defendant honestly believed.

Under an objective standard of self-defense, the fact finder determines what a reasonable person would believe was necessary to protect herself in the same or similar circumstances. Using this standard, a woman is justified in using deadly force to protect herself if a reasonable person in the same situation would have acted in the same manner. Under this standard, evidence regarding what the particular woman believed may be irrelevant and expert testimony regarding her individual state of mind may not be admissible at trial.

Not surprisingly, the traditional defense for women who have killed their husbands has been the insanity plea. An excuse defense such as NGRI is fundamentally different from a justification defense because an excuse defense focuses upon the victim instead of the victim's act. Obviously, the use of an insanity plea has a serious impact on women because acquittal may lead to involuntary commitment in a mental health institution (Duncan, 1992).

In *State v. Kelly* (1984) it was held that in asserting self-defense the defendant may offer expert testimony on battered woman syndrome to aid a jury in understanding how a history of abuse may support a woman's claim that she believed she was in imminent danger and that her belief was reasonable. In particular, the Kelly court declared that the subject was "beyond the ken of the average juror and thus suitable for explanation through expert testimony." The court also held that the syndrome had sufficient scientific basis to fulfill an expert witness reliability requirement. Recently, however, in *State v. McClain* (1991), a court limited the applicability of battered woman syndrome evidence by holding that, because the defendant was not in imminent danger, such evidence was irrelevant to the question of reasonableness (Lustberg & Jacobi, 1992). In *Bechtel v. State* (1992) the court defined self-defense as being based on reasonableness and imminence: "The key to the defense of self-defense is reasonableness. A defendant must show that she had a reasonable belief as to the imminence of great bodily harm or death...." In *Ibn-Tamas v. US* (1979) expert testimony relating to "battered woman" in support of the defendant's self-defense claim in the killing of her husband was ruled inadmissible on the grounds that it would invade the province of the jury and that its probative value was outweighed by its prejudicial impact. In contrast, in New Jersey expert PTSD testimony was permitted to explain the inability of battered women to escape forced prostitution (*US v. Winters,* 1984).

Other courts have accepted battered woman syndrome as a scientifically recognized theory. Thirty-two jurisdictions throughout the country have addressed the admissibility of testimony regarding battered woman syndrome. Of these, 22 jurisdictions allow the testimony through judicial decision or legislation; two jurisdictions prohibit the testimony and do not provide clemency for women convicted of killing their abusers; two jurisdictions (Louisiana and Wyoming) do not allow the testimony but do provide clemency for women convicted of killing their abuser; and in six others—Indiana, Massachusetts, Montana, Nevada, North Carolina, and Oregon—the courts have not ruled on the admissibility issue, deciding the cases on other grounds (Duncan, 1992). Of the 22 jurisdictions that address the issue, the majority allow testimony regarding battered woman syndrome to determine whether the affirmative justification of self-defense is appropriate. Jurisdictions, however, differ on whether a defendant is entitled to claim self-defense when she has killed her abuser in his sleep. Courts allowing testimony have ruled that it does not establish that a battered woman is insane or

suffering from some other mental disability. Some states have even allowed testimony regarding battered woman syndrome when the woman is the complaining victim of an assault as opposed to the defendant in a murder trial.

Jurisdictions vary on the requisite qualifications of a testifying expert and the allowable content of the expert's testimony. In some jurisdictions, an expert testifying about battered woman syndrome must be a qualified psychologist or psychiatrist. In others, the person may simply work with battered women or be familiar with the subject. Some courts have held that an expert may not testify to the specifics of the case (Duncan, 1992). The state of Minnesota limits expert testimony regarding battered woman syndrome to a general description of the syndrome, thereby relieving the defendant of the need to submit to an adverse psychiatric examination (Williams, 1991).

For a successful claim, a battered woman generally must satisfy each of the self-defense doctrine's elements. First, the battered woman must show that she reasonably believed that she was in imminent danger of serious bodily harm or death at the time of the killing. Second, the woman must show that she used only reasonable force to prevent the danger. Third, a woman must establish that she did not instigate the violence. Finally, in some jurisdictions, the woman must prove that she had no safe avenue of retreat from danger.

The element requiring battered women to show that they reasonably feared imminent danger of serious bodily harm poses the most difficulty for defendants. Under traditional self-defense doctrine, a defendant reasonably must believe that the aggressor poses an immediate danger. Although some women who kill their spouses in the midst of battering incidents can show an imminent threat of serious injury or death, many battered women kill their spouses during a lull in the violence. Under a strict imminence interpretation, therefore, there is no threat of immediate bodily injury or death and, as a result, battered women's self-defense claims often fail. Talbott (1988) contends that narrow self-defense interpretations do not address fairly or adequately the circumstances surrounding battered women's actions. A partial solution to the problem of defending battered women would be for courts to interpret the imminence requirement more broadly so that a defendant could show that although her spouse may not have posed an immediate threat, she reasonably feared that death or serious bodily injury was inevitable (Talbott, 1988).

Dr. Lenore Walker (1984) defines a battered woman as 18 years of age or older, who is or has been in an intimate relationship with a man who repeatedly subjects or has subjected her to forceful physical and/ or psychological abuse. The abuse element includes behavior such as excessive jealousy, extreme verbal harassment, restriction of activity, non-verbal or verbal threats of punishment, sexual assault, and physical attack. The presence of children in the home exacerbates stress and increases the chances of a violent response, especially if the children themselves are threatened by the abuser. The abuser's threat to kill the woman, or to find her if she leaves, increases her fear of deadly attack and similarly increases the risk of a violent response. Other factors include the presence of weapons in the home, the woman's jealousy triggered by the abuser's open extramarital affairs, and alcohol or drug abuse by the abuser. Finally, it appears that a deadly response by the woman is more likely to occur later in the relationship when the severity of the abuse escalates (Williams, 1991).

The attacker's history of abuse, progressive cycle of violence, and threats of imminent abuse are all relevant to the issue of reasonableness. Many commentators note that traditional self-defense doctrine presumes a single encounter in public between adversaries of approximately equal strength (Maher, 1988; Mihajlovich, 1987). These commentators thus criticize the standard as representative of the male viewpoint, and propose changing the reasonableness standard (Williams, 1991).

A reduced charge of manslaughter based on evidence of provocation might be an option in cases involving battered women. A person only commits first- or second-degree murder by killing with intent and without significant provocation. A lesser charge of manslaughter is applicable if the perpetrator was provoked into a "heat of passion" that precipitated the killing. Another defense available in some states is diminished capacity if it can be shown that the defendant suffered from an "abnormal mental condition" (e.g., PTSD) while committing the crime. Like a provocation defense, this defense reduces the severity of the offense to manslaughter, as it establishes that the defendant did not have the requisite criminal intent for first- or second-degree murder. In particular, the defense should focus on the intense anger the battered woman felt at the time of the killing. This defense shares the disadvantage of a "heat of passion" defense because it does not result in an acquittal (Williams, 1991).

Cutler (1989) notes that scholarly commentary has overwhelmingly endorsed the use of battered woman syndrome evidence. In part, he says, this is linked to the legal system's frequent inability to effectively intervene in escalating domestic violence disputes. A study conducted at Chicago's Cook County Jail shows that many women are convicted and sentenced for having murdered husbands or boyfriends who were physically and sexually abusive. Of 132 women serving time for murder or manslaughter, 40 percent had killed lovers who had subjected them to physical abuse (Cutler, 1989).

Although not perfect, self-defense is usually the best defense strategy for battered women accused of murder. Most courts now allow the use of expert testimony, seemingly giving legal acceptance to the syndrome. Along with the defense's success, however, has come criticism and public concern that "husband killing" has gotten out of hand. Some have suggested that use of the syndrome as a defense excuses the killing simply because of the victim's evil character (Cutler, 1989). Others see the defense as a juxtaposition of the insanity defense and self-defense (Vaughn & Moore, 1983). Most courts use either the objective or subjective test but some use both tests. In North Carolina, imminence is measured by a subjective standard and reasonableness by an objective standard (*State v. Norman,* 1988).

In summary, courts have placed a greater emphasis on the probability that a physical attack will occur and the impending nature of the attack, and placed less emphasis on the immediacy of an attack or whether an attack was actually occurring. In finding "the decedent's sleep was but a momentary hiatus in a continuous reign of terror," the court of appeals in

State v. Norman (1988) ruled in accordance with other jurisdictions in finding sufficient provocation. The realities of an abusive relationship force most courts to apply the basic elements of self-defense subjectively. This ultimately raises questions regarding self-defense criteria and whether a special defense has been or should be created for battered women (Cutler, 1989).

CIVIL

Workers' Compensation

Each state has its own workers' compensation statutes. Most were passed in the early 1900s, around the time of World War I. In some basic respects, the various state statutes are similar and provide compensation to injured workers for certain consequences of their work injuries. Compensation includes medical expenses, lost wages during recuperation, and any permanent loss of earning capacity (Sersland, 1984).

Before the first compensation law in 1911, employers were liable only for injuries resulting from negligence; hence, employees had to prove fault to receive an award for an injury arising in the workplace. To facilitate recovery and a quick return to work, injured workers were relieved from a legal burden of proof by workers' compensation laws, and, without fault, employers were responsible for all injury costs. Borrowing from the doctrine of proximate cause in tort law (see next section), workers' compensation law creates a two-part requirement for workplace causation; the injury must arise out of, and occur in, the course of employment (London et al., 1988).

The 1960 landmark Michigan case, *Carter v. General Motors* (1961), was the first case to compensate for a mental disorder precipitated solely by a mental stimulus. In common jargon, three basic terms are used to describe workers' compensation claims: *physical/mental, mental/physical,* and *mental/mental.* In a physical/mental claim, a physical injury leads to some sort of mental distress (e.g., depression or anxiety following a back injury). A mental/mental claim, of course, means that mental stress has resulted in a mental problem (Colbach, 1982).

The injury must arise from the course of employment, but the employment contribution does not need to be the sole cause for the injury to be compensable. It is usually thought to be sufficient if the employment contribution is one cause among several. Moreover, the relative importance of the various causes is usually not weighted (Sersland, 1984).

Physical/mental claims appear to be the most straightforward. The physical component refers to instances where there is an injury or an occupational disease that is—at least, in most cases—compensable. As a consequence of the initial, disabling condition, the employee develops a mental condition that itself is further disabling. Claims for physical/mental cases are compensable in all states. One reason that these claims seem more straightforward is that the injury that triggered the mental disorder may be well-identified, at a single time and place. If the employee manifested no signs of mental impairment prior to the originating injury, the issue may not be complex. Suppose, however, the injury or disease that triggered the mental condition developed without a circumscribed incident. Clearly, that complicates the physical compensability issue which in turn clouds mental injury compensation.

In mental/physical cases the key problem is often the causality issue. Unlike physical/mental claims (or mental/mental for that matter) where the critical issues are both etiology and assessment of impairment, mental/physical claims can be problematic because of the need to prove that the condition arose out of, and in the course of, employment. The physical types of diseases that could emerge as a consequence of psychological stress have received mixed scientific support. Though these cases are regularly litigated and may be difficult to resolve, they are currently of small consequence. Observers, however, are concerned about the potential weight of claims for cardiovascular disorders. There are two elements of this type of mental/physical claim that are ominous. First is the possible volume of claims. Every year almost a million Americans die from cardiovascular diseases. The second critical element is that they tend to be expensive both in terms of indemnity benefits and medical expenses, which are high because the period of recuperation can be extended and because these cases are more likely to occur in older and better paid employees (Barth, 1990).

A common concern about the mental/mental case category is preexisting vulnerability to mental illness. Since a significant percentage of adults in the United States have suffered from at least one psychiatric disorder (Robins et al., 1984), the potential exists for greater liability under workers' compensation laws for mental disabilities than has ever existed for physical disabilities. Both in personal injury cases and workers' compensation, a claimant's predisposition to, or preexisting, mental illness is legally irrelevant. The worker is taken as is. As Justice Oliver Wendell Holmes remarked: "The law is not for the protection of the physically sound alone" (Modlin, 1983).

Throughout the United States, workers' claims for stress-related disorders have proliferated (Appleson, 1983). While stress claims represented only 4.7 percent of the occupational disease cases in 1980, they more than doubled in the following three years and have continued to rise ever since (Blodgett, 1986). If the number of work stress claims can be viewed as a valid index, psychological disorders have become one of the fastest growing occupational illnesses in recent years. The National Council on Compensation Insurance reports that stress accounted for 14 percent of all occupational disease claims by the end of the 1980's, a jump from 5 percent at the beginning of the decade. Even more startling are statistics in specific states. In California, for example, stress claims "increased forty-seven times faster than disabling injury claims" (Pattison, 1994, p. 146). The financial implication of this can be profound. It has been estimated that the overall health care costs of stressful work places might be as high as $300 billion annually, a figure that exceeds the net income of all Fortune 500 companies combined (Pattison, 1995).

The fact that employers and insurers often contest stress claims exacerbates the problem because litigation expenses siphon money away from legitimately injured workers (Matsumoto, 1994). The economy is moving away from claims for physical injury—the kind that often occur working with machines—to stress claims arising out of office work. In the state of Oregon, from 1980 to 1986, the number of disabling mental stress claims rose from 159 to 683, an increase of more than 300 percent; in the same time period, to-tal claims decreased (Department of Insurance and Finance, 1987). Mental stress claimants are typically younger than other claimants, and a significantly higher proportion are female (National Council on Compensation Insurance, 1985). Stress claims are increasing as the work force continues to shift from manufacturing to service sector jobs.

In California, stress-related workers' compensation claims increased 700 percent between 1981 and 1991, and an additional 12 percent between 1991 and 1992. Although changes in California workers' compensation laws are expected, existing workers' compensation laws require that only actual events of employment be responsible for at least 10 percent of the total causation from all sources contributing to a psychiatric injury (deCarteret, 1994). As a result of this broad definition, claims became easy to promulgate. A prime example occurred when a restaurant closed permanently, and 115 of its 119 employees filed stress claims. Attorneys had stationed themselves outside the door the day of the layoff to intercept the newly unemployed, influencing them to file claims (Schut, 1992). The laws in California have been so liberal that one worker was awarded compensation because of the stress caused by working in a multi-ethnic environment. In another case, a state judge was awarded compensation after claiming he suffered a stroke as a result of being overworked by the increased caseload of workers' compensation claims (deCarteret, 1994)! In 1990, the California courts held that an employee performing poorly on the job and appropriately disciplined may file a stress claim against the employer. The courts also ruled that a worker had the right to workers' compensation for stress resulting solely from job loss (Stevens, 1992). This provided financial incentive for many workers to file stress claims rather than accept unemployment benefits (deCarteret, 1994)!

It has been suggested that highly publicized workers' compensation claims spur similar claims. This may be particularly important in mental stress claims because stress is acknowledged to be a universal condition. Since dissatisfaction with working conditions commonly underlies mental stress, some of the recent claim increases may be related to increases in unemployment, plant closings, and relocations. A portion of the increase in mental stress claims may simply reflect the increasing legal recognition of compensation for mental injuries in contexts other than workers' claims. There is an increasing legal tendency to allow tort recovery for both intentional and negligent infliction of emotional distress. Tort recoveries, which were previously limited to narrow and extreme situations, have also expanded considerably (National Council on Compensation Insurance, 1985).

Basically there are four categories of reasoning adopted by courts regarding mental/mental compensability standards (National Council on Compensation Insurance, 1985); (1) no compensation; (2) compensation if the stress is a sudden frightening, or shocking event (such as may be implicated in the causation of PTSD); (3) compensation if the stress exceeds the stress of everyday life or employment; and (4) compensation even if the stress is not in excess of the stress of everyday life or employment.

In some states, if there is no physical stimulus, compensability is denied. There are 10 states that quite clearly apply this requirement; 29 states do not impose a physical injury requirement; and the remainder have not clearly addressed the issue. In 14 states, the standard for compensability in the mental/mental category requires that the mental injury result from greater than day-to-day on-the-job stress. There is a requirement in seven states that the mental stimulus be a sudden or dramatic event. In a few states, to be compensable, the mental disability must be peculiar to the unique facets of the employment and not due to such factors as on-the-job interpersonal relationships (deCarteret, 1994).

In Maine, if the claimant is predisposed to mental illness and might succumb to ordinary work stress, it must be proved that his or her employment predominated in producing the mental disorder. In Oregon, when employment conditions are compared with non-employment factors, the major contributing causes of the claimant's disorder must be job related. The stressful conditions, however, must be real and not imaginary (Sersland, 1984; Matsumoto, 1994). A handful of states have been granting compensation for workers' stress caused by job termination, demotion, or disciplinary action (Blodgett, 1986). This has caused considerable controversy; in California recently, an amendment was written to the state employer's liability insurance specifically excluding claims due to termination of employment, demotion, reassignment, or disciplinary action (California Employer's Liability Insurance Amendment, 1988).

In 1987, with almost four times as many stress claims as the national average, Oregon implemented reform laws limiting the compensability for mental stress claims to illness with "clear and convincing evidence" that the disorder arose "out of and in the course of employment." The law also required that the injury be established by medical evidence supported by objective findings (Bussey, 1993). As a result of the amendment to the definition of occupational illness, stress claims dropped 38 percent from 1987 to 1988 (deCarteret, 1994). In Pennsylvania, there has been a decrease in the number of mental/mental cases over the years due to a heightened burden of proof (Grezlak, 1996a; 1996b). California now requires the use of DSM psychiatric diagnoses; however, there is still a liberal subjective interpretation of mental injury (Matsumoto, 1994).

Acceptance of stress claims varies considerably by state. A worker may be compensated for a job-related mental disability in one state, while a worker with a similar disability will be denied compensation in another. In states with more restrictive criteria, a worker with a legitimate work-related mental disability may have to bear the burden individually and personally for disabling mental injury. On the other hand, states that use more liberal criteria not only have awarded benefits to more workers with legitimate claims, but may have also opened the doors to abuse and fraud. Because most stress claims are litigated, decisions coming from the courts can keep state compensation laws in constant flux. So many state workers' compensation laws are in revision that it is nearly impossible to keep current on criteria for compensability for all state systems.

Personal Injury (Torts)

In a personal injury lawsuit or tort action, the plaintiff claims that a trauma has caused damages that have resulted from the defendant's negligent or intentional action and asks for a money award in reparation for the damage. The law on torts is concerned with the allocation of losses arising out of human activities (Slovenko, 1985). Most personal injuries are pursued under the theory of negligence, that is, unintentional breach of tort.

To press a lawsuit successfully, the plaintiff must assume the burden of proof and show that the defendant had a legal duty of care that was fulfilled negligently, and that, as a result, the plaintiff experienced substantial damage. A psychiatrist's legal involvement in such cases is usually occasioned by a victim's decision to bring suit against another individual or individuals for damages due to psychic injury. The plaintiff's attorney must be satisfied on the first two points of liability before the mental health professional is called on to determine the extent of psychic damage to the claimant. This third point is crucial: If there is no damage, there is no case. The testimony of medical experts, whether expressed in written report, deposition, or trial appearance, makes or breaks the plaintiff's lawsuit (Modlin, 1983).

In the past, liability for psychic impairment was contingent on physical impact or physical injury. Other than that, there was no tort liability for a "broken mind." In a famous English case, *Lynch v. Knight* (1861), the judge said: "The law does not pretend to redress mental pain when the unlawful act complaint consists of that pain alone." The first case that involved the intentional infliction of "extreme mental suffering" was litigated in 1897 (*Wilkinson v. Downton*). In this seminal case, the defendant was held liable for intentional infliction of mental suffering in "outrageous circumstances" that exceeded the bounds of decency. This has come to be called the tort of "outrage" (Lambert, 1978). The law then moved from intentional infliction of extreme mental distress to the area of negligent infliction. At first it was not possible to recover for mental distress from fright or shock without physical impact—the so-called impact rule (*Spade v. Lynn,* 1897). The theory seemed to be that the impact afforded the desired guarantee that the mental disturbance was genuine.

In the past twenty years, the courts have been tracing a somewhat irregular line between compensable and noncompensable psychic impairment. With psychic injury becoming more widely recognized, the courts have become increasingly willing to compensate for emotional distress in the absence of physical injury or impact. Three types of rulings have resulted (Lambert, 1978): (1) zone of danger cases, in which the plaintiff is within the radius of risk from negligent physical contact and suffers emotional disturbance but without impact; (2) bystander recovery (e.g., *Dillon v. Legg,* 1968), in which the plaintiff is outside the zone of physical impact, but suffers emotional distress from witnessing the peril or harm of a third person such as a spouse, child, or near relative; and (3) beyond bystander (e.g., *Prince v. Pittston,* 1974), in which the plaintiff does not actually see the physical injury of a third person (e.g., child) but suffers severe shock when hearing of it or seeing the results.

In consideration of the above situations, the trend of the law has been to give increasing and extensive protection to feelings and emotions of injured parties and to enlarge redress in reparation for psychic injury. Tort claims related to PTSD that have been growing by "leaps and bounds" are psychological injury/sexual harassment claims (Levy, 1995, p. 27; Vinciguerra, 1994).

These cases, as well as workers' compensation cases, often involve complex scientific issues of causation. Lawyers usually divide the idea of causation into two parts: (1) cause in fact, or factual cause, and (2) proximate cause, or legal cause. It is the former that is closely related to the concept of medical causation that would encompass, for example, the scientific question of whether cigarette smoking causes lung cancer. Cause in fact can be formulated by the "but for" rule, which states that one event is a cause of another when the first event would not have occurred but for the second event. Another rule for cause in fact is the "substantial factor" test, which states that a defendant's action is the cause of the damage if it was a material element in bringing it about (Goldstein, 1987).

Proximate cause, on the other hand, often revolves around the question of whether or not the defendant has a legal duty of care. If the defendant has a legal duty to protect the plaintiff, the defendant would then be held liable for any damages. Once the plaintiff suffers any foreseeable injury, even if relatively minor, as a result of the defendant's negligent conduct, the defendant is then liable for any additional consequences. This consideration extends liability to encompass injury that causes a disability, activates a latent condition, or worsens a preexisting condition (Modlin, 1983). An example is the hypothetical case of a plaintiff who, unbeknownst to the defendant, has a skull of eggshell thinness. If the defendant inflicts even a minor impact on this skull, the defendant will then be liable for any injury. The rule is sometimes expressed by saying the defendant "takes his plaintiff as he finds him" (Goldstein, 1987).

Fortunately for defendants, some jurisdictions do not extend the eggshell plaintiff reasoning to claimants with an eggshell psyche. While jurisdictions differ, some distinguish between ordinarily sensitive and super sensitive persons. For instance in *Theriault v. Swan* (1989), the Supreme Judicial Court of Maine held *when the harm reasonably could affect only the hurt feelings of the super sensitive plaintiff—the eggshell psyche—there is no entitlement to recovery. If, however, the harm reasonably could have been expected to befall the ordinary sensitive person, the tortfeasor must take his victim as he finds her—extraordinarily sensitive or not.* Brown (1996) states that conventional wisdom aside, legal causation in a PTSD case can be just as difficult to prove as cases involving other disorders. There are multiple psychosocial and environmental stressors unrelated to the alleged traumatic incident that may operate to produce PTSD symptoms. From a defense attorney's viewpoint, perhaps, the most effective method to attack a PTSD claim is not to challenge the symptoms, but to prove or at least plant a question in the fact finder's mind that the defendant's actions did not bring about the symptoms. For instance, if the symptoms are valid, they pre-existed the alleged traumatic incident or were caused by something other than the defendant's alleged negligence (Brown, 1996). Lawyers have been warned that the most important factor in defending against a PTSD claim is to start the defense early and immediately seek retention of a qualified expert.

On March 22, 1990, the fish-processing vessel, Aleutian Enterprise, with a crew of 31, sank in the relatively calm Bering Sea. Nearby vessels recovered 22 persons. The remaining nine persons were missing at sea and presumed dead. Nineteen survivors of the ma-

rine disaster were seen by mental health professionals while pursuing personal injury claims and received a PTSD diagnosis that was maintained for more than six months. This yielded an incidence rate for chronic PTSD of no less than 86 percent, a rate in excess of practically any previously recorded percentage for any type of trauma. The partial explanation of this is the influence of attorney advice and symptom sharing, plus the inexperience of mental health professionals making the diagnosis (Rosen, 1995).

Physicians sometimes have difficulty understanding legal approaches to causation that include not only the initiation of physical or psychological injury, but also the production of additional damage or dysfunction in individuals with preexistent problems. A causal role may be legally significant if it can be shown to have played some part, not necessarily the major one, in initiating, contributing to, accelerating, or aggravating the plaintiff's injury. Many jurists also have difficulty empathizing with this view. An astute defense attorney, therefore, endeavors to draw opinions from expert witnesses about the plaintiff's preexistent susceptibility to stress in an effort to influence the jury despite the letter of the law (Modlin, 1986).

In personal injury litigation, psychiatrists typically offer opinions about whether or not a traumatic event—physical injury, psychological stress, and/or exposure to a noxious substance—is the proximate cause of the plaintiff's ensuing psychic injury. The court follows the reasoning that the test for allowing a plaintiff to recover in a tort suit is not scientific certainty but legal sufficiency. Thus a cause in fact relationship need not be conclusively proven before a psychiatrist can testify that, in his or her opinion, a causal relationship exists. The following case (*Wotalewiez v. Gallagher,* 1986) is illustrative.

The plaintiff, a 33 year-old female parking patrol officer, was involved in an altercation with an irate male citizen after issuance of a parking ticket. The defendant grabbed the plaintiff's right arm and verbally abused her for writing the ticket. The plaintiff, suing for $150,000 with punitive damages of $100,000, asserted that the defendant intentionally and willfully attempted to do violence to her. Furthermore, "as a direct and proximate result of the defendant's assault and battery, plaintiff was caused to suffer permanent injuries including acute PTSD with some associated regression, partial personality decompensation, depressive reaction, pain, suffering, stress and anxiety." The defendant's anger and physical force reminded the plaintiff of previous physical and sexual abuse that she had sustained as a child. The developmental history indicated that the plaintiff's mother had died when she was a young girl and that she also had lost a child several years earlier from medical complications of a premature birth. Medical history included a right shoulder injury in an auto accident 3 years prior, with subsequent surgery for thoracic outlet syndrome. The clinical evaluations by several mental health professionals described a variety of symptoms and signs such as tearfulness, wringing of hands, stuttering, and a pervasive helpless feeling. Although there was no systematic inquiry for objective symptoms, all clinicians for the plaintiff diagnosed PTSD. At trial, the defendant was found negligent, but there was no battery and no intentional tort established. The final financial settlement was approximately 10 percent of what the plaintiff had originally requested.

EVALUATION AND EXPERT TESTIMONY

Expert Witness

Courts are skeptical of psychological evidence because it rarely rises to the level of "beyond a reasonable doubt," the proof necessary to sustain a criminal conviction (Boresi, 1989). PTSD has provided fuel for the periodic firestorm about psychiatric and psychological expert testimony. In 1988, Faust and Ziskin took psychiatry to task for its difficulties in achieving "reliable" diagnostic classifications and for the gap between determination of clinical criteria and satisfaction of legal criteria. They maintained that there is generally considerable heterogeneity among individuals who fall within the same psychiatric diagnostic categories which limits forensic value, and that, when a jury considers a criminal defense such as diminished capacity, "a diagnosis such as PTSD offers little guidance" (Faust & Ziskin, 1988, p. 32). Taking this notion to the extreme, the West Virginia supreme court recently held that despite expert opinion to the contrary, lay testimony

was sufficient to find that a first-degree murder defendant was sane beyond a reasonable doubt (*West Virginia v. Walls,* 1994). In this case several witnesses testified that Walls "appeared normal to them" before and after the crime, and the jury gave more weight to their testimony than to the three experts (two psychologists and a psychiatrist) who diagnosed paranoid schizophrenia and agreed that Walls was not criminally responsible. This bias against psychiatric testimony is an example of frequently held lay belief that ordinary common sense has more validity than "psychobabble."

Most assuredly, the specific use of PTSD in the courtroom has been abused, but as Hoge and Grisso (1992) point out, the test in the courtroom is not scientific certainty but legal sufficiency. The fact that scientific experimentation would require more evidence before reaching a conclusion is irrelevant. In fact, the most common problem with the general acceptance of psychiatric testimony is that the judicial system seems to have an "unquenchable thirst" for its use, often asking mental health professionals to exceed their knowledge base. Indeed, in the current legal climate, psychiatric testimony is alternatively valued and devalued. On one hand it is seen as soft exculpatory and imprecise; on the other hand, it is in demand because it offers insight into criminal psychopathology (Perlin, 1994). Mental health experts "do not have to answer legal questions of competence or criminal responsibility in order to provide valid assistance to courts.... Their proper role is to describe the relative abilities, disabilities, symptoms, and diagnostic conditions in clinical and behavioral terms, leaving the court to weigh the observations in the context of legal concepts and standards" (Hoge & Grisso, 1992, pp. 73,74).

All scientific courtroom testimony including psychiatric evidence is governed by expert witness rules. The first important standard is called the Frye rule, which was laid down in a 1923 decision by a federal appellate court in a case that involved a lie detector test. The Frye rule states that any scientific evidence given in trials must be "generally accepted by the scientific community." Since the 1920s, with the increasing litigation involving scientific issues and a broader appreciation of scientific controversy, lawyers and others have argued that a strict application of the Frye rule was becoming less relevant (Marwick, 1993a). One of the major problems with the Frye test is that the term "general acceptance" is vague and difficult to define. Because Frye is a relatively strict standard, there was concern that it could deprive courts of relevant evidence, particularly new information that had not had a chance to diffuse throughout the scientific community. Some courts, however, see the test's conservative nature as its primary advantage because it offers more protection against "junk science" testimony (Huber, 1991).

The US Federal Rules of Evidence also apply to expert testimony. Rule 702 putatively broadens the Frye admissibility standard by allowing an expert witness to offer any evidence that will aid the trier-of-fact in determining a question. All evidence is relevant and admissible unless its probative value is "substantially outweighed by the danger of unfair prejudice, confusion of the issues, misleading the jury, or by considerations of undue delay, waste of time, or needless presentation of cumulative evidence" (Federal Rules of Evidence 403). By 1990, 34 American states had adopted a code of evidence patterned directly after the Federal Rules (Steinberg, 1993).

The liberalization of evidentiary rules and the adoption of the Federal Rules of Evidence in 1975 have eroded conservative attitudes toward psychological testimony in the past two decades. The rules established a new and less restrictive approach to expert testimony of all sorts. The new evidentiary environment has opened the door to psychological testimony on issues such as battered woman syndrome and rape trauma syndrome. As new forms of expert testimony have appeared, some jurisdictions have responded by limiting their admissibility, and/or invoking venerable evidentiary cases that predate the adoption of more liberal evidentiary rules.

There are three primary issues. First, courts are concerned with reliability, particularly because courts have long experience with a litigant's ability to find experts to support virtually any position. Second, courts are extremely concerned with the "aura of special reliability and trustworthiness" that surrounds an expert's testimony. Third, courts would like to restrict testimony in some manner so that the courtrooms will not be overrun with experts. Expert testimony has added substantially to the length and cost of some trials; and courts may resist using it unless they are convinced it will aid the trial process (Murphy, 1992).

The latest development comes from a 1993 US Supreme Court decision, *Daubert v. Merrill Dow*, when the Court granted certiorari in light of the sharp divisions among lower courts regarding the proper standard for admission of scientific expert testimony. The Court essentially handed down a strict interpretation of the Federal Rules of Evidence stating that the testimony of an expert must pertain to "scientific knowledge" and that validity disputes should be resolved by the trial judge by taking into account, among other things, peer review and publication of underlying theory or technique (Steinberg, 1993; *Daubert v. Merrill Dow*, 1993; Marwick, 1993b). This is a more restrictive approach to the admissibility of expert testimony at the Federal level than has been taken at any time since the adoption of the Federal Rules twenty years ago (Shuman, 1995).

These standards have had variable influence on PTSD testimony which, although generally accepted, has been considered prejudicial, irrelevant, and/or non-probative by some courts. For example, an Alaska appeals court recently reversed a murder conviction because expert evidence about PTSD had been improperly excluded from the trial (*Shepard v. Alaska*, 1993). The defendant, a Vietnam veteran, had attempted to call two experts to bolster his case. One, a psychiatrist, was the Director of a Veterans Administration (VA) PTSD treatment program and a specialist in PTSD. Outside the presence of the jury, he testified that PTSD is a generally accepted medical condition, discussed its technical definition, its causes and its common symptoms. He noted that avoidance, denial, and fear or distrust of authority figures are among the symptoms. He indicated that the kind of stress the defendant experienced in Vietnam was typical of the stress that caused PTSD, and that members of his hospital staff had treated many such patients. He stated that physical attack is the type of event capable of bringing about recurrence of PTSD symptoms, and thought it plausible that the defendant's effort to cover up his crime resulted from PTSD. Although the trial court allowed another defense expert to testify generally about PTSD, it excluded the VA psychiatrist's testimony because it amounted to "questionable" psychological profile evidence that might induce a decision by the jury on a purely emotional basis. Prosecution experts, on the other hand, who had never served in Vietnam were allowed to testify about conditions there, to opine that the defendant's remaining expert was rather naive about criminal defendants, and to assert that PTSD had become a fad in legal defenses.

Because PTSD has a specific, easily identifiable stressor causing equally identifiable symptoms, it is sometimes concluded that the syndrome's existence or absence is well within the ordinary man's understanding. PTSD expert testimony has usually been allowed when aspects of the posttraumatic behavior are thought to be outside the realm of common knowledge or when there are atypical considerations such as a dissociative state.

Finally, the risk of misuse of a psychiatric diagnosis is heightened when the diagnosis is based largely on subjective symptoms. Whenever a patient gains a great deal (either excuse from blame or monetary award) by receiving a diagnosis (such as PTSD) that is largely based on self-report, the use of that diagnosis in the courtroom requires scrutiny. Abuse of the PTSD diagnosis by forensic psychiatric experts stems from three major causes: (1) inadequate forensic evaluation of the claimant; (2) failure to properly apply the PTSD criteria to the claimant; and (3) advocacy or bias. It is misleading for the expert to imply that making this diagnosis clarifies any legal issue unless the precise relationship between the symptoms and the stressful event is carefully documented (Halleck et al., 1992).

Retrospective Forensic Assessment

History. An evaluation process might well begin with an attempt to sort claims into those that involve a PTSD diagnosis and those that do not. The plaintiff's condition may not meet PTSD criteria for any of several reasons generally related to a lack of severity of either the stressor or the symptoms. Does the plaintiff have another mental disorder? There are diagnoses in DSM-IV other than PTSD that should be considered before resorting to nonstandardized nomenclature such as "traumatic depression." The further from the PTSD diagnosis the evaluator strays, the more speculative the causation opinion will become. It is also more likely that problems of preexisting injury will be significant. The DSM-IV PTSD criteria are the starting point for psychiatric evaluation of a claim of negligent infliction of emotional distress whether the context is criminal or civil (Spaulding, 1988).

It has been previously observed (Sparr & Atkinson, 1986) that, in criminal proceedings such as NGRI and diminished capacity, establishing a valid link between PTSD and criminal behavior is an imposing task. At least two levels of causation have to be investigated: (1) causal link between the traumatic stressor and the psychiatric symptoms and (2) causal connection between psychiatric symptoms and the criminal act. No one argues whether mental health experts know the symptoms of PTSD. At issue is whether their professional abilities extend to deciding whether the stressor occurred, if it was sufficiently traumatizing, and whether the designated stressor or some preceding or subsequent stressor or provocation is the cause of the complainant's symptoms (Raifman, 1983). When PTSD is a factor in a criminal case, the diagnosis itself may not be questioned; however, the contribution of the PTSD to the defendant's mental state at the time of the alleged criminal act may be disputed. Opposing attorneys will often point to secondary factors such as financial problems, interpersonal conflicts, or drug and alcohol abuse as proximate motivations for criminal activity. Although these factors may be related to PTSD, they are not generally regarded as sufficient to relieve an individual from criminal responsibility (Marciniak, 1986).

There are good reasons to place greater emphasis on outside information sources in legal evaluations than during other psychiatric examinations. For example, malingering is uncommon in routine clinical practice, but special care is needed to diagnose it in a forensic setting. The subject of evaluation often has something to gain by a finding of mental illness and may attempt to exaggerate or even feign a psychiatric disturbance (Halleck et al., 1992). Ultimately, the most effective tool for detecting fabricated PTSD symptoms may be those that verify and quantify the stressor and its impact through eyewitness accounts or by other collateral sources. Direct psychiatric examination should always include a trauma history. Unresolved psychological reactions to previous trauma may predispose an individual to dissociative reactions, and to other effects of subsequent trauma. Because of the tendency of PTSD patients to avoid painful memories, superficial questioning may fail to elicit bona fide symptoms. On the other hand, direct inquiry regarding PTSD diagnostic criteria may be treated by motivated respondents as a series of leading questions evoking answers that too readily bring about a PTSD diagnosis.

These are formidable obstacles to reliable evaluation. The skilled evaluator, however, is not without tools to overcome them. The first device is non-directive interviewing. The interviewer should begin by asking the claimant to describe the problems he/she has been experiencing and then allow time to talk with as little interruption as possible. A claimant who talks for fifteen or thirty minutes hardly mentioning a PTSD symptom, but who answers positively to almost all PTSD symptoms during subsequent direct questioning, should be regarded with suspicion. Another tool is insistence on detailed illustration. Knowledgeable or coached claimants may know which PTSD symptoms to report, but being able to illustrate them with convincing personal life details is another matter. Invented symptoms have a vague and stilted quality. The interviewer must determine whether the history being presented has the quality of a personal autobiography, or merely a textbook. While eliciting the history, the evaluator should pay close attention to the claimant's behavior. Some PTSD symptoms (e.g., irritability, difficulty concentrating, or exaggerated startle) may be directly observed. Also relevant is whether the claimant's behavior and affect are consistent with the history he/she is providing. The display of genuine emotion, or lack of it, during rendition of a traumatic event and its sequelae can be revealing.

Structured Interview Instruments. Following the non-directive portion of the interview, the evaluator should conduct a directive interview that inquires into each PTSD diagnostic criterion in turn, as well as into the criteria of other Axis I and II mental disorders that could enter into the differential diagnosis. Psychiatric researchers are now required to determine the presence or absence of diagnostic criteria in a systematic manner, usually by means of structured interview instruments. Forensic evaluations call for a similar approach. Suitable structured interview instruments for PTSD have been reviewed by Wilson and Keane (1997). An instrument available for the detection of malingering is the Structured Interview for Reported Symptoms, or SIRS (Rogers, Bagby, & Dickens, 1992). A number of psychometric questionnaires also yield numerical scores pertinent to the presence or absence, as well as severity, of PTSD (Wilson & Keane, 1997). The Minnesota Multiphasic Personality Inventory-II (Litz et al., 1991) incorporates validity scales as checks for symptom exaggeration. However, research has indicated that even the MMPI can fail to detect fabricated PTSD (Lees-Haley, 1990; Perconte & Goreczny, 1990). This consideration makes psychometric tests useful only for screening, or as ancillary tests to confirm or call into question an evaluator's total impressions.

Psychophysiological Testing. Laboratory measurement of physiologic responsivity during exposure to cues related to traumatic event has been described as "the best and most specific biological diagnostic test for PTSD" (Friedman, 1991, p. 74). Pitman et al. (1993) have recently proposed that such measurement "has the potential to redeem the PTSD diagnosis from its current subjectivity and to help separate the wheat from the chaff in the forensic evaluation of PTSD claims" (p. 40). As with psychometric testing, those proposing the utility of psychophysiologic testing emphasize that the results do not stand on their own but serve as one component of a comprehensive forensic PTSD evaluation. To date, physiologic testing has been utilized in several forensic PTSD evaluations and admitted into evidence in at least two cases (Pitman, 1993; Pitman et al., 1993).

Criminal Evaluation. Finally, in evaluating a defendant with alleged PTSD who is charged with a crime, the following factors may have particular applicability to the determination of authenticity (Auberry, 1985; Blank, 1985; Marciniak, 1986): (1) the criminal act should represent spontaneous unpremeditated behavior uncharacteristic of the individual; (2) the choice of a victim may be fortuitous or accidental; (3) the crimes should recreate in a psychologically meaningful way elements of the traumatic stressor; (4) the defendant is mostly unaware of the specific ways he has repeated and reenacted traumatic experiences; (5) seemingly benign incidents may result in bouts of violence; (6) there may be amnesia for all or part of the episode; (7) there is inability to explain the reason for the behavior; (8) there is no previous criminal record; (9) crimes are generally precipitated by events and circumstances that realistically or symbolically force the individual to face unresolved conflicts; (10) the behavior lacks current motivation; and (11) coherent dialogue appropriately related to time and place are not found in dissociative states. In assessment of combat trauma, discharge papers, combat history, and access to military records may be necessary. Evaluation protocols for Vietnam veterans have been offered by various authors (Sparr & Atkinson, 1986; Marciniak, 1986; *Physician's Guide,* 1985; Sparr & Pankratz, 1983). In addition, Simon (1995) has established comprehensive guidelines for forensic PTSD assessment, and Motherway (1987) has provided specific guidance to attorneys with PTSD clients.

CONCLUSION

The DSM criteria often define the thin membrane separating a diagnosable psychiatric disorder from the ordinary travails of life. Although some forensic assessments require a DSM-IV psychiatric diagnosis such as PTSD, others may only need to address the issue of whether or not a claimant has experienced psychic injury of any kind. PTSD should be diagnosed if the facts fit, but only if they fit. To do otherwise dilutes and trivializes the diagnosis. In some situations where PTSD is inappropriately diagnosed, one wonders whether or not we are questioning whether human beings can adapt to anything. If a worker is unfairly treated, unjustly terminated, or displeased with his lack of promotion, he is not thereby necessarily mentally ill. Stress is not necessarily bad for people, and the absence of its challenge, be it physical or mental, can sometimes be as serious a detriment as the presence of too much stress (Savodnik, 1991).

Nevertheless, because the experiences of many individuals such as battered women, rape victims, or combat soldiers are outside the mainstream, expert psychiatric testimony at times is a valuable resource to the legal system. There have been concerns about psychiatric input because it may infringe on the jury's fact-finding duty, or because the experts may venture outside their area of expertise and state conclusions that are actually their own value judgments. Generally, however, our justice system is too protective of individual rights to allow gross infringements. Moreover, psychiatric testimony has always been greeted skeptically. Despite these difficulties, legal advocates are expected to continue to request assistance from mental health professionals familiar with PTSD to provide opinions that will help their cases. The vicissitudes of forensic assessment of traumatized adults have been explored in this chapter. Trauma may be significantly disabling and may be the result of negligence, violence, or some other misdeed that could require prosecution and/or reparation. As awareness of the aftereffect of traumatization increases, its use in the legal system also increases. It is important for mental health professionals to understand the basic ground rules of any forensic venue they plan to enter. In doing so, they more effectively aid themselves, their patients, and the judicial process.

REFERENCES

American Psychiatric Association. *Diagnostic and statistical manual of mental disorders,* (4th ed.). Washington, DC: Author, 1994, xxiii.

Appelbaum, P. S., Jick, R. Z., Grisso, T., Giveler, D., Silver, E., & Steadman, H. J. (1993). Use of posttraumatic stress disorder to support an insanity defense. *American Journal of Psychiatry, 150(2),* 229–234.

Appleson, G. (1983). Stress on stress: Compensation cases growing. *American Bar Association Journal, 69,* 142–143.

Astin, M. C., Lawrence, K. J., & Foy, D. W. (1993). Post-traumatic stress disorder among battered women: Risk and resiliency factors. *Violence and Victims, 8,* 17–28.

Atkinson, R. M., Henderson, R. G., Sparr, L. F., & Deale S. (1982). Assessment of Vietnam veterans for post-traumatic stress disorder in Veterans Administration disability claims. *American Journal of Psychiatry, 139,* 1118–1121.

Auberry, A. R. (1985). PTSD: Effective representation of a Vietnam veteran in the criminal justice system. *Marquette Law Review, 68(4),* 648–675.

Barth, P. S. (1990). Workers' compensation for mental stress cases. *Behavioral Sciences and the Law, 8,* 349–360.

Bechtel v State 840 P.2d 1 (Okl. cr., Sep 2, 1992) (NO. F-88–887).

Blank, A. S. (1985). The unconscious flashback to the war in Viet Nam veterans: Clinical mystery, legal defense, and community problem. In S. M. Sonnenberg, A. S. Blank, & J. A. Talbott (Eds.), *The Trauma of war: Stress and recovery in Viet Nam veterans* (293–308) Washington, DC: American Psychiatric Press.

Block, A. P. (1990). Rape trauma syndrome as scientific expert testimony. *Archives of Sexual Behavior, 19,* 309–322.

Blodgett, N. (1986). Legal relief from tension—work-induced stress spurs workers' compensation claims. *American Bar Association Journal 17,* 17–18.

Bohnert v State, 312 Md 266, 539 A.2d 657 (1988).

Boresi, K. O. (1989). Syndrome testimony in child abuse prosecutions: The wave of the future? *Saint Louis University Public Law Review, 8(1),* 207–231.

Bownes, I. T., O'Gorman, E. C., & Sayers, A. (1991). Assault characteristics and posttraumatic stress disorder in rape victims. *Acta Psychiatrica Scandinavica, 83,* 27–30.

Breslau, N., Davis, G. L., Andreski, P., & Peterson, E. (1991). Traumatic events and posttraumatic stress disorder in an urban population of young adults. *Archives of General Psychiatry, 48,* 216–222.

Brown, J. T. (1996). Compensation neurosis rides again: A practitioner's guide to defending PTSD claims. *Defense Counsel Journal 63(4),* 467–482.

Buchele, B. J., & Buchele, J. P. (1985). Legal and psychological issues in the use of expert testimony on rape trauma syndrome. *Washburn Law Journal, 25,* 26–42.

Burge, S. K. (1988). Post-traumatic stress disorder in victims of rape. *Journal of Traumatic Stress, 1,* 193–210.

Burgess, A., & Holmstrom, L. (1974). Rape trauma syndrome. *American Journal of Psychiatry, 131,* 980–986.

Bussey, G. D. (1993). Mental "stress" claims and workers' compensation: The problems and suggestions for change. *Federation of Insurance and Corporate Counsel Quarterly 43(2),* 99–115.

California Employer's Liability Insurance Amendment 413181, State Compensation Insurance Fund, January 13, 1988.

Calise, A. (1993). Workers' compensation mental-stress claims in decline. *National Underwriter 8,* 3, 31.

Carter v General Motors, 106 NW2d (361 MI 1961).

Cling, B. J. (1988). Rape trauma syndrome: Medical evidence of nonconsent. *Medical Trial Technique Quarterly, 35,* 154–181.

Colbach, E. M. (1982). The mental-mental muddle and work' comp in Oregon. *Bulletin of the American Academy of Psychiatry and the Law, 10,* 261–217.

Commonwealth v Mulcahy, No. 460–464 (Phila Ct. C. P. PA Dec 1978).

Cotton v Alabama, 639 So. 2d 577 (Ala. Crim. App. 1993).

Cutler, J. M. (1989). Criminal law—battered woman syndrome: The killing of a passive victim—a perfect defense or a perfect crime?—*State v Norman. Campbell Law Review, 11,* 263–278.

Daubert v Merrill Dow, 92–102 US Supr Ct, 125 L Ed 2d 469 (1993).

Davidson, J. R. T. (1991). Clinical efficacy shown in pharmacologic treatment of post traumatic stress disorder. *Psychiatric Times 26 (September),* 62.

deCarteret, J. C. (1994). Occupational stress claims: Effects on workers' compensation. *American Association of Occupational Health Nurses Journal, 42,* 494–498.

Delia S. v Torres, 134 Cal. App. 3d 471 (1982).

Department of Insurance and Finance. (1987). Mental stress claims in Oregon 1980–1986. Salem OR, Department of Insurance and Finance, Research and Statistics Section.

Dillon v Legg, 441 P2d 919 (Cal 1968).

Duncan, M. J. (1992). Battered women who kill their abusers and a new Texas law. *Houston Law Review, 29(1),* 963–990.

Dutton, M. A., & Goodman, L. A. (1994). Posttraumatic stress disorder among battered women: Analysis of legal implications. *Behavioral Sciences and the Law, 12,* 215–234.

Dwyer, D. A. (1988). Expert testimony on rape trauma syndrome: An argument for limited admissibility. *Washington Law Review, 63(4),* 1063–1086.

Erlinder, C. P. (1984). Paying the price for Vietnam: Posttraumatic stress disorder and criminal behavior. *Boston College Law Review, 25(2),* 305–347.

Falk, C. E. (1995). Criminal law—*State v. Phipps:* The Tennessee Court of Criminal Appeals accepts diminished capacity: Evidence to negate *mens rea. Memphis State University Law Review, 26(4),* 373–392.

Faust, D., & Ziskin, J. (1988). The expert witness in psychology and psychiatry. *Science, 241,* 31–35.

Faust, D. & Ziskin, J. (1989). Challenging post-traumatic stress disorder claims. *Defense Law Journal 38(3),* 407–424.

Federal Bureau of Investigation. (1988). Uniform Crime Reports: Crime in the United States. Washington DC: Government Printing Office, 1988:46–48.

Federal Rules of Evidence 403.

Federal Rules of Evidence 702.

Fielder v State 683 S. W. 2d 565, 595 (Tex, Ct, App. 1985) rev'd 756 S. W. 2d 309 (Tex. Crim. App. 1988).

Foa, E. B., & Riggs, D. (1994). Posttraumatic stress disorder and rape. In R. Pynoos, (Ed.), *Posttraumatic stress disorder* (pp. 133–163). Lutherville, MD: Sidran Press.

Frazier, P., & Borgida, E. (1985). Rape trauma syndrome evidence in court. *American Psychologist, 40(9),* 984–993.

Frazier, P., & Borgida, E. (1988). Juror common understanding and the admissibility of rape trauma syndrome evidence in court. *Law and Human Behavior, 12,* 101–122.

Friedman, M. J. (1991). Biological approaches to the diagnosis and treatment of posttraumatic stress disorder. *Journal of Traumatic Stress, 4,* 67–91.

Frye v United States, 293 F, 1013 (DC Cir. 1923).

Goldstein, R. L. (1987). The twilight zone between scientific certainty and legal sufficiency: Should a jury determine the causation of schizophrenia? *Bulletin of the American Academy of Psychiatry and the Law 15,* 95–104.

Grant, B. L., & Coons, D. J. (1983). Guilty verdict in a murder committed by a veteran with post-traumatic stress disorder. *Bulletin of the American Academy of Psychiatry and the Law, 11(4),* 355–358.

Green, B. L. (1995). Recent research on findings of diagnosis of post traumatic stress disorder. In R. I. Simon, (Ed.), *Posttraumatic stress disorder in litigation: Guidelines for forensic assessment* (pp. 13–30). Washington DC: American Psychiatric Press.

Grezlak, H. (1996a). No benefits for 'downsizing' depression: Forced move to lower-status job not compensable, justices rule. *Pennsylvania Law Weekly, 19 (January 24),* 3.

Grezlak, H. (1996b). Proctor & Gamble worker denied benefits for depression. *Pennsylvania Law Weekly, 19 (July 29),* 14, 31.

Hall, H. V., & Hall, III, F. L. (1987). Post-traumatic stress disorder as a legal defense in criminal trials. *American Journal of Forensic Psychology, 5,* 45–53.

Halleck, S. L., Hoge, S. K., Miller, R. D., Sadoff, R. L., & Halleck, N. H. (1992). The use of psychiatric diagnoses in the legal process: Task force report of the American Psychiatric Association. *Bulletin of the American Academy of Psychiatry and the Law, 20(4),* 481–499.

Hermann, D. H. (1986). Criminal defenses and pleas in mitigation based on amnesia. *Behavioral Science and the Law, 4(1),* 5–26.

Hoge, S. K., and Grisso, T. (1992). Accuracy and expert testimony. *Bulletin of the American Academy of Psychiatry and the Law, 20(1),* 67–76.

Huber, P. W. (1991). *Galileo's Revenge: Junk Science in the Courtroom.* New York, NY: Basic Books.

Hutton v State, 339 Md 486, 663 A.2d 1289 (1995).

Ibn-Tamas v United States, 407 A 2d 626 (DC 1979).

Illinois v Wheeler, 602 N.E.2d 826 (Ill. Sup. Ct. 1992).

Karpay, K. (1986). Maryland accepts stress-disorder evidence. *National Law Journal, 9(26),* 3,10.

Kelner, J., & Kelner, R. S. (1989). Rape trauma stress syndrome in criminal and civil cases. *New York Law Journal, (April 19), 201(74),* 3, 5.

Kemp, A., Green, B. L., Hovanizt, C., & Rawlings, E. I. (1995). Incidence and correlates of posttraumatic stress disorder in battered women: Shelter and community samples. *Journal of Interpersonal Violence, 10,* 43–55.

Kiev, A. (1993). Conveying psychological pain and suffering: Juror empathy is key. *Trial 29(10),* 16–21.

Koss, M. P., Gidycz, C. A., & Wisniewski N. (1987). The scope of rape: Incidence and prevalence of sexual aggression and victimization in a national sample of higher education students. *Journal of Consulting and Clinical Psychology 55,* 162–170.

Lambert, T. F. (1978). Tort liability for psychic injuries: Overview and update. *Journal of the Association of Trial Lawyers of America, 37,* 1–31.

Leavitt, S. S. (1980). Determining compensable workplace stressors. *Occupational Health and Safety, 49,* 38–46.

Lees-Haley, P. R. (1990). Malingering mental disorder on the Impact of Event Scale (IES): Toxic exposure and cancerphobia. *Journal of Traumatic Stress, 3,* 315–321.

Lees-Haley, P. R. (1986). Pseudo post-traumatic stress disorder. *Trial Diplomacy Journal, 9,* 17–20.

Levy, M. I. (1995). Stressing the point: Post traumatic stress disorder claims. *For the Defense 37(11),* 27–31.

Litz, B. T., Penk, W. E., Walsh, S., Hyer, L., Marx, D., Blake, D. D., Keane, T., & Bitman, D. (1991). Similarities and differences between MMPI and MMPI-2 applications to the assessment of posttraumatic stress disorder. *Journal of Personality Assessment, 57(2),* 238–253.

London, D. B., Zonana, H. V. & Loeb, R. (1988). Workers' compensation and psychiatric disability. In R. Larson (Ed.), *Psychiatric injury in the workplace.* Philadelphia, PA: Hanley and Belforth.

Lustberg, L. S., & Jacobi, J. V. (1992). The battered woman as reasonable person: A critique of the appellate division decision in *State v. McClain. Seton Hall Law Review, 22,* 365–388.

Lynch v Knight, 11 Eng. Rep. 854, 863 (HL 1861).

Maher, V. M. (1988). The skeleton in the closet: The battered woman syndrome, self-defense and expert testimony. *Mercer Law Review 39,* 545–547.

Marciniak, R. D. (1986). Implications to forensic psychiatry of post-traumatic stress disorder: A review. *Military Medicine, 151,* 434–437.

Maremaa, T. (1981). Defending Vietnam vets: How attorney Bob Bell helped protesting Vietnam vets. *California Lawyer, 1(1),* 16–17.

Marwick, C. (1993a). Court ruling on 'junk science' gives judges more say about what expert witness testimony to allow. *Journal of the American Medical Association, 270(4),* 423.

Marwick, C. (1993b). What constitutes an expert witness? *Journal of the American Medical Association, 269 (16),* 2057.

Matsumoto, A. V. (1994). Reforming the reform: Mental stress claims under California's workers' compensation system. *Loyola of Los Angeles Law Review, 27,* 1327–1365.

Mihajlovich, M. (1987). Does plight make right: The battered woman syndrome, expert testimony and the law of self-defense. *Indiana Law Journal 62,* 1253–1254.

Modlin, H. C. (1983). Traumatic neurosis and other injuries. *Psychiatric Clinics of North America, 6,* 661–682.

Modlin, H. C. (1986). Compensation neurosis. *Bulletin of the American Academy of Psychiatry and the Law 14,* 263–271.

Morris, G. H. (1975). *The insanity defense: A blueprint for legislative reform.* Lexington, MA: DC Heath and Company.

Moscarello, R. (1991). Posttraumatic stress disorder after sexual assault: its psychodynamics and treatment. *Journal of the American Academy of Psychoanalysis, 19(1),* 235–253.

Motherway, N. J. (1987) Post-traumatic stress disorder. *American Jurisprudence Proof of Facts 2nd, 49,* 73–124.

Murphy, S. (1992). Assisting the jury in understanding victimization: Expert psychological testimony on battered woman syndrome and rape trauma syndrome. *Columbia Journal of Law and Social Problems, 25(2),* 277–312.

National Council on Compensation Insurance. (1985). Emotional stress in the workplace: New legal rights in the 80's. *National Council on Compensation Insurance.*

National Victims Center and Crime Victims Research and Treatment Center. (1992). Rape in America: A report to the nation (Research Report #1992–1). Washington, DC: National Victims Center and Crime Victims Research and Treatment Center.

Neal, L. A. (1994). The pitfalls of making a categorical diagnosis of post traumatic stress disorder in personal injury litigation. *Medicine, Science and the Law, 34,* 117–122.

Nordheimer, J. (1971, May 26). From Dakota to Detroit: Death of a troubled hero. *New York Times,* 1, 16.

Norris v State, 490 So. 2d 839 (Miss. 1986).

Olson, W. K. (1991). *The litigation explosion.* New York, NY: Dutton.

Pattison, P., & Varca, P. E. (1994). Workers' compensation for mental stress claims in Wyoming. *Land and Water Law Review 29(1),* 145–173.

People v Bledsoe, 681 P 2d 291 (Cal. 1984).

People v Reid, 475 N. Y. S. 2d 741 (1984).

People v Taylor, 536 NY 536 NY52d 825 (App Div. 2d Dept. Dec. 30, 1988).

People v Wells, 202 P.2d 53 (Cal. 1949).

People v Wood, No 80–7410 (Cir Ct. Cook County Ill. May, 1982).

Perconte, S. T., & Goreczny, A. J. (1990). Failure to detect fabricated posttraumatic stress disorder with the use of the MMPI in a clinical population. *American Journal of Psychiatry, 147,* 1057–1060.

Perlin, M. L. (1994). *The jurisprudence of the insanity defense.* Durham, NC: Carolina Academic Press.

Peterson, A. F. (1996). Restricting expert testimony on post traumatic stress disorder. *Maryland Law Review, 55(3),* 677–695.

Physician's guide for disability evaluation examinations Psychiatric sequelae of military duty in a war zone. (Chapter 20). (1985). Washington, DC: Department of Veterans Affairs.

Pitman, R. K., Orr, S. P., & Bursztajn, H. J. (1993). *Vinal v. New England Telephone:* Admission of PTSD psychophysiologic test results in a civil trial. *American Academy of Psychiatry and the Law Newsletter, 18(3),* 67–69.

Prince v Pittston, 63 FRD 28 (SD WVa 1974).

Pub. L. No. 98–596, §§402, 404, 406, 98 Stat. 3134 (Oct 12, 1984).

Raifman, L. J. (1983). Problems of diagnosis and legal causation in courtroom use of posttraumatic stress disorder. *Behavioral Science and the Law, 1,* 115–130.

Robins, L. N., Helzer, J. E., Weissman, M. M., et al. (1984). Lifetime prevalence of specific psychiatric disorders in three sites. *Archives of General Psychiatry 41, 949–958.*

Rogers, R., Bagby, R. M., & Dickens, S. E. (1992). *Structured interview for reported symptoms.* Odessa, FL: Psychological Assessment Resources, Inc.

Rosen, G. M. (1995). The *Aleutian Enterprise* sinking and posttraumatic stress disorder: Misdiagnosis in clinical and forensic settings. *Professional Psychology: Research and Practice, 26,* 82–87.

Rosen, G. M., Sparr, L. F., McFall, M. Aronson R., & Fergueson, J. F. (1995). PTSD in the courtroom: Have our fears come true? 26th Annual Meeting. American Academy of Psychiatry and the Law. CME Syllabus 26:83–34. Seattle, WA. October 22, 1995.

Sadoff, R. L. (1992). In defense of the insanity defense. *Psychiatric Annals, 22(11),* 556–560.

Sanders, R. C. (1986). Criminal law—evidence—expert testimony that rape victim suffered post traumatic stress disorder is admissible to rebut a defense of consent. *University of Baltimore Law Review, (1),* 141–153.

Savodnik, I. (1991). The concept of stress in psychiatry. *Western State University Law Review, 19,* 175–189.

Schornhorst, F. T. (1988). Don't be cowed by scientific evidence: A pretrial primer for prosecutors and defense attorneys. *Criminal Justice, 3(2),* 18–21; 44–46.

Schut, J. H. (1992). From the folks who brought you the hot tub. *Institutional Investor 26(11),* 171.

Sersland, S. J. (1984). Mental disability caused by mental stress: Standards of proof in worker's compensation cases. *Drake Law Review, 33,* 751–816.

Shepard v Alaska, 847 P.2d.75 (Alaska St. App. 1993).

Shulze, T. (1987). Vietnam post traumatic stress disorder and criminal behavior. *Society Journal, 25(7),* 38–40.

Simon, R. I. (Ed.) (1995). *Posttraumatic stress disorder in litigation: Guide for forensic assessment.* Washington, DC: American Psychiatric Press.

Slovenko, R. (1985). Law and psychiatry. In H. I. Kaplan & B. J. Sadock (Eds.), *Comprehensive textbook of psychiatry* (4th ed.) Baltimore, MD: Williams & Williams.

Slovenko, R. (1992). Is diminished capacity really dead? *Psychiatric Annals, 22(11),* 566–570.

Slovenko, R. (1994). Legal aspects of post-traumatic stress disorder. *Psychiatric Clinics of North America 17(6),* 439–446.

Spade v Lynn, 47 NE 88 (Mass 1897).

Sparr, L. F. (1990). Legal aspects of posttraumatic stress disorder: Uses and abuse. In M. E. Wolf, A. D. Mosnaim (Eds.), *Posttraumatic stress disorder: Etiology, prenomology, and treatment.* Washington, DC: American Psychiatric Press.

Sparr, L. F. (1995). Post-traumatic stress disorder: Does it exist? *Neurologic Clinics of North America 13(2),* 413–429.

Sparr, L. F., & Atkinson, R. M. (1986). Posttraumatic stress disorder as an insanity defense: Medicolegal quicksand. *American Journal of Psychiatry, 143(5),* 608–613.

Sparr, L. F., & Pankratz, L. D. (1983). Factitious posttraumatic stress disorder. *American Journal of Psychiatry, 140(8),* 1016–1019.

Sparr, L. F., Reaves, M. E., & Atkinson, R. M. (1987). Military combat, posttraumatic stress disorder, and criminal behavior in Vietnam veterans. *Bulletin of the American Academy of Psychiatry and the Law, 15(2),* 141–162.

Spaulding, W. J. (1988). Compensation for mental disability. In R. Michels (Ed.), *Psychiatry* (Vol 3, Chapter 33, pp. 1–27). Philadelphia: J.B. Lippincott Co.

State v Allewalt, 308 Md. 89, 91, 517 A.2d. 741,742 (1986).

State v Black, 109 Wash. 2d 336, 398, 745 P.2d 12,18 (1987).

State v Heads, No. 106–126 (1st Jud. Dist. Ct. Caddo Parish La. Oct 10, 1981).

State v Kelly, 97 N.J. 178,478 A.2d 364 (1984).

State v Liddell, 685 P.2d 302 (Mont. 1984).

State v Marks, 647 P.2d 1292 (Kan, 1982).

State v McClain, 248 N.J. Super. 409,591 A.2d 652 (App. Div. 1991).

State v McGee, 324 N. W. 2d 232 (Minn, 1982).

State v McQuillen, 236 Kan. 161,172,689 P.2d 822,830 (1984).

State v Norman, 89 NC App.389,366 SE.2d 586 (1988).

State v Ogle, 668 S. W. 2d 138 (1984).

State v Phipps, 883 S. W. 2d 138,139 (Tenn. Crim. App. 1994).

State v Saldana, 324 N. W. 2d 227 (Minn. 1982).

State v Taylor, 663 S.W. 2d 235 (Mo, 1984).

Steinberg, C. E. (1993). The Daubert decision: An update on the Frye Rule. *American Academy of Psychiatry and the Law Newsletter, 18(3),* 66–69.

Stevens, M. J. (1992). Stress in California. *Risk Management 39(7),* 40–43.

Talbott, J. S. (1988). Is "psychological self-defense" a solution to the problem of defending battered women who kill? *Washington & Lee Law Review 45(4),* 1527–1547.

Terrio v McDonough, 450 N.E. 2d 190 (1983).

Theriault v Swan 588 A2d 369,372 1982,(Me 1989).

Trethewy, C. (1996). Senate Bill 369: Another chapter in the political saga of workers' compensation in Oregon. *Willamette Law Review, 32(1),* 217–248.

Trosch, L. A., Jr. (1991). *State v Strickland:* Evening the odds in rape trials! North Carolina allows expert testimony on post traumatic stress disorder to disprove victim consent. *North Carolina Law Review 69(3),* 1624–1643.

United States v Cantu, 12F. 3d 1506 (9th Cir. 1993).

United States v Tindall, CR 79376 (D Mass, Sept 19, 1980).

United States v Winters, 729 F 2d 602 (9th Circ 1984).

Vaughn, E., & Moore, M. L. (1983). The battered spouse defenses in Kentucky. *Kentucky Law Journal 10,* 399–419.

Vinciguerra, J. L. (1994). The present state of sexual harassment law: Perpetuating post traumatic stress disorder in sexually harassed women. *Cleveland State Law Review, 42(2),* 301–337.

Walker, L. E. (1980). *The battered woman.* New York, NY: Harper Collins.

Walker, L. E. (1984). *The battered woman syndrome.* New York, NY: Springer Publishing Company.

Walker, L. E. (1993). Legal self-defense for battered women. In M. Hansen & M. Harway (Eds.), *Battering and family therapy: A feminist perspective.* Newbury Park: Sage Publications.

West Virginia v Walls, 445 S.E. 2d 515 (W. Va. Sup. Ct. 1994).

Wilkinson v Downton, 2 QB 57 (1897).

Williams, K. M. (1991). Using battered woman syndrome evidence with a self-defense strategy in Minnesota. *Law and Inequality, 10,* 107–136.

Wilson, J. P. & Keane, T. M. (Eds.). (1997). *Assessing psychological trauma and PTSD.* New York: Guilford Press.

Wotalewiez v Gallagher, CR 831–207779 (Mult. County, or Cir. Ct., 1986.)

CHAPTER 15

PREVENTION OF POSTTRAUMATIC REACTIONS: DEBRIEFING AND FRONTLINE TREATMENT

YUVAL NERIA, PH.D. & ZAHAVA SOLOMON, PH.D
Tel Aviv University
The Bob Shapell School of Social Work

OVERVIEW

Exposure to traumatic stress may result in either or both immediate and long-term impairment of mental health. The most prevalent effects are acute stress disorder in the short run, and posttraumatic stress disorder in the long run (APA, 1994). Traditionally, clinicians treated these and other trauma disorders *after* their appearance and *in* their office or clinic. Prevention, however, is no less important than treatment. In recent years, greater awareness of its importance has led to the search for ways of reducing the risk of long-term disorders by intervening soon after the exposure to traumatic stress, before they become apparent (e.g., Brom & Kleber, 1989; Solomon & Shalev, 1995).

Three basic types of prevention have been conceptualized (Caplan, 1964; Mausner & Bahn, 1974; Williams, 1993). Primary prevention involves preparing the individual or the community to cope with an expected traumatic event before it occurs. Secondary prevention refers to early intervention, right after the exposure, in order to limit its long-term damage. Tertiary prevention means helping those who sustain or are at very high risk for sustaining long-term damage to reduce its chronicity and return to optimal functioning.

In the field of trauma, prevention generally refers to secondary prevention (Freedy & Donkervoet, 1995; Norris & Thompson, 1995), that is, efforts to keep persons who were exposed to traumatic stress from developing long-term disorders (Armfield, 1994; Lundin, 1994; McCarroll, James, Ursano, Fullerton, & Lundy, 1995). Without in any way impugning the value of primary and tertiary intervention in cases of trauma, this chapter focuses on secondary prevention. Before discussing this, however, a brief discussion of the possible outcomes of exposure to traumatic stress is in order.

REACTIONS TO TRAUMATIC STRESS

Exposure to traumatic stress may result in any combination of immediate and long-term responses, as shown in Table 15.1.

TABLE 15.1 Responses to Traumatic Exposure: Acute and Posttraumatic Stress Disorders

1 No ASD No PTSD	3 ASD No PTSD
2 No ASD PTSD	4 ASD PTSD

Immediate Responses

Close to the time of exposure, a person may or may not have an identifiable acute response. Acute reactions to traumatic stress have been found among victims of terrorist attack (Shalev, 1992), of a factory explosion (Weisaeth, 1989a; 1989b), of motor vehicle accidents (Malt, Hoivik, & Blikra, 1993; Mayou, Bryant, & Duthie, 1993), and of natural and technological disasters (Green & Solomon, 1995).

Most of the studies of acute reaction were carried out in connection with war, and the bulk of them focused on combatants in a range of different confrontations. Findings in different countries and over a number of different wars indicate that between about ten and thirty percent of all combatants suffer from a psychological breakdown on or near the battlefield (Solomon, 1993). Today termed "Combat Stress Reaction (CSR)," the breakdown is a labile, polymorphic disorder, characterized by high variability and rapid changes in manifestation (Solomon, 1993), the most prevalent ones being restlessness, irritability, psychomotor retardation, apathy, psychological withdrawal, sympathetic activity, startle reactions, anxiety and depression, constriction of affect, confusion, abdominal pain, nausea and vomiting, aggressive and hostile behaviors, paranoid reactions and ill-concealed fearfulness (Bar-On, Solomon, Noy, & Nardi, 1986; Bartemeier, 1946; Grinker, 1945; Solomon, 1993). These symptoms are universal and have been observed among combatants of different wars, at different times, and from different cultures (Bar-On et al., 1986). Various taxonomies of the breakdown that were drawn up—by Bailey, Williams, Komora, and Salmon and Fenton (1929) on Americans soldiers in World War I, by Bartemeier (1946) and by Grinker (1945) on American soldiers in World War II, by Cavenar and Nash (1976) on Americans soldiers in Vietnam war, and by Solomon, Mikulincer, and Benbenishty (1989) on Israeli soldiers in the Lebanon War—similarly show a great deal of resemblance, with anxiety, depression, and disassociation being major features of virtually all of them.

Civilians have also been found to respond with strong immediate psychological distress to the stresses of war. Rachman (1990) found acute responses among residents of London during the German blitz in the second World War (Rachman, 1990). Saigh (1984) found that Lebanese students in Beirut responded with anxiety reactions. A study of Israeli civilians in the Gulf War (Bleich, Dycian, Koslowsky, Solomon & Wiener, 1992; Solomon, 1995) found that 51 percent of the 1,059 war-related hospital emergency room admissions came with symptoms of acute psychological distress. Another study showed that Israelis who were evacuated from their homes that were damaged or destroyed by Scuds had not only an inordinately high level of psychiatric symptomatology and high levels of the intrusion and avoidance (IES, Horowitz, Wilner & Alvarez, 1979) that characterize persons' attempts to deal with traumatic events, but also a very high level of what is identified as posttraumatic symptomatology (PTSD). A full 80 percent of those assessed displayed a constellation of symptoms consistent with DSM-III-R criteria for the disorder (APA, 1987). While a formal diagnosis of PTSD cannot be considered so soon after a traumatic event (according to the DSM-IV, a minimum of one month's duration for symptoms is required), the finding does indicate that the vast majority of people respond to traumatic events with a level of stress and a constellation of symptoms that would be deemed pathological if they persisted.

The various findings regarding the immediate responses to traumatic stress among both soldiers and civilians under a range of circumstances have resulted in a new formulation of acute stress disorder by the American Psychological Association. As it is defined, ASD combines the strong anxiety and dissociation found in CSR with manifestations of stress after the traumatic event, such as the intrusion and avoidance symptoms that are characteristics of PTSD. It is a broader concept than CSR, must last longer (at least two days) for a diagnosis, and can last up to four weeks before its symptoms are defined as posttraumatic stress disorder.

Long-Term Responses

In the long term, there are also two possible responses. One, again, is a non-response. The person shows no pathological residuals of the exposure to trauma. The other is pathology; the most common and conspicuous long-term sequela is posttraumatic stress disorder (PTSD). PTSD is a complex of distressing emotional responses that ensue directly from a breakdown in the course of traumatic event, or it can develop independently after the event has come to an end, and the victim is no longer in the dangerous exposure. In either case PTSD casualties remain embroiled in the traumatic event. They continue to suffer from the anxiety it induced, reliving its horrors in frequent intrusive manifestations that bring back the painful emotions of the traumatic experience. Continuing to live the trauma, most PTSD casualties lose interest in activities they had previously found pleasurable and meaningful, withdraw from social contact, and shut themselves emotionally. They tend to be irritable, nervous, and to have sundry sleeping, concentrating, and remembering disorders.

Relationship between Acute and Long-Term Stress Responses: Problems of Prediction

The relationship between immediate and long-term stress responses is of paramount interest to all who are concerned with the prevention of long-term trauma sequelae. Acute stress response is conceptualized as a short-term, transient disorder, and in some cases it indeed passes without leaving pathological residuals. Analogously, PTSD can develop whether or not the individual showed immediate signs of pathology. Indeed, many persons exposed to traumatic stress develop posttraumatic symptomatology without having had prior acute reactions (Ingraham & Manning, 1986; Kulka et al., 1990). On the other hand, research suggests that the existence of an acute reaction is a good predictor of long-term disorders. The Lebanon study (Solomon, 1993) shows that nearly half of the soldiers who sustained a CSR in the battlefield were still suffering from diagnosable PTSD three years after their participation in battle. Similarly, the study of the Gulf War evacuees cited above (Bleich, et al., 1992) shows that a year after their homes were bombed, three quarters of those who had initially responded with a high level of

PTSD symptomatology actually met the DSM criteria for the disorder.

But what determines whether or not an ASD will abate and become a passing event or, alternatively, develop into long-term psychopathology is little understood. A major source of the confusion may be the difficulty of distinguishing normal from pathological immediate responses to stress in the first place. Strong distress responses following a catastrophe are quite commonplace and normal. The high psychiatric symptomatology, intrusion and avoidance, and, above all, the startling 80 percent "PTSD rate" among the Scud evacuees a week after the event all suggest as much.

Despite the clear criteria, the diagnosis of ASD, as of CSR before it, is something of a conundrum. Both CSR and ASD are diagnosed functionally rather than clinically. That is, the existence of symptoms alone does not warrant a diagnosis. For a diagnosis of CSR to be made, the soldier must cease to function militarily and act in a manner that may endanger himself and/or his fellow combatants (Kormos, 1978). For a diagnosis of ASD, the individual must show not only a clinical level of distress but the inability to function normally and to carry out necessary tasks.

There are a number of reasons for the functional definition. One is that some of the major manifestations are both normal and adaptive in catastrophes and not limited to people who can be considered psychiatric casualties. For example, anxiety and feelings of vulnerability are realistic responses to life threatening perils, which will keep people attuned to danger signals under circumstances where that is very much needed (Eberly, Harkness, & Engdahl, 1991). Another is a reluctance to stigmatize the afflicted individual with a pathological label.

The use of functional definitions is problematic. The loose behavioral criterion is relative, dependent on the identification threshold of those making the judgment, that is, on the level of psychopathology that the individual or those in his/her environment can tolerate without labeling the person a stress casualty (Moses & Cohen, 1984). This level is determined by the suffering that the individual can bear, by the judgment of either the individual or those around him/her of what constitutes normal or acceptable functioning under conditions of stress, and by the ability of the person's family, friends, workmates, military unit, and so forth to serve as a holding environment, to name only some of the factors involved. Diagnosis thus tends to vary from situation to situation.

The problem of diagnosis has numerous implications. For the individual, a low identification threshold may result in normal reactions to stress being labeled, and stigmatized, as pathological, while a high threshold may leave persons who have serious emotional disturbances unidentified, as well as untreated (Solomon, 1993). On the theoretical level, the uncertainties of identification blur the path between immediate and long-term reactions to traumatic events. While findings show a clear correlation between the two, the problem of identifying an ASD means that in many cases one can probably not be sure whether or not it actually preceded a posttraumatic response and, if it did, what specific features of the ASD are predictive of PTSD, and what treatment foci would be likely to be most effective in reducing the likelihood of its developing. Among other things, the problem of diagnosing ASD and the uncertainties of its link with PTSD raises the question of who preventive efforts should be directed to: everyone who is exposed to a traumatic event or only those who show severe, pathological distress in its course or immediate aftermath? We now turn to these issues.

PREVENTION OF LONG-TERM STRESS REACTIONS

A variety of early interventions have been designed to ameliorate the immediate distress following exposure to trauma and/or to try to prevent the development of long-term stress disorders. The two that we will discuss here are debriefing and frontline treatment. Although some of their principles and practices overlap, the first is designed to help all persons exposed to a traumatic situation and has been practiced following a large variety of potentially traumatic events; the second is designed to help only those identified as traumatized and is generally associated with the military. Neither is defined as therapy as such. In this they are unlike both crisis intervention (Bargess & Baldwin, 1981; Caplan, 1961; 1964;

Greenstone & Leviton, 1981; Lindemann, 1944) and Horowitz' brief therapy (Horowitz & Kaltreider, 1995), which are also aimed at preventing the development of long-term stress reactions (among individuals who suffer from acute trauma reactions and acute grief reactions).

Debriefing

Debriefing has been used to try to attenuate the detrimental impact of traumatic stress among a variety of groups, including combat soldiers, emergency workers, rescue teams, accident victims, and hostages (Dunning & Silva, 1980; Jones, 1985; Melton, 1985; Mitchell, 1981; 1982; 1983; 1986; Raphael, Singh, Bradbury, & Lambert, 1983; Shalev, 1994). It is a group-oriented intervention in which the major elements of the stressful event are examined by the participants shortly after their exposure. All those who were exposed to the event participate in the debriefing, whatever their immediate psychological response to it. There is great variety in what is actually done in debriefing sessions, but they generally combine elements of emotional expression with cognitive appraisal, and counseling with instruction. One of the major assumptions behind this method is that peers can assist the individual's healing and that a person's traumatic experiences are better worked through with others who shared them. The model for debriefing is humanistic rather than psychiatric. That is, all the reactions to the event are considered normal responses to traumatic stress, and no reaction, however bizarre, is labeled deviant, abnormal or pathological. Among the reasons for this is that spontaneous recovery has been observed in many individuals who suffer from quite severe immediate reactions (Shalev, 1996; Solomon, 1993).

The idea of debriefing has intuitive appeal and can draw support from a variety of theories (Shalev, 1994). Theories of traumatization provide reason to believe that the ventilation and abreaction included in debriefing help the individual to discharge the emotional overload experienced in traumatic events; that the verbalization that is encouraged facilitates the processing of the traumatic event; and that both may help to release susceptible individuals from the freezing of affect and surrender to the threat that may follow upon their exposure. Theories of cognitive processing emphasize the role of cognitive schemata in modulating stress reactions. Similarly, there is considerable evidence that social support—which may be obtained from the debriefing group—both buffers stress and moderates its pathological impact (Fullerton, Ursano, Kao, & Bhartiya, 1992; Green, Grace, & Gleser, 1985; Turner, 1981).

Preventive debriefing falls under the heading of what is known as "psychological debriefing." Psychological debriefing has its roots in various forms of instrumental briefing designed for the purpose of gathering information about and drawing lessons from a variety of tasks. Instrumental debriefing is aimed, first and foremost, at improving the performance of the task in the future, through a combination of analysis of how the task had just been performed and the enhancement of group cohesion that comes from the joint review and clarification of the event. A type of instrumental debriefing in current use in both military and non-military settings is "task oriented debriefing." For example, the Israel Defense Forces routinely and systematically debriefs soldiers and commanders after every mission. Many non-military institutions, such as fire fighting and rescue organizations, also hold debriefing meetings following operations.

Needless to say, cognitive and educational elements take precedence over emotional and expressive ones in this type of debriefing. At the same time, the discussion of the event by the participants may bring a good deal of emotion to the surface, give order and meaning to what was probably a rather chaotic experience, and help the individual to integrate the experience into more stable frameworks, both his own and that of the institution to which he belongs.

The potential emotional benefits of even instrumental debriefing are apparent from the historical group debriefing developed in World War II by the Chief Historian of the U.S. Army, Brig. Gen. S.L.A. Marshall (Marshall, 1944; 1956; Shalev, 1994; Spiller, 1980). This consisted of a highly detailed, comprehensive reconstruction of the battle by the surviving soldiers carried out in its immediate wake. Marshall's debriefing was not conceived as a form of psychological intervention, but as a method of maintaining the cohesion and morale of the fighting forces by filling in, post facto, the information that the individual soldier rarely has when he is fighting. The idea was that if the soldiers could make sense of the chaos of the battle in which they had participated, they would regain much of the sense of control and mastery that are lost in the turmoil of battle, would get a better handle on their fear, and would function better both individually and as a unit. Marshall claimed that his debriefings had a profound psychological impact, providing release, increasing self-esteem, and improving unit cohesion.

Marshall's historical group debriefing is an important precursor of current psychological debriefing. Indeed, it included many elements that are familiar to psychotherapy. The data that were gathered included the soldiers' thoughts and feelings as they engaged in the fighting, so that the process involved reliving the experience. Premature closure was avoided, high levels of ambiguity tolerated, and contradictory renditions accepted until the information permitted a conclusion. Attention was paid to rendering the contributions of the soldiers who had been killed, and the leaders of the debriefing sessions, who were military men, were instructed to be uncritical and encouraging and not to pull rank.

Psychological Group Debriefing. Modern psychological debriefing was developed in the 1980s to help rescue workers and other persons in high risk occupations deal with the inevitable stresses of their jobs so as to moderate the development of stress reactions in the future. Fitting this aim, the balance of cognitive and emotional elements was reversed, with the latter taking precedence, and a variety of procedures may be employed: cognitive rehearsal, ventilation, and "resource mobilization" (Mitchell, 1983), sharing and education (Raphael, 1986), active counseling and teaching (e.g., Wagner, 1979), and reframing (e.g., Bergman & Queen, 1986).

The two main developers of the approach are Raphael and Mitchell. Raphael (1986) formulated guidelines for helping teams of rescue workers and helpers in the Granville rail disaster (Raphael et al., 1983). She recommended formal group sessions in which "The experience is given a cognitive structure and the emotional release of reviewing helps the worker to a sense of achievement and distancing" (Raphael, 1986, p. 255). Great weight is placed to the workers' expression of their feelings, ranging from the helplessness and frustration they felt during their work through their nightmares, intrusive images, and fear of dying afterwards. Also discussed are the workers' relationships with the families of the disaster victims and their relations with one another.

Mitchell (1981, 1982, 1986) devised a method he termed Critical Incident Stress Debriefing (CISD), to be carried out by teams consisting of especially trained professional peers (e.g., fire personnel, police personnel) with the support of mental health professionals. The idea is that the people involved in a potentially traumatogenic event be given the opportunity to discuss their experiences in a rational, structured manner, to diffuse their emotions, and to see that they are not alone. The CISD is carried out in a series of stages, beginning with a factual discussion of each participant's role in the event and an exploration of their thoughts about their experience; moving to a discussion of their emotional reactions; and then moving back to the cognitive plane, with a discussion of the participants' stress symptoms and instruction on the normalcy of the symptoms and ways of managing them. For mass disasters, Mitchell modified the model somewhat, so as to include a reframing stage and end up with a summary that emphasizes the lessons learned and the positive things the participants can take away from the disaster. In both cases, the solicitation of the participants' emotional reactions is carefully enclosed in a cognitive framework, presumably to keep them from getting out of hand.

Effectiveness of Debriefing

Despite the intuitive soundness and theoretical grounding of debriefing, its effectiveness is far from clear. As can be seen in Table 15.2, there are relatively few studies of the impact of debriefing and a good portion are not controlled. Comparison and evaluation are hampered by the variety of the groups studied, the variety of measures and timeframes used, the failure of most scholars to describe how the debriefing they evaluated was conducted, and the inevitable inconsistency in the skill of the persons who carry out the debriefing.

Strikingly, there is a consistent difference in the findings of the controlled and the non-controlled studies. Virtually all the non-controlled studies report findings that point to the effectiveness of debriefing. Raphael and colleagues (1983) report that debriefed rescue workers were able to assimilate their stressful experience. Robinson and Mitchell (1993) report a reduction of stress symptoms following debriefing in 60 percent of debriefed emergency service, welfare, and hospital personnel who experienced symptoms. Mitchell and Bray (1990) similarly report that emergency personnel who underwent CISD debriefing showed diminishing job turnover, less early retirement, and fewer mental health problems. The pattern of findings among Gulf War veterans is similar. Fitzgerald, Braudway, Leeks, Padgett, and colleagues (1993) contend that debriefing facilitated integration and decreased emotional reactivation among soldiers who had been physically injured in Saudia Arabia. Ford and colleagues (1993) claim that veterans and their spouses who underwent a variety of short-term interventions which they labeled "debriefing" were able to resolve the symptoms of psychosocial malfunctioning prevalent among returning soldiers and their families. In another study, Stallard & Law (1993) found that adolescent survivors of a minibus accident who were screened immediately before their debriefing (three months after the event) and again three months later had significantly fewer PTSD symptoms in the second screening.

The controlled studies yield very different results. At best they show no improvement. Deahl, Gillham, Thomas, Searle, and Srinivasan (1994) found that at a nine-month follow-up debriefed and non-debriefed British soldiers charged with handling and identifying dead bodies in the Gulf War scored similarly on the IES and GHQ-28. Hytten and Hasle (1989) found that firefighters who had undergone formal psychological debriefing after a hotel fire scored the same on the IES as those who had talked informally. The latter findings suggest that the value of debriefing may lie not in its technique or content but in the opportunity it affords for expression and review, which can occur in any number of settings, but often

TABLE 15.2 Effectiveness of Debriefing

AUTHOR	GROUP STUDIED	DESCRIPTION OF INTERVENTION	TYPE OF STUDY	RESULTS
Raphael, Singh, Bradbury, & Lambert, 1983	Rail disaster rescue workers	Psychological debriefing	Non-controlled	Assimilation of stressful experience.
Hytten & Hasle, 1989	Firefighters dealt with hotel fire	Psychological debriefing	One group participated in formal debriefing sessions and other group talked informally.	Majority reported that debriefing was helpful. But no difference in the groups' IES scores.
Mitchell & Bray, 1990	Emergency personnel	CISDN	Non-controlled	Diminishing problems as job turnover, early retirement, and mental and health problems.
Griffiths & Watts, 1992	Emergency personnel	Psychological debriefing	Controlled	Debriefed subjects had higher levels of intrusive and avoidant symptoms at 12 months than non-debriefed.
Fitzgerald, Braudway, Leeks, Padgett et al., 1993	Injured soldiers returning from Saudi Arabia	Psychological debriefing	Non-controlled	Facilitation of integration and decreased emotional reactivation.
Ford et al., 1993	Veterans from Operation Desert Storm	Psychological debriefing	Non-controlled	Reduction of symptoms of psychosocial malfunctioning.
Robinson & Mitchell, 1993	Emergency service, welfare, and hospital personnel	Psychological debriefing	Non-controlled	Reduction of stress symptoms in 60% of the participants who experienced "stress symptoms." 34% reported that the debriefing was "helpful."
Stallard & Law, 1993	Young survivors (14–15 years) of a minibus accident	Debriefing	Non-controlled	Significant reductions of all measures.
Carlier, Van Uchelen, Lamberts, & Gersons, 1994.	Police officers in Holland	Psychological debriefing	Controlled	More PTSD symptoms, depression, agoraphobic complaints, and anger manifestations among debriefed compared to their non-debriefed counterparts.
Deahl, Gillham, Thomas, Searle, & Srinivasan, 1994	British soldiers (duties of handling and identification of dead bodies) in the Gulf War	Psychological debriefing	Controlled	After 9 months no difference between debriefed and non-debriefed soldiers on IES and measures of general psychological health (GHQ-28).
Turner, Thompson, & Rosser, 1993	Survivors of the 1987 King's Cross fire	Spontaneous debriefing	Non-controlled	Spontaneous debriefing associated with subjective benefit.
Kenardy et al., 1996	Policeman, emergency services, welfare volunteers, and counselors that debriefed following the Newcastle earthquake in Australia	CISD	Controlled	The non-debriefed showed lower general psychological morbidity (on the GHQ-12) and less intrusion and avoidance (on the IES).

does not. At worst, the controlled studies reveal higher vulnerability and more severe psychopathology among the debriefed subjects. The debriefed police officers studied by Carlier, Van Uchelen, Lamberts, and Gersons (1994) reported more PTSD symptoms, depression, agoraphobic complaints, and anger than their non-debriefed counterparts. Kenardy and colleagues (1996) similarly found that policemen, emergency workers, welfare volunteers, and counselors who received CISD debriefing following the Newcastle earthquake in Australia showed greater general psychological morbidity and more intrusion and avoidance than those who were not debriefed.

The consistent disparity in the findings of the controlled and uncontrolled studies over different types of traumatic encounters and in different populations makes it very difficult to determine how effective debriefing is or is not as a preventive instrument. The uncontrolled studies, by their very nature, cannot provide sufficient evidence for the effectiveness of debriefing. On the one hand, various of the uncontrolled studies report that a good portion of the participants found the debriefing "helpful" (Hytten & Hasle, 1989; Robinson & Mitchell, 1993; Turner, Thompson, & Rosser, 1993) or were otherwise satisfied with it (Flannery, Fulton, Tausch, & Deloffi, 1991). If these are not social desirability responses, they suggest that the debriefing made at least some people feel better and answered needs that they had. On the other hand, there is no necessary connection between satisfaction and mental health. Moreover, it is impossible to know whether the symptom reduction these studies report is the outcome of the debriefing or of spontaneous recovery over time, which would occur in any case.

The findings of the controlled studies showing that debriefed groups suffer from more PTSD, more anxiety, and more depression are also ambiguous. Although they seem damning, they do not necessarily mean that debriefing is in fact damaging. The negative effects may be as much the result of reporting bias as of real damage. Because debriefing raises negative emotions and stress symptoms to awareness, debriefed subjects may simply be more prone to report the symptoms than subjects who have not been debriefed and who might also suffer from them. This possibility points to the need for clinical assessment, including physiological measures (Orr & Kaloupek, 1997), and not only the self-report measures used in the studies to date.

The negative findings may also stem from the possibility that the debriefed groups were, to begin with, more distressed than their non-debriefed counterparts. The persons undergoing debriefing were not necessarily a random sample but may have been self-selected. Those who were less distressed by their exposure or felt more capable of coping on their own or with the help of their families or friends may not have joined debriefing groups.

At the same time, the possibility that debriefing can be damaging cannot be ruled out. Debriefing opens up wounds, but it is not certain that it can heal them. As currently practiced, debriefing is a very short process, lasting no more than a few hours, and sometimes no more than one hour. This short time contrasts markedly with the unlimited time allotted by Marshall for his historical group debriefings, which did not end until the entire reconstruction of the event was completed, and lasted anywhere from several days to a week. It is questionable whether the benefits Marshall reported after days of debriefing can be obtained after a few hours.

Although the debriefings whose results are assessed here are rarely described in full, it may be suggested that they suffer from a problem of closure. In Mitchell's CISD, for example, the discussion of the participants' emotional reactions is sandwiched between fact finding and cognitive reframing, which suggests that not enough attention is paid to the tumultuous and scary feelings aroused by the traumatic exposure. On the one hand, they seem to be given short shrift and their expression firmly contained. On the other hand, there might not be effective closure of those feelings that are aroused. This combination might account for the lingering anxiety, depression, and PTSD symptoms among debriefed subjects. So might the possibility that the debriefing reactivated unresolved traumas. Rescue teams, police officers, firefighters, disaster workers, and others in similar professions are repeatedly exposed to potentially traumatogenic events. The debriefing may open up former wounds in addition to current ones.

Another problem may be a failure to identify vulnerable individuals and provide them with the continuing treatment they require. The group nature of the debriefing, the absence of prior screening, the prescribed format, the short time allotted, and the built-in refusal to label any symptom as pathological all impede the identification of persons with acute stress disorders. It is doubtful that such persons should participate in debriefing in the first place. When they do, they run the risk of having their anxieties stirred up and being inundated by them, in a situation which provides inadequate means for alleviating them afterwards. The education and reframing that are part of debriefing as conceived by both Mitchell and Raphael may be well enough for people whose distress is readily containable, but not an answer to the needs of individuals who are overwhelmed by anxiety.

Implications for Debriefing Research and Intervention

Research on the effectiveness of debriefing is beset by two major difficulties. The first stems from the ethical problems that would be involved in attaining a random sample for a controlled study. To obtain such a sample, half of those who wanted debriefing would have to be denied it, or half of those who did not want it would have to be compelled to undergo it. Without a random sample, however, we are left with the confounding resulting from self-selection.

The other problem involves the weighing and evaluation of the results of the various studies. Although the studies cited above all termed the intervention that was examined "debriefing," the fact is that the interventions were quite different from one another. Many of the studies did not trouble to describe the method and content of their interventions. But the little they said suggests that these diverged widely both from the Raphael and Mitchell models and from one another. They varied in their temporal proximity to the traumatic exposure, in the method, content, and duration of the intervention and the size of the group, and in the professional qualifications (professionals versus non-professionals) of the people who conducted them. Results are obviously difficult to gauge and compare when the independent variable is as shifting as this one.

The actual implementation of debriefing must take into consideration the possibility that it may cause damage. The possibility that some persons—such as those with an ASD or a history of former unresolved traumatogenic encounters—should not participate in debriefing should be considered. Research to investigate contraindications for debriefing would be helpful to this end. The introduction of screening of the participants in debriefing sessions would naturally follow from a decision to exclude individuals at high risk for harm. Screening and ongoing assessment might also be considered to monitor possible reactivation once people are in the debriefing group. Equally important, individuals who may show signs of heightened distress in the debriefing sessions should not be left to work out their emotions on their own, but should be closely watched and referred to continuing treatment.

Along somewhat different lines, care should be taken both to allow enough time for disclosure and emotional ventilation, on the one hand, and for adequate closure on the other. Provisions for closure are made in Mitchell's and Raphael's debriefing protocols, but, as noted above, these are not consistently followed. Nor has their effectiveness been tested.

FRONTLINE TREATMENT

In contrast to debriefing, frontline treatment, as its name suggests, was devised for military contexts and to address the needs of persons requiring "treatment"—that is, identified CSR casualties. It has the advantage of focusing on a high risk group for the development of PTSD and the disadvantage of having nothing to offer to the many vulnerable soldiers who escape identification, to people in other high risk occupations, or to disaster or accident victims.

The frontline treatment approach was developed by the military psychiatrist T. W. Salmon (1919), based on the experience of the British and the French armies during World War I. Until then, battlefield breakdowns were viewed either as madness or malingering, and the unfortunate soldier was evacuated to the rear and either treated or punished. Salmon viewed the breakdown, which came to be called a CSR, as stemming from the combatant's inner conflict between his values of commitment, patriotism, honor, and loyalty and his wish to save his life by fleeing. He formulated his frontline treatment method to help the casualty resolve the conflict, weighting the odds in the favor of the soldier's moral values. In somewhat moralistic terms, Salmon's aim was to bend the soldier's will to returning to his duties on the front. To this end, Salmon stipulated that the intervention should be administered close to the front, as close in time as possible to the symptoms' appearance, and with the expectation of rapid recovery and return to the original unit. These stipulations removed the possibility of flight through a tranfer to the rear and long-term treatment in civilian facilities and avoided rupturing the soldier's connection with his fellow fighters. Preserving the soldier's identity as a combatant and keeping him in contact with his unit became essential elements of all subsequent frontline treatment.

Later, Artiss (1963), rephrased Salmon's recommendations to encompass the following three principles: (1) Proximity: treatment should be administered close to the incident; insofar as possible, the victim must not be sent out of the war zone for hospitalization; (2) Immediacy: treatment must be given as close as possible to the time of the onset of the symptoms; and (3) Expectancy: the victim must understand that his crisis is transient, and that he is to return to his unit immediately after the short intervention.

Like the idea of debriefing, these principles also have intuitive validity and sound theoretical justification. Proximity of the treatment to the front is seen as facilitating the casualty's continuing contact with comrades and commanders, strengthening his commitment to his unit, and maintaining his identity as a soldier (Grinker & Spiegel, 1945; Marlowe, 1978). The presence of battle stimuli (e.g., sound of helicopters and artillery) may effect desensitization and reduce the connection between combat stimuli and fear (Enoch, 1996). Moreover, the unit is more likely to welcome back a soldier with whom they remained in contact than one who had left the front altogether. Similarly, the clinician on the front is seen as more likely to identify with the needs of the military and thus more readily promote and recommend a return to the unit than the clinician behind lines (Glass, 1954). Immediate treatment conveys the message that the soldier belongs to his unit, is only on temporary leave,

and is both expected and wanted back in his unit. Moreover, it has the advantage of enabling the problem to be tackled before ossification sets in. Expectancy conveys to the soldier the message that he is not ill and has only had a temporary, normal reaction to the stress, which has the benefit of preserving his self-esteem and reducing the stigma of the breakdown (Kormos, 1978; Mullins & Glass, 1973).

Frontline principles have been adopted by western armies (e.g., Johnson, Cline, Marcum, & Intress, 1992; Solomon, 1993): Where possible, the casualty is kept on the front but removed from the fire. The first priority is to meet the exhausted casualty's physiological needs for food, drink, and sleep. No less important is to prevent him from becoming isolated, lonely, and detached. Group therapy, where the casualty learns that others felt the same helplessness and fear that he did; a high ratio of mental health professionals to casualties; and maintenance of contact with the unit are means to this end. The idea that the CSR is a transient, normal response to the extreme stress of battle and expectations of a rapid return to combat are reinforced by both social pressure and the maintenance of a military atmosphere, with casualties remaining in uniform and expected to function responsibly and autonomously. Any change in the soldier's status as a member of a combat team is avoided until appropriate efforts to reverse the traumatic effects of the stress have been made and proven unsuccessful. Only then is the soldier to be moved for treatment to a hospital in the rear.

Like debriefing, the frontline treatment framework allows for significant variations in implementation. Though most descriptions of frontline treatment since its inception in World War I confirm more or less to the above description, the actual distance from the front and the type of installation (i.e., first aid station, field hospital) where the treatment is provided vary. So do the form and content of the treatment. In World War I, the French Army included electric shock as part of its frontline treatment, to cite an extreme example (Hausman & Rioch, 1967). After World War II, medication for those who needed it became a standard part of most—but not all—frontline treatment, and group therapy was added to the treatment repertoire.

Because it is designed specifically for identified stress casualties, frontline treatment naturally gives more place than debriefing to the therapeutic aspects of the intervention. The very fact that the treatment generally lasts from three to five days rather than a few hours makes greater attention to the casualty's mental state possible. Nonetheless, the relative proportion of therapy to the other activities involved in frontline treatment (i.e., relaxation, physical fitness, non-combat tasks) varies from program to program, as do the aim and orientation of the therapy itself. It is generally agreed that the therapy emphasize the soldier's experiences in the battle and his current emotions and avoid delving into his personal history, and most of the therapeutic endeavors seem to allow for the ventilation of emotions. While some emphasize behavioral techniques and goals, others have a stronger psychodynamic orientation.

The variations can be illustrated by the frontline treatment programs in the field hospitals of the Israel Defense Forces in the 1982 Lebanon War (Enoch, 1996; Toubiana, Milgram, & Noy, 1986) and of the U.S. Army in the 1991 Persian Gulf War (Johnson, Cline, Marcum, & Intress, 1992). In the Lebanon War, a mixture of psychodynamic (Goren, Triest, & Margalit, 1986) and behavioral (Nardi, Wozner, & Margalit, 1986) forms of group and individual therapy was applied. Treatment was given by a variety of mental health personnel (social workers, psychologists, psychiatrists), some army professionals, and others who had been called up for reserve duty and donned army uniforms. The twice daily group sessions combined reconstruction of the main events immediately before, during, and after the battle and the ventilation of the feelings associated with the experience. The mutual revelations of shared helplessness and anxiety were conceived as bringing a reduction of the guilt and shame that overwhelmed the soldiers when they were evacuated. Return to the unit was encouraged by emphasis on active coping and mutual responsibility and solidarity. Individual therapy was similarly to focus on the recent traumatic event and the anticipated functioning in the immediate future.

In the Gulf War (Johnson et al., 1992), treatment was provided by psychiatric personnel, while the casualties were informed that they were not ill, just fatigued. The treatment consisted of group therapy conducted by psychiatrists and educational sessions led by a psychiatric nurse. Individual therapy was not provided. The group therapy seems to have been used for the ventilation of the soldiers' anger, fears, and concerns, but otherwise is not described. The educational sessions seem to have provided a strong cognitive component, in contrast to the stronger emotional component of the Israeli program. The educational sessions are said to have covered six topics—fear, anxiety, and the stress response; guilt and shame; grief and loss; mood and affect; positive thinking; and self-esteem and communication—which, in the Israeli program were dealt with in the group therapy. Fuller comparison is impossible because of the limited information in the paper (for example, we do not know how much time was allotted to therapy and how much to education). But, it is clear that for all that the two programs adhered to the basic frontline principles of proximity, immediacy, and expectancy, their implementation was not entirely the same.

Effectiveness of Frontline Treatment

The evidence for the effectiveness of frontline treatment is somewhat stronger than that for debriefing. As in the case of debriefing, most of the support comes from non-controlled studies. Other than the study by Johnson and colleagues (1992), which measured symptoms before and after the treatment, the data for these studies is based on the impressions of the clinicians who decided whether or not the soldier in their care was fit to return to his unit. As can be seen in Table 15.3, most of the clinical impressions from a variety of wars support the effectiveness of frontline treatment. Most reports from WWI (Hausman & Rioch, 1967; Panagapoulos, 1980), WWII (Artiss, 1963; Hausman & Rioch, 1967; Wagner in Bourne, 1969), the Korean War (Hausman & Rioch, 1967), and the Vietnam War (Allerton in Bourne, 1969; Bloch, 1969; Pettera, Johnson, & Zimmer, 1969; Strange in Bourne, 1969) indicate high rates of return to combat roles, ranging from 50 percent to 100 percent. Some studies suggest lower rates of return (Glass, 1957, on WWII; Noy, 1985, on the 1973 Yom Kippur War), ranging from 15 percent to 20

TABLE 15.3 Effectiveness of Frontline Treatment

AUTHOR	GROUP STUDIED	WAR	ASPECTS OF TREATMENT BEYOND PRINCIPLES OF PROXIMITY, IMMEDIACY, AND EXPECTANCY	TYPE OF STUDY	RESULTS
Hausman & Rioch, 1967	Combat neurosis among French forces	WW I	Persuasion, both by the professional staff and group pressure, used to get soldiers to meet their obligations. Use of aversive techniques, such as painful electric shock and threat of isolation and loss of privileges, to eliminate secondary gains.	Clinical reports	65% of treated returned to non-combat units within 7 days. Of those, 4% were later evacuated.
Panagapoulos, 1980	British and French psychiatric casualties	WW I	Rest, relaxation, support, and suggestion in psychiatric installations on the division level. Opportunity to vent feelings through psychotherapy was provided.	Survey of reports made on the basis of clinical experience	91% of those treated returned to military functioning, and of those, 66% to combat assignments.
Glass, 1957	American psychiatric casualties	Second half of WW II	Short psychotherapy dealing with the soldier's combat experiences and feelings about them, and including relaxation, ventilation, and suggestion that the soldier return to his unit. Medication. Casualties performed non-combat tasks. Treatment carried out in army installations (tents) that provided a therapeutic atmosphere.	Clinical impressions	Despite improvement in the soldiers' condition, only about 15% returned to military functioning.
Artiss, 1963	American psychiatric casualties	WW II prior to 1943	Recommendation to permit injured to continue their work in their units at their former level of functioning.	Survey of clinicians' experiences	70%–80% returned to adequate functioning. Rates of psychiatric hospitalization reduced from 24 per 1000 to 6 per 1000 casualties.
Hausman & Rioch, 1967	American psychiatric casualties	WW II, North African front, 1943	No details.	Survey of military experience	70% returned to functioning.
Wagner in Bourne, 1969	American combat fatigue casualties	WW II, Normandy	Treatment based on proximity. Separation of lightly injured from seriously injured soldiers. Opportunity for rest, warmth, shelter, food, relative physical security, sleep, abreaction. Expectancy. Treatment administered in the unit for between 48–72 hours and includes rest and sleeping pills.	Clinical experiences	59% returned to combat tasks. 25% returned to non-combat tasks. 16% referred to rear for further treatment. An estimated 15% of those returned to their units continued to suffer from disturbing symptoms.

TABLE 15.3 Continued

AUTHOR	GROUP STUDIED	WAR	ASPECTS OF TREATMENT BEYOND PRINCIPLES OF PROXIMITY, IMMEDIACY, AND EXPECTANCY	TYPE OF STUDY	RESULTS
Hausman & Rioch, 1967	American soldiers	Korean War	The casualty remained in uniform, under supervision of the military authorities. Treatment simple and limited in time. The soldier should be enabled to retain his identification with his unit and his sense of obligation to it.	Survey of military experience	65% to 70% returned to their units, most of them to non-combat tasks. Of those who returned, 10% had a relapse of distressing symptoms.
Allerton in Bourne, 1969	American psychiatric casualties	Vietnam 1963–1968	Emphasized early detection and treatment. Maintenance of military, as opposed to hospital, atmosphere, and a limited use of medication.	Clinical experience	Approximately 12 evacuees per 1000 soldiers.
Pettera, Johnson, & Zimmer, 1969	Combat fatigue casualties following long-term combat	Vietnam 1967–1968	Reassuring the soldier that his fear and anxiety are appropriate and that there is no danger of insanity. Medication; physical exercise through sports.	Clinical experience	70% returned to functioning, 15% transferred to non-combat assignments.
Bloch, 1969	American CSR casualties	Vietnam 1967–1968	Relaxation; meeting physiological needs; encouraging the injured to re-enact the traumatic experience; attention to proximity, immediacy, and expectancy.	Clinical experience	100% returned to unit.
Noy, 1985	Battle fatigue casualties	Yom Kippur (1973) War	Frontline treatment implemented only towards the end of the fighting, in field hospital and in the rear.	Clinical experience	Fewer than 20% were returned to the front.
Solomon & Benbenishty, 1986	CSR casualties	Lebanon (1982) War	A mixture of psychodynamic and behavioral forms of group and individual therapy.	Controlled study with matched controls	60% of the soldiers treated with all the three principles of frontline treatment returned to their unit, and had lower rates of long-term PTSD compared to combatants who did not get frontline treatment.
Johnson, Cline, Marcum, & Intress, 1992	American combatants with combat fatigue	1991 Persian Gulf War	Immediate treatment in a recovery unit (including military routines, educational sessions, and group therapy).	Before-after comparison of stress symptoms.	21 (out of 22) returned to duty after 1–10 days. Reduction in all distress measures.

percent. These variations may be accounted for by such factors as differences in the stress of the battles and the condition of the soldiers to begin with, in the readiness of the units to accept the injured soldier, in the predisposition of the clinicians to send soldiers who broke down back to the fire, and in the way the frontline treatment was implemented.

In their largely positive evaluations of the success of frontline treatment, these uncontrolled studies are much like the uncontrolled investigations of debriefing, and share some of their weaknesses. Their findings are derived mostly from clinical impressions and from small-scale surveys. There was little long-term follow-up. Outcome measures are almost entirely rate of return, with little attention to psychiatric symptoms (exceptions are Glass, 1954; 1957; Johnson et al., 1992; Kardiner, 1947). The differences in the programs and the inadequacy of description add to the difficulty of assessment, as they do to the evaluation of the debriefing.

What adds weight to the evidence for the effectiveness of frontline treatment are the positive findings of a carefully controlled study carried out by the Israel Defense Forces on the treatment outcomes of CSR casualties of the Lebanon War, the first war in which the Israeli military made a consistent effort to implement frontline treatment. War conditions generally do not provide a setting conducive to systematic study, but the circumstances in the Lebanon War allowed comparison between CSR soldiers treated on the front and those treated in civilian facilities in the rear. The location and treatment method were determined solely by logistic considerations; and because frontline and civilian services were in close geographic proximity, confounding by transfer time was negligible. These conditions enabled the design of a quasi-experimental study of all the identified Israeli CSR casualties of that war (Solomon & Benbenishty, 1986). The study investigated the impact of the three frontline principles of proximity, immediacy, and expectancy on the soldiers' return to their units and on their PTSD status one year later. The three principles were dealt with separately because they were not always applied together as a single package.

Findings showed that the more consistent the treatment was with the three principles, the better the outcome. On the whole, soldiers who were treated in Lebanon immediately upon their arrival at a treatment station and who understood that they were expected to resume their combat duties showed more positive outcomes than those treated either in a field hospital on the Israeli side of the border or well within Israel, more time after their breakdown, and who did not understand that they were expected to return to their units. The more principles of frontline treatment that were applied, the more frequently the clinician recommended a return to unit, the more the soldier actually returned to his unit and resumed his previous tasks, and the lower the subsequent PTSD rates. While 60 percent of the soldiers treated with all three principles went back to their units, only 22 percent of the soldiers who were not treated with any of the principles did. And while 70 percent of the soldiers who were not treated with any of the principles suffered from PTSD a year later, only 40 percent of those who were treated with all the principles did.

Implications for Research and Intervention

Of all the many studies of the impact of frontline treatment, only one is a controlled study, which investigates long-term psychological outcomes as well. In fact, this is the only study that touches on the preventive powers of frontline treatment. The paucity of controlled study stems from both the great difficulty of planning and carrying out systematic empirical investigations in wartime and from the relative infrequency with which frontline treatment is actually applied. Although frontline treatment is the recommended treatment for CSR in many armies, it is rarely given to all the casualties. For example, in the Lebanon War only 7 percent of the Israeli CSR casualties received frontline care. Both logistic problems and the moral uneasiness that some battalion physicians feel about keeping an obviously distressed soldier on the front contribute to the inconsistency (Solomon, 1993).

The findings of the Solomon and Benbenishty study also raise questions. How frontline treatment promotes a return to the unit is clear enough. How it reduces the incidence of PTSD is less clear. One possibility may have to do with the intensive treatment followed by the return to the unit of a large majority of the casualties. Both the treatment on the front and the rapid resumption of combat activity appear to mitigate the guilt and shame of the battlefield breakdown and strengthen the injured soldier's self-structure and thereby increase his resilience. Treatment in the rear carries the stigma of mental illness and may thereby foster regression, increasing the vulnerability to long-term disorder. On the other hand, it may well be that those soldiers who were returned to their units had the better prognosis to begin with.

The apparent success of frontline treatment in war makes its adaptation to other traumatic events appealing. Recently, the principles of frontline treatment have been applied to caring for ASD casualties following terrorist attacks in Israel. The outcomes are as yet unpublished. When more information is available, it may be worth considering applying "frontline treatment" to non-military trauma casualties. The approach clearly cannot be applied to victims of repetitive traumas (such as captivity or torture, sexual abuse or family violence), where the person is not returned to the scene. But victims of accidents and natural disasters who show signs of ASD, as well as persons who have serious illnesses or who have undergone drastic surgery may benefit from the approach.

CONCLUSIONS

For all of its ambiguities, the differential picture of the effectiveness of debriefing and of frontline treatment is rather curious. While frontline treatment seems to prevent the development of long-term trau-

matic reactions in a fair proportion of cases, the limited evidence suggests that debriefing may not do so. Yet, debriefing strives to use the same frontline principles of proximity, immediacy, and expectancy that were associated with frontline treatment's preventive power. The apparently differential outcomes may have a number of sources. One may be the fact that frontline treatment focuses on identified casualties, while debriefing is provided to all persons exposed to a traumatogenic event, with the resulting risk to persons who are particularly vulnerable. A related, and deeper, source may be the relatively large therapeutic component of frontline treatment in comparison to debriefing. Even where therapy is intentionally kept to a minimum and other activities are emphasized, there is still more attention to persons' emotional states in frontline treatment than in debriefing. The military milieu that is part of frontline treatment today is, after all, created by mental health professionals in uniform, who bring their training and experience to the front. It is worth trying to formulate debriefing protocols that incorporate the therapeutic elements that are part of frontline treatment, though they are not named with the principles. In particular, it might be helpful to screen out persons with ASD, monitor for stress reactions in the course of the debriefing, and increase the therapeutic component of the intervention for these individuals. While debriefing of low-risk individuals might be conducted by trained laymen along educational lines, vulnerable individuals might do better being debriefed by mental health professionals along therapeutic lines.

REFERENCES

American Psychiatric Association (APA). (1987). *Diagnostic and statistical manual of mental disorders* (3rd ed. Rev.). Washington, DC: Author.

American Psychiatric Association (APA). (1994). *Diagnostic and statistical manual of mental disorders* (4th ed.). Washington, DC: Author.

Armfield, F. (1994). Preventing post traumatic stress disorder resulting from military operations. *Military medicine, 159,* 739–746.

Artiss, K. L. (1963). Human behavior under stress: From combat to social psychiatry. *Military Medicine, 128,* 1011–1015.

Bailey, P., Williams, F. E., Komora, P. O., & Salmon, T. W., & Fenton, N. (1929). *The Medical Department of the United States Army in the World War: Vol. X. Neuropsychiatry.* Washington DC: Government Printing Office.

Bargess, A. W., & Baldwin, B. A. (1981). *Crisis intervention theory and practice: A clinical handbook.* Englewood Cliff, NJ: Prentice-Hall.

Bar-On, R., Solomon, Z., Noy, S., & Nardi, C. (1986). The clinical picture of combat stress reactions in the 1982 war in Lebanon: Cross-war comparisons. In N. A. Milgram (Ed.), *Stress and coping in time of war: Generalizations from the Israeli experience* (pp. 103–109). New York: Brunner/Mazel.

Bartemeier, L. H. (1946). Combat exhaustion. *Journal of Nervous and Mental Disease, 104,* 359–425.

Bergman, L. H. & Queen, T. (1986). *Critical incident stress: Part 1. Fire command,* April, 52–56.

Bleich, A., Dycian, A., Koslovsky, M., Solomon, Z., & Weiner, M. (1992). Psychiatric implications of missile attacks on civilian populations. *Journal of the American Medical Association, 268,* 613–615.

Bloch, H. S. (1969). Army clinical psychiatry in the combat zone. *American Journal of psychiatry, 126,* 289–298.

Brom D. & Kleber, R. J. (1989). Prevention of posttraumatic stress disorders. *Journal of Traumatic Stress, 2,* 335–351.

Bourne, P. G. (1969). *The psychology and physiology of stress.* New York: Academic Press.

Caplan, G. (1961). *An approach to community and mental health.* London: Tavistock.

Caplan, G. (1964). *Principles of preventive psychiatry.* New York. Basic Books.

Carlier, I. V. E., Van Uchelen, J. J., Lamberts, R. D., & Gersons, B. P. R. (1994). The effect of debriefing. A study at the Amsterdam police after the Bijlmer plane-crash. Internal report, Academic Medical Center at the University of Amsterdam.

Cavenar, J. O., & Nash, J. L. (1976). The effects of combat on the normal personality: War neurosis in Vietnam returnees. *Comprehensive Psychiatry, 17,* 647–653.

Deahl, M. P., Gillham, A. B., Thomas, J., Searle, M. M., & Srinivasan, M. (1994). Psychological sequelae following the Gulf War: Factors associated with subsequent morbidity and the effectiveness of psychological debriefing. *British Journal of Psychiatry, 165,* 60–65.

Dunning, C. & Silva, M. (1980). Disaster-induced trauma in rescue workers. *Victimology, 5:*287–297.

Eberly, R. E., Harkness, A. R., & Engdahl, B. E. (1991). An adaptational view of trauma response as illustrated by the prisoner of war experience. *Journal of Traumatic Stress, 4,* 363–380.

Enoch, D. (1996). *An indigenous military community as a therapeutic agent.* Unpublished manuscript.

Fitzgerald, M. L., Braudway, C. A., Leeks, D., Padgett, M. B. et al., (1993). Debriefing: A therapeutic intervention. *Military Medicine, 158,* 542–545.

Flannery, R. B., Fulton, P., Tausch, J., & Deloffi, A. Y. (1991). A program to help staff cope with psychological sequelae of assaults by patients. *Hospital and Community Psychiatry, 42,* 935–938.

Ford, J., Shaw, D., Sennhauser, S., Greaves, D., Thacker, B., Chandler, P., Schwartz, L., & McClain, V. (1993). Psychological debriefing after Operation Desert Storm: Marital and family assessment and intervention. *Journal of Social Issues, 49,* 73–102.

Freedy, J. F. & Donkervoet, J. C. (1995). Traumatic stress: An overview of the field. In J. R. Freedy and S. E. Hobfull (Eds.), *Traumatic stress: From theory to practice* (pp. 3–28). New York: Plenum Press.

Fullerton, C. S., Ursano, R. J., Kao, T., & Bhartiya, V. (1992). The chemical and biological warfare environment: Psychological responses and social support in a high stress environment. *Journal of Applied Social Psychology, 22,* 1608–1623.

Glass, A. J. (1954). Psychotherapy in the combat zone. *American Journal of Psychiatry, 110,* 725–731.

Glass, A. J. (1957). Observations upon the epidemiology of mental illness in troops during warfare. *Symposium on preventive and social psychiatry.* Walter Reed Army Institute of Research, Washington, D.C.

Green, B. L., Grace, M. C., & Gleser, G. C. (1985). Identifying survivors at risk: Long term impairment following the Beverly Hills supper club fire. *Journal of Consulting and Clinical Psychology, 53,* 672–678.

Green, B. L., & Solomon, S. D. (1995). The mental health impact of natural and technological disasters. In J. R. Freedy and S. E. Hobfull (Eds.), *Traumatic stress: From theory to practice* (pp. 163–180). New York: Plenum Press.

Greenstone, J. L., & Leviton, S. C. (1981). Crisis management. In R. J. Corsini (Ed.), *Handbook of innovative psychotherapies* (pp. 216–228). New York: Wiley.

Griffiths, J., & Watts, R. (1992). *The Kempsaey and Grafton bus crashes: The aftermath.* East Lismore, Australia: Instructional Design Solutions.

Grinker, R. R. (1945). Psychiatric disorders in combat crews overseas and in returnees. *Medical Clinics of North America, 29,* 729–739.

Grinker R. R. & Spiegel, J. P. (1945). *Men under stress.* Philadelphia: Blakiston.

Hausman, W. & Rioch, D. (1967). Military psychiatry. *Archives of General Psychiatry, 16,* 727.

Horowitz, M. J., & Kaltreider, N. B. (1995). Brief therapy of the stress response syndrome. In G. E. Everly and J. M. Lating (Eds.), *Psychotraumatology* (pp. 231–244). New York: Plenum Press.

Horowitz, M., Wilner, N., & Alvarez, M. (1979). Impact of Event Scale: A measure of subjective stress. *Psychosomatic Medicine, 41,* 209–218.

Hytten, L., & Hasle, A. (1989). Firefighters: A study of stress and coping. *Acta Psychiatrica Scandinavica, 80* (Suppl. 355), 50–55.

Ingraham, L. & Manning, F. (1986). American military psychiatry. In R. A. Gabriel (Ed.), *Military psychiatry* (pp. 25–65). New York: Greenwood Press.

Johnson, L. B., Cline, D. W., Marcum, J. M., & Intress, J. L. (1992). Effectiveness of a stress recovery unit during the Persian Gulf War. *Hospital and Community Psychiatry, 43,* 829–831.

Jones, D. R. (1985). Secondary disaster victims: The emotional impact of recovering and identifying human remains. *American Journal of Psychiatry, 142,* 303–307.

Kenardy, J. A., Webster, R. A., Lewin, T. J., Carr, V. J., Hazell, P. L. & Carter, G. L. (1996). Stress debriefing and patterns of recovery following a natural disaster. *Journal of Traumatic Stress, 9,* 37–49.

Kormos, H. R. (1978). The nature of combat stress. In C. R. Figley (Ed.), *Stress disorders among Vietnam veterans.* New York: Brunner Mazel.

Kulka, R. A., Schlenger, W. E., Fairbank, J. A., Hough, R. L., Jordan, B. K., Marmar, C. R., & Weiss, D. A. (1990). *Trauma and the Vietnam War generation.* New York: Brunner Mazel.

Lindemann, E. (1944). Symptomatology and management of acute grief. *American Journal of Psychiatry, 101,* 141–148.

Lundin, T. (1994). The treatment of acute trauma: Post traumatic stress disorder prevention. *Psychiatric Clinics of North America, 17,* 385–391.

Malt, U. F., Hoivik, B., & Blikra, G. (1993). Psychosocial consequences of road accidents. *European Psychiatry, 8,* 227–228.

Marlowe, D. H. (1978). Cohesion, anticipated breakdown, and endurance in battle: Considerations for severe and high intensity combat. Department of Military Psychiatry, Walter Reed Army Institute of Research, Washington, DC.

Marshall, S. L. A. (1944). *Island victory.* New York: Penguin Books.

Marshall, S. L. A. (1956). *Park Chop Hill.* William Morrow & Co.

Mausner, J. S. & Bahn, A. K. (1974). *Epidemiology: An introductory text.* Philadelphia, PA: W. B. Saunders Company.

Mayou, R., Bryant, B., & Duthie, R. (1993). Psychiatric consequences of road traffic accidents. *British Medical Journal, 307,* 647–651.

McCarroll, J. E., James, E., Ursano, R. J., Fullerton, C. S., & Lundy, A. C. (1995). Anticipatory stress of handling human remains from the Persian Gulf War: Predictors of intrusion and avoidance. Journal of Nervous and Mental Disease, 183, 698–703.

Melton, C. (1985). The days after: Coping with after effects of the Delta 1–1022 crash. *Firehouse,* December, 49–50.

Mitchell, J. T. (1981). *Emergency response to crisis: A crisis intervention guidebook of emergency service personnel.* Bowie, MD: Brady Co.

Mitchell, J. T. (1982). Recovery from rescue. *Response Magazine.* Fall, 7–10.

Mitchell, J. T. (1983). When disaster strikes. *Journal of Emergency Medical Services, 8,* 36–39.

Mitchell, J. T. (1986). Critical incident stress management. *Response, 5,* 24–25.

Mitchell, J., & Bray, G. (1990). *Emergency services stress.* Englewood Cliffs, NJ: Prentice-Hall.

Moses, R. & Cohen, I. (1984). Understanding and treatment of combat neurosis: The Israeli experience. In H. J. Schwartz (Ed.), *Psychotherapy of the combat veteran* (pp. 269–303), New York: Spectrum Publications.

Mullins, W. S., & Glass, A. J. (1973). *Neuropsychiatry in World War II, Vol. 2: Overseas theaters.* Washington, DC: Army Medical Department.

Norris, F. H. & Thompson, M. P. (1995). Applying community psychology to the prevention of trauma and traumatic life events. In J. R. Freedy and S. E. Hobfull (Eds.), *Traumatic stress: From theory to practice* (pp. 3–28). New York: Plenum Press.

Noy, S. (1985). Combat stress reactions: Correlations, manifestations, prevention and treatment. Technical report, Department of Mental Health, Medical Corp., IDF [Hebrew].

Orr, S. P. & Kaloupek, D. G. (1997). Psychophysiological assessment of posttraumatic stress disorder. In J. P. Wilson & T. M. Keane (Eds.), *Assessing psychological trauma and PTSD* (pp. 69–97). New York: Guilford Press.

Panagapoulos, M. C. (1980). *Psychiatric Casualties in Battle.* Lecture delivered at the 9th International Advanced Course for Young Medical Officers, Athens, Greece.

Pettera, R. L., Johnson, B. M., & Zimmer, R. (1969). Psychiatric management of combat reactions with emphasis on a reaction unique to Vietnam. *Military Medicine, 134,* 673–678.

Rachman, S. (1990). *Fear and courage.* New York: Freeman.

Raphael, B. (1986). *When disaster strikes.* New York: Basic Books.

Raphael, B., Singh, B., Bradbury, L., & Lambert, F. (1983). Who helps the helpers? The effects of disaster on rescue workers. *Omega, 14*(1), 9–20.

Robinson, R., & Mitchell, J. (1993). Evaluation of psychological debriefings. *Journal of Traumatic Stress, 6*(3), 367–382.

Saigh, P. (1984). Pre- and postinvasion anxiety in Lebanon. *Behavior Therapy, 15,* 185–190.

Salmon, T. W. (1919). War neuroses and their lesson. *New York Medical Journal, 109,* 993–994.

Shalev, A. Y. (1992). Posttraumatic stress disorder among injured survivors of a terrorist attack: Predictive value of early intrusion and avoidance symptoms. *Journal of Nervous and Mental Disease, 180,* 505–509.

Shalev, A. Y. (1994). Debriefing following traumatic exposure. In R. J. Ursano, B. G. McCaughey, & C. S. Fullerton (Eds.), *Individual and community responses to trauma and disaster: The structure of human chaos* (pp. 201–219). Cambridge: Cambridge University Press.

Shalev, A. Y. (1996). Stress versus traumatic stress: From acute homeostatic reactions to chronic psychopathology. In B. A. van der Kolk, A. C. McFarlane, & L. Weisaeth (Eds.), *Traumatic stress: The effects of overwhelming experience on mind, body, and society.* (pp. 77–101). New York: Guilford Press.

Solomon, Z. (1993). *Combat stress reaction: The enduring toll of war.* New York: Plenum Press.

Solomon, Z. (1995). *Coping with war-induced stress: The Gulf War and the Israeli response.* New York: Plenum Press.

Solomon, Z. & Benbenishty, R. (1986). The role of proximity, immediacy, and expectancy in frontline treatment of combat stress reaction among Israelis in the Lebanon War. *American Journal of Psychiatry, 143,* 613–617.

Solomon, Z., Mikulincer, M., & Benbenishty, R. (1989). Combat stress reaction: Clinical manifestations and correlates. *Military Psychology, 1,* 35–47.

Solomon, Z., & Shalev, A. Y. (1995). Helping victims of military trauma. In J. R. Freedy and S. E. Hobfoll (Eds.), *Traumatic stress from theory to practice* (pp. 241–262). Plenum Press.

Spiller, R. J. (1980). S. L. A. Marshall and the ratio of fire. *The Royal United Service Institute for Defense Studies Journal, 133,* 63–71.

Stallard, P., & Law, F. (1993). Screening and psychological debriefing of adolescent survivors of life-threatening events. *British Journal of Psychiatry, 163,* 660–665.

Toubiana, Y., Milgram, N., & Noy, S. (1986). A therapeutic community in a forward army field hospital: Treatment, education, and expectancy. In N. A. Milgram (Ed.), *Stress and coping in time of war: Generalizations from the Israeli experience* (pp. 117–129). New York: Brunner/Mazel.

Turner, R. J. (1981). Social support as a contingency in psychological well being. *Journal of Health and Social Behavior, 22,* 357–367.

Turner, S. W., Thompson, J., & Rosser, R. M. (1993). The King's Cross fire: Early psychological reactions and implications for organizing a "phase-two" response. In J. P. Wilson & B. Raphael (Eds.), *International handbook of traumatic stress syndromes* (pp. 451–459). New York: Plenum Press.

Wagner, M. (1979). Airline disaster: A stress debrief program for police. *Police Stress, 2*:16–20.

Weisaeth, L. (1989a). The stressors and post traumatic stress syndrome after an industrial disaster. *Acta Psychiatrica Scandinavica, 80* (Suppl. 355), 25–37.

Weisaeth, L. (1989b). A study of behavioral responses to an industrial disaster. *Acta Psychiatrica Scandinavica, 80* (Suppl. 355), 13–24.

Williams, T. (1993). Trauma in the workplace. In J. P. Wilson & B. Raphael (Eds.), *International handbook of traumatic stress syndromes* (pp. 925–933). New York: Plenum Press.

CHAPTER 16

PHARMACOLOGICAL TREATMENT OF POSTTRAUMATIC STRESS DISORDER

SUZANNE M. SUTHERLAND, M. D.
JONATHAN R. T. DAVIDSON, M. D.
Duke University Medical Center

INTRODUCTION

Posttraumatic stress disorder is a complex illness which often demands a multidimensional approach to treatment. The use of pharmacological intervention is consistent with our increasing knowledge of the various neurobiological systems that are implicated in this disorder and has been supported by a growing number of studies and reports demonstrating the beneficial effects of medication. It is becoming increasingly evident that psychoactive drugs can be a powerful treatment for many persons who suffer from this debilitating illness (Friedman, 1988; Solomon, Gerrity, & Muff, 1992), and pharmacotherapy has now found a place as a viable treatment alongside the more traditional approaches such as individual and group psychotherapy utilizing cognitive-behavioral techniques and psychodynamically oriented therapy.

Recently, there has been a wealth of new publications concerning PTSD, most of them generated since our revived interest in this issue after the Vietnam War and then its entry into the DSM nomenclature in 1980 (APA, 1980). Although this may suggest a new and comprehensive understanding of the disorder in terms of etiology, epidemiology, psychobiology, comorbidity, and treatment, it is clear that there is a long history of understanding of these various areas on the part of practitioners who worked with victims of trauma. Alexandra Adler wrote compellingly of the effects of trauma on victims of Boston's famous Cocoanut Grove fire in an article published in the Journal of the American Medical Association (Adler, 1943). In 1945 Grinker and Spiegel published a book

which documented the extensive psychological and neuropsychiatric effects of combat trauma in United States military personnel. Further understanding of trauma in the civilian population was provided by John Nemiah in a 1963 article concerning the psychological effects of industrial injuries. Each of these authors was concerned with the mind/body relationships in psychological health and saw that the illness resulting from severe trauma involved both a psychological and a biological component. "Traumatic neurosis" was referred to in the medical literature as early as 1890 by Oppenheim in an issue of *Lancet* where it was pointed out that trauma has wide-ranging consequences, and that it is often difficult to separate this functional disease from organic disease, as they often appear together. Even earlier, the physician Weir Mitchell wrote about the posttraumatic features seen in American Civil War veterans and also in female civilians who had been traumatically abused (Weir Mitchell, 1885). He noted the tendency of these patients to self-medicate with alcohol and opiate drugs, a phenomenon which continues to be one of the complicating factors of PTSD.

As indicated above, many writers referred to the physioneurological effects of trauma, but most of these writers did little to elaborate on the specific changes that may occur. In the 1940s, Kardiner and Spiegel described the biological disorganization that they saw occurring in soldiers on the battlefield and then haunting them for the rest of their lives. They recognized the generalized physiological arousal that remained present in these victims of trauma and questioned the possibility of reversing the profound biological changes that underlay this symptomatology. In their book, *War Stress and Neurotic Illness* (1947), they addressed the significant disturbances of the autonomic nervous system that are seen in "soldier's heart" or "effort syndrome" and noted that chronic disturbances of this type may cause the development of organic sequelae. Referring to the disorganization present in the adaptation of the ego following trauma, they viewed the traumatic neurosis as concerning predominantly body-ego action systems and applied the term "physioneurosis" to this condition which they viewed as "an entity which lies between pure disturbances in adaptation and organic 'disease'" (Kardiner & Spiegel, 1947, p. 337). In the last two decades, various researchers have begun to identify and describe some specific organic changes found in the brains of persons with PTSD, lending support to this early theory. Kardiner and Spiegel also connected disturbances in the gastrointestinal tract, skin, lungs and kidneys, as well as endocrine abnormalities such as Graves' disease to autonomic disturbances associated with traumatic neurosis and even suggested that there may be some connection to allergies. These observations also continue to be supported by such findings as higher rates of peptic ulcer disease, gastrointestinal disturbances, bronchial asthma, and hypertension in trauma populations (Davidson, Hughes, Blazer, & George, 1991). These early researchers had a good understanding of the components of the biopsychosocial illness that develops in many individuals following exposure to severe trauma, and our understanding of the symptomatology has changed little over the last several decades. However, we are beginning to describe the physiology that underlies some of these symptoms and to be able to apply our current knowledge of biological treatments in psychiatry to this disorder which in its fullest presentation has components of anxiety, affective, and psychotic illnesses.

BIOLOGICAL ISSUES IN PTSD

Autonomic Nervous System Dysregulation

As indicated above, it has long been apparent that the autonomic nervous system is dysregulated in persons with PTSD. Evidence of these disturbances supports both the view that PTSD is characterized by tonic autonomic hyperarousal and that there are reactive increases in autonomic system activity in response to trauma-relevant stimuli. Several studies have looked at physiological differences between veterans with PTSD and veterans from the same era without PTSD and also between individuals with PTSD and non-veteran control populations when they are exposed to trauma-relevant stimuli (Blanchard, Kolb, Pallmeyer, & Gerardi, 1982; Gerardi, Blanchard, & Kolb, 1989; Orr, Pitman, Lasko, & Herz, 1993). Although most of these studies have involved veterans, there are also a few studies which assess civilian populations with PTSD. The measures most frequently used are electrodermal activity as represented by skin conductance (SC) levels; skin temperature; responses such as heart rate (HR), systolic and diastolic blood pressure (BP); and electromyographic (EMG) activity of various facial muscles such as the frontalis, zygomaticus, corrugator, and orbicularis oculi.

Prins and colleagues reviewed the literature on autonomic arousal and found some variability in the reports (Prins, Kaloupek, & Keane, 1995). Researchers in the late 1940s documented higher resting HR and SC levels in veterans with "operational fatigue" as compared with a group of "psychoneurotics" and a control group. Both "decompensated" and "compensated" WWII veterans and Vietnam veterans with PTSD have been found to have significantly higher resting HRs as compared with noncombat control subjects, while no significant differences were found between the "decompensated" and "compensated" veteran groups. A more recent study of both World War II and Korean veterans by Orr and colleagues (1993) also found no difference in resting HR between those with PTSD and those without. However, of six studies comparing Vietnam veterans with PTSD to those with no mental disorder, four reported that the PTSD subjects had significantly higher resting HRs (Blanchard, Kolb, Gerardi, Ryan, & Pallmeyer, 1986; Gerardi et al., 1989; Pallmeyer, Blanchard, & Kolb, 1986; Pitman, Orr, Forgue, de-Jong, & Claiborn, 1987), while two found no difference (Blanchard, Kolb, Taylor, & Wittrock, 1989; Malloy, Fairbank, & Keane, 1993). One other study of Vietnam veterans comparing those with PTSD to a group with other anxiety disorders also found no difference in resting HR and no difference in SC between the two groups (Pitman et al., 1990). Although this study had no control group and each of the study groups consisted of only seven subjects, the results suggest that consideration should be given to the possibility that a higher resting HR could be characteristic of veterans with an anxiety disorder rather than specifically PTSD. Another study which casts doubt on the theory that PTSD is associated with a higher resting heart rate was reported by McFall, Murburg, Ko, and Veith (1990). In this study a group of Vietnam veterans with PTSD showed no difference in resting HR when compared with a mixed control group of non-PTSD subjects. Although to date most of the studies assessing physiological characteristics in PTSD have been conducted with veteran subjects, there is one study reported by Shalev, Orr, and Pitman in 1993 which found no difference in HR between Israeli civilians with and without PTSD, but found a significantly *lower* SC in the group with PTSD. Another study comparing civilians with PTSD resulting from motor vehicle accidents (MVAs) with a second group of civilians who had experienced MVAs but did not develop PTSD also showed no difference in resting HR (Blanchard, Hickling, Taylor, Loos, & Gerardi, 1994). While it remains unclear as to whether PTSD is characterized by a baseline higher autonomic arousal, it is a phenomenon that clearly is present in at least some subgroups of this population. The evidence for phasic changes in autonomic arousal in PTSD is more consistent across studies. There are significant differences in HR reactivity to trauma-relevant stimuli reported in 11 of 13 studies reviewed by Prins et al. (1995). Heart rates in combat veterans with PTSD and also in non-veterans with PTSD have been consistently reported to be much more reactive to trauma-related stimuli than in control groups.

Another commonly recognized symptom of PTSD is the exaggerated startle response. This occurs in reaction to various nonspecific stimuli which are unexpected, e.g., loud noises, unanticipated touch, or the sudden appearance of another person. Howard and Ford (1992) describe this reaction as consisting of two components. The first stage has a duration of 0.3—1.5 seconds and begins with an eye-blink response and facial grimace and then continues with flexion of the upper and lower limbs and trunk. The second stage is quite variable and may include postural adjustments and orientation toward the stimulus source, accompanied by a rise in systolic blood pressure and an increased HR and a fall in GSR. This latter characteristic may be related to the findings of a lower skin conductance in PTSD civilian patients. The authors describe the secondary component, which is not prominent in infancy, as "voluntary and socially-conditioned," and suggest that the hyperstartle of the neuropsychiatric syndromes of PTSD and generalized anxiety disorder represent an extreme end of the normal startle response. In the process of their review, these authors note that the motor component of the startle response consists of two neuronal systems, the cerebral noradrenergic pathway, which is inhibited by serotoninergic activity, and a serotoninergic spinal system. The inhibitory effect of serotonin which is a component of the first neuronal system may be enhanced by serotoninergic medications and may be the mechanism that underlies the improvement in exaggerated startle response seen with these drugs. They also suggest that overactivity or overreactivity of the dopaminergic mesolimbic system may be a common factor in conditions in which an exaggerated startle response is a prominent symptom, a theory that is consistent with the increase in plasma dopamine found in some PTSD subjects (Hamner, Diamond, & Hitri, 1990).

Locus Coeruleus Activation

It is well-documented in animal studies that the noradrenergic neurons of the locus coeruleus (LC) play a central role in the organism's response to stress. The findings from laboratory investigation of this role are summarized by Zigmond, Finlay, and Sved (1995) in *Neurobiological and Clinical Consequences of Stress* (Friedman, Charney, & Deutch, 1995). While noradrenergic neurons are present within several cell groups of the reticular formation, they are chiefly found in the LC, which is located within the brain stem and has widespread connections to rest of the brain. It is hypothesized that acute stress causes an increase in the synthesis, release, and breakdown of NE in neurons projecting from the LC. Electrophysiological studies in conscious animals have demonstrated that these neurons do in fact increase their firing rate in response to all stimuli that the organism attends to, with stressful or noxious stimuli eliciting greater responses which are also more sustained. This global activation of the cells in the LC is analogous to the response of the peripheral noradrenergic neurons of the sympathetic nervous system in reaction to stress. However, there also may be significant functional heterogeneity in these LC neurons as evidenced by conditioned stressors evoking response in only a subset of these neurons and also by the demonstration of distinct behavioral syndromes following selective lesioning of different noradrenergic projections of the LC.

Less is known about the response of noradrenergic neurons in the LC to chronic stress, but emerging evidence suggests that it may be quite different from that in acute stress. Whereas acute stress that is sufficiently severe may actually cause a reduction in tissue NE, when the stress is repetitive or protracted, there is no depletion and there may actually be an increase in basal levels of NE (Zigmond et al., 1995). Accompanying this increase is a decline in the typical stress-induced increase in LC firing rate in response to the same stressor, which is reflective of the reduction in stress-evoked release of NE from sympathetic nerves with repetitive exposure to a stressor. However, when the chronically stressed organism is exposed to an acute and novel stressor, the response is enhanced in comparison to control animals. This phenomenon of stress-induced sensitization appears to be a function of duration of exposure to the stressor and/or the passage of time following the exposure. This is consistent with our understanding of the development of PTSD being more likely to occur with prolonged exposure to trauma and also with the somewhat puzzling occurrence of delayed-onset PTSD.

Although it is clear that noradrenergic neurons found in other brainstem regions also respond to various stressors, the focus on the LC as of primary importance in understanding the role of these neurons in stress is based on (1) its being the site of most of the body's noradrenergic cell bodies, (2) its ability to influence widespread areas of the CNS, and (3) the findings that LC neurons receive sensory input of all types and respond to virtually all stressful stimuli. This implies a central role in vigilance and has implications for the hypervigilance found in PTSD. Laboratory studies involving stimulation of LC neurons produce behaviors normally associated with stress and also show that these behaviors are reduced with lesions of the LC, lending support to the hypothesis that the noradrenergic neurons of the LC play an important role in the response of the organism to stress (Zigmond et al., 1995).

There are many unanswered questions in our understanding of the role of the LC and its noradrenergic cells. The changes that occur in the system in response to multiple or prolonged exposure may be adaptive initially, but with increasing levels of exposure may become maladaptive and result in some of the hyperarousal and also the numbing symptoms of PTSD. As it becomes more clear what the actual mechanism of adaptation and maladaptation is, it may be possible to develop more specific approaches to the treatment of the symptoms of psychiatric disorders caused by severe stress. For a more detailed discussion, please see the chapter on the autonomic nervous system elsewhere in this volume.

Hypothalamic-Pituitary-Adrenal Axis

Our understanding of the stress response syndrome has been challenged in the last decade in light of accumulating evidence that alterations seen in the hypothalamic-pituitary-adrenal (HPA) axis in PTSD are distinctly different from those found in other psychiatric disorders. The symptoms of PTSD have historically been conceptualized as representing a normative response to extreme stress, and consequently, many of the biological studies of PTSD were conducted with the expectation that the alterations that would be found in symptomatic individuals would reflect the prior findings observed in studies of animals and humans subjected to acute and chronic stressors. Part of the documented psychoneuroendocrine response to stress was a consistent finding of an increase in the release of pituitary-adrenocortical hormones. The basic stress response is still generally defined by the strength of the pituitary-adrenocortical activity in spite of more recent knowledge of multiple cellular and molecular changes induced by stress. However, it is also now understood to be modulated by various hormonal and neuronal factors, as well as additional factors such as the nature of the current stressor, a history of prior stressful events in the affected individual, and various other genetic and environmental factors.

While findings of HPA axis dysregulation have been reported in most studies of PTSD, the direction of the system alterations has been found to be opposite of that which was predicted. Individuals with PTSD have been found to have low cortisol levels as measured by 24-hour urinary excretion in comparison with normal controls and also patients with other psychiatric conditions including major depression, bipolar mania, schizophrenia, and panic disorder. This finding is present in Vietnam veterans with PTSD studied 20 to 25 years after their combat exposure and also in Holocaust survivors with PTSD who were studied 50 years after their trauma, indicating that low cortisol levels may exist for decades in symptomatic individuals (Yehuda, Giller, Levengood, Southwick, & Siever, 1995). Basal plasma cortisol excretion has been found to be lower in PTSD subjects as compared with normal controls and patients with major depression, while these same subjects show evidence of a higher degree of cortisol fluctuation over a 24-hour diurnal cycle relative to the lower excretion levels and also a greater degree of circadian rhythm, suggestive of a more dynamic HPA axis in PTSD.

Further evidence of differences in the HPA axis dysregulation in PTSD have been found in various HPA axis challenge tests. As contrasted with major depressive disorder, in which there have been consistent findings of cortisol "nonsuppression" in response to a dexamethasone challenge test, patients with PTSD do suppress cortisol following dexamethasone and have even been shown to hypersuppress cortisol following exposure to low doses of dexamethasone (0.50 mg and 0.25 mg as contrasted with the typical challenge test dose of 1 mg). This enhanced suppression of cortisol has not been described in other psychiatric disorders and has been suggested to have the

potential for being useful as a specific biological marker for PTSD (Yehuda et al., 1995).

Additional findings of HPA axis dysregulation involve abnormal ACTH levels in response to challenge tests. PTSD patients have been found to have a significantly lower ACTH response to CRF in comparison to control subjects in the presence of normal evening plasma cortisol levels (Smith, Davidson, Ritchie, & Kudler, 1989). Yet they have been found to have substantially higher increases in ACTH response to abrupt discontinuation of cortisol synthesis via the administration of metyrapone, in a challenge test designed to examine pituitary sensitivity. Taken together, these findings suggest that in PTSD subjects the pituitary may receive excessively high levels of CRF stimulation when the negative feedback influence of cortisol is interrupted, enabling it to produce substantially higher levels of ACTH as compared to the increases found in normal subjects. A third observation of an increased number of glucocorticoid receptors in lymphocytes, possibly reflecting increases in the pituitary gland, may explain the blunted ACTH response to CRF in the face of normal levels of cortisol, wherein the pituitary gland becomes hyperresponsive to the negative feedback of the circulating cortisol.

Yehuda and colleagues have suggested a model of an enhanced negative feedback inhibition in PTSD which accounts for the various HPA axis abnormalities detailed above (Yehuda et al., 1995). This model can accommodate the view of PTSD as an illness in which there is a hyperresponsiveness to stress as seen in the stronger circadian rhythm of cortisol as well as the stronger signal-to-noise ratio of cortisol (i.e., cortisol fluctuations that are high relative to the baseline lower level of cortisol excretion in PTSD patients). This model is also consistent with the accepted clinical view of PTSD patients being exceptionally responsive to acute stressors with both exaggerated behavioral and biological responses commonly seen in reaction to internal and external stimuli.

The cause of the increased number of glucocorticoid receptors in the pituitary gland in PTSD may parallel the "early handling" paradigm in the animal stress literature, wherein neonatal animals exposed to stress of daily handling for several weeks exhibit permanent upregulation of hippocampal glucocorticoid receptors and resultant decrease in cortisol following exposure to subsequent stress. It is hypothesized that there is a developmentally sensitive period in which exposure to environmental events leads to the establishment of this different type of stress response. This is consistent with the findings of lower basal excretion of cortisol and higher numbers of glucocorticoid receptors in PTSD. The model also may have clinical relevance in that the early handling of neonatal animal subjects may parallel those combat veterans who have had a higher exposure to stressful events during childhood and are then more likely to develop PTSD following combat trauma (Bremner, Southwick, Johnson, Yehuda, & Charney, 1993; Yehuda et al., 1995).

Neurotransmitter Alterations

Neurotransmitters which have been found to be altered in posttraumatic stress disorder and that may have implications for biological treatments include the catecholamines, glucocorticoids, serotonin, and endogenous opioids. Although research in this area remains limited, some of the findings have begun to illuminate our understanding of the broad and complex neurobiological mechanisms involved in PTSD.

The sympathetic nervous system neurotransmitters, norepinephrine, epinephrine, and dopamine, and the opiate and serotonergic systems will be reviewed separately, but it must be remembered that these systems are closely interrelated and also that there are probably other neurotransmitter systems involved in the acute and ongoing response to trauma that have not yet been elucidated. It is clear in the light of our current knowledge that it is not possible to clearly determine the specific effects of a single neurotransmitter.

Catecholamine System. The alterations in the sympathetic nervous system in PTSD have been described above and clearly are a primary factor in the development of the symptomatology of PTSD. Researchers have begun to investigate the actions of the key sympathetic nervous system neurotransmitters that underly the sympathetic activation found in victims of trauma.

In an attempt to demonstrate evidence of autonomic hyperarousal in PTSD, researchers have also looked at catecholamine levels in the urine and in plasma. While no differences have been found in baseline plasma NE, the studies reported typically use NE values obtained by venipuncture and may be contaminated by the stress of the venipuncture itself. Studies measuring urinary NE have found elevated 24-hour urinary excretion in combat veterans with PTSD (Kosten, Mason, Giller, Ostroff, & Harkness, 1987; Pitman et al., 1987; Svensson, 1987) and also in combat veterans without PTSD (Pitman & Orr, 1990) as compared to normal controls. A community study of residents living closer to (5 miles) as compared to those living farther from (80 miles) Three Mile Island was done 5 years after the accident at the nuclear power station and revealed higher urinary NE levels in the more proximal group without regard to PTSD diagnosis. As suggested by Southwick, Yehuda, and Morgan (1995), these alterations in NE excretion may be a function of trauma and not specifically of PTSD.

Southwick and colleagues (1995) also summarized the studies involving dopamine (DA) and epinephrine (EPI) measurements in PTSD subjects. Both DA and EPI urinary excretion have been reported as elevated in PTSD, although some researchers have failed to replicate the finding of EPI elevation. Plasma DA has also been found to be elevated in PTSD patients as compared to healthy controls and patients with major depression, while elevated plasma EPI has not been reported. In a study measuring severity of PTSD symptomatology, Yehuda and colleagues found that urinary NE and DA both correlated with symptom severity, especially intrusive symptoms, while EPI excretion showed no pattern in relation to symptoms (Yehuda, Southwick, & Giller, 1992).

Alpha-2-adrenergic receptors, which play a role in translating the neurochemical messages of the catecholamines and may reflect overall sympathetic tone, have been found to be decreased in number in subjects with PTSD as compared to controls and also as compared to patients with major depression and generalized anxiety disorder. Of note, decreased alpha-2-adrenergic receptor number has also been shown in patients with borderline personality disorder. It may be that these two disorders share a common alteration of the noradrenergic system that is different from other depressive and anxiety disorders.

Studies of catecholamine levels in response to acute stimuli are also limited, but suggest increased responsivity of brain catecholamine systems. Administration of both lactate and yohimbine, substances which are believed to stimulate the noradrenergic system, both cause an increase in intrusive symptomatology in PTSD patients as represented by the induction of flashbacks with administration of these substances (Rainey et al., 1987; Southwick et al., 1993). Animal models which have demonstrated increased responsiveness of LC neurons in response to chronic stress have shown increased release of NE in the LC and the hippocampus as well as other brain regions in response to acute stress in chronically stressed animals, as well as increases in DA in both chronic and acute stress. Several studies of PTSD patients subjected to trauma-related stimuli also show increases in the circulating catecholamines EPI and NE in parallel with increased blood pressure, heart rate, and reported subjective distress. Exaggerated startle response, known to be a cardinal symptom in PTSD, has also been shown to be present in laboratory conditions of fear and during hyperadrenergic states but not in the absence of stressful test conditions in PTSD subjects.

Clinically, a possible role for the implication of the mesocortical dopaminergic system in memory and attention alterations has been suggested by Bremner and colleagues (1993). Many of the symptoms of chronic PTSD such as exaggerated startle, hypervigilance, exaggerated physiological responsiveness to trauma-related stimuli and often full-blown panic attacks, and generalized autonomic hyperarousal are related to increased noradrenergic function. In animal studies the yohimbine-induced increased startle and increased circulating NE have been attenuated by the administration of clonidine (Davis, Redmond, & Baraban, 1979), suggesting a possible role for this drug in the treatment of the PTSD symptoms related to hyperresponsiveness of brain catecholamine systems. Recognizing the role of this system in creating and maintaining many of the symptoms of PTSD may help clinicians to understand the frequent abuse of alcohol, opiates, and benzodiazepines in patients with this disorder. Each of these drugs has been shown to reduce stress-induced increases in NE in various parts of the brain and use of these substances, which often leads to abuse, may represent an attempt to relieve the symptoms induced by the hyperactive catecholamine system.

Opioid System.   The endogenous opioid system also appears to be dysregulated in PTSD. Van der Kolk and associates (1989) noted the similarities between opioid withdrawal and PTSD symptoms and suggested that chronic PTSD is associated with a chronic lowering of opioid levels, as well as a stress-induced analgesia suggestive of hyperreactivity (van der Kolk, Greenberg, Orr, & Pitman, 1989). It has been noted that Vietnam veterans with combat-related PTSD have high rates of heroin abuse and dependence (Kulka, Schlenger, Fairbank, Jough, & Jordan, 1990) and that, in general, these veterans appear to prefer opiates to other substances of abuse such as cocaine and alcohol, a finding which may relate to the existence of abnormally low opioid levels as well as to the above-mentioned attenuation of exaggerated adrenergic responsiveness with opiates. Studies documenting a decrease in endogenous opiates in chronic stress are limited, but there is some evidence suggesting a chronic baseline opiate depletion in such patients. Additional evidence of dysregulation of the opioid system was found in the reversal of stress-induced analgesia by naloxone in PTSD combat veterans during exposure to trauma-related stimuli (Pitman, van der Kolk, Orr, & Greenberg, 1990). Taken together, these limited findings suggest that there may be chronically lower opiate levels along with enhanced opiate release in acutely stressful situations involving trauma-related stimuli. It has been hypothesized that the avoidance and numbing symptoms of PTSD may be related to this dysregulation of the opioid system in PTSD and that the use of opiates by those persons with chronic PTSD may be a form of self-medication (Richardson & Zaleski, 1983; Charney, Deutch, Krystal, Southwick, & Davis, 1993). Opiates have been shown in animal studies to be powerful suppressants of noradrenergic activity and may serve to reduce the well-documented hypersensitivity in these patients. Finding a more appropriate substitute to address this sensitivity is one of the challenges in the pharmacological treatment of PTSD.

Serotonin System. Evidence for serotoninergic (5-HT) activity playing a significant role in the pathophysiology of PTSD is found in animal models and also in a large amount of indirect evidence implicating this transmitter system in the development of several PTSD symptoms. The rapidly accumulating evidence of the usefulness of serotonin reuptake inhibitors in the treatment of PTSD symptoms also lends credence to the inclusion of this neurotransmitter in the short list of substances of primary importance in the neurobiology of PTSD.

Low serotonin functioning has been associated with destructive or aggressive and impulsive behaviors (Brown & Linnoila, 1990; Van Praag et al., 1990) and also with suicidal behavior (Stanley & Stanley, 1990). Serotonergically related dysregulation in corticostriatal-thalamocortical circuits may be relevant in the pathophysiology of both poor impulse control (Goldman-Rakic & Solomon, 1990) and non-associative learning (Kandel, 1983). Successful stress adaptation in animals has been associated with increased central 5-HT function (Joseph & Kennett, 1983) and a 5-HT pathway which arises in the median raphe and innervates the hippocampus appears to mediate resilience and adaptation to stress (Deakin, 1983). Another 5-HT pathway, arising from the dorsal raphe nucleus and innervating the amygdala, mediates the development of conditioned avoidance behaviors via postsynaptic $5-HT_2$ receptors.

The above observations suggest a possible role for the use of serotonergic drugs in the treatment of such symptoms of PTSD as poor impulse control, difficulty with concentration and short-term memory, exaggerated startle response, and avoidance behaviors. Some support for this role is found in recent clinical studies which report at least partial efficacy in treating PTSD avoidance/numbing and hyperarousal symptoms as well as intrusive memories (reviewed below). Further indirect support for the usefulness of serotonergic drugs is provided by a recent study which examined paroxetine binding in blood platelets of combat veterans with PTSD and found that platelet 5-HT uptake was significantly decreased under baseline conditions (Arora, Fitchner, & O'Connor, 1993).

A more recent study, moreover, reported PTSD symptoms induced by the administration of the 5-HT agonist m-chloro-phenyl-piperazine (MCPP). In this study of 14 combat veterans with PTSD, five subjects had a panic attack and four had a flashback in response to MCPP, as contrasted with only one flashback in response to administration of the placebo saline (Southwick et al., 1995). This may reflect hypersensitivity of postsynaptic receptors that respond to an acute influx of serotonin, resulting in an acute aggravation of symptoms, and suggests that, at least in some patients, serotonergic drugs may at least initially cause an exacerbation in intrusive symptoms. Clearly, further studies are needed to clarify the role of serotonin in this disorder.

Thyroid Function

It has been established that thyroid function tests are frequently abnormal in PTSD and that these abnormalities tend to be in an opposite direction from the abnormalities found in major depressive disorder. Patients with depression are likely to have hypothyroidism when this system is disturbed, whereas PTSD patients have been shown to have elevated thyroid function (Mason et al., 1995). As contrasted with patients with major depression who exhibit a blunted thyroid-stimulating hormone (TSH) response to thyroid-releasing hormone (TRH), some patients with PTSD have exhibited an augmented response to TRH (Kosten, Wahby, Giller, & Mason, 1990). PTSD patients also may exhibit elevated mean serum total thyroxine (T4), thyroid-binding globulin, total and free triiodothyronine (T3), and T3/T4 ratios, in some patients approaching the thyrotoxic range. The markedly elevated levels of total T3 reflect the increase in conversion of thyroxine to T3 which is mediated by peripheral catecholamines and probably reflects the increase in adrenergic activity found in PTSD. While these alterations in thyroid function may at times be striking, most patients with PTSD and major depression are likely to have thyroid function tests within the normal clinical range, but at the high and low end, respectively.

Hyperarousal and Sleep Dysfunction

A unique biological pattern of sleep has been noted in PTSD. Unlike the abnormal sleep disturbances of depression, the atypical sleep patterns in PTSD include increased rapid eye movement (REM) latency, decreased REM and stage 4 sleep, and reduced sleep efficiency. Traumatic nightmares are one of the cardinal symptoms of PTSD and occur in various sleep stages, including, but not confined to, REM sleep. These nightmares are not characteristic of typical REM-related dream anxiety attacks nor of stage 4 night terror/ nightmare syndrome as they characteristically involve trauma-related content, are temporally set in the past, and have an absence of distortion, in addition to having a high threat content. Woodward discusses the recurrent trauma-related nightmares as being related to the trauma content of the individual's memories and comments on the frequently drawn analogy between these memories and fear conditioned responses in animals (Woodward, 1995). He suggests that the recurrence of this trauma content during sleep may imply that the noradrenergic mechanisms which mediate the conditioned fear responses in PTSD may play a part in the production of these nightmares via the locus coeruleus/noradrenergic axis in sleep. The generic arousal found in PTSD may therefore also include a specific sleep-related arousal that is related to the noradrenergic response to traumatic stress. These unusual sleep patterns in PTSD help support the view of this disorder as essentially one of abnormal arousal and are frequently a major source of distress and frustration for patients suffering from PTSD and the treating clinicians as these sleep abnormalities often respond poorly to treatment.

BIOLOGICAL TREATMENT APPROACHES TO PTSD

Pharmacotherapy of PTSD— Review of the Literature

Although the published data on use of drug treatment in PTSD remains limited, there are some emerging patterns that can help the clinician to initiate a particular course of treatment. Antidepressant medications remain the mainstay of treatment and are the most studied in controlled clinical trials, but there are many reports in the literature of alleviation of specific symptoms of PTSD with the use of various other medications such as sympatholytic agents, mood-stabilizers such as lithium and anticonvulsants, benzodiazepines, and drugs which affect the dopamine, opioid, and serotoninergic systems (reviewed below). It is important to bear in mind that PTSD is a complex disorder involving multiple neurobiological systems, with evidence implicating the adrenergic, dopaminergic, hypothalamic-pituitiary-adrenocortical, opioid, and thyroid systems, and also suggestions of involvement of the serotoninergic and gamma-aminobutyric acid systems. We do not know the extent to which treatment approaches addressing individual systems are likely to be effective, thus hampering the ability of treatment trials, which are generally limited to single medications which often affect one or two specific systems, to show remission of the total cluster of PTSD symptoms. Likewise, the clinician may find only partial response in individual patients with a single medication and will find it necessary to consider addressing the multiple symptom clusters with a combination of medications. The review which follows should help in the selection of these appropriate medications to address the symptom patterns of PTSD.

Antidepressants. Antidepressant drugs utilized in PTSD controlled clinical trials include tricyclic antidepressants (TCAs), monamine oxidase inhibitors (MAOIs), and selective serotonin reuptake inhibitors (SSRIs). The MAOIs were first used in the treatment of PTSD in the late 1970s and there are two early case series reports. Hogben and Cornfield (1981) treated five inpatients with chronic "traumatic war neurosis" who had not responded to various TCAs, antipsychotics, or psychotherapy, given singly and in combination. Each of these patients responded quickly to phenelzine, with calmer mood reported as early as one day, reduction of nightmares and daytime intrusive thoughts within one to two weeks, and cessation of startle reactions and violent outbursts and lifting of depressive symptoms after two to four weeks. A second report by Walker (1982) showed similar positive effects in three patients treated with phenelzine. An open trial by Milanes, Mack, Dennison, and Slater (1984) reported on outpatients who had failed various forms of psychotherapy and pharmacotherapy over at least three years and who then completed eight weeks of treatment with phenelzine; 10 of the original group of 11 patients met DSM-III criteria for PTSD and also generalized anxiety disorder and/or dysthymia, and 1 had comorbid schizophrenia. Four of the patients failed to follow through and the patient with comorbid schizophrenia was hospitalized with an increase in psychotic symptoms and suicidality; the remaining 6 patients were evaluated over an eight-week treatment period and, as in the earlier study, 6 patients showed rapid improvement in hyperarousal and depressive symptoms without severe side effects from the medication. Two prospective open trials of phenelzine were published in 1987, both with combat veterans meeting DSM-III criteria. Davidson and colleagues observed rapid symptomatic improvement in 8 of 11 Vietnam veterans (Davidson, Walker, & Kilts, 1987). Lerer and colleagues (1987) found only partial or transient symptomatic improvement in 22 Israeli combat veterans who participated in at least four weeks of phenelzine treatment, but did report substantial improvement in insomnia symptoms and statistically significant, though not clinically impressive, improvement in several intrusive and numbing symptoms. Because of these early promising reports of phenelzine, researchers utilized this medication in two of the early placebo-controlled studies, both published in 1988. Shestatzky, Greenberg, and Lerer (1988) conducted a brief crossover study of 13 Israeli patients with varied trauma histories who met criteria for DSM-III PTSD and found no differences in response between phenelzine and placebo. Positive findings were reported by Frank and colleagues (Frank, Giller, Kosten, & Dan, 1988) in their larger study involving 46 male veterans, who were randomized to treatment with phenelzine, imipramine, or placebo. Over an average treatment period of 6.4 weeks, there was a significant reduction in symptoms of the intrusive category with both drugs, and a slight, but not significant, improvement in avoidance symptoms, with phenelzine showing a greater effect than imipramine.

Reversible MAOIs which promise greater safety, tolerability, and freedom from the potentially dangerous and life-threatening interaction with tyramine have been studied in the United States and in Europe in various anxiety disorders including PTSD. Two large trials investigated brofaromine, a selective reversible inhibitor of monoamine oxidase type A (RIMA) and the uptake of serotonin. In the U.S. study there was inconsistent evidence for efficacy, with the PTSD scales indicating no difference between drug and placebo in a population of mainly combat veteran subjects. In the European study, which treated both combat veterans and patients with other trauma histories, there was a more marked drug effect. Unfortunately, despite its obvious promise, brofaromine has since been abandoned by its manufacturer and is not available, while moclobemide, the other RIMA which has been studied in anxiety disorders, is not available in the United States.

There have been no further controlled trials with any MAOIs, but clinicians continue to consider these drugs in difficult cases that are unresponsive to other medications. A recent case series report describes positive results in five Indochinese refugees with PTSD and depression who were treated with tranylcypromine (4) and isocarboxazid (1) after failure to respond to TCAs (Demartino, Mollica, & Wilk, 1995). Although the data remains too limited to definitively assess the usefulness of MAOIs in treating PTSD, these drugs may continue to be an important part of the armamentarium and should not be ignored.

The literature on treatment of PTSD with TCAs includes three double blind placebo-controlled trials, one the above-mentioned study of imipramine with phenelzine and placebo, one with amitriptyline, and one with desipramine. Imipramine was not found to be effective in the treatment of avoidant symptoms but was better than placebo in treating intrusive symptoms, confirming Burstein's (1984) earlier report of effectiveness in treating flashbacks, and showed overall statistically significant drug effect as measured on the IES scale. However, imipramine did not have as powerful an effect as phenelzine in alleviating symptoms. A second placebo-controlled trial that studied a larger number of veterans with PTSD over an 8-week treatment period (Davidson et al., 1990) found that amitriptyline modestly alleviated distress of some of the trauma-induced symptoms, with avoidance symptoms being somewhat more reduced than intrusive symptoms, a finding that has not been replicated in other controlled trials of TCAs. The third placebo-controlled randomized trial treating 18 male veterans with TCAs was a 4-week crossover study with desipramine and placebo which showed significant improvement only in the seven patients with both PTSD and major depression and only in intrusive and depressive symptoms, not in overall anxiety and PTSD symptoms (Reist et al., 1989). An open label study of amitriptyline treatment reported the highest success occurring after 6 months of treatment (Bleich, Siegel, Garb, & Lerer, 1986), which speaks to the need for longer-term treatment in this disorder. Taken together, the results of these studies and of the other published clinical reports suggest that, as with MAOIs, the beneficial effects of TCA treatment appear to be limited in scope and to show only modest alleviation of the symptoms that are responsive to these drugs.

Southwick, Yehuda, Giller, and Charney (1994) undertook an analysis of all published reports on the use of TCAs and MAOIs in PTSD treatment in an attempt to evaluate the varied results and clarify which, if any, of the specific symptoms of PTSD respond to antidepressant intervention. They concluded that only the "reexperiencing" category of symptoms, such as flashbacks, nightmares, and intrusive memories, showed significant improvement and that phenelzine was more beneficial than TCAs. Although the symptoms of avoidance and hyperarousal were not found to respond well overall, insomnia, a prominent symptom in the hyperarousal cluster, did show moderate improvement with these antidepressants. Furthermore, the concurrent symptoms of anxiety, including panic attacks, and depression also failed to respond to treatment, a curious finding in light of the known efficacy of antidepressant treatment in major depression and panic disorder. It was also noted that, in general, global improvement was rated high overall with drug treatment. The authors suggest that this may reflect positive effects in such areas of functioning as social relationships, family, and work in ways that are not measured in these studies. Also, they note that improvement in even one symptom cluster in these often chronic and treatment-resistant patients can be viewed by the clinician as making a substantial difference in the patient's overall presentation.

One TCA medication that is of particular interest in the potential treatment of PTSD due to its serotonergic properties is clomipramine. There is one report of an open trial of seven Vietnam veterans with PTSD and accompanying OCD symptoms, in which marked reduction in both the intrusive symptoms of PTSD and in the Yale-Brown obsession score was noted in six of the seven patients (Chen, 1991). This author points out the similarity between the intrusive thoughts of PTSD and the obsessions of OCD. We have also seen clinically that many PTSD patients engage in brief periods of compulsive behavior, often in response to reminders of their prior trauma, when they appear to be in a highly agitated state. The possible relationship between these two illnesses may carry implications for the choice of drugs and also the dosage range, as OCD generally requires high doses of the SSRI drugs in order to have a good response.

The class of antidepressants that shows promise in being more globally effective in treating all categories of PTSD symptoms is the SSRIs. These agents are probably the most widely used currently in the treatment of PTSD and have recently become the best studied. The open trials of SSRIs include three using sertraline, all of which show promising results. A small study of rape victims by Rothbaum, Ninan, and Thomas (1996) and a second small study which included nine patients with comorbid alcoholism (Brady, Sonne, & Roberts, 1995) showed positive results in sertraline treatment of civilian PTSD. The Brady and colleagues study included six women and three men and found significant improvement in all three PTSD symptom clusters as well as improvement in alcohol usage in the six patients who completed the 12-week trial. A third trial by Kline and colleagues (Kline, Dow, Brown, & Matloff, 1994) treated combat veterans who had failed other agents and reported positive responses in 12 (63 percent) of the 19 patients. There is now underway a very large double-blind, multi-center controlled trial comparing sertraline to placebo. The more than 200 patients in this study represent the largest data set to date, but the results of this study are not yet available.

A second SSRI which shows promise for the treatment of PTSD is fluvoxamine. Our center has recently seen very positive results with this drug in treating civilians while Marmar and colleagues had good results with veterans (Marmar et al., 1996). A European study used fluvoxamine in the treatment of a group of Dutch World War II Resistance veterans, both male and female, with PTSD or partial PTSD (meeting criteria for either the intrusive or avoidance cluster of symptoms). At four weeks there was significant change on the PTSD self-rating scale in these elderly patients who had suffered from intractable PTSD complaints for decades, and at the end of the 12-week study the gains were maintained (DeBoer et al., 1992). Although the quantitative improvement for the group as a whole was limited, 5 of the 11 subjects who completed the trial reported substantial improvement, especially in sleep quality, and insisted on continued use of the drug. The specific symptoms that improved for the group as a whole were survival guilt, insomnia, nightmares, intrusive recollections, explosiveness, and fear; and interestingly, there was little effect on avoidance symptoms and on depressive symptoms.

The evidence for efficacy of fluoxetine in various psychiatric disorders, including PTSD, has grown rapidly since its introduction in the United States in 1987. Several case series reports were published in the early 1990s and reported positive results with this drug for both veterans and several nonveteran men and women. The civilian patients had been exposed to sexual assault or industrial/motor vehicle trauma (Davidson et al., 1991). Two studies carried out at the National Center for PTSD found marked improvement in intrusive, avoidant, and arousal symptoms in 13 of 20 Vietnam veterans (McDougle, Southwick, Charney, & Saint James, 1991) and moderate to marked improvement overall in 12 of 19 military veterans (Nagy, Morgan, Southwick, Steven, & Charney, 1993). Shay (1992) treated 18 depressed Vietnam veterans with fluoxetine at a dose of 20 to 80 mg and found that, in addition to helping with mood, the treatment resulted in a marked decline in explosiveness and decreased duration of rageful episodes as well as a greater ability to think before acting on anger. Those who had been treated with neuroleptics also reported better relief from explosive rages, fewer problematic side effects, and a greater sense of being in contact with themselves and the world when treated with fluoxetine.

The one published placebo-controlled trial of an SSRI was with fluoxetine and included 64 patients, 31 military veterans and 33 civilian adult survivors of childhood sexual abuse (van der Kolk et al., 1994). In this 5-week treatment study, fluoxetine significantly reduced overall PTSD symptomatology, especially in the numbing symptoms of the numbing/arousal cluster with the civilian patients, who overall had a lower level of symptomatology than the veterans. The improvement from drug was due to the inclusion of civilians, and the authors found no difference between drug and placebo in veterans. Of note, the improvement in PTSD symptoms was also accompanied by a decrease in depressive symptoms. Results of a recently completed controlled trial of fluoxetine and placebo at our center are now undergoing comprehensive analysis and demonstrate a robust drug effect in civilians with chronic PTSD treated over a 12-week treatment period, with significant improvement seen in all symptom clusters.

In summary, although there is only one published placebo-controlled trial of SSRI treatment in PTSD, there are several case reports and open trials which have consistently reported efficacy in treating symptoms of the avoidance/numbing cluster and in the intrusive and hyperarousal clusters as well (see Table 16.1). We anticipate that more positive findings from our own recent study and from other sites will continue to be published, lending further support for the use of these drugs in PTSD treatment, at least in civilians.

Additional Drugs with Serotonergic Effects. Buspirone is a unique anxiolytic agent, which acts as a 5-HT_{1A} partial agonist and is most often used in the treatment of generalized anxiety disorder. There is one report in the literature of three combat veterans treated with doses ranging from 35 to 60 mg (Wells et al., 1991). All three reported marked reductions in anxiety, insomnia, flashbacks, and also depressed mood. No patient showed improvement in avoidant/numbing symptoms.

A drug which has been used to treat PTSD-related nightmares is cyproheptadine, a 5-HT antagonist. This was reported to be effective in suppressing recurrent traumatic nightmares in case reports of two (Harsch, 1986) and four (Brophy, 1991) PTSD pa-

TABLE 16.1   Controlled Drug Trials for Treatment of Posttraumatic Stress Disorder

INVESTIGATOR	SUBJECTS	AGENT(S)/DOSE	TREATMENT LENGTH/ DESIGN	RESULTS
Shestatzky et al., 1988	13 pts, DSM-III PTSD, varied trauma	Phenelzine, 45–75 mg	Greater than 4-week/ crossover	No difference in response between phenelzine and placebo
Frank et al., 1988	46 male veterans, DSM-III-R PTSD	Imipramine, 50–300 mg Phenelzine, 15–75 mg	Mean 6.4 weeks	Intrusive scores on IES decreased substantially with phenelzine, also decreased with imipramine; some decrease in avoidance subscale with phenelzine; no difference in measures with placebo group
Reist et al., 1989	18 male veterans DSM-III PTSD, most with other concurrent diagnoses	Desipramine, 100–200 mg	4 week/ crossover	Significant improvement on IES intrusion subscale and depressive symptoms only for group (n=7) with concurrent major depression; no change overall in anxiety, PTSD symptoms
Davidson et al., 1990, 1993	62 male veterans DSM-III	Amitriptyline, 50–300 mg	8 weeks	Amitriptyline superior to placebo on Hamilton anxiety and depression; marginally significant improvement on IES avoidance and intrusive scales
Braun et al., 1990	16 Israeli patients DSM-III PTSD, varied trauma	Alprazolam, 2.5–6 mg	5 weeks	Alprazolam superior to placebo on Hamilton anxiety; no difference on IES, Hamilton depression
van der Kolk et al., 1994	31 veterans; 33 civilian trauma victims	Fluoxetine, 20–40 mg	5 weeks double-blind; 5 weeks open	Significant reduction in symptoms, including intrusive/numbing; one half no longer met PTSD criteria

tients. This may be of particular interest in light of the increasingly common usage of cyproheptadine in treating the sexual dysfunction associated with the SSRIs.

A recent case series of a small number of combat veterans treated with trazodone (Hertzberg, Feldman, Beckham, & Davidson, 1996), a serotonergic antidepressant with alpha-adregnergic blocking activity, which also is known for its sedative effects and its ability to enhance sleep quality, demonstrated, as expected, significant improvement in sleep, with sleep duration doubling, on average, over the treatment period. Moderate improvement in PTSD symptoms, especially reexperiencing and hyperarousal, were reported, but only

after four months of treatment as contrasted with the two to three months required for sleep to improve. This data offers further evidence of the extended treatment period necessary for PTSD symptoms to respond, in addition to lending support for serotonin involvement in this disorder.

Anxiolytics. It seems logical that patients with sleep problems who are very anxious, jittery, hyperaroused, easily startled, and autonomically unstable would benefit by the use of benzodiazepine drugs, which affect the GABA-benzodiazepine system. These drugs have also been shown in animal studies to reduce LC activity and stress-induced increases in NE turnover and in prefrontal dopamine activity, two of the biological factors involved in PTSD. However, there is limited evidence for their efficacy as single agents in treating even the hyperarousal symptoms of this disorder. DeBoer and colleagues (1992) noted that most of the Dutch World War II Resistance fighters with chronic PTSD symptoms who participated in a fluvoxamine study had a long treatment-seeking history and many had been treated with benzodiazepines without satisfactory outcome. These medications, particularly the more potent short-acting ones, also can be the cause of uncomfortable and even dangerous withdrawal symptoms. A report of alprazolam use in PTSD detailed severe reactions in eight combat veterans who were gradually withdrawn from the medication after receiving doses ranging from 2 to 9 mg/day over periods of one to five years (Risse et al., 1990). This clinic had treated a total of 116 patients with alprazolam over a 5-year period, with 79 of the patients having been tapered or discontinued from the medication during that period. While no difficulties were reported in 45 of the 79 patients, 34 had some degree of clinically significant withdrawal reactions with at least mild rebound symptoms. Of these 34 patients, 8, all of whom had prior history of alcohol abuse or benzodiazepine dependence, had severe reactions, including anxiety, sleep disturbance with increased nightmares, rage reactions, hyperalertness, and increase in intrusive thoughts to a level not experienced before, 6 reported homicidal ideation, and 4 reported dissociative symptoms for the first time. These results suggest that, at least in some PTSD patients with a substance abuse history, the benefit of alprazolam may be outweighed by its risks. Another open trial by Feldman (1987) reported reduced insomnia, anxiety, irritability, and hyperarousal in 16 of 20 veterans with PTSD, but cautioned that 4 patients exhibited benzodiazepine-induced disinhibition marked by increased outbursts of anger.

The only randomized, double-blind study reported with this class of drugs was a 5-week crossover trial with a 2-week interim phase which compared alprazolam to placebo in a group of 10 Israeli patients, including both combat veterans and civilians with DSM-III PTSD (Braun, Greenberg, Dasberg, & Lerer,

1990). Because alprazolam, a triazolobenzodiazepine, has been reported to have antianxiety, antidepressant, antipanic, and possibly antiphobic properties, the authors expected that it might be useful in PTSD, which has a spectrum of symptoms encompassing these elements. Although it did modestly relieve some anxiety and depressive symptoms, it had no effect on core PTSD symptoms.

Lowenstein, Hornstein, and Farber (1988) reported on an open label study of clonazepam in a group of patients with PTSD and multiple personality disorder. Clonazepam is a long-acting, high-potency benzodiazepine with antikindling properties, originally used in treatment of epilepsy, and has also been reported to have an effect on serotonin systems in the CNS possibly causing an increase in serotonin at central sites in addition to its agonist effects on benzodiazepine receptors (Chouinard, 1985; Chouinard, Young, & Annable, 1983; Greenblatt, Miller, & Shader, 1987; Lowenstein et al., 1988). In the five cases described, the length of treatment ranged from 6 to 21 months and doses ranged from 1 to 6 mg/day in standing doses with occasional addition p.r.n. doses. The group demonstrated long-lasting improvement in nightmares, early insomnia, intrusive recollections, panic and severe anxiety, and also in intensity of flashbacks. The authors also report successful treatment of PTSD symptoms in a number of additional MPD patients, with nightmares and insomnia showing the greatest improvement, and flashbacks, anxiety, hyperarousal, and panic symptoms improving as well. They caution, however, that several other patients responded in a manner more typical of MPD patients taking other benzodiazepines, exhibiting an initial brief decrease in symptoms followed by return to baseline and lack of response to increasing doses.

It remains unclear as to whether benzodiazepines should have a prominent role in the treatment of PTSD. Friedman and Southwick (1995) point out a great disparity in prescribing practices for this class of medications. In some settings up to 71 percent of PTSD patients have received benzodiazepines, while in other settings, few PTSD patients receive them, as many clinicians are reluctant to prescribe them in this population which is known for having high rates of alcoholism and chemical dependency. These authors suggest that benzodiazepines may actually be of particular value in the treatment of those PTSD patients who also suffer from alcoholism/substance abuse, and point out that these drugs have been reported to be safe in use with alcoholics when prescribed rationally (Ciraulo, Sands, & Shader, 1988). As these authors suggest, clonazepam, with its low abuse potential and its assumed greater safety with regard to rebound anxiety/withdrawal, and its potential efficacy, may be the benzodiazepine that should be further studied in the treatment of PTSD symptoms. Our clinical experience with patients leads us to support further study of this potential role for clonazepam in the treatment of PTSD.

Mood-Stabilizing Agents. Lithium is well-known as a mood-stabilizing agent in recurrent affective disorders and has also been advocated as a possible treatment for impulsivity. There are two open trials of lithium in PTSD, the first by van der Kolk (1983) in which 14 of 22 patients without bipolar disorder experienced marked reduction in autonomic arousal, a greater capacity to cope with stress, and reduced alcohol consumption, and the second reporting improvement in irritability, inappropriate anger, anxiety, and insomnia in 5 patients (cited in Friedman & Southwick, 1995).

Anticonvulsants with mood-stabilizing properties and anti-kindling effects have been used effectively in bipolar illness and may also prove to be of particular value in the treatment of PTSD. There are several published reports of the successful use of the anticonvulsants, valproate and carbamazepine. Lipper and colleagues (1986) reported on 10 veterans with PTSD, all of whom had normal EEGs and only 1 of whom had an additional Axis I diagnosis of generalized anxiety disorder. In a 5-week open study, this group of 10 veterans showed significant improvement in the reexperiencing symptoms of nightmares, flashbacks, and intrusive recollections, and also had a significant reduction in hostility. The authors hypothesize that the kindling model, which has been proposed to explain the action of carbamazepine in bipolar disorder (Post & Uhde, 1985), may also be applicable to PTSD, wherein the initial traumata are viewed as having produced biochemical or bioelectric

changes in the CNS, resulting in abnormal neuronal sensitization and increased susceptibility to the arousal caused by memories, dreams or environmental reminders. Another open trial of 10 Vietnam veterans with PTSD and with normal EEGs reported improvement in impulsivity, irritability, and violent behavior, but did not report on PTSD symptomatology (Wolf, Alavi, & Mosnaim, 1988). There are also three case reports reporting reduction in flashbacks, traumatic nightmares, and insomnia with carbamazepine in a total of five patients with PTSD and abnormal EEGs consistent with complex partial seizures (cited in Friedman & Southwick, 1995). An interesting recent report of treatment with carbamazepine of 26 children and adolescents with PTSD secondary to sexual abuse reported total remission of PTSD symptoms in 22 and significant improvement in the other 6 patients during an average 35-day hospital stay (Looff, Grimley, Kuller, Martin, & Shonfield, 1995). Unfortunately, the authors do not report on followup after discharge to the community.

Valproate appears to have a different effect on PTSD symptoms, suggesting a different mechanism of action, in spite of its sharing antikindling properties with carbamazepine. Fesler (1991) reported on an open trial of valproate in 14 Vietnam veterans who could not tolerate lithium or carbamazepine due to unacceptable side effects. In contrast with carbamazepine, none of the patients reported significant improvement in reexperiencing symptoms, but 11 reported significant improvement in hyperarousal and 9 in avoidant symptoms. Five patients in this group were also taking antipsychotic medications for paranoia, psychotic symptoms, or thought disorder, and 1 discontinued the antipsychotic while the other 4 decreased the dosage. Only 1 had been taking a benzodiazepine (clonazepam) and this was discontinued after stabilization with valproate. The veterans were followed over an average of 13.6 months. Three who discontinued valproate after 12, 14, and 16 months, respectively, did not experience withdrawal symptoms nor a return to the prior level of PTSD symptomatology over a 2-month followup period.

Two other potentially useful anticonvulsants which have only recently been applied to the treatment of psychiatric disorders are lamitrogine and gabapentin. In considering these agents, we have noted reports in the literature of mood-enhancing properties, as well as reports of reduced irritability and anxiety, with these agents when they have been utilized in the treatment of epilepsy and also in some instances of application to bipolar illness (Calabrese, Fatemi, & Woyshville, 1996; Dimond, Pande, Lamoreaux, & Pierce, 1996; Ryback & Ryback, 1995).

In summary, these various anti-kindling agents have been reported to be effective in reducing impulsivity, irritability, and violent behavior, as well as relieving hyperarousal and intrusive symptoms in PTSD patients, and may prove to be useful at least as adjunctive treatment and perhaps even as single agents for some patients.

Antipsychotics.   There is little evidence of efficacy of antipsychotics in treatment of PTSD, and many clinical case reports explicitly relate failure of symptomatic relief with this class of drugs. Although it is less common now with our better appreciation of the symptoms of PTSD, many patients have been given various diagnoses during encounters with the mental health system before finally being identified as victims of PTSD. Hogben and Cornfield (1981) refer to the failure to diagnose traumatic war neurosis and relate a history of other diagnoses, most often chronic paranoid schizophrenia in their patients who responded to phenelzine after failure of other psychotropic medications, including neuroleptics. They suggest that accurate diagnosis is difficult as symptoms can mimic substance abuse disorder, schizophrenia, and phobic and depressive states. The hallmark reexperiencing symptoms of nightmares and flashbacks may be difficult and painful for patients to relate, while the constricted affect which reflects emotional numbing, the social isolation, and the periodic rageful and aggressive outbursts can be observed by others and may be interpreted as schizophrenic symptoms. Another confounding factor is that patients may refer to their vivid daytime visualizations and flashback experiences as "hallucinations" even though these reflect specific past traumatic events and are unlike the bizarre hallucinations of the schizophrenic patient. Yet PTSD patients

do at times display psychotic features which may respond to brief intervention with neuroleptic agents, and those patients with borderline personality features that exhibit prominent ego disorganization may benefit by ongoing treatment with low dose neuroleptics, at least during periods of high stress.

Other Medications.   Given the excessive adrenergic activity present in patients with PTSD, it would be logical to use sympatholytic agents in the treatment of the disorder. In spite of promising results reported by Kolb and associates (Kolb, Burris, & Griffiths, 1984) with both clonidine, an alpha-2 adrenergic agonist, and propranolol, a postsynaptic beta adrenergic blocking agent, very little attention has been given to these medications in the literature. The few open trials of clonidine report some reduction in both reexperiencing and hyperarousal symptoms. Kolb and colleagues (1984) reported reduction of nightmares and intrusive thoughts and also in the symptoms of hypervigilance, insomnia, exaggerated startle, and angry outbursts in nine Vietnam veterans. Improvement in nightmares, insomnia and startle reactions was noted in Cambodian refugees with both depression and PTSD when clonidine was added to the TCA imipramine (Kinzie & Leung, 1989).

Propranolol has been reported to reduce intrusive and arousal symptoms in Vietnam veterans (Kolb et al., 1984), but was not found to be effective in an open trial with Cambodian refugees (Kinzie, 1989). A more promising study that was an open label, but an A-B-A design with 6-weeks off–6-weeks on–6 weeks off medication, demonstrated significant reductions in both intrusive and arousal symptoms in the majority of a group of 11 children with PTSD precipitated by physical and/or sexual abuse (Famularo, Kinscherff, & Fenton, 1988).

With no controlled studies and very limited case report data, it is difficult to asses the usefulness of these sympatholytic agents, but given the prominent sympathetic arousal in many patients with PTSD, it would be appropriate to further consider these agents, at least as adjunctive treatment. We are hopeful that there will be further study to help guide clinicians in this area.

Selection of Pharmacological Agents in Treatment of PTSD

It is apparent that clinicians have found many different medications from various classes to be useful clinically in treating the various symptoms of PTSD. Our review of both controlled trials and case reports suggests that most medications affect only some of the symptoms and have not been proven to effect a cure of the disorder. As clinicians dealing with the whole person, it would be a mistake to limit our approach to the alleviation of specific symptoms without assessing the overall effect of treatment in reducing the disability resulting from the illness and allowing the patient to resume a more normal life. But it is also clear that much suffering can be reduced by targeting those symptoms which may be alleviated by medications in an attempt to relieve some of the pain and distress of the illness. Sargant and Slater (1972), pioneers in biological treatments of PTSD, who worked with acute PTSD patients in World War II, expressed their positive view of antidepressants as contrasted with one form of psychotherapy, abreaction, which was used widely during the middle years of this century. They asserted that the TCA and MAOI antidepressants were more valuable than the traditional abreactive therapies with their patients. They explained that as the patients improved with medication they were able to repress their fears, which were eventually forgotten without the need to "ventilate" them, as happens with human beings in general when they are well.

Sargant and Slater (1972) seemed to suggest that drug therapy is a sufficient treatment in itself and is, in fact, a better approach than psychotherapy for the patient populations that they treated. However, psychotherapeutic approaches for PTSD were poorly developed during the time period that these authors were practicing, and the abreactive (uncovering) approach to therapy, which has now been abandoned by the majority of clinicians treating PTSD patients, was the predominant method. But clearly, pharmacotherapy may be a cost-effective treatment for those patients for whom this approach is effective and sufficient, and may be successful in "sealing over" the symptoms and enabling the patient to resume normal functioning.

A different understanding of the usefulness of pharmacotherapy was portrayed by Hogben and Cornfield (1981) in their case series report of veterans who had benefitted from phenelzine treatment. They observed that the medication "actually seemed to enhance psychotherapy...by stimulating an intense abreaction that had not been achieved in earlier therapies with or without psychotropic medication" (Hogben & Cornfield, 1981, p. 444). They described a "period of emotional outpouring" which included three distinct phases, the first consisting primarily of rage, followed by depression, and then a final brief period of elation. The patients processed old memories from various time periods of their lives, including traumatic war scenes, and exhibited more intensity and better integration of associated affect with the latter memories during treatment with phenelzine.

The individual clinician must decide the approach that is appropriate to each individual patient and then carefully apply the drug treatment that is most likely to achieve the best results. Table 16.2 summarizes the findings of the main classes of drugs which have been used in treatment of PTSD and may serve as a general guide to the initial selection of pharmacotherapeutic agents.

Factors in Response to Treatment

Although various therapeutic approaches to the treatment of PTSD, including behavior, dynamic, and group therapies, as well as pharmacotherapy, have been found to be efficacious, PTSD continues to prove to be an illness that is extremely difficult to treat (Burstein, 1984; Friedman, 1988; Giller, 1990; Solomon, et al., 1992). It is a heterogeneous condition that is frequently accompanied by psychiatric comorbidity in patients with widely variable trauma histories. Drugs that are effective with one sub-group of patients may have little or no effect in another, as, for example, was demonstrated in the studies with phenelzine cited above which showed great benefit in reducing intrusive symptoms in U.S. veterans, but

TABLE 16.2 Reported Drug Efficacy in Alleviating PTSD Symptoms

| | ADRENERGIC INHIBITORS[1] | BENZODIAZEPINES | ANTIDEPRESSANTS | | | MOOD STABILIZERS | |
			MAOI	SSRI[2]	TCA	Lithium[1]	Anticonvulsants[1]
Cluster B: Reexperiencing/ Intrusive	Positive results with propranolol and clonidine in adults and children	No effect demonstrated in controlled trials Clonazepam may be beneficial in some patients.	Positive results in veteran populations Promising results with reversible MAOIs	Positive effect	Some reduction, especially with imipramine, clomipramine Not as effective as phenelzine	No effect	Positive effects
Cluster C: Avoidant/ Numbing	No measurable effect	No effect	No significant effect	Positive effect on both avoidant and numbing symptoms	Little effect perhaps some with amitriptyline	No effect	Some decrease in avoidance
Cluster D: Hyperarousal	Positive results with propranolol and clonidine in adults and children	No effect on core PTSD symptoms Some reduction in general anxiety	Some reduction, with insomnia the most significant clinically	Significant effects in all symptoms, also reduction in rageful episodes	No effect	Perhaps helpful with irritability, insomnia	Reduction in insomnia and irritability as well as hostility and violent behavior

[1]Open trials and case reports only.

[2]The only antidepressants clearly efficacious in clusters B, C, and D.

less effect in Israeli veterans. Understanding the factors that may predict response can help the clinician in determining treatment.

In a study of 62 veterans treated with the TCA amitriptyline, Davidson and colleagues evaluated several possible predictors that included general measures of age, exposure to trauma, anxiety, personality traits, severity of PTSD symptoms, and psychiatric comorbidity (Davidson et al., 1993). They observed better response with lower baseline levels of depression, neuroticism, combat intensity, anxiety, impaired concentration, somatic symptoms, and feelings of guilt. A lower level of autonomic arousal as indicated by fewer panic symptoms, as well as less avoidance of thoughts and feelings related to the trauma and lower baseline levels of intrusive emotional reactions, was associated with a good outcome. The factor which had the greatest effect on outcome measures of PTSD symptoms was found to be combat intensity, with the subjects with the highest amount of exposure having the poorest response to medication. This suggests that understanding and quantifying the extent of the trauma history is an important part of the evaluation process. This may prevent both the clinician and the patient from having too high a level of expectation for a course of treatment and can help to better plan the treatment course.

Dosages of Medication. Selecting dosages of medications in the treatment of PTSD may at times be challenging. Many patients exhibit prominent side effects, especially those reflecting sympathetic arousal, with the use of typical doses of antidepressants, while some patients also exhibit a higher tolerance for medications. Often a longer treatment course, as well as higher doses of medication, are necessary in order to begin to see response to the PTSD symptoms in patients, even though there may be some initial improvement in mood and sense of well-being reported by patients and their families. Table 16.3 provides a list of medications that may be used and dosage ranges. The clinician must bear in mind that the response to medication may be slow and that, barring intolerable side effects, a trial of a medication should last at least 8 to 12 weeks before determining that it is ineffective, and that higher doses than typically used to treat depressive illnesses

TABLE 16.3 Medications in Posttraumatic Stress Disorder: Dose Rangers

DRUG CATEGORY	DOSE RANGE (MG/D)
Antidepressants	
Selective serotonin reuptake inhibitors	
Fluoxetine	10–60
Fluvoxamine	50–300
Sertraline	50–200
Paroxetine	10–60
Tricyclic Antidepressants	
Amitriptyline	50–300
Impramine	50–300
Monoamine Oxidase Inhibitors	
Phenelzine	15–90
Tranylcypromine	20–60
Triazolopyridine	
Trazodone	150–300
Phenylpiperazine	
Nefazodone	200–600
Anticonvulsants	
Carbamazepine	200–1500
Valproic Acid	125–2000
Mood Stabilizers	
Lithium Carbonate	300–1200
Antiadrenergic Drugs	
Propranolol	20–160
Clonidine	0.1–0.4
Anxiolytics	
Benzodizepines	
Clonazepam	0.5–6
Lorazepam	0.5–4
Chlordiazepoxide	5–40
Diazepam	2–40
Azapirones	
Buspirone	5–60

and other anxiety disorders may be necessary to achieve results.

Comorbidity.   Another factor which contributes significantly to the difficulty in effecting a cure for patients with PTSD is that it often is comorbid with other psychiatric disorders. In fact, some authors have concluded that it is a clinical entity that rarely occurs alone, that an individual who meets criteria for PTSD will likely also meet criteria for another major mood or anxiety disorder, for alcoholism or other substance abuse disorder, or a personality disorder (Friedman & Yehuda, 1995). Each of these additional diagnoses must be considered in determining the treatment course and may influence the choice of medication as well as the approach to psychotherapy.

One of the most common and most recognized comorbid conditions in PTSD is that of substance abuse, including alcohol and drug abuse and dependence. Studies have estimated the prevalence of PTSD among populations seeking treatment for alcohol dependence to be between 30 percent and 50 percent, and substance abuse or dependence approaches 80 percent in some veteran populations with PTSD (Cottler, Compton, Mager, Spitznagel, & Janca, 1992). It remains unclear as to what causal relationship may exist between these disorders, but it is clear that each of them causes difficulty in emotional and behavioral regulation and has a detrimental effect on social relationships. The fragility of emotional and biological homeostasis and difficulties in self-regulation common to these disorders may also compromise the individual's ability to benefit from treatment. Both illnesses must be addressed and the typical substance abuse treatment that involves individual and group psychotherapy and utilizes cognitive-behavioral techniques may also be useful in some of the PTSD-related issues. For example, the learning model that is commonly used in substance abuse treatment to deal with self-regulation involves identifying and extinguishing automatic and impulsive responses to drug-related cues. This method may also help patients to deal with the automatic responses triggered by trauma-related stimuli. A multi-phase approach to these combined disorders is suggested, in which the first phase is one of stabilization and safety and the establishment of solid motivation before continuing into a period of more focused PTSD and substance abuse treatment, often in group format. As reviewed above,

there is some promise in treating PTSD and comorbid alcohol dependence with sertraline and, by extrapolation, with the other SSRIs. Medications may be helpful in solidifying the stabilization period and may continue to stabilize the patient through the more intense working-through period of therapy.

Other Axis I disorders that are commonly found to exist with PTSD include panic disorder and generalized anxiety disorder and also major depression. Some of the symptoms of these disorders overlap with PTSD, such as the impaired concentration and insomnia of GAD and depression, the physiological symptoms such as trembling, shortness of breath, heart palpitations, dizziness, and nausea that occur in panic and GAD, and the generalized hyperarousal symptoms of irritability, edginess or hypervigilance that may occur in GAD. Some of these symptoms, when occurring only in a single illness, may respond well to a single intervention such as a TCA antidepressant or a benzodiazepine, but appear to be more resistant to medication treatment when they occur in the context of multiple diagnoses. It remains imperative that the clinician must do a complete diagnostic assessment in order to select appropriate medication and to monitor response to treatment.

Other conditions comorbid with PTSD include personality traits and disorders, especially Cluster B. Although we have seen some responsiveness in personality traits with medication, the treatment of these disorders generally requires extensive psychotherapy and must be considered a confounding factor in treatment.

Female Gender Issues in PTSD.   A population survey of 2,663 men and women in the St. Louis area asked about traumatic events and PTSD symptoms as well as substance use. After controlling for other variables, the data analysis found that female gender was one of the predictors of PTSD (Cottler et al., 1992). The lifetime prevalence of DSM-III-R PTSD in the National Comorbidity Survey was found to be twice as high in women as in men, with a rate of 10.4 percent and 5.0 percent, respectively (Kessler, Sonnega, Bromet, & Nelson, 1995). In light of these findings, the increasing recognition by clinicians of PTSD in this segment of the population is encouraging. Also, the data on the responsiveness to SSRIs in female civilians with PTSD is promising.

Females of childbearing age may present a special treatment challenge. Response to medication may be different during pregnancy and potential side effects may be more of an issue for women who are pregnant and/or who are breastfeeding. The increase in metabolism that accompanies these conditions should be considered in assessing medication dosages, and clinicians may find that an increase in dose is frequently warranted. Clinicians should also be knowledgeable about potential teratogenic effects of the various classes of medication used in PTSD, and should be prepared to discuss any potential risks with a patient who is pregnant or is considering pregnancy. In approaching these discussions, the clinician should be aware of the distrust of authority figures that is often prominent in patients with PTSD and should be respectful of the woman's concern not only about her own health, but also the health of her baby.

A recent review of the literature by Baum and Misri (1996) on the use of SSRIs during pregnancy and lactation recommended a conservative approach to their use, especially avoiding them during the first trimester and then tapering them prior to delivery and also discouraged their use during breastfeeding. Although they found no evidence of teratogenesis with in utero exposure to fluoxetine, the one SSRI that has been studied, they note that behavioral teratogenesis has not been addressed. A prospective study of 128 pregnant women found that the rate of miscarriage with fluoxetine treatment (13.5 percent) approximated that in women treated with TCAs (12.2 percent) and was higher than the nondepressed control group (6.8 percent) (Pastuszak et al., 1993). Other authors have cited the spontaneous abortion rate as 15 percent for the general population (Goldstein & Marvel, 1993).

Wisner and Wheeler (1994) reviewed the literature on antidepressant treatment during breast-feeding. They point out that the decision to use medication while breast-feeding is an individual one and that the risks and benefits should be carefully considered. If the decision is made to use a medication, they recommend that the antidepressant chosen be one of the group which were not found in quantifiable amounts in nurslings and for which no adverse effects were reported. This group includes amitriptyline, nortriptyline, desipramine, clomipramine, and sertraline. As adverse effects of sedation and respiratory depression were reported with doxepin use and colic with fluoxetine use, these two antidepressants are not recommended during lactation.

Cultural Factors. Data from treatment of the many refugees from Southeast Asia who have suffered varying degrees of trauma before emigrating to the United State has begun to accumulate. Clinical observation suggests that slightly lower doses of medications may be therapeutic in the treatment of PTSD and depressive symptoms, although there are no pharmacokinetic studies to support this hypothesis (Demartino et al., 1995).

Other cultural factors should be borne in mind when selecting psychotropic medications. For example, Indochinese populations eat a tyramine-rich diet (soy sauce, pickled food, fish sauces) and also commonly use various herbal remedies, many of which have anticholinergic properties which may exacerbate side effects of TCAs and MAOIs. Also, in some cultures and subcultures, it is common to share medications and patients should be educated about the possible dangers of doing so with many of the drugs used in PTSD treatment as there could be serious and even life-threatening consequences of combining these medications with other substances.

Phasic Changes in Symptoms with Ongoing Treatment of PTSD. The clinician frequently finds that the status of an individual patient may vary widely from visit to visit, especially if the visits are spaced far apart. The concept of tonic and phasic alteration first identified and elaborated on by Horowitz (1973) is a typical pattern in patients with chronic PTSD. Symptoms of hyperarousal and intrusive symptoms may predominate for a period of time and then be replaced by prominent numbing and avoidance symptoms. This phasic pattern may occur without reference to external factors or may reflect such things as anniversary dates of losses or of especially disturbing traumatic memories. Trauma-related memories and emotions may be triggered by events that are directly related to the traumatic incident(s), such as court dates for those who have been assaulted and have pressed charges, requiring that they face the assailant in court and revisit the details of the trauma. Certain seasons or specific types of weather may cause an increase in reexperiencing symptoms for those whose trauma may not have a specific anniversary date, but may have occurred only during a certain time of year. For those for whom a pattern can be identified, the clinician can anticipate the increase in a particular symptom or symptom-complex and may be able to ameliorate the distress by planned changes in medication. Alternatively, the expectation that this symptom change will occur and the knowledge that it may be brief may prevent the clinician from making unnecessary medication changes.

SUMMARY

We have begun to understand some of the physiological underpinnings of PTSD and have acquired a significant amount of information about biological therapies for this disorder. Although clearly this knowledge is still in the preliminary stages, we now have some structure with which to approach psychopharmacologic treatment. We know that the reexperiencing symptoms respond to all of the major types of antidepressants, including the monoamine oxidase inhibitors, the tricyclics, and the serotonin reuptake inhibitors, with nightmares, intrusive memories during waking, and even flashback experiences being alleviated in many patients. Although not as well documented, the sympatholytic medications such as clonidine and propranolol and the anticonvulsant carbamazepine also appear to be helpful for this symptom cluster.

The symptoms of avoidance and numbing have been the least responsive to treatment, but the SSRIs appear to be somewhat effective, and the anticonvulsant valproate has also been shown to significantly decrease these symptoms.

The hyperarousal symptoms as a group are generally unresponsive to the antidepressants with the exception of SSRIs, although insomnia appears to respond also to the TCAs and MAOIs. Propranolol and clonidine may be particularly useful for this symptom cluster. Other potentially useful agents include the benzodiazepines, especially the longer-acting agents, and valproate and lithium. Insomnia may be helped by all of these agents that are useful for the hyperarousal symptoms, as well as being responsive to cyproheptadine and trazodone.

The clinician who takes a thoughtful approach to medication treatment and who also considers the many complicating factors in PTSD treatment is likely to succeed in alleviating many of the disturbing symptoms of this disorder and to help restore the patient to a pre-trauma level of functioning. An initial careful evaluation and ongoing assessment of symptoms and functioning as well as attention to the more global assessment of well-being are important in optimizing treatment. Providing a safe therapeutic environment and constantly attending to the therapeutic alliance with these traumatized individuals is also a critical factor in successful treatment. The healing power of the therapeutic relationship is one of the factors that remains constant even when the treatment approach is purely biological. The constancy and reliability of this relationship is especially germane for this patient population where the world has been experienced as inconstant, unsafe, and unpredictable. Work with these patients can be difficult and tiring, while watching these damaged individuals begin to heal and to resume their rightful place as functioning members of society can be intensely rewarding.

REFERENCES

Adler, A. (1943). Neuropsychiatric complications in victims of Boston's Cocoanut Grove disaster. *Journal of the American Medical Association, 123,* 1098–1101.

American Psychiatric Association (1980). *Diagnostic and statistical manual of mental disorders* (3rd ed.). Washington, DC: Author.

Arora, R. C., Fitchner, C. G., & O'Connor, F. (1993). Paroxetine binding in the blood platelets of posttraumatic stress disorder patients. *Life Science, 53,* 919–928.

Baum, A. L., & Misri, S. (1996) Selective serotonin-reuptake inhibitors in pregnancy and lactation. *Harvard Revised Psychiatry, 4,* 117–125.

Blanchard, E. B., Hickling, E. J., Taylor, A. E., Loos, W. R., & Gerardi, R. (1994). The psychophysiology of motor vehicle accident related posttraumatic stress disorder. *Behavior Therapy, 25,* 453–467.

Blanchard, E. B., Kolb, L. C., Gerardi, R. J., Ryan, P., & Pallmeyer, T. P. (1986). Cardiac response to relevant stimuli as a tool for diagnosing posttraumatic stress disorder in Vietnam veterans. *Behavior Therapy, 17,* 592–606.

Blanchard, E. B., Kolb, L. C., Pallmeyer, T. P., & Gerardi, R. J. (1982). A psychophysiological study of posttraumatic stress disorder in Vietnam veterans. *Psychiatric Quarterly, 54,* 220–229.

Blanchard, E. B., Kolb, L. C., Taylor, A., & Wittrock, D. (1989). Cardiac response to relevant stimuli as an adjunct in diagnosing post-traumatic stress disorder: Replication and extension. *Behavior Therapy, 20,* 535–543.

Bleich, A., Siegel, B., Garb, B., & Lerer, B. (1986). Posttraumatic stress disorder following combat exposures of clinical features and psychopharmacological response. *British Journal of Psychiatry, 149,* 365–369.

Brady, K. T., Sonne, S. C., & Roberts, J. M. (1995). Sertraline treatment of comorbid posttraumatic stress disorder and alcohol dependence. *Journal of Clinical Psychiatry, 56*(11), 502–505.

Braun, P., Greenberg, D., Dasberg, H., & Lerer, B. (1990). Core symptoms of posttraumatic stress disorder unimproved by alprazolam treatment. *Journal of Clinical Psychiatry, 51,* 236–238.

Bremner, J. D., Southwick, S. M., Johnson D. R., Yehuda, R., & Charney, D. S. (1993). Childhood abuse in combat-related posttraumatic stress disorder. *American Journal of Psychiatry, 150,* 235–239.

Brophy, M. H. (1991). Cyproheptadine for combat nightmares in posttraumatic stress disorder and dream anxiety disorder. *Military Medicine, 156*(2), 100–101.

Brown, G. L., & Linnoila, M. I. (1990). CSF serotonin metabolite (5-HIAA) studies in depression, impulsivity, and violence. *Journal of Clinical Psychiatry, 51,* 31–41.

Burstein, A. (1984). Treatment of posttraumatic stress disorder with imipramine. *Psychosomatics, 25,* 681–682.

Calabrese, J. R., Fatemi, S. H., & Woyshville, M. J. (1996). Antidepressant affects of lamotrigine in rapid cycling bipolar disorder. *American Journal of Psychiatry, 153*(9), 1236.

Charney, D. S., Deutch, A. Y., Krystal, J. H., Southwick, S. M., & Davis, M. (1993). Psychobiologic mechanisms of posttraumatic stress disorder. *Archives of General Psychiatry, 50*(4), 295–305.

Chen, C-J. (1991). The obsessive quality and clomipramine treatment in PTSD. *American Journal of Psychiatry, 148*(8), 1087–1088.

Chouinard, G. (1985). Antimanic effects of clonozepam. *Psychosomatics, 26* (Suppl), 7–12.

Chouinard, G., Young, S. N. & Annable, L. (1983). Antimanic effects of clonozepam. *Biological Psychiatry, 18,* 451–466.

Ciraulo, D. A., Sands, B. F., & Shader, R. I. (1988). Critical review of liability for benzodiazepine abuse among alcoholics. *American Journal of Psychiatry, 145,* 1501–1506.

Cottler, I. B., Compton, W. M., III, Mager, D., Spitznagel E. L., & Janca, A. (1992). Post-traumatic stress disorder and substance abusers for the general population. *American Journal of Psychiatry, 149,* 664–670.

Davidson, J. R. T., Hughes, D., Blazer, D. G., & George, L. K. (1991). Posttraumatic stress disorder in the community: An epidemiological study, *Psychological Medicine, 21,* 713–721.

Davidson, J. R. T., Kudler, H. S., Saunders, W. B., Erickson, L., Smith, R. D., Stein, R. M., Lipper, S., Hammett, E. B., Mahorney, S. L., & Cavenar, J. O. (1993). Predicting response to amitriptyline in posttraumatic stress disorder. *American Journal of Psychiatry, 150,* 1024–1029.

Davidson, J. R. T., Kudler, H. S., Smith, R. D., Lipper, S. L., Mahorney, S. L., Hammett, E. B., Saunders, W. B., & Cavenar, J. O. (1990). Treatment of posttraumatic stress disorder with amitriptyline and placebo. *Archives of General Psychiatry, 4,* 259–269.

Davidson, J. R. T., Roth, S. & Newman, E. (1991). Fluoxetine in posttraumatic stress disorder. *Journal of Traumatic Stress, 4*(3), 419–423.

Davidson, J., Walker, J. I., & Kilts, C. (1987). A pilot study of phenelzine in the treatment of posttraumatic stress disorder. *British Journal of Psychiatry, 150,* 252–255.

Davis, M., Redmond, E., & Baraban, J. M. (1979). Noradrenergic agonists and antagonists: Effects on conditioned fear as measured by the potentiated startle paradigm. *Psychopharmacology, 65,* 1111–1118.

Deakin, J. F. W. (1983). Roles of serotoninergic systems in escape, avoidance, and other behaviors. In S. J. Cooper (Ed.), *Theory of psychopharmacology* (pp. 149–193). London: Academic Press.

DeBoer, M., Op den Velde, W., Falger, P. R., Hovens, J., DeGroen, J., & Van Dujin, H. (1992). Fluvoxamine treatment for chronic PTSD: A pilot study. *Psychotherapy Psychosomatics, 57*(4), 158–163.

Demartino, R., Mollica, R. F., & Wilk, V. (1995). Monamine oxidase inhibitors in posttraumatic stress disorder. *Journal of Nervous and Mental Diseases, 183,* 510–515.

Dimond, K. R., Pande, A. C., Lamoreaux, L., & Pierce, M. W. (1996). Effect of gabapentin (neurontin) on mood and well-being in patients with epilepsy. *Neuro-Psychopharmacological and Biological Psychiatry, 20,* 407–417.

Famularo, R., Kinscherff, R., & Fenton, T. (1988). Propranolol treatment for childhood posttraumatic stress disorder, acute type: A pilot study. *American Journal of Diseases of Children, 142,* 1244–1247.

Feldman, T. B. (1987). Alprazolam in the treatment of posttraumatic stress disorder [letter]. *Journal of Clinical Psychiatry, 48,* 216–217.

Fesler, F. A. (1991). Valproate in combat-related posttraumatic stress disorder. *Journal of Clinical Psychiatry, 52*(9), 361–364.

Frank, J. B., Giller, E. L., Kosten, T., & Dan, E. (1988). A randomized clinical trial for posttraumatic stress disorder: An interim report. *American Journal of Psychiatry, 145,* 1289–1291.

Friedman, M. J. (1988). Toward rational pharmacotherapy for posttraumatic stress disorder: An interim report. *American Journal of Psychiatry, 145,* 281–285.

Friedman, M. J., Charney, D. S., & Deutch, A. Y. (Eds.) (1995). *Neurobiological and clinical consequences of stress: From normal adaptation to PTSD.* Philadelphia: Lippincott-Raven Publishers.

Friedman, M. J., & Southwick, S. M. (1995). Towards pharmacotherapy for posttraumatic stress disorder. In M. J. Friedman, D. S. Charney, and A. Y. Deutch (Eds.), *Neurobiological and clinical consequences of stress: From normal adaptation to PTSD* (pp. 465–481). Philadelphia: Lippincott-Raven Publishers.

Friedman, M. J., & Yehuda, R. (1995). Posttraumatic stress disorder and comorbidity: Psychobiological approaches to differential diagnosis. In M. J. Friedman, D. S. Charney, & A. Y. Deutch (Eds.), *Neurobiological and clinical consequences of stress: From normal adaptation to PTSD.* Philadelphia: Lippincott-Raven Publishers.

Gerardi, R. G., Blanchard, E. B., & Kolb, L. C. (1989). Ability of Vietnam veterans to dissimulate a psychophysiolgical assessment for post-traumatic stress disorder. *Behavior Therapy, 20,* 229–243.

Giller, E., Jr. (Ed.) (1990). *Biological assessment and treatment of posttraumatic stress disorder.* Washington, DC: American Psychiatric Press.

Goldman-Rakic, P. S., & Solomon, L. D. (1990) New frontiers in basal ganglia research. *Trends in Neuroscience, 13,* 241–244.

Goldstein, D. J., & Marvel, D. E. (1993). Psychotropic medications during pregnancy: Risk to the fetus [letter]. *Journal of the American Medical Association, 270,* 2177.

Greenblatt, D. J., Miller, L. G., & Shader, R. I. (1987). Clonazepam pharmacokinetics, brain uptake, and receptor interactions. *Journal of Clinical Psychiatry, 48* (10, Suppl.), 4–9.

Grinker, R. R., & Spiegel, J. P. (1945). *Men under stress.* Philadelphia: Blakiston.

Hamner, M. B., Diamond, B. I., & Hitri, A. (1990). Plasma dopamine and prolactin levels in PTSD. *Biological Psychiatry, 27,* 72A.

Harsch, H. H. (1986). Cyproheptadine for recurrent nightmares. American *Journal of Psychiatry, 143,* 1491–1492.

Hertzberg, M. A., Feldman, M. E., Beckham, J. C., & Davidson, J. R. T. (1996). Trial of trazodone for posttraumatic stress disorder using a multiple baseline group design. *Journal of Clinical Psychopharmacology, 16*(4), 294–298.

Hogben, G. L., & Cornfield, R. B. (1981). Treatment of traumatic war neurosis with phenelzine. *Archives of General Psychiatry, 38,* 440–445.

Horowitz, M. J. (1973). Phase oriented treatment of stress response syndromes. *American Journal of Psychotherapy, 27,* 506–515.

Howard, R., & Ford, R. (1992). From the jumping Frenchmen of Maine to posttraumatic stress disorder: The startle response in neuropsychiatry. Psychological Medicine, 22(3), 695–707.

Joseph, M. H., & Kennett, G. A. (1983). Corticosteroid response to stress depends on increased tryptophan availability. *Psychopharmacology, 79,* 79–81.

Kandel, E. R. (1983). From metapsychology to molecular biology: Explorations into the nature of anxiety. *American Journal of Psychiatry, 140,* 1277–1293.

Kardiner, A., & Spiegel, H. (1947) *War stress and neurotic illness.* New York: Medical Book Department of Harper & Brothers.

Kessler, R. C., Sonnega, A., Bromet, E., & Nelson, C. B. (1995). Posttraumatic stress disorder in the national comorbidity survey. *Archives of General Psychiatry, 52,* 1048–1060.

Kinzie, J. D. (1989). Therapeutic approaches to traumatized Cambodian refugees. *Journal of Traumatic Stress, 2,* 75–91.

Kinzie, J. D., & Leung, P. (1989). Clonidine in Cambodian patients with posttraumatic stress disorder. *Journal of Nervous and Mental Disease, 177*, 546–550.

Kline, N. A., Dow, B. M., Brown, S. A., & Matloff, J. L. (1994). Sertraline efficacy in depressed combat veterans with posttraumatic stress disorder [letter]. *American Journal of Psychiatry, 15*(4), 621.

Kolb, L. C., Burris, B. C., & Griffiths, S. (1984). Propranolol and clonidine in the treatment of the chronic posttraumatic stress disorders of war. In B. A. van der Kolk (Ed.), Post traumatic stress disorder: Psychological and biological sequelae (pp. 97–107). Washington, DC: American Psychiatric Press.

Kosten, T. R., Mason, J. W., Giller, E. L., Ostroff, R. B., & Harkness, L. (1987). Sustained urinary norepinephrine and epinephrine elevation in post-traumatic stress disorder. *Psychoneuroendocrinology, 12*, 13–20.

Kosten, T. R., Wahby, V., Giller, E. Jr., & Mason, J. (1990). The dexamethasone suppression test and thyrotropin-releasing hormone stimulation test in posttraumatic stress disorder. *Biological Psychiatry, 28*(8), 657–664.

Kulka, R. A., Schlenger, W. E., Fairbank, J. A., Jough, R. L., & Jordan, B. K. (1990). *Trauma and the Vietnam War generation.* New York: Brunner/Mazel.

Lerer, B., Bleich, A., Kotler, M., Gorb, R., Hertzberg, M., & Levin, B. (1987). Post-traumatic stress disorder in Israeli combat veterans. Effect of phenelzine treatment. *Archives of General Psychiatry, 44*(11), 976–981.

Lipper, S., Davidson, J. R. T., Grady, T. A., Edingar, J. D., Hammett, E. B., Mahorney, S. L., & Cavenar, J. O. (1986). Preliminary study of carbamazepine in posttraumatic stress disorder. *Psychosomatics, 27*, 849–854.

Looff, D., Grimley, P., Kuller, F., Martin, A., & Shonfield, L. (1995). Carbamazepine for PTSD [letter]. *American Academy of Children and Adolescent Psychiatry, 34*(6), 703.

Lowenstein, R. J., Hornstein, N., & Farber, B. (1988). Open trial of clonazepam in the treatment of posttraumatic stress symptoms in MPD. *Dissociation, 7*(8), 3–12.

Malloy, P. F., Fairbank, J. A., & Keane, T. M. (1993). Validation of a multimethod assessment of posttraumatic stress disorders in Vietnam veterans. *Journal of Consulting and Clinical Psychology, 51*, 488–494.

Marmar, C. R., Schoenfeld, F., Weiss, D. S., Metzler, T., Zatzick, D., Wu, R., Smiga, S., Tecott, L., & Neylan, T. (1996). Open trial of fluvoxamine treatment for combat-related posttraumatic stress disorder. *Journal of Clinical Psychiatry, 57* (Suppl 8), 66–72.

Mason, J. W., Wang, S., Yehuda, R., Bremner, J. D., Riney, S. J., Lubin, H., Johnson, D. R., Southwick, S. M., & Charney, D. S. (1995). Some approaches to the study of the clinical implications of thyroid alterations in post-traumatic stress disorder. In M. J. Friedman, D. S. Charney, & A. Y. Deutch (Eds.), Neurobiological and clinical consequences of stress: From normal adaptation to PTSD (pp. 367–379). Philadelphia: Lippincott-Raven Publishers.

McDougle, C. J., Southwick, S. M., Charney, D. S., & Saint James, R. L. (1991). An open trial of Fluoxetine in the treatment of posttraumatic stress disorder. *Journal of Clinical Psychopharmacology, 11*(5), 325–327.

McFall, M. E., Murburg, M., Ko, G., & Veith, R. (1990). Automatic responses to stress in Vietnam combat veterans with post-traumatic stress disorder. *Biological Quarterly, 27*, 1165–1175.

Milanes, F. J., Mack, C. N., Dennison, J. & Slater, V. L. (1984). Phenelzine treatment of post-Vietnam stress syndrome. *Veteran Affairs Practitioner, 40*–49.

Nagy, L., Morgan, C. A., Southwick, S., Steven, M. & Charney, D. S. (1993). Open prospective trial of Fluoxetine for posttraumatic stress disorder. *Journal of Psychopharmacology, 13*(2), 107–113.

Nemiah, J. C. (1963). Psychological complications in industrial injuries. *Archives of Environmental Health, 7*, 481–486.

Oppenheim (1890, August). Proceedings from the International Medical Conference in Berlin. *Lancet*, 470–471.

Orr S. P., Pitman, R. K., Lasko, N. B. & Herz, L. R. (1993). Psychophysiological assessment of post-traumatic stress disorder imagery in World War II veterans. *Journal of Abnormal Psychology, 102*, 152–159.

Pallmeyer, T., Blanchard, E., & Kolb, L. (1986). The psychophysiology of combat induced post-traumatic stress disorder in Vietnam veterans. *Behaviour Research and Therapy, 24*, 645–652.

Pastuszak, A., Schick-Boschetto, B., Zuber, C., Feldkamp, M., Pinelli, M., & Shin, S. (1993). Pregnancy outcome following first-trimester exposure to fluoxetine (Prozac). *Journal of the American Medical Association, 269*, 2246–2248.

Pitman, R. K. & Orr, S. (1990). Twenty-four hour urinary cortisol and catecholamine excretion in combat-related post-traumatic stress disorder. *Biological Psychiatry, 27*, 245–247.

Pitman, R. K., Orr, S. P., Altman, B., Forgue, D. F., Herz, L. R. & deJong, J. B. (1990). Psychophysiologic response to combat imagery of Vietnam veterans with posttraumatic stress disorder vs. other anxiety disorders. *Journal of Abnormal Psychology, 99,* 49–54.

Pitman, R. K., Orr, S. P., Forgue, D. F., deJong, J. B., & Clairborn, J. M. (1987). Psychophysiologic assessment of posttraumatic stress disorder imagery in Vietnam combat veterans. *Archives of General Psychiatry, 44,* 970–975.

Pitman, R. K., van der Kolk, B. A., Orr, S. P. & Greenberg, M. S. (1990). Naloxone-reversible analgesic response to combat-related stimuli in posttraumatic stress disorder. *Archives of General Psychiatry, 47,* 541–544.

Post, R. M., & Uhde, T. W. (1985). Are the psychotropic effects of carbamazepine in manic-depressive illness mediated through the limbic system? *Psychiatric Journal of the University of Ottawa, 10*(4), 205–219.

Prins, A., Kaloupek, D. G., & Keane, T. M. (1995). Psychophysiological evidence for autonomic arousal and startle with traumatized adult populations. In M. J. Friedman, D. S. Charney, & A. Y. Deutch (Eds.), Neurobiological and clinical consequences of stress: From normal adaptation to PTSD (pp. 335–349). Philadelphia: Lippincott-Raven Publishers.

Rainey, J. M., Aleem, A., Ortiz, A., Yeragami, V., Pohl, R., & Bereliou, R. (1987). Laboratory procedure for the induction of flashbacks. *American Journal of Psychiatry, 144,* 1317–1319.

Reist, C., Kauffman, C. D., Haier, R. J., Sangdahl, C., Demet, E. M., Chicz-Demet, A., & Nelson, J. N. (1989). A controlled trial of desipramine in 18 men with posttraumatic stress disorder. *American Journal of Psychiatry, 146,* 513–516.

Richardson, J. S., & Zaleski, W. A. (1983). Naloxone and self mutilation. *Biological Psychiatry, 18,* 99–101.

Risse, S. C., Whittlers, A., Burke, J., Chen, S., Scurfield, R. M., & Raskind, M. A. (1990). Severe withdrawal symptoms after discontinuation of alprazolam in eight patients with combat-induced posttraumatic stress disorder. *Journal of Clinical Psychiatry, 51*(5), 206–209.

Rothbaum, B. O., Ninan, P. T., & Thomas, L. (1996). Sertraline in the treatment of rape victims with posttraumatic stress disorder. *Journal of Traumatic Stress, 9*(4), 865–871.

Ryback, R. & Ryback, L. (1995). Gabapentin for Behavioral Dyscontrol [letter]. *American Journal of Psychiatry, 152*(9), 1399.

Sargant, W. W. & Slater E. (1972). The use of drugs in psychotherapy. In Sargant, Iver, & Slater (Eds.), *An introduction to physical methods of treatment in psychiatry* (pp. 144–162). New York: Science House.

Shalev, A. Y., Orr, S. P., & Pitman, R. K. (1993). Psychophysiological assessment of traumatic imagery in Israeli civilian patients with posttraumatic stress disorder. *American Journal of Psychiatry, 150,* 620–624.

Shay, J. (1992). Fluoxetine reduces explosiveness and elevates mood of Vietnam combat veterans with PTSD. *Journal of Traumatic Stress, 5,* 97–101.

Shestatzky, M., Greenberg, D., & Lerer, B. (1988). A controlled trial of phenelzine in posttraumatic stress disorder. *Psychiatry Research, 24,* 149–155.

Smith, M. A., Davidson, J., Ritchie, K. C., & Kudler, H. (1989). The corticotropin releasing hormone test in patients with posttraumatic stress disorder. *Biological Psychiatry, 26,* 349–355.

Solomon, S. D., Gerrity, E. T., & Muff, A. M. (1992) Efficacy of treatments for posttraumatic stress disorder: An empirical review. *Journal of the American Medical Association, 260,* 633–638.

Southwick, S. M., Krystal, J. H., Morgan, C. A., Johnson, D., Nagy, L. M., & Nicolaou, A. (1993). Abnormal noradrenergic function in posttraumatic stress disorder. *Archives of General Psychiatry, 50,* 266–274.

Southwick, S. M., Yehuda R., Giller, E. L., & Charney, D. S. (1994). Use of tricyclics and monoamine oxidase inhibitors in the treatment of PTSD: A quantitative review. In M. M. Murburg (Ed.), Catecholamine function in post-traumatic stress disorder: Emerging concepts (pp. 293–305). Washington, DC: American Psychiatric Press.

Southwick, S. M., Yehuda, R., & Morgan, A. C. (1995). Clinical studies of neurotransmitter alterations in posttraumatic stress disorder. In M. J. Friedman, D. S. Charney, & A. Y. Deutch (Eds.), *Neurobiological and clinical consequences of stress: From normal adaptation to PTSD* (pp. 335–349). Philadelphia: Lippincott-Raven Publishers.

Stanley, M. & Stanley, B. (1990). Postmortem evidence for serotonin's role in suicide. *Journal of Clinical Psychiatry, 51,* 22–28.

Svensson, J. H. (1987). Peripheral autonomic regulations of locus coeruleus noradrenergic neurons in the brain: Putative implications for psychiatry and psychopharmacology. *Pscyhopharmacology, 92,* 1–7.

van der Kolk, B. A. (1983). Psychopharmacological issues in posttraumatic stress disorder. *Hospital and Community Psychiatry, 34,* 683–691.

van der Kolk, B. A., Dryfuss, D., Michaels, M., Berkowitz, R., Saxe, G. & Goldenberg, I. (1994). Fluoxetine in posttraumatic stress disorder. *Journal of Clinical Psychiatry, 55,* 517–522.

van der Kolk, B. A., Greenberg, M., Orr, S. P. & Pitman, R. K. (1989). Endogenous opioids, stress induced analgesia, and posttraumatic stress disorder. *Psychopharmacology Bulletin, 25*, 417–421.

Van Praag, H. M., Asnis, G. M., Kahn, R. S., Brown, S. L., Korn, M., Friedman, J. M., & Wetzler, S. (1990). Monamines and abnormal behavior: A multiaminergic perspective. *British Journal of Psychiatry, 157*, 723–734.

Walker, J. L. (1982). Chemotherapy of traumatic war stress. *Military Medicine, 147*, 1029–1033.

Weir Mitchell, S. (1885). *Fat and blood*. Philadelphia: Lippincott.

Wells, G. B., Chu, C., Johnson, R., Nasdahl, C., Ayubi, M. A., Sewell, E., & Statham, P. (1991). Buspirone in the treatment of posttraumatic stress disorder. *Pharmacotherapy, 11*(4), 340–343.

Wisner, K. L & Wheeler, S. D. (1994). Prevention of postpartum major depression. *Hospital and Community Psychiatry, 45*, 1191–1196.

Wolf, M. E., Alavi, A., & Mosnaim, A. D. (1988). Posttraumatic stress disorder in Vietnam veterans clinical and EEG findings. Possible therapeutic effects of carbamazepine. *Biological Psychiatry, 23*, 642–644.

Woodward, S. H. (1995). Neurobiological perspectives on sleep in posttraumatic stress disorder. In M. J. Friedman, D. S. Charney, & A. Y. Deutch (Eds.), *Neurobiological and clinical consequences of stress: From normal adaptation to PTSD* (pp. 315–333). Philadelphia: Lippincott-Raven Publishers.

Yehuda, R., Giller, Jr., E. L., Levengood, R. A., Southwick, S. M. & Siever, L. J. (1995). Hypothalamic-pituitary-adrenal functioning in posttraumatic stress disorder: Expanding the concept of the stress response spectrum. In M. J. Friedman, D. S. Charney, & A. Y. Deutch (Eds.), Neurobiological and clinical consequences of stress: From normal adaption to PTSD (pp. 351–365). Philadelphia: Lippincott-Raven Publishers.

Yehuda, R., Southwick, S. M., & Giller, E. L. (1992). Urinary catecholamine excretion and severity of PTSD symptoms in Vietnam combat veterans. *Journal of Nervous and Mental Diseases, 180*, 321–325.

Zigmond, M. J., Finlay, J. M., & Sved, A. F. (1995). Neurochemical studies of central noradrenergic responses to acute and chronic stress: Implications for normal and abnormal behavior. In J. J. Friedman, D. S. Charney, & A. Y. Deutch, (Eds.), *Neurobiological and clinical consequences of stress: From normal adaption to PTSD*. Philadelphia: Lippincott-Raven Publishers.

CHAPTER 17

BEHAVIORAL TREATMENT OF CHILD-ADOLESCENT POSTTRAUMATIC STRESS DISORDER

PHILIP A. SAIGH, PH.D.
City University of New York Graduate Center

ANASTASIA E. YASIK, PH.D.
Columbia University School of Public Health

RICHARD A. OBERFIELD, M.D.
New York University School of Medicine

SUBHASH C. INAMDAR, M.D.
New York University School of Medicine

HISTORICAL BACKGROUND

Although exposure-based procedures have gained recognition as effective treatments for a number of anxiety disorders, different forms of these regimens have been employed for centuries (Saigh, 1992a). Goethe's autobiography provides a clear account of his successful self-induced treatment of acrophobia (Boudewyns & Shipley, 1983). Malleson (1959) described an imaginal or *in vitro* exposure procedure that was used to reduce emotional reactivity of a test-phobic student. The student was described as being "...classically panic stricken...sobbing and fearful, bewailing his fate, and terrified of the impending examination..." (1959, p. 225). Malleson instructed the student to "tell of the awful consequences that he felt would follow his failure—derision from his colleagues...disappointment from his family and financial loss" (1959, p. 225). The student was also told that whenever he "felt a little wave of spontaneous alarm, he was not to push it aside, but was to augment it, to try to experience it more profoundly and more vividly" (Malleson, 1959, p. 225). Although

this regimen was associated with a degree of discomfort, the student followed Malleson's instructions and subsequently reported that he was almost unable to experience test-related anxiety as the date of the examination approached. As it were, he was able to pass the test with apparent ease.

In 1961 Stampfl coined the expression "implosive therapy" to describe a treatment modality that "may be regarded as a synthesis between Freudian oriented and Mowerian approaches to psychotherapy" (p. 1). Stampfl and Levis (1967) developed an elaborate description of the procedure as well as a theoretical explanation to account for its efficacy. They reported that the initial objective of implosive therapy involves the identification of exteroceptive and interoceptive conditioned stimuli or cues that are being avoided. They hypothesized that fear-inducing stimuli are apparent in a variety of forms (e.g., auditory, tactile, and cognitive). It was also proposed that these cues are interdependent and ordered in a serial hierarchy according to the degree of avoidance. Cues are said to be selected from subjective experiences wherein "objects or situations are known to have high-anxiety eliciting value, as in specific traumatic situations, material produced by dreams or symbolism of a psychoanalytic nature" (Stampfl & Levis, 1967, p. 502). Once identified through clinical interviewing, cues are presented in a sequential order by instructing patients to repeatedly imagine and verbalize symptom contingent cues until extinction occurs.

Shortly thereafter, Rachman (1966) introduced the term "flooding" to the clinical literature. Rachman ascribed the term to Pollin (1959) who used it to describe the aversive component of an infrahuman laboratory experiment involving extinction. While Rachman's (1966) paper determined that systematic desensitization was more effective than flooding in reducing the symptoms of a phobic sample, he also reported that the "disparate results can be accounted for by differences in method" (p. 5). It was acknowledged that the cases that were treated had not received more than two minutes of anxiety inducing exposure at a time and that it was "possible therefore that the crucial element omitted in the present technique is prolonged exposure" (Rachman, 1966, p. 6). Following the initial reports by Stampfl (1961), Stampfl and Levis (1967), and Rachman (1966), a number of reports involving longer intervals of therapeutic exposure (i.e., 40–60 minutes of stimulation) were carried out (Hogan & Kirchner, 1967; Levis & Carrera, 1967). Unlike Rachman's (1966) initial paper, these reports denoted anxiety reduction with a variety of simple and social phobics.

By 1972, flooding studies had been carried out by different investigators across a wide-range of subjects and settings. Following a review of the extant flooding literature, Marks (1972) formulated an important definition of the flooding process. According to this definition,

> Flooding is at one end of a continuum of approach to distressing situations, at the opposite end of which is desensitization. The difference between the two is largely one of degree. The more sudden the confrontation, the more it is prolonged, and the greater the emotion that accompanies it, the more apt is the label "flooding" for that procedure (Marks, 1972, p. 154).

Continuing from the 1970s to date, a considerable number of clinicians have utilized flooding techniques to effectively treat a wide-range of phobic patients (Boudewyns, 1975; Chaplin & Levine, 1981; Hogan & Kirchner, 1967; Jacobson, 1991; Mannion & Levine, 1984; Sellick & Peck, 1977; Yule, Sacks, & Hersov, 1974). Although it is beyond the parameters of this chapter to present a thorough review of this literature base, it may be said that flooding, in one modality or another, has been successfully used to treat a wide-range of phobic individuals.

THE USE OF FLOODING WITH TRAUMATIZED YOUTH

Historically, Fairbank, DeGood, and Jenkins (1981) were the first to use a multi-faceted flooding package in the treatment of a traumatized patient, a 32-year-old female survivor of a motor vehicle accident. Keane and Kaloupek (1982) went on to publish a frequently cited paper involving "imaginal flooding in the treatment of posttraumatic stress disorder" (p. 321). The paper described the treatment of a 36-year-old Vietnam veteran who developed PTSD. Analogously, imaginal flooding has been utilized to treat adults following exposure to stressors including incest (Rychtarik, Silverman, & Van Landingham, 1984), a fatal helicopter crash, and a motor vehicle accident (McCaffery & Fairbank, 1985). For more information regarding the use of imaginal flooding with adult populations the reader is referred to the chapter by Meadows and Foa (1998).

Given the absence of empirically derived information involving the use of flooding with traumatized youth and the need to provide psychological services for traumatized patients during the Lebanese crisis, Saigh conducted a series of single-case flooding trials at the American University of Beirut Medical Center. Initially, Saigh (1987a) evaluated and treated a 14-year-old Lebanese boy who had been abducted and tortured. Six months after his ordeal, the boy met diagnostic criteria for PTSD as determined by an administration of the Children's PTSD Inventory (Saigh, 1989a). The youth presented with trauma-related thoughts and nightmares, reduced ability to concentrate, and impaired short-term recall, as well as anger, trauma-related avoidance behaviors, and feelings of depression. A series of clinical interviews were instrumental in identifying four anxiety-inducing scenes. These scenes reflected the chronological sequence of the actual events that the boy had experienced during his ordeal (e.g., being stopped, forced into a vehicle at gun point, blindfolded, driven away, interrogated, beaten, deprived of food and water).

Prior to treatment, the boy completed the State Trait Anxiety Inventory (STAI; Spielberger, Gorsuch, & Lushane, 1968), the Rathus Assertiveness Schedule (RAS; Rathus, 1973), and the Beck Depression Inventory (BDI; Beck, Ward, Mandelson, Mock, & Erbaugh, 1961). The WISC-R Coding and Digit Span subtests were also administered as these indices denote concentration and short-term memory. A 12-item Behavioral Avoidance Test (BAT) was constructed in order to evaluate the quantitative aspects of trauma-specific avoidance behaviors. The BAT involved a 10-minute behavioral walk wherein the patient left his home and followed the route that he had taken to the site where the abduction actually occurred. Emotional reactivity relative to the traumatic scenes that were presented during the imaginal stimulations was evaluated through the use of subjective units of disturbance (SUDS) ratings. Each scene was rated on a 0–10 point continuum with 0 denoting "no discomfort" and 10 denoting "maximum discomfort."

The imaginal flooding sessions involved 10 minutes of therapist directed deep muscle relaxation exercises. At this point, 60 minutes of therapeutic stimulation were presented wherein the boy was urged to imagine the components of the anxiety-evoking scenes according to a multiple baseline across traumatic scenes design (Fairbank & Keane, 1982). SUDS ratings were recorded at two-minute intervals during the aversive scene presentations. As may be noted from Figure 17.1, the boy's SUDS levels markedly decreased after seven flooding sessions. A four-month follow-up revealed that the youth experienced almost no distress as measured by trauma-specific SUDs ratings.

Post-treatment and four-month follow-up assessments reflected clinically significant posttreatment gains with respect to self-reported anxiety, depression, and misconduct. Although the youth only completed one-third of the BAT items before the treatment, all of the BAT tasks were accomplished after the last treatment session. These improvements were also apparent during a four-month follow-up evaluation. Clinically significant post-treatment gains were observed on measures of concentration and short-term memory as denoted by WISC-R Coding and Digit Span scaled scores.

Saigh (1986, 1987b, 1987c, 1989b) went on to carry out four single-case replications wherein *in vitro* flooding was used in the treatment of traumatized youth. In each case, traumatic scenes were established through clinical interviews and verbally presented according to a multiple-baseline across traumatic scenes design. Stimulus and response imagery cues (Levis, 1980) were used throughout the flooding process. Stimulus cues involved the auditory, olfactory, visual, and tactile components of each scene. Response cues involved the cognitive and behavioral aspects of the scenes.

In two of the Lebanese reports (Saigh, 1987b, 1987c), the frequency of intrusive trauma-related ideation (excluding the ones that were induced in therapy) was self-monitored on a pocket frequency counter (i.e., the Knit Tally, Boyle Needle Company). Figure 17.2 presents the frequency of spontaneous trauma-specific thoughts that were self-monitored by the youth who experienced an artillery barrage (Saigh, 1987b). As may be noted from the figure, treatment was associated with a brief exacerbation of intrusive trauma-related thoughts. It may also be noted that the frequency of traumatic memories appreciably decreased over time. A comparable sequence of arousal and habituation was noted in a follow-up study involving three Lebanese children with war-related PTSD (Saigh, 1987c).

Clinically significant pre- and posttreatment differences were observed on the WISC-R Digit Span and Coding subtests in all of the Saigh single-case studies indicating improvements in short-term memory and concentration following treatment. Significant reductions in self-reported reactivity to the traumatic scenes were evident on the SUDs ratings that were recorded before therapy, during the course of therapy, at post-treatment, and at follow-up assessments. Moreover,

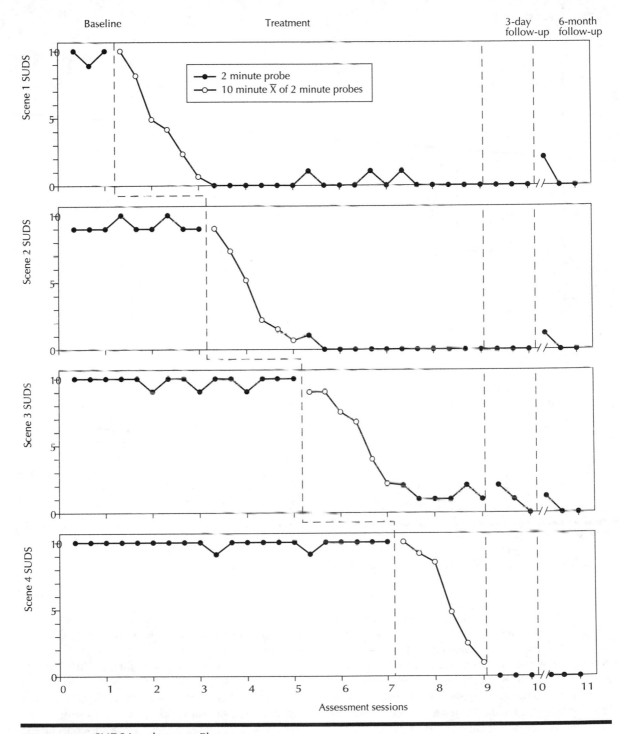

FIGURE 17.1   SUDS Levels across Phases

From Saigh, P. A. (1987a). *In vitro* flooding of an adolescent's posttraumatic stress disorder. *Journal of Clinical Child Psychology, 16,* 147–150. Copyright 1987 by Lawrence Erlbaum Associates. Reprinted with permission.

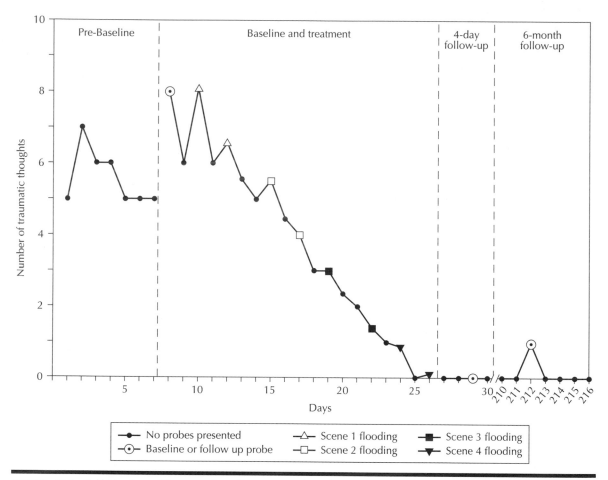

FIGURE 17.2 Self-Monitored Frequencies of Traumatic Thoughts across Phases
From Saigh, P. A. (1987b). *In vitro* flooding of a childhood posttraumatic stress disorder. *School Psychology Review, 16*, 203–211. Copyright 1987 by Lawrence Erlbaum Associates. Reprinted with permission.

clinically significant gains were observed across a number of self-report measures of anxiety and depression. Four of the Lebanese child-adolescent reports (1987a, 1987b, 1987c, 1989b) employed behavioral performance measures. In each of these investigations, appreciably fewer avoidance behaviors were evident as measured by BAT performance at posttreatment and follow-up assessments. Finally, the subjects' anecdotal comments supported the social validity (Schwartz & Bear, 1991; Wolf, 1978) of the interventions as they reported that the treatment

come was well worth the temporary distress that they experienced.

Yule (1998) employed a slightly different approach in the treatment of a traumatized 16-year-old British male. The youth developed PTSD following the sinking of a cruise ship (Yule & Udwin, 1991). The adolescent presented with elevated scores on the Revised Children's Manifest Anxiety Scale (RCMAS; Reynolds & Richmond, 1978), Impact of Event Scale (IES; Horowitz, Wilner, & Alverez, 1979), and the Birleson Depression Inventory (Birleson, 1981). Yule's treatment regimen involved asking the youth to describe what he saw, heard, smelled, felt, and thought during the incident. The boy was also asked to listen to an audio recording of his account of the sinking of the ship between treatment sessions. Following exposure therapy, significant gains were observed on the RCMAS, Birleson Depression Inventory, and IES. Yule also reported that the youth was able to remain in trauma-reminiscent situations (e.g., a crossing of the English channel) without distress.

While these reports demonstrated clear treatment effects across divergent subjects, measures, settings, and therapists, they involved within-subject single-case trials. Although single-case trials have traditionally controlled for the effects of history, maturation, and testing, they do not provide the equivalent degree of external validity that is associated with true experimental designs (Kazdin, 1992). As the efficacy of flooding with child-adolescent PTSD subjects only rested on a limited number of single-case investigations, Saigh and Fairbank (1995) performed a quasi-experimental analysis of the research involving Lebanese youth (see above). The subject pool involved 8 patients (5 males and 3 females) with a mean age of 11 years. The mean duration between stress exposure and treatment was 2 years. While different outcome measures such as the RCMAS, STAI, Reynolds Adolescent Depression Scale (RADS; Reynolds, 1987), Children's Depression Inventory (CDI; Kovacs, 1981), and BDI had been administered to different subjects, all of the Lebanese subjects received administrations of the WISC-R Digit Span and Coding subtests and expressed SUDs ratings. Moreover, all of the Lebanese trials used therapeutic packages that involved relaxation (10–15 min.), imaginal exposure to traumatic scenes (24–60 min.), and additional relaxation (5–10 min.). Data analysis revealed that imaginal flooding was associated with statistically significant gains on the Digit Span and Coding subtests. Statistically significant posttreatment reductions were also evidenced when the pre- and posttreatment SUDs ratings were compared. Four to six-month follow-up assessments were also associated with statistically significant WISC-R Digit Span and Coding gains and significant SUDs reductions.

While an experimental study involving the use of flooding with traumatized youth has not appeared in the clinical literature, it is of considerable relevance to note that three experimental studies involving adult veterans of the Vietnam conflict have been conducted (Boudewyns & Hyer, 1990; Cooper & Clum, 1989; Keane, Fairbank, Caddell, & Zimering, 1989). In addition, Foa, Rothbaum, Riggs, and Murdock (1991) examined the effects of imaginal exposure among adult female sexual assault victims. These reports consistently indicated that flooding successfully reduced trauma-related symptomology.

THEORETICAL EXPLANATIONS FOR THERAPEUTIC EFFICACY

Whereas a number of treatments rely on an equivocal theoretical foundation (c.f., Jensen, 1994; Shapiro, 1989), behavioral scientists have developed two well-documented theoretical frameworks to explain the therapeutic effects of flooding. The first of these involves a variant of Mowrer's (1939) classical two-factor formulation and the second reflects an out growth of information processing theory. Despite the apparent conceptual differences between these theoretical frameworks, it will be seen that these theoretical frameworks are not orthogonal.

Behavioral Models

Mowrer's (1939) two-factor theory applies the principles of classical and instrumental conditioning to explain the development of fear. According to the classical conditioning model a neutral stimulus is closely followed by the presentation of an aversive stimulus (UCS) that serves to evoke a fear reaction (UCR). After repeated trials, the neutral stimulus becomes a conditioned stimulus (CS) that may independently evoke a fear response (CR). Mowrer (1939) went on to note that fear "may effectively motivate human beings" (p. 565) and that the reduction of fear "may serve powerfully to reinforce behavior that brings about such a state of anxiety relief or security" (p. 565). Given this foundation, Mowrer's theory has been applied to explain the etiology of PTSD as well as the efficacy of exposure based treatments (c.f., Keane, Fairbank, Caddell, Zimering, & Bender, 1985).

Extending Mowrer's model, Solomon, Kamin, and Wynne (1953) devised a scheme for infrahuman traumatic conditioned avoidance and extinction. Solomon and his colleagues conditioned dogs to jump (CR) over a gate at the sound of a buzzer (CS) in order to avoid electric shocks (UCS). Whereas the electric shocks were eliminated after conditioning, the animals continued to jump over the gate when the buzzer was presented (i.e., the CR did not extinguish). To prevent escape, Solomon et al. constructed a glass partition in front of the cage and forced the animals to remain in the previously electrified section of the cage. Extinction was established and maintained, following several presentations of the buzzer (CS) without electrical stimulation (UCS).

Interestingly, Solomon et al. (1953) drew an analogy between the experimental animals' reactions and the chronic avoidance exhibited by phobic individuals. Solomon et al. also proposed that "arranging the situation in such a way that an extremely intense emotional reaction takes place in the presence of the CS" (1953, p. 299) is the most effective way to extinguish a maladaptive habit (e.g., avoidance). This was considered to be analogous to a reinstatement of the initial acquisition paradigm. As the UCS was withheld, reduced conditioned reactivity was anticipated.

In a similar vein, Levis and Boyd (1979) developed an infrahuman serial conditioning model. In this model a sequence of neutral stimuli (e.g., buzzer or blinking light) took place before the presentation of an electric shock (UCS). After several trials, the series of neutral stimuli came to act as CS that were capable of evoking avoidance (CR). Interestingly, the conditioned animals consistently evidenced this response (to avoid the previously neutral stimuli) for hundreds of trials.

Keane and his colleagues (1985) utilized information gleaned from various infrahuman conditioned avoidance trials (e.g., Levis & Boyd, 1979; Mineka, 1979) to formulate an etiological model for PTSD as well as a rationale for the efficacy of flooding with traumatized individuals. The etiological model contends that individuals with PTSD have become conditioned to various stimuli that were present as the traumatic sequence of events unfolded. According to Keane et al., "other people present, the time of day,

and even cognitions become associated with the anxiety from the event and are capable of evoking extremely high levels of arousal" (1985, p. 263). They also advanced that cues may serve to induce (i.e., condition) similar stimuli to elicit the same fear responses through the process of higher order conditioning. Stimulus generalization may also serve to explain the number of stimuli that can induce trauma-related thoughts and physiological reactivity. The probability of inducing a trauma-related response (CR) to a novel stimulus (CS) varies as a function of the degree of similarity between a novel stimulus (e.g., the sound of an automobile backfiring) and the complex of stimuli that comprise the traumatic event (e.g., the sound of a rifle shot).

Within this theoretical foundation, Keane and his colleagues (1985) established a conceptual rationale to account for the effectiveness of flooding. Keane et al. (1985) focused their attention on explaining the apparent paradox between the intrusive trauma-specific ideations that fail to independently remit and the efficacy of exposure-based therapeutic stimulations. Given that individuals with PTSD evidence reexperiencing symptoms of traumatic experiences through intrusive nightmares or cognitions, it would seem that these spontaneous or naturally occurring exposures (in the absence of actual consequences) should serve to induce extinction. Keane and his colleagues (1985) suggested that stress-exposed individuals without PTSD review their experience in order to identify trauma-specific facts that are crucial for memory consolidation and subsequent adaptation. For individuals without PTSD, this process is considered a non-aversive method for the consolidation of trauma-related thoughts. However, for individuals with PTSD, this process is believed to involve recollections that have acquired a highly aversive valence. Keane et al. contend that traumatic memories "are so aversive and anxiety-provoking that the motivation to enhance the consolidation of the memory is compromised by the extreme aversion associated with the memory" (1985, p. 265). The authors also suggested that individuals with PTSD purposely attempt to stop, avoid, or interrupt trauma-related recollections which in turn prevents the needed exposure to induce extinction. In contrast to systematic desensitization, flooding requires prolonged and uninterrupted aversive stimulation. Keane and his colleagues (1985) contend that the duration of therapeutic stimulations that occur during exposure-based treatments expedite the formation of traumatic memories in the absence of the original unconditioned stimulus. They also contend that this process induces long-term extinction.

Keane and his colleagues (1985) also suggest that the process of affective state dependent retention (Bower, 1981) significantly influences the retrieval of traumatic memories. Whereas traumatic events are accompanied by increased levels of arousal, they theorized that memory storage which occurs during a traumatic event involves emotional and physical states that are not in synchrony with the level of arousal that is generated when traumatic memories are reviewed (e.g., intrusive nightmares or cognitions). Information supportive of the state dependent retention model (Keane, 1976) indicates that "memories stored in one affective state can best be recollected only when that state is stimulated" (Keane et al., 1985, p. 266). In view of this, it is suggested that access to traumatic memories is limited by differences between past and current levels of emotional and psychophysiological arousal. For individuals with PTSD, this offers limited opportunities for exposure and successful resolution (i.e., extinction). In contrast, the prolonged therapist directed stimulations (an integral component of the flooding process) evoke elevated levels of emotional and psychophysiological arousal which serve to facilitate comprehensive exposures to the overall CS complex.

Emotional Processing

In seeming contrast to Mowrer's (1939) classical two-factor model and its recent application to PTSD, several cognitive models have been presented to account for the effects of exposure based techniques. Lang's (1977, 1979) bioinformational theory warrants exceptional consideration inasmuch as it influenced the development of a number of anxiety reduction models. From this theoretical viewpoint, the most accurate measures of cognitive processing are psychophysiological parameters of anxiety (e.g., heart rate, galvanic skin resistance, and body temper-

ature). According to Lang (1977), images of traumatic experiences should be regarded as propositional structures rather than unrefined sensory representations. Lang indicates that "the image is a finite set of propositions. Such propositions are assertions about relationships, descriptions, interpretations, and labels which prompt percept-like verbal reports, but which are more basically the units of a perceptual set to respond" (1977, p. 864). These emotional complexes are comprised of "stimulus," "response," and "meaning" propositions. Stimulus propositions are defined by the visual, auditory, tactile, or olfactory properties of an event. Response propositions include three independent yet interactive modalities of behavior (i.e., self-statements, overt behavior, and psychophysiological responses). Meaning propositions consist of subjective interpretations attributed to a particular stimulus and a specific response. In view of these points, verbal instructions to imagine trauma-related activities and associated emotional reactions may be capable of eliciting stored propositions.

Although Lang's model had a significant influence on subsequent models, his theory did not provide an explanation for the therapeutic effects of flooding. As such, other theorists (Foa & Kozak, 1986; Rachman, 1980) have attempted to bridge this conceptual gap by formulating more detailed explanations for therapeutic efficacy. The term "emotional processing" was utilized by Rachman to denote "a process whereby emotional disturbances are absorbed and decline to the extent that other experiences and behaviours can proceed without disruption" (1980, p. 51). Rachman proposed that clinical symptoms will become evident if an emotional disorder is not satisfactorily processed. Intrusive thoughts are indicative of unsatisfactory emotional processing. Similarly, concentration impairment, hypervigilance, and irritability (i.e., cardinal symptoms of PTSD) were said to reflect secondary signs of unsatisfactory emotional processing. Analogous to Lang's (1977) theory, Rachman's formulation maintains that an individual must first experience anxiety before it can be effectively reduced. Drawing on research by Mathews (1971) and Borkovec and Sides (1979), Rachman observed that physical relaxation augments the clarity of fear-evoking images. A number of factors that could facilitate or inhibit adequate emotional processing were subsequently identified by Rachman. Factors which were reported to facilitate emotional processing included extended scene presentations, repeated practice, a sense of perceived control, and involved exposure to arousing material. In contrast, distractibility, avoidance, poorly presented material, inadequate practice, irregularity of stimulation, and unresponsive psychophysiological reactions were reported to impede emotional processing.

Drawing on the theoretical models that were formulated by Lang (1977) and Rachman (1980), Foa and Kozak (1986) constructed a framework to account for the efficacy of flooding. After an extensive review of treatment outcome literature (e.g., Anderson & Borkovec, 1980; Borkovec & Sides, 1979; Foa & Chambless, 1978; Lang, Melamed, & Hart, 1970), Foa and Kozak specified a number of characteristics predictive of treatment efficacy. Successful treatments were characterized by increased psychophysiological arousal within therapeutic sessions and decreased psychophysiological reactivity across therapeutic sessions. In addition, Foa and Kozak indicated that information which evokes a fear reaction may be routed through different sensory modalities (e.g., visual, auditory, olfactory, and tactile cues). Furthermore, the affective valence of cues varies as a function of how closely the cues approximate an existing fear structure. As the interval of exposure that is necessary for habituation to develop was reported to vary across anxiety disorders, it is apparent that more pervasive fear structures will require longer stimulations.

Foa and Kozak (1986) proposed that effective exposures provide a source of new information that is in direct opposition to the existing stimulus, response, and meaning propositions. They suggested that the reduced psychophysiological arousal that occurs during therapeutic stimulations may lead to the establishment of "interoceptive information about the absence of psychophysiological arousal. This information is available for encoding as response propositions that are inconsistent with those of existing structures, thereby weakening the preexisting links between stimulus and response" (Foa & Kozak, 1986, p. 27). This interoceptive information provides the basis for the construction of a new fear configuration that is

less readily accessed by incongruent information. Similarly, the tendency to avoid fear stimuli may be reduced by revised meaning propositions. Finally, Foa and Kozak observed that the habituation that occurs across treatment sessions (Anderson & Borkovec, 1980; Borkovec & Sides, 1979; Foa & Chambless, 1978) provides an additional avenue of evidence that serves to modify patient efficacy expectations during anxiety-evoking situations.

CLINICAL APPLICATIONS

As noted in the historical review, flooding regimens have been used to treat a wide-range of traumatized children, adolescents, and adults since 1978. Despite the marked variations between ages, cultural backgrounds, precipitating stressors, and psychiatric comorbidity of the cases that were seen, the actual procedures that have been employed are very similar. In effect, these procedures involve two interactive phases. The first entails the administration of multiple-component assessment packages and the second involves the provision of imaginal flooding regimens.

Phase One: Assessment

The assessment of traumatized individuals has three essential goals (Caddell & Drabman, 1992; Saigh, 1992a). These goals involve the: (a) identification of pathological behaviors, (b) determination of etiological variables that maintain distress, and (c) establishment of baseline data to determine treatment efficacy over time. In order to realize these goals, a multi-axial multi-model assessment paradigm (Keane et al., 1985; Litz, Penk, Gerardi, & Keane, 1992) is recommended. The term "multi-axial" denotes that different sources of information (e.g., clinical interviews, standardized self-report inventories, reports by significant others, psychophysiological ratings, and behavioral avoidance tests) should be used. The term "multi-model" is based on Lang's (1977, 1978) tripartite theoretical model that regards anxiety as being comprised of three interacting response parameters (behavioral, cognitive, and psychophysiological).

Interviews.   Interviews have traditionally been used to formulate inferences in clinical settings. In effect, an interview "involves a series of interactions, frequently in question and answer format, that are used in formulating inferences" (Saigh, 1992b, p. 142). Interviews generally adhere to an unstructured or structured format. Unstructured interviews entail non-standardized questions or probes that are indicative of the examiner's knowledge and on-going clinical observations. Standardized interviews involve a standardized process wherein examiners present questions according to a specified protocol. Although unstructured interviews may yield a wealth of clinically valuable information, they are associated with information variance (i.e., variations in the information that is derived from the same subject by different examiners) (Spitzer, Endicott, & Robins, 1978). Although standardized interviews may appreciably increase reliability, the exclusive reliance of this modality may preclude the use of clinically meaningful questions (Saigh, 1992b). As such, the position advocated herein is to formulate a diagnosis on the basis of unstructured interviews as well as structured interview data.

Structured Interviews. As noted by March (1998) in the earlier chapter on child-adolescent assessment, a number of structured interviews have been developed to assess the wide-range of psychiatric conditions that affect children and adolescents. By way of example, the Diagnostic Interview for Children and Adolescents (DICA) was developed for clinical and epidemiological research with children and adolescents (Reich, Leacock, & Shanfeld, 1994). Currently three versions of the DSM-IV (APA, 1994) based DICA are available. The DICA-R-C (ages 6–12 years) and DICA-R-A (ages 13–17 years) are interviews administered directly to the child or adolescent respectively. Parents of youth may be interviewed utilizing the DICA-R-P (a parental interview). These instruments yield diagnostic information relative to the majority of psychiatric disorders (including PTSD) that apply to children and adolescents. Although the DICA-R-C, DICA-R-A, and DICA-R-P PTSD modules appear to be content valid relative to the DSM-IV, the sensitivity and specificity of the modules have not been established.

As in the case of the omnibus structured interviews, a number of interviews have been expressly developed for diagnosing PTSD in children and adolescents. Viewed in this context, Saigh (1997) developed the Children's PTSD Inventory on the basis of the DSM-IV criteria for formulating an Axis I PTSD diagnosis. The instrument presents four subtests that are scored on a dichotomous basis (i.e., 1 for presence and 0 for absence of symptoms). The first subtest assesses traumatization through experiential or vicarious mediation (e.g., "Has a very scary thing happened to you?"). The second assesses unwanted trauma-related ideation (e.g., "Do you sometimes feel as if your bad experience is happening all over again?"). The third assesses for avoidance and numbing symptoms (e.g., "Have you become less interested in seeing friends or being with people since you had the experience?"), and the fourth assesses for symptoms of increased arousal (e.g., "Has it been difficult to go to sleep or stay asleep at night?") that were not apparent before the trauma. A fifth section of the interview assesses for the presence of significant impairment in important areas of functioning. In terms of interrater reliability with a preliminary outpatient sample of 28 consecutive stress-exposed cases (age range 7–18 years) with documented histories involving sexual or physical assaults or serious injuries, 100 percent interrater agreement (*kappa* = 1.00, p < .001) was observed (Saigh et al., 1997). Preliminary data indicate a *kappa* coefficient of .92 (p < .001) between clinician derived diagnoses and diagnoses that were obtained utilizing the Children's PTSD Inventory. Further data analyses indicated a sensitivity of 1.00, a specificity of .92, and an overall diagnostic efficiency of .96. A positive predictive power of .93 and a negative predictive power of 1.00 were also noted. Additional data collection involving incarcerated juveniles, war victims, and special education referrals is in progress. For a fuller review of the structured interviews that have been developed for children and adolescents, the reader is referred to the earlier chapter on the assessment of child-adolescent PTSD by March (1998).

Unstructured Interviews. Having made a formal diagnosis (i.e., PTSD positive or negative diagnosis) on the basis of a DSM-IV structured interview, additional information should be secured. As the flooding process entails imagining specific aspects of the actual stressor as well as the context in which it occurred, additional information (i.e., the setting, other people present, and the time of day) should be obtained. It must be emphasized in this context that this sort of interviewing almost invariably induces considerable discomfort and several sessions may be needed to obtain a comprehensive account of this all important information. Although unstructured interviews by their very nature are not intended to follow a set pattern of interactions, examiners should strive to establish the specific event(s) that the patient is unable to prevent from coming to mind. Likewise, trauma-related stimuli that are being avoided or situations that are inducing distress should be specified. Questions like "What went through your mind as this happened?" are recommended. In addition, information from significant others (e.g., parents, teachers, siblings, physicians, or mental health practitioners) should be considered as this form of data may provide important insights as to the exact nature of the precipitating stressor(s). As based on Saigh's (1987a) case of the 14-year-old Lebanese boy who had been abducted and tortured, Table 17.1 presents a chrono-logical description of the stressful sequence of events. It should be noted that the traumatic sequence was broken down to denote four thematically congruent scenes.

Quite frequently, children and adolescents are reluctant to discuss traumatic experiences inasmuch as they may fear their personal reactions to these accounts (e.g., incest or witnessing the violent death of a parent). Certainly, examiners should proceed with the realization that the acquisition of this type of information will induce a good deal of situational distress. Although this sort of reactivity may not be avoided, it may help to remind the patient that the details of his or her experience will constitute an integral feature of the treatment that he or she will receive. The use of relaxation exercises or positively valenced relaxing mental images (see Phase Two: Intervention) may also serve to offset situational distress. Certainly, the therapist should express his or her appreciation for the effort that was made. The child's parents as well as the therapist should also explain that the reactivity that the child may experience is understandable and that they are not angry with the child for having described the traumatic sequence.

Treatment Outcome Measures.   In line with Lang's tripartite model of anxiety, a multi-axial assessment paradigm is recommended. Whereas psychophysiological measures for traumatized youth are limited, a number of measures assessing the cognitive and behavioral correlates of anxiety are of particular relevance to the determination of treatment outcome in cases involving traumatized youth. Viewed along these lines, case-control studies (Saigh, 1987b, 1987c, 1989b, 1992a) clearly determined that the following measures discriminate between child or adolescent PTSD cases and matched clinical and non-clinical controls. For children (age range 6–12 years), these measures include the CDI, Connors Teacher Rating Scale (CTRS; Connors, 1969), and RCMAS. In a similar vein, the BDI, Beck Hopelessness Scale (Beck, 1978), and RADS are utilized for older youth. Analogously, preliminary data from Saigh and colleagues (1997) indicate that the Child Behavior Checklist (Achenbach, 1991), Children's Future Orientation Scale (Saigh, 1995), Piers-Harris Children's

TABLE 17.1   Traumatic Scenes

SCENE NUMBER	PROPERTIES
1	Approaching the area where the abduction occurred, being stopped, forced into a car at gun point, blindfolded, and driven away.
2	Walking into a building while blindfolded, being questioned, accused, and listening to the militia argue over the merits of his execution.
3	Being interrogated, responding, receiving repeated blows to the head and body, and experiencing intermittent periods of isolation.
4	Learning that he was going to be released and not trusting the militia to keep their word.

From Saigh, P. A. (1987a). *In vitro* flooding of an adolescent's posttraumatic stress disorder. *Journal of Clinical Child Psychology, 16*, 147–150. Copyright 1987 by Lawrence Erlbaum. Reprinted with permission.

Self-Concept Scale (Piers, 1969), Wide Range Assessment of Memory and Learning (Sheslow & Adams, 1990), and WISC-III discriminated amongst urban youth who developed or failed to develop PTSD after exposure to traumatic events (e.g., physical assaults, sexual assaults, motor vehicle accidents). It is of interest to note that clinical gains were reflected on the CDI, BDI, RCMAS, FSS, STAI, and CTRS as well as the WISC-R Digit Span and Coding subtests (measures of concentration and memory impairment) following several flooding trials with traumatized youth (Saigh, 1986, 1987a, 1987b, 1987c, 1989b).

Of course, the utility of BATs should not be overlooked as this device presents an important index of trauma-related avoidance and as significant treatment gains were reflected on the BATs that were employed in the aforementioned studies (Saigh, 1986, 1987a, 1987b, 1987c, 1989b). It should also be noted that as repeated trauma-related ideation is one of the primary and most disturbing symptoms of PTSD, pre- and posttreatment frequencies of these aversive thoughts and images can only be regarded as important parameters of treatment efficacy. With this in mind, it is also advised that patient's should self-monitor trauma-related ideation before, during, and after flooding. Saigh (1987a, 1987b, 1987c, 1989), for example, trained traumatized youth to self-monitor traumatic thoughts with the aid of pocket frequency counters. Whereas flooding was initially associated with more trauma-related thoughts relative to pre-treatment baselines, continued stimulation was associated with clinically significant and long lasting reductions in traumatic ideation.

Although the adult PTSD treatment literature is replete with examples of psychophysiological reactivity, this modality has not been used to determine treatment efficacy in studies involving traumatized children or adolescents. Given that the cost of psychophysiological monitoring equipment has appreciably decreased in recent years and as this mode of assessment presents a unique index of reactivity to trauma-related stimuli, the inclusion of cardiovascular and related measures of muscular tension and skin conductance can only be regarded as viable and clinically significant parameters of treatment efficacy.

Phase Two: Intervention

The treatment of traumatized individuals involves five basic steps. It is important to note that these steps should be presented in the sequential order that is described herein. Moreover, it should be understood that therapists who employ flooding regimens with traumatized youth should be trained in controlled settings (e.g., doctoral internships) by qualified supervisors. It should also come without saying that effective flooding requires the establishment of a positive therapeutic alliance between the therapist, the patient, and the patient's family.

Education.   Therapists may decrease the probability of attrition or non-compliance by instructing youth and their families about the procedures that will be utilized. Before treatment is attempted, it is extremely important to obtain the informed consent of the affected youth as well as his or her parents or guardians. In effect, the therapist should accurately describe each component of the flooding process and candidly answer questions that may arise. It should be conveyed that flooding is an aversive process and that PTSD symptoms may increase during the initial stages of therapeutic exposure. Medical staff and mental health practitioners (e.g., school counselors) should be informed about the anticipated treatment and the possible time-limited reactivity.

Imagery Training.   Following the educational phase, the youth should receive instruction on how to establish and maintain relaxing images. In addition, the child or adolescent should be taught how to establish and maintain aversive mental images.

Endemic Images.   Saigh's (1980) endemic image procedure involves asking youth to read a series of statements that describe potentially relaxing scenes. Table 17.2 presents Saigh's endemic images.

Patients should be asked to denote their image preference by rating each statement according to a 5-point Likert-type scale with 5 denoting that the patient prefers the scene "very much" and 1 denoting "not at all." Following this, the therapist should review the evaluations and identify the scene that received the highest rating. This process serves to

TABLE 17.2 Endemic Image Questionnaire

The items in this questionnaire reflect images and scenes that may be appealing to you. Please indicate your image preference.

1. Imagine that you are sitting on a balcony on a sunny winter afternoon and that all the surroundings are covered with snow. In the distance you can see a mountain peak partially covered with snow.

5	4	3	2	1
Very Much	Much	A Fair Amount	A Little	Not at All

2. Imagine being in a mountain cabin and that you are listening to soft music as you gaze up at the moon.

5	4	3	?	1
Very Much	Much	A Fair Amount	A Little	Not at All

3. Imagine that you are in a sailboat during a quiet afternoon and that you are watching the ripples made by the wake.

5	4	3	2	1
Very Much	Much	A Fair Amount	A Little	Not at All

4. Imagine that you are wading out of the sea on a summer day and that you approaching a white towel. Imagine lying down on the towel and looking up at a while cloud as the sun radiates toward your body.

5	4	3	2	1
Very Much	Much	A Fair Amount	A Little	Not at All

5. Imagine that you are on a balcony overlooking the sea and that you can see a small boat in the distance. Concentrate on the white sails against the blue background as they gently move toward the horizon.

5	4	3	2	1
Very Much	Much	A Fair Amount	A Little	Not at All

6. Imagine that you are seated in a comfortable chair overlooking the desert on a quiet afternoon. Imagine looking directly at the sun as it slowly sets over the distant dunes.

5	4	3	2	1
Very Much	Much	A Fair Amount	A Little	Not at All

7. Imagine that you are in a warm room on a winter day and that you are looking out at a pine tree as the snow gently settles on its branches.

5	4	3	2	1
Very Much	Much	A Fair Amount	A Little	Not at All

8. Imagine that you are sitting under a tree by a lake and that you see a child throwing pebbles into the water. Concentrate on the ripples that the pebbles are making.

5	4	3	2	1
Very Much	Much	A Fair Amount	A Little	Not at All

TABLE 17.2 Continued

9. Imagine that you are looking out of a window after a heavy rain and that you see a rainbow. Concentrate on the colors of the rainbow.

5	4	3	2	1
Very Much	Much	A Fair Amount	A Little	Not at All

10. Imagine that you are in a mountain cabin and that you are comfortably seated in an armchair by a fireplace. Concentrate on the glowing embers and try to imagine that you almost feel the heat as it radiates toward you.

5	4	3	2	1
Very Much	Much	A Fair Amount	A Little	Not at All

From Saigh, P. A., & Antoun, F. (1984). Endemic images and the desensitization process. *Journal of School Psychology, 22,* 182–183. Reprinted with permission from Elsener Science.

identify scenes that are indicative of the patient's actual preferences. As such, this process decreases the possibility that therapist selected scenes may be less pleasing or aversive relative to the actual preferences of the patient.

Once image preferences have been established, children and adolescents should be advised that it is necessary to determine if they are capable of establishing and maintaining the image in question. This is accomplished by asking the patient to gently shut their eyes and keep their eyes closed until they are instructed to open them. At this point, the therapist should slowly and systematically encourage the patient to concentrate on the various aspects of the scene. After approximately 3 minutes, the therapist should inquire "Were you able to imagine the scene?". If the youth indicates that he or she was able to do so, then the therapist should ask the patient to rate the clarity of material that he or she imagined according to a 10-point Likert-type scale (e.g., 10 = "very clear" and 1 = "not at all clear"). If the youth reports lower ratings (1–4), these ratings should be discussed in order to determine why the patient was not able to clearly imagine the scene. In some instances, children and adolescents benefit from additional practice. In other instances, the particular components of the endemic image that was selected may be too complex for the youth to imagine. Should this oc-

cur, the therapist should review the endemic imagery ratings and present a different scene. If the patient continues to report that he or she is unable to imagine the positively valenced material, the therapist may revert to the use of relaxation exercises.

Aversive Images. Having trained the patient to imagine relaxing mental images, the therapist should proceed with training regarding the establishment of aversive (i.e., fear-evoking) images. As in the case of the endemic imagery training, the patient should be advised that it is important to determine that he or she can actually imagine aversive material inasmuch as the effectiveness of the later phases of treatment will depend on the ability to imagine traumatic images. Clinical interviews should be conducted with the patient to identify a fear-evoking (but not traumatic) scene.

Circumscribed fears involving insects, dogs, snakes, and rats are frequently reported by children and adolescents (Miller, Barrett, & Hempe, 1974). Once a clear description of a fear-evoking object or situation has been obtained, aversive imagery training may proceed. The patient should be advised to close his or her eyes and imagine the therapist's description of the fear-evoking scene. The patient should be asked to open his or her eyes after approximately 3 minutes. Based on a 10-point Likert-type scale the patient should rate the clarity of the aversive scene. As previously noted, ratings of 4 or less should be discussed in order to identify what factors have interfered with the clarity of scenes. In some cases, young children may report that their attention wandered. In such instances, the exercise may be repeated with verbal prompts (e.g., "Don't drift off!" or "Try to imagine what I'm saying and don't think about anything else.") that may facilitate the formation of an aversive image. In other instances, visual or auditory prompts (e.g., color photographs, audio, or video tapes) may facilitate image formation.

The therapist should also train the patient to recognize and rate his or her reactivity to the aversive material according to a 10-point SUDS scale with 10 denoting "very much" and 1 denoting "not at all." It should be recalled in this context that this form of the treatment is an analog exercise. As such, SUDS ratings of 5 or less are appropriate inasmuch as they are not indicative of traumatic material.

Relaxation Training.   An integral part of the flooding process is relaxation training. This procedure facilitates the ability to imagine trauma-related images and decreases residual anxiety following the presentation of these images (Keane et al., 1985). Although a number of approaches have been used to induce deep muscle relaxation (Bernstein & Borkoveck, 1973; Jacobson, 1938), a sequence of tensing and relaxing images that consists of three basic procedures has been successfully used in the treatment of traumatized youth (Saigh, 1987a, 1987b, 1987c, 1989b).

Initially, the patient is seated in a comfortable armchair with a headrest and asked to gently shut his or her eyes. Then the patient is asked to make a fist with both hands and urged to contract the muscles of both hands for 8–10 seconds. The patient is subsequently told to "STOP!", open his or her hands, and encouraged to concentrate on relaxing the muscles that were contracted. After 1 minute of muscle relaxation, the exercise is repeated. Pursuant to four sets of these exercises, the patient is directed to simultaneously make a fist with both hands and contract the muscles that surround the eyes and forehead (i.e., the levatator and frontalis muscles) for 8–10 seconds. At this point the therapist instructs the patient to stop the

contractions and quietly urges the patient to develop a feeling of deep muscle relaxation in both hands. After 1 minute of this, the patient should be asked to shift his or her attention to relaxing the muscles that surround the eyes and forehead for approximately 1 minute. After four sets of hand-eye contractions and guided relaxation instructions, the patient is asked to concurrently tense his or her hands, the muscles that surround the eyes and forehead, as well as the muscles of the jaw (i.e., the patient is instructed to occlude the maxillary molars against the mandibular molars)[1] for 8–10 seconds. Following this, the patient is instructed to "STOP!" and urged to concentrate on the sequential and orthogonal relaxation of the hands (1 minute), the muscles that surround the eyes and forehead (1 minute), and the jaw (1 minute). As in the case of the earlier sets, this sequence is repeated four times.

Having completed the entire sequence, the therapist should assess the patient's level of arousal by asking the patient to rate his or her level of physical relaxation according to a 10-point scale wherein 10 denotes feeling "very calm" and 1 denotes feeling "very tense." Whereas the aforementioned sequence has been found to be very effective with traumatized youth, a modicum of cases may not be able to comply with the regimen due to physical infirmities. In these instances, the therapist will have to exclusively rely on the endemic image procedure in order to induce relaxation.

Presentation of Traumatic Scenes.   Following the introduction of deep muscle relaxation, the therapist should slowly and systematically instruct the patient to imagine the first of the traumatic scenes that were compiled during the unstructured interview. To begin, the patient is asked to imagine that he or she is at the location of the traumatic event shortly before the traumatic sequence unfolded. Specifically, the patient is asked to imagine exactly what he or she was doing at the time. To facilitate this process, visual, auditory, tactile, and olfactory cues may be pre-

---

[1]Children and adolescents with dental or orthodontal problems should forgo this exercise.

sented. Using the present tense, the therapist goes on to ask the patient to imagine what he or she saw, heard, smelled, felt, and thought as the first scene took place. Throughout this process, it is of the utmost import to keep the patient's attention focused on the memory of the traumatic event. Table 17.3 presents an example of this process as based on an imaginal course of flooding that a 14-year-old male adolescent received after he observed the shooting of a close friend (Saigh, 1987a).

An important aspect of this treatment phase involves the regular monitoring of the patient's self-reported distress relative to the traumatic scenes that are being imagined. SUDS ratings should be monitored approximately every 5 minutes. As it is of considerable clinical utility to have a continuous record of treatment efficacy, this information should be entered in the patient's chart. Each of the traumatic scenes that were devised should be presented and rated until 0 SUDS ratings are reported on three con-

secutive occasions. Only then should the therapist proceed to the next scene in the sequence.

Debriefing. After approximately 60 minutes of stimulation, the relaxation procedure is reintroduced for 10 minutes. Then 5 to 10 minutes of endemic imagery should be presented. It should be noted in this regard that relaxation exercises coupled with positively valenced scenes are of considerable utility in reducing high levels of emotional distress and psychophysiological reactivity that are invariably experienced in the previous stage of the treatment. Following this, the patient should be asked to open his or her eyes and the therapist should slowly obtain information regarding the cognitive and psychophysiological reactivity that was experienced. It should come without saying that the therapist should demonstrate considerable emotional support throughout this process. Likewise, parents should clearly acknowledge that they are cognizant of how distressing

---

TABLE 17.3 Example of the *In Vitro* Flooding Process

Therapist 1	"Imagine that you and Robert are walking in the direction of the video store." (15-sec pause) "Imagine the cars going by." (15-sec pause) "The summer heat." (15-sec pause) "Can you do this?"
Tony 1	"Yes."
Therapist 2	"According to the scale that we talked about, how much does it bother you?"
Tony 2	"A lot. I don't like it a 10."
Therapist 3	"Good. Let's go on. I want you to imagine that you and Robert are slowly approaching the video store." (15-sec pause) "Imagine how the cars look and sound as they pass by."(15-sec pause) "Imagine the buildings that you are passing." (15-sec pause) "Now imagine that you are looking at Robert's face as the two of you are slowly walking toward the video store." (15-sec pause) "Imagine the expression on his face as he says 'What films do you want to get?' Just think of this and nothing else." (15-sec pause) "Do these images bother you?"
Tony 3	"Yes. Very much."
Therapist 4	"How much?"
Tony 4	"Ten."

From Saigh, P. A. (1989b). The use of an *in vitro* flooding package in the treatment of traumatized adolescents. *Journal of Developmental and Behavioral Pediatrics, 10,* 17–21. Copyright 1989 by Williams & Wilkins. Reprinted with permission.

the flooding process must have been. The therapist as well as the parents should also emphatically express their appreciation for the effort that was made. Finally, parents should be advised to be particularly sensitive and supportive of their child's emotional needs throughout the flooding process.

CLINICAL AND ETHICAL CONCERNS

Although this chapter is not intended to serve as a clinical manual (a detailed description of flooding procedures with children and adolescents was reported by Saigh, 1992a), a number of clinical and ethical concerns warrant attention. As flooding is a challenging procedure, clinicians must insure that the rights of children and adolescents are protected. Therapists should inform affected youth and their parents about the actual procedures and honestly answer questions that may develop. Clearly, the informed consent of the children-adolescents and their parents or guardians must be obtained before flooding is implemented. Families, mental health practitioners, and medical staff should be advised that PTSD symptoms may increase during the initial stages of therapy (c.f., Saigh, 1987a, 1992a).

The Association for the Advancement of Behavior Therapy's (AABT) ethical guidelines (AABT, 1977) are of import in this context as they provide operational recommendations that address several of the concerns that are germane to the needs of children and adolescents. The AABT recommends that clinicians should ensure that a client's participation is voluntary by examining possible sources of coercion and by ensuring that clients can withdraw from the treatment without reprimand. Likewise, when the competence of a subordinate client (e.g., a child or adolescent) is limited or questionable, efforts should be made to ensure that the "client as well as the guardian participate in treatment discussions to the extent that the client's ability permits" (AABT, 1977, vi). The AABT further advocates that the client's understanding of the treatment goals should be established by having the client verbally restate the goals (a highly recommended procedure with young children) or in writing. The AABT guidelines further recommend that the choice of treatment methods should

be adequately reviewed. Given that PTSD may spontaneously remit over time (Saigh, Fairbank, & Yasik, 1998; Saigh, Green, & Korol, 1996), therapists may wish to initially consider the time-limited use of supportive counseling (Scott & Stradling, 1992).

Examined from a more clinical perspective, it should be understood that exposure based paradigms for PTSD should occur within the context of a supportive therapeutic relationship (Fairbank & Nicholson, 1987; Resick & Schnicke, 1993; Saigh, Yule, & Inamdar, 1996). It should also be understood that flooding regimens for PTSD have been conducted within broad treatment plans that targeted the multiple dimensions of PTSD (Saigh, 1992a). Whereas flooding has been associated with favorable outcomes, supportive counseling and educational interventions may serve to offset pathological self-efficacy expectations (Saigh, Mroueh, Zimmerman, & Fairbank; 1995) and impaired academic achievement (Saigh, Mroueh, & Bremner, 1997) that may develop over time. In a similar vein, the use of behavioral anger management techniques (Feindler & Ecton, 1987) and assertion training procedures (Wolpe, 1990) may be of value in treating associated symptoms of irritability.

Young children may not be able to imagine traumatic scenes, follow complex relaxation instructions, or tolerate prolonged *in vitro* presentations. In these instances, asking traumatized children to prepare sketches of their stressful experience and verbally report the content of their work may present an effective adjunct to the more orthodox form of flooding. Likewise, the use of trauma-reminiscent prompts may facilitate the ability to imagine stressful material. By way of example, Saigh (1987c) reported that a 12-year-old Lebanese boy whose home had been destroyed was not able to imagine a scene involving a shelling incident that led to the loss of his home. In this case, the sounds of increasingly closer shell and rocket bursts that occurred during a particularly trying episode of the Lebanese war were audiotaped. The sound track was amplified by two 50 watt speakers and played as the therapist instructed the youth to imagine the shelling incident. As it were, the boy reported that the recording was very realistic and this, coupled with verbal instructions to imagine the traumatic scenes, was associated with a positive therapeutic outcome.

Although the flooding literature has been largely associated with favorable outcomes, flooding may not always be the treatment of choice (Saigh, 1992a; Saigh, Yule, & Inamdar, 1996). Flooding may be contraindicated in instances involving co-morbidity (i.e., psychosis, limited mental ability, depression, conduct disorder, attention deficit hyperactivity disorder, or substance abuse). A history of non-compliance, focused compensation-seeking efforts, difficulty in establishing mental images, and limited reexperiencing symptoms were listed by Litz, Blake, Gerardi, and Keane (1990) as reasons for not employing flooding. It is of relevance to note that all of the subjects in the Lebanese trials were carefully selected before treatment to insure that they could establish and maintain positive and negative mental images and follow instructions. Moreover, their mental ability was within or slightly above normal limits as denoted by standardized norm referenced tests. In situations where flooding is not advisable, alternative procedures such as general supportive counseling, family therapy, or psychopharmacological regimens are recommended alternatives.

SUMMARY AND FUTURE DIRECTIONS

Exposure-based therapeutic regimens have had a long and colorful history. Dating from Goethe's 1770 autobiography to date, actual or imaginal exposure has been effectively used to treat an assortment of phobic reactions. Shortly before PTSD was recognized as an independent psychiatric classification, Fairbank and his associates (1981) successfully implemented an imaginal course of flooding to eliminate the "persistent post-traumatic startle response" of a 32-year-old accident victim. Given the marked absence of research involving the use of flooding with traumatized children or adolescents, Saigh conducted a series of single-case multiple-baseline trials with Lebanese children and adolescents (Saigh, 1987a, 1987b, 1987c, 1989b). Building on an earlier flooding trial with a noise phobic 11-year-old boy (Yule et al., 1974), Yule (1998) successfully applied a flooding regimen in the treatment of a 16-year-old British survivor of a shipping disaster.

Given the apparent success of the single-case trials and experimental trials among traumatized adults (Meadows & Foa, 1998), experimental flooding studies involving traumatized youth would be of exceptional interest as the child-clinical literature is currently limited to a modicum of single-case trials and one quasi-experimental report. As the assignment of traumatized youth to no treatment, waiting-list, or non-specific control conditions may not be feasible or ethically defensible, the use of randomized active treatment designs (Kazdin, 1992) is regarded as the recommended way to proceed. Investigators may wish to compare the effects of flooding (i.e., the treatment of interest) to a variety of well-established behavioral procedures such as systematic desensitization. It would also be of interest to examine the comparative effects of *in vitro* participant modeling (Bandura, Jeffery, & Wright, 1974) as this therapeutic technique does not call for imaginal exposure. As such, young children who are unable to imagine traumatic material may benefit from this form of exposure.

Experimental research designed to detect child-adolescent PTSD patient, treatment, family, and therapist factors that are associated with successful outcomes is obviously needed. Morris and Kratochwill's (1983) review of the systematic desensitization and flooding literature concluded that investigators should attempt to identify child-adolescent factors that are associated with treatment efficacy (i.e., age, ability to adhere to verbal instruction, ability to imagine, quality of visual imagery, ability to relax, and fatigue threshold). Likewise, there is a need to identify co-morbid psychiatric disorders that occur during the developmental period (e.g., conduct disorder, oppositional defiant disorder, other anxiety disorders, or attention deficit hyperactivity disorder) which may influence therapeutic outcomes. Likewise, the influence of moderator variables such as the quality of therapeutic relationships and parental support are worthy of systematic exploration. Investigators should also attempt to illustrate the integrity of these treatments as experimental investigations with adults have not controlled for this form of variance.

The Lebanese and British children and adolescents who successfully responded to flooding regimens were the victims of war-related events and a maritime disaster. Although these subjects met diagnostic criteria for PTSD, they did not present with symptoms of shame, guilt, or loss of trust. Given that child sexual and physical abuse victims frequently report these symptoms (Wolfe, 1991), it would be of interest to test the efficacy of regimens that combine therapeutic exposure and cognitive interventions as described in recent studies involving adult rape victims (c.f., Resick & Schnicke, 1993; Rothbaum & Foa, 1992).

REFERENCES

Achenbach, J. M. (1991). *Manual for the Child Behavior Checklist: 4–18 and 1991 profile.* Burlington, VT: University of Vermont Department of Psychiatry.

American Psychiatric Association. (1994). *Diagnostic and statistical manual of mental disorders* (4th ed.). Washington, DC: Author.

Anderson, M. P., & Borkovec, T. D. (1980). Imagery processing and fear reduction during repeated exposure to two types of phobic imagery. *Behaviour Research and Therapy, 18,* 537–540.

Association for the Advancement of Behavior Therapy. (1977). Ethical issues for human services. *Behavior Therapy, 8,* v–vi.

Bandura, A., Jeffery, R. W., & Wright, E. (1974). Efficacy of participant modeling as a response to instructional aids. *Journal of Abnormal Psychology, 83,* 56–64.

Beck, A. T. (1978). *Beck Hopelessness Scale.* San Antonio, TX: Psychological Corporation.

Beck, A. T., Ward, C. H., Mandelson, M., Mock, J., & Erbaugh, J. (1961). An inventory for measuring depression. *Archives of General Psychiatry, 4,* 561–571.

Bernstein, D. A., & Borkoveck, T. D. (1973). *Progressive relaxation training.* Champaign, IL: Research Press.

Birleson, P. (1981). The validity of depressive disorder in childhood and the development of a self-rating scale: A research report. *Journal of Child Psychology and Psychiatry, 22,* 73–78.

Borkovec, T. D., & Sides, J. (1979). The contribution of relaxation and expectance to fear reduction via graded imaginal exposure to feared stimuli. *Behaviour Research and Therapy, 17,* 529–540.

Boudewyns, P. A. (1975). Implosive therapy and desensitization therapy with inpatients: A five-year follow-up. *Journal of Abnormal Psychology, 84,* 159–160.

Boudewyns, P. A., & Hyer, L. (1990). Physiological response to combat memories and preliminary treatment outcome in Vietnam veteran PTSD patients treated with direct therapeutic exposure. *Behavior Therapy, 21,* 63–87.

Boudewyns, P. A., & Shipley, R. H. (1983). *Flooding and implosive therapy.* New York: Plenum Press.

Bower, G. H. (1981). Mood and memory. *American Psychologist, 36,* 129–148.

Caddell, J. M., & Drabman, R. S. (1992). Post-traumatic stress disorder in children. In T. Ammerman & M. Hersen (Eds.) *Handbook of behavioral therapy with children and adults: A longitudinal perspective* (pp. 219–235). Boston: Allyn & Bacon.

Chaplin, E. W. & Levine, B. E. (1981). The effects of total exposure duration and interrupted versus continuous exposure in flooding therapy. *Behavior Therapy, 12,* 360–368.

Conners, C. K. (1969). A teacher rating scale for use in drug studies with children. *American Journal of Psychiatry, 126,* 884–888.

Cooper, N. A., & Clum, G. A. (1989). Imaginal flooding as a supplementary treatment for PTSD in combat veterans: A controlled evaluation. *Behavior Therapy, 20,* 381–391.

Fairbank, J. A., DeGood, D. D., & Jenkins, C. W. (1981). Behavioral treatment of a persistent post-traumatic startle response. *Journal of Behavior Therapy and Experimental Psychiatry, 12,* 321–324.

Fairbank, J. A., & Keane, T. M. (1982). Flooding for combat-related stress disorders: Assessment of anxiety reduction across traumatic memories. *Behavior Therapy, 13,* 499–510.

Fairbank, J. A., & Nicholson, R. A. (1987). Theoretical and empirical issues in the treatment of posttraumatic stress disorder in Vietnam veterans. *Journal of Clinical Psychology, 43,* 44–55.

Feindler, E. L., & Ecton, R. B. (1987). *Adolescent anger control training: Cognitive-behavioral techniques.* New York: Pergamon.

Foa, E. B., & Chambless, D. L. (1978). Habituation of subjective anxiety during flooding in imagery. *Behaviour Research and Therapy, 16,* 391–399.

Foa, E. B., & Kozak, M. J. (1986). Emotional processing of fear: Exposure to corrective information. *Psychological Bulletin, 99,* 20–35.

Foa, E. B., Rothbaum, B. O., Riggs, D., & Murdock, T. (1991). Treatment of posttraumatic stress disorder in rape victims: A comparison between cognitive behavioral procedures and counseling. *Journal of Consulting and Clinical Psychology, 59,* 715–723.

Hogan, R. A., & Kirchner, J. H. (1967). Preliminary report on the extinction of learned fears via short term therapy. *Journal of Abnormal Psychology, 72,* 106–109.

Horowitz, M. J., Wilner, N., & Alverez, W. (1979). Impact of Event Scale: A measure of subjective stress. *Psychosomatic Medicine, 41,* 209–218.

Jacobson, E. (1938). *Progressive relaxation.* Chicago: University of Chicago Press.

Jacobson, P. B. (1991). Treating a man with a needle who requires daily injections of medication. *Hospital and Community Psychiatry, 42,* 877–879.

Jensen, J. A. (1994). An investigation of eye movement desensitization and reprocessing (EMD/R) as a treatment for posttraumatic stress disorder (PTSD) symptoms of Vietnam combat veterans. *Behavior Therapy, 25,* 311–325.

Kazdin, A. (1992). *Research designs in clinical psychology* (2nd ed.). New York: Macmillan.

Keane, T. M. (1976). *State-dependent retention and its relationship to psychopathology.* Unpublished manuscript, State University of New York at Binghamton.

Keane, T. M., Fairbank, J. A., Caddell, J. M., & Zimering, R. T. (1989). Implosive (flooding) therapy reduces symptoms of PTSD in Vietnam combat veterans. *Behavior Therapy, 20,* 245–260.

Keane, T. M., Fairbank, J. A., Caddell, J. M., Zimering, R. T., & Bender, M. E. (1985). A behavioral approach to assessing and treating post-traumatic stress disorder in Vietnam veterans. In C. R. Figley (Ed.), *Trauma and its wake* (pp. 257–294). New York: Brunner/Mazel.

Keane, T. M., & Kaloupek, D. G. (1982). Imaginal flooding in the treatment of post-traumatic stress disorder. *Journal of Consulting and Clinical Psychology, 50,* 138–140.

Kovacs, M. (1981). *The Children's Depression Inventory.* Pittsburgh, PA: University of Pittsburgh Press.

Lang, P. J. (1977). Imagery in therapy: An information processing analysis of fear. *Behavior Therapy, 8,* 862–886.

Lang, P. J. (1978). Anxiety: Towards a psychological definition. In A. S. Akiskal & W. L. Webb (Eds.), *Psychiatric diagnosis: Exploration and biological criteria.* New York: Spectrum.

Lang, P. J. (1979). A bioinformational theory of emotional imagery. *Psychophysiology, 16,* 495–512.

Lang, P. J., Melamed, B. G., & Hart, J. (1970). A psychophysiological analysis of fear modification using an automated desensitization procedure. *Journal of Abnormal Psychology, 76,* 220–234.

Levis, D. J. (1980). Implementing the technique of implosive therapy. In A. Goldstein & E. B. Foa (Eds.), *Handbook of behavioral interventions: A clinical guide* (pp. 92–151). New York: Wiley.

Levis, D. J., & Boyd, T. J. (1979). Symptom maintenance: An infrahuman analysis and extension of the conservation of anxiety principle. *Journal of Abnormal Psychology, 88,* 107–120.

Levis, D. J., & Carrera, R. N. (1967). Effects of ten hours of implosive therapy in the treatment of outpatients: A preliminary report. *Journal of Abnormal Psychology, 72,* 504–508.

Litz, B. T., Blake, D. D., Gerardi, R. G., & Keane, T. M. (1990). Decision making guidelines for the use of direct therapeutic exposure in the treatment of posttraumatic stress disorder. *The Behavior Therapist, 13,* 91–93.

Litz, B. T., Penk, W. F., Gerardi, R. J., & Keane, T. M. (1992). Assessment of posttraumatic stress disorder. In P. A. Saigh (Ed.), *Posttraumatic stress disorder: A behavioral approach to assessment and treatment* (pp. 50–84). Boston: Allyn and Bacon.

Malleson, N. (1959). Panic and phobia: A possible method of treatment. *Lancet, 1,* 225–227.

Mannion, N. E. & Levine, B. A. (1984). Effects of stimulus representation and cue category on exposure (flooding) therapy. *British Journal of Clinical Psychology, 23,* 1–7.

March, J. (1999). Assessment of pediatric posttraumatic stress disorder. In P. A. Saigh & J. D. Bremner (Eds.), *Posttraumatic stress disorder: A comprehensive textbook* (pp. 199–218). Needham Heights, MA: Allyn and Bacon.

Marks, I. A. (1972). Flooding (implosion) and allied treatments. In S. Argas (Ed.), *Behavior modification: Principles and clinical applications* (pp. 151–211). Boston, MA: Little, Brown, & Co.

Mathews, A. (1971). Psychophysiological approaches to the investigation of desensitization. *Psychological Bulletin, 76,* 73–83.

McCaffery, R. J., & Fairbank, J. D. (1985). Post-traumatic stress disorder associated with transportation accidents: Two case studies. *Behavior Therapy, 16,* 406–416.

Meadows, E. A., & Foa, E. B. (1999). Cognitive-behavioral treatment of traumatized adults. In P. A. Saigh & J. D. Bremner (Eds.), *Posttraumatic stress disorder: A comprehensive textbook.* Needham Heights, MA: Allyn and Bacon.

Miller, L. C., Barrett, C. L., & Hempe, E. (1974). Phobias of childhood in a prescientific era. In A. Davids (Ed.), *Child personality and psychopathology: Current topics* (pp. 89–134). New York: Wiley.

Mineka, S. (1979). The role of fear in theories of avoidance learning, flooding, and extinction. *Psychological Bulletin, 86,* 985–1010.

Morris, R. J., & Kratochwill, T. R. (1983). *Treating children's fears: A behavioral approach.* New York: Pergamon.

Mowrer, O. H. (1939). Stimulus response theory of anxiety. *Psychological Review, 46,* 553–565.

Piers, E. V. (1969). *Piers-Harris Children's Self-Concept Scale.* Los Angeles, CA.: Western Psychological Corporation.

Pollin, A. T. (1959). The effects of flooding and physical suppression as extinction techniques on an anxiety motivated avoidance locomotor response. *Journal of Psychology, 47,* 235–245.

Rachman, S. J. (1966). Studies in desensitization-II: Flooding. *Behaviour Research and Therapy, 4,* 1–6.

Rachman, S. J. (1980). Emotional processing. *Behaviour Research and Therapy, 18,* 51–60.

Rathus, S. A. (1973). A 30-item schedule for assessing assertive behavior. *Behavior Therapy, 4,* 398–406.

Reich, W., Leacock, N., & Shanfeld, C. (1994). *Diagnostic Interview for Children and Adolescents-Revised-Parent Version (DICA-R).* St. Louis, MO: Washington University.

Resick, P. A., & Schnicke, M. K. (1993). *Cognitive processing therapy for rape victims. A treatment manual.* Newbury Park, CA: Sage

Reynolds, C., & Richmond, B. O. (1978). *Revised Children's Manifest Anxiety Scale.* Los Angeles, CA: Western Psychological Services.

Reynolds, W. M. (1987). *Reynolds Adolescent Depression Scale.* Odessa, FL: Psychological Assessment Resources, Inc.

Rothbaum, B. O., & Foa, E. B. (1992). Cognitive-behavioral treatment of posttraumatic stress disorder. In P. A. Saigh (Ed.), *Posttraumatic stress disorder: A behavioral approach to assessment and treatment* (pp. 85–110). Boston: Allyn & Bacon.

Rychtarik, R. G., Silverman, W. K., & Van Landingham, W. P. (1984). Treatment of an incest victim with implosive therapy: A case study. *Behavior Therapy, 15,* 410–420.

Saigh, P. A. (1980). The use of endemic images as a means of inducing relaxation and desensitization. *Mediterranean Journal of Social Psychiatry, 1,* 11–16.

Saigh, P. A. (1986). *In vitro* flooding in the treatment of a 6-year-old boy's posttraumatic stress disorder. *Behaviour Research and Therapy, 24,* 685–688.

Saigh, P. A. (1987a). *In vitro* flooding of an adolescent's posttraumatic stress disorder. *Journal of Clinical Child Psychology, 16,* 147–150.

Saigh, P. A. (1987b). *In vitro* flooding of a childhood posttraumatic stress disorder. *School Psychology Review, 16,* 203–211.

Saigh, P. A. (1987c). *In vitro* flooding of childhood posttraumatic stress disorders: A systematic replication. *Professional School Psychology, 2,* 133–145.

Saigh, P. A. (1989a). The development and validation of the Children's Posttraumatic Stress Disorder Inventory. *International Journal of Special Education, 4,* 75–84.

Saigh, P. A. (1989b). The use of an *in vitro* flooding package in the treatment of traumatized adolescents. *Journal of Developmental and Behavioral Pediatrics, 10,* 17–21.

Saigh, P. A. (1992a). The behavioral treatment of child and adolescent posttraumatic stress disorder. *Advances in Behaviour Research and Therapy, 14,* 247–275.

Saigh, P. A. (1992b). Structured clinical interviews and the inferential process. *Journal of School Psychology, 30,* 141–149.

Saigh, P. A. (1995). *The Future Orientation Scale.* New York: City University of New York Graduate School.

Saigh, P. A. (1997). The *Children's Posttraumatic Stress Disorder Inventory.* New York: City University of New York Graduate School.

Saigh, P. A., & Antoun, F. (1984). Endemic images and the desensitization process. *Journal of School Psychology 22,* 679–682.

Saigh, P. A., & Fairbank, J. A. (1995, November). The effects of therapeutic flooding on the memories of child-adolescent PTSD patients. In J. D. Bremner (Chair), *Memory and cognition in PTSD.* Symposium conducted at the annual meeting of the International Society of Traumatic Stress Studies, Boston, MA.

Saigh, P. A., Fairbank, J. A., & Yasik, A. E. (1998). War-related posttraumatic stress disorder among children and adolescents. In T. Miller (Ed.), *Stressful life events* (2nd ed.) (pp. 119–140). Madison, CT: International Universities Press.

Saigh, P. A., Green, B., & Korol, M. (1996). The history and epidemiology of posttraumatic stress disorder with special reference to children and adolescents. *Journal of School Psychology, 34,* 107–131.

Saigh, P. A., Inamdar, S. C., Oberfield, R. A., McHugh, M., Spencer, K., Yasik, A. E., Rubenstein, H., &

Nester, J. (1997). [A comparative analysis of the affective, behavioral, and cognitive ratings of stress exposed adolescents]. Unpublished raw data.

Saigh, P. A., Mroueh, A., & Bremner, J. D. (1997). Scholastic impairments among traumatized adolescents. *Behaviour Research and Therapy, 35,* 429–436.

Saigh, P. A., Mroueh, A., Zimmerman, B., & Fairbank, J. A. (1995). Self-efficacy expectations among traumatized adolescents. *Behaviour Research and Therapy, 33,* 701–705.

Saigh, P. A., Yule, W., & Inamdar, S. C. (1996). Imaginal flooding of traumatized children and adolescents. *Journal of School Psychology, 34,* 163–183.

Schwartz, I. S., & Bear, D. M. (1991). Social validity assessments: Is current practice the state of the art? *Journal of Applied Behavior Analysis, 24,* 189–204.

Scott, M. J., & Stradling, S. G. (1992). *Counseling for posttraumatic stress disorder.* London: Sage.

Sellick, K. J. & Peck, C. L. (1977). Behavioral treatment of a child with cerebral palsy using a flooding treatment *Archives of Physical Medicine and Rehabilitation, 62,* 398–400.

Shapiro, F. (1989). Eye movement desensitization: A new treatment for post-traumatic desensitization. *Journal of Behaviour Therapy and Experimental Psychiatry, 51,* 199–223.

Sheslow, W., & Adams, D. (1990). *Wide Range Assessment of Memory and Learning.* Wilmington, DE: Jastak Associates, Inc.

Solomon, R. L., Kamin, S., & Wynne, L. C. (1953). Traumatic avoidance learning: The principles of anxiety conversation and partial irreversibility. *Psychological Review, 61,* 353–385.

Spielberger, C. D., Gorsuch, R. L., & Lushane, R. E. (1968). *Manual for the State Trait Anxiety Inventory.* Palo Alto, CA: Consulting Psychologist Press.

Spitzer, R. L., Endicott, J., & Robins, E. (1978). Research diagnostic criteria: Rational and reliability. *Archives of General Psychiatry, 23,* 45–55.

Stampfl, T. G. (1961). *Implosive therapy a learning theory derived psychodynamic technique.* Unpublished manuscript, John Carroll University at Cleveland.

Stampfl, T. G., & Levis, D. J. (1967). Essentials of implosive therapy: A learning-based psychodynamic behavioral therapy. *Journal of Abnormal Psychology, 72,* 496–503.

Wolf, M. M. (1978). Social validity: The case of subjective measurement or how applied behavior analysis is finding its heart. *Journal of Applied Behavior Analysis, 11,* 315–329.

Wolfe, D. A. (1991). *Preventing physical and emotional abuse of children.* New York: Guilford.

Wolpe, J. (1990). *The practice of behavior therapy* (4th ed.). Elmsford. Pergamon.

Yule, W. (1998). Posttraumatic stress disorder in children and its treatment. In T. Miller (Ed.), *Stressful life events* (2nd ed.) (pp. 219–243). Madison, CT: International Universities Press.

Yule, W., Sacks, B., & Hersov, L. (1974). Successful flooding treatment of a noise phobia in a 11-year-old boy. *Journal of Behaviour Therapy and Experimental Psychiatry, 5,* 209–211.

Yule, W., & Udwin, O. (1991). Screening child survivors for symptoms of post-traumatic stress disorder: Experiences from the *Jupiter* sinking. *British Journal of Clinical Psychology, 30,* 131–138.

CHAPTER 18

COGNITIVE-BEHAVIORAL TREATMENT
OF TRAUMATIZED ADULTS

ELIZABETH A. MEADOWS, PH.D.,
Central Michigan University

and

EDNA B. FOA, PH.D.,
Center for the Treatment and Study of Anxiety
Department of Psychiatry
Allegheny University of the Health Sciences
(formerly Medical College of Pennsylvania and
Hahnemann University)

Traumatic experiences and their psychological sequelae are alarmingly prevalent in our society. Epidemiological studies suggest that 39 percent of individuals in the United States experienced at least one traumatic event in their lifetimes (Breslau, Davis, Andreski, & Peterson, 1991). Such traumas include assault, natural disasters, accidents, and combat. Each of these has been associated with the development of posttraumatic stress disorder (PTSD). Estimates of PTSD in the general U.S. population have ranged from 1 percent (e.g., Helzer, Robins, & McEvoy, 1987) to 9 percent (e.g., Breslau et al., 1991). Given this high prevalence, it is clear that PTSD is a problem of significant proportion, rendering the development of effective treatments for this disorder crucial. Since the recognition that traumatic events may result in chronic psychological difficulties, mental health providers have utilized various interventions including crisis intervention programs, group psychotherapy, hypnosis, psychodynamic psychotherapy, and cognitive-behavioral therapy (for a review, see Foa & Meadows, 1997). In this chapter we will focus on the cognitive-behavioral therapies that have been developed to treat PTSD. These include exposure procedures, cognitive therapy, anxiety management techniques, and programs combining these procedures. Each of these treatments will be discussed, focusing on theoretical underpinnings, descriptions of the treatments, a review of the efficacy literature, and a discussion of potential treatment obstacles.

EXPOSURE THERAPY

Exposure techniques involve confronting one's fears. These techniques are derived from learning theory, primarily from Mowrer's (1960) two-factor theory. According to this theory, fear is acquired via classical conditioning, when a neutral stimulus is paired with an aversive stimulus (or unconditioned stimulus; UCS). Following such pairing, the neutral stimulus (now a conditioned stimulus, or CS) comes to elicit a conditioned fear response (CR). This acquired fear is then maintained via operant conditioning, in which avoidance and escape are used to alleviate anxiety through negative reinforcement. Even when the UCS is terminated, the persistent avoidance of the CS prevents the realization that the CS no longer leads to negative consequences, and so the avoidance serves to maintain the fear and anxiety. Exposure techniques were developed as a way of intervening in this process, forcing the fearful individual to realize that the CS is no longer dangerous and avoidance no longer necessary.

Expanding on these notions, Foa and Kozak (1986) posited that the fear reduction observed during exposure is mediated by cognitive changes, referring to these changes as emotional processing. Drawing from Lang's (1979) bioinformation theory of emotion, Foa & Kozak viewed pathological fear as a cognitive structure that includes erroneous associations among representations of stimuli, responses, and their meaning. They then suggested that exposure reduces fear by correcting these erroneous associations via the activation of the fear structure (through exposure to the feared stimuli) and the presentation of corrective information (e.g., that the feared consequences do not occur). This conceptualization of emotional processing is compatible with Rescorla's (1988) view of conditioning as a change in meaning.

Within the emotional processing conceptualization of PTSD, exposure therapy is thought to ameliorate symptoms by introducing information that challenges the erroneous cognitions underlying the disorder (Foa & Jaycox, in press). The corrective information includes the notion that thinking about the trauma is not dangerous, that the act of remembering is not equivalent to actually reexperiencing the trauma, and that even without avoidance/escape the anxiety associated with the feared stimuli gradually decreases. Further, exposure serves to teach clients that experiencing PTSD symptoms does not lead to a loss of control.

Exposure techniques vary along several dimensions, including those of exposure medium (imaginal versus in vivo), exposure length (short versus long), and arousal level (low versus high). Thus, different exposure methods share the common feature of confronting feared stimuli, but vary on these dimensions as to how exposure is conducted. (For more details, see Foa, Rothbaum, & Kozak, 1989).

Systematic Desensitization

Systematic Desensitization (SD) falls on one extreme of the dimensions of exposure methods, using brief, imaginal, and minimally arousing exercises. SD, pioneered by Wolpe (1958), was among the earliest behavioral treatments studied for PTSD. It involves pairing imaginal exposure with relaxation, so that the anxiety elicited by the confrontation with the feared stimuli is inhibited by relaxation. First, the client is instructed in muscle relaxation exercises. When a state of relaxation is achieved, the feared stimuli are introduced, via imagined scenarios, in a graded, hierarchical manner with the least anxiety-provoking scenarios presented first. When the client begins to feel anxious, the client is instructed to erase the scene, focus on relaxation, and then imagine the scenario again. This scenario is repeated until it no longer elicits anxiety, at which point the next most difficult scenario is introduced. This process continues until the stimuli on the hierarchy no longer elicit anxiety.

As noted earlier, SD was one of the first behavioral methods utilized to treat combat reactions and post-rape sequelae. Case reports and uncontrolled studies (e.g., Bowen & Lambert, 1986; Frank & Stewart, 1983, 1984; Schindler, 1980; Turner, 1979; Wolff, 1977) showed SD to be effective in reducing PTSD symptoms, although definitive conclusions about its efficacy cannot be drawn from such studies. Frank et al. (1988) also found SD efficacious, relative to a group of untreated women, in decreasing symptoms in women who had been raped. However, the untreated comparison group was obtained from two separate studies conducted at other sites and thus did not constitute an adequate control group. A large experimental study by Brom, Kleber, and Defares (1989) supported the efficacy of SD in victims of mixed traumas (including many who were not directly traumatized themselves, but had lost a loved one). Specifically, clients were randomly assigned to either SD, psychodynamic therapy, hypnotherapy, or a wait-list control group; all active treatments produced greater symptom improvement than did the wait-list control.

Although short imaginal exposure in SD was proven to be somewhat effective in ameliorating pathological anxiety, it has been repeatedly demonstrated to be inferior to long exposures, in which the anxiety-provoking stimuli are not removed when the client becomes anxious (e.g, Stern & Marks, 1973). Additionally, Barlow, Leitenberg, Agras, and Wincze

(1969) conducted an analog study comparing systematic desensitization with real versus imagined stimuli with snake-fearful students. Subjects confronting the live snakes performed significantly better on a subsequent behavioral approach test than subjects who confronted only imagined snakes. In recent years, the interest in SD as a treatment for PTSD has waned, with studies focusing increasingly on prolonged exposure.

Imaginal and In Vivo Exposure

Both prolonged imaginal and *in vivo* exposure demonstrated considerable efficacy in several controlled studies following promising results from case reports and uncontrolled studies (e.g., Fairbank & Keane, 1982; Johnson, Gilmore, & Shenoy, 1982; Keane & Kaloupek, 1982). Currently, most of the well-controlled studies of PTSD treatments involve imaginal and/or in vivo exposure treatments.

Description of Exposure Treatment.   *Imaginal exposure* is generally conducted by having the client relive the traumatic event in memory, by recounting it in detail aloud. To enhance the vividness of the memory, clients are instructed to visualize the scene as they describe it, to focus on the events as well as on their thoughts and emotions, and to talk about it as if it was happening now, rather than telling a story about a past event. Instructions for a client with assault-related PTSD are as follows:

> *"I want you to close your eyes and begin to talk about the assault. Talk about it in the first person, as if it is happening to you right now. As you're talking, picture the story in your mind, and describe what is happening. Describe it in as much detail as possible, including what you're doing, what he's doing, what you're thinking and feeling. Try not to let go of the image, even if it's upsetting to you, and we will talk about it after the exposure is finished."*

Depending on the length of the trauma narrative, the traumatic event may be recounted several times within one exposure session, to ensure that the exposure is sufficiently prolonged to allow adequate processing (generally a minimum of 30 minutes). Clients are told in advance that the discussion about their experiences during exposure will be delayed until the exposure portion of the session is completed. In this way, the full exposure time can proceed uninterrupted.

In vivo exposure consists of the client's confronting objectively safe situations that have become associated with the traumatic event and thus have acquired (erroneous) fearful properties. Typically, a hierarchy of such situations is developed, and exposure begins with those situations rated as moderately fear-inducing. As in imaginal exposure, clients confront their fears, this time by placing themselves in situations that remind them of the trauma. For example, a man who was assaulted in a parking lot might include on his hierarchy staying in a parked car at the lot, walking in the lot with a friend, and walking in the lot by himself. Situations that do involve realistic danger, such as walking around a deserted parking lot at night, are not appropriate targets for *in vivo* exposure, and thus decision-making regarding the development of the hierarchy becomes critically important. In the above example, the first exposure exercise might include sitting in the parked car for an hour daily. When this exercise no longer elicits severe anxiety, the next hierarchy item is confronted. It is usually unnecessary to confront every feared stimulus due to the generalization that often occurs during exposure.

Review of the Literature.   A number of studies have demonstrated the efficacy of imaginal and *in vivo* exposure for PTSD. As was true for the SD studies, to date imaginal and *in vivo* exposure have been studied primarily with veterans and assault victims, although the treatment has been employed recently with other trauma populations.

Studies of exposure treatments in veteran populations have typically compared such treatments either with a wait-list control group or with "standard treatment" conducted at VA hospitals and clinics. Cooper and Clum (1989) examined imaginal exposure as an adjunct to standard outpatient treatment (psychosocial and pharmacological) in combat veterans with PTSD. Results showed that the addition of exposure to standard treatment enhanced improvement on some PTSD symptoms. Keane, Fairbank, Caddell, and Zimering (1989) compared imaginal exposure (flooding) with a wait-list control group. In this study, exposure was found to reduce fear and depression, as well as the reexperiencing symptoms of PTSD, although the other PTSD symptom clusters were not affected. Finally, Boudewyns and colleagues (Boudewyns & Hyer, 1990; Boudewyns, Hyer, Woods, Harrison, & McCranie, 1990) studied exposure as an adjunct to standard milieu treatment on a special PTSD inpatient unit. This program was compared with individual counseling, also as an adjunct to standard milieu treatment. These two reports noted that exposure was somewhat superior to the control condition on self-reports of psychological symptoms. On the other hand, no significant differences were seen on physiological responding.

All of the veterans studies just reviewed suffered from methodological difficulties, and thus caution must be exercised in drawing definitive conclusions; however, the combined studies suggest that imaginal exposure is at least somewhat efficacious in alleviating PTSD symptoms in veterans.

Two well controlled studies (Foa, Dancu, Hembree, Jaycox, & Meadows, 1997; Foa, Rothbaum, Riggs, & Murdock, 1991) examined the use of prolonged exposure (PE) in female assault victims. Unlike the veterans studies, these studies focused on *in vivo* as well as on imaginal exposure. In the first, PE was compared with stress inoculation training (SIT) and supportive counseling (SC), as well as with a wait-list control condition. The second study compared PE, SIT, and their combination, also with a wait-list control condition. Both of these studies showed that PE was efficacious in reducing PTSD symptoms. In the first study, PE appeared superior to the other treatments at follow-up evaluations of up to one year. In the second study, PE consistently outperformed the other two treatments, although these differences did not always reach significance.

Three other studies, conducted with victims of a variety of traumas, also showed evidence for the efficacy of exposure. Richards, Lovell, and Marks (1994) examined two treatment programs: imaginal exposure followed by *in vivo* exposure, and *in vivo* followed by imaginal exposure. Both these programs were quite effective in reducing PTSD symptoms; *in vivo* exposure appeared more effective than imaginal exposure in reducing avoidance regardless of the or-

der in which it took place. Thompson, Charlton, Kerry, Lee, and Turner (1995) also conducted an open trial of exposure treatment, both imaginal and *in vivo,* with a mixed trauma population. Although the lack of a control group precludes definitive conclusions, this study provides additional support for the efficacy of exposure; in addition to a reduction in PTSD symptoms, post-treatment results indicated improvement on measures of general health symptoms and general psychological symptoms. Finally, Marks, Lovell, Noshirvani, Livanou, and Thrasher (1997) compared the efficacy of exposure (imaginal and *in vivo*), cognitive restructuring, and their combination, to a relaxation treatment. Exposure, cognitive restructuring, and the combination treatment were more effective than relaxation in reducing PTSD symptoms. However, clients in the relaxation group evidenced modest improvement as well.

Taken together, the exposure studies provide consistent evidence for the efficacy of imaginal and *in vivo* exposure in the treatment of PTSD. The results appear to be stronger in civilian populations. It should be noted that the two studies examining the efficacy of exposure in assault-related PTSD come from the same research group. However, Resick and her colleagues are currently conducting a study that examines the efficacy of PE, with initial results supporting its use (Resick, Nishith, & Astin, 1996).

Eye-Movement Desensitization/Reprocessing (EMDR)

EMDR is a form of imaginal exposure accompanied by saccadic eye movements. It is conducted by having a client focus on a disturbing image or memory while the therapist moves a finger across the client's visual field (Shapiro, 1995). The saccadic eye movements result from the client's tracking the therapist's finger. Since its inception, EMDR has been the focus of much controversy (Tolin, Montgomery, Kleinknecht, & Lohr, 1996). Positive results of EMDR have been reported in a number of case studies (for a review, see Lohr, Kleinknecht, Tolin, & Barrett, 1996) but studies incorporating at least minimal controls have demonstrated mixed results.

A number of studies (Boudewyns, Stwertka, Hyer, Albrecht, & Sperr, 1993; Jensen, 1994; Pitman et al., 1996; Renfrey & Spates, 1994; Rothbaum, 1995; Shapiro, 1989; Silver, Brooks, & Obenchain, 1995; Vaughan et al., 1994; Wilson, Becker, & Tinker, 1995) have been conducted to examine the efficacy of EMDR in reducing posttrauma reactions. In some studies EMDR was compared to a wait-list control, standard treatment, or alternative treatment such as relaxation. Other studies compared EMDR to a variant of the technique, such as imagery without the eye movements or with a different form of focus on the eye. Some studies included both comparisons. These studies typically showed that clients treated with EMDR reported lower subjective anxiety ratings during session than did clients in other treatment groups, but did not evidence any differences on objective standardized outcome measures. Additionally, almost all of these studies suffered from methodological flaws that rendered their results inconclusive. Two exceptions are the Rothbaum (1997) and Pitman et al. (1996) studies. In Rothbaum's well-controlled study, 21 female rape victims were randomly assigned to either EMDR or a wait-list control group. Those who received EMDR improved significantly on both subjective and objective measures of PTSD symptoms compared to wait-list, suggesting that EMDR can effectively reduce PTSD symptoms. Participants in the Pitman et al. study were 17 male veterans with PTSD who received EMDR with and without eye movements in a crossover design. Results indicated that both treatments demonstrated decreased symptoms on self-report measures, but not on independent assessor ratings. The lack of differences between the two procedures suggests that the eye movements, the feature that differentiates EMDR from other exposure treatments, do not appear relevant to treatment outcome. Overall, the EMDR studies provide mixed evidence as to the efficacy of the therapy. Well-controlled studies are needed to determine if the treatment is effective, and whether differences in efficacy exist between EMDR and more established exposure treatments.

Summary of Exposure Treatments

Taking all the exposure studies together, there is clear evidence for the efficacy of exposure. The bulk of the well-controlled studies have focused on prolonged imaginal and *in vivo* exposure, with scantier evidence for the efficacy of SD and EMDR. The consistency of the positive results of exposure, demonstrated in a variety of trauma populations, suggests that exposure might be considered the treatment of choice for PTSD. Not only has this treatment been demonstrated to be effective, but it is also relatively easy to learn, making it particularly suitable for dissemination to clinicians who do not specialize in PTSD or in cognitive-behavioral treatments.

Special Considerations

Despite the strong support for the use of exposure therapy, the clinician needs to consider several issues when conducting this treatment (see Jaycox & Foa, 1996, for a fuller discussion). For example, anger has been shown to interfere with imaginal exposure, by impeding emotional engagement with the traumatic memory that is necessary for emotional processing of the trauma to occur (Foa, Riggs, Massie, & Yarczower, 1995). Intense anger during exposure may be addressed in several ways. First, clients can be informed about the detrimental effect of anger on the effectiveness of exposure and instructed to delay discussion about the anger until later in treatment. Often, following symptom reduction clients become less angry. For clients who seem unable to delay working on their anger, the use of cognitive therapy is recommended to deal directly with this emotion.

Dissociation can also interfere with exposure. On rare occasions, clients are unable to titrate their emotions during imaginal exposure and enter a dissociative state (i.e., have prolonged flashbacks of the trauma). For exposure to be successful, the client needs to engage in the traumatic memory and concurrently realize that the exposure experience is occurring in the present, in a safe environment, and when the client is in full control. These elements are missing when the client enters a dissociative state. In these instances, exposure is unlikely to provide corrective information and consequently, modify the pathological associations underlying PTSD. To overcome such dissociative states the therapist can instruct the client to keep his or her eyes open rather than closed, and can frequently introduce reminders that the client is in the therapist's office, that remembering the trauma does not mean being retraumatized, and that the client is currently safe.

Some clients are unable to emotionally engage in the trauma memory and report being numb rather than anxious. These clients, as well as those having difficulty with imagery, may need additional prompting and questioning to enhance the vividness of their images. The introduction of concrete cues, such as playing music that elicits memories of the trauma, may also enhance vividness. Some clients use numbing as a coping strategy; a reiteration of the rationale for emotional engagement during exposure may help the client overcome this problem. Few clients cannot engage emotionally at all during in-session exposure, especially when the necessity for doing so has been adequately explained; however, if this occurs other treatments should be implemented.

Some clients refuse to enter exposure therapy because of anticipated fear and strong avoidance habits. In these cases, beginning therapy with less anxiety-provoking treatments such as SIT can provide the client with sufficient coping strategies that he or she might become willing to try exposure once these strategies are in place.

Finally, there is some evidence that exposure treatment is not advisable when the client's PTSD symptoms focus on acts of perpetration rather than of victimization (Pitman et al., 1991). Such clients may not only fail to benefit from exposure, but may even deteriorate, and thus alternative treatments should be implemented.

COGNITIVE THERAPY

Description of the Procedure

Cognitive therapy was pioneered by Beck (1972, 1976) and further developed by others (e.g., Clark, 1986) to help clients modify dysfunctional cognitions. The basic assumption in this therapy is that dysfunctional thoughts drive negative emotional states such as fear or anger. Thus, a given situation may lead to different emotions depending on the interpretation of the situation. Accordingly, pathological emotions are being generated by distorted, dysfunctional thoughts. Typically, cognitive restructuring (CR) aims to teach clients to identify dysfunctional thoughts, to evaluate their validity, to challenge erroneous or unhelpful thoughts, and to replace them with more beneficial ones. For example, a person who hears a noise in the night might think, "Oh, the cat's playing in the living room again." This person would likely feel at most mild annoyance at having been woken, and return to sleep. Alternatively, the person might think, "Oh no! Someone is breaking into my house!" In this case, the person would likely have a strong emotional reaction of fear, despite having been exposed to the same noise as in the first case. Cognitive restructuring would initially focus on identifying the thoughts that precede strong emotions, such as "I'm going to be attacked." Then the validity of this belief or its usefulness would be evaluated. Erroneous or unhelpful beliefs are replaced by rational responses suggested by the evidence reviewed in the previous step (i.e., "there are many sources of noise in my house").

Review of the Literature

CR has been incorporated into several treatment programs for PTSD, including SIT, which will be discussed in the next section, and PE/CR, which will be discussed in the section on combination programs. In this section we will review studies that evaluated CR only.

As noted in the section on SD, Frank et al. (1988) randomly assigned women who had been raped to SD or cognitive therapy, and found that both treatments were effective in alleviating post-assault symptoms. However, as Kilpatrick and Calhoun (1988) noted, the inclusion of recent victims rendered these results inconclusive; indeed symptoms decrease in the process of natural recovery even if treatment is not provided. Because of this possible confound of natural recovery shortly following assault, Frank et al. (1988) conducted a separate analysis including only "delayed treatment-seekers," or a subsample of 24 women who sought treatment several weeks to several months after the rape. These women also showed significant improvement on measures of depression, fear, anxiety, and self-esteem, with no differences being observed between the two treatments, suggesting that both SD and cognitive therapy were effective in reducing symptoms of chronic post-rape reactions. As noted earlier, this study did not include an appropriate control group. Therefore, extraneous factors such as expectancy cannot be ruled out as a cause of symptom reduction.

The efficacy of CR in treating PTSD clients was also examined in the Marks et al. (1997) study reviewed earlier, which compared CR, exposure, their combination, and relaxation. Exposure, CR, and their combination were equally effective in reducing PTSD symptoms, although inspection of the means suggest that cognitive therapy was somewhat inferior to exposure and the combination treatment.

In summary, the efficacy of cognitive therapy in ameliorating chronic PTSD has not been studied as extensively as that of exposure therapy. However, the few studies that have examined CR attest to its efficacy. At minimum, CR may be useful as an adjunct to exposure treatments, especially in cases such as those described in the preceding section in which emotional or behavioral responses interfere with the exposure. It remains to be seen if CR is a useful alternative for those cases in which exposure is contraindicated, such as traumas of perpetration.

Special Considerations

Because of the limited experience with the use of cognitive therapy for PTSD, less is known about what issues require special attention. Clinical observations suggest that clients with abstraction or intellectual deficits may have difficulty grasping the concepts of CR and using them to identify and modify trauma-related cognitive distortions. Using more concrete forms of CR, such as index cards of rational responses to common cognitive distortions, may address this problem.

ANXIETY MANAGEMENT THERAPIES

The assumption that seems to underlie the rationale for anxiety management programs centers on the notion that pathological anxiety stems from skills deficits. As such, it is thought that providing anxious clients with appropriate skills will enable them to manage their anxiety. These skills include relaxation training, positive self-statements, breathing retraining, biofeedback, social skills training, and distraction methods. Unlike the therapies reviewed previously, which aim at preventing pathological anxiety from occurring by correcting the mechanisms thought to underlie it, anxiety management treatments focus on managing the anxiety when it does occur.

Stress Inoculation Training (SIT)

One of the most commonly used anxiety management treatments for PTSD is SIT. SIT was developed by Meichenbaum (1974) as a treatment for anxious clients and was adapted by Veronen, Kilpatrick, and Resick (1979) for treating rape-related disturbances. The modified SIT includes psychoeducation, muscle relaxation training, breathing retraining, role-playing, covert modeling, guided self-dialog, and thought-stopping. As described in Kilpatrick, Veronen, and Resick (1982), the SIT package used with rape victims begins with an educational phase in which responses to the rape are explained in terms of learning principles such as classical conditioning, stimulus generalization, and avoidance behavior. The three-component model is discussed in this phase as well, so that clients can begin to see their responses as falling in the physiological, behavioral, and cognitive domains.

Breathing retraining and muscle relaxation address the physiological manifestations of fear. In breathing retraining, clients are taught to breathe more slowly and deeply, while in muscle relaxation training various muscle groups are systematically tensed and released. This training may also include a discussion of other means of relaxation, such as engaging in activities one has found to be relaxing.

Role-playing and covert modeling address the behavior component of fear. These strategies are used to encourage the client to practice various behaviors such as gradual exposure to fear-provoking situations, with the therapist serving as a model for the client to imitate and providing opportunities for the client to practice in session.

Finally, thought stopping and guided self-dialog address the cognitive component of fear. In thought-stopping, clients are taught to suddenly say "STOP" to themselves when an upsetting thought arises. This statement can be accompanied by a loud handclap, snap of a rubberband or other adjunct to increase its salience. Guided self-dialog is more aligned with cognitive restructuring methods, with clients taught to identify negative thoughts and employ self-statements to offset these thoughts.

Review of the Literature

The efficacy of SIT for female rape victims was first examined in two uncontrolled studies (Kilpatrick et al., 1982; Veronen & Kilpatrick, 1982). In one study (Kilpatrick et al., 1982) the women were allowed to choose among three conditions offered, SIT, SD, and peer counseling, because one of the goals of the study was to assess treatment preferences. Seventy percent of the participants chose SIT, with 30 percent choosing peer counseling and none choosing SD, suggesting that SIT is a palatable program. Both studies indicated that SIT was efficacious in reducing symptoms such as rape-related fears, anxiety, and depression; PTSD symptoms were not assessed in their entirety as the diagnosis had only recently entered the psychiatric nosology. Two additional case reports (Kilpatrick & Amick, 1985; Pearson, Poquette, & Wasden, 1983) also attested to the success of SIT in alleviating post-rape symptoms. Because of the uncontrolled nature of these studies, conclusions from these results are limited.

The first experimental study examining the efficacy of SIT for rape victims was conducted by Resick, Jordan, Girelli, Hutter, and Marhoefer-Dvorak (1988). As in the previous studies, PTSD diagnostic status was not assessed and the treatment targeted rape-related fear and anxiety. The SIT treatment conducted in this study varied somewhat from that described by Kilpatrick et al. (1982). Specifically, components such as assertiveness training were removed due to their constituting alternative treatment conditions. In this study, the order of the treatments (SIT, assertiveness training, or supportive psychotherapy, all conducted in group format) was pre-determined and clients were assigned to the next available therapy group in the order of their enrollment. The efficacy of these treatments were compared to one another and to a naturally occurring wait-list control group. All three treatments were effective in reducing symptoms relative to the wait-list condition, although this improvement was generally of modest proportions, and no differences were observed between the three treatments.

Two other controlled studies, both reviewed in the section on exposure therapy, examined the efficacy of SIT in treating female assault victims with chronic PTSD. In these studies, SIT was conducted in individual sessions rather than in the group format used in the previous study. Foa et al. (1991) compared SIT with PE, supportive counseling, and a wait-list condition, with results indicating that SIT and PE were equally effective in reducing PTSD symptoms at post-treatment. At follow-up (M=three months post-treatment), however, there was a slight difference between these two groups, with PE showing superior outcome. The second study (Foa et al., 1997) compared SIT, PE, the combination of SIT/PE, and a wait-list condition. Results from this study also demonstrated SIT to be effective in reducing PTSD symptoms, with all three active treatments producing significant improvement in PTSD, depression, and anxiety symptoms relative to the wait-list condition. As noted earlier, on some measures PE showed superiority to the other two active treatments.

In summary, the available studies on the use of SIT in treating PTSD suggests that it is an effective treatment. However, it should be noted that all of these studies were conducted with female assault victims, and thus the efficacy of SIT with other trauma populations remains unknown.

Biofeedback

Another anxiety management treatment, biofeedback, has also been used in the treatment of PTSD. Biofeedback is a procedure in which clients learn to gain control over their physiological processes. This control is achieved by having clients observe displays of their physiological activity (i.e., electromyographic activity or EMG) and then try to change the display.

Three studies have examined the efficacy of biofeedback in treating trauma clients. In an early case report, Blanchard and Abel (1976) noted that biofeedback training was effective in helping a rape victim control her physiological reactivity (tachycardia). This report, of course, predated the diagnosis of PTSD but does suggest improvement of the major symptoms of PTSD.

Hickling, Sison, and Vanderploeg (1986) treated six veterans with PTSD by a combination of biofeedback and relaxation training and reported improvement on all symptom measures. Peniston (1986) examined the efficacy of a program that included biofeedback combined with desensitization versus a no-treatment condition in 16 veterans with PTSD. Again biofeedback was found to be helpful, being superior to no treatment on measures of muscle tension, nightmares, and flashbacks. Thus, there is some evidence that biofeedback may be effective in alleviating symptoms of PTSD, but the limited data precludes endorsing this technique as a treatment of choice for this disorder.

Summary of Anxiety Management Treatment

SIT is the most studied program of the anxiety management treatments for PTSD, and has been shown to be effective in treating this disorder. Biofeedback has also been found to be of potential utility although it was less rigorously studied. Therefore, among the anxiety management therapies, the evidence for SIT clearly outweighs that for other treatments.

Special Considerations for SIT

A difficulty in evaluating the utility of SIT stems from the absence of dismantling studies. Although the program includes a number of components and thus is quite labor intensive for both therapists and clients, sufficient data is not yet available to guide us in deciding which components are necessary and which can be deleted. Additionally, some SIT components, such as thought-stopping, have been shown to be ineffective in treating other anxiety disorders such as obsessive-compulsive disorder (e.g., Stern & Marks, 1973), and may detract from the efficacy of

the SIT program by occupying time that could be devoted to components with proven efficacy such as cognitive restructuring. Until results from dismantling studies are available, therapists will need to rely on clinical judgment to make case-by-case decisions regarding the inclusion of individual SIT components.

One problem that may arise during SIT treatment involves relaxation-induced anxiety. Some anxious individuals have adverse reactions to relaxation and become more rather than less anxious during the procedure (Heide & Borkevec, 1983, 1984). In some cases, the relaxation-induced anxiety stems from cognitive distortions, such as a fear of losing control if one becomes too relaxed; these problems may be addressed via the cognitive component of SIT. For other clients, relaxation triggers anxiety by enhancing attention to anxiety-evoking thoughts and sensations. These problems may also be addressed via cognitive restructuring, although in clients with more severe anxiety it may be preferable to forego relaxation training.

As in the case of cognitive therapy, clients with abstraction or intellectual deficits may have difficulty with the more cognitive components of SIT. A more detailed discussion that deals with the modification of these components was provided in the earlier section on cognitive therapy.

PROGRAMS COMBINING EXPOSURE AND ANXIETY MANAGEMENT TREATMENTS

Because exposure therapy, cognitive therapy, and SIT were all shown to be effective in reducing PTSD symptoms, researchers began to examine whether programs that combine several techniques would enhance the efficacy that has been found for single programs. In this section we will examine the efficacy of combination programs. These include programs that simply combine existing treatments, many of which were already described in preceding sections, as well as new programs that incorporate aspects of different treatments.

Foa et al. (1997) compared the efficacy of a combined SIT/PE program with SIT alone, PE alone, and a wait-list control condition in reducing assault-related

PTSD. Results of this study indicated that the combined treatment was not superior to either individually. Unexpectedly, clients who received exposure only showed more improvement on some measures, with other measures indicating that the three treatments were equivalent, all outperforming the wait-list group equally well.

Similar results were observed in the Marks et al. (1997) study, which included a comparison of CR alone, PE alone, and the combination of CR and PE (as well as a relaxation control group). The authors noted that all three treatments were equally effective and superior to relaxation with respect to PTSD symptoms, depression, work and social adjustment, and a self-reported "main problem." However, at 6-month follow-up, the means of the groups seem to indicate the superiority of PE alone and PE/CR over CR alone. The relaxation group was followed only to three months post-treatment, with means at that follow-up point indicating the superiority of PE and PE/CR relative to relaxation.

Hickling and Blanchard (1997) examined a modified version of the Foa et al. (1997) SIT/PE program to treat 10 motor vehicle accident victims with either full-blown or subsyndromal PTSD. In addition to the SIT and PE components included in the Foa et al. program, the Hickling and Blanchard treatment also included pleasant events scheduling and discussion of existential issues. Preliminary results indicated that this open trial of SIT/PE was effective in reducing symptoms of PTSD. However, due to the lack of control and comparison treatments, it is not clear which aspect or aspects of the treatment were instrumental in effecting this change.

Another combined treatment approach, cognitive processing therapy (CPT), was developed by Resick and Schnicke (1992a) specifically to treat rape victims. This treatment draws from cognitive and information processing models, using both exposure and cognitive therapy techniques. However, both these procedures are conducted somewhat differently than in traditional exposure and cognitive therapies. The exposure component of CPT consisted of the client writing an account of the rape, and then reading this account. In contrast to traditional CR, which does not specify in advance which themes will be addressed in any given session, the cognitive restructuring component of CPT focuses on five themes identified a priori, with each discussed at designated sessions. These themes are described by McCann and Pearlman (1990) as the core difficulties observed in female rape victims and include safety, trust, power, esteem, and intimacy.

The efficacy of CPT was examined by Resick and Schnicke (1992a). Treatment was conducted in group format with 19 rape victims. Using a quasi-experimental design, outcomes of treated clients were compared to those of a naturally occurring wait-list control group. Clients in the CPT group improved significantly with regard to symptoms of PTSD and depression. These promising outcomes were supported by an updated report of this study (Resick & Schnicke, 1992b), in which 54 participants (those included in the first report plus additional clients) showed improvement in both PTSD and depressive symptoms. Prior to treatment, 96 percent of clients met criteria for PTSD; 88 percent of these clients no longer received a PTSD diagnosis following CPT. These results suggest that CPT is an effective treatment for rape-related PTSD. However, as in the case of the Hickling and Blanchard study, the lack of comparison groups and dismantling studies do not permit conclusions about the relative efficacy of each CPT component.

Overall, the initial hopes of improved efficacy by combining treatment approaches have not been borne out. One possible explanation for this failure of combination treatments to outperform single-treatment programs is that the combined treatments short-change the individual components by allowing less time to learn and practice any one technique. Additionally, because the combined approaches have not been subjected to dismantling studies, we do not know which components of such treatments are active, or even which may be detrimental. Research currently being conducted may help answer these questions. For example, Foa and her colleagues are currently testing a simplified version of their SIT/PE treatment, comparing PE alone with PE plus CR. Resick and her colleagues are also continuing to study combination treatments, currently comparing CPT, PE, and a wait-list control group.

CONSIDERATIONS FOR SPECIFIC TRAUMA POPULATIONS

Veterans

As noted in the section on exposure treatment, studies of veteran populations have reported lower rates of improvement following PTSD treatment than have studies of nonveteran populations. This may indicate that veterans do not respond as well as nonveterans to treatment. However, it may also be an artifact of the studies themselves. For example, most studies of veterans are conducted through the VA system. This system, by virtue of compensating for service-connected disability, introduces significant secondary gains for its patients to remain ill. In addition, many veterans may never enter studies based in military systems, as those with more resources have access to private treatment; however, it is these same clients who might be expected to respond most to treatment due to their higher level of functioning. Also, the studies of Vietnam veterans were conducted 10–20 years following the trauma, in contrast to studies of other trauma populations which typically include more recently traumatized clients. Thus, it is possible that over the years, the veterans' PTSD symptoms may have become more pervasive and less amenable to treatment. Associated difficulties, such as substance use, might also have become more entrenched over the additional years. Studies of more recently traumatized veterans, such as those who fought in the Persian Gulf or served in peacekeeping missions, may begin to address these issues.

A more clinical issue in the treatment of veterans arises when considering the specific nature of the traumatic events. While guilt and shame are common reactions among trauma survivors (e.g., rape victims who blame themselves for not having prevented the rape), the triggers for guilt and shame in veterans may be realistic when the distress is related to being perpetrators. Thus, the veteran who killed innocent civilians, for example, might rightly resist attempts to challenge the justification for this guilt. Dealing effectively with such issues may require going beyond the traditional cognitive-behavioral treatment strategies described in this chapter. Several such alternative strategies include exploring ways of making reparations, such as performing volunteer work with veterans' families, and bearing witness to the events of the past. Kubany (1994) also addresses the issue of guilt in combat-related PTSD, and has developed a model of different guilt types, each associated with different errors in logic. He suggested that combat-related guilt is amenable to change via cognitive therapy targeting these specific errors.

Sexual Assault Victims

Victims of assault, unlike combat veterans upon return to peace zones, must face the reality that they may confront a similar trauma. Thus, issues of daily safety play a critical role in the treatment of assault victims. Some clients may need guidance in discriminating safe from unsafe situations. Therapists may notice areas of possible poor risk recognition as clients recount their experiences during imaginal exposure, and can use such examples in training clients to recognize potential dangers early on. Similarly, in developing the hierarchy to be used for *in vivo* exposure, therapists may help clients to differentiate situations that remind them of the trauma but are objectively safe (e.g., shopping in the store they had been in the day of the assault) from those that are reminders but are also realistically dangerous (e.g., walking alone at night in deserted areas). Thus, delineating PTSD-related avoidance versus realistic precautions is particularly important in this population.

Childhood Abuse Victims

A diagnosis of PTSD requires that symptoms represent a change from pre-trauma functioning. However, it may not be possible to assess such changes in childhood abuse victims, either because they may not remember their pre-trauma level of functioning or because their lives have not included a time without trauma. In these cases, the therapist must rely on inferences regarding the association between observed symptoms and the traumatic experiences. Child abuse victims also face the additional complication that the trauma and subsequent recovery overlap with normal developmental processes. Thus, such clients may never have experienced "normal" relationships;

adjunct techniques, such as education regarding interpersonal interactions, may prove helpful in such cases.

CONCLUSIONS

Considering the treatment outcome literature reviewed in this chapter, it seems clear that several cognitive-behavioral treatments are effective for post-traumatic stress disorder. Exposure treatments have enjoyed the largest number of controlled studies to date, with the evidence converging to demonstrate the efficacy of these treatments in a variety of trauma populations. Given the proven efficacy and relative simplicity of exposure therapy, exposure might be considered the treatment of choice for PTSD. However, as noted earlier, not all clients are able or willing to tolerate the distress generated by exposure therapy.

There is also evidence that SIT, CPT, and cognitive therapy are effective for PTSD, although these studies are fewer in number and more limited in target population relative to the exposure studies. However, for clients who have difficulty accepting exposure therapy, these treatments may be preferable. EMDR has been the subject of a number of studies, but due to the methodological flaws of most of these studies, the efficacy of EMDR cannot be ascertained at this time.

Based on the degree of improvement seen in veteran versus nonveteran studies, there is some evidence suggesting that civilians respond more strongly than veterans to PTSD treatments. It should be noted that we do not have data that compare responses of different trauma populations to treatment within the same study. As such, we can not recommend different treatment approaches based on type of trauma at this time. However, therapists may need to attend to specific issues that are more likely to arise in treatment with respect to the type of trauma experienced by the client.

REFERENCES

Barlow, D. H., Leitenberg, H., Agras, W. S., & Wincze, J. P. (1969). The transfer gap in systematic desensitization: An analogue study. *Behavior Research and Therapy, 7,* 191–196.

Beck, A. T. (1972). *Depression: Causes and treatment.* Philadelphia: University of Pennsylvania Press.

Beck, A. T. (1976). *Cognitive therapy and the emotional disorders.* New York: International Universities Press.

Blanchard, E. B., & Abel, G. G. (1976). An experimental case study of the biofeedback treatment of a rape induced psychophysiological cardiovascular disorder. *Behavior Therapy, 7,* 113–119.

Boudewyns, P. A., & Hyer, L. (1990). Physiological response to combat memories and preliminary treatment outcome in Vietnam veterans PTSD patients treated with direct therapeutic exposure. *Behavior Therapy, 21,* 63–87.

Boudewyns, P. A., Hyer, L., Woods, M. G., Harrison, W. R., & McCranie, E. (1990). PTSD among Vietnam veterans: An early look at treatment outcome using direct therapeutic exposure. *Journal of Traumatic Stress, 3,* 359–68.

Boudewyns, P., Stwertka, S., Hyer, L., Albrecht, W., & Sperr, E. (1993). Eye movement desensitization for PTSD of combat: A treatment outcome pilot study. *Behavior Therapy, 16,* 29–33.

Bowen, G. R., & Lambert, J. A. (1986). Systematic desensitization therapy with post-traumatic stress disorder cases. In C. R. Figley (Ed.), *Trauma and its wake* (Vol. II, pp. 280–291). New York: Brunner/Mazel.

Breslau, N., Davis, G. C., Andreski, P., & Peterson, E. (1991). Traumatic events and posttraumatic stress disorder in an urban population of young adults. *Archives of General Psychiatry, 48,* 216–222.

Brom, D., Kleber, R. J., & Defares, P. B. (1989). Brief psychotherapy for posttraumatic stress disorders. *Journal of Consulting & Clinical Psychology, 57,* 607–612.

Clark, D. M. (1986). A cognitive approach to panic. *Behaviour Research and Therapy, 24,* 461–470.

Cooper, N. A., & Clum, G. A. (1989). Imaginal flooding as a supplementary treatment for PTSD in combat veterans: A controlled study. *Behavior Therapy, 3,* 381–391.

Fairbank, J. A., & Keane, T. M. (1982). Flooding for combat-related stress disorders: Assessment of anxiety reduction across traumatic memories. *Behavior Therapy, 13,* 499–510.

Foa, E. B., Dancu, C., Hembree, E., Jaycox, L. H., & Meadows, E. A. (1997). Efficacy of prolonged exposure and stress inoculation training for chronic PTSD. Manuscript in preparation.

Foa, E. B., & Jaycox, L. H. (in press). Cognitive-behavioral treatment of post-traumatic stress disorder. In D. Spiegel (Ed.), The practice of psychotherapy. Washington, DC: American Psychiatric Press.

Foa, E. B., & Kozak, M. J. (1986). Emotional processing of fear: Exposure to corrective information. *Psychological Bulletin, 99,* 20–35.

Foa, E. B., & Meadows, E. A. (1997). Psychosocial treatments for post-traumatic stress disorder: A critical review. In J. Spence, J. M. Darley, & D. J. Foss (Eds.), *Annual Review of Psychology* (Vol. 48, pp. 449–480). Palo Alto, CA: Annual Reviews Inc.

Foa, E. B., Riggs, D. S., Massie, E. D., & Yarczower, M. (1995). The impact of fear activation and anger on the efficacy of exposure treatment for PTSD. *Behavior Therapy, 26,* 487–499.

Foa, E. B., Rothbaum, B. O., & Kozak, M. J. (1989). Behavioral treatments of anxiety and depression. In P. Kendall & D. Watson (Eds.), *Anxiety and depression: Distinctive and overlapping features* (pp. 413–454). New York: Academic Press.

Foa E. B., Rothbaum B. O., Riggs D., & Murdock T. (1991). Treatment of post-traumatic stress disorder in rape victims: A comparison between cognitive-behavioral procedures and counseling. *Journal of Consulting and Clinical Psychology, 59,* 715–723.

Frank, E., Anderson, B., Stewart, B. D., Dancu, C., Hughes, C., & West, D. (1988). Efficacy of cognitive behavior therapy and systematic desensitization in the treatment of rape trauma. *Behavior Therapy, 19,* 403–420.

Frank, E., & Stewart, B. D. (1983). Physical aggression: Treating the victims. In E. A. Bleckman (Ed.), *Behavior modification with women* (pp. 245–272). New York: Guilford Press.

Frank, E., & Stewart, B. D. (1984). Depressive symptoms in rape victims. *Journal of Affective Disorders, 1,* 269–277.

Heide, F. J. & Borkevec, T. D. (1983). Relaxation-induced anxiety: Paradoxical anxiety enhancement due to relaxation training. *Journal of Consulting and Clinical Psychology, 51,* 171–182.

Heide, F. J., & Borkevec, T. D. (1984). Relaxation-induced anxiety: Mechanisms and theoretical implications. *Behaviour Research and Therapy, 22,* 1–12.

Helzer, J. E., Robins, L., & McEvoy, L. (1987). Post-traumatic stress disorder in the general population. *New England Journal of Medicine, 317,* 1630–1634.

Hickling, E. J. & Blanchard, E. B. (1997). The private practice psychologist and manual-based treatments: Posttraumatic stress disorder secondary to motor vehicle accidents. *Behavior Research and Therapy, 35,* 191–203.

Hickling, E. J., Sison, G. F. P., & Vanderploeg, R. D. (1986). Treatment of posttraumatic stress disorder with relaxation and biofeedback training. *Behavior Therapy, 16,* 406–416.

Jaycox, L. H., & Foa, E. B. (1996). Obstacles in implementing exposure therapy for PTSD: Case discussions and practical solutions. *Clinical Psychology and Psychotherapy, 3*(3), 176–184.

Jensen, J. A. (1994). An investigation of Eye Movement Desensitization and Reprocessing (EMD/R) as a treatment for posttraumatic stress disorder (PTSD) symptoms of Vietnam combat veterans. *Behavior Therapy, 25,* 311–325.

Johnson, C. H., Gilmore, J. D., & Shenoy, R. Z. (1982). Use of a feeding procedure in the treatment of a stress-related anxiety disorder. *Journal of Behavioral Therapy & Experimental Psychiatry, 13,* 235–237.

Keane, T. M., Fairbank, J. A., Caddell, J. M., & Zimering, R. T. (1989). Implosive (flooding) therapy reduces symptoms of PTSD in Vietnam combat veterans. *Behavior Therapy, 20,* 245–260.

Keane, T. M., & Kaloupek, D. G. (1982). Imaginal flooding in the treatment of post-traumatic stress disorder. *Journal of Consulting and Clinical Psychology, 50,* 138–140.

Kilpatrick, D. G., & Amick, A. E. (1985). Rape trauma. In M. Hersen & C. G. Last (Eds.), *Behavior therapy casebook.* New York: Springer.

Kilpatrick, D. G., & Calhoun, K. S. (1988). Early behavioral treatment for rape trauma: Efficacy or artifact? *Behavior Therapy, 19*(3), 421–427.

Kilpatrick, D. G., Veronen, L. J., & Resick, P. A. (1982). Psychological sequelae to rape: Assessment and treatment strategies. In D. M. Dolays & R. L. Meredith (Eds.), *Behavioral medicine: Assessment and treatment strategies* (pp. 473–497). NY: Plenum Press.

Kubany, E. S. (1994). A cognitive model of guilt typology in combat-related PTSD. *Journal of Traumatic Stress 7,* 3–19.

Lang, P. J. (1979). A bio-informational theory of emotional imagery. *Psychophysiology, 6,* 495–511.

Lohr, J. M., Kleinknecht, R. A., Tolin, D. F., & Barrett, R. H. (1996). The empirical status of the clinical application of Eye Movement Desensitization and Reprocessing. *Journal of Behavior Therapy and Experimental Psychiatry, 26,* 285–302.

Marks, I., Lovell, K., Noshirvani, H., Livanou, M., & Thrasher, S. (1997). Exposure and cognitive restructuring along and combined in PTSD: A controlled study. Manuscript in preparation.

McCann, I. L., & Pearlman, L. A. (1990). *Psychological trauma and the adult survivor: Theory, therapy, and transformation.* New York: Brunner/Mazel.

Meichenbaum, D. (1974). Self-instructional methods. In F. H. Kanfer & A. P. Goldstein (Eds). *Helping people change* (pp. 357–391). New York: Pergamon Press.

Mowrer, O. A. (1960). *Learning theory and behavior.* New York: Wiley.

Pearson, M. A., Poquette, B. M., & Wasden, R. E. (1983). Stress inoculation and the treatment of post rape trauma: A case report. *Behavior Therapy, 6,* 58–59.

Peniston, E. G. (1986). EMG biofeedback-assisted desensitization treatment for Vietnam combat veterans' posttraumatic stress disorder. *Clinical Biofeedback Health, 9,* 35–41.

Pitman, R. K., Altman, B., Greenwald, E., Longpre, R. E., Macklin, M. L., Poire, R. E., & Steketee, G. S. (1991). Psychiatric complications during flooding therapy for posttraumatic stress disorder. *Journal of Clinical Psychiatry, 52,* 17–20.

Pitman, R. K., Orr, S. P., Altman, B., Longpre, R. E., Poire, R. E., & Macklin, M. L. (1996). Emotional processing during Eye-Movement Desensitization and Reprocessing therapy of Vietnam veterans with chronic post-traumatic stress disorder. Comprehensive Psychiatry, 37, 419–429.

Renfrey, G., & Spates, C. R. (1994). Eye movement desensitization: A partial dismantling study. *Journal of Behavioral Therapy & Experimental Psychiatry, 25,* 231–239.

Rescorla, R. A. (1988). Pavlovian conditioning: It's not what you think it is. *American Psychologist, 43,* 151–160.

Resick, P. A., Jordan, C. G., Girelli, S. A., Hutter, C. K., & Marhoefer-Dvorak, S. (1988). A comparative victim study of behavioral group therapy for sexual assault victims. *Behavior Therapy, 19,* 385–401.

Resick, P. A., Nishith, P., & Astin, M. C. (1996, November). Preliminary results of an outcome study comparing cognitive processing therapy and prolonged exposure. In P. A. Resick (Chair), *Treating Sexual Assault/Sexual Abuse Pathology: Recent Findings.* Presented at the annual meeting of the Association for Advancement of Behavior Therapy, New York, NY.

Resick, P. A., & Schnicke, M. K. (1992a). Cognitive processing therapy for sexual assault victims. *Journal of Consulting and Clinical Psychology, 60,* 748–756.

Resick, P. A., & Schnicke M. K. (1992b, October). Cognitive processing therapy for sexual assault victims. In E. B. Foa (Chair), *Treatment of PTSD: An update.* Presented at the Eighth Annual Meeting of the International Society for Traumatic Stress Studies, Los Angeles, CA.

Richards, D. A., Lovell, K., & Marks, I. M. (1994). Posttraumatic stress disorder: Evaluation of a behavioral treatment program. *Journal of Traumatic Stress, 7,* 669–680.

Rothbaum, B. O. (1997). A controlled study of eye movement desensitization and reprocessing in the treatment of postraumatic stress disorder. *Bulletin of the Menninger Clinic, 61,* 317–334. Poster presented at the Association for Advancement of Behavior Therapy, Washington, DC.

Schindler, F. E. (1980). Treatment by systematic desensitization of a recurring nightmare of a real life trauma. *Journal of Behavior Therapy & Experimental Psychiatry, 11,* 53–54.

Shapiro, F. (1989). Eye movement desensitization: A new treatment for post-traumatic stress disorder. *Journal of Behavior Therapy & Experimental Psychiatry, 20,* 211–217.

Shapiro, F. (1995). *Eye Movement Desensitization and Reprocessing: Basic principles, protocols, and procedures.* New York: Guilford Press.

Silver, S. M., Brooks, A., & Obenchain, J. (1995). Treatment of Vietnam war veterans with PTSD: A comparison of Eye Movement Desensitization and Reprocessing, biofeedback, and relaxation training. *Journal of Traumatic Stress, 8,* 337–342.

Stern, R. S., & Marks, I. M. (1973). Brief and prolonged flooding: A comparison in agoraphobic patients. *Archives of General Psychiatry, 28,* 270–276.

Thompson, J. A., Charlton, P. F. C., Kerry, R., Lee, D, & Turner, S. W. (1995). An open trial of exposure therapy based on deconditioning for post-traumatic stress disorder. *British Journal of Clinical Psychology, 34,* 407–416.

Tolin, D. F., Montgomery, R. W., Kleinknecht, R. A., & Lohr, J. M. (1996). An evaluation of Eye Movement Desensitization and Reprocessing (EMDR). In T. Jackson (Ed.), *Innovations in clinical practice, Vol. 15.* Sarasota, FL: Professional Resources Press.

Turner, S. M. (1979, November). *Systematic desensitization of fears and anxiety in rape victims.* Paper presented at the annual meeting of the Association for Advancement of Behavior Therapy, San Francisco, CA.

Vaughan, K., Armstrong, M. S., Gold, R., O'Connor, N., Jenneke, W., & Tarrier, N. (1994). A trial of eye movement desensitization compared to image habituation training and applied muscle relaxation in post-traumatic stress disorder. *Journal of Behavior Therapy and Experimental Psychiatry, 25*(4), 283–291.

Veronen, L. J., & Kilpatrick, D. G. (1982, November). *Stress inoculation training for victims of rape: Efficacy and differential findings. Presented in a symposium entitled "Sexual Violence and Harassment."* Paper presented at the annual meeting of the Association for Advancement of Behavior Therapy, Los Angeles, CA.

Veronen, L. J., Kilpatrick, D. G., & Resick, P. A. (1979). Treating fear and anxiety in rape victims: Implications for the criminal justice system. In W. H. Parsonage (Ed.), *Perspectives on victimology* (pp. 148–159). Beverly Hills, CA: Sage Publications.

Wilson, S. A., Becker, L. A., & Tinker, R. H. (1995). Eye Movement Desensitization and Reprocessing (EMDR) treatment for psychologically traumatized individuals. *Journal of Consulting and Clinical Psychology, 63*(6), 928–937.

Wolff, R. (1977). Systematic desentization and negative practice to alter the after effects of a rape attempt. *Journal of Behavior Therapy and Experimental Psychiatry, 8,* 423–425.

Wolpe, J. (1958). *Psychotherapy by reciprocal inhibition.* Stanford: Stanford University Press.

Wolpe, J., & Abrams, J. (1991). Post-traumatic stress disorder overcome by eye-movement desensitization: A case report. *Journal of Behavior Therapy and Experimental Psychiatry, 22*(1), 39–43.

CHAPTER 19

GROUP AND MILIEU THERAPY FOR VETERANS WITH COMPLEX POST-TRAUMATIC STRESS DISORDER

BY JONATHAN SHAY, M. D., PH.D.
Department of Veterans Affairs Outpatient Clinic,
Veterans Improvement Program (VIP),
Tufts Medical School Departments of Psychiatry, Boston

AND JAMES MUNROE, ED.D.[1][2][3][4]
Department of Veterans Affairs Outpatient Clinic,
Veterans Improvement Program (VIP),
and National Center for PTSD Behavioral Sciences Division, Boston.

INTRODUCTION

In this chapter we do not claim to address treatment issues for all trauma survivors, nor do we aspire to see the world through the tiny keyhole of the clinical population with which we work: American male combat veterans of the Vietnam War (hence the masculine pronoun throughout) with chronic posttraumatic stress disorder (PTSD) and "enduring personality change after catastrophic experience" (WHO, 1992, p. 209). If what we say translates to the reader's other clinical or public health populations, we are gratified, but the reader must make the translation. In part, this reflects our philosophic position that we should not pretend to universal, eternal scientific knowledge about these things, nor shall we covertly claim this knowledge through the use of an unlocated authoritative textbook "voice." We have worked together for almost ten years, and speak from a specific time and place with lives and works in progress. When later in this chapter we speak of our treatment program called "VIP," it is not to advertise

---

[1]Neither author has past, present, or anticipated relationship to the manufacturer of any medication or class of medications mentioned in this chapter.

[2]The views expressed here are those of the authors, and should not be taken as official views of any governmental or academic institutions.

[3]The authors wish to thank the veterans of the VIP and the rest of the VIP clinical team, Lisa Fisher, and Christine Makary. We acknowledge valuable critical input from a number of Professors of Philosophy, who have been kind enough to vet an earlier draft of this chapter for "howlers." Thanks (in alphabetical order) to Eugene Garver, Jennifer Radden, Amélie Rorty, and Charles Young. We also thank the following for their critical advice: J. Douglas Bremner, Susan Brock, Michelle Citron, Vicki Citron, Greg Febbraro, Faris Kirkland, Hannah Shay, and Tamar Shay. Thanks also for insights from classicist, Professor Erwin F. Cook.

[4]Editors' Note: In view of the comprehensive nature of this book, and, as many clinicians have an interest in group interventions that are intended to address the problems of Vietnam veterans, this chapter describes a highly regarded multi-faceted program that deals with the psychopathology of traumatized veterans. While the efficacy of the treatment that is described has not been subjected to scientific scrutiny, it is hoped that this information may stimulate efficacy-based research involving group therapy for traumatized veterans.

for patients nor even to offer it as a model to be cloned, but rather as an example to be assimilated to the character of the reader's patients, colleagues, and institutions.

Personality ("character") changes have made these veterans huge consumers of resources for hospitalization, incarceration, family and workplace disruption, and clinical crisis management. Of all aspects of these veterans' psychological injuries, their enduring posttraumatic personality changes—damage to good character—impose the greatest social, economic, political, and clinical costs. In our opinion, these veterans' damaged characters can be restored—well enough, at least, to provide a safer world for their families, employers, and communities—and well enough to enhance the quality of life as they themselves experience it. However, as we shall describe below, this restoration entails clinical practices at odds with much of our culture's normative value pattern for the professional.

Our patients were all participants in the exercise of state military power in and around Vietnam between 1965 and 1972, and trace their injuries to this participation. Because of the dominating element of power, the context of their injury is thus in every sense political; we shall argue that important features of their injury are political. We shall take the position that the treatment we provide is political—we consciously foster an empowered community among the veterans that we treat. Our position with respect to the veterans is one defined by a very ancient term. We aspire to be "*rhêtor*" (i.e., democratic persuader) in the rich form laid out by Aristotle in the *Rhetoric:* Our task is to create trust (*pístis*) for fellow citizens. As Aristotle uses "*pístis*" in the *Rhetoric,* it means variously, trust, persuasion, proof, credibility, belief, and the processes or means that bring about persuasion (Garver, 1994b, p. 142; Carey, 1996, p. 299). For Aristotle, the contrasting opposite to the *rhêtor* was the sophist. The sophist was, in quite modern terms, a professional who applied a *technê,* that is, a teachable, ends-rational skill available for hire from the holder of credentials certifying mastery (Garver, 1994b, pp. 206–231).

This chapter addresses the encounter of the psychologically injured Vietnam combat veteran and the mental health professional.

The Core Treatment Issue Is Social Trust

We regard the key manifestation of the veterans' psychological injuries in the treatment setting is destruction of the capacity for social trust. How the veterans' incapacity for trust plays out in the family, workplace, government office, commercial establishment, has been well described elsewhere (Lifton, 1973; Mason, 1990; Matsakis, 1996; Shatan, 1985). In the clinic, social trust is the readiness to repose trust in professional credentials, institutional position, and the value pattern of the professional. We shall explain below what we mean by the value pattern of the professional. But at this point it suffices to say that the veterans we work with have had the real experience of being exploited and betrayed by people holding the right professional credentials, in fulfillment of their institutional positions, in a context of 24-hour-a-day danger that meant that there was "no safe place." Our veterans live in perpetual expectation of physical attack, interpersonal coercion, and institutional exploitation, deceit, and betrayal. Because their psychological injuries have destroyed social trust, the most severely injured veterans are least able to get and retain access to treatment.

The combination of PTSD symptoms (American Psychiatric Association, *Diagnostic and Statistical Manual,* 1980, 1987, 1994, hereafter collectively "DSM") plus personality changes has been well characterized by others under the terms "complex PTSD," "DESNOS," and other locutions reviewed by Herman (1993). We offer nothing new here in nosology. This combination has not been accepted in the DSM, but not for lack of its being described and studied. In the rest of this chapter we shall use Judith Herman's term "complex PTSD" for our patients with post-combat complex PTSD. Many veterans who have served in war do not have even "partial" PTSD, and many who meet the full diagnostic criteria for PTSD do not have complex PTSD. Our patients meet the DSM criteria for PTSD and have in addition other bio-psycho-social changes that Herman (1992b, 1993) describes. These changes encompass:

- Altered affect regulation, such as persistent dysphoria, chronic suicidal preoccupation, explosive or extremely inhibited anger, which may alternate

- Altered consciousness, such as transient dissociative episodes, amnesia or hypermnesia for traumatic events
- Altered self-perception, including a sense of helplessness, paralysis of initiative, shame, guilt, and self-blame, a sense of defilement or stigma, a sense of complete difference from others, which may include sense of elite specialness
- Altered perception of the perpetrator, including preoccupation with revenge and/or idealization or paradoxical gratitude toward the perpetrator
- Altered relations with others, such as repeated search for a rescuer, which may alternate with isolation and withdrawal, persistent distrust, repeated failures of self-protection
- Altered systems of meaning, including loss of sustaining faith, sense of hopelessness and despair
- Somatization

Destruction of Normal Narcissism

Mental health professionals who have casually encountered combat veterans with PTSD are often unpleasantly struck by their "narcissism," as manifested by some of the following:

- Demands for honor and acknowledgment
- "Entitlement"
- Self-important claims to having been players in the most significant events in human history
- Readiness with which they take offense at what they take to be slights
- Occasional insistence that they will deal only with the Chief of Service ("the head of the snake")
- "Global" destructiveness of their fantasies, wishes, and, occasionally, behavior
- Vulnerability to collapses of morale which leave them so apathetic that they cannot want or will anything at all
- Hypochondriacal preoccupations and psychosomatic disorders

This unappealing portrait of "narcissistic" combat veterans has important roots in reality, which if properly understood, teach us much about working with them and much about ourselves. The word "narcissism" was introduced in the writings of late nineteenth century psychologists and sexologists, primarily to talk about auto-erotic phenomena. It was used theoretically by Freud in several ways including his developmental theory of normal infancy. The generation of psychoanalysts after Freud, most notably Kohut, but many others as well, decisively broke the concept away from its sexological roots and associated the word with the rise and fall of self-esteem, self-confidence, and self-respect. More generally the term came to be associated with a psychology of the experience of the self in general, including healthy self-esteem, self-confidence, and self-respect. The concept also broadened beyond the valuative sense of pride and shame, to include the strength or weakness of the self's coherence, continuity in time, moral agency, creative efficacy, and the capacity for empathic grasp of other people as real and significant (Pulver, 1970). Thus narcissism is not exclusively an infantile or pathological phenomenon, but infuses essential elements in human flourishing. When clinicians use the term "narcissistic" to damn veterans who are easily enraged, boastful, or demanding, it is as though they have utterly forgotten the importance of narcissism in any good life.

In the post-Freud sense of the word, the psychological issues involved in combat trauma, and in recovery from it, are in the territory of narcissism. We strongly agree that narcissism is part of the psychic economy of the healthy adult, and wish to point out that it is intimately bound up with the moral and social world that the adult inhabits. As such, "narcissism" is simply the most recent term for a notion with a long history in the attempts to understand the human being. Working backwards in time, this notion has been called "desire for recognition" (Hegel), "*amour-propre*" (Rousseau), pride or vainglory (Hobbes), "*thumoeidés*" (Plato), and "*thumós*" (Homer).

The features of the normal adult world which control narcissistic emotions and moods are ideals, ambitions, and affiliations. Here, when we use the word "character," we refer descriptively to the following, taken together—

- The historically and socio-culturally constructed content of the commitments embodied in ideals, ambitions, and affiliations

- The intensity with which the commitments are energized
- The narcissistic emotions aroused by cognitive appraisal of the condition (particularly improvement or deterioration) of these commitments in the world

How stable character is, depends largely on the ecology of social power, upon the good-enough fulfillment of the culture's moral order by those who hold power. The normal adult's cloak of safety and guarantor of narcissistic, hence characterologic, stability is the normative structure of the society, its implementation by powerholders, and the concrete social support of a face-to-face community. Good-enough realization in the world of these commitments is the foundation of ordinary self-respect and of the sense of self-worth that we expect in the normal adult. Sudden, undreamed of fulfillment in any of these three realms will usually make a healthy adult euphoric. And serious, high-stakes destruction in any of these three realms—especially when the threat originates in betrayal of the moral order by powerholders or in abandonment by those to whom one is attached and socially affiliated—is the basis of the damaging changes to character which are the principal subject of this chapter. We do not offer character stability as a goal or good in itself—the posttraumatic changes in character we attempt to reverse are sometimes horrifyingly robust—and it is only the continuing fluidity of adult character that provides an opportunity for treatment.

Some readers will reflexively reject the very idea that good character, once formed by good upbringing in childhood, can ever be damaged by any events that merely happen to the adult. The idea that adult good character is inviolable is an old and disputed philosophic position or a useless tautology, not a scientific fact (Shay, 1995b).

Narcissism, the allegedly most "primitive" of psychological phenomena, much entwined with the body, is therefore deeply enmeshed with the social, moral, and political. Social betrayal and isolation in a high-stakes situation has profound physiological, as well as psychological, consequences. To chronically live in "no safe place," made unsafe by other people, damages the body.

In ancient Greece, the emotions and commitments embodied in ideals, ambitions, and affiliations were subsumed under the single Homeric word *thumós* (i.e., spirited self-respect). This has often been unhelpfully translated as the single word "spirit." It has also been translated as "temper," "*animus*," "spiritedness," "aspiration." Professor Amélie Rorty (personal communication, 1996) has been kind enough to provide a more informative translation: "the energy of spirited honor." To be entirely deprived of honor has been described as "social death" (Patterson, 1982). It was Achilles' "large" *thumós* (*Iliad* 9:255) that led him to become so enraged with Agamémnon when the latter betrayed the shared military norms of their culture by dishonoring him and seizing the prize of honor awarded to him by acclaim of the troops. Plato's Socrates posits the "high-spirited principle" (*thumoeidés*) as one of the three divisions of every human psyche in his famous tripartite division of the soul (*Republic* IV, 435e–444e). In *Politics* VII.6.1327b39ff Aristotle says, "*Thymos* is the faculty of our souls which issues in love and friendship—it is also the source—of any power of commanding and any feeling for freedom." (Garver trans. 1994a, p. 177n8) The normal narcissism of the healthy adult can now help us understand characterological changes in complex PTSD after combat.

We hold that the conditions which cause complex PTSD (persistent human betrayal and rupture of community in high-stakes situations of captivity) destroy *thumós* and normal narcissism. Modern battle is a condition of captivity (even when it has been entered voluntarily), a fact that has escaped notice because the captives move about in the open carrying powerful weapons, and because the role of captor is cooperatively shared by the two enemy military organizations which are presumed to cooperate in nothing (Shay, 1994). Modern combat itself is a condition of enslavement and torture. Until we end the practice of war itself, this will be the case.

What replaces normal narcissism when it is impaired? Our own answer to this must be taken as limited by the patient population we work with, who over the decades have sought treatment and been involuntarily enrolled in the mental health system. Most have cycled repeatedly through several of the following, sometimes quickly, sometimes slowly—

- Demoralization [*athumía*], death to the world, apathy, ennui, and aboulia, anhedonia, dysthymia— sickened *thúmos*
- Loss of self-respect
- Self-loathing
- Social withdrawal
- Pervasive "raw" feeling of vulnerability
- Blind obedience, which may turn into a fanatical "mission"
- Grandiosity and entitlement
- Rage at small slights, disappointment, lapses
- Coercive attempts to establish power dominance
- Coercive demands for respect, honor, acknowledgment
- Danger-seeking, fight-seeking
- Mortal risk-taking to divine the status of one's "luck"

It is possible that most men who remained in only one of these would never have come to our attention in a specialized PTSD clinic, because they would be dead, incarcerated, stably reclusive, famous and powerful on a small or large scale, or misdiagnosed as schizophrenic. If complex PTSD after combat appears to be marked by repetitive cycling, it may be because the veterans themselves and the social system direct elsewhere those who do not cycle.

"Combat Ages You"

Several pieces of the personality pattern we have described here were touched on with painful clarity by Aristotle when he sketched his portrait of the elderly in the *Rhetoric* II.13.1389b13ff:

> *"Because they have...been deceived many times... they are malignant...[that is, they] interpret everything in the worst light. Furthermore, they are* excessively suspicious *because of their* lack of trust (apistían), *and* lacking in trust because of their experience.... And they are small of soul.... And they are* self-loving *more than is appropriate; for this too is a kind of smallness of soul.... [T]hey think every suffering is waiting for them.... For this reason they are given to grieving, and are neither charming nor fond of laughter." (Nussbaum translation, 1986, p. 338, emphasis added)*

It is not mere word-association to quote what we have often heard veterans say: "Combat ages you. You get old real fast."

Rupture of community and "betrayal of what's right" (Shay, 1994) are responsible for layering the characterologic, narcissistic injury onto PTSD that the intrinsic terror, grief, privation, and horror of war inflicts on those who fight. In the discussion that follows, we focus on community, because restoration of community is the core of our treatment model.

Destruction of the Combatant's Community

Destruction of Unit Cohesion. In Vietnam, whatever group cohesiveness developed within small units was left behind as soldiers rotated home quickly by air, as individuals rather than as a unit (Shay, 1994). They returned truly alone, in planes packed with strangers. There was no "debriefing," no opportunity to communalize the terrors, the losses, the might-have-beens and should-have-dones. A recent paper by a leading military historian and two active duty Army officers in *Parameters: Quarterly Journal of the US Army War College* speaks of debriefing, decompression, and three forms of validation (substantive, institutional, and memorial) as essential for soldiers returning from combat duty (Kirkland, Halverson, & Bliese, 1996). These protective practices of cohesive military units were systematically denied to American combatants returning from Vietnam, through a combination of neglect, ignorance, culturally driven blindness, and unintended consequences of well-intended policies. We shall return to these practices of cohesive units in our discussion of the VIP treatment model for combat veterans.

Aversion to Returning Veterans Is an Old Story. Acts of war generate a profound gulf between the combatant and the community he left behind. The veteran carries the taint of a killer, of blood pollution, that many cultures other than our own recognize in purification rituals. Both he and his community may question the wisdom of return. The community worries about his control. The veteran, knowing what he is capable of, may also fear losing control. He may fear that if people knew what he had done, they would reject him or even lock him up. Both the veteran and the community collude in the belief that he is "no longer one of us." Many veterans express the feeling that they died in Vietnam and should not have returned.

Both the trauma of war, and recovery from it, are social, not individual events. Many authors have emphasized the importance of social supports and community in recovery from traumatic events (Catherall, 1989; Erikson K. T., 1976; Figley, 1988; Janoff-Bulman, 1985; Keane, Scott, Chavoya, Lamparski, & Fairbank, 1985; Lifton, 1967, 1979; Shatan, 1985; van der Kolk, Brown, & van der Hart, 1989). Janoff-Bulman (1992) proposed that trauma undermines the survivor's basic assumptions that the world is benevolent, meaningful, and that the self is worthy. Erik Erikson's (1959; 1963) theory of normal psychosocial development describes "basic trust" as the first of eight stages. It is at this stage that the child develops a sense of community which then allows further development to occur. The parents give the child "a firm sense of personal trustworthiness within the trusted framework of their community..." (Erikson, 1959, p. 63). The parents also communicate "a deep, almost somatic conviction that there is meaning to what they are doing," (Erikson, 1963, p. 249) and a belief in "Fate's store of good intentions" (Erikson, 1959, p. 62). Collectively, these authors describe the link between trauma and loss of community. It is not the loss of a specific community, but the loss of the ability to belong to any community. Belonging to a community requires the mutual belief that members will look out for each other.

Some of the disconnection and alienation between returning Vietnam veterans and their home communities came from the rapid social changes at the time and the gulf of experience that separated veterans from their peers. However, it is more nearly typical for returning U.S. war veterans to be shunned by the communities they returned to (Severo & Milford, 1990), than to be celebrated by them. The experience of the World War II veterans—the fathers of the Vietnam veterans—is the historical anomaly. At the end of World War II, politicians, with fresh memories of the Bonus Army of World War I veterans, worried about so many returning soldiers looking for jobs.

Congress appropriated unprecedented benefits, which then declined in real terms to half their value by the time of the Vietnam War.

Farmers from the Revolutionary War returned to find banks foreclosing their farms because the money the government gave them was no good. Civil War veterans had trouble finding employment and were accused of being drug addicts. Supposedly, our word "hobo" comes from homeless Civil War veterans—called "hoe boys"—who roamed the lanes of rural America with hoes on their shoulders, looking for work. World War I veterans who marched on Washington and camped on the Mall to demand their bonuses had their camp burned and were driven out with tanks and bayonets. Korean veterans were accused of being too weak to win, and in the wake of McCarthyism, were suspected of communist sympathies from brainwashing as POWs.

With increasing polarization over the Vietnam War, veterans returned home to protesters who accused them of being torturers, perpetrators of atrocities, and baby killers. For every returning veteran who encountered this personally, there were many more who saw highly selected scenes of it in the news or heard nth-hand stories. The media presented a barrage of images portraying the Vietnam veteran as crazy, drug addicted, and violent. For many veterans who had joined up because it was their duty as citizens, who had grown up on John Wayne and Audie Murphy, and because they thought what they would be doing was right, rejection by the community was infuriating. In their fathers' VFW and Legion posts, some were greeted with derision even more devastating than the criticisms leveled by the war protesters: "We won our war. What is wrong with you?"

The supposedly traditional idea of honoring returning veterans ran afoul of deep divisions over the justice and wisdom of the war as a whole, making honor to the veterans seem an endorsement of the war policy. From the hawks on the political right to the doves on the political left, the nation as a whole lost sight of the fundamental importance of social esteem—embodied no less in private gestures of respect than in public rituals of honor and recognition—in rebuilding the capacity for social trust in a person who has come home from war.

Consequences of Shattered Trust—No Safe Place.
When "basic trust" is destroyed, what replaces it is perpetual mobilization to fend off attack and to figure out other people's trickery. In the world of Homer's warriors, the world was seen primarily in two dimensions, *biê,* (might) and *mêtis* (cunning); Achilles embodied the former and Odysseus the latter. Our patients construct the world similarly. Civil society, founded in a third dimension of trust and trustworthy restraints, seems to them a deceptive veneer to hide a violent and exploitative reality (Munroe, 1991). Alertness and suspicion anticipate attack and deception. This is easily mistaken for paranoia, but in our patients it is the persistence into civilian life of a valid adaptation to the real environment of war that they have experienced. Lying and deceit are valuable military skills, for which Odysseus boasted, "Men hold me formidable for guile…this fame has gone abroad to the sky's rim." (Homer, ca. 800 B. C. E./1961, Book 9, Lines 20f). In war, "they"— the enemy—really are out to kill you. The modern soldier's own military organization propels him, terrified, into the presence of that enemy. After such experience, friendliness and cooperation may only look like manipulations to trick inexperienced rubes into a position where they can be exploited or injured.

What Community Offers. Communities offer safety. At the crudest level of physical security, other people share alertness to threat, so that each individual does not have to be constantly vigilant. Within the defensive group, safety lies in the predictability of boundaries and normative restraints of behavior. But beyond this there may be some as-yet unclarified aspect of human brain biology at work in the subjective sense of safety that accrues when there is mutual social recognition and esteem. To be secure in the esteem of your community and of your identity within it—basic satisfaction of *thumós*—reads as being secure, *simpliciter.* In our ancestral environment where the human brain evolved to its present form, this connection may have prevailed at the most basic level of survival. Contrawise, moral danger of betrayal and abandonment are read in the body as physical danger. Moral betrayal, social isolation, and lack of social support enter into a self-feeding cycle with fear and suspicion of other people.

How Lack of Social Trust Becomes a Problem for Mental Health Professionals

We believe that the lack of social trust leads to a characteristic impasse between mental health professionals and combat veterans with complex PTSD. We also believe that this impasse is the main obstacle to treatment.

We maintain that the veteran is, by reason of injury inflicted by real experience in war of betrayal by those with credentials and institutional position, unable to trust clinicians on the basis of their credentials and institutional position. The veteran enters the relationship with a big question mark after the word "trust"—Should I trust you?"—and sets about making observations and setting up tests of trust to answer the question.

On the other hand, the clinician has ideals of professional conduct, feels justifiably proud of having fulfilled ambitions to attain a responsible job title, usually aspires to advancement in his or her institution and profession, and draws a sense of personal value from membership (affiliation) in the collectivity of the profession. In a word, the clinician is a normal adult of the modern world with *thumós*—ideals, ambitions, and affiliations. The normal mental health professional takes offense at being treated as a question mark—is this person trustworthy?—rather than as an established certainty, what the clinician is entitled to as a matter of credentials and institutional title. The predictable result is a counter-transference narcissistic rage. The clinician's hurt feelings in encounters with combat veterans make it easy to apply derogatory labels, such as "borderline," "character disordered," "anti-social," which, despite precise operational definition, mostly function as synonyms for troublesome, bad, vile, evil—and hopelessly untreatable. Diagnoses of personality disorders may carry less information about the veteran than about the way the clinician relates to the veteran.

The Paradox of Therapy for Trauma

Complex PTSD destroys the resources necessary for its successful treatment. Therapy requires that the trauma survivor trust the therapist. We believe that the veterans have reason, based on their experience, to distrust therapists and to expect to be exploited. They will assume, for example, that a therapist is only interested in them to get a graduate degree, to earn VA salary money, or to write a book. (In the last ten years, J. M. did earn his doctorate, and J. S. did publish a book. Periods of intense anxiety followed both of these events, with veterans watching to see if we each would leave, having accomplished our "real" purpose in being there.)

Therapists usually find that their efforts are not well received. Such "resistance" by combat survivors results in their being declared poor treatment candidates in the medical record, in the informal institutional memory, and often to the veterans' faces. This is a form of blaming the victim. Therapists who demand "compliance" prior to the establishment of trust and terminate resistant veterans simply add one more layer of violated trust and rejection. Severe trauma requires an infrastructure of trust before traditional therapies can proceed.

We believe that the requirement for trust for treatment to begin is doubly true of randomized treatment trials. In order for a veteran to give informed consent to participate in a randomized trial he must, among other things (a) view written disclosure documents as truthful, (b) believe assurances that he can withdraw from the trial without justification, penalty, or institutional prejudice ("in his record"), (c) believe that the randomization is honest and not rigged, (d) believe assurances that if the active treatment is found beneficial, he will ultimately receive it, (e) be willing to be assessed and, in some studies, even treated by people he has never met and tested, and (f) believe that if something goes wrong, he will not be sacrificed to the goals of the researchers.

We maintain that participation in blind trials requires a degree of trust beyond what many nontraumatized people will extend. Because American Psychiatric Association nosology lumps together simple and complex PTSD, lumps together trauma survivors with and without personality changes, conclusions have been drawn that purport to apply to all patients with PTSD. We believe that veterans with complex PTSD have systematically been excluded and excluded themselves from blind clinical trials.

We submit that we know virtually nothing from blind studies about what works with the very patients who cause us the most worry, the most effort, expense, and trouble.

VIP TEAM TREATMENT MODEL

Our Posture toward New Members

Our daytreatment VA staff have treated a large number of veterans with complex PTSD at our Veterans Improvement Program (VIP). Compared to ten years ago, the amount of provocative and dangerous behavior thrown off by members of our program has declined very sharply. The VIP has been running now for almost twenty years and we are unable to parcel out the effect of our good reputation among local veterans, the effects of aging on the veterans, FDA approval of selective serotonin uptake inhibitors, the settling presence of old hands among the veterans in VIP—who function as unofficial peer counselors—and what comes from incremental improvement in our ongoing practices and philosophy. Here are some of the things that we either make explicit or simply have in mind when a new member joins the program:

- We do not expect blind, automatic trust
- We expect that we have to earn trust through time, observation, and testing
- We are not angry back at him for not trusting us
- We expect that trust will be based on observation of how we treat other veterans
- We expect that trust will be based on observation of how we treat each other
- We are willing to be observed and judged

Just as in a military unit, where there is no privacy in the leader's qualities of trustworthiness—the troops are always watching—the team has no privacy in the way it deals with individual veterans and in the way team members deal with each other. Veterans will mostly do as we do, and little of what we say.

We find the VIP team treatment model is well suited to work with chaotic, crisis-ridden patients and with people who have learned to survive through violence and intimidation. It provides both physical safety, through its moral effect in veteran community support—the VIP veterans do not tolerate even the smallest threat against the team—as well as psychological safety. The model presupposes that trauma survivors must test the trustworthiness of anyone claiming good intentions, particularly where power is involved. Most of the "acting out" by combat veterans is a test of the team's trustworthiness. We maintain that trust can only be earned, never assumed from job titles or degrees.

The VIP team treatment model aims at building community among the veterans, demonstrating that they do not have to go through it alone, establishing the value of each veteran's life to others. In parallel, the treatment team strives for a strong community within itself, and to create a partnership of mutual respect between the veterans' community and the team community.

Among ourselves and in speaking with veterans we use the three-stage description of recovery, developed by Judith Herman (1992b): Stage I, establishment of safety, sobriety, and self-care; Stage II, trauma centered work of constructing a personal narrative and of grieving; Stage III, reconnecting with people, communities, ideals, and ambitions. Although we think and speak of these stages, the VIP is not programmatically built around them, and each veteran progresses at his own pace.

Stage I: Safety, Sobriety, Self-Care

We ask the veteran to start with the body and move outward by laying down weapons, maintaining sobriety, terminating current violence as perpetrator and/or victim, meeting health needs, and terminating danger-seeking behaviors. These are goals and results of successful Stage I recovery.

In group therapies with Stage I veterans, we are active and didactic as group leaders, assisting members in gaining authority over the pacing of traumatic disclosure, so it is safe. Meanwhile, we build the theme, "You are not alone; you don't have to go through it alone." Like-trauma peer recognition is central at this stage, but disclosure of new trauma history is not an active goal. We relate the inevitable disclosures back to the you-are-not-alone theme and to

the individual veteran's recognition of links to trauma-driven failures of safety and self-care. We seek the delicate balance between silencing the veteran and allowing him to become flooded by re-living the trauma, which only retraumatizes the patient. We establish the VIP culture of mutual respect for all veterans. No individual's branch of service, military function, battles, suffering is more "significant" than any other's.

From the beginning, other veterans provide what Kirkland and his colleagues (1996, p.86) call "substantive validation," a knowledgeable audience (even if they were not in the same specific units or operations) to whom the veteran's experience matters, and who are able to support him through the confusion, doubt, and self-criticism that seem intrinsic to having survived the chaos of battle. The team provides practical support for veterans to obtain their military records, unit diaries, and after-action reports when the situation demands. Surprisingly, this often provides the first "institutional validation" that the veterans have been able to take in, sometimes learning for the first time of awards and decorations for valor that they had earned, but had never been personally presented. VIP runs an annual trip to the Vietnam Veterans Memorial ("The Wall") in Washington, DC, which provides a focus for "memorial validation"—the opportunity to grieve for and commune with dead comrades in a safe and sober fellowship, where the importance of keeping faith with the dead through authentic emotion and respectful remembrance is understood without explanation or justification.

With each other's support, the veterans finally, decades later, experience the three forms of validation that current U.S. Army doctrine on "combat stress control" declares that every soldier should receive promptly after combat (Headquarters, Department of the Army, 1994). Need this be said? Prevention is better than treatment.

Aside: Pharmacotherapy of Combat PTSD

An integral part of Stage I is the achievement of safety. This means safety for one's self and safety of others from one's self. Together, violence and the avoidant strategies that veterans use to protect others from themselves have blighted the lives of most of the men in VIP. Past pharmacotherapeutic attempts have sometimes been literal chemical straight-jackets, such as dosing with anti-psychotics to the point that extrapyramidal rigidity made assaults physically impossible, or heavy daytime dosing with sedating drugs, such as trazodone. These treatments cut veterans off from themselves and from the world, and have been almost universally rejected by them. We rely more on the moral power of the veteran community in VIP as a robust restraint on violence both in and out of the program, than on such medication. One of us (Shay, 1992, 1995a) has written on our experiences with medication and violence in this group.

Pharmacotherapy provides valuable benefits to men with combat PTSD, providing that a basic principle of the treatment program is followed: Return control to the veterans. In practice this means the following—

We provide a strong, honest educational component on the effects of the various available drugs on combat PTSD. Education includes both prescribed and non-prescribed drugs. The goal is to increase the veteran's intelligent choice on what drugs he is going to ingest. The VIP veteran milieu provides a setting in which veterans who have benefited from medication can pass on this information. Our goals for every veteran who takes medication are that (a) he has made the decision to take it (b) on the basis of trustworthy reasons to suppose that it may improve some aspect of his life and (c) that the drug is worth the risk of side-effects and adverse reactions. We do not force medication on anyone.

The psycho-educational component gives the reasons why certain categories of prescription drugs are relatively contraindicated in combat PTSD, such as opiates, barbiturates, benzodiazepines, and yohimbine (which is absolutely contraindicated). Here, too, the role of other veterans is critical. The purpose is to empower the veterans to speak. In traditional one-on-one medication consultations in a private office behind a closed door, veterans are frequently too mistrustful, or simply afraid. Medication evaluation and consultation in the presence of the other men creates the safety to talk about side-effects and complications, fear of being experimented on, fear of medical

incompetence, despair and shame at the idea of taking psychiatric medications, and so forth. The shift in the power balance in favor of the patients has been an unqualified success, in our experience.

In our experience, the single most useful family of medications for complex PTSD after combat has been the serotonin reuptake inhibitors, of which fluoxetine (Prozac®) is the best known. The principal benefit that the veterans report is a many-faceted change in the economy of anger. A number of our veterans regard fluoxetine as having saved the lives of other people in civilian life, whom these veterans say that formerly they would, literally, have killed. Quite apart from the benefit that the patients themselves receive from reduced explosiveness, the public health benefit in reduced family, workplace, and public violence is one that we dare not ignore.

Stage II: Constructing a Cohesive Narrative and Grieving

When a veteran has tested the community and the team sufficiently, he is often able to venture beyond the safety of we-all-went-through-the-same-thing into the particularity of his own experience, and his partial responsibility for both events and the course that his life has taken. The catalyst for construction of a personal narrative is sometimes the practical requirements of applying for a disability pension. The process of constructing a narrative invariably arouses intense emotions, particularly of grief, not only for comrades lost during and since the war, but almost always some mix of (a) irretrievable losses of pre-war relationships after return to civilian life, (b) ambitions, ideals, and relationships blighted by alcohol and drug abuse, and their consequences, (c) ambitions, ideals, and relationships blighted by violence and its consequences, (d) lost innocence, and (e) lost youth and health, waste.

This is not a smooth process, but one that cycles through periods of renewed testing, sometimes with breaks in safety, sobriety, and self-care, which must then be restored. In the group therapies leaders serve to assure "air time," and safeguard the VIP culture that every person's suffering is significant and cannot be measured against any other person's suffering. The

VIP tradition strongly discourages "pissing contests." We monitor the emotional state of the veteran making the disclosure, as well as that of other veterans who may be triggered by it. Very often, the first disclosure of traumatic material occurs in individual therapy, and is only later taken into a group. In imparting fragments of trauma narrative to the group, veterans experience, "My story has meaning and value to others. I can trust them to understand and remember it. They are trustworthy witnesses to my grief, rage, and guilt and experience enough of these emotions with me that I know I am understood."

Stage III: Reconnection

The first two stages of recovery turn the veterans inward both toward themselves and toward the other veterans in the VIP. In the third stage, veterans selectively reconnect with people, activities, ideals, ambitions, and group identities from which they had become isolated, or make new connections. The core of this is the negotiation of safe, non-violent attachments in the family. This often entails reunion with, or renegotiation of relationships with, long-estranged children and parents. Sometimes the ruptures are irretrievable, or have been rendered so by death. When Odysseus meets the ghost of his dead mother in the underworld, he learns she died of grief during his long inexplicable vagrancy after the end of the Trojan War. This can be taken as a metaphor of such irretrievable losses that veterans must now face after their protracted, tormented *nóstoi,* "homecomings." The veterans of VIP strongly support a therapeutic culture in the program aimed at preventing the intergenerational transmission of trauma (Ancharoff, Munroe, & Fisher, 1998)—support born of guilt and sorrow at the damage that they did in past years to parents, spouses, and children.

Some veterans, by no means all, have taken satisfaction in educating youngsters on war, or in active peace advocacy. Several engage in regular volunteer work with homeless veterans, particularly those who have recently been homeless themselves. A great many have participated in educational activities for mental health professionals at various levels, as well as medical students.

We have already spoken of "validation," which plays important and varying roles in all three stages of recovery. The veteran community offers other resources that cut across all three recovery stages. These stages involve (a) "venting" the full range of feelings associated with trauma and its aftermath, (b) "value" that comes from having something to give to others, and (c) "views" that are disparate from and even contradictory to those of any given traumatized veteran, but held and expressed by someone the veteran nonetheless continues to treat with respect, usually another veteran.

One of us (Munroe, 1996) has called these four—validation, venting, value, views—the "four Vs" offered by the veterans' community. We have been influenced in the way we conceptualize the dimensions of recovery by Mary Harvey's account (1996) wherein she stresses authority over the remembering process, integration of memory and affect, affect tolerance, symptom mastery, self-esteem and self-cohesion, safe attachment, and meaning-making. We do speak to our patients of these dimensions as future, expected results of treatment—in concrete language arising from the veteran's own experience. All of our patients struggle against chronic despair. One cannot "give hope" of recovery, without giving understandable content to that hope. Over a period of time, veterans readily understand Harvey's dimensions of recovery.

DEFINING CONCEPTS AND PRACTICES OF THE VIP TEAM TREATMENT MODEL

Restoration of Community

Community Is More Than Any Number of Dyads. Basic trust (J. M.'s preferred term), social trust (J. S.'s preferred term), the capacity to attach to a community, requires at least three people. We are not playing logical games when we say that the dyadic trust between two people, no matter how many times it is pair-wise created, does not make a community. A community begins with the addition of the third person, and with the belief of each individual that when alone together the other two will continue to safeguard the interests of each even when that person is absent. The trauma-world assumption is that they will plan some exploitation or attack. Good-enough nurturance in childhood produces basic trust as a matter of course; bad-enough trauma *at any age* destroys it. We feel that the main task in treating combat complex PTSD is to create a family of re-origin (Munroe, Shay, Makary, Clopper, & Wattenberg, 1989) where the veteran can relearn basic trust.

Suspicion of Words. It is not enough to talk about trust and tell patients verbally what they need to do. Vietnam combat veterans, like veterans of many other wars and other traumatized populations, were deceived by words as part of their trauma. Our patients were told many idealistic things about the war, but were not told of the horrors. They were told about codes of conduct, but they quickly saw that the rules did not apply. They were told the enemy was weak and ill equipped, but they saw how competent the enemy's tactics and weapons were. They were told in many voices that it was noble to be a warrior and that they would come home as heroes, but they learned they were not wanted. Veterans learned not to trust words, but to observe behavior. They observe the behavior of therapists who profess to offer therapy. They observe how well the therapist models basic trust.

Tests of Trust

Our patients with complex PTSD, like good researchers, skeptically assume that there is no trust among professionals, and proceed to test this assumption. This is their "null hypothesis." The veterans replicate and re-test any finding that there *is* trust with many variations before they draw firm conclusions. The trauma worldview—"expectancy of exploitation"—is well-founded for survivors. They view evidence to the contrary with suspicion.

These testing procedures are well known to therapists—impatiently endured as obstacles to therapy. For combat trauma survivors with complex PTSD, these tests are the therapy. Therapists who are in a hurry and expect the survivor to be past this stage will guarantee their own ineffectiveness, missing opportunities to establish the infrastructure of trust nec-

essary for further therapy. Once the survivor "experimentally" confirms that the therapist is untrustworthy, the perceived relationship reverts, by default, to mutual exploitation. Survivors then cycle endlessly through suspicion and testing. The survivor will manipulate to get whatever is expedient, such as a medication that makes him feel good, a letter to divert bill collectors, help with disability compensation, getting him out of trouble, or a place to vent out rage. In our experience, without basic trust, therapy will never move beyond these points.

Tests of trust generally fall into four categories: (1) boundary maintenance, (2) professional trust, (3) secondary trauma ("compassion fatigue," Figley, 1995), and (4) therapist self-care (Munroe, 1995; Yassen, 1995).

Boundary Maintenance. The traumatized combat veteran, who has observed the repeated violation of rules and boundaries without sanction, is keenly interested in whether the professional community can police its boundaries. Tests might revolve around the time that sessions start or stop, times outside of scheduled sessions, how threats or intimidation are handled, or whether violations of rules are condoned. Wherever lines are drawn, veterans venture across them. The test is not so much about where the lines are drawn but rather, how the community deals with violations. Are the consequences clear, and will the community enforce them? Veterans also test to determine whether the rules are fair and how the team responds if rules are demonstrated to be unfair. Can the team acknowledge error and correct it or will clinicians deny it and blame the patient? For the veteran, unclear boundaries, irrational rules, and inflexible authorities who will not listen are reminiscent of the war zone and become triggers for intrusive and hyperarousal symptoms.

Professional Trust. Veterans observe how treaters treat each other. Our patients create tests to discover if we trust the other members of the team. It is very difficult for civilians to grasp the mortal stakes that enlisted men have in their officers and NCOs trusting each other in combat: When it's not safe for a junior leader to tell his boss the truth, people die.

Control of information (including disinformation) and of emotional self-presentation are powerful social techniques for survival in extreme situations. These are the principal means by which trauma survivors split therapists from each other and from their institutional setting (Munroe, Shay, Fisher, Makary, Rapperport, & Zimering, 1995). Splitting maneuvers usually seek out the actual ecology of power in the treatment setting. These often include trying to get one therapist to agree that another is incompetent or uncaring. They may also give conflicting information to different team members to see if they will communicate. Sometimes veterans engage one therapist to disagree with the treatment plan of another, or they ask about various theories or treatment approaches favored by others. Members of the team are pitted against one another on whatever issue is convenient.

These maneuvers can be directed at existing staff tensions, such as occupational or gender rifts, or treatment issues where there is plenty of room for different approaches. The content is secondary to testing whether professionals trust each other and can work out disagreements. It is an excellent opportunity for clinicians to model trust by openly dealing with splits. VIP team practices require forthright exchange of information and expression of feelings among team members and aim to make it safe for team members with different degrees and kinds of power to struggle together.

Splitting is a fundamental survival skill in a situation of captivity—which, modern combat is. As an adaptive move it plays one powerholder against another and gets them to fight with each other, or gets one to ally with the captive against the other. Splitting moves are complex strategies that control the information (and disinformation) the splitter gives on both fact and emotion, presenting one picture to one person, and another picture to another. The usual aim is to insert a wedge into an already existing fault line in the ecology of power and open it up into a chasm. The veteran who splits is not evil—he is simply applying his survival skills.

The team, when working well, assists its members in managing the powerful emotions aroused by splits. Falling for the "positive" side of a split is intensely pleasurable and inflating—almost everyone

doing this work for any length of time has experienced near hypomania from being on the "positive" side of a split. A clinician who buys into this loses the veteran's trust as surely as the angry, counterattacking clinician on the "negative" side of the split, who has fallen into that. The clinician who takes in the "negative" side of a split as a valid judgment, can descend into painful despondency and self-doubt. Clinicians who have known and liked each other for years find themselves flaring in naked hatred. The tensions and animosities that successful splitting creates can injure therapists and are a major cause of secondary trauma.

Here we want to remind readers that they should critically examine whether our experience in a long-term outpatient setting is suited to the character of their population, staff, and institutional setting. It is entirely possible, for example, that the staff of an inpatient setting with little control over their own intakes, a short length of stay devoted to "stabilization," and with no meaningful enduring relationships among the veterans or between the veterans and staff, would be much better served by a clear and rigid hierarchy of power than the fluid, egalitarian structure that works well for us. We are not recruiting disciples.

There is no possibility of removing the differences among team members that veterans exploit to create splits. This would deprive the team and veterans of diversity, even if it were possible. Working alone in private practice cannot eliminate splits, because splits can always be engineered between the therapist and other patients, health insurers, police, the therapist's family.

Secondary Trauma ("Compassion Fatigue"). Secondary trauma, psychological injury to the caregivers from doing the work, is intrinsic in the work itself. In our view, no degree of training, no degree of personal maturity, no perfection in the termination of a personal psychoanalysis, no perfected personal virtue or religiosity can protect an isolated mental health worker in any discipline from secondary trauma. A workplace community of trust, support, and safe struggle confers protection. And even that is not absolute. In public health terms, a well-functioning team provides secondary prevention of secondary trauma:

It prevents injury from becoming permanent and disabling by supporting recovery *pari passu* with the injury, but does not remove the injurious factor from the environment (which would be primary prevention).

Work with trauma survivors may injure therapists through three mechanisms:

1. The patients' narrative of traumatic life events make the therapist a witness to atrocities. The VIP model of team function allows its members to communalize these trauma disclosures with the team. Therapists' emotional and physical reactions to things heard are expected and normal, and are valuable clinical data. Unless the patients' material is "processed," i.e., communalized, it will injure the therapist. This is an Occupational Health and Safety practice in the workplace, not "group therapy."

2. Veterans with complex PTSD perceive the clinic in terms of situations in which they were injured and apply survival skills and strategies that were adaptive in the past traumatic situation. Common examples of these strategies are intimidation and splitting. Taken together, trauma-based ways of perceiving and adaptive strategies add up to re-enactment of trauma themes. As they play themselves out, these can be extremely damaging to the therapist.

3. When a treatment team is in continuous contact with a community of veterans, processes occurring in the veteran community develop in the treatment team as well. Because these processes manifest a worldview that assumes exploitation and victimization—sees everything in an us-against-them light—the worldview of the therapists can be damaged.

Occupational psychological injury to trauma workers has also been called vicarious trauma (McCann & Pearlman, 1990), secondary trauma (Catherall, 1992; Munroe, 1991; Rosenheck & Nathan, 1985), and countertransference (Wilson & Lindy, 1994). Danieli, a pioneer in demonstrating the importance of countertransference and secondary trauma in work with Holocaust survivors since 1980, has reviewed this subject in 1994.

Trauma survivors are well aware that reporting their stories affects those that hear them (Munroe, Makary, & Rapperport, 1990). They are very interested to see how therapists protect themselves from this exposure. They look for ways to do this, as a model for how they should deal with their own trauma. They will often say such things as "I can't tell my wife about these things," or "my last therapist cried or changed the subject when I brought these things up." We often see a veteran vacillate between overexposing others to his traumas—so someone will understand—and keeping it all to himself to protect others from the fate of experiencing these events. How the clinician handles this is of primary interest to combat survivors. If they observe that therapists deny the impact and keep it to themselves, therapy is unsuccessful. If they observe that professionals acknowledge the effects and help each other as a community, they have a model for recovery.

Trauma survivors frequently test whether the therapist is isolated or engages the support of a community. We regard the standard image of the expert clinician who acts alone and is not bothered by trauma material to be detrimental to the veteran because it implies that if he were as well-informed, well-educated, or otherwise as strong and fortunate as the therapist, there would be no symptoms of PTSD. There is good empirical evidence that therapists are not immune from the effects of their patients' trauma material (Chrestman, 1994; Kassam-Adams, 1995; Munroe, 1991; Pearlman & MacIan, 1995; Schauben & Frazier, 1995) and therefore an image of invulnerability is counter-factual. Knowingly to pass it on to students and trainees is unethical.

Therapist Self-Care. For war veterans, trustworthiness in combat was measured by whether one would risk his life for the other. In the clinic, veterans frequently induce therapists to move toward extremes of demonstrating the sacrifices they will make. Therapists often get caught up in trying to rescue trauma survivors at their own expense. However, in doing so they model devaluing their own worth and they reenact the trauma theme of exploitative or lethally self-sacrificial relationships. This can take the obvious form of placing the clinician in the position of rescuing the patient from a suicide attempt, or more subtle forms such as moving appointments around, bringing up important material at the end of sessions, or calling the therapist at home or on week-ends. The test is whether the therapists will allow themselves to be abused. Crises do occur in the normal course of treatment, and this is often where the real therapy begins. If clinicians are unable to practice self-care, the survivor is unlikely to take them seriously. Crisis intervention may be necessary, but the issue is safety, not therapy.

Survivors may also ask self-care questions directly, such as when the therapist takes vacation, or how he or she handles all the trauma material, or what the therapist does to relax. Conventional training in most mental health disciplines teaches us to turn away these questions as diversions from therapy or inappropriate intrusiveness into the life of the clinician. However, these are opportunities for direct modeling of self-care. Survivors require that therapists practice what they preach. In VIP, we can truthfully answer these questions by reference to the team.

Team as Community and Team Plus Community

The VIP veterans now have a strong system of rules, devoted primarily to safety, sobriety, and self-care, developed over many years by the veterans, and mainly enforced by them in cooperation with the treatment team. The community rules are continuously a work in progress. The core of VIP is its group therapies. However, we use a "behavioral" point system as well, which awards points for attendance, constructive participation, and other pro-recovery activities. The point system embodies the principle that each veteran earns his place in VIP by his efforts toward recovery and by the contributions he makes to the recovery of others. Failure to make point requirements leads to mandatory meetings with the team as a whole. Persistent non-participation leads to discharge from the program. Despite periodic complaints that the point system is childish, petty, "chickenshit," or demeaning, the veterans support it as a means of making sure that the team is paying attention, and that the veterans have not been forgotten as members of the community.

We believe that rebuilding the capacity for trust is a process of re-socialization. Like the child's socialization in his original family, the ways team members conduct themselves toward each other—their

capacity to negotiate, the uses and abuses of power, mutual accommodation through expression and understanding of emotion, the trustworthiness of words, how they support or defeat each other's self-care—are an essential part of the VIP team treatment model. The famous aphorism of Sarah Haley (1974), "The therapeutic alliance is the therapy," can be adapted as "The team *is* the treatment."

The Rhetoric of Treatment for Combat PTSD

We see ourselves engaged with the veterans as our fellow citizens of a democratic polity, which puts us squarely in the territory described by Aristotle in the *Rhetoric* (Rorty, 1996). We are going for the veterans' trust, to establish ourselves as trustworthy. In this context of free citizenship, Aristotle says—correctly in our experience—we have three interrelated means of achieving their trust. This involves appeal to their reason (*lógos*), appeal to their character (*êthos*), and appeal to their emotions (*páthos*). These are not separate, because reason pertains primarily to means, while the ends of action arise from the ideals, ambitions, and affiliations—which is to say, the character—of the veterans, and their emotions arise primarily from their cognitive assessments of the improvement or deterioration of these commitments. In this context, how we formulate our appeals gives evidence to them for our character, and in particular gives the veterans evidence of our good sense (*phronêsis*), personal integrity and competence (*aretê*), and good will for and toward the veterans we are persuading (*eunoia*). The centrality of persuasion, rather than coercion or deception, is a manifestation of the team's respect for our fellow citizens, these veterans, an aspect of our good will. What arguments and examples we choose from the infinity available, and how we develop them, provide evidence for our *phronêsis* and *aretê* and overall provide evidence for our own character. The persuasive power of sincere appeals to reason comes more from the evidence which it provides for our respect toward the veterans than from any intrinsic ability of reason to compel assent, or having compelled assent, to guide or restrain behavior. This, too, is one of the points Aristotle makes in the *Rhetoric* (Garver, 1994b, pp. 139–171, "Why Reasoning Persuades").

One aspect of *aretê,* integrity, and competence—excellence in general—calls for comment here, both because it seems critical to a combat veteran's feeling safe in the treatment program, and because it throws light on the clash between the ethos of the professional and what it takes to work with this patient population. This dimension of *aretê* in the clinician is a matter of the clinician's *thumós.* To trust the person offering care, combat veterans need to feel that this person is his or her "own person," not a slave to the rules, goals, and authorities of the institution in which he or she serves. (The word "slave" is not used lightly as a cheap hyperbole here—see Garver, 1994a.) The veterans' fearful sensitivities on this are understandable in terms of their real experience in war, when a leader who gives blind obedience to an irrational or illegal order can get the soldier killed or irretrievably tainted by commission of atrocities. Many tests of trust are set up as splits between the clinician and his or her boss, institution, professional code of ethics, licensure, and reimbursement rules. While there is an occasional veteran who appears to be saying, in effect, "I can never trust you unless you are an outlaw like me," most are satisfied with knowing that we personally and freely (not slavishly) support the substance of the rules.

We are open in our persuasion and also open to persuasion, when what we recommend, or an action that we take, seems wrong-headed or unjust to the veteran. Aristotle's account of persuasion, of reaching for trust, is useful and unsentimental—so long as we look back to the context in which we seek trust: We are in this together and are parts of each other's future as fellow citizens.

What we do is political in the richest senses of the word. We foster community among the veterans and join that community to the community of the treatment team. In doing so we establish the possibility of attachment to the larger social world because we (the treatment team) sincerely believe in that larger world and show that it is possible to participate in it with perceptive good judgment. We must do this as *rhêtor*—a citizen openly and undeceptively seeking the trust of fellow citizens and sharing in their fate—not as hireling sophist or as a slave of the institution and its rules. We speak to the veterans as free fellow citizens, not hired agents of social control or slaves of the state. The veterans know that we all receive VA salaries, and are more or less currently dependent on them for our livelihoods, but all team members have truthfully made it clear that we could be working elsewhere, and do this work because we want to, and choose to, not because "it's a paycheck."

Our work is political also in the sense that we encourage the veterans' participation in the democratic political life of the country that they fought for. As one of us has pointed out (Shay, 1995c), unhealed combat trauma disables the basic social and cognitive capacities required for democratic participation. As such, we strive to enable our patients to keep appointments, experience the world as trustworthy, explore the possibility of persuasion, negotiation, compromise, to explore the possibility of winning without killing and losing without dying, and to see the future as real and meaningful.

The team is also publicly and politically active in education of other mental health professionals on trauma treatment in general, and work with combat veterans in particular. The veterans have participated with great satisfaction in video education projects for mental health professionals—one such video formed a presentation at a professional meeting. As a whole team we have published and presented at professional meetings, with full knowledge of the veteran community. One of us (J. S.) publicly testifies on veterans' concerns at Congressional hearings, lectures and organizes conference panels on prevention of psychological injury for active duty military audiences, writes for the trade press, and does media appearances on the themes of combat trauma and on prevention of psychological injury in military service. The veterans in VIP are particularly supportive of these "missionary" educational and hortatory activities to the active duty military. They don't want other young kids to be wrecked the way they were wrecked.

We see these public and political activities as integral to the treatment; in terms of Aristotle's analysis, as a team we achieve trust on the basis of our character, and our public activities are one evidence of our character.

Summary of VIP Team Practices

In effect, our VIP stresses the following precepts:

- Authority resides in the team, not in any single individual.
- Functional roles among team members are intentionally blurred and traded from time to time.
- Hierarchy empowers some to speak and silences others, empowers some for the possession of information and forbids it to others. The team acknowledges *no* hierarchy within itself, and strives for working equality of team members.
- Feelings are essential discourse among team members. These include feelings and countertransference experiences aroused by the patients' traumatic material, feelings toward the patients, and, most important, feelings aroused between team members. The latter is essential to uncover and heal splits.
- The goal of team process is clarity, not unanimity. A team accustomed to safe, affectively honest struggle will not remain split. A team has been successfully split when there is an unacknowledged disagreement, negative emotion, or adverse value judgment within it.
- Team members with different degrees and kinds of power are encouraged to struggle together. The goal of the team culture is to render this safe. The slogan, "Safe Struggle," places equal emphasis on both words.
- Veteran information is shared among the team, along with the feelings aroused in the clinician toward the information, toward the veteran, and toward others working with the veteran.
- More than one team member is always actively working with the veteran—this is important protection for both the therapist and the veteran.
- Therapist self-care is essential to work with survivors of severe trauma. The team culture encourages this self-care. It actively works against the constant pressure on therapists to become rescuers who are out there all alone with the veterans. The by-word is "I need to know you are taking care of yourself, for me to do my work."

- Multiple relationships and value commitments outside the team are essential to individual well-being and to prevent the team from becoming a totalitarian cult. The team strongly supports value-richness and views workaholism as a failure of self-care, a sign of injury.
- The team model is inherently vulnerable to impairment by *any* of its members, regardless of the degree and kinds of power that person has from institutional or other sources. Team trust is thus fundamentally dependent upon unanimity of support for the team model itself—even though the team model encourages forthright disagreement over any other issue.

DIVERGENCES IN THE TEAM MODEL FROM THE VALUE PATTERN OF THE PROFESSIONAL

The VIP team model for long-term treatment of complex PTSD after combat is difficult for mental health professionals to carry out because it diverges from the psychologically internalized and socially institutionalized value pattern of the professional in our society. Most parts of this value pattern seem so pervasively "true" that they are as invisible to us as water is to a fish. We shall attempt to bring them to awareness using the classic description given by Talcott Parsons (1951, p. 343 and other references indexed under "pattern variable"). His description is still on the nose, as not much has changed.

Parsons analyzed this professional value pattern through a series of dichotomous variables, and claimed that any given social position (such as "doctor") could usefully be characterized by the particular pattern of value commitments the person in that position is expected to fulfill. Parsons' dichotomous value "pattern variables" were universalism/particularism, functional specificity/functional diffuseness, collectivity orientation/self-orientation, achievement/ascription, affective neutrality/affectivity. We shall take up each one in turn and show how it obstructs the creation of trust in our population of combat veterans for whom the destruction of the capacity for trust is the most disabling aspect of their injury. Centuries of historical change and struggle lie behind each pattern variable, not only institutionalizing norms that serve the interests of powerholders in modern industrial societies, but also often institutionalizing fairness, rationality, and protection for the powerless. Why should combat veterans react so badly to clinicians' loyal adherence to them?

Universalism (Opposite: Particularism)

A mental health professional is expected to relate to a patient on the basis of technical rules governed by having identified the patient as a subsumable example of an abstractly defined category. Once the VA has applied the rules declaring a man or woman to be a "veteran" and "eligible," the mental health professional applies an institutionalized set of rules known as "diagnosis" to the patient's history and current life. We believe that these abstract, universalistic standards are claimed to "transcend" the particularity of the patient's history, situation, and future. Many combat veterans (especially at the beginning of their treatment when trust is absent) vocally resent being lumped with incest survivors, concentration camp survivors, auto wreck survivors, battered women, who are all conceived as having the "same" diagnosis. The veteran's angry insistence upon the therapist knowing the specifics of his military service, upon knowing who the 1st Battalion, 9th Marine Regiment were, is often taken by clinicians as a repellent narcissistic claim of "specialness." According to their professional training in the abstract universalistic system of diagnosis, and in the treatments claimed to be applicable to any exemplar of a diagnostic class, the clinicians are doing the right thing. Why does this veteran so perversely insist upon "being treated like an individual," when in the mind of the clinician, the veteran "ought to know" that scientific professionalism will provide him with the best possible outcome based on his universalistically defined diagnosis, not on the accidental particulars of his life? Is this just ignorance, or narcissism?

The answer is usually fear. These veterans have had the real experience of lives being lost, and people maimed, when a person in a position of power "went by the book," rather than looking first very sharply at the particulars, and then applying the book to them with flexibility and good sense. (Aristotle: "The doctor cures a particular [i.e., not universal] man" EN I.61097a13.). Most veterans will not insist that a therapist be or become a subject-matter expert on every technical detail of the Vietnam era military, but only that the therapist be willing to "listen." Universal rules were sometimes—in reality—what got people killed.

Functional Specificity (Opposite: Diffuseness)

"Division of labor" and "specialization" are often thought to be crowning achievements of the historic process of modernization. It is deeply ingrained in our common sense and institutionalized in law and in work rules. The voice of common sense says, "You do your job, and I'll do mine, and together we'll get the work done." Functional specificity is largely invisible to us as a value posture; we experience it more like a feature of the natural landscape, like gravity. Many readers may be scratching their heads wondering how the division of labor between, say, psychiatrists, psychologists, nurses, and social workers, could possibly be a trust issue for combat veterans.

In fact, the division of labor is a key element in the processes that support state-sponsored atrocities and torture (Kelman, 1994). Veterans who had the misfortune of witnessing or participating in these were told, "none of your business," or "not my job," or "just do your job" if they raised questions. Many of those who crossed into the heart of darkness are now dead by their own hand.

Probably the most frequent "boundaries" that combat veterans openly or subtly demand we cross—as a test of trust—are the boundaries of functional specificity, professional specialization, division of labor. Masters-level counseling psychologists are importuned for advice on medication; psychiatrists are pressured to locate Section 8 housing, and so on. No wonder well-socialized mental health professionals see these patients as demanding and narcissistic. However, the engine behind these demands is fear, not vanity. In the VIP team we intentionally blur disciplinary lines, and each of us strives to see the whole veteran as significant, with no predetermined limits to the dimensions of his welfare that are our concern.

Functional specificity is deeply institutionalized in licensure, departmental organization of the VA, and career paths in the professions. For many combat veterans with complex PTSD, the careerism of officers, the career management systems of the military services (manifested then as six-month rotations in troop command positions), were the visible sources of their betrayals.

Collectivity Orientation (Opposite: Self-Orientation)

In the professionalized, bureaucratic society of "modernity," *thumós* (i.e., spirited self-respect) is not completely erased, it is tamed and channeled into the institutions (collectivities) of the society. One expects to find identity, satisfaction, pride, recognition, accomplishment, solidarity—but also material compensation—embodied in these institutions. Collectivity orientation channels ideals, ambitions, and affiliations through collectivities, not through personal relationships. The dichotomous opposite that Parsons chose for his jargon, "self-orientation," begs to be read simply as "selfishness," even though he carefully defines it in less moralizing terms. The moralizing is not completely off-base. Examples of corrupt self-orientation would be personally taking money from a VA patient to perform a clinical or administrative service one ought to be doing anyway. Under the normative value pattern variable, the mental health professional may receive his material compensation only from the collectivity. Or if a clinician became romantically, sexually, or narcissistically involved with a veteran, this would be a clear example of self-orientation, taking gratification from the specific relationship with the veteran rather than channeling all gratification through the collectivity and in the licit forms that the collectivity grants. These are the easy cases.

It gets murky when the veterans' welfare matters to the clinician more than that of his or her employer, or the veterans' esteem matters more than the esteem of professional colleagues. Such a mental health professional is likely to find him- or herself under suspicion by colleagues and supervisors, even if no steps have been taken in the real world that impair the insti-

tution or reject the colleagues. It's not hard to detect the lack of a collectivity-orientation; the professional who lacks it is "not with the program."

During the Vietnam War, officers who resisted rotation out of dangerous troop command billets at the end of their six months were labeled as having "gone native," that is, having developed more commitment to the troops than to the officer corps and to personal career advancement. This label was a career-ending stigma. Ironically, in some instances it was ideals of purely professional competence that led to such refusals, because the six-month rotation policy guaranteed that no one in command of a company or battalion had the time to learn what they had to learn to do the job well—in purely military terms.

The veterans we treat, who are all enlisted men, treasure the memories of the officers who were more devoted to their substantive military tasks and to the men under their command than to the reward system of their military service. More to the point clinically, any sign of collectivity-orientation by a clinician is liable to be a traumatic trigger, bringing back memories of having been put in lethal danger to get body count—or worse, to fill out the denominator of a kill ratio, where the presence of American casualties was rated as positive evidence of the commander's "aggressiveness" and "balls."

The urgency of fear lies behind the veterans' need to know that we are working in VIP because we want to, because it gives us personal pleasure and satisfaction for its own sake. Parsons would probably have called this "self-orientation" rather than "collectivity-orientation."

This pattern variable also has a subtle influence on the interactive style of clinicians. Normative avoidance of "self-orientation" seems to call for a degree of modesty in dealing with trauma survivors that may not serve the patients best. The narcissistic dimension of the veterans' injuries not only drives them to demand *timê* (Homer's heavy-freighted word for honor), but calls for the clinician to be able to accept with graceful good humor the idealizing, admiring reactions that veterans develop toward those whom at long last they have come to trust. Kohut (1971) was the first to point this out, and it accords with our experience. A clinician's professional colleagues are liable to react negatively not only to the idealization itself, but to the reluctance of the clinician, the object of the idealization, to disparage and rebuff it as pathological.

Achievement (Opposite: Ascription)

Modern clinicians attain to their professional credentials and institutional position through achievement of the standards of their respective disciplines. No one, least of all the injured veterans in the VA, wants to be treated by people whose only qualification is that they are a relative of someone powerful in the government, by some accident of birth. Such nepotism would be a textbook example of "ascription." "Achievement" is institutionalized in examinations, training program standards for accreditation, credentialing laws, and rules. The veterans do insist on competence—one dimension of the *aretê* (i.e., competence and integrity) on which they found their trust—so how does this normative value pattern variable get the mental health professional into a bind with combat veterans?

Again, fear is the problem. Veterans experienced lethal incompetence at the hands of officers and bureaucrats who had all the right credentials but whose competency in examinations and management science did not equip them for the reality of war against a resourceful human enemy who progressively figured out how to turn each textbook solution into a death trap. The veterans insist that there is something personal (read "ascribed") that makes someone trustworthy as a combat leader or as a clinician. Our institutions treat professionals who have the same "achieved status" evidenced by the same credentials as fungible—absolutely substitutable—for one another. The veterans reject this. Their trust is personal, non-transferable.

When you ask what personal quality made trustworthy officers worthy of trust, the most frequent answer is their willingness to listen. In the combat situation, it was willingness to listen to the particularity of the local and current knowledge of the most experienced person in the unit, regardless of rank. In the clinician, it is the willingness to listen to the particularity of the veteran's own experience. They don't ask us to be universal experts, and will be less trusting of a widely read clinician who is smug about this knowl-

edge, than of someone who knows the limits of what he or she knows.

Affective Neutrality (Opposite: Affectivity)

The normative expectation that the professional will be emotionally detached, coldly rational, has been under attack for a long time and from many quarters, not the least of them being the recognition that even the simplest rational social judgments and self-restraints are flatly impossible for someone truly devoid of emotion (Damasio, 1994). The problem for our work lies less in some official insistence that professionals be affectively neutral, than in the difficulty of allowing emotions a full place at the table with our patients and our colleagues. One of us (Shay, 1994) has argued elsewhere that the communalization of trauma requires authentic emotion in the hearer of traumatic material. Even harder to overcome is the posture of affective neutrality in the presence of and toward professional colleagues. Yet, as we have explained above, treatment team members must make the emotions stirred toward each other by the veterans' splitting maneuvers a part of the team's work. The emotions stirred by veteran narratives, re-enactments, and tests of trust carry valuable clinical information, which is lost at everyone's peril.

Are We Kicking Sacred Cows?

Some readers may wonder if a delight at kicking sacred cows is at work here. While neither of us is above such perverse pleasures, the main point of this review of Talcott Parsons' classic sociological analysis is to bring home the mismatch between our acculturation to professional norms and the psychological make-up of combat veterans with complex PTSD, and perhaps of any severe, human-caused prolonged trauma in a condition of captivity.

In her lucent analysis of the relationship of complex PTSD to the ecology of power, Judith Herman (1992b) has pointed out that professionals who devote themselves to the care of these patients risk becoming tainted and stigmatized by association with those whom the powerholders have victimized. In countries ruled by tyrants, this can be literal and life-threatening, as when a general practitioner is questioned by the political police for setting the broken bone of the wife of an executed enemy of the state. In less extreme conditions it can be simple social ostracism, lack of otherwise merited recognition or advancement, and embarrassed discomfort of colleagues, such as Freud experienced when he took seriously the childhood sexual exploitation of his female patients. Judith Herman's observations stand firmly as the most important single thing to know about this matter, if we were limited to knowing but one thing about it.

Here, we have added a different sort of insight on the difficulties arising in the treatment of combat veterans with complex PTSD. These veterans may suffer unbearable terror when they encounter unthinking obedience by their caregivers to the normative value pattern of the professional. Even when these terrors can be allayed, the normative value pattern promotes the illusion of the invulnerable expert, able to work in social and emotional isolation—a Lone Ranger. This is a poor role model for the veterans, to whom we advocate the support and nourishment of a community.

Aristotle Again—Human Is *Politikón Zôon*

We take seriously that the human being is a bio-psycho-social-cultural whole at every moment. This restates Aristotle's (4th century, BCE) zoological observation that the human is the animal of the political community. Body, mind, society, culture are not separate "realities," even less are they hierarchical "levels," which underlie each other, making some fundamental and others epiphenomenal. Our physical brains are biologically evolved to make us culture bearers and users; it is our biological nature to live in relation to culturally constructed moral codes; our social lives remodel our brains; cognitive assessments and their related emotional states influence bodily health, and so on. The very fact that we speak in terms of body, mind, society, culture is no more than a reflection of the methodological and institutional history of our intellectual worlds. They are temporary guides to perception and communication. They are throwaways, not eternal realities existing beyond the Platonic veil. What we do at this moment of writing and what you do at this moment of reading is at one and the same moment physiological, psychological, social, and cultural.

Given our experiences with traumatized Vietnam veterans, we believe that there is no conclusive and comprehensive theory of the human that sanctions the hegemony of any one mental health discipline's approach to our patients. As a clinical matter, our bio-psycho-social-cultural understanding is in harmony with our multi-modal treatment that incorporates the practices of numerous schools of thought. To offer settings in which veterans can communalize despair and grief does not contradict offering the same veterans serotonin reuptake inhibitors, or making the group in which grief is communalized part of a "behavioral point system," or offering concrete assistance with public transport passes and disability pension hearings. This is not flabby eclecticism—it's the best we can do with the knowledge that we have. The distinction between "real treatment" and "mere support" blurs when we treat the whole person.

REFERENCES

American Psychiatric Association. (1980). *Diagnostic and statistical manual of mental disorders* (3rd ed.). Washington, DC: Author.

American Psychiatric Association. (1987). *Diagnostic and statistical manual of mental disorders* (3rd ed. Rev.). Washington, DC: Author.

American Psychiatric Association. (1994). *Diagnostic and statistical manual of mental disorders* (4th ed.). Washington, DC: Author.

Ancharoff, M. R., Munroe, J. F., & Fisher, L. M. (1998). The legacy of combat trauma: Clinical implications of inter-generational transmission. In Y. Danieli (Ed.), *Intergenerational handbook of multigenerational legacies of trauma.* New York: Plenum.

Carey, C. (1996). Rhetorical means of persuasion. In A. O. Rorty (Ed.), *Essays on Aristotle's Rhetoric.* Berkeley: University of California Press.

Catherall, D. R. (1989). Differentiating intervention strategies for primary and secondary trauma in post-traumatic stress disorder: The example of Vietnam veterans. *Journal of Traumatic Stress, 2*(3), 289–304.

Catherall, D. R. (1992). *Back from the brink: A family guide to overcoming traumatic stress*. New York, Bantam Books.

Chrestman, K. R. (1994). *Secondary traumatization in therapists working with survivors of trauma*. Unpublished doctoral dissertation, Nova University.

Damasio, A. R. (1994). *Decartes error: Emotion, reason, and the human brain*. New York: Grossett/Putnam.

Danieli, Y. (1980). Countertransference in the treatment and study of Nazi Holocaust survivors and their children. *Victimology: An International Journal. 5*, 355–367.

Danieli, Y. (1994). Countertransference, trauma and training. In J. P. Wilson and J. Lindy (Eds.), *Countertransference in the treatment of post-traumatic stress disorder.* (pp. 368–388). New York: Guilford Press.

Erikson, E. H. (1959). Identity and the life cycle. *Psychological Issues, 1*(1, Whole No. 1).

Erikson, E. H. (1963). *Childhood and society*. New York: Norton & Company.

Erikson, K. T. (1976). *Everything in its path: Destruction of community in the Buffalo Creek Flood*. New York: Simon and Schuster.

Figley, C. R. (1988). Post-traumatic family therapy. In F. M. Ochberg (Ed.), *Post-traumatic therapy and victims of violence* (pp. 83–110). New York: Brunner/Mazel.

Figley, C. R. (Ed.). (1995). *Compassion fatigue: Secondary traumatic stress disorder from treating the traumatized*. New York: Brunner/Mazel.

Garver, E. (1994a). Aristotle's natural slaves. *Journal of the History of Philosophy 32,*173–195.

Garver, E. (1994b). *Aristotle's Rhetoric: An art of character*. Chicago: University of Chicago Press.

Haley, S. A. (1974). When the patient reports atrocities. *Archives of General Psychiatry, 30,* 191–196.

Harvey, M. R. (1996). An ecological view of psychological trauma and trauma recovery. *Journal of Traumatic Stress, 9,* 3–23.

Headquarters, Department of the Army. (1994). *FM 22–51: Leader's Manual for Combat Stress Control*. Washington, D.C.

Herman, J. L. (1992a). Complex PTSD: A syndrome in survivors of prolonged and repeated trauma. *Journal of Traumatic Stress, 5*(3), 377–392.

Herman, J. L. (1992b). *Trauma and Recovery*. New York: Basic Books.

Herman, J. L. (1993). Sequelae of prolonged and repeated trauma: Evidence for a complex posttraumatic syndrome (DESNOS). In J. R. T. Davidson and E. B. Foa (Eds.), *Posttraumatic stress disorder: DSM-IV and beyond*. Washington, D.C.: American Psychiatric Press.

Homer (ca. 800 B. C. E./1961). *The Odyssey,* Translated by R. Fitzgerald. New York: Random House.

Janoff-Bulman, R. (1985). The aftermath of victimization: Rebuilding shattered assumptions. In C. R. Figley (Ed.), *Trauma and its wake* (pp. 15–35). New York: Brunner/Mazel.

Janoff-Bulman, R. (1992). *Shattered assumptions: Towards a new psychology of trauma*. New York: The Free Press.

Kassam-Adams, N. (1995). *The risks treating sexual trauma: Stress and secondary trauma in psychotherapists*. Unpublished doctoral dissertation, University of Virginia.

Keane, T. M., Scott, W. O., Chavoya, G. A., Lamparski, D. M., & Fairbank, J. A. (1985). Social support in Vietnam veterans with post-traumatic stress disorder: A comparative analysis. *Journal of Consulting and Clinical Psychology, 53*(1), 95–102.

Kelman, H. C. (1994). The social context of torture. In Ronald D. Crelinsten and Alex P Schmid (Eds.), *The politics of pain: Torturers and their masters*. Boulder, Colorado: Westview Press.

Kirkland, F., Halverson, R. R., & Bliese, P. D. (1996) Stress and psychological readiness in post-cold-war operations. *Parameters: Quarterly Journal of the U.S. Army War College 26,* 79–91.

Kohut, H. (1971) *The analysis of the self*. Madison, Connecticut: International Universities Press.

Lifton, R. J. (1967). *Death in life: Survivors of Hiroshima*. New York: Simon & Schuster.

Lifton, R. J. (1973). *Home from the war: Vietnam veterans, neither victims nor executioners*. New York: Basic Books.

Lifton, R. J. (1979). *The broken connection*. Simon & Schuster: New York.

Mason, P. H. C. (1990). *Recovering from the war: A woman's guide to helping your Vietnam vet, your family and yourself*. New York: Viking.

Matsakis, A. (1996). *Vietnam wives*. (2nd ed.). Woodbine House, Kexisington, MD.

McCann, I. L. & Pearlman, L. A. (1990). Vicarious traumatization: A framework for understanding the psychological effects of working with victims. *Journal of Traumatic Stress, 3*(1), 131–150.

Munroe, J. F. (1991). *Therapist traumatization from exposure to patients with combat related post-traumatic stress disorder: Implications for administration and su-*

pervision. Unpublished doctoral dissertation, available from Dissertation Abstracts, Ann Arbor, Michigan.

Munroe, J. F. (1995). Ethical issues associated with secondary trauma in therapists. In B. Stamm, (Ed.), *Secondary traumatic stress: Self care issues for clinicians, researchers, and educators.* Lutherville, MD: Sidran.

Munroe, J. F. (1996). The loss and restoration of community: The treatment of severe war trauma. *Journal of Personal and Interpersonal Loss 1,* 393–409.

Munroe, J. F., Makary, C., & Rapperport, K. (1990). *PTSD and twenty years of treatment: Vietnam combat veterans speak.* Videotape presentation at the Sixth Annual Meeting of the Society for Traumatic Stress Studies, New Orleans, LA.

Munroe, J. F., Shay, J., Fisher, L., Makary, C., Rapperport, K., & Zimering, R., (1995). Preventing compassion fatigue: A team treatment model. In C. Figley, (Ed.), *Compassion fatigue: Coping with secondary traumatic stress disorder in those who treat the traumatized.* New York: Brunner/Mazel.

Munroe, J. F., Shay, J., Makary, C., Clopper, M., & Wattenberg, M., (1989). Creating a family of re-origin: A long term outpatient PTSD unit. Presented at the Fifth Annual Meeting of the Society for Traumatic Stress Studies, San Francisco, CA.

Nussbaum, M. C. (1986). *The fragility of goodness: Luck and ethics in Greek tragedy and philosophy.* New York: Cambridge University Press.

Parsons, T. (1951). *The social system.* Glencoe, IL: Free Press.

Patterson, O. (1982). *Slavery and social death.* Cambridge: Harvard University Press.

Pearlman, L. A. & MacIan, P. S (1995). Vicarious traumatization: An empirical study of the effects of trauma work on trauma therapists. *Professional Psychology: Research and Practice, 26,* 558–565.

Pulver, S. (1970). Narcissism: The term and the concept. *Journal of the American Psychoanalytic Association 18,* 319–341.

Rorty, A. O. (1996). Structuring rhetoric. In A. O. Rorty (Ed.), *Essays on Aristotles' Rhetoric.* Berkeley: University of California Press.

Rosenheck, R. & Nathan, P. (1985). Secondary traumatization in children of Vietnam veterans. *Hospital and Community Psychiatry, 36*(5), 332–344.

Schauben, L. J., & Frazier, P. A. (1995). Vicarious trauma: The effects on female counselors of working with sexual violence survivors. *Psychology of Women Quarterly, 19,* 49–54.

Severo, R. & Milford, L. (1990). *The wages of war: When American's soldiers came home—from Valley Forge to Vietnam.* New York: Simon & Schuster.

Shatan, C. F. (1985). Have you hugged a Vietnam veteran today? The basic wound of catastrophic stress. In W. D. Kelley (Ed.), *Post-traumatic stress disorder and the war veteran patient* (pp. 12–28). New York: Brunner/Mazel.

Shay, J. (1992). Fluoxetine reduces explosiveness and elevates mood of Vietnam combat veterans with PTSD. *Journal of Traumatic Stress 5,* 97–101.

Shay, J. (1994). *Achilles in Vietnam: Combat trauma and the undoing of character.* New York: Atheneum. Also (1995), New York: Simon & Schuster Touchstone.

Shay, J. (1995a). About medications for combat PTSD. [On-line] Robert Hsiung (Ed.), *Psychopharmacology tips home page.* World Wide Web URL: http://uhs.bsd.uchicago.edu/~bhsiung/tips/tips.html.

Shay, J. (1995b). Achilles: Paragon, flawed character, or tragic soldier figure? *Classical Bulletin, 71,* 117–124.

Shay, J. (1995c). The birth of tragedy out of the needs of democracy. [On-line] *DIDASKALIA: ANCIENT THEATER TODAY* Vol. 2 No. 2, April 1995. World Wide Web URL. http://www.csv.warwick.ac.uk/cgi-bin/mfs/01/didaskalia/issues/vol2no2/Shay.html.

van der Kolk, B. A., Brown, P., & van der Hart, O. (1989). Pierre Janet on post-traumatic stress. *Journal of Traumatic Stress, 2*(4), 365–378.

Wilson, J. P. & Lindy, J. D. (Eds.) (1994). *Countertransference in the treatment of PTSD.* New York: Guilford Press.

WHO [World Health Organization]. (1992). *The ICD-10 classification of mental and behavioral disorders: Clinical descriptions and diagnostic guidelines.* Geneva, WHO.

Yassen, J. (1995). Preventing secondary traumatic stress disorder. In Charles Figley, *Compassion Fatigue.* New York: Brunner/Mazel.

Author Index